Annals of Lincoln County, North Carolina:
Containing Interesting and Authentic Facts of Lincoln County History through the Years 1749 to 1937

William L. Sherrill

HERITAGE BOOKS
2008

HERITAGE BOOKS
AN IMPRINT OF HERITAGE BOOKS, INC.

Books, CDs, and more—Worldwide

For our listing of thousands of titles see our website at
www.HeritageBooks.com

Published 2008 by
HERITAGE BOOKS, INC.
Publishing Division
100 Railroad Ave. #104
Westminster, Maryland 21157

Copyright © 1937 William L. Sherrill

All rights reserved. No part of this book may be reproduced or transmitted in any form or by any means, electronic or mechanical, including photocopying, recording or by any information storage and retrieval system without written permission from the author, except for the inclusion of brief quotations in a review.

International Standard Book Numbers
Paperbound: 978-0-7884-0871-7
Clothbound: 978-0-7884-7075-2

To my wife, now for fifty-three years a devoted companion and constant inspiration, this volume is affectionately inscribed.

TABLE OF CONTENTS

	Page
Foreword	3
Introduction	5
Chapter I. First Pioneers to Country West of the Catawba	7
Chapter II. 1759 to 1774	13
Chapter III. 1775 to 1779	23
Chapter IV. 1779 to 1780	29
Chapter V. The Battle of Ramsour's Mill	36
Chapter VI. 1780 to 1781	41
Chapter VII. 1782 to 1800	52
Chapter VIII. 1801 to 1811	62
Chapter IX. 1812 to 1819	74
Chapter X. 1820 to 1829	84
Chapter XI. 1830 to 1839	102
Chapter XII. 1840 to 1849	122
Chapter XIII. 1850 to 1859	147
Chapter XIV. 1860 to 1869	167
Chapter XV. 1870 to 1879	206
Chapter XVI. 1880 to 1889	229
Chapter XVII. 1890 to 1899	254
Chapter XVIII. 1900 to 1909	284
Chapter XIX. 1910 to 1919	324
Chapter XX. 1920 to 1929	362
Chapter XXI. 1930 to 1936	398
Chapter XXII. Something about the Colored Folks	434
Chapter XXIII. Industrial Growth in Lincoln County	436
1. Iron Manufacture	436
2. Cotton Manufacture	442
3. Pottery	444
4. Paper Mills	445
5. Tanneries	446
6. Furniture	447
7. Workers in Iron	447
8. Coach Makers	448
9. Corn and Flour Mills	448
10. Miscellaneous	448
Chapter XXIV. The Progress of Education	450
Chapter XXV. Newspapers, Authors, Physicians, Lawyers	460
Newspapers	460
Authors	462
Physicians	464
Lawyers	465
Chapter XXVI. The Church in Lincoln County	466
Emanuel's Church	466
Daniel's Church	473
Salem Church	474
St. Matthew's Church	474
The Episcopal Church	477
The Prebyterian Church	481
The Baptist Church	485
The Methodist Church	490
Appendix—Officials of Lincoln County	499
Office Holders from Lincoln County	

ILLUSTRATIONS

The Author ....Frontispiece

Signers of Tryon Association ....Opposite page 20

Pleasant Retreat Academy, Lincolnton High School,
McKendree Methodist Church, Machpelah Presbyterian Church ....Opposite page 80

Four Notable Marriages in Lincoln ....Opposite page 174

Gen. Robert F. Hoke, Gen. Stephen D. Ramseur,
Gen. John H. Forney, Gen. Robert D. Johnston,
Lt. William E. Shipp, Capt. R. Z. Johnston..................Opposite page 181

James Graham, William H. Forney, Henry W. Connor,
William Lander, Charles A. Jonas ....Opposite page 187

Court House, 1870; Court House, 1910;
Court House, 1930 ....Opposite page 206

Gov. J. P. Henderson, Gov. J. F. Johnston, Gov. W. A.
Graham, Sen. W. L. Hill, Gov. Hoke Smith..................Opposite page 220

Dr. Albert M. Shipp, Dr. R. L. Abernethy, Dr. R. H.
Morrison, Dr. Alfred J. Fox, Rev. P. F. W. Stamey....Opposite page 251

Dr. Samuel Lander, Dr. R. Z. Johnston, Dr. W. R.
Wetmore, Dr. R. A. Yoder, Rev. W. S. Bynum............Opposite page 294

Vardry McBee, Maj. W. A. Graham, Col. William
Johnston, J. F. Reinhardt, Ambrose Costner................Opposite page 335

Judge W. M. Shipp, Judge David Schenck, Judge W. P.
Bynum, Judge W. A. Hoke, Judge M. L. McCorkle......Opposite page 376

Daniel E. Rhyne, James A. Abernethy, John M.
Rhodes, Robert S. Reinhardt, D. P. Rhodes,
Isaac C. Lowe ....Opposite page 442

Prof. D. Matt Thompson, Maj. S. M. Finger,
Miss Kate C. Shipp, Dr. Charles L. Coon,
Prof. James M. Bandy ....Opposite page 450

Dr. Michael Hoke, Dr. C. L. Hunter, Dr. R. B. Killian,
Dr. J. R. Gamble, Dr. L. A. Crowell,
Dr. W. L. Crouse ....Opposite page 464

ANNALS OF LINCOLN COUNTY

FOREWORD

THESE ANNALS appeared serially in the *Lincoln Times* from June, 1935, to November, 1936. They are the product of prolonged and diligent research on the part of the author. Many facts were obtained from the *Colonial* and *State Records;* from *The Life of General Joseph Graham* and *The History of the South Fork Baptist Association*, both written by the late Major William A. Graham; from Dr. Charles L. Coon's *Documentary History of Schools in North Carolina;* from *Marriage Bonds of Tryon and Lincoln Counties* by Curtis Bynum; from Dr. Coon and Mr. Bynum personally; from many old newspapers, including the news items pertaining to Lincoln County as they appeared in the *Charlotte Journal* covering the period from 1830 to 1860; from the late Miss Kate C. Shipp and from my father, both of whom were thoroughly conversant with the County history since the early days; from Miss Maude R. Mullen, Mrs. George A. Brown, and others; from tombstone records found in many cemeteries; and from personal knowledge and recollection of many events as they occurred.

The original articles published in the *Times* have been carefully revised and many newly discovered facts added. Many items which may seem of minor importance are included, and the ANNALS would be incomplete without them. Events of both small and great importance appear, in order that the reader may obtain a clearer knowledge of the life of the people and of the things they were interested in through each decade of our history. No history was ever complete, and this is certainly true of the ANNALS; but no item of interest has been purposely omitted. Many things were done which are not written in this book; much history not written has faded from memory because no record was made of it; this volume is written to preserve much of the splendid history of our County of Lincoln so that the succeeding generations may know more about what the fathers did.

This work, long and tedious, has been a labor of love for one who is proud to claim Lincoln as the county of his nativity, and who has, without expectation of fee or reward, striven to preserve some of the history made by its people.

In conclusion it should be said that the author has been encouraged to publish the volume by the following public-spirited citizens of Lincolnton:

CHARLES A. JONAS	E. H. REECE	F. H. CHAMBERLAIN
O. A. COSTNER	DR. W. F. ELLIOTT	F. H. CHAMBERLAIN, JR.
M. H. KUHN	F. P. BARKLEY	W. M. LENTZ
C. L. GOODSON	G. B. GOODSON	L. E. MCQUINN
S. R. WARLICK	JOHN P. JONES, JR.	M. L. SIPE
T. F. CORRIHER	B. C. LINEBERGER	DR. J. R. GAMBLE
W. M. PICKENS	DR. I. R. SELF	C. GUY RUDISILL, JR.

These loyal men have agreed to share with the author the financial risk involved in the publication of the ANNALS.

WILLIAM L. SHERRILL.

INTRODUCTION

Those of us who hunger for facts rather than myths will value these ANNALS OF LINCOLN COUNTY. Since the publication of the *Colonial Records* and of *Ashe's History* the facts for the State as a whole are safe. But a vast amount of work remains to be done in collecting the facts of county history. That work is difficult and tedious. Only a generous and devoted soul will undertake the necessary research. The sole reward that need be expected is gratitude. In the case of the ANNALS I am certain that reward will be forthcoming.

It is like Mr. Sherrill to have undertaken this work for our county of Lincoln. He has prepared for it through all his active life. He has with painstaking care preserved every fragment of local history that has come within his eager reach. Patiently he has filled a storehouse with valuable facts. And here he has opened the doors to all of us.

Everybody knows what the Sherrill family has meant to Lincoln County. A characteristic modesty has led the author of the ANNALS to touch lightly upon the achievements of those who bore his name. I can not and would not change that. But I think I can quite properly say a word about the author himself.

William Lander Sherrill was born February 9th, 1860. All of us will remember with respect and affection his father, Samuel Pinckney Sherrill, and many will in like manner remember his mother, Sarah Catherine Lander Sherrill; modest reference to them has been made in the ANNALS. Mr. Sherrill was schooled in the Lincolnton Academy, then an institution of collegiate standards. When nineteen years old he ventured into business with a pharmacy in Dallas, then county-seat of Gaston County. In 1884, when but twenty-four, he was mayor of the town of Dallas. In that year he was married to Luetta Connor, daughter of the gallant Lieutenant whose tragic death is recounted in the ANNALS. In 1890 Mr. Sherrill was ordained to the self-sacrificing life of a minister of the Methodist Episcopal Church, South. Obedient to the laws of his church he has held ten several pastorates. In addition to his pastoral duties he has done useful work as co-editor of the *Christian Advocate* and as Secretary-Treasurer of the Board of Education of the Western North Carolina Conference, and has been Secretary of the Conference since 1894. His home is now in Charlotte. He has been a member of the General Conference and of the General

Board of Church Extension. He appears in *Who's Who in America* as one of the nation's widely known clergymen. Mr. Sherrill's son, Henry Connor Sherrill, is a business man of high standing in Charlotte. There, in 1917, he organized the Morris Plan Bank, and he is now President and active manager of that institution. He was married June 3, 1914, to Betty D. King, of Georgia; two children, Betty and Connor Marie, promise to carry on the honored record of the Sherrill name.

The author of the ANNALS has, without knowing it, written his own character upon every page of his book. You will find there his accuracy and his sense of duty; his kindliness and his generosity; above all his Christianity. Even the simple truth about him cannot now be told. I must be content to say that he has done his duty as a loyal son of Lincoln County. I am confident that his people, our people, will see what I see, and will continue to value the man and his work.

CURTIS BYNUM.

Asheville, N. C.
March, 1937.

CHAPTER I

THE FIRST PIONEERS TO THE COUNTRY WEST OF THE CATAWBA RIVER

We have no record of civilized man in America prior to its discovery by Columbus in 1492. From the morning of creation it had been a wild country where the bear and the buffalo, the panther and the wolf contested with the savage Indians for supremacy.

Through the milleniums the seasons came in order and the fruits of the earth wasted, save that consumed by wild beasts and wilder men. The birds sang the same songs they sing today but their melodies fell upon ears that knew not harmony; the fragrance of native flowers was wasted on the desert air; the streams, fresh and pure from the heart of nature, silently journeyed to the sea and only an occasional savage halted by the shore to fish, or to drink from the flowing stream. Through the long centuries the virgin land had been reserved by Providence for a new and mighty people to dwell upon.

It was full 250 years after Columbus came that the white man first beheld the beauty of the Catawba valley and the hills to the west of it. When counties were first organized on the seacoast their western boundaries reached to the Mississippi River, which was the British frontier. Thus New Hanover, established in 1728 included all the wilderness to the west, until Bladen, organized in 1734, fell heir to it. Later Anson, formed in 1749, embraced all the western country until Rowan in 1753 and Mecklenburg in 1762 absorbed that territory. In 1769 Tryon County, named for the Royal Governor, William Tryon, was established and included all the territory west of the Catawba River except the section north of the Earl Granville line which was attached to Rowan until absorbed by Burke in 1777.

It is not known for certain who were the first settlers west of the Catawba. The late Alfred Nixon to whom we are all indebted for valued service in preserving our County history, stated that "the first pale face to set foot on Lincoln soil was John Beatty," who crossed the Catawba in 1749 at the ford which bears his name, and settled near the present Unity Presbyterian Church. We feel sure that when he made that statement he had in mind the present county of Lincoln and not the territory covered by the larger county as organized in 1779.

It is claimed by some that Henry Weidner (Whitener) came from Pennsylvania in 1742, while the *Colonial Record* states that he came about 1745.

The late Judge M. L. McCorkle, at a memorial service held at the original Weidner home in Catawba County, May 30, 1884, stated that Weidner came about 1745 and that he started west from Adam Sherrill's at Sherrill's Ford, without pilot or companion, to explore an unknown land inhabited by wild beasts and hostile savages. Going west from Sherrill's Ford he discovered the South Fork at the point where the two streams come together. He was armed with a gun, the barrel about six feet long, while a tomahawk and long knife were in the scabbard. Elsewhere Judge McCorkle stated that Henry Weidner, John Perkins, several Robinsons and others, came to Sherrill's Ford with Adam Sherrill, the pioneer, and the tradition is that Sherrill with his eight sons in company with John Perkins, the Robinsons, Weidner and others, crossed the Catawba at Sherrill's Ford in 1747.

John Beatty's land grant bears date July, 1749.

The first Sherrill grant is dated April 5, 1749, while the Weidner grant was issued in 1750.

The first settlers lived far from the County seat of Anson and for lack of neighbors had choice of the best lands which they occupied probably for some time prior to the dates given in their land grants. It matters little who came first. The records do not determine the fact but the Beattys, Sherrills and Weidners were certainly among the first to settle west of the Catawba River.

Volume 8 of *Colonial Records* states that Henry Weidner came from Pennsylvania about 1745 and settled on Henry River, named for him, that he lived at peace with his Indian neighbors and was a trapper. Later he went back to Pennsylvania, married to Mary Mull, and returned to Henry River with her and a youth named Conrad Yoder. These were certainly the first Dutch settlers in the larger Lincoln County.

Jacob Forney, another of the earlier pioneers, came in 1752, and then followed multitudes of new people, including the names of Johnston, Abernethy, McCorkle, McLean, Howard, Reid, Dickson, Munday, Thompson, Gabriel, Wilkinson, and later

Burton, Brevard, Graham, Fulenwider, Luckey, King, Cherry, Kincaid, Barclay, Brotherton, Lockman, Little, Cornelius, Shelton, Asbury, Nixon, Connor, Hager, Hutchison, Bell, Goodson, Ballard, Burch, Long, Proctor, Hayes, Paine, Lowe, Robinson, Rutledge, Moore, Chronicle, Hambright, Rankin, Jenkins, Henderson, Davenport and many other early settlers came, reaching along the eastern part from Lookout Shoals to the South Carolina line.

Then following Henry Weidner there came into the Central and Western portion of old Lincoln a steady stream of Dutch pioneers from Pennsylvania, among whom were the following families: Ramsour, Wilfong, Mull, Yoder, Schenck, Cansler, Hoke, Coon, Costner, Quickel, Shrum, Conrad, Rudisill, Finger, Seagle, Yount, Hoover, Killian, Loretz, Rhyne, Reinhardt, Lineberger, Hoffman, Carpenter, Miller, Friday, Rendleman, Shuford, Bandy, Dellinger, Houser, Motz, Setzer, Hauss, Heavner, Hoyle, Crouse, Sigmon, Lowrance, Rhodes, Cline, Stroupe, Reep, Coulter, Lutz, Boyd, Summerow, Smith and many others worthy and true, so that by 1775 there was a considerable population west of the Catawba. The County of Tryon was organized in 1769 and it was these people and those who came with them, who laid the foundations upon which we have builded, and it is their history that we would preserve, for if we should fail to write down their deeds, other people will not preserve them.

North Carolinians have always been modest, and when they chose the State motto, "Esse Quam Videri," which being interpreted means "to be, rather than seem to be," modesty and sincerity, two lofty virtues, have been woven warp and woof, into the character of our citizenship. While our people have done more than their share in all the struggles of the Nation, they have without boasting, left the results to posterity and our historians until recent years have been silent about their achievements. They preferred "to be, rather than seem to be," knowing that virtue is its own reward. We should, however, want to know where we came from and what were the characteristics of our forebears. We should not be so broad as to obliterate all local attachments. The land of our nativity should be dearest to us. North Carolina is the State and Lincoln County that part of the State to which we are most intimately related.

The pioneer settlers of this section were hardy and brave. Those who crossed the Catawba found no shelter but a wintry sky and the cold stars looked down pitilessly upon them as the howling wolves serenaded them through the lonely nights. We can never know the sacrifices those men made nor the suffering they endured, but the soil was watered by the tears and enriched by the graves of their women.

The primitive life of the pioneers in the wilderness and the privations and perils they were forced to endure developed in them the spirit of manly independence and self-reliance, which gave them a vision of human equality devoid of the caste spirit. The original settlers were in the main plain people, honest, conscientious and religious. In the old country they had been oppressed by the government and persecuted by the church, so that they braved the perils of the sea to find freedom in the western wilds. They were strong-minded and untrained but here they found opportunity for the development of their latent powers. There were no principal citizens, for every citizen was one. They were men of iron, with faith and fortitude. It is such as these that history should magnify. They hewed down the forests, developed the plains, fought our battles and taught their children to fear God, and to tell the truth. We can never pay these men and women the debt we owe for their love and sacrifice.

These pioneers, as Bancroft says: "Came from civilized life and scattered among forests; hermits with wives and children, resting upon the bosom of nature in perfect harmony with the wilderness and the gentle climate; careless of religious sects and unmolested by oppressive laws, they enjoyed liberty of conscience and personal independence, freedom of the forest and the river. The children of nature listened to the inspirations of nature. They desired no greater happiness than they enjoyed."

In the solitude of the wilderness they were self-dependent. When their rights were imperilled they resisted taxation without representation in the days which tried men's souls. They faced perils, endured suffering and conquered difficulties. They were apt scholars in the school of self-denial. They accepted a hard situation with the spirit that would put to shame the "tenderfoot" of the twentieth century, who, living in a period of extravagance and self-indulgence, knows nothing of sacrificial devotion to duty as the fathers did. When the hardy pioneers first crossed the Catawba, most probably in winter, they faced the pitiless elements with faith and courage, built rude cabins and lacked every comfort which their children have today. The furnishings were scant, and generally the cabin had but one room in which they cooked, ate, slept and entertained, and they lived on such food as the wilderness supplied. They had burned every bridge behind them. They were here to stay and fight back the savages, the wild beasts and the unkindly elements which were to be conquered before they could find peace and security.

On the journey from the far north they brought meagre supplies for they had only pack horses to carry the burdensome loads, and when they settled west of the Catawba, the cabins were built without nails, the cracks were daubed with mud, split slabs were used for roofing with stones to weight them down lest the roof be torn away by storm and wind, the doors were secured by wooden hinges and there was no glass for the windows. The houses were built in valleys close to the spring. They hewed down the forests, built rail fences to protect crops from cattle and hogs, worked through the long days and kept watch by night, lest prowling savages might do them violence.

The women endured hardships even greater than the men, for they helped to clear the forests and work the crops, and besides performed all the household duties. They not only cooked the food, made the meagre garments, patched them often until they were as many colored as Joseph's coat, but they worked the garden, milked the cows, washed the clothes, worked the cotton patch and then with their fingers separated the cotton from the seed, spun the cotton and wool into thread and wove the thread into cloth for garments and blankets. Indeed the women worked at all tasks and never complained. It must have been one of like experience who wrote the old couplet:

A man's work is from sun to sun,
But a woman's work is never done.

These pioneer women were strangers to the modern beauty parlor and had no need for one for the sign of health was written upon their faces. They lived so close to nature that their ruddy cheeks bespoke their health and vigor. They exercised the body, lived in the great out of doors, breathed invigorating air, basked in the life giving sunshine and had poor reason to use lip sticks or other superficial methods of converting ugliness into beauty. There were no stores, and fashion plates were never seen outside the seaport towns. The pioneers left the comforts of life to seek finally a better life.

On the frontier neighbors learned the meaning of neighborliness. They had log rollings, house raisings, corn shuckings and quilting parties, and those who refused to help in neighborly deeds lost caste. They were industrious and possessed varied gifts which served them well in their new environment. They had learned to work with their hands. There were blacksmiths, carpenters, cabinet makers, millwrights, tanners, shoemakers, saddlers, tailors, hatters, skilled workers in iron. These all worked their farms and also worked at their trades when needed. So the people were not only farmers but manufacturers from the start, and supplied their neighbors with such as they could produce by hand. Necessity being the mother of invention, it was wonderful how they found substitutes for many things. They used honey or sorghum for sugar, parched rye for coffee, ashes and waste grease combined were converted into soap. Corn and wheat were ground by hand and the people never heard of appendicitis.

Back of all their splendid traits there shone a radiant faith, for they brought the Church with them and never lost the habit of congregational worship. The Lutheran, German Reformed, Presbyterian and Baptist Churches were the first to be established, and later on the Episcopal and Methodist Churches all combined to preserve righteousness among the people. They had the Bible and worshipped God in the wilderness, "where the groves were God's first temples."

These first settlers were not ignorant people, even if, for lack of schools many of their children could not read. Many of the pioneers could write legibly and spell fairly well, but the children were busy at the task of keeping the wolf from the door, and had no teachers to instruct so that many really well to do, even as late as 1860, could not write their names.

CHAPTER II

1759-1774

1759. Uriah (Ute) Sherrill, of Rowan (later Lincoln) allowed 1 pound and 15 shillings for cows killed by Indians and for provisions going to war. C. R. 6-211-13.

1767. St. Thomas Parish was created west of the Catawba River but the country was too sparsely settled to make provision for a minister. C. R. 7-541.

1768. The Colonial Assembly of North Carolina in 1768 created a new county out of that part of Mecklenburg west of the Catawba River and South of the Earl of Granville line and named it Tryon County in honor of William Tryon who had been appointed Governor of the Province by the British Crown.

December 12, 1768. From a letter of Governor Tryon to Lord Hillsborough: "If South Carolina boundary line be changed as suggested, the South government boundary would take from this province, independent of what it would rob from Earl Granville's district, a tract of country, now Tryon County, of 45 miles in breadth, due North and South and 80 miles due East and West, it having been found that distance, from Catawba River to the Western boundary line, which was run last year between the Cherokee hunting grounds and this province." C. R. Vol. 7.

1768. That all taxes in the following counties: Anson, Mecklenburg, Orange, Rowan and Tryon be paid as in other counties of the province, and warehouses shall be erected in same. C. R. 8-xvi.

1768. Marriage: That every denomination of people may marry according to their respective mode. C. R. 8-xvi.

1769. Reward by the Assembly of 7 shillings, 6 pence for every wolf or panther killed.

1769. The poll tax was fixed at 6 pence. C. R. 23-784.

1769. The Assembly appointed Thomas Neel, Henry Clark, William Yancey, Daniel Warlick, Jacob Forney, John Gordon and William Watson Commissioners to contract for the building of court house, prison and stocks for Tryon County and to levy a tax of two shillings on each taxable poll to meet this expense.

1769. At the first session of the Tryon County court the record shows that Ezekiel Polk produced his commission as Clerk and John Tagart his commission as Sheriff and Alexander Martin was appointed Attorney for the Crown. It appears also that Waightstill Avery, John Quinn, Samuel Spencer and John Forsyth were present and were sworn in as Attorneys.

(Ezekiel Polk was the grandfather of James K. Polk, 11th President of the United States.)

According to Alfred Nixon the first session of the Tryon County Court was organized at the home of Charles McLean and the sessions for the years 1769, 1770 and 1771 were held in the McLean home; the sessions of 1772 at Christian Reinhardt's and those of 1773 and 1774 at Christian Carpenter's.

From Records in Office of Secretary of State

1769. At a council held at Newbern, November 10, 1769, it was ordered that the following be added to the Commission of Peace and dedimus for Tryon County: John Robeson, Francis Adams, George Blanton, John Thomas, Robert Ewart, Robert Blackburn, James McIntyre and Timothy Riggs, and that the chairman of the County Court be directed to insert the names of the several gentlemen above mentioned in the Commission of peace and dedimus in open court in the order they now stand. C. R. 8-149.

1769. At the October term of Court the Tryon County expenses for the year were reported to be L71—16s—10d, equivalent to about $355.00 of our money. There were 1,226 taxable polls in the County and tax assessment of three shillings, two pence was levied on each taxable person.

William Moore, Coroner of Tryon County was allowed forty shillings for holding inquest of John Gilmore as per account filed. C. R. 22-861.

The Assembly appointed and empowered William Moore to collect Tryon County taxes for 1768. C. R. 8-293.

1770. At the January term of the County Court Charles McLean, Zachary Bullock, Thomas Beatty and Ephraim McLean were presented with commissions as Captains of Tryon regular troops. At the April term commissions as Captains of Militia were presented to Andrew Hampton, Abram Kurkendall, Henry Clark and Joseph Green and for Lieutenants, to Patrick McDavid and Daniel Simpson; as Ensigns, to Perrygreen Magness and

THE ANNALS OF LINCOLN COUNTY

John Branson. Captain Robert Blackburn was assigned to regiment of foot soldiers, commanded by Thomas Neel.

The Assembly of 1770 appointed Thomas Neel, William Moore, Robert Adams, Ephraim McLean and John Beard, a new set of Commissioners to build a court house for Tryon County and were required to agree upon and select within three months a proper and convenient place whereon to erect court house and other buildings and to have the same completed within twelve months after the passage of this act. C. R. 8-344.

1771. In his autobiography, David Crockett states that he was born in Lincoln County, N. C. The following written by Alfred Nixon, April 2, 1912, confirms the above statement of Crockett.

Mr. Nixon wrote: "I find names in record of David and William Crockett as March 11, 1771, Thomas Yeates of Berkley County province of South Carolina conveyed to David Crockett of Tryon County, N. C., in consideration of 110 pounds current money of said province, 250 acres of land on south side of Catawba River, being part of a tract of land granted to John Killian, September 13, 1759."

1771. The Public of North Carolina indebted to Frederick Hambright for going against the Cherokee Indians to the express from the commanding officer of Tryon County, March 15, 1771.

	No. Days	Ration	Total Amt.
Frederick Hambright, Captain	8 @ 7s6d	5s4d	3- 5-4
John Hoyle, Lieutenant	8 @ 5s	5s4d	2- 5-4
James Cozart, Sergeant	8 @ 4s	5s4d	1-17-4
Andrew Hoyle, Sergeant	8 @ 4s	5s4d	1-17-4

Peter Conner, Jacob Rodes (Rhodes), Conrad Kinder, James Wyatt, Jacob Vanzant, Andrew Goforth, Richard Gullet, James French and Daniel McCarty, each 8 days @ 2s, rations—5s5d, total for each 1 pound 1s 4 pence.

I do hereby certify that the above Company of men were on the expedition by my orders under Captain Hambright.

(Signed) THOMAS NEEL.

This day came Frederick Hambright and made oath that the above account is just and true. Certified before me this 29 April, 1772.

(Signed) FREDERICK HAMBRIGHT.

(Witness) JACOB COSTNER.

1771. Petition presented by Presbyterians of Tryon County that authority be given to Presbyterian ministers to solemnize marriages. C. R. 23-80b.

1771. (Vol. 8-630-632). Petition of German Lutherans of Rowan County granted for Christopher Lyerly and Christopher Randleman to solicit aid for church work in the colony. (1772). C. R. 8-630-2.

Note: They went on horseback through the wilderness to Charleston and there sailed for Germany and brought back Rev. Adolphus Nussman to preach and John Gottfried Arndt to teach. Later Nussman ordained Arndt to the ministry and he became the pioneer Lutheran preacher in Tryon (now Lincoln) County, and when he died his sacred dust was buried beneath the Old White Church in Lincolnton.

1771. John Tygart, Sheriff, due 734 pounds and 7 shillings on taxes. C. R. 9-575.

1771. The assembly exempted William Logan and Robert Davis from public taxes and public duties. C. R. 9-145.

1772. Andrew Neel appointed Clerk of Inferior Court, Bond 1,000 pounds, signed by John Ritzhaupt and Thomas Neel, and witnessed by Robert Blackburn. C. R. 9-350.

1772. Ezekiel Polk was chosen Clerk and Thomas Neel Register, for Tryon County. C. R. 9-298.

1773. John Nuckles late under Sheriff. C. R. 9-502; 9-56.

1773. Commissioners appointed by the Assembly to build court house, jail and stocks for Tryon County. C. R. 9-760.

1773. John Tygart and Francis Adams, late Sheriffs. C. R. 9-477.

1773. Robert Blackburn, Assemblyman. C. R. 9-491.

1773 and 1774. William Moore and Christian Reinhardt. C. R. 9-734.

1773, February 23. Captain William Sherrill was allowed by the Assembly 27 pounds and 15 shillings for service rendered by himself and ten other men on expedition to Silver Creek and Quaker Meadows (located now in Burke County). C. R. 9-257. Compare C. R. 22-878.

In an earlier record is found a petition signed by the same William Sherrill, of Anson County (later Tryon and afterward

Lincoln) with others asking for a land grant of 600 acres for himself. (1752). C. R. 4-1014.

1774. The Provincial Congress met in Newbern, August 25, 1774. The delegates from Tryon were David Jenkins and Robert Alexander.

When the Assembly met in 1774, Tryon County was still without a court house, the Commissioners hitherto appointed having failed to agree upon the site for it, and William Moore, John Walker, Abram Kurkendall, Charles McLean, Christopher Carpenter and John Hill were appointed Commissioners with full authority to use all taxes collected for that purpose to build court house, jail and stocks at the point they may agree upon, and to levy additional tax if needed to complete the work.

The permanent county seat was not chosen until 1774 when the report following was approved by the Assembly:

"North Carolina,
Tryon County.

We, the Commissioners appointed by act of the Assembly, for laying and constituting and appointing the place whereon to erect and build the Court House, Prison and Stocks of Tryon County, having maturely considered and deliberated on the same, are of the opinion that the place called the "Cross Roads," on Christian Mauney's land, between the heads of Long Creek, Muddy Creek and Beaver Dam Creek in the county aforesaid, is most central and convenient, for the purpose aforesaid for the inhabitants of this county.

"Therefore, agreeable to the directions of the said act, we have and by these presents, do lay off, constitute and appoint the said place as the most proper whereon to erect and build the Court House, Prison and Stocks of the said County."

"As witness our hands and seals the 26th day of July, 1774.

(Signed)
CHARLES MCLEAN (SEAL)
WILLIAM MOORE (SEAL)
JOHN HILL (SEAL)
CHRISTOPHER CARPENTER (SEAL)

It seems that the building of the court house, prison and stocks was postponed indefinitely, as it was ordered that the county courts be held at the home of Christian Mauney at the "Cross Roads" on his land and space in his house was secured for a jail and the courts were held here until 1783 when the county seat was moved to Lincolnton.

The old County Court of Pleas and Quarter sessions obtained in all the Counties of the Province. It was presided over by three Justices of the Peace. It was continued as the County Court in North Carolina after the Revolution until the adoption of the Constitution of 1868. The duties of that Court are now performed by the Recorders Court, the Clerk of the Superior Court and the County Commissioners. It appears from the Records that licenses were granted by this Court to William Wray, James Patterson, John Dellinger and Henry Dellinger to keep hotels or inns, then known by the name of Ordinary, and the prices to be charged for entertainment at such public houses were fixed by law. A specimen of the prices fixed is as follows:

Lodging in good feather bed and clean sheets per night....4 pence
Breakfast and supper, each..3 pence
Every dinner with not less than two dishes of meat......1 shilling
Pasturage for horse or mare for 24 hours......................4 pence
Stabling per night, hay and fodder for horse or mare......1 shilling
Maderia or Port Wine, per quart..................................3 shillings
Claret Wine, per quart..4 shillings
Punch and loaf sugar and West India rum, per
 quart ....1 shilling, 6 pence
Toddy and loaf sugar..1 shilling, 4 pence
Toddy with New England rum..8 pence
Brandy and whiskey toddy, per quart..............................8 pence
Beer, per quart..4 pence
Cider, per quart..6 pence
West India rum, per ½ pint ....10 pence
New England rum, per ½ pint..6 pence
Brandy or whiskey, per ½ pint..6 pence

As shown by the records, roads in different directions from Tryon Court House were ordered to be built or laid out as follows:

1. "Ordered by the Court that Christy Carpenter, Lawrence Kiser, Jacob Ramsour, Adolphus Reep and John Eaker be appointed Commissioners to lay out and mark a road from Burke County line to Ramsour's Mill, and from there, the nearest and best way to Tryon County Court House.

2. "Ordered that William Moore, Abram Scott, Zack Spencer, Fred Hambright, Michael Hoyle, Thomas Costner, Jacob Mauney, Peter Laboon, Michael Huffstetler and John Hoyle to be a jury to lay out and mark a road, the nearest and best way from Tryon Court House to Tuckaseege Ford.

3. "Ordered that Christy Mauney be appointed overseer of the road from Tuckaseege to Tryon Court House as far as Peter Laboon's, and Peter Laboon from his house to the South Fork river and Samuel Martin from the Forks to the Tuckaseege Ford.

4. "Ordered that Henry Dellinger be appointed overseer of the road leading from Tryon Court House to Beatty's Ford."

(This site of Tryon County Court House is about five miles North of Bessemer City on the highway leading from Bessemer to Cherryville.)

District Court in Salisbury June 1, 1775. The jurors from Tryon were William Moore, Fred Hambright, Moses Moore, William Gilbert, James McIntire, John McKinney, James Johnston and Abram Kerkindall. C. R. 10-1.

Moses Moore and William Gilbert were grandjurors.

1775. "North Carolina,

"Tryon County.

"Committee of Public Safety, Tryon County, proceedings:

"Organization.

"At a meeting of the freeholders of the County of Tryon at the Court House of said County on 26th July, 1775, in order to select a Committee for said County, the following persons were chosen, to-wit:

"Military Committees elected: Captain Beatty's Co.: Thomas Beatty, David Jenkins, James Johnston, Jacob Forney; Captain Carpenter's Co.: Thomas Espey, Nicholas Friday, Valentine Mauney; Captain Hardin's Co.: Joseph Hardin, Benjamin Hardin, Davis Whitesides; Captain Coburn's Co.: James Coburn, Robert Alexander; Captain Hambright's Co.: Fred Hambright, James Logan; Captain Hampton's Co.: Andrew Hampton, John Morris, George Russell; Captain Magness' Co.: Perigreen Magness, William Graham, George McAfee; Captain Paris' Co.: George Paris, Ambrose Mills; Captain Aaron Moore's Co.: John Walker, John Beeman, George Black; Captain Baird's Co.: James Baird, Andrew Neel, William Patterson; Captain McKinney's Co.: John McKinney, Jonas Bedford; Captain Kuykendall's Co.: Abram Kuykendall, William Thompson, Robert McMinn; Captain Barber's Co.: John Barber, Charles McLean, John Robeson."

(See Vol. 10-120 and 124 for Military Committees).

1775. Representatives from Tryon County to Provincial Congress at Hillsboro August 20, 1775: John Walker, Robert Alexander, Joseph Hardin, William Graham, Fred Hambright and William Kennon. C. R. 10-166.

1775. August 14. Tryon County Safety Committee—Minutes: Met according to adjournment. Present John Walker, Chairman, Thomas Beatey, David Jenkins, Jacob Forney, Thomas Espey, Valentine Mauney, James Coburn, Robert Alexander, Joseph Harden, Benjamin Harden, Fredk Hambright, James Logan, Andrew Hampton, John Morris, Charles McLean, John Robison, William Graham, Jas. McFee, George Paris, John Beeman, George Black, Andrew Neel, James Baird and Davis Whitesides, who took the necessary oaths for their qualification.

Resolved that Colonel Chas. McLean serve as Deputy Chairman in the absence of Col. Walker.

Resolved that Each Company elect three members of Committee for this County who on a Debate are each man to have his vote.

Resolved that this association be Signed by the Inhabitants of Tryon County.

An Association

The unprecedented, barbarous and bloody actions committed by the British Troops on our American Brethren near Boston on the 19th of April and 20th of May last, together with the Hostile operations and Traiterous Designs now Carrying on by the Tools of Ministerial Vengeance and Despotism for the subjugating all British America, suggest to us the painful necessity of having recourse to Arms for the preservation of those Rights and Liberties which the principles of our Constitution and the Laws of God, Nature and Nations, have made it our duty to defend.

We, therefore, the Subscribers, Freeholders and Inhabitants of Tryon County do hereby faithfully unite ourselves under the most sacred ties of Religion, Honor and Love to Our Country, firmly to Resist force by force, in defense of our Natural Free-

Signers of Tryon Association—August 14, 1775.

dom and Constitutional Rights against all Invasions, and at the same time do solemnly engage to take up Arms and Risque our lives and fortunes in maintaining the Freedom of our Country, whenever the Wisdom and Council of the Continental Congress or our Provincial Convention shall declare it necessary, and this Engagement we will continue in and hold sacred till a Reconciliation shall take place between Great Britain and America on Constitutional principles, which we most ardently desire.

And we do firmly agree to hold all such persons Inimical to the liberties of America, who shall refuse to subscribe to this Association. Signed by:

John Walker
Charles M'Lean
Andr Neel
Tomas Beatty
James Cobun
Frederick Hambright
Andr Hampton
Benjamin Hardin
George Pearis
William Graham
Robt. Alexander
David Jenkins
Thomas Espey
Perygren Mackness
James McAfee
William Thomason
Jacob Farny (Forney)
Davis Whiteside
John Beeman
John Morris
Joseph Hardin
John Robinson
Vallentine Mauny
George Black
Jas. Logan

Jas. Baird
Christan Carpinter
Abel Beatty
Jacob Turner
Jonathan Price
Jas. Miller
Petter Sides
William Whitesides
John Dellinger
Georg Dellinger
Samuel Karbender (Carpenter)
Jacob Moony Junr
John Wells
Jacob Castner (Costner)
Robert Haselip
Fried Mauser
James Buchanan
Moses Moore
Joseph Kuykendal
Adam Sims
Richd Walker
Samuel Smith
Joseph Neel
Samuel Lofton

Resolved *nem con* that we will continue to profess all Loyalty and attachment to our Sovereign Lord, King George the Third, His Crown & Dignity, so long as he secures to us those Rights and Liberties which the principles of Our Constitution require.

* * * *

Signed by JOHN WALKER, *Chairman.* C. R. 10-161-3.

Tablet placed at home site of Christian Mauney and Tryon Court House, 5 miles north of Bessemer City on road to Cherryville.

> "HOME OF CHRISTIAN MAUNEY
> PIONEER AND PATRIARCH, 1770
>
> SITE OF TRYON COURT HOUSE
> 1774-1783
>
> Camp of Lord Cornwallis and British Army
> January 23, 1781
>
> Erected by descendants of Christian Mauney and their friends
> 1919
>
> W. A. MAUNEY, *Chairman*."

The bronze plate on reverse side of the monument contains the following:

"Here, in August, 1775, was formulated and signed the Tryon Declaration of Rights and Independence from British Tyranny. The following were signers."

Then appear the names of 48 signers, including also, the name of James McEntire.

"Tablet Contributed by Col. Frederick Hambright Chapter D. A. R., 1919."

CHAPTER III

1775-1779

1775. The Tryon County Committee of Public Safety spoke on August 14, 1775, in plain and patriotic protest against British tyranny and a bronze tablet with the names of the heroic signers should be placed on the wall of the Lincoln County Court room to perpetuate the patriotic stand they took on that historic day.

1775. William Moore and William Alston were the Assemblymen from Tryon in 1775. C. R. 9-1189.

1775. Aquilla Sherrill, Constable was in court and released of fine imposed at last court. C. R. 10-3.

September, 1775. William Graham was elected Colonel, Charles McLean, Lt. Colonel, Thomas Beatty, 1st Major and Frederick Hambright, 2nd Major, of Tryon County.

September 14, 1775. The Committee of Public Safety met according to adjournment. Present: Charles McLean, Chairman; Thomas Espey, Fetty Mauney, Frederick Hambright, Geo. Russell, John Morris, Robert McMinn, Abram Kurkendall, John Robinson, John Barber, George Black, James Logan, James McAfee, Andrew Neel, Andrew Hampton, William Thompson, Nicholas Friday, Benjamin Hardin and Perrygreen Mackness.

Captain Andrew Hampton was authorized to apply to the Council of Safety at Charleston for what gunpowder, lead and flints as can be bought with 8 pounds, 17 shillings and 6 pence, proclamation money of North Carolina for the protection of those living on the frontiers of Tryon County, against attacks of savage Indians. C. R. 9-647.

1776, January. Safety Committee in Tryon County met according to adjournment. Present: William Graham, Chairman; and Andrew Hampton, George Paris, Robert Parks, Robert Alexander, Robert Porter, Alexander Gilliland, John McKinney, John Ashley, Thomas Townsend, William Yancey, Frederick Hambright, Joseph Hardin. Resolved, that no person or persons of the County of Tryon, shall sell or dispose of Salt, Iron or Steel to any person within the County for more than two hundred per cent from the first Cost purchased in Charles Town, Cross Creek or port where salt is to be got, upon the forfeit of paying Ten Shillings Proc. Money for every Twenty Shillings worth they shall sell or dispose of contrary to this Resolve.

Resolved that no person or persons shall bring us Rum from any place into this County and sell it for more than Eight Shillings per Gallon. Such persons as have license to Retail Liquors only excepted. C. R. 10-424.

January, 1776. William Graham, James Logan, Frederick Hambright, Robert Alexander, Robert Parks, Alexander Gilliland and David Jenkins were appointed a Committee of Secrecy. C. R. 10-424.

1776. The Tryon County Militia System was reorganized on account of promotions and other causes and Thomas Beatty was elected Colonel; Andrew Hampton, Lt. Colonel; Andrew Long, 1st Major, and Jacob Costner, 2nd Major.

1776, January. Safety Committee of Tryon County met according to adjournment. Present: William Graham, Chairman; and Andrew Hampton, George Paris, Robert Parks, Robert Alexander, Robert Porter, Alexander Gilliland, John McKinney, John Ashley, Thomas Townsend, Wm. Yancey, Frederick Hambright, Joseph Hardin. It was

RESOLVED, That no person or persons of the County of Tryon shall sell or dispose of Salt, Iron or Steel to any person within the County for more than Two hundred per cent from the first Cost, purchased in Charles Town, Cross Creek, or port where salt is to be got, upon the forfeit of paying Ten Shillings Proc. Money for every Twenty Shillings worth they shall sell or dispose of contrary to this Resolve.

RESOLVED, That no person or persons shall bring us Rum from any place into this County and sell it for more than eight shillings per Gallon . . . Such persons as have License to Retail Liquors only excepted. C. R. 10-424.

1776. William Grimes and Robert Alexander were appointed to procure and purchase fire arms for the use of troops. C. R. 10-525.

1776. Tryon County Militia elected by Halifax Convention William Graham, Colonel; Thomas Beatty, Lt. Colonel; Andrew Hampton, 1st Major; Jacob Costner, 2nd Major. C. R. 10-532.

1776. George Wilfong was elected 2nd Major of the Second Regiment of Rowan troops. C. R. 10-532.

1776. Delegates from Tryon to Halifax Convention, November, 1776, were Joseph Hardin, Robert Abernethy, William Graham, William Alston and John Barber. C. R. 10-915.

1776. John Sevier, Samuel Sherrill, Adam Sherrill and 150 other petitioners to the Assembly, asked that they be annexed to the Carolina Province.

THE ANNALS OF LINCOLN COUNTY 25

These petitioners lived in the Watauga Valley in what is now East Tennessee. (1772.)

1776. Joseph Hardin, Captain of Company of Light horse of Tryon on Cherokee expedition was allowed 789 pounds on his claim. C. R. 10-949.

1776. Charles McLean and James Johnston, of Tryon, took their seats in Provincial Congress. C. R. 10-556.

1777. Tryon County Jurors at Salisbury Court, March, 1777, Samuel Spencer, Judge, and Adlai Osborne, Clerk, were: George Lambkin, Sr., James McFadden, William Cronakle, John Hoyle, Richard Singleton, John Hill, John Stanford and Jacob Costner. Matthew Locke was Foreman of grand jury and George Lambkin, Sr., and Jacob Costner were grand jurors from Tryon County. S. R. 22-502.

1777. Charles McLean was Senator from Tryon in 1777. S. R. 12-2. James Johnston and John Barber, the Assemblymen.

1778. William Graham was the Senator and William Gilbert and Joseph Hardin, Assemblymen from Tryon County in 1778.

1778. A call was made by the Assembly for troops; 83 was the quota for Tryon County. S. R. 13-411.

1778. Tryon County was ordered to furnish army with 55 hats; 231 yards linen; 110 yards woolen cloth; 110 pairs shoes and 110 pairs stockings. S. R. 12-639.

1778. Petition to the Assembly for the creation of a new County west of the Catawba River, signed by Francis McCorkle, Moses Sherrill, and others. S. R. 13-352-3.

1779. Roll of Company of Lt. Col. W. L. Davidson, April 23, 1779. Pension office, Book entitled "North Carolina," not paged. Copied from Orderly book of Sergeant Isaac Rowel.

Edward Yarborough, 1st Lt.; Reuben Wilkinson, 2nd Lt. Among privates were Adam Brevard, William Wilkinson; Sergeant Isaac Rowel, Sergeant John Godwin, Sergeant John Horton; Corporal Dempsey Johnson, Corporal Jesse Baggett, Corporal James Tharp.

James Goodson died in hospital at New Windsor.

Peter Valentine died in hospital in Philadelphia. S. R.14-294.

1778. At the next session of the Assembly (1778) Tryon County was abolished and the Counties of Lincoln and Rutherford erected out of the Tryon territory.

Samuel Lambkin, Benjamin Hardin, John Walker and Jonathan Gullick were appointed as Commissioners to run the dividing line between the new counties agreeable to the act creating the counties.

Benjamin Hardin, Thomas Welch, John Earls, Abram Kurkendall and John Potts were appointed Commissioners to lay off the site for court house, jail and stocks.

The fires of discontent among the people of the west began prior to 1773 and grew to be a conflagration by August, 1775, when patriotic citizens of Tryon County assembled at Tryon Court house, adopted resolutions which the powers that be could not misunderstand, protesting against the policy of the British as cruel and unjust, and provision was made to resist oppressive laws and taxes. This spirit grew throughout the Colony until April 1776 the people of North Carolina in Convention assembled at Halifax, declared themselves independent of British rule and joined the other Colonies in the war for complete independence. The name of William Tryon, the Royal Governor was held in derision and in 1778 the Assembly abolished the County (Tryon) which bore his name and established in place of it two new counties, Lincoln and Rutherford.

1779. William Gilbert expelled from Assembly for intentionally defrauding the public by passing sundry erroneous accounts in former sessions of the Assembly. (These charges were later proved to be groundless.) C. R. 16-707.

1779. Col. Charles McLean writing from Crowders Mountain in Tryon County early in February 1779, reported on information that John Moore, a Tory, had raised 300 men and claimed it would grow to 2,000. To quell insurrection 2,000 militia and 750 light horse were called out to meet in Salisbury. Gen. Rutherford being absent in South Carolina, Matthew Locke was appointed General of the Salisbury district pro tempore. C. R. 14-611.

1779. In another letter written by Col. Charles McLean to the Assembly and dated Feb. 6, 1779, he stated that John Moore and his troops robbed Timothy Riggs of all his horses, saddles, etc., and robbed Robert McMann of saddle, gun and other valuables. C. R. 14-261.

1779. Order was given in favor of Robert Alexander, Commissioner of Tryon County, for 100 bushels of salt. C. R. 14-470.

1779. The officers of Tryon County from its organization to the establishment of Lincoln County were:
1. Clerks of County Court:
   April, 1769, to October, 1772.............................Ezekiel Polk
   October, 1772, to April, 1776.........................Andrew Neel
   April, 1776, to July, 1777..........................William Graham
   July, 1777, to April, 1780.............................Andrew Neel
2. Sheriffs:
   April, 1769, to April, 1771..........................John Taggart
   April, 1771, to April, 1773..........................Francis Adams
   April, 1773, to July, 1777...........................Jacob Costner
   July, 1777, to July, 1778............................James Holland
   July, 1778 ....James Miller
3. Public Registers:
   October, 1771, to October, 1772...................Thomas Neel
   October, 1772, to July, 1777........................Andrew Neel
   July, 1777, to April, 1779..................Jonathan Hampton
4. Coroners:
   January, 1770, to April, 1773...................William Moore
   January, 1773, to January, 1778..................John Walker
   January, 1778, to January, 1779..................James White
   January, 1779 ....Thomas Espey

The complete list of representatives from Tryon County to the Colonial Assembly follows:
1769. William Moore and Thomas Neel.
1770. William Moore and Thomas Neel.
1771. William Moore and Thomas Neel.
1773. Robert Blackburn.
1773-74. William Moore and Christian Reinhardt.
1775. William Moore and William Alston.
1777. Charles McLean, Senator; James Johnston and John Barber, Assemblymen.
1778. William Graham, Senator; William Gilbert and Joseph Hardin, Assemblymen.
1779. Robert Abernethy.

To the Provincial Congress:
   August, 1774, David Jenkins and Robert Alexander.
   April, 1775—
   August, 1775, John Walker, Robert Alexander, Joseph Hardin, William Graham, Fred Hambright and William Kennon.

To Halifax Convention:
April, 1776, Charles McLean and James Johnston.
November, 1776, Joseph Hardin, Robert Abernethy, William Graham, William Alston and John Barber.

According to Tryon County Court Records, the following were Justices of the Peace between the years of 1769 and 1778, because they appear as Justices present at various meetings of the County Courts:

Thomas Neel, William Moore, William Watson, William Twitty, John Retzhough, Jacob Costner, James McLean, Henry Clark, Jonas Bedford, John Gordon, John Walker, Henry Holman, Robert Harris, David Anderson, Francis Adams, Robert Blackburn, George Blanton, John Robeson, James McEntire, Timothy Riggs, John Thomas, James McElwaine, Alex Gilliland, John Sloan, John Moore, Robert Alexander, Jonathan Gullick, James McAfee, Jonathan Hampton, John McKinney, James Logan, James Johnston, Francis Quinn, Ezekiel Polk, Jacob Randall, Thomas Espey, Joseph Hardin, Charles McLean, William Graham, George Lambkin, William Yancey, Robert Johnston, Frederick Hambright, Valentine Mauney, George Black, Davis Whitesides and William Neville.

CHAPTER IV

1779-1780
LINCOLN COUNTY

Lincoln County, named for Gen. Benjamin Lincoln, a hero of the American Revolution, was established out of a part of Tryon County, by the General Assembly at Halifax, in January, 1779. Tryon was abolished and Lincoln and Rutherford Counties organized out of its territory, according to the act, to make it easier for its inhabitants in its remote parts to perform public duties, but another reason was to eliminate the name of Royal Governor, William Tryon, whose record was odious to the patriots of the Revolution.

The General Assembly named Sampson Lambkin, Benjamin Hardin, John Walker, Jonathan Gullett, as Commissioners, to run the dividing line between the newly organized Counties. The Justices of Tryon were continued in these positions in their respective counties, without new commissions.

Further, Christopher Carpenter, Valentine Mauney, James Reid, John Patrick and William Grimes were commissioned to buy 100 acres of land in the most central and convenient part of Lincoln, for a court house, prison and stocks, and to contract for the erection of same and to pay for these buildings, an additional tax for two years of two shillings on the 100 pounds value of taxable property, and one shilling on every free man was levied. The money previously raised for the Tryon court house and jail was ordered divided between Lincoln and Rutherford. A bill introduced that year by William Graham, the Senator, to establish a county seat town on lands of Valentine Mauney, failed to pass.

The County was assigned to the Salisbury Superior Court district. The County Court for several years was held at old Tryon court house.

In December, 1782, the General Assembly added part of Burke to Lincoln County and named Daniel McKissick, Henry Thompson, James Lytle, John Dickson, John Wilson, John Caruth, Frederick Hambright and Nicholas Friday, Commissioners, to fix a place for the court house for Lincoln County, and levied a tax of six pence specie on each 100 pounds value of property for two years. In 1783 the courts were held upstairs at the home of Christian Mauney, 9 miles southwest of Lincolnton; in 1784, at the homes of Nicholas Friday and Henry Dellinger, east of Lincolnton.

In 1784, the General Assembly established a new boundary line between Burke and Lincoln and appointed Joseph Dickson, John Caruth, John Wilson, Joseph Steele and Nicholas Friday, to buy 100 acres of land "as near the center of the county as may be and to contract with proper workmen to build a court house, prison and stocks thereon." The Commissioners acted and early in 1784, the Assembly set forth in an Act that they had entered 300 acres of vacant and unappropriated land between the lines of Phillip Kanceller (Cansler) and Christian Reinhardt, and had laid off 50 acres for a town and sold lots. This site the Assembly "established into a town which shall be called Lincolnton." Joseph Dickson and the other Commissioners named in 1784 were continued as "Town Trustees and Directors."

The Commissioners reserved an acre of land for the court house and jail and in 1785 these buildings were erected of logs. In 1788, a new frame court house was built, the space between the planks being filled with earth. The outside was painted red and was known as the "red court house." It was removed in 1810, and a third court house erected in its place. This building was abandoned about 1855, when a structure of brick and stone of attractive design was built and used until 1923 when the present handsome court house, built of concrete and stone, was erected on the same site at a cost of about $225,000.00.

The original Wills and Deeds and the County Court Minutes all begin in 1769 for Tryon, and 1779 for Lincoln County.

The first United States census, taken in 1790, gave the county 1405 heads of white families. The census was taken by the Militia districts (now called townships) 12 in number, covering the country which then embraced the present counties of Catawba, Gaston, Lincoln and half of Cleveland County.

(The above information was largely supplied by Col. Fred A. Olds, of Raleigh.)

On January 11, 1841, the General Assembly finally passed the bill signed by Andrew Joyner, Speaker of the Senate, and Robert B. Gilliam, Speaker of the House of Commons, creating the County of Cleaveland, from parts of Rutherford and Lincoln Counties. It was named in honor of Benjamin Cleaveland, a brave soldier of the Revolution who took part in the battle of

Kings Mountain, October 7, 1780. The bill reads that "Cleaveland County is to be composed of parts of the counties of Rutherford and Lincoln, beginning at a point in the South Carolina line and running a north course so as to tap within 14 miles east of Rutherfordton until it strikes the Burke County line; thence with the dividing line of Burke and Rutherford to the Lincoln line; thence to the 13-mile post on the Lucas ford road; thence to the 12-mile post on the new post road leading from Rutherford to Lincolnton; thence to the 12-mile post leading from Lincolnton to Quinn's ferry; thence to the 12-mile post leading from Morganton to Yorkville (S. C.); thence with the road tapping Abernethy's store by the Gold Mine at Kings Mountain to the South Carolina line, then with it to the beginning.

The bill provided also that "Robert H. Burton, Alexander McCorkle, Henry Cansler, Eli Hoyle, Ed Bryant, Achilles Durham, John McDowell, Samuel Andrews and David Gray, be a committee to designate some point in said county of Cleaveland, not more than four miles from Thomas Wilson's mineral springs (now Cleaveland Springs) which shall be the county seat of said County," and the site of the present town of Shelby (named for Isaac Shelby, another hero of Kings Mountain) was selected for the county seat, by the aforesaid commissioners appointed to locate same.

This left Lincoln a large county, the majority of the inhabitants lived far from the county seat with poor highways and many of the citizens wanted to divide the county. Nathaniel Wilson, one of the leaders of the new county movement, was elected to the House of Commons on that issue in 1842. The Lincolnton opposition to Wilson aroused his ire and he advocated division line to run through the center of the town of Lincolnton when Catawba County was established in 1842. A compromise resulted in the placing of the boundary line one mile north of Lincolnton, and it remained so until Gaston County was organized in 1846, when the southern boundary of Catawba was moved five miles north of Lincolnton and the northern boundary of Gaston five miles south of Lincolnton, leaving the present County of Lincoln ten miles wide and thirty miles long. Gaston was named for Judge William Gaston and the county seat for George M. Dallas, at that time Vice-President of the United States.

Catawba County, as well as the Catawba River, was named for the Catawba tribe of Indians. Newton, the county seat, was named for Sir Isaac Newton, the philosopher.

The three counties voted together for members of the General Assembly after the division, until 1854, when they voted separately for members of the House of Commons.

Jacob Forney the pioneer was born in Alsace about 1721 and came with his wife Maria Bergner to what is now Lincoln County in 1754.

Joseph Dickson, the patriot, was born in Chester County, Pa., in April, 1745.

John Beatty, the pioneer, in 1749, crossed the Catawba at the ford which bears his name and Alfred Nixon said he was the first white settler in the present county of Lincoln.

Col. Frederick Hambright was born in Germany. He came to North Carolina about 1755 and was a gallant soldier at Kings Mountain where Col. Patrick Ferguson, the commander of the British troops was killed October 8, 1780.

Adam Sherrill, the pioneer, with his eight sons, and John Perkins, Henry Weidner and several Robinsons crossed the Catawba at Sherrill's Ford and were among the first settlers west of the Catawba River.

Col. James Johnston, son of Henry Johnston, the pioneer, was born in 1742, and came with his parents to this section in 1755.

Rev. Humphrey Hunter, the patriotic soldier and pioneer Presbyterian preacher, was born in Ulster County, Ireland, May 14, 1755.

Gentleman John Perkins who came to this section with Adam Sherrill in 1747 was born, (son of Elisha Perkins) in Virginia, September 15, 1733, and died in Burke County, N. C., Friday morning, April 13, 1804, at five minutes of seven o'clock. His daughter, Mary Perkins, married to Rev. Robert Johnson Miller, the pioneer Episcopal preacher, who was generally called "Parson" Miller. John Perkins is the forebear of a long line of notable descendants, many of whom lived in Burke, Caldwell and Lincoln Counties.

Peter Hoyle, the pioneer was born in Germany, May 14, 1710, married to Catherine Dales April 7, 1736, came to America, landing in Philadelphia, September 11, 1738. Later he came to North

Carolina, crossed the Catawba about 1747 and settled at Hoylesville about three miles east of the present town of Dallas, where he entered 770 acres of land on South Fork River. He reared a large family there and died in 1761.

Robert Johnston Miller was born in Angusshire, Scotland, July 11, 1758. Came when quite young to Charlestown, Mass., where his elder brother was a merchant. He was a soldier of the Revolution. Later he became identified with the Methodists and accompanied Bishop Coke to Franklin County, N. C., when the Conference was held at the home of Green Hill. Some years after he became a Lutheran minister and finally took orders in the Protestant Episcopal Church and was the pioneer preacher of that denomination in Lincoln and Burke counties. He was ordained to the priesthood in Raleigh in May, 1821, when about 63 years old. He married a daughter of Gentleman John Perkins, the pioneer, and has many descendants in Western Carolina.

James Connor was born in Ireland in 1754, and his brother, Henry Connor (Senior) in 1758.

General Peter Forney was born in what is now Lincoln County on April 21, 1756, son of Jacob and Maria Bergner Forney.

Major William Chronicle, the brave soldier who gave his life for his country in the battle of Kings Mountain, was born in what is now Gaston County, about 1755.

Dr. William McLean was born in Rowan April 2, 1757.

Major Abram Forney who fought at Ramsour's Mill and Kings Mountain was born in the present County of Lincoln in 1758.

Gen. Joseph Graham, a distinguished citizen of Lincoln, was born in Pennsylvania October 13, 1759.

William Rankin, a patriot of the Revolution, was born in Pennsylvania January 10, 1761. Married to Mary Moore, sister of General John Moore. Col. Richard Rankin, late of Gaston County was a son of that marriage.

Capt. Alexander Brevard, one of the early settlers of Lincoln County, was born in April, 1755.

1779—Colonial Records—Lincoln County

Bill introduced to create Lincoln and Rutherford Counties out of Tryon County, 1778. (Vol. 24: 236-238.)

That the Counties of Rutherford and Lincoln shall be considered a part of the Salisbury district and the County Court of each shall appoint three jurors to attend the General Court at Salisbury. (Vol. 24: 235-238).

Jurors failing to attend court to be fined 200 pounds unless good cause is shown by next court why they failed to attend. Jurors allowed $10.00 for every day they shall attend or travel to and from court. (Vol. 24: 273.)

October 19, 1779. Bill introduced by Senator William Graham to annex a part of Burke to Lincoln and it passed Senate and was sent to the House of Commons and passed.

October 22, 1779. A petition was received from County Court of Lincoln that Samuel Elder was a proper person to be exempted from taxation.

November 20, 1779. The bill introduced by William Graham to establish in Lincoln County a town on lands of Valentine Mauney was rejected by the House.

1779. Manuscript Records in the office of the Secretary of State, Raleigh.

At a County Court of Pleas and Quarter Sessions was begun and held for the County of Lincoln on Monday, the 19th day of April, 1779, before the Worshipful James Johnston, Thomas Espey and Robert Alexander, Justices of the County aforesaid, it was ordered that George Pee, an inhabitant of the said county, a very poor infirm man, be recommended to the General Assembly of this State as a proper subject to be exempted from the payment of taxes. (Vol. 14: 292.)

(Signed) ANDREW MCNEEL, C. C.

Excerpt from a letter from Col. Thomas Wade written from Salisbury, to Gov. Nash, complains of Tories who he classes as foragers and rioters, endangering the welfare of the people of the Counties of Anson, Rowan, Surry, Burke, Rutherford and Lincoln. In Lincoln he states that a large body of them are on South Fork of Catawba. He urges the appointment of Judge Spencer to hold courts in those counties in the hope that their depradations on farms and stores might be stopped. (Vol. 14: 865.)

See Vol. 14: 685, for letter of Gen. William Davidson to Gen. Jethro Sumner on Battle of Kings Mountain.

Upon the division of Tryon County all the County records fell to the new County of Lincoln.

In April, 1779, at the first session of the County Court of Lincoln, John Wilson was elected to the office of Register.

CHAPTER V

THE BATTLE OF RAMSOUR'S MILL

The years were long and dreary even to the hardy pioneers, from 1770 to the end of the American Revolution. The differences which separated the Whigs and Tories developed a bitterness which continued for many years after the long war, but time, the great healer has drawn all the factions together. Among the Dutch there had been a strong Tory element, but at the same time, a vigorous and determined party of Whigs. When, in August, 1775, at Tryon court house the resolutions of protest against British tyranny were adopted, Jacob Forney, Valentine and Jacob Mauney, Christopher Carpenter, James Miller, John and George Dellinger, Samuel Carpenter, Jacob Costner, Adam Sides and others were strong advocates of independence and among the brave men who fought at Ramsour's Mill and Kings Mountain were Peter and Abram Forney, Adam and Michael Reep, John Wilfong, Jacob and John Hoffman, Thomas Costner, Peter Eddleman, William Elmore, Casper Bolick, Martin Coulter, Mitchel Cline, Jacob Plonk, Peter Shrum and many others who braved every peril to establish independence.

There were many of the Dutch, however, who, conservative by nature, were opposed to the war, counted prudence the better part of valor and were slow to take up arms against Britain because they felt ours to be a losing cause, with after effects more intolerable than the galling tyranny we were so anxious to throw off.

When early in 1780 the Tories captured the City of Charleston, and were hastening to wipe out rebellion in the South, it was Col. John Moore (son of Moses Moore who lived about six miles west of Ramsour Mill) and Major Welch, of the British Army who came up from South Carolina and persuaded these Dutch Loyalists that Washington's troops were without supplies and would soon be completely conquered, and to make sure the early defeat of the Whigs, that the local Tories join in with the British then in South Carolina to end the war. The result was that on June 13, 1780, about 200 local Tories were assembled at Ramsour's Mill to make ready for military service. This number by June 20 increased to 1,300 men. The very next day this important news reached the ears of Gen. Rutherford who forthwith sent word to Col. Francis Locke, of Rowan, to gather forces to disperse these Tories. Whereupon Col. Locke organized some 400 men from Rowan, Mecklenburg and Lincoln to join with Gen. Rutherford against the group located at Ramsour's Mill.

Gen. Rutherford on June 19, encamped with about 1,000 men at Col. Dickson's, two miles west of the present town of Mt. Holly, and sent a message to Col. Locke, who with his force was in camp on Mountain Creek, 20 miles away. Rutherford sent word for Locke to join him at Dickson's while Locke sent word to Rutherford that he would proceed to Ramsour's Mill on the 19th, but neither received the message. So Locke on the night of June 19, marched some fifteen miles to a point near the Tory camp, where the troops were met by Adam Reep, a local patriot, who made known to Locke the lay of the land and the strength and courage of the enemy.

With Reep for a guide, at daylight they approached the battle field from the east side. The fog was so thick they could not see over 50 feet ahead and the struggle began with heavy firing by the cavalry companies of Captains Brandon, Falls and McDowell that preceded the footmen on the march. The suddenness of the attack dumbfounded the Tories at the start but they rallied and fought bravely until the end of the battle which was concluded in less than two hours, according to Abram Forney, one of the Whig soldiers, when the Tories fled down the hill toward Ramsour's Mill located on Clark's Creek below.

It was a signal victory for the Whigs, who with 400 men overcame the 1,300 Tories. It was a desperate struggle, neighbor against neighbor, and brother against brother, and at times a hand to hand battle which resulted in 70 killed, equally divided between the two armies; with 100 wounded and the capture of 50 Tories. They wore no uniforms. The only way to distinguish the troops was by the white paper pinned on hats of the Whigs and green twigs on hats of the Tories. The Whig officers killed were Captains Falls, Knox, Dobson, Smith, Bowman, Sloan and Armstrong. Captain James Houston was seriously wounded and never fully recovered, while Captain Daniel McKissick was wounded but not seriously.

Several non-commissioned officers were killed and 13 men from Fourth Creek neighborhood of Rowan were found dead on the battlefield. Joseph Wasson of Snow Creek received five wounds and carried one bullet for forty years to the day when it came out.

The brick structure on the hillside in sight of the road contains the bodies of the six Whig captains who were killed in action, besides the bodies of Wallace Alexander and his wife, (who was a daughter of Captain Dobson).

Among the Tory losses were Captains Nicholas Warlick, Cumberland and Murray. Captain Warlick's brother, Philip, and Israel Sain were also among the killed, while Captain Carpenter was seriously wounded.

Among the many other Whig soldiers who took part in the battle were Hugh Brevard, Abram Forney, Wallace Alexander, Hugh Torrence, David Caldwell, John Reid, Robert Ramsey, of Rowan, David Vance, grandfather of Governor Vance; John Duckworth, William Feimster, of Iredell, Francis McCorkle, Adam Brevard, John Stamey, Jeremiah Munday and William Simpson, of Lincoln County. Of course, Adam Reep of Lincoln bore an important part both before and during the battle, along with some thirty picked men who were with him and who met Col. Locke and his forces upon their arrival some two miles east of the battleground on that eventful morning.

This was indeed a Civil War, without a British soldier in the ranks of the loyalists. Brother fought brother and neighbor was against neighbor and there has been but little boasting by the descendants of either side out of respect of the one for the other. The local community has never known much about the struggle which resulted in consternation and complete disorganization of the loyalists and along with that such a heartening of the Whigs that the defeat of Ferguson at Kings Mountain in October following was made possible with the final memorable result that complete victory for the American cause was effected at Yorktown October 19, 1781, when Cornwallis surrendered to Washington and the way was prepared for the establishment of the American Government.

Had the loyalists won at Ramsour's Mill it is very probable that America today would be an English province along with Canada. This seemingly insignificant battle of which little note has ever been taken, has in fact changed the history of the world.

The first monument ever placed upon that field, where the blood of brothers battling against each other commingled in the same furrows, was erected June 20, 1934, (one hundred and fifty-four years after the battle was fought), to commemorate the courage of three loyalist soldiers, natives of Lincoln County, Captain Nicholas Warlick, his brother Philip Warlick, and their neighbor Israel Sain, who fought to the death to defend what they thought was a righteous cause. Their bodies are entombed in one grave which is now marked with a handsome stone erected by R. A. Ramsour of Lincolnton, J. M. Barnhardt of Lenoir and three brothers, David, Jacob and Henry Warlick of Lincoln County, all descendants of the brave Captain Nicholas Warlick, a loyalist who died on that battlefield with his face to the front 154 years before.

It must have been these three who fought so valiantly that they attracted the attention of Col. Francis Locke the Commander of the Whig forces, for it is a fact that the bodies of three brave loyalists were decently buried in one tomb by order of Col. Locke, who stood reverently by the grave side while the bodies were laid to rest after the storm of that battle had ceased. Two hours after the victory, Gen. Rutherford with a thousand troops arrived, but too late to have a part in the contest.

The loyalist soldiers who went down in defeat on that dismal morning were honest, brave, and true to their convictions and they proved true to the new government that followed the war. Their descendants have made as fine citizens as the nation can boast and have never flinched in perilous times but bravely fought in every war since and proved themselves as courageous as were the three men who sleep secure under the newly erected stone in the local battlefield.

Captain W. A. Day who lives at Sherrill's Ford recently told me that he had two great uncles, William Simpson, a Whig, and Reuben Simpson, a Tory. They lived a few miles south of Sherrill's Ford on the Catawba River. They were on opposite sides at Ramsour's Mill. Just before the battle, William Simpson, the Whig, was sent out on a scouting expedition, but as soon as he heard the firing, he rushed back as fast as his horse could run and when the horse was exhausted, he ran afoot, determined to kill his Tory brother in the battle but before he reached the battleground the victory was gained by the Whigs. This shows the bitter feeling which brothers had for brothers who thought the other way in the days which tried men's souls.

Francis McCorkle who lived on Mountain Creek where Locke had camped the night before he marched to Ramsour's Mill was a soldier in that battle, and it was rumored that he was among the killed. He later, however, got home and when it was so reported in the neighborhood some of his friends went to his house by night pretending to be Tories who came to kill him. They called him out and when they asked how he stood he replied, "I won't die with a lie in my mouth, for I stand for Liberty." Then the visitors made themselves known as his friends and neighbors who had come to rejoice with him over the victory which he had helped to win.

This battle was fought one-half mile north of Lincolnton on the lands of Christian Reinhardt, the pioneer and ancestor of a long line of notable descendants, some of whom have been prominent in the history of the County and State.

It is said that when Adam Reep was striving to learn the secrets of the Tories on the battleground before the arrival of the Whigs that Mrs. Reinhardt, who by the way was Barbara Warlick before her marriage and closely related to some of the Tory troops, secreted Adam Reep in the cellar of her home and that Adam, a heavyweight, found it a hard job to squeeze through the narrow cellar door but finally got through with the help of Mrs. Reinhardt. Later he squeezed himself out in time to meet Locke upon his arrival on the morning of June 20th. Full reports of this battle may be found in *Hunter's Sketches* and in *Wheeler's History*, so that only a few of the important facts are embraced in this sketch.

Later on when Cornwallis visited the battleground he approved of the plan made by Col. John Moore for defense but unforeseen conditions, the heavy fog, and the surprise attack made the best laid plans of no effect.

On June 14, 1780, Gen. Rutherford, below Charlotte, watching Lord Rawdon at Hanging Rock, learned that John Moore with 1,300 Tories were assembled at Ramsour's Mill near Lincolnton. Gen Rutherford directed Col. Francis Locke, Capt. Falls and others to raise men and attack. They acted promptly and on June 20, Col. Locke, with 400 men, after a severe fight, dispersed this formidable body of Tories and put new life in the patriots of that section, which helped toward the great victory at Kings Mountain, October 7, 1780.

CHAPTER VI

1780-1781

Christian Reinhardt, the pioneer, married Elizabeth, daughter of Daniel Warlick, the pioneer.

Among his children were three sons:

1. Christian Reinhardt, Jr., who married Mary, daughter of Gen. Peter Forney. They had several children and all moved West and remained there, except one son, Franklin M. Reinhardt who returned to North Carolina, engaged in the iron business and married Sarah, daughter of David Smith (See 1869). His son, J. F. (Jack) Reinhardt represented Lincoln six terms in General Assembly (See 1913). Abram Forney Reinhardt, a grandson, was Sheriff of Lincoln County, 1928 to 1936.

2. Michael Reinhardt, who represented Lincoln in the State Senate four terms. He married Mary, daughter of Alexander Moore, and among their children was Wallace M. Reinhardt, an honored and popular citizen of Lincolnton, who for six years was Clerk of Superior Court. He married Frances Ann, daughter of Benjamin S. Johnson of Lincolnton. Among their children were Benjamin who went to Missouri and died there. Jennie married Dr. Pollock and went to Colorado; Mary married Melvin Reinhardt and went to the West; Annie married Stephen D. Smith; Pinkie married W. Locksley Long. They had two sons, Thurman B. Long of Charlotte, and Dr. Wallace Long of Rutherfordton. Irva married Major W. A. Fair and they live in Lincolnton.

3. John Reinhardt married Annie, another daughter of Alexander Moore. He represented Lincoln in House of Commons, 1799 and 1800. His son, Franklin D. Reinhardt, married Frances Perkins, was a member of House of Commons four terms from 1844 to 1850, and State Senator in 1858. Robert P. Reinhardt, son of Franklin D., married Susan Ramsour, and they were the parents of W. A. Reinhardt, State Senator for two terms, 1919 and 1921. W. P. Reinhardt, another son of John, represented Catawba in the Legislature from 1862 to 1867. The Reinhardts have always been noted for courage, thrift and popularity with the people, and every generation from Christian Reinhardt they have represented Lincoln or Catawba Counties in both branches of our State Legislature.

Adam Sherrill, the pioneer, settled one mile west of the Catawba River in 1747 near the ford which bears his name. He had eight sons: William, Samuel, Uriah, Adam, Aquilla, Isaac, Jacob and Moses, all of whom came from Virginia with their parents.

Many of the name now living in the Sherrill's Ford section are descendants of the eldest son, Captain William Sherrill (1723-1786). His son, Jacob, born in 1748, moved up the river into what is now Caldwell County and most of the Sherrill name in that section are his descendants.

Samuel, the second son, born in 1725, went from Sherrill's Ford to the Watauga Valley in what is now Tennessee. Among his seven children was Catherine (known as Bonny Kate), who was the second wife of John Sevier, married August 14, 1780, by Joseph Wilson, J. P. Three of her brothers, Samuel, Adam and George were among the mountain boys who fought under Col. John Sevier at Kings Mountain. Uriah, the third son of the pioneer was the ancestor of Rev. R. E. Sherrill, Presbyterian minister, who was active in church work in West Tennessee, and Texas; Rev. Dr. Lewis J. Sherrill, now Professor in Presbyterian Theological Seminary, Louisville, Ky.; and Dr. Fraser Hood of the Davidson College faculty (1936).

Among other descendants of Adam Sherrill, the pioneer, not elsewhere mentioned in this volume, were Rev. R. D. Sherrill; Rev. M. V. Sherrill, Methodist minister of note, who spent much time in preparation of the extensive family genealogy; his son John B. Sherrill, founder and until his death, editor of the *Concord Tribune;* William M. Sherrill who succeeded his father as editor of the *Tribune;* Rev. C. F. Sherrill and his son Frank O. Sherrill, a widely known business man; Dr. Bruce R. Payne, President of Peabody Normal College of Nashville who died April 21, 1937; and Dr. George R. Sherrill, who now (1936) fills the Chair of Economics and Government in Clemson College, S. C.; Rev. Leonidas B. Hayes of the Methodist Church; the descendants of Dr. R. L. Abernethy through his wife, Mary Hayes; Rev. George W. Ivey through his wife, Selina Neal; and Rev. L. E. Stacy through his wife, Rose Ann Johnson.

Diedrich Ramsour, the pioneer, died in 1780 and his will was probated in March of that year. He had several sons, two of whom were Jacob and David.

1. Jacob operated the Ramsour mill in 1780, the year the attle was fought on the nearby hill. His son, David, married arah Wilfong and they were the parents of Jacob A. Ramsour nd Mrs. John F. Phifer of Lincolnton.

His son Jacob, II, married Barbara Summey and they were he parents of Edmund G., William, Dr. Alexander Ramsour, Irs. L. E. Thompson, Mrs. B. H. Sumner and others.

Both Jacob A. and Jacob, II, were prominent Lincolnton 1erchants for many years.

2. David, son of Diedrich the pioneer, was the father of ohn Ramsour who married Elizabeth Heedick and represented he County in House of Commons, 1797 and 1798, and among his ons were:

(1) Jacob Ramsour (commonly known as Millwright Jake), ather of Theodore J., Oliver A., Melvin and Walter.

Theodore lost a leg in the Civil War and Walter died from younds received in battle in 1863.

(2) Daniel married Frances Shuford and they were the ,arents of the late Thomas J. Ramsour.

(3) Andrew married Sarah Ramsour and they had two aughters, Isabella, who married Col. W. H. Michal, and Anne, vho married John E. Boger. (See 1842-1862-1863, and 1880.)

(4) Henry (1770-1828) married Magdelene Shuford; heir son, Solomon, married Elizabeth Warlick and they were the ,arents of Henry E. Ramsour.

The Battle of Kings Mountain fought October 7, 1780, hanged the tide of war sentiment in the South, and made possible the final victory at Yorktown a year later, when Cornwallis urrendered to Washington and American freedom was secured.

John Wilfong was born, son of George Wilfong, April 8, 762. Enlisted in the Whig army September 1, 1780, under Japtain Sigmon and Lt. Vanhom in Col. McDowell's regiment. Marched to Morganton, then to Cane Creek in Burke, then to Vatauga. Returned with Colonels Sevier, Campbell and Shelby o Cane Creek, thence to the Cowpens where they were joined by Jolonels Cleveland and Williams and Lincoln troops. Crossed 3road River and fought at Kings Mountain. The same day Ferruson was killed and his whole army captured. Wilfong was younded in the left arm and returned home next day, October

8, 1780. In July, 1781, he volunteered for ten months with Captain Cowan and marched from Lincolnton to near Augusta, Georgia, there joining General Greene, and was in the Battle of Eutaw Springs, September 6, 1781. In March, 1782, he marched to the Cherokee nation under Captain Jesse Johnson, then returned to Gen. Pickens in South Carolina, where he served the residue of his time. Colonial Records, Vol. 22-158.

Major William Chronicle was born near the present town of Belmont in 1755. He lived where the present Chronicle Cotton Mill is located in Belmont. His mother married first to a Mr. McKee in Pennsylvania and came to North Carolina. By this marriage there was one son, James McKee, a soldier of the Revolution and the ancestor of the McKee family of Gaston County. After the death of her first husband, Mrs. McKee married to a Mr. Chronicle, and Major Chronicle, who was killed in the Battle of Kings Mountain, was a son of that marriage. He was first a Captain, but when a regiment was organized in Lincoln in 1780, with William Graham, Colonel, and Fred Hambright, Lieut. Colonel, William Chronicle was elected Major. On account of sickness in his family Col. Graham did not appear at Kings Mountain, so that Col. John Dickson and the other officers of the regiment led the troops in that memorable battle.

Chronicle was prudent and brave, leading in the charge and encouraged his troops with the command, "Come on, boys, never let it be said that a Fork boy fled." That nerved every trooper to do his best. Forward they went, Chronicle in the lead, to within gun shot of the British, when he fell mortally wounded in the breast, being 25 years old. His sword and spurs passed into the hands of his half brother, James McKee. (See *Hunter's Sketches*.)

Lincoln County, N. C., December, 1780.

To the Honorable the Speaker and the Gentlemen of the Senate and House of Commons. The petition of your faithful subject hereby sheweth:

That in February last there was a number of the inhabitants of the said County and from other Counties, most secretly collected together and being embodied, forceably marched off, plundering and robing (robbing) and taking prisoners as they went, bosting themselves that they would soon be victorious after joining the King's forces.

Your humble petitioner being by duty bound raised a number of the militia for to purshua and interrupt the march of the insurgents, but their march being so pressed could not overtake them. The people employed in pershute being disappointed in overtaking them and being cautious of a reward due them from those treators of the said State, and finding nothing else but some of the property of the saide insurgents laide hold of several horses creaters and fetched them in with them, and your humble petitioner not knowing how to proceed for the safety of the people that was thus concerned, I thought best to put those articles to sale and took bond to the governor in name of the State. These I lay before your Honorable body, for your wisdom and mercy to me to save me from the persecution of these, your humble petitioner, with submission to your honorable body, would lay down his Commis and take up his musket, and to convince your honorable body that it is not any disappointment to said State or County, there is a gentleman ready to make application for the same.

I am your humble servant to command.

CHARLES McLEAN.

C. R. 15: 213.

1781

In January, Cornwallis spent three days at Ramsour's Mill. Gen. O'Hara camped at the Reep place two miles from the mill and Tarleton crossed the South Fork in Cobb's bottom and marched over the hill on which Lincolnton now stands to join Cornwallis at the mill.

On January 28th, Cornwallis with his forces marched east to Jacob Forney's where he camped for three days and foraged on the Forney cattle, hogs, sheep and chickens until it was safe to cross the swollen Catawba River.

February 1st, he broke camp at Forney's and marched to Cowan's Ford six miles below Beatties Ford, where the battle of Cowan's Ford took place. (See *Hunter's Sketches*, pages 220-227 for full account of Cornwallis in Lincoln.)

General William Davidson was killed in battle at Cowan's Ford, February 1st, 1781.

Judge Robert H. Burton was born in Granville County, N. C., in 1781.

William Armstrong declared in Caldwell County, Kentucky, November 20, 1833, that "during the Revolutionary War I lived in Lincoln County, North Carolina, and was a Militia Captain in 1780. While out on service in 1781, the Tories destroyed nearly all my property in Lincoln and took five of my horses." (C. R. 22: 107.)

Assembly, October, 1781

"Whereas, it is absolutely necessary that the pay due, or which may hereafter be due for militia duty and all other claims against the State for articles furnished or impressed or which hereafter may be furnished or impressed should be speedily settled and certificates granted for the same, therefore: be it enacted that a Board of Auditors be appointed in each of the districts, for the Salisbury district, Matthew Locke, William Cathey and David Wilson, for the Lower Board and John Brown, Daniel McKezick and Alexander Irwin for the Upper Board."

Then follows the allowance in specie for the articles furnished: Salt beef per barrel, 7 pounds; fresh beef per 100, 2 pounds, 4 shillings; pork per barrel, 8 pounds, 16 shillings; bacon per pound, 1 shilling 4d; fresh pork per 100, 2 pounds, 16 shillings; sheep, 1 pound, 12 shillings; wheat per bushel, 12 shillings; flour per 100, 1 pound, 16 shillings; oats per bushel. 4 shillings; sheaf oats per bundle, 4d; rye per bushel, 8 shillings; salt per bushel, 2 pounds; salt in Salisbury district, 4 pounds per bushel; good brandy per gal., 10 shillings; good whiskey per gal., 8 shillings; West India Rum per gal., 14 shillings; molasses, 10 shillings; good cyder per barrel, 1 pound and 10 shillings; brown sugar per pound, 1 pound 6d; bar iron per pound, 1 shilling 4d; wagon, driver and 4 horses per day, 24 shillings. C. R. 24:387.)

"THE ROSTER OF SOLDIERS FROM NORTH CAROLINA DURING THE AMERICAN REVOLUTION"

Published in 1933 by the North Carolina Daughters of the American Revolution contains the following list of Lincoln County men who were soldiers of the Revolution, and by permission this authentic record is published in these ANNALS, with certain changes:

Tryon County Companies: William Graham, Colonel; Charles McLean, Lt. Col.; Thomas Beatty, Major; Frederick Hambright, 2nd Major.

The Annals of Lincoln County

Gaston County (then Lincoln) soldiers who fought at Kings Mountain:

1—Col. Frederick Hambright, at time of battle lived near Long Creek. (Hunter 325.)
2—Major Frederick Hambright, family record.
3—John Hambright, son of Col. Fred Hambright (Hunter 325).
4—Major William Chronicle, South Fork, (Hunter 290). (Schenck 167-8 and 175.)
5—Dr. William McLean, South Fork (Hunter 285-6).
6—Alex McLean, Jr., (Hunter 285-6).
7—George McLean (Hunter 285-6).
8—John McLean (Hunter 286).
9—Matthew Leeper (Family Bible and tomb. Buried at Smith graveyard).
10—Capt. John Mattocks (Wheeler 158 and Hunter 291, 295).
11—Captain Charles Mattocks (Wheeler 158 and Hunter 291, 295).
12—Lt. William Rabb (Wheeler 158 and Hunter 291, 295).
13—James McKee (half brother of Chronicle) (Wheeler 158).
14—Col. William Davenport (Draper 333-4, 340, 473).
15—Robert Henry (Draper refers often to him).
16—William Caldwell (Hunter 294, Wheeler 158).
17—Captain Samuel Caldwell (Hunter 294, Wheeler 158).
18—Hugh Erwin (Draper 365).
19—Andrew Barry (Draper 365).
20—Enoch Gilmer (Schenck 158) (Draper 225).
21—William Gilmer (Draper 257).
22—John Chittim (Draper 258).
23—Capt. Samuel Martin (Hunter 291 to 294).
24—Lt. John Boyd (Hunter 289 and 291).
25—John Glenn (Family Bible). Buried at Goshen.
26—William Gregory (Family Bible). Buried in Bethel section.
27—Capt. Samuel Espey (Schenck 167).
28—Capt. Isaac White (Draper 476).
29—Lt. James White (Draper 476).
30—Capt. James Johnston (Hunter 244-7).
31—Moses Henry (Draper 319).
32—James Henry (Draper 319).
33—Isaac Holland, Jr., (Hoffman's *Our Kin*, 521).
34—Felix Walker (His *Memoirs* indicate he was not in the battle).
35—Jacob Hoffman, fought at Kings Mountain, died 1860.
36—John Hoffman, buried at Earl Summey place.
37—Major John Dickson (Hunter 29 and Schenck 107-8).
38—Matthew Armstrong (Court House records). Fought at Kings Mountain. Buried at Smith's graveyard near Belmont.
39—Capt. John Kincaid (family Bible record). Buried at Olney.
40—Adam Baird, an officer unable to give his rank. His granddaughter, Mrs. W. E. Weatherly, Gastonia, has the gun he carried at Kings Mountain.
41—James Baird, brother of Adam (record in family history). (Capt.).
42—Jesse Lane (record in family history).

KINGS MOUNTAIN MEN—LINCOLN COUNTY

Pensioned—Robert Abernethy, Pt.
    Elias Alexander (Rutherford).
Pensioned—Vincent Allen, Pt.
    Matthew Armstrong, pensioned by N. C., 1783.
    William Armstrong.
    William Blackburn.
    William Bradley.
    Richard Bradley.
    William Carroll (pensioned by N. C. in 1833).
    John Chittim, pensioned in Lincoln County.
    James Clark, pensioned in Lincoln County.
    Michael Clark, pensioned in Lincoln County.
Pensioned—James Collins, Pt., from Lincoln.
Pensioned—Samuel Collins, Pt., from Lincoln.
Pensioned—Thomas Costner, pensioned in Lincoln, 1833.
Pensioned—Bartholemew Thompson, pensioned in Lincoln.
    Joseph Dickson, commanded Lincoln County men.
    John Crockett, father of David Crockett, was with Lincoln County militia.
    George Dameron, pensioned in Lincoln.
    Peter Eddleman, pensioned in Lincoln, 1835.
    William Elmore, pensioned in North Carolina.
    Samuel Espey, Lincoln County. Wounded at Kings Mountain.
    James Ewart and Robert Ewart.
    James Farewell, with Lincoln County men.
    Enoch Gilmer and William Gilmer, brothers from Lincoln.
    Joseph Godwin, Robinson Godwin, Samuel Godwin, from Lincoln pensioned in Lincoln, 1833.
Pensioned—John Gregory, William Gregory, Nathan Gwaltney, Nicholas Hofner, Simon Hager, John Helm, pensioned in Lincoln, 1833.
    James Gabriel, Pt. and Sgt. (S. R. 22-67).
Pensioned—James Hill, Lt., from Lincoln.
Pensioned—James Hill, Pt., born in Lincoln, 1742.
Pensioned—Robert Johnston, Pt., pensioned in 1835.
Pensioned—Lt. William Johnson, pensioned by N. C.
    John Kidd, Lincoln, pensioned, fought with Lincoln men.
    Robert Knox, pensioned in 1833.
    Joseph Logan, Lincoln, in Mattocks Company.
    William Logan, Lincoln, in Mattocks Company.
    Francis McCorkle, in 1774, Com. Pub. Safety, Rowan, died in Lincoln, 1802. Fought at Ramsour's Mill and Kings Mountain.
    Shadrich Lefy, Lincoln man, pensioned.
    William McCarthy, was under Cleveland, pensioned in Lincoln, 1833.
Pensioned—Patrick Mason and Thomas Mason of Lincoln County, pensioned 1833.
Pensioned—Alexander Moore, Pt., Lincoln, pensioned 1833.
    Nathan Mendenhall, with Lincoln men, pensioned 1833.

THE ANNALS OF LINCOLN COUNTY 49

Pensioned—Captain John Moore, born 1759 in Lincoln; Alexander Moore, James Moore, William Moore, Pt. and Capt., brothers of John, all claimed as Kings Mountain men.
Pensioned—Jeremiah Munday, a Lincoln soldier, pensioned there in 1833.
Humphrey Parker, from Lincoln, where he was pensioned.
William Potter, of Lincoln Militia, claimed to be a Kings Mountain soldier.
Pensioned—Adam Reep, lived 2 miles west of Lincolnton.
Michael Reep, pensioned in Lincoln.
Charles Regan, pensioned in Lincoln.
Henry Rumfelt (Remfeldt?), pensioned in Lincoln in 1833.
Adam Sherrill, born on Catawba 1758.
Philip Tillman, Lincoln soldier pensioned in Lincoln, 1833.
Elisha Withers, pensioned in Lincoln.
Charles Whit, pensioned in Lincoln.
James Alexander, born in Rowan, 1756, entered army from Lincolnton.
John Turbyfill, Pt., pensioned.

LINCOLN PENSIONERS

Age
Not given, John Chittin, Pt., $286.73, Revolutionary War, Jan. 1, 1815.
Not given, Samuel Espey, Pt., $125.90, Revolutionary War, Sept. 4, 1808.
Not given, Samuel Espey, $777.44, Revolutionary War, April 24, 1816.
Not given, Samuel Espey, $200.00, Revolutionary War, July 4, 1832.
Not given, David Miller, $332.63, U. S. Army, Sept. 4, 1808.
Not given, David Miller, $537.01, U. S. Army, April 24, 1816.
Not given, David Miller, $383.30, U. S. Army, Sept. 4, 1824.
Not given, Mitchell Reep, $150.00, Revolution, Apr. 20, 1811.
Not given, Mitchell Reep $857.07, Revolution, Apr. 24, 1816.
82 Robert Abernethy, $40.00, N. C. Militia, March 4, 1831.
78 Vincent Allen, $240.00, Va. Militia, March 4, 1831.
85 Christian Arney, $169.98, N. C. Militia, March 4, 1831.
71 Mathew Armstrong, $99.99, N. C. Militia, March 4, 1831.
78 Casper Bolick, $109.98, N. C. Militia, March 4, 1831.
75 Jonas Bradshaw, $120.00, N. C. Continental Line, March 4, 1831.
72 Robert Berry, $60.00, N. C. Militia, March 4, 1831.
75 Samuel Caldwell, $160.00, N. C. Continental Line, March 4, 1831.
74 Martin Coulter, $64.68, N. C. Militia, March 4, 1831.
73 Mitchell Cline, $88.02, N. C. Militia, March 4, 1831.
82 William Carroll, $120.00, N. C. Militia, March 4, 1831.
87 Thomas Costner, $64.95, N. C. Militia, March 4, 1831.
Not given, Samuel Collins, $78.48, Maryland Militia, March 4, 1831.
75 William Elmore, $114.99, N. C. Continental Line, March 4, 1831.
69 Peter Edleman, $94.98, N. C. Militia, March 4, 1831.
76 Sam'l Espey, Corp. and Capt., $296.16, N. C. Militia, March 4, 1831.
76 Abram Forney, Sgt. and Capt., $436.80, N. C. Militia, March 4, 1831.
77 William Gregory, Pt., $60.00, N. C. Militia, Nov. 9, 1831.
75 Joseph Graham, Sergeant, Adjutant, Captain and Major, $870.00, N. C.

Continental Line, March 4, 1831.
- 69   Robinson Goodwin, $139.98, N. C. Continental Line, March 4, 1831.
- 71   Simeon Hager, $99.99, N. C. Continental Line, March 4, 1831.
- 75   James Hill, Lieut., $360.00, N. C. Militia, March 4, 1831.
- 81   James Henry, Pt., $210.00, S. C. Continental Line, March 4, 1831.
- 78   Nicholas Hofner, Pt., $90.00, N. C. Militia, March 4, 1831.
- 72   John Harmon, Pt., $117.00, N. C. Militia, March 4, 1831.
- 73   John Helm, Pt., $120.00, Va. Continental Line, March 4, 1831.
- 79   Simon Hager, Pt., $79.32, N. C. Militia, March 4, 1831.
- 76   John Kidd, Pt., $159.99, N. C. Continental Line, March 4, 1831.
- 92   Robert Knox, Pt., $80.00, N. C. Militia, March 4, 1831.
- 85   John Kincaid, Pt., $229.98, S. C. Militia, March 4, 1831.
- 80   Alexander Moore, Pt., $101.64, N. C. Militia, March 4, 1831.
- 72   Tapley Mahanas, Pt., $240.00, Va. Continental Line, March 4, 1831.
- 83   William Moore, Capt., $210.00, N. C. Militia, March 4, 1831.
- 100 Samuel Martin, Capt., $750.00, S. C. Militia, March 4, 1831.
- 75   John Moore, Pt., $66.65, N. C. Militia, March 4, 1831.
- 74   George Oliver, Pt., $150.00, N. C. Militia, March 4, 1831.
- 85   Jacob Plunk, Pt., $90.00, N. C. Militia, March 4, 1831.
- 84   Hiram Pendleton, Pt., $197.27, N. C. Continental Line, died Aug. 27, 1833.
- 84   William Potter, Corporal, $74.49, N. C. Militia, March 4, 1831.
- 72   Humphrey Parker, $99.99, N. C. Militia, March 4, 1831.
- 79   Adam Reep, $163.29, N. C. Militia, March 4, 1831.
- 71   James Robeson, $99.99, N. C. Militia, March 4, 1831.
- 73   William Rankin, $148.90, N. C. Militia, March 4, 1831.
- 74   Joshua Roberts, $69.99, N. C. Militia, March 4, 1831.
- 76   Charles Regan, $150.00, N. C. Continental Line, March 4, 1831.
- 72   Peter Shrum, $136.66, N. C. Militia, March 4, 1831.
- 72   John Stamey, $210.00, N. C. Militia, March 4, 1831.
- 89   Conrad Tippong, $90.00, N. C. Militia, March 4, 1831.
- 93   John Turbyfill, $120.00, Va. Militia, March 4, 1831.
- 72   Bartholomew Thompson, $199.98, Georgia Militia, March 4, 1831.
- 72   Charles Thompson, $124.98, N. C. Militia, March 4, 1831.
- 87   Philip Tillman, $90.00, N. J. Militia, March 4, 1831.
- 79   Joseph Willis, $76.98, N. C. Militia, March 4, 1831.
- 70   Charles Whit, $225.24, S. C. Militia, died Dec. 28, 1833.
- 75   Elisha Weathers, $137.49, N. C. Militia, March 4, 1831.
- 72   John Wilfong, $112.62, N. C. Militia, March 4, 1831.
- 71   James Wilkinson, $84.63, Va. Militia, March 4, 1831.
- 88   Nathan Mendenhall, $109.98, Penn. Militia, March 4, 1831.
- 76   William McCarthy, $199.98, S. C. Militia, March 4, 1831.

John Wilfong, Lincoln County, enlisted 1780, pensioned U. S. A. Sept. 4, 1808, $152.81.

John Wilfong, Lincoln County, enlisted 1780, pensioned U. S. A., April 24, 1816, $571.59.

The patriotic Daughters of the American Revolution deserve our thanks for the valuable information found in the foregoing pages, which they have carefully prepared and published from official records, giving the part many Lincoln men took in the struggle for American freedom.

Due to the fact that many were called temporarily into military service from civil life, to resist invasions of the enemy, and after the battle returned to private pursuits, with no record kept of their service, it is easy to understand how the sacrifice made by many brave patriots was forgotten. The above list was taken largely from pension rolls and is correct, even though it does not give the name of every Lincoln County soldier who lived through the war, nor the great number who were slain in battle. Gen. Peter Forney and his brother, Jacob Forney, Peter Smith and William Simpson, as well as Captain Daniel McKissick, who was severely wounded at Ramsour's Mill, rendered conspicuous service, and John Hoyle, youngest son of Peter Hoyle, the pioneer, served as Lieutenant under Colonel Hambright against the Indians and was a gallant soldier of the Revolution. The John Hoyle Chapter, Daughters of the American Revolution (of Hickory, N. C.) was named in his honor and a large number of the members of that chapter are his lineal descendants, but none of these were on pension rolls.

CHAPTER VII

1782-1800

May 4, 1782. House received from Senate, bill to amend the act entitled, An Act for Dividing Tryon County.

John Moore was granted leave to absent himself from the House for the balance of session. (Vol. 16:99).

At the same session 1782. The Morgan district was organized out of that part of Salisbury district embraced in Wilkes, Burke, Rutherford, and Lincoln Counties. (Vol. 24: 451.)

Sunday, May 5, 1782

The House in session received from Senate, bill for adding a part of Burke County to Lincoln; for appointing commissioners for the purposes therein mentioned, and for laying a tax to complete the buildings therein. Endorsed in Senate May 4, and read first time and passed. (Vol. 16: 102.)

David Vance and John Caruth were appointed Commissioners to run the new line between Burke and Lincoln Counties.

Daniel McKissick, Henry Thompson, James Lyttle, John Dickson, John Wilson, John Caruth, Frederick Hambright and Nicholas Friday were named as Commissioners for fixing a place for court house and other public buildings. (Vol. 24: 472.)

Gov. Alexander Martin (23rd July, 1782) orders Gen. McDowell to organize an expedition against Cherokee Indians or the hostile tribes of that nation called "Chicammoggys." To have by August 20, next 500 volunteer horsemen to march against the valley settlements of Cherokees, so as to form a junction with Col. Shelby and Brig. Gen. Pickens at a place called Shumack. That if a sufficient number of volunteers are not enrolled by the time aforesaid you will order a draft from the Counties of Burke, Wilkes, Rutherford and Lincoln. (Vol. 16: 697.)

Letter From Gov. Martin, August 4, 1782

I am informed that there are some Cherokee prisoners in Rutherford or Lincoln Counties, or somewhere in Morgan district.

That the Indians may have no excuse in surrendering the white prisoners among them, you will please to order such Indian prisoners be given up to Colonel Martin, that he may send them to the Nation in exchange for ours.

ALEX MARTIN.

To General McDowell. (Vol. 16: 800.)

Sheriff's Petition

Referred to Mr. Hawkins, Mr. Montford, Mr. Tripp, Mr. Wilson, Mr. Rowan, Mr. Phifer.

State of North Carolina, Lincoln County.

To the Honorable the House of Sinnet and to the worshipful the house of burgesses in assembly:

The petition of George Lamkin, late sheriff of Tryon County, humbly sheweth that your petitioner in the year 1772, ye 27 day of October, entered into the office of sheriff, and Law did not continue over three months in full force, and after Law Dropt your petitioner indeavoured to collect the taxes due for that year, and got a little over 100 pounds as will appear by the settlement with Tryon Court. At that time Law stopt, no trade nor money to be got, so that people could not pay there dues. I made destress on sum persons goods, but could not sell. Soon after there was a committee appointed in the county. Complaint being made to your committee, thought fit to stop your petitioner from collecting or making distress. Soone after, your petitioner moved to examine the Sheriff's list before them, that I might know how many persons was gone out of the county since the settlement with Tryon Court and there was wanten 107 persons that was taxt in your sheriff's list. Soone after this the Indians broke out and did drive all the county as lo as Buffalo Creek 50 miles in. Sum few got into forts, sum went to Virginia, sum went to ye South and sum down in this State to the amount by my list 257 taxable persons and now the Tory party has broke out, being ye upper part of said County. What feu was left after ye Indians is now gone, so that it is impossible for your petitioner to make any collection. Now therefore I humbly pray you will take into your consideration that your petitioner may be discharged, as I have none of the publick money in my hands but what I have accounted for and a ticket I tuck after of Robert

Blackburns, one of ye Burgesses, which I have sent down, and your petitioner as in duty bound shall pray.

(Signed) GEORGE LAMKIN.

(Vol. 15: 219) 1782.

1783

1783. Robert Abernethy was married to Sarah Nicols on June 23, 1783. He was a member from Tryon County to the Halifax Convention of 1776 and grandfather of Rev. Dr. Robert L. Abernethy, the great educator who founded Rutherford College.

Peter Forney was married to Nancy Abernethy February 27, 1783.

Resolution in Commons permitting Frederick Hambright, Jonathan Gullick, James Johnston and John Moore to resign as Justices of the Peace and Frederick Hambright, Lt. Colonel of Lincoln County to resign his commission. (Vol. 19: 289.) Journal Gen. Assembly, 30 April, 1783.

Col. Alexander presented bill for levying a tax on every 100 pounds value of taxable property in County of Lincoln for building court house, jail and stocks for the use of said County. May 5, 1783. (Vol. 19: 179.)

Read in Senate, a receipt for 30 bushels corn and 60 dozen sheaf wheat furnished by Benjamin Orman, of Lincoln, for the use of a British flag of truce, whereupon,

RESOLVED that the Auditors of the District of Salisbury do grant a Certificate to the said Orman for amount thereof, and charge the same to his Brittanic Majesty, and transmit a copy of said charge to Commissary of Prisoners in this State. (Vol. 19: 53.)

1784

1784. James Rutledge was appointed by General Assembly, Tax Collector for Lincoln County.

1784. Jurors for the Morgan District were increased and secured as follows: From Burke 16; Lincoln 13; Rutherford 10; and Wilkes 9 Jurors.

Daniel M. Forney was born in Lincoln County in May, 1784.

1785

McKissick in Commons of 1785 moved and presented bill for erecting and establishing a town in County of Lincoln. It was read and sent to Senate. (Vol. 17: 297.)

The Commissioners appointed to build court house, jail and stocks for Lincoln County entered 300 acres of vacant land, lying and being between lines of Philip Kanceller (Cansler) and Christian Reinhardt, the same being a healthy pleasant situation, well watered and the inhabitants of the County are desirous that a town should be established thereon and the said Commissioners having laid off 50 acres into squares, streets, and lots of half-acre each and sold same.

Be it enacted by the General Assembly of North Carolina, that the said 50 acres so laid off, be and the same is hereby constituted, erected and established into a town and shall be called by the name of Lincolnton.

That Joseph Dickson, John Caruth, John Wilson, Joseph Steele and Nicholas Friday be trustees and directors, for designing, building and carrying on said town and the said Commissioners are empowered to fill vacancies caused by death or removal of any of their number. 1785. (Vol. 24: 778.)

Legislation authorizing a tax levy for bounties to those who kill wild beasts was passed.

The bounty for each wolf shall be 20 shillings and for each wildcat 3 shillings. 1785. (Vol. 24: 750.)

By order of General Assembly Thomas Espey of Lincoln was suspended as a Justice of Peace. (See Vol. 17: 325.)

The resignation of John Alexander, a Justice of Peace, was referred by Daniel McKissick and Robert Alexander. (See Vol. 17: 405.)

William Graham, a Colonel of the Militia of the County of Lincoln, was discharged and Joseph Dickson was appointed by the General Assembly Colonel for the said County of Lincoln. (See Vol. 17: 667.)

1786

The General Assembly honored those officers who distinguished themselves in the capture of the British commanded by Major Ferguson at Kings Mountain when it "Resolved that an elegant mounted sword be presented to each of the following officers, viz: Col. Cleaveland, of Wilkes; Col. Campbell, of Virginia; Col. Shelby, of Sullivan County; Lt. Col. Lewis, of Washington County; Lt. Col. Hambright, of Lincoln County; Major Winston, of Surry, and Major Shelby of Sullivan County, for their voluntary and distinguished service in defeat of Ferguson at Kings Mountain." (Vol. 17: 697.)

December 30, 1786. Daniel McKissick tendered his resignation as Justice of the Peace and it was accepted. (See Vol. 18:179.)

Bartlett Shipp was born in Stokes County, March 6, 1786.

1787

Thomas Beatty, son of John Beatty, the pioneer, Lieut. Col. of Tryon County Militia in 1776, died in 1787.

1788

It is claimed that first church deed recorded in Lincoln County bears the date January 10, 1788, and was made to Christian Reinhardt and Andrew Heedick, Trustees for the Societies of the Dutch Presbyterians (German Reformed) and Dutch Lutherans.

Two acres in Southeast square of Lincolnton, the consideration being ten shillings (about $2.50). It is stated in the deed that a Dutch meeting house was on the said lot.

The first preachers were John Gottfried Arndt, Lutheran, and Andrew Loretz, German Reformed.

In 1819 the old log church was raised a story higher. The Southeast corner was "carried up" or fitted by Philip Cansler and Adam Reep. It was weather boarded, ceiled, refurnished and galleries built in. In 1830 it was painted white and ever afterwards called the old White Church until it was destroyed by fire in 1893. Every denomination now in Lincolnton worshipped in this meeting house until they built churches of their own.

From the death of Andrew Loretz in 1812 until 1828 the Reformed congregation had no pastor but from 1828 to 1859 the pastors were in order named, Rev. J. G. Fritchey, Rev. J. H. Crawford, Rev. S. S. Middlekauf and Rev. David Crooks.

After the death of Mr. Loretz many of the members enrolled as Presbyterians and were charter members of the Presbyterian Church in Lincolnton, which was organized in 1823.

The German Reformed preachers held no meetings after the church was burned until 1910. In 1911 Rev. W. H. McNairy came from Lexington as pastor and organized a congregation of 26 members and now (1934) they have an attractive church building on East Main Street.

THE ANNALS OF LINCOLN COUNTY 57

In 1830 the Lutherans ceased to use the old church for about 60 years until they organized a new congregation in Lincolnton about 1890. After the fire in 1893 the Lutherans built a brick church on the same site at a cost of about $2,500.00 and now (1934) this building is used as a funeral home.

In 1900 the interest of the Dutch Presbyterians in this property was sold to the Emanuel Lutherans for $75.00. Since then the Lutheran pastors were: W. P. Cline, J. C. Deitz, H. J. Mathias, R. A. Yoder, Enoch Hite, W. J. Roof, V. C. Ridenhour, Voigt Cromer and John Allen Arndt (a lineal descendant of Rev. John Gottfried Arndt, the pioneer Lutheran preacher) who was the pastor in 1928.

1789

Colonel Charles McLean was a leader of the patriots in the days of the Revolution, in council and in camp, for he was active not only as an official but also as a soldier.

He was a member of the Committee appointed by the Assembly of 1774 to choose the county seat for Tryon County; member of the Tryon County Committee of Public Safety; Chairman at Tryon Court House, August 14, 1775, of the patriotic meeting, which adopted the ringing resolutions protesting against British oppression, and one of the signers of that immortal document.

He, with James Johnston, was a delegate from Tryon to the Halifax Convention in April, 1776, and was a member of the Assembly of 1777. He was a Tryon County magistrate and Lieut. Colonel of Tryon County Militia. In peace and war he was loyal and true.

In 1789 Peter Forney, Abram Forney, Abram Earhardt and Turner Abernethy took advantage of the land grant act passed by the Assembly of 1788 to encourage iron manufacture and erected a forge at Big Ore Bank, in Lincoln County and were the pioneer iron manufacturers in Lincoln County, and in fact in this section. A little later Peter Forney sold an interest in the business to Gen. Joseph Graham, Alexander Brevard and their father-in-law, John Davidson. Later they erected Vesuvius and Mt. Tirzah forges. Finally Peter Forney sold his interest to his partners who continued the business under the firm name of Joseph Graham and Company. Brevard later built Rehoboth and Graham built Spring Hill forge.

1790

Turner Abernethy built Mt. Carmel forge on Mountain Creek and it was later operated by Isaac E. Paine.

J. Madison Smith operated for many years the Rough and Ready forge on Mountain Creek and during the Civil War built Stonewall furnace on Anderson Creek and worked it until his death about 1873.

Alexander Brevard left Mount Tirzah forge to his son, Robert A. Brevard, who operated it until 1870, and Rehoboth forge to his son, Ephraim Brevard, who operated it until 1852, when he sold it to F. M. Reinhardt and Bartlett Shipp when it was known as Reinhardt furnace.

Peter Forney left Mount Welcome forge to his son-in-law, Dr. William Johnston, who with his sons operated it until 1860, when Jonas W. Derr bought and ran it until his death in 1881. The Mariposa Cotton Mill is now operated on this site.

In the early days lime was hauled a long distance from Kings Mountain, but later abundant supply was found in Ironton township, in the mine which was operated many years by Lawson W. Keener. Iron was a medium of exchange among furnace employees and merchants from afar brought goods to Lincoln to exchange for iron. The country to the west bought cooking utensils and other iron products and a market was found for the metal as far east as Hillsboro and Fayetteville. The coming of the railroad brought competition from Pennsylvania which discouraged the local industry and the iron business was abandoned in Lincoln, after the death of Jonas W. Derr in 1881.

June 12, 1790, Philip Cansler, Jr., was married to Mary Quickel, daughter of Michael Quickel.

When the first pioneers crossed the Catawba River (from 1747 to 1790) they marched into a wilderness, but forty years later in 1790, the population increased as shown by the Federal Census taken in that year to 9,234. Of those, 8,289 were white and 935 were negro slaves.

The Federal Constitution had been adopted by all the States except Rhode Island and North Carolina, and George Washington was chosen as the first President of the United States. North Carolina and Rhode Island were too late in giving approval to participate in that election. Washington was inaugurated President in New York City, April 30, 1789.

Gen. Benjamin Hawkins, of Warren, and Samuel Johnston of Chowan were the first Senators to represent North Carolina in the Federal Congress.

Rev. Jacob Hill, Methodist minister and many years a resident of Lincoln, was born in Anson County, December 21, 1790.

In 1790 Daniel Asbury, a Methodist preacher, came from Virginia to a colony of Methodists who settled in Lincoln County near the present village of Terrell and there organized Rehoboth, the first Methodist church west of the Catawba River.

Daniel Asbury was married to Nancy Morris on January 4, 1790. She professed faith in Christ at a Methodist meeting in Virginia and joined the church with William McKendree and Enoch George, both of whom became great preachers and bishops of the Church.

Over the pulpit in Rehoboth church is the following tablet: "Rev. Daniel Asbury, the pioneer of Methodism in Western North Carolina, was born February 18, 1762. Died May 15, 1825. He organized the circuit 1789 and the same year organized here the first Methodist church in the State, west of the Catawba River. The first church building was erected here in 1791. The first camp meeting was held here in 1794." See further about Daniel Asbury, 1825.

1792

Peter Hoyle, Jr., was married to Sarah Hovis on January 23, 1792.

Dr. William McLean, a native of Rowan, but from early life a citizen of Lincoln County, was married June 19, 1792 to Mary Davidson, daughter of John Davidson, of Mecklenburg. Among his descendants were the late Dr. William B. McLean, of the Beatties Ford section, Major Augustus A. McLean, of Lincolnton and Dr. John D. McLean, later of Gaston County.

1793

Eli Whitney (1765-1825), a Yale graduate, went to Georgia to teach, about 1790, and there made the world his debtor when, in 1793, he invented the Whitney Cotton Gin. Before that time one man could grow 25 bales of cotton and it took 25 slaves one hundred days to seed the cotton. Whitney's invention at the first did the work of ten men but the modern gin does the work of 100 men, and does it better.

The cotton gin encouraged southern farmers to grow cotton extensively giving them a crop which always found ready sale for cash in the days of barter. After the gin was introduced Lincoln County farmers grew cotton and hauled the crop over bad roads to Fayetteville, Cheraw, Camden, Columbia and sometimes to Charleston, until the railroad came and brought the market to their doors.

The invention of the cotton gin transformed southern agriculture, bringing to this section a world market for all the surplus cotton crop. The present textile growth of the South would never have been possible without the cotton gin.

James Graham, son of Gen. Joseph Graham, was born January 7, 1793.

Alexander Sherrill was married to Ruanna Gabriel January 24, 1793.

Maj. Henry W. Connor was born in Prince George County, Virginia, August 5, 1791, son of Captain Charles Connor and wife, Ann (Epps) Connor.

1794

The oldest Baptist church in old Lincoln County is said to have been organized somewhere between 1772 and 1777. It was Long Creek church about a mile east of Dallas. There are no records of its earliest history. It was reorganized in 1794. The death of James Lewis, one of the early members and sometime pastor of this church, is recorded in the minutes of 1834. He was the grandfather of the late James R. Lewis, a leading Baptist and merchant of Dallas until his death in 1928.

Ephraim Perkins, son of Gentleman John Perkins, the pioneer, was married February 1, 1796, to Elizabeth Abernethy.

Gen. John Moore, a soldier of the Revolution, was married August 4, 1797, to Polly Goodwin.

Joseph Dickson, Federalist, defeated James Holland for Congress in this district in 1798.

Rev. Dr. R. H. Morrison, Presbyterian minister and first president of Davidson College was born on Rocky River in what is now Cabarrus County in 1798.

Lawson Henderson, son of James Henderson, the pioneer, was married to Elizabeth Caruth July 25, 1798.

After the death of George Washington in December, 1799, according to facts published by the late Judge David Schenck, a very eloquent sermon was preached by Rev. Andrew Loretz, the pioneer Reformed preacher, at a memorial service held in the old White Church, in honor of General Washington.

Rev. Henry Asbury, son of Daniel Asbury, the pioneer Methodist preacher, was born in Lincoln County, May 29, 1799.

CHAPTER VIII

1801-1811

Major Francis McCorkle, son of Matthew McCorkle, of Scotch Irish descent, was an early settler in Rowan (now Lincoln) and was a member of Rowan Committee of Public Safety in 1774-75. He lived on Mountain Creek about two miles north of Denver and never failed to attend a Public Safety meeting thirty miles away in Salisbury. (See *Wheeler's History* idem.) He was a brave patriot of the Revolution and fought at Ramsour's Mill, Kings Mountain, and was with Peter Forney in the skirmish against Tarleton at Torrence Tavern. He married first to Sarah, daughter of Alexander Work, by whom he had five children:

1. Matthew McCorkle (1769-1844). Bachelor.

2. Isabella (1771-1842) married William Beatty, son of John Beatty, the pioneer.

3. Jane, born June 15, 1773, married Abram Alexander of Mecklenburg County, March 3, 1808.

4. Alexander Work McCorkle, born July 25, 1775, was an influential man in Lincoln County and while never an office holder, was active in politics as a Whig. He died January 26, 1854. Bachelor.

5. Rebecca, born May 21, 1777, married Gilbert Milligan on October 6, 1804, and died October 31, 1863.

They are all buried in the McCorkle family graveyard and death dates are found on their tombstones. The birth and marriage dates are taken from family records.

His second marriage was to Elizabeth (Betsy) Brandon, daughter of Richard and Margaret Locke Brandon of Rowan. She was the Betsy Brandon who served the breakfast to President Washington and several of his aides in 1791 at the Brandon home six miles south of Salisbury, as the party was en route from Charlotte to Salisbury.

On June 14, 1933, a marker erected by the Elizabeth Maxwell Steele Chapter, D. A. R. of Salisbury, commemorating the event, was placed by the roadside in front of the original homesite of her father, Richard Brandon.

Among the children of Francis McCorkle and his second wife, Betsy Brandon, were:

Sarah, born October 21, 1784, married John Wilkinson.

Elizabeth, born July 31, 1786, married Jeptha Sherrill.

Francis, Jr., born October 22, 1787, married Elizabeth Abernethy.

Richard, born January 26, 1790, married Agnes Sherrill.

Thomas, born April 20, 1793, married Casey Sherrill.

William Brandon, born, November 19, 1794, married Mary Marshall of Wadesboro.

John, born June 30, 1796, married .... Turbyfill.

Among their descendants were:

Judge Matthew Locke McCorkle; Colonel James Marshall McCorkle, a brilliant lawyer of Salisbury; his brothers, Dr. John R., Dr. Wm. A. and Dr. Francis M. McCorkle; S. P. Sherrill of Lincolnton; Dr. J. A. Sherrill, Powell Sherrill, Henderson Sherrill and Dr. Josephus Turner of Catawba, all deceased; George McCorkle of Washington; Judge Wilson Warlick of Newton; Dr. Watson S. Rankin, a noted physician of Charlotte; S. J. and J. L. Blythe, progressive business men of Charlotte; Rev. L. D. Thompson; Howard R. Thompson; J. W. A. Paine; Rev. H. R. Cornelius; Rev. C. E. Murray; and others including Reinhardts, Beattys and Gabriels of this section.

Major McCorkle had a large landed estate and many slaves and exerted a fine influence in his day, but never held public office, other than above mentioned. He died October 9, 1802, in his sixtieth year, and his body is buried in the old McCorkle graveyard some fifteen miles from Lincolnton near highway leading to Mooresville.

1801. The first church, called Unity, erected near Beatties Ford by the Presbyterians was a log building, but in 1801 additional ground was deeded to James Connor, Alex Brevard, John Reid and Joseph Graham, Trustees for the erection of a new and larger church.

1803. Captain Charles Connor, father of Major Henry W. Connor, died at his home near Beatties Ford in 1803.

February 27, 1803, Abram Forney was married to Rachel Gabriel.

Christian Reinhardt, Jr., married to Polly Forney, January 25, 1803.

1803

Henry Connor of County Antrim, Ireland, an elder of the Presbyterian Church, married Miss Workman.

They had four sons:

1. John, who married in Ireland and had two daughters. He did not come to America.

2. Captain Chas. Connor, merchant and Captain on ships plying between Liverpool and Norfolk, was the first of the family to come to America; was wealthy, served in Revolutionary Army in Virginia and received his title as an active soldier of the Revolution. Married Ann, daughter of Peter Epps of Prince George County, Virginia, came to Mecklenburg County, N. C., and settled near Beatties Ford where he died in 1803.

He had two children:

(1) Major Henry William Connor (1793-1866), who lived and died at Beatties Ford, Lincoln County.

(2) Elizabeth (called Betsy) (1797-1836) married John D. Graham, son of General Joseph Graham. (See *Life of Gen. Joseph Graham* by Maj. W. A. Graham.)

3. James Connor (1754-1835) came to America in 1772, married Lilis Wilson of Mecklenburg County, N. C., and lived and died there, across the river from Beatties Ford. He was a soldier of the Revolution and represented Mecklenburg in the House of Commons two terms. Among his children were:

(1) Chas. D. Connor, who represented Iredell in State Senate four terms from 1817 to 1820, and then went to Mississippi where he died.

(2) Henry Workman Connor settled in Charleston, S. C., and was a banker, married into the prominent Courtney family of that city. Was Mayor of the city and member of the Secession Convention held in Columbia in December 1860. He died about 1861.

Among his children were:

a. Gen. James Connor of the Confederate Army, a lawyer and elected Attorney General of South Carolina on the ticket headed by Gov. Wade Hampton in 1876.

b. Henry Workman Connor, Jr., was a banker in New Orleans and died about 1890. One daughter, Mrs. L. R. Staudenmyer, at one time lived in Lincolnton.

c. Margaret, daughter of James Connor, married Franklin Brevard (1788-1829), son of Captain Alexander Brevard of Lincoln County; their daughter, Rebecca, married Robert I. McDowell and were parents of Franklin Brevard McDowell, prominent Charlotte citizen, Mayor of the city, and one time State Senator from Mecklenburg.

4. Henry Connor, the youngest brother (1758-1821), was a wealthy and influential citizen of Lincoln County. The name of his wife inscribed on tombstone is Nancy (maiden name not entered).

Among his children were: Dr. Samuel Connor; Harriet, who married Dr. Sidney X. Johnston; Eliza, who married W. S. Simonton; James married Mary Simonton, moved to Alabama; Henry never married; he died in Charleston, S. C.

1804

Gov. William A. Graham was born September 5, 1804.

John Fulenwider erected a forge on Maiden Creek, near the present town of Maiden, in 1804, and for some years manufactured iron there. Later it was operated by A. F. and E. J. Brevard and later still by William Williams, until about 1880. John Fulenwider was also the founder of the High Shoals Iron Works. He manufactured there cannon balls during the war of 1812 and shipped them in flat boats to Charleston. He also made wagon tire, plows, horse shoes, chain iron, nails and various farm tools. After the Civil War this property was owned and operated by Admiral Charles Wilkes of the United States Navy. Nails were made there as late as 1872, when it ceased to be operated. About 1900 the High Shoals Cotton Mill was built on the same site by D. A. Tompkins.

Philip W. Cansler the pioneer was one of the early settlers west of the Catawba River. The record shows that he owned land near High Shoals in 1767. Later he lived one-half mile south of Lincoln Court House where he had large landed interests and was a frugal and sturdy citizen.

The town of Lincolnton was in 1785 located on land between the Cansler home and the home of Christian Reinhardt (another pioneer), one-half mile north of the town, near Ramsour's Mill.

Mr. Cansler married Barbara, daughter of Michael Rudisill (another pioneer). He later moved to land on Leeper's Creek, east of Lincolnton, and died there in 1804, and his body was buried in a graveyard (now neglected) near his Leeper's Creek home. His marble gravestone bears a German inscription, which translated would read:

"Here rests a father of many children, a friend of men and a Christian, who through the cross is now perfect. He is well known to us; he served his people and his country. His name is with all honor the (our) father, Philip W. Cansler."

His wife was buried by his side, but with no stone to mark her grave.

M. L. Hoffman in *Our Kin* says:

"About the time of the founding of the town of Lincolnton he, by sale or gift, transferred this home place to his son, Philip Cansler, and he himself with his family moved to Leeper's Creek in the Rudisill-Arndt neighborhood where he built his house and a mill on the west bank of the creek on the slope of the hill facing the creek and adjoining the lands of the Rev. Jno. Gottfried Arndt and in the neighborhood of the ancestral home of the Rudisills. His house was of the regulation style for those Indian days with a high basement wall of stone and the upper house built of very large hewed logs. This house stood till recently when it was torn down and a new and more modern one erected on the same site. The old logs of the house were moved a short distance from their old position and rebuilt as a barn or some sort of outhouse. The mill is still in use. In later years it has been known as the Hammerschold Mill."

They had ten children:

Catherine married ....Cline.

Margaret (1759-1833) married Philip Davenpaugh (1751-1825).

Katie married John Finger.

Mary married ....Garden.

Elizabeth never married.

Barbara married Henry Troutman, 1802.

John married .... and moved to Rutherford County.

Philip married Mary Quickel. (See 1870.)

George married Margaret, daughter of Peter Finger.

Conrad married Barbara Rudisill.

Mr. Cansler's original will on file in the Clerk's office of Lincoln County, N. C., follows:

"In the name of God, Amen. I, Philip Cancelor, of the County of Lincoln and State of North Carolina, being sick and weak in body but of perfect memory and sound understanding, and calling to mind the mortality of my body, do make, constitute, appoint and ordain this to be my last will and testament, and as touching my worldly estate desire to dispose of it in manner and form following:

"1st. I desire that my debts should be paid and that I may be buried in a decent Christianlike manner at the discretion of my executors hereinafter named.

"2nd. I give and bequeath to my well beloved wife, Uly Cancelor, as much of the furniture belonging to the house as she may choose and likewise of my stock of horses and cattle as she shall choose during her widowhood and the remainder to be sold with all my movable property to me anyways belonging.

"3rd. I give and bequeath to my daughter, Catherine Cline, one hundred acres of land on the waters of Indian Creek and forty pounds of money arising from the Vandue.

"4th. I give and bequeath to my daughter, Margaret Devepaugh, one hundred and twenty acres of land out of a tract on waters of Leeper's and Hoyle's Creeks and forty pounds.

"5th. I give and bequeath to my daughter, Caty Finger, same as the above daughters.

"6th. I give and bequeath to my daughter, Mary Garden, the same as the above.

"7th. I give and bequeath to my daughter, Elizabeth, the same as above.

"8th. I give and bequeath to my daughter, Barbara, the same as above; and I also do give to my two last named daughters three cows apiece.

"9th. I give and bequeath unto my son, John Cancelor, five shillings.

"10th. I give and bequeath to my son, Philip Cancelor, five shillings.

"11th. I give and bequeath to my son, George Cancelor, three hundred and fifty acres of land more or less lying on Leeper's Creek, including the place whereon I now live.

"12th. I give and bequeath to my son, Conrade Cancelor, two hundred and seventy-five acres more or less lying on the waters of the South Fork, near Lincolnton, on the pine field branch and twenty pounds. And the remainder of my whole estate to my aforesaid wife during her widowhood and then to be equally divided between my aforesaid wife and all my children equally. And I do appoint my wife and Philip Cancelor, my son, executors of this my last will and testament and I do disannul and revoke all wills and testaments by me heretofore made and confirm this to be my last will and testament. In witness whereof I have hereunto set my hand this 25th day of May, 1801.

PHILIP GANTZLER.

Witness:
Jos. Abernethy,
Philip Devepaugh."

1805

Henry Johnston (Scotchman) settled very early in Lincoln County with his young wife, when the Indians and wild beasts held full sway. His wife died comparatively young, leaving two children, Mary and James. Mary married Moses Scott, who lived near Goshen church in what is now Gaston County. The son, James Johnston (1742-1805), was a prominent figure in the history of the county. He entered the military service in 1776 as a Captain in the patriot army and was a brave soldier under Col. William Graham against the Tories in South Carolina. He was a delegate from Tryon County, with Charles McLean, to the Halifax Convention April 12, 1776. He was also a member of the Senate from Lincoln in 1780, 1781 and 1782 and a member of the convention held in Hillsboro in 1788.

Ephraim Perkins was Senator from Lincoln in 1805, occupying the seat which his father, Gentleman John Perkins, held when he was Senator from Lincoln in 1795.

David Ramsour was married to Sarah Wilfong July 12, 1805.

1806

Green W. Caldwell was born in Lincoln County near Belmont, April 13, 1806.

General John Moore of Lincoln, John Steele of Rowan and James Welborn of Wilkes, were appointed Commissioners in 1806 to settle the Southern boundary line of the State and they completed the task in 1808. (See John Steele, Vol. 2: 468-566-789.)

John Moore, Brig. Gen. N. C. State Militia and Speaker of the House of Commons, 1806, was instrumental in bringing Joseph Glass, Robert Clary, Abraham Collins and Allen Twitty to trial for counterfeiting and they in turn attempted to blackmail Gen. Moore, charging that he too was a counterfeiter, but upon investigation Moore was completely vindicated. (See John Steele, Vol. 1: 453, and Vol. 2: 798.)

Robert Williamson, a notable lawyer and State Senator was married to Elizabeth, daughter of Capt. John Reid of Catawba Springs on November 24, 1806.

Jacob Forney was born in Alsace about 1721. When 14 years old he sailed from Amsterdam for Philadelphia, and when of age returned to Alsace to secure a legacy. On the return voyage to America he met Maria Bergner and they married later in Philadelphia. They migrated to North Carolina about 1754 and settled in what is now Lincoln County. He was one of the earlier pioneers in Lincoln and became a loyal patriot of the Revolution, a member of the Tryon County Committee of Safety, a signer of the resolutions of protest against British tyranny which were adopted at Tryon Court House in August, 1775, and one of the Committee appointed by the Assembly to locate court house and jail for Tryon County.

Few patriots suffered heavier losses on account of British invasions and Indian depredations. By industry and frugality he had more of comforts and supplies than the average citizen, and when Cornwallis invaded the county he used the Forney home for headquarters, forcing the old people to occupy the cellar, while the British troops literally stripped the plantation, and also that of his son, Gen. Peter Forney, who was away from home fighting for his country. They butchered the sheep and cattle, fowls and hogs for food and confiscated all the grain and provender. Forney's three sons, Jacob, Peter and Abram were all in the patriot army. His four daughters were Catherine, Elizabeth, Christina and Susan. When 85 years old he died in 1806, a Lutheran in faith. The graves of Jacob and Maria (Bergner) Forney are in the old Dutch Meeting House graveyard, about three miles from the Forney homestead. Many of their descendants were distinguished people.

George Lohr and Susan Hasselbarger were married December 10, 1806.

Prior to 1782 Lincoln was attached to the Salisbury district and all Superior Court sessions were held in Salisbury. In 1782 the Morgan district was created including Burke, Lincoln, Rutherford and Wilkes Counties, and the courts were held in Morganton. In 1806 the Legislature changed the plan for the convenience of the people by providing sessions of Superior Court in each county and the first session of Superior Court was convened in Lincolnton, April 13, 1807, with Judge Francis Locke, of Rowan presiding. Judge Locke was a son of Col. Francis Locke, who commanded the Whig forces at the battle of Ramsour's Mill. Lawson Henderson was then appointed Clerk of the Superior Court for life and served in that capacity until he resigned in 1837.

1807

George Ramsour died in 1807 and his wife, Sarah Ramsour, died May 26, 1832. Their graves are in the White Church cemetery.

Alfred M. Burton was licensed as an attorney in 1807.

John Gottfried Arndt was born December 11, 1740, in Goettingen; graduated from the Teachers Seminary in Hanover, Germany, and his Certificate as a school teacher to North Carolina bears date, October 16, 1772, indicating that he was aged 32 years when he came to America. For two years he taught the children of the old Organ Church in Rowan County and then upon recommendation of the congregation and the pastor, Rev. Adolphus Nussman, he was ordained as a minister of the Lutheran church on the 11th Sunday after Trinity, 1775, by Joachim Beulow, missionary and inspector over North and South Carolina Lutherans.

He was the first minister ordained in North Carolina and the second pastor of Organ Church, which he served for 11 years until about 1786 when he moved to Lincoln County, where he preached for 21 years until his decease July 9, 1807. He was one of the organizers of the North Carolina Lutheran Synod and its first president. He is said to have been a Chesterfield in manners; was blue-eyed with fair complexion and auburn hair which reached to his shoulders.

The Annals of Lincoln County 71

He married Hannah Rudisill, daughter of Michael Rudisill, the pioneer. Their children were:

John, born October 12, 1780, married Susan Bisaner.

Catharine, born January 8, 1778, married Solomon Hoover.

Hannah, born April 19, 1786, married Lewis Hafer.

Elizabeth, born January 27, 1783, married David Smith, son of Peter Smith and Hannah Bess.

Susan, born January 30, 1789, married John Sadler.

Jacob, born April 3, 1791, married Jane Rutledge.

Frederick, born April 10, 1794, married Holly Robinson.

Mary, born June 25, 1799, married Henry Cansler, son of Philip W. Cansler, the pioneer.

Rev. Geo. H. Cox in *The Beginning of the Lutheran Church in North Carolina*, says: "He was very particular as to his personal appearance and always neatly dressed according to the fashions of the day, and wearing gloves wherever he went, something very unusual among the hardy people of that time." Also: "During his latter years he was blind but continued in the ministry until, worn and weary, he passed triumphantly into the land of eternal bliss, leaving as a legacy to the church and his posterity an enduring reputation for piety, humility and zeal."

His body was buried under the old "Dutch Meeting House" in Lincolnton and the German inscription on the tombstone translated into English is: "Here rests the body of the Rev. John Gottfried Arends. Having been a true evangelistic preacher, and died July the 9th at the age of 66 years, six months and 28 days, of a kind of consumption disease, after faithfully administering the office of preacher for 32 years."

"*Blessed are all those that die like thou
They to the rest of heaven shall come.*"

Below in English is written:

"*Remember man as you pass by,
As you are now, so once was I;
As I am now, you soon shall be,
Therefore prepare to follow me.*"

An eagle, 13 stars and "E pluribus unum," the motto of the United States, is proof of his patriotism. The late Miles L. Hoffman, in *Our Kin*, classed him as a patriot and Whitsett, in *Founders of the Church and State*, says: "Rev. John G. Arndt was bold in his stand for liberty."

After coming to Lincoln County he formed a warm friendship with the Rev. Andrew Loretz, of the Reformed Church, and it is said they agreed that the one who died first should be buried by the other. Mr. Loretz lived until 1812, five years after the death of Mr. Arndt.

The influence of this great preacher and citizen still abides and many of his descendants have reflected honor upon the name.

Robert Johnston married to Mary Reid, daughter of Capt. John Reid, April 21, 1807. They were the parents of Col. William Johnston, Dr. Sidney X. Johnston, John R., and Rufus M. Johnston.

1808

Thomas Dews, Jr., son of Thomas Dews, was born at Saint Peter's Port, Isle of Guernsey, on May 10, 1808, and later came with his parents to America and to Lincolnton. His father lived and had a cabinet shop on the lot where the Baptist church now stands.

At a court trial in Rutherford sometime in the 1830's the attorneys were Col. James R. Dodge, Samuel Hillman, Governor Swain and Thomas Dews. Col. Dodge placed the following lines on Dews' table:

> *"Here lies a Hillman and a Swain*
> *Their lot let no man choose;*
> *They lived in sin and died in pain*
> *And the Devil got his Dews."*

Immediately Dews wrote:

> *"Here lies a Dodge who dodged all good*
> *And dodged a deal of evil,*
> *But after dodging all he could*
> *He could not dodge the Devil."*

John Hoke was married January 9, 1808, to Barbara Quickel, daughter of Michael Quickel, the pioneer.

1809

Daniel Finger was married to Catherine Summerow, January 28, 1809. They were the parents of Major Sidney M. Finger, the educator and State superintendent of Public Instruction, 1884 to 1892.

John Motz was married November 16, 1809, to Catherine Loretz, daughter of Rev. Andrew Loretz, the pioneer minister of the German Reformed church in Lincoln.

Elias Alexander, a notable citizen of Lincolnton in the earlier days, died in 1809.

1810

On July 12, 1810, Paul Kistler was married to Amy Smith.

Joseph Dickson of Rutherford County, Tenn., was married to Ellen Rankin on October 11, 1810.

1811

Alfred M. Burton was married to Elizabeth Fulenwider, daughter of John Fulenwider, June 1, 1811.

CHAPTER IX

1812-1819

D. P. Loretz, a descendant of the Rev. Andrew Loretz, writing from Centre, Ala., February 12, 1877, "To the Honorable Members of Classis and other friends of the German Reformed church," says:

"I herewith submit the following short sketch of the life of the Rev. Andrew Loretz taken from notes and papers in my possession.

"Rev. Andrew Loretz, born in the town of Chur, which is the capital of the Canton of Graubuenden, (Grisons, Switzerland), in the year 1761. He was educated at Kaufbeuren, Bavaria, and was a professor in the college there, as the translation from the German on the fly leaf in his album would indicate, which translation I herewith note:
'To Patrons, Friends and Acquaintances,
This book shall dedicated be. Write
herein your respective names, as I request,
for thus shall the remembrance of you, deep
in my heart prevail, and I'll the honor have
Ever your obedient servant to remain.'
Kaufbeuren, May 6, 1779.   (Signed) Andrew Loretz."

"But little is known of his early history. His passport, which I have in possession, is dated from Chur, Switzerland, August 7, 1784, and is signed by the Mayor (Der Burgermeister). He landed in Baltimore after a voyage of three months and from there went to Meyerstown, Penn. About the year 1786 he married to a Mrs. Schaffer (who was formerly Miss Lehman, of Hagerstown, Md.). The latter part of the year 1786 or 1787 he moved to Lincoln County, North Carolina.

"He was a man of thorough education. His native language was German, although he was familiar with French and Latin. It must have been more difficult for ministers to travel in those days than now, for it took two horses to serve him in his labors, as he had also a large congregation in Lancaster, S. C. He was a man of very polished manners and of a jovial nature. At one time he is said to have remarked to a friend that he had three sons, of whom he was going to make a thief, a liar and a beggar (a doctor, a lawyer and a preacher). But he died too soon to accomplish his desire as he left his sons all quite young and they had to use great economy to succeed. His library was valuable but was sold at his sale for a trifling sum.

"He now lies buried at Daniel's church, a tombstone over his grave bearing his name and dated 1812.

"I have been informed by Consul General Hiltz, of Switzerland that several families bearing the name of Loretz are now living in the town of Chur.

(Signed) D. P. Loretz.

Centre, Cherokee Co., Ala., Feb. 12, 1877."

Judge David Schenck in the *Lincoln Progress*, July 12, 1873, wrote:

"Rev. Andrew Loretz died March 31, 1812, aged 59 years, and his body was buried at Daniels church, four miles northwest of Lincolnton, where many of his family are also buried. He was a man of remarkable energy and great endurance, and zealous in the performance of duty. He was also a man of extraordinary talent and well educated. He preached a funeral sermon on the death of General Washington, which was so original and eloquent that it was published in pamphlet form and widely distributed. As a speaker he is said to have been very powerful and attractive and his people were greatly attached to him. During his entire pastorate at Emanuel Church (the old White Church) in Lincolnton and the pastorate of the Rev. John Gottfried Arndt, of the Lutheran church the services were always conducted in German, this being the only language then in use among the Dutch people, and in which their records were kept until 1822. After the death of Mr. Loretz the Presbyterians seem to have occupied the church jointly with the Lutherans, and were organized under the ministration and pastoral care of Rev. Humphrey Hunter. We have no record of his pastorate and have only the memory of those living, who heard him preach there. An ancient relic is a silver sacramental cup, which is the only remaining part of a silver service bequeathed by Philip Anthony (Grandfather of John P. Anthony) to the church. It is now (1873) in the possession of Mrs. J. C. Cobb, who received it from her father, Mr. John Butts, an elder of the church. Mrs. Cobb keeps it for the use of the proper owners when called for."

The Rev. Mr. Loretz filled a high niche in the church history of Lincoln County and left a posterity which honored the name. One son, Andrew H. Loretz, was prominent in the public life of the County and was its representative in the State Legislature for three terms, 1828, 1829, and 1830. One daughter, Catherine, became the wife of John Motz, an influential citizen, and they were the parents of Caleb, Wade H., Andrew, and George W. Motz, all well-known and highly respected in their day.

The Raleigh Star of May 1, 1812, paid high tribute to the memory of the Rev. Andrew Loretz.

Mr. Loretz purchased in 1792 nearly two thousand acres of land near the present Daniels Church for which he paid fourteen pounds, North Carolina currency. After his death this land was divided between seven of his children:

1. Catherine, who married John Motz, November 16, 1809.
2. Elizabeth, who married Charles Reinhardt, October 6, 1812.
3. Mary, who married David Ramsour, September 15, 1814.
4. Andrew H. Loretz, who married Elizabeth Ramsour, May 1, 1822.
5. Daniel, who married Elizabeth Reinhardt, October 23, 1828.
6. & 7. Frederick and Sarah.

Rev. O. B. Michael who recently wrote a sketch of the Loretz family says: "There were evidently other children besides the above as follows:

Barbara, who married John Hallman, March 21, 1814.
Salome, who married Henry Roseman, March 12, 1816.
Anne, who married Jacob Michael, November 13, 1820.
John F., who married Polly Ramsour, August 21, 1827.

"Marriage records show that other Loretz girls, doubtless granddaughters of Rev. Andrew Loretz and probably daughters of Frederick or Andrew H. Loretz as follows:

Polly married Daniel Hallman, February 5, 1824.
N_____ married Thomas Wilkinson, June 25, 1835.
Judith married Joseph Clay, May 3, 1837.
Mary J. E. married Marcus L. Bost, September 7, 1849.
Mary H. married Lawson Henry, April 1, 1835."

Jacob Brem married Eve Hoover, May 9, 1812. He was a skilled worker in wood and it is said that he constructed the beautiful spiral stairway in the old Hoke residence in Lincolnton, now known as Inverness Inn. Mr. Brem moved to the Beatties Ford section and among his children was Colonel Thomas H. Brem, for many years a prominent Charlotte merchant.

Col. Brem had three sons, Thomas H. Brem, Jr., a lawyer, Dr. Charles F. Brem, a physician, both bachelors, and Walter

THE ANNALS OF LINCOLN COUNTY 77

Brem an active Charlotte business. man who married Hannah, daughter of Gov. Tod R. Caldwell of Morganton.
Their children are (1936): Dr. Walter Brem of California, T. R. Brem, Mrs. Robert A. Mayer, and Mrs. Robert R. Beatty all of Charlotte.

On July 7, 1812, "Gentleman" Jonas Rudisill was married to Polly Seagle.

David Ramsour, son of Diedrich Ramsour, the pioneer, died in his fiftieth year on February 23, 1812.

MUSTER ROLLS OF THE SOLDIERS OF THE WAR OF 1812, detached from the Militia of North Carolina in 1812 and 1814. Published in pursuance of the resolutions of the General Assembly of North Carolina, January 21, 1851.

SIXTH COMPANY DETACHED FROM THE FIRST LINCOLN REGIMENT

Edward Boyd, Captain
Edwin S. Lingles, Lieutenant
John Hill, Ensign
Mason Harwell, 1st Sergeant
Joshua Abernethy, 2nd Sergeant
David Lineberger, Corporal
John Club, Corporal
Sherod Little, Corporal
John Ganny, Corporal

Samuel Harwell
Gardner Myers
Levi Perkins
Frederick Abernethy
Thomas Long
Michel Sides
Henry Eddleman
Moses Abernethy
Jacob Eddman
Joseph Burke
Peter Evans
George Club, Jr.
Ezekiel Abernethy
James McGinnis
Robert Ramsey
Martin Gruson
Robert McCullock
Henry Holland
Matthew Holland, Jr.
William Robertson, Jr.
Robert Huggins, Jr.
James Rhodes
David Rhyne, Jr.
John Rhyne
Joseph Senter
Frederick Hovis
Jacob Totherow
Jonathan Nardike
Nicholas Dillin
John Friday
Samuel Armstrong
Matthew Armstrong
John Neagle
Alexander Irwin
George Irwin
George Oliver
John Henderson
William Hawkins
John Lineberger
Archibald Cathey
Daniel Morrison
Alexander Moore
Adam Cloninger, Jr.
Jonathan West
George Hager
William Stephenson
Thomas Henry
Andrew Ferguson
William Falls
Samuel Carson
John Hager
Daniel Tucker
Robert Beal
Levi Sides
William Hinkle
William Hunt
John Blalock
John Little
Miles Farrer

SEVENTH COMPANY, DETACHED FROM FIRST LINCOLN REGIMENT

Henry Rudisill, Captain
Robert Oates, Lieutenant
Philip Hains, Ensign
Moses Herring, 1st Sergeant
Peter Crites, 2nd Sergeant
Christopher Lewis, 3rd Sergeant
William Fulbright, 4th Sergeant
Abram Wyatt, Corporal
Linus Shuford, Corporal
David Cline, Corporal
Samuel Edgin, Corporal

John Master
John Tucker
Jepthah Sain
James Clark
Henry Barclay
Jesse Wheeler
John Ballard
George Sifford
Meacum Shelton
George Freet
William Sifford
John Sifford
Isaac Fleming
Gatlin Sifford
Adam Hopper
Martin Dellinger
Robert Williams
William Lowe

Isaiah Abernethy
Drury Baggett
Abram Baggett
Absalom Bumgarner
George Moore
William Walker
Nicholas Lowrance
Thomas Ashe
Moses Bumgarner
Colbert Sherrill
Isaac Robertson
Jacob Burns
John Caldwell
Frederick Summey
Jacob Finger
Jacob Rudisill
Solomon Cline
Elijah Call
John Wilson

Alfred Moore
Aaron Moore
William Johnston
Francis Asbury
John Kistler
James Martin
Samuel Turner
John Brim
Thomas Hannon
Edward Sneed
William Bennett
Jacob Miller
Robert Wilson
John Craig
John Murphy
James Lindsay
Adam Speight
Christy Speight

EIGHTH COMPANY DETACHED FROM SECOND LINCOLN REGIMENT

George Hoffman, Captain
David Bailey, Lieutenant
Daniel Cline, Ensign
John Jarrett, 1st Sergeant
Jacob Connor, 2nd Sergeant

Thomas Bandy, 3rd Sergeant
Robert H. Simpson, 4th Sergeant
Philip Fry, Corporal
Thomas Simpson, Corporal
John Norman, Corporal
Christopher Acer, Corporal

Daniel Shuford, Jr.
Daniel Whitener, Jr.
Adolph Fadz
Michael Propts
David Bost
John German
Andrew Setzer
Adam Killian
Jacob Rink
Daniel Peterson
Abram Setzer
George Fisher
Payton Vaughn
Conrad Yoder
George Mosteller
Silas Wilson
Jacob Thorne
George McIntosh
Thomas Huskey
Reuben Copelin

William Harrison
Peter Herman
Ephraim Davis
James Patterson
Solomon Gladden
Benjamin Waterson
William Scoggins
Solomon Harmon
Abner Camp
David Wier
Perry G. Reynolds
Uell Reynolds
John Rudisill
John Turner
Cyrus Peed
Isaac Williams
Benjamin Edwards
Jacob Raugh
Michael Hefner
John Miller

John Taylor
William Caldwell
William Hull
William Bird
William Carroll
John Trout
Peter Houser
Jacob Speagle
James Center
John Edwards
Wiley Harris
John Heavner
Robert Watts
Joseph Kyson
Thomas Lawing
Adam Husslatter
Peter Beam
John Vickers
Joseph Carpenter
Peter Kiser

LINCOLN COUNTY, FIRST REGIMENT

James Finley, Captain
William J. Wilson, 1st Lieutenant

Richard Cowan, 2nd Lieutenant
Andrew Barry, 3rd Lieutenant
John Beard, Ensign

Ambrose Gaultney
Andrew Slinkard
John Hogan
Henry Salder
George Berry
Jacob Troutman

Red Errowood
Robert Luckey
Charles Edwards
Anthony Long
Freeman Shelton
Reuben Grice

David Costner
Jacob Smith
George Houser
Amos Robeson
Alex McCullock
Reece Price

THE ANNALS OF LINCOLN COUNTY

William Short
James Graham
Isaac Murrell
John Hunt
Benedict Jetton
Benjamin Proctor
John Lutz
William Little
Richard Proctor
William Nance, Jr.
James White
William Nance
William Tucker
Ambrose Cobb
Jacob Cloninger
Samuel Pew
Thomas Sadler
Needam Wingate
David Smith, Jr.
Robinson Moore
William McGinnis
John McGinnis
William Sutton
John Mayhew
Bedford Childers
Thomas Tucker
Samuel Abernethy

John Bynum
William Hill
Willie Ballard
William Killian
Robinson Harris
Anthony Hinkle
Ashman Gwin
James Hicks
Daniel Killian
Frederick Killian
Edward Carroll
John Jenkins
Thomas Dickson
John Venable
Austin Ford
Peter Titman
James McCarver
William McCarver
William Rockford
Robert Alexander
Wiert Jenkins
Reuben Jenkins
Jacob Rhyne
Adam Rhyne
Solomon Rhyne
John Rhodes

Moses Grissom
Thomas Groves
Hiram Harris
James Shannon
Jacob Fite
Ezekiel McClure
James McClure
John Merner
Samuel Williams
William Lattimore
John Damon
Anderson Wells
William Hamilton
John Leeper
John Glover
Alexander Rankin
William Reid
Stuart Jenkins
William Bluford
John Hanks
Ebner Rumfelt
John Cathey
Jacob Kennedy
John Oates
John Palmer
William Adams
John Blackwood

LINCOLN COUNTY, SECOND REGIMENT

Daniel Hoke, Captain Gilbert Millegan, 2nd Lieutenant
John B. Harris, 1st Lieutenant Isaac Mauney, 3rd Lieutenant
Peter Hoke, Ensign

John Carpenter
Henry Huffstettler
Moses Barr
Jacob Plonk
William Carpenter
Joseph Black
William Ferguson
Cadias Smith
Jonas Rudisill
Peter Mauney
David Kizer
Peter Eaker
Geo. Seller
Peter Costner
John Huffstettler
Wm. Guntlessey
Daniel Clodfelter
Elias Clodfelter
George Clodfelter
Rudolph Clodfelter
John Teague
Lewis Huitt
Philip Ekerd
Thomas Smith
John Bumgarner
William Hope
Archibald Cobb
Elisha Saunders

Robert Barber
Young Marden
Thomas Black
David Dickson
Hardy Long
Solomon Childers
Christopher Carpenter
James Ensley
Anthony Clark
David Bookout
Archibald Ensley
John Wright
Thomas Craig
Philip Haynes
John Whitworth
Joshua Howell
Samuel Collins
John Mouser
Casper Bolick
George Bowman
Henry Lockman
Matthew Poovey
Charles Ward
William Harmon
David Hunley
Martin Lockman
George Turner
Abraham Gray

Joseph Ashe
John Earney
Sefred Sherrill
Elias Shine
Conrad Ward
Avery Grunt
Andrew Yount
Philip Hedrick
Benedict Levant
John Cowan
George Shook
Jacob Fulbright
Leonard Kagle
Ephraim Christopher
William Ekerd
John Hedrick
Aaron Downson
Peter Keller
Gabriel Isaac
Samuel Peterson
Frederick Knup
Francis King
Peter Rabey
Michael Sattonfield
Jonathan Robinson
Miles Abernethy
David Hawn
Valentine Taylor

Joshua Hunter
Conrad Hildebrand
Peter Reymer
Bostian Best
John Houser
Solomon Shoup
Samuel Bingham
William Willis
Chas. Williams
James Chapman
Nathaniel Pew
Jacob Houser
John Watterson
Joseph Wear
James Patterson
Preston Goforth
Hugh Spruling
Isaac Mullinax
James Elliott
Thos. Earwood
George Goforth
Jacob Harmon

Henry Lockman, Jr.
Samuel Sullivan
Christian Dellinger
Christian Hope
Michael Ingle
William Cline
John Shafer
Henry Houser
Ransom Husky
Matthias Barringer
Michael Dellinger
Daniel Blackburn
Jacob Havner
Aaron Moore
David Dick
Joseph Hildebrand
Joseph Leonhart
James Lemons
David Fulbright
Francis Summit
Daniel Summit
Nicholas Carpenter
Peter Lowrance

John Stamey
Peter Frey
James Hildebrand
John Snyder
James Bridges
James Jones
Benjamin Newman
Sterling Singleton
John Ward
John Clodfelter
James Fisher
Samuel Jetton
William Black
David Warlick
Elisha Winson
Nimrod Winson
Henry Killian
Solomon Killian
Daniel Coulter
Henry Coulter
John Shuford
James Henderson

SEVENTH COMPANY DETACHED FROM 10TH BRIGADE

Henry Ramsour, Captain
William Green, 1st Lieutenant
Jacob Summers, 2nd Lieutenant
John Zimmerman, Cornet
John Falls, 1st Sergeant

John Slagle, 2nd Sergeant
Henry Smith, 3rd Sergeant
Moses Sides, 4th Sergeant
George Fry, Saddler
Ezekiel Hazlitt, Trumpeteer

Elias Bost, Dragon

William Bost
Jacob Smoyer
Hiram Harbison
Alexander Neal
Henry Smith
Charles Reinhardt
Edward Saunders
Mathew Haynes
Absalom Taylor
Allen Wetherly

William Price
John Henry
Moses Heron
John Rhyne, Jr.
Edward Scarboro
David Ramsour
James Grist
Richard Maze
James Knox
Samuel McMinn
John Wilkinson

Alexander McCorkle
John Cornelius
Hardy Abernethy
William Porter
Frederick Rimmy
Benjamin Suttle
William Hannon
Jeremiah Runyan
Timothy Hauny
Isaac Vanzant

1813

Robert H. Burton was married May 11, 1813, to Mary Fulenwider, daughter of John Fulenwider.

Pleasant Retreat Academy, in Lincolnton, for boys, was chartered by the Legislature December 10, 1813. A school site of four acres was secured on the north side of the town. A long line of notable people have been educated there. The original Trustees were Rev. Philip Henkel, Rev. Humphrey Hunter, Lawson Henderson, Joseph Graham, John Fulenwider, John Hoke, Peter Forney, Robert Williamson, Daniel Hoke, John

Top: Pleasant Retreat Academy, established 1813. Probably the oldest building in Lincolnton. Now Memorial Hall.
Center: Lincolnton High School building, erected in 1924.
Lower left: McKendree Methodist Church, established in 1836. (See 1936)
Lower right: Machpelah Presbyterian Church. (See 1847)

Reinhardt, Vardry McBee, David Ramsour, Peter Hoyle, Henry Y. Webb, George Carruth, William McLean, Robert H. Burton, John Reid and David Reinhardt, altogether a very remarkable body of men.

John Phifer, of Cabarrus, was defeated for Congress in 1813 by Gen. Peter Forney, of Lincoln County.

1814

Dr. William McLean was elected to the State Senate from Lincoln in 1814.

1815

Dr. William McLean delivered the address at the first celebration of the battle of Kings Mountain, held on the battleground, October 7, 1815, and had erected there at his own expense a plain stone with an epitaph on one side as follows: "Sacred to the memory of Major William Chronicle, Capt. John Mattocks, William Rabb and John Boyd, who were killed here on the 7th of October, 1780, fighting in defense of America." On the other side of the stone the inscription reads: "Col. Ferguson, an officer belonging to his Brittanic Majesty was here defeated and killed." This was the first marker ever placed on that historic battleground.

1816

The first cotton factory operated south of the Potomac River was built in 1816 by Michael Schenck, the pioneer, near the McDaniel spring, one and one-half miles east of Lincolnton. Some of the machinery was bought in Providence, R. I., but portions of it were made by Absalom Warlick, a skilled worker in iron, and a relative of Mrs. Michael Schenck. Michael Beam made some of the machines as shown by the following contract dated April 27, 1816:

"Articles of agreement made and entered into this 27th April, 1816, between Michael Schenck and Absalom Warlick of the County of Lincoln, N. C., of the one part and Michael Beam, of County and State aforesaid, of the other part. WITNESSETH: That the said Michael Beam obliges himself to build for the said Schenck and Warlick, within 12 months from this date, a spinning machine with 154 fliers, with 3 sets of flooted rollers, the back to be set of wood, the other 2 sets to be iron; the machine to be made in two frames with 2 sets of wheels, one carding machine with 2 sets of cards to run 2 ropings, each to be one foot wide, with a picking machine to be attached to it with as many saws as may be necessary to feed the carding machine; one rolling (or roping) with 4 heads; all the above machinery to be completed in a workmanlike manner. And the said Beam is to board himself and find all the material for the machine and set the machinery going on a branch on Ab Warlick's land below where the old machine stood. The said Schenck and Warlick are to have the house for the machine and the running gears made at their expense, but the said Beam is to fix the whole machinery above described thereto. The wooden cans for the roping and spinning, and the reel to be furnished by said Schenck and Warlick together with all the straps and bands necessary for the machinery. In consideration of which the said Schenck and Warlick are to pay the said Beam the sum of $1,300.00, to-wit: $300.00 this day, $200.00 three months from this date, $100.00 six moths from this date, and the balance within twelve months after said machine is started to spinning. In testimony whereof we have hereunto set our hands and seals the day and year above written.

ABSALOM WARLICK (SEAL)
MICHAEL SCHENCK (SEAL)
MICHAEL BEAM (SEAL)

TEST: ROBERT H. BURTON."

1817

Dr. Alfred J. Fox was born at Staley, N. C., September 6, 1817; came to Lincoln County in 1854 as a Lutheran minister, served as pastor of Daniel, Trinity and Salem Churches until he died in 1884.

William Lander was born in Ireland May 9, 1817.

Daniel M. Forney was married October 18, 1817, to Harriet Brevard, daughter of Alexander Brevard, of Lincoln County.

Jacob Forney, Jr., was married to Sarah Hoke, daughter of Daniel Hoke, March 5, 1817.

1818

Bartlett Shipp married 29th November, 1818, to Susan Forney, daughter of Gen. Peter Forney.

Michael Quickel, the pioneer, married Anna Mariah Friday, who died in 1826, aged 78 years. He first settled two miles east of Lincolnton on land which Boger City was built.

His children were:

1. Michael (1781-1850). He married Elizabeth, daughter of Henry Hoke.

2. Barbara married Col. John Hoke.
3. Anna Mariah married Philip Cansler.
4. Elizabeth married David Carpenter and their daughter, Catherine, married Henry Rhodes, whose daughter, Nancy, married to Sheriff J. A. Robinson.
5. Catherine married Jacob Carpenter.

Vardry A. McBee was born in Lincolnton, April 17, 1818, in a house which stood on the lot now occupied by the Methodist church.

Henry Y. Webb, lawyer and legislator from Lincoln, appointed Territorial Judge in Alabama by President Monroe, later elected to the same position by the State Convention of 1819, and died September, 1823.

Winchester Pegram was married to Mary Stowe, sister of Larkin Stowe, in 1818.

1819

The Schenck factory though small was so profitable that Michael Schenck, John Hoke, a Lincolnton merchant, and Dr. James Bivens, in 1819 built the Lincoln Cotton Mill with 3,000 spindles at the old Laboratory site two miles south of Lincolnton. People came long distances to buy yarn or to exchange cotton for yarn. Later they attached an axe factory and other mechanical industries, and the axes were in great demand because of their fine quality. Later Schenck and Bivens sold their interest to Hoke who conducted it until his death in 1844. Later it was operated by Col. L. D. Childs, until destroyed by fire in 1863.

CHAPTER X

1820-1829

In 1820, David Smith, son of Peter Smith, the pioneer and soldier of the Revolution, bought the Henry Dellinger place, 6 miles east of Lincolnton. The County Court in 1784 was held in the Dellinger home and the spring house was used as the county jail. Dellinger later moved to Lincolnton and resided on northwest corner of the square now known as the Robinson corner.

On June 19, 1780, Gen. Rutherford camped overnight on the Dellinger farm en route to Ramsour's Mill, and reached the battleground next morning after the battle was won by the troops commanded by Col. Francis Locke.

When David Smith bought the 900-acre tract in 1820 he built the substantial brick residence which now stands there and kept public house. In the old days many travelers stopped overnight there. James K. Polk and Mrs. Polk spent the night there before he was President and the bed they slept on is still in the same room.

David Smith married Elizabeth Arndt, daughter of the pioneer Lutheran preacher, John Gottfried Arndt, and reared a large family among whom were John Barnett Smith and Mrs. F. M. Reinhardt. The home was called Magnolia Grove for the handsome magnolia trees which surrounded the house. The property is still held by the Smith family, is kept in good repair and is an interesting historical place to visit.

1820

William Preston Bynum born in Stokes County, June 16, 1820.

Dr. William Johnston married to Nancy Forney, daughter of Gen. Peter Forney, October 3, 1820. They were the parents of Gov. Joseph Forney Johnston, of Alabama, and Gen. Robert D. Johnston, of the Confederate Army.

Lincolnton Academy

The Trustees of this Academy wish to employ an assistant teacher who is a good classical scholar, capable of teaching Latin

THE ANNALS OF LINCOLN COUNTY 85

and Greek languages, and who can produce satisfactory certificates of his moral and character qualifications.

D. REINHARDT, *Sec'y to Bd. of Trustees.*

Lincolnton, August 12, 1820.
The Star, August 25, 1820.

1821

Captain John Reid was a brave soldier of the Revolution and an influential citizen of Lincoln County; was State Senator for four terms (1810-11 and 1817-18). He was for many years proprietor of the Catawba Springs. Rufus Reid, his son, settled in Iredell County and was a member of the House of Commons in 1844 and 1846. The wives of Robert Johnston and Robert Williamson were daughters of Captain Reid. He died January 28, 1821, aged 65 years, and was buried in Unity graveyard.

The Legislature on April 21, 1821, granted a charter to the Western College to be established in the western part of the State for the convenience of those living so far from the State University. Trustees were elected and it was their decision to locate the school in Lincolnton. Subscriptions were made by citizens of Lincoln, Burke, Mecklenburg, Iredell and Cabarrus; $15,000.00 of these pledges were made unconditionally, while $45,000.00 was subscribed with the condition that the college be located where these subscribers wanted it built. This meant that only $15,-000.00 was available should the school be located in Lincolnton.

A meeting of the Trustees was then held in Lincolnton, July 24, 1824, and the resolution following offered by Maj. Lawson Henderson was passed: "That, as sufficient funds had not been obtained to put this institution in operation at the site which is fixed on, the site of the Western College be transferred to Mecklenburg County, and that all subscriptions heretofore made to the Trustees of the Western College be held void and that all subscribers be discharged from the payment thereof."

Major Henderson then tendered his resignation as Trustee and reported that he had never received any funds but had paid out for a book and carriage thereof $6.25. Vardry McBee then resigned as Secretary to the Board. The program for a Western College for the State was thus abandoned, but this effort bore fruit in that the agitation for a college in this section continued until finally Davidson College was established in 1837 under the control of the Presbyterian church.

The Lincolnton Female Academy was chartered by the Legislature December 21, 1821, with James Bivins, Vardry McBee, David Hoke, John Mushatt, Joseph E. Bell and Joseph Morris, as Trustees. Four acres on the south side of the town were conveyed to the Trustees for the school site.

1822

Robert Laban Abernethy, the great educator, was born in Lincoln County, April 3, 1822.

Andrew H. Loretz, son of Rev. Andrew Loretz, was married May 1, 1822, to Elizabeth Ramsour.

Philip Cansler, a man of wealth and influence, son of Philip W., the pioneer, married Mary, daughter of Michael Quickel, and his wife, who was a sister of Nicholas and Martin Friday, all prominent in their day.

They had two children:

1. Elizabeth Cansler, who married Philip Rudisill, son of Philip, Sr., and brother of Gentleman Jonas Rudisill.

Their children were Marcus, who married Fanny Killian; Philip, died single; Eliza, married Eli Deihl; William, married Fanny Hallman; Mary, married Gen. Joseph Barringer; Anne, married Robert Powell; and Fanny, married Jacob Deal.

2. Henry Cansler married on June 13, 1822, Fanny Shuford (1801-1866), and developed into a citizen of wide influence and distinguished in Lincoln County history. (See 1870.)

Among the students at Lincolnton Male Academy in 1822 were Samuel Abernethy, Robert and Washington Ballard, William Boyd, Theodorus W. Brevard, Richard Brumby, James and Samuel Connor, George L. Davidson, Thomas Dews, Charles C., Hugh L., and James Pinckney Henderson, John Hoke, Michael Hoke, John Huggins, Ransom Hunley, James and Sidney Johnston, John and George Motz, William Mushat, Luther and Silas McBee, Henry Fulenwider, Daniel and Jacob Ramsour, James Rudisill, Robert and Rufus Williamson, Moses White and William Work, several of whom became distinguished in public life.

1823

The First Presbyterian church, in Lincolnton, was organized February 14, 1823. Rev. Joseph E. Bell was Moderator and John Hoke, David Ramsour, Peter Summey and Michael Reinhardt were elders.

Charles E. Reinhardt was elected elder in 1828. Rev. Mr. Bell came to Lincolnton from Tennessee to teach in the Lincolnton Academy, was ordained as a Lutheran minister, later joined the Presbyterian church and was the first pastor and organizer of that church in Lincolnton.

During the seven years from 1827 to 1834, Rev. Patrick J. Sparrow and Rev. W. B. Davis served as pastors. Rev. A. W. Watts was supply pastor for two years (1834-36). Up to this time the Presbyterians worshipped in the Old White Church. About 1836 Paul Kistler conveyed to David Ramsour and J. T. Alexander, Trustees, part of lot 19 on Water Street in the middle of the block west of the county jail. Here the first Presbyterian church was built. The elders in 1839 were David Ramsour, Charles E. Reinhardt and Isaac Ervin. Rev. R. N. Davis served as pastor from 1850 until his death in 1870. Rev. R. Z. Johnston succeeded Mr. Davis as pastor and served until his death in 1908. He was in the later years assisted by Rev. W. A. Murray.

In 1890 the Presbyterians built a new church on West Main Street. Later it was enlarged and remodelled.

The pastors since 1908 served in the following order: Rev. W. R. Minter, Rev. W. S. Wilson, Rev. W. W. Akers and Rev. W. S. Wilson again, who now (1935) is the pastor.

William H. Forney, son of Jacob Forney, Jr., and his wife, Sarah Hoke Forney, was born in Lincolnton, November 9, 1823.

Catawba School, 1823

"The subscribers having had the experience of Nathaniel N. Smith for the last session feel confidence in recommending him as a teacher qualified to discharge his duties. Under his instruction young gentlemen can be prepared to enter any college in our country.

"While due attention is paid to the classics, particular pains will be taken in teaching the English language critically, penmanship, arithmetic, geography, composition and history.

"Students for the future will be required to attend school on Saturday forenoon, for the purpose of reciting English grammar, reading, parsing, composition and declamation.

"It often happens that boys who have neglected those previous studies enter college and graduate, without being able to write a tolerable letter, much less to arrange their thoughts in a clear, pure and eloquent style. The reason of the above regulation is to obviate this fault.

ROBERT JOHNSTON.
HENRY CONNOR.
JOHN HAYES."

Western Carolinian,
Dec. 2, 1823.

This school was conducted near Beatties Ford.

1824

Gen. Daniel Seagle, on March 3, 1824, was married to Mary Bolinger.

At a meeting of the Trustees of the Lincolnton Female Academy held at the home of Vardry McBee, May 24, 1824, Dr. James Bivens, Vardry McBee, Joseph E. Bell, Jacob Forney, Charles E. Reinhardt and John Zimmerman being present with Dr. James Bivens in the chair, the question: Shall the Academy house be long or square? was decided by vote as follows: For a long house—Jacob Forney, Charles E. Reinhardt, J. E. Bell and John Zimmerman (4); For a square house—Vardry McBee (1).

The vote was then taken for and against a portico: For portico—Jacob Forney, Charles E. Reinhardt and John Zimmerman; Against portico—Vardry McBee and J. E. Bell.

It was unanimously agreed to build it of brick, two stories high, size 40 by 25 feet. At a meeting of Trustees held June 19th, it was decided not to add the portico to the building because of the extra cost of same.

"On June 19, 1824, Trustees of Female Academy met. Present: Dr. James Bivens, Daniel Hoke, J. E. Bell, Vardry McBee, John Zimmerman and Jacob Forney. Bonds from contractors were secured from Samuel Yundt, Philip Hines, Michael Reinhardt, John Williams and Lemuel Moorman.

"Philip Hines is to furnish all the scantling at $1.69 per 100 feet.

"Daniel Hoke is to furnish all the hewn timber for $35.00.

"Thomas Webster is to furnish all the window sills of good soap stone at .62½ per foot, and door sills of granite at $1.00 per foot, neatly hewn.
JOSEPH E. BELL, Sec'y."

1825

"Trustees of Female Academy met in called sessions at Vardry McBee's, March 21, 1825. Dr. James Bivens, C. E. Reinhardt, Daniel Hoke, Vardry McBee, Jacob Forney and John Zimmerman were present.

"Resolved: that the seasoned plank now at the Academy site be hauled to the shop of Andrew Ramsour at the expense of the Board and that if necessary, John Zimmerman purchase plank for the scaffolds for the carpenters.

"Further, that the Secretary furnish Col. Daniel Hoke with a bill of the hewn timber for the Academy.

"Also, that the Secretary publish that a contract will be let for furnishing doors and window sills for the Academy on April 2nd.

"Jacob Forney is authorized to contract for the delivery of 450 bushels of lime at the Academy as soon as possible.
VARDRY MCBEE, Sec'y protem."

Daniel Asbury, the pioneer Methodist preacher west of the Catawba River, was born in Fairfax County, Virginia, February 18, 1762. When about 16 years old, he went to Kentucky, following the tide of emigrants to that section. He was captured by the Shawnee Indians and held in captivity for several years; was carried to Canada and there captured by the British and brutally treated; confined in irons and imprisoned in Detroit. He finally escaped and found his way back to Virginia and to his father's home. He there came in contact with the pioneer preachers and under their influence "came to himself" and joined the Methodist church. In 1786 he became a traveling preacher and from that date most of the time to the end of his life preached the gospel over the wide range of territory from Virginia to Georgia, serving Amelia and Halifax in Virginia; Holstein in Tennessee; Yadkin, Lincoln, Union and Onoee in North Carolina as pastor, and served for 12 years, from 1810 to 1822, as presiding elder, the Savannah, Camden, Catawba and Broad River districts in the order named.

In 1790 he first preached west of the Catawba near the present village of Terrell, where he found a colony of Methodists who had just migrated from Old Brunswick, Va., and here he organized Rehoboth, the first Methodist church established west of the Catawba. It was there he met and married Nancy Morris, a devout woman and a member of the Virginia colony, which had just settled in that community. His bitter experiences during the period of his early captivity served in good stead in the after years of his ministerial life. In many places he met with ridicule and persecution but "endured hardness as a good soldier." Dr. Albert M. Shipp in *The History of Methodism in South Carolina* gives account of a ruffian band led by one Permenter Morgan, who seized Asbury and brought him before Jonathan Hampton, a worthy Magistrate in Rutherford County, on the charge that he was going about preaching the gospel without authority, and the good magistrate dismissed the case as one inspired by malicious persecution.

Daniel Asbury did not possess high scholarship, but with a rare knowledge of the pioneer people, among whom he labored, and with a deep religious experience and a spiritual discernment of the truth which was marvelous, his fervent appeals to unconverted seemed irresistible and his ministry was abundantly blessed. He was a moving spirit in the great spiritual awakening of 1802 when the Presbyterians and Methodists combined to overcome the iniquity of the times, and a great spiritual wave swept over this section of the country. With all of his seriousness he had a fine sense of humor as once shown while preaching in Columbia; some of the congregation showed decided signs of drowsiness when he said, "These people want to hear the gospel but the Devil is trying to put them to sleep."

On Sunday, April 15, 1825, at his home in Lincoln County, he died suddenly and his body was buried in the graveyard of Rehoboth church, in the present County of Catawba, nearby the Lincolnton and Mooresville highway. It is a coincidence that he was born, captured by the Indians, returned from captivity, converted and died on the Sabbath day. It was this good man who laid the foundation of the Methodist church in this section of the State and his burial spot deserves an imposing marker to commemorate the priceless service he rendered as a minister of Christ.

A petition, signed by William Henderson, Jacob Ramsour, Robert Williamson, G. McCulloh and Vardry McBee was sent to the General Assembly, setting forth that legislative authority was given several years ago to sell town lots to raise money to build the Male Academy and of the amount secured by the sale of the lots, there still remains a balance of money in the hands of Jacob Ramsour, not otherwise appropriated, for which we petition for authority to use this balance still in the hands of Jacob Ramsour to meet expense of repairing said Academy from time to time as the Trustees may deem wise.

Received in House of Commons, November 29, 1825, and referred to committee.

Ambrose Costner was born June 14, 1825.

1826
O'Reilly's School

"The subscribers having engaged Mr. M. O'Reilly to take charge of a school, beg leave to inform those who may be disposed to educate their children that a school will be opened March 1; boarding can be had at reasonable terms and a few scholars taken in.

"Mr. O'Reilly is highly recommended for moral character and as being well qualified to teach the English, Latin and Greek languages; and we feel confident will give satisfaction to such as may entrust their children to his charge.

"The situation is healthy, being one mile and a half from Beatties Ford and within three miles of Catawba Springs, in Lincoln County.

ROBERT ABERNETHY.
ALFRED M. BURTON.
ROBERT H. BURTON."

Catawba Journal, Feb. 7, 1826.

Mrs. Sabina Hoke, whose husband, John Hoke, died in Lancaster County, Penn., came to Lincoln County with her children about 1797 or 1798. She died in Lincolnton, August 9, 1826.

Their children were:
1. Sarah, born 1772, married Conrad Michal, father of Jacob Michal, father of Col. William H. Michal, prominent Lincolnton merchant, who married Isabella Ramsour.
2. Daniel, born 1773, married Barbara Ramsour. (See 1835.)
3. Frederick married four times. (See Bynum's *Marriage Bonds*.)
   (1) Catherine Smith.
   (2) Elizabeth Lowrance.
   (3) Elizabeth Stirewalt.
   (4) Rebecca Kibler.

4. Henry married Catherine Ramsour.
5. John, born 1778, married Barbara Quickel.
(See 1844, 1888, 1925, 1931.)

Col. Joseph Dickson was born in Chester County, Pennsylvania, in April, 1745; moved with his family to Rowan County, North Carolina, where he was reared and educated. He married Margaret McEwen. Engaged in cotton and tobacco planting. Member Rowan Committee of Public Safety, 1775. Commissioned as a Captain and served under Gen. Rutherford in 1780, and at battle of Kings Mountain as a Major in Regiment of Lincoln County men. Opposed Gen. Cornwallis and for bravery was made Colonel. Clerk Lincoln County Court 1781-88; Senator from Lincoln, 1788 to 1795; was delegate from Lincoln to the convention held in Fayetteville in 1789, when North Carolina officially approved the Federal Constitution; member of the Commission that established the University of North Carolina and was one of the forty original trustees and one of the seventeen members present when the Board of Trustees was organized on December 18, 1798. Was elected to the sixth Congress of the United States from the Lincoln district over James Holland (1799-1801). Some years after the war he was elected General of the State Militia.

In 1803 he moved to Burke County and then to Rutherford County, Tennessee, in 1806. Was elected to the Tennessee House of Representatives from Rutherford County in 1807, and served for two terms (1807-1811) and was speaker of the house during the last two years. On October 11, 1810, he was married (second time) to Ellener Rankin, daughter of William Rankin, of Lincoln County, North Carolina. He died in Tennessee, April 14, 1825. He had nine children, six of whom were boys. One grandson, John B. Dickson, was a Lieutenant under Gen. Andrew Jackson in the Creek and Seminole Wars, was wounded in the battle of New Orleans in 1813 and died in Texas in 1878, aged 85 years.

Jacob Ramsour, son of Diedrich Ramsour, the pioneer, died January 11, 1826.

John Fulenwider, a native Swiss, was born about 1756. As a very young man he came to America and to Rowan County, North Carolina, fought with the Rowan men at Ramsour's Mill and

Kings Mountain. After the war he was attracted to Lincoln County on account of the rich iron deposits. Was one of the first manufacturers of pig iron from iron ore, using charcoal in the process of its manufacture. He also operated a gold mine on his own land, but his signal success was in the manufacture of pig iron, and as stated elsewhere he furnished the goverment with cannon balls, manufactured from iron which he mined, for use in the War of 1812. He was a man of mark in his day, was founder of the High Shoals Iron Works, and his will, probated in 1828, indicates that he possessed some 20,000 acres of land in Lincoln County, many slaves and personal property besides, of great value. Had he lived in our day he would, no doubt, have been a great captain of industry.

His wife was Elizabeth Ellis of Rowan, and an aunt of the late Governor Ellis. He had four sons and four daughters. John, Jr., married Lavinia, daughter of Peter Forney; Henry married Ann, daughter of David Ramsour; William married Martha, daughter of John Hayes; Jacob married Mary, daughter of Andrew Hoyle; Sarah married George Phifer, of Cabarrus; Esther married John Phifer, brother of George; Elizabeth married Alfred M. Burton; Mary married Judge Robert H. Burton (brother of Alfred M.).

He died September 4, 1826. The executors of his will were his son, Henry Fulenwider, and his son-in-law, Judge Robert H. Burton. When he died his body was buried at High Shoals and the tomb bears the following inscription:

> "Sacred to the memory of
> John Fulenwider
> who died on the 4th day of September, 1826,
> in the 70th year of his age.
> Beloved in life,
> Regretted in death."

"The Trustees of the Female Academy met January 3rd, 1826, to consider the application of Mrs. Lucretia Matthews for the principal of the school. The letter of Mrs. Matthews was read. Col. Daniel Hoke moved that the Board decide whether or not they would employ Mrs. Matthews. A vote was taken. C. E. Reinhardt, Daniel Hoke and V. McBee voted yea: John Zimmerman and J. E. Bell voted nay.

"It was then resolved that Mrs. Matthews be tutress of Lincolnton Female Academy until the Board can procure another tutress and no longer, and that as soon as another is selected Mrs. Matthews shall give up the Academy and its pupils.

JOSEPH E. BELL, *Sec'y*."

1827

Peter Hoyle, the Pioneer, and Some of His Descendants

Peter Hoyle, to whom reference has been made, and who settled at Hoylesville in the present County of Gaston about 1747, had notable descendants in various fields of endeavor. Among them were Andrew Hoyle, A. A. Shuford, L. J. Hoyle and Eli Warlick, prominent business men; Rev. Jacob Hoyle, Rev. M. H. Hoyle, Rev. R. M. Hoyle, and Rev. E. M. Hoyle, prominent ministers of the Methodist church, and Rev. Polycarp Henkel, a distinguished Lutheran minister; Dr. John F. Miller, a distinguished physician; Poindexter Shuford, one time Attorney General of Texas, Edwin T. Cansler, of Charlotte, Judge Wilson Warlick, of Newton, and Robert L. Ryburn, of Shelby, who died in 1935, all lawyers of first rate ability; and Dr. Bruce R. Payne, president of Peabody Normal College, of Nashville, Tenn.

Among the children of Peter Hoyle, the pioneer, were:

1. His eldest son, Jacob Hoyle, married to Elizabeth Brooks, by whom he had three children. He died early. The Rev. Robert M. Hoyle (1850-1929), who died in Cleveland County and Rev. E. M. Hoyle, who died at Cornelius in 1917, were descendants of this couple. The widow of Jacob Hoyle married later to Major Jacob Costner in 1764, and by this marriage there were three children. Major Costner was sheriff of Tryon County in 1774; was a patriot of the Revolution who signed the Articles of Independence at Tryon Court House in August, 1775. He and his wife were drowned November 16, 1779, as they attempted to cross a swollen stream near the present city of Gastonia. The late Ambrose Costner, of Lincoln, was an honored grandson of Major Costner.

2. Michael Hoyle, the second son of Peter Hoyle, the pioneer, married to Elizabeth Carpenter, and their son, Peter Hoyle, the politician (1762-1827), was a popular and influential citizen of Lincoln, who represented the county in the House of Commons from 1802 to 1817 (except 1809 and 1814) fourteen terms, and was State Senator in 1819. He lived near Daniels church and

was a Lutheran in faith. Two of his daughters married Lutheran ministers.

Fanny married to Rev. Ambrose Henkel, October 3, 1827, and Catherine married Rev. David Henkel, a distinguished Lutheran divine, on May 17, 1814.

3. Andrew Hoyle (1771-1857), third son of Peter, the pioneer, is referred to elsewhere in these ANNALS.

4. John Hoyle, the youngest son of Peter, the pioneer, served as a Lieutenant under Col. Hambright in the march against the Indians, and was a brave soldier of the Revolution. The John Hoyle Chapter, Daughters of the American Revolution (of Hickory), was named in his honor and most of the members of that chapter are his lineal descendants. His wife was Margaret Costner, who was a sister of Major Jacob Costner, and they had 13 children. Two of the sons became Methodist ministers of note:

1. Rev. John Hoyle, who moved to Tennessee.

2. Rev. Jacob Hoyle, of Cleveland County, whose son, Rev. Abel Hoyle, was the father of the late Capt. Lemuel J. Hoyle, of Shelby, who was Senator from Cleveland in 1875, and later for some years Clerk of the Superior Court of that County. Rev. Jacob Hoyle, married to Catherine Summey and they were the grandparents of the late Rev. Maxwell H. Hoyle (1841-1908) (son of Noah Hoyle) of the Methodist Conference and who died in Charlotte, March 24, 1908. To his daughter, Mrs. Elizabeth Hoyle Rucker, of Charlotte, a lady of rare historical knowledge, I am indebted for the facts stated in this Hoyle sketch. The late Philip Hoyle, a prominent citizen of Catawba County, was also a grandson of Rev. Jacob Hoyle.

3. Mary Hoyle, daughter of John Hoyle, married to Lewis Warlick (born 1765). Their son, Solomon Warlick, married Barbara, sister of Maxwell Warlick and they were the parents of Eli A. Warlick, who married Catherine Seagle, and grandparents of Judge Wilson Warlick. They were also parents of Lewis Franklin Warlick, who married Sarah Robinson, and grandparents of Dr. Bruce R. Payne, president of Peabody Normal College, of Nashville, Tenn.

4. Margaret Hoyle (1769-1840), another daughter of John Hoyle, married to Jacob Shuford, son of Martin, son of John Shuford, the pioneer, in 1789. Their daughter, Fanny Shuford, married to Henry Cansler, and they were the grandparents of

Edwin T. Cansler, a noted lawyer of Charlotte. Jacob Shuford, Jr., who died in 1874, was the father of A. A. Shuford, pioneer merchant, banker and manufacturer of Hickory.

L. M. Hoffman, in *Our Kin*, says:

"Margaret Hoyle Shuford had a brother, Eli Shuford (1803-1874), who died in Quitman, Texas. His son, Poindexter Shuford, known as "Deck" was a lawyer, opposed to the Civil War, and one of seven delegates to the Texas Convention, of 1861, who voted against Secession. After the war Gov. Hamilton appointed him Attorney General. He died in his prime in 1875.

"Gov. Hogg said of him: 'He was a fine lawyer, a gentle, kind-hearted man and a Republican for whom the people, regardless of political persuasion, had respect as a lawyer and honest man.'

"He was educated at Catawba College, Newton, where Prof. H. H. Smith taught."

Thomas R. Shuford and Elizabeth Butts were married May 30, 1827.

"The Board met at Mr. McBee's office July 8, 1827, to settle with Mr. Burton respecting the building of the Female Academy. It appears that he had received $2,801.67 from sale of lots, against which he produced the following vouchers, leaving a balance in his hands of $82.69.

	Dr.	Cr.
Debit amount of sale of lots	$2,801.67	
Credit by amount paid Jacob Forney		$2,622.73
Credit by amount paid Henry Cansler, surveyor		33.25
Credit by amount paid B. S. Johnson, crying sale		4.00
Credit by amount paid Jacob Reinhardt, work		2.00
Credit by amount paid Taxes, 1823 & 1824		1.00
Credit by amount paid Printing advertisements		1.00
Credit by amount paid Mr. Burton, commissions		55.00
	$2,801.67	$2,718.98
	2,718.98	
	$ 82.69	

Note of Michael Schenck	$63.69
Cash	19.00
	$82.69

"Which amount was ordered turned over by Mr. Burton to Major Lawson Henderson to be accounted for in his settlement between the Trustees of the Male and Female Academies.

JOHN D. HOKE, *Secretary*."

Buffalo Academy

Major Lawson Henderson and David Kiddoe, in *Catawba Journal* of January 2, 1827, recommended Buffalo Academy in Lincoln County as a school of high grade with P. J. Sparrow as principal.

"This Academy is situated in a healthy place, about 17 miles southwest of Lincolnton, in a respectable and plentiful neighborhood where boarding can be had on ready terms."

The Rev. Humphrey Hunter was born in Ulster County, Ireland, May 14, 1755. Four years later his father died and soon thereafter the boy came with his mother to America, arriving at Charleston, August 27, 1759, after a voyage of over three months. From there they journeyed to Poplar Tent in the present County of Cabarrus, where she settled and reared her son. He was in Charlotte May 20, 1775, when the Mecklenburg Declaration was adopted and saw that document signed. When over twenty years old he entered Queens College in Charlotte, and his plans for study were broken up on account of the war, but he entered the Whig army as a Lieutenant under Captain Thomas Givens, and proved his courage as a soldier. Resuming his studies after the war, he graduated from Mount Zion College, Winnsboro, S. C., in June, 1787, and after two years more of preparation he was licensed to preach by the South Carolina Presbytery, October 15, 1789. Then for six years he was pastor of Hopewell and Aimwell churches in South Carolina.

In 1795 he moved to Lincoln County to accept the pastorate of Unity and Goshen Presbyterian churches, which he served until 1805, when he accepted the call to the Steele Creek and Hopewell congregations in Mecklenburg County and continued in this pastorate until his death August 21, 1827. For several years during this latter period, after the death, in 1812, of Rev. Andrew Loretz, the German Reformed preacher, Mr. Hunter had regular appointments and preached in the old White Church and ministered to the Presbyterians of the Lincolnton community, in addition to his work in Mecklenburg County.

His body was buried in Steele Creek cemetery and the monument erected by that congregation bears the following high tribute to this sainted minister:

"For nearly 38 years he labored as a faithful and assiduous Ambassador of Christ, strenuously enforcing the necessity of repentance and pointing out the terms of salvation. As a parent he was kind and affectionate; as a friend, warm and sincere, and as a minister persuasive and convincing."

He was all of that as well as a preacher of unusual gifts, and completely consecrated to his task. He was the pioneer Presbyterian preacher in Lincoln County, and the two congregations, Unity and Goshen, which he organized, have long exercised a fine influence on the western side of the Catawba River from Beatties Ford to the South Carolina line. His son, Dr. Cyrus L. Hunter, was an honored citizen of Lincoln County, where he married and spent all of his active life.

1828

The following sketch of Felix Walker was written by R. F. Cope of Gastonia, N. C.

Col. John Walker came from Delaware and settled about 1756 on Lee Creek which was in *old* Lincoln County. His eldest son, Felix Walker, was born in Hampshire County, Virginia, July 19, 1753, and came with his parents to this section three years later.

Felix attended such schools as the county then afforded and worked on his father's farm. Having an unsettled and roving nature he soon gave up farm work and ventured into the wilds of Kentucky with Daniel Boone and Richard Henderson, and the settlement of Boonesboro was established about that time.

He was twice married, first to Susan Robinson, January 8, 1778; second to Isabella Henry, January 10, 1780. He took an active part in the struggle for American Independence and was a soldier in several battles of that war.

According to his *Memoirs*, which he wrote in 1826, he was not a participant in the Battle of Kings Mountain for he says:

"A battle was fought at Kings Mountain, October 7, 1780, where a complete victory was obtained by the Americans, being all militia, over the British Regulars and Tories, commanded by Major Ferguson, who was shot from his horse while bravely leading his men. Seven bullets went through his body, it was said. He was a brave and gallant officer from Scotland, and it was well he was killed to prevent his doing more mischief."

He had five brothers who engaged in military service during the Revolutionary War: John, Jr., James Reuben, William,

Thomas and Joseph. Most all of the Walker family were born in Lincoln County, excepting Felix and John, Jr.

In the fall of 1763 the Walker family moved to a farm about four miles from Kings Mountain on Crowder's Creek, in the present County of Gaston. In 1768 they moved to Rutherford County.

Felix Walker later settled in Haywood County and was elected to the United States Congress from the Mountain district in 1817, and served until 1823, when he was defeated for re-election by Robert B. Vance by a small majority.

He then moved to Clinton, Mississippi where he died in 1828.

Dr. William McLean, son of the pioneer, Alexander McLean, was born in Rowan County on Sunday, April 2, 1757. He was educated at Queen's Museum in Charlotte and read medicine under Dr. Joseph Blythe. He served under the 1st N. C. Regiment commanded by Colonel Archibald Lytle, at Charleston, James Island, Kings Mountain and elsewhere, and was appointed Surgeon's Mate in that Regiment.

After the war he completed his medical education at the University of Pennsylvania in 1787 and settled in the South Point section of what is now Gaston County, where he was for many years a successful physician.

On June 19, 1792, he married Mary, daughter of Major John Davidson, of Mecklenburg. Among their children were Dr. John D. McLean, who succeeded his father as a physician at South Point and Major Augustus A. McLean, who married Catherine Schenck, of Lincolnton, and lived there during his active life.

Dr. William McLean was a skilled physician and had a large practice. He was also a patriotic and progressive citizen. He was a member of the Constitutional Convention of 1788 at Hillsboro, and the convention at Fayetteville in 1789, which adopted the Federal Constitution. He was also a member of the House of Commons four terms, 1788 to 1791 inclusive, and was the Senator from Lincoln in 1814. In the same year he delivered the oration at the first celebration of the Battle of Kings Mountain and had erected there, at his own expense, a monument to the memory of the brave South Fork boys who died there for liberty.

He was one of the original members of the North Carolina Society of the Cincinnati, organized by the officers of the Continental line at Hillsboro, October 25, 1783. He was a Presbyterian in faith and when he died October 25, 1828, his body was buried in the Bethel Presbyterian graveyard in York County, South Carolina.

Rev. James Hill, a Methodist minister, who died in 1828, was the first person to be buried in the Methodist graveyard in Lincolnton.

1829

Captain Alexander Brevard, son of John Brevard, the pioneer, was born in Rowan (now Iredell) County. Was a soldier who fought under Washington in New Jersey and in 1779, on account of feeble health, was advised by Washington to return home to recuperate. As soon as his health was restored he joined the Southern Army under General Gates and was transferred later to the command of General Greene, and was active as a soldier during the greater part of the war. After the war he married to Rebecca, daughter of Col. John Davidson. In 1791 Captain Brevard and Gen. Joseph Graham came to Lincoln County and bought from Gen. Peter Forney an interest in the iron business and engaged in iron manufacture. Brevard engaged in the manufacture of iron and in agricultural pursuits until his death November 1, 1829. He had large landed interests and many slaves and by his industry and frugality he amassed a large estate.

He was a man of lofty character and a prominent and influential citizen of the County. A Presbyterian in faith he was for long years an elder in that church and when he died was buried at Machpelah.

He had five sons, Ephraim, Franklin, Robert, Joseph and Theodorus W. Brevard, all of whom honored the name, and two daughters, Harriet, who married Hon. Daniel M. Forney, and Mary, who was the wife of Richard T. Brumby.

Buffalo Shoals School

"An enfeebled constitution renders it impossible for me to take an extensive circuit in the practice of my profession as a Lawyer and I propose therefore, assisted by my brother, to open a school at my house in Lincoln County on Catawba River, 9 miles from Statesville, and 24 miles from Lincolnton, on March 1, by which time my buildings will be completed. No scholar will be taken who cannot board with me as a member of my family. I now have one law student and am anxious to get a few more.

"All applications must be made to me in person or by letter directed to Thomas Ferry of Statesville.

"For particulars as to my qualifications I refer to Judge Badger, Raleigh, or to Major Henderson, of Lincolnton.

RICHARD T. BRUMBY."

Raleigh Register, December 14, 1829.

Richard T. Brumby was born in Sumter County, South Carolina, August 4, 1804, and died near Athens, Ga., October 6, 1875, the day after the death of his wife, Mary Brevard Brumby, and the bodies were buried in Oconee cemetery, Athens, Ga.

NOTE: The record shows that Richard Brumby was a student at the Lincolnton Male Academy in 1822; that he graduated from the University of South Carolina in 1825; married April 18, 1828, to Mary Brevard, daughter of the pioneer, Alexander Brevard, who was one of the wealthy and influential citizens of Lincoln County. Mr. Brumby, after his graduation, was licensed to practice law, but on account of ill health established the Buffalo Shoal School in 1829.

Later he removed to Alabama and became one of the first Professors in the University of that State. He is said to be the discoverer of the iron and coal deposits in Alabama. He had a daughter, Harriet Brevard Brumby, who married to Lewis J. Russell, and one son by that marriage is Richard Brevard Russell, the present (1935) Chief Justice of the Georgia Supreme Court. This Judge Russell is the father of Richard Brevard Russell, Jr., late Governor of Georgia, and now Senator in Congress from that State.

J. Franklin Brevard died February 13, 1829, aged 41 years, and was buried in the Baker graveyard in Iredell County. He was a son of Alexander and Rebecca Davidson Brevard, and grandfather of the late F. Brevard McDowell, of Charlotte. He represented Lincoln in the Legislature in 1818.

James Pinckney Henderson was licensed as an Attorney in 1829, and practiced law in Lincolnton until he went to Texas in 1836.

CHAPTER XI

1830-1839

Col. John Zimmerman, a prominent and early citizen of Lincolnton, died in 1830, and his body rests in the Old White Church graveyard.

June 22nd. A meeting was held at South Point to plan for the July 4th celebration. Larkin Stowe, chairman, W. A. Wilson, Secretary. Capt. B. Thomason was chosen as orator, Larkin Stowe to read the Declaration. Gen. R. D. S. McLean and Col. J. G. Hand, Marshals; Committee of Arrangements: Col. J. G. Hand, Major T. B. McLean, Capt. J. L. McArver, Larkin Stowe and Dr. A. L. Barry.

Rev. Stephen Frontis, of the Presbyterian Church, was married in Lincolnton, June 29, 1830, to Martha Dews, a sister of the brilliant and versatile Thomas Dews, Jr.

June 29th. From the *Raleigh Register* we learn that Michael Hoke, of Lincoln, was granted County Court license to practice law.

James M. Burton will deliver the 4th of July address at Catawba Springs.

Among the toasts at South Point celebration of July 4th, was one by J. L. McAver to "H. W. Connor, member of Congress and a candidate for re-election," and one by Dr. Cyrus L. Hunter to "The State of North Carolina—the first to frame a Declaration of Independence—May she be found the last to violate the sanctity of that political maxim: The Federal Union, it must be preserved."

July 6th. Bartlett Shipp issues address to the freemen of Lincoln, Mecklenburg and Cabarrus Counties as a candidate for Congress.

July 13th. James Bivens & Company, owners of the Lincoln Cotton Manufacturing Company, advertise yarn and cloth for sale. This mill was operated on South Fork River at the Laboratory.

August 17th. Major Henry W. Connor, of Lincoln, was re-elected to Congress by 854 majority, over Bartlett Shipp. The vote stood as follows:

	Connor	Shipp
Lincoln	1676	966
Mecklenburg	1023	648
Cabarrus	362	593
Total	3,061	2,207

In the County election of 1830, Daniel Hoke was chosen for the Senate and Bartlett Shipp and Andrew Loretz for the Commons. Thomas Ward was elected Sheriff.

October. It is with regret we learn that Judge George E. Badger, on Tuesday last, was thrown from his sulky between his place and Louisburg, and it is feared his leg was broken by the fall.—*Charlotte Journal.* (He was an uncle of Rev. W. R. Wetmore of the Episcopal church.)

November 8th. Mail contract from Fayetteville through Charlotte to Lincolnton let to Emanuel Reinhardt; the mail to be carried twice a week in four-horse stages.

December 6th. A large vein of gold has been discovered in the Henderson and Wilson mine in Lincoln County near Kings Mountain and the ore is worth $3.20 per bushel.

Robert H. Burton, of Lincoln, has been elected Treasurer of the State by the Legislature now in session. The vote stood 100 for Burton and 92 for William S. Mahoon of Bertie.

We have received from Hon. H. W. Connor, member of Congress, the President's message with reports of the Navy, War and Post Office Departments. (Charlotte Journal.)

Advertisement: Charlotte Hotel, J. D. Boyd, Proprietor, offers the best table and bar which the market in the back country can afford. Beds and bedding are inferior to none. Ostlers are employed and stables abundantly furnished.

1831

May 18th. William S. Simonton, who recently purchased the Catawba Springs property near Beatties Ford, from Charles Jugnot, has had this water analysed by Professor Olmsted who recommends its use for all complaints of liver or debility.

June 18th. A meeting was held in Lincolnton to arrange for the 4th of July celebration. Dr. S. P. Simpson was Chairman and George Hoke, Secretary. James P. Henderson was selected Orator; Dr. George Hoke, reader of the Declaration of Independence; Major John Michael and Capt. John Taylor Alexander, Marshals; Charles Leonard, B. S. Johnson, Isaac Irwin, Jacob Propst, J. Reinhardt, V. McBee, D. Ramsour and John Hoke, Committee on Arrangements and Thomas Williamson, P. Dewey, Jacob Ramsour, Michael Hoke, John D. Hoke and Dr. Simpson, Committee on Toasts.

Hannah Arndt widow of John Gottfried Arndt, the pioneer Lutheran preacher, died in 1831.

Advertisement. December 7th. Lincolnton Female Academy, Miss Amelia Thompson has the assistance of two ladies from New York.

(Signed) V. McBee, Daniel Hoke, Peter Summey, Jacob Ramsour, C. E. Reinhardt, John D. Hoke and C. Leonard, Trustees.

December 22nd. Married in Charlotte by Rev. R. H. Morrison, Dr. Pinckney C. Caldwell to Sarah R. Wilson, daughter of the late Joseph Wilson. (They were parents of the late Mrs. B. S. Guion.)

1832

Rev. James Richardson was married in Lincolnton, January 16, 1832, to Catherine Schenck, daughter of Michael Schenck.

April 24th. James King died near Beatties Ford, aged 87 years.

May 15. A new post office has been established in Lincoln County to be called Catawba Springs, and William S. Simonton has been appointed postmaster.

In 1832 a Paper Mill was established on the site of the Long Shoals Cotton Mill, four miles south of Lincolnton on the South Fork River, by George Mosteller. It seems that about 1857 it was taken over by Samuel Oates, who managed it until about 1867 when James Banister and a Mr. Grady took charge. In 1868 A. C. Wiswall, of Massachusetts, who was skilled in that business formed a co-partnership with William Tiddy until 1872 when William and Richard Tiddy took this mill over, together with the paper mill located on the site of the present Lincoln Cotton Mill, a mile below the Laboratory. They also built a third mill on Buffalo Creek in Cleveland County and carried on the business until about 1882 when it was abandoned. The paper was manufactured from old rags which the merchants over a wide section bought for three cents a pound in barter and sold to the manufacturers. The Tiddy Brothers operated many wagons to haul rags to the mills. About 1873 William Tiddy solicited an order for paper from the well-known Harper Publishers, of New York. Harper gave a "trial" order which it took three months to fill. Many of the old Lincoln County Record books were manufactured at these mills.

June 24th. Hon. Henry W. Connor, will please accept our thanks for the report on steam carriages and other Congressional documents. (Charlotte Journal.)

July. The Supreme Court has licensed Michael Hoke to practice law in Superior Courts and M. W. Reinhardt to practice in County Courts.

July 10th. In the vicinity of Knoxville, Tenn., June 12, 1832, Richmond M. Pearson, Attorney at Law of Rowan and late member of the House of Commons from that County, was married to Miss Margaret C., daughter of Col. John C. Williams, of Tennessee.

Note: He later became Chief Justice Pearson, of North Carolina, whom President Grant would have appointed Chief Justice of our Federal Supreme Court to succeed Salmon P. Chase, but for the fact that Pearson was more than 70 years old at the time.

The late Dr. E. B. Holland, of Dallas, a versatile man, told the writer that his father-in-law, the late Hon. Daniel W. Courts, in his early days was intimate with Pearson and that when some of the Williams family of Knoxville visited their Williams kin on the Yadkin about 1831, Pearson fell in love with one of the daughters and said to Courts, "Dan, if I had the money I would follow that girl to Tennessee and marry her." Courts offered him the money, as a loan, he accepted it and the result was the marriage above recorded.

They were the ancestors of Richmond Pearson, Congressman from the Asheville District and Minister to Persia, Richmond Pearson Hobson, of the Spanish-American War and General Richmond Pearson Davis, of the United States Army.

Miss Louvenia Schenck, daughter of Michael Schenck, of Lincolnton, was married October 23, 1832, to Rev. Angus McPherson of the South Carolina Conference.

1833

On January 30, 1833, the South Carolina Methodist Conference met in Lincolnton. Bishop James O. Andrew, president, and Dr. W. M. Wightman, the secretary, was in 1866 elected Bishop. Among those who attended that Conference were Whiteford Smith, who later developed into a great preacher and educator, and James J. Richardson, who married a daughter of Michael Schenck, the pioneer cotton manufacturer. Rev. Mr. Richardson was the father of Dr. J. M. Richardson, the long time beloved physician of Lincolnton. Rev. Dr. Samuel Lander, the preacher and educator, was born in Lincolnton the day this Conference convened in the town.

Rev. Daniel G. McDaniel, on February 7, 1833, was married to Elizabeth Schenck, daughter of Michael Schenck, of Lincolnton.

The Lincoln County Grand Jury, at the 1833 spring term of Superior Court with John Wilfong, Foreman, and Cornelius Connor, Alexander Sherrill, Robert Baird, James Reid, James Lofton, Hiram Sherrill, Aaron Jenkins, Jeptha Sherrill, George Helderman, John Earney, Henry Mull, Henry Grant, Ephraim Young, David Troutman, Charles Beatty, Henry Whitener and Christian B. Reinhardt, pledged themselves individually and severally to support for office no candidate who before or at election treats with ardent spirits.

May 8th. Married at Beatties Ford, Michael Hoke, to Frances, eldest daughter of Robert H. Burton by Rev. Robert J. Miller.

June 22nd. The Supreme Court has granted Law license to Hugh L. Henderson of Lincolnton. (Raleigh Register.)

All the Trustees of the Female Academy met at Mr. McBee's office, July 1, 1833. On motion of Jacob Ramsour, ordered that the Treasurer pay the amount of Daniel Shuford's bill and to pay Mr. McBee his bill for fire wood.

John D. Hoke, Sec'y.

July 24th. A Henry Clay meeting was held at Pleasant Retreat Academy in Lincolnton. Gen. Joseph Graham presided and Robert H. Burton and D. Reinhardt were Secretaries. Major Lawson Henderson, Robert H. Burton and W. J. Wilson were appointed to meet with delegates from Mecklenburg and Cabarrus to choose Presidential Elector. A Correspondence Committee composed of D. J. Coulter, Hugh Quinn, D. Ramsour, Rev. Hartwell Spain, Col. E. A. Brevard and D. Reinhardt, was appointed.

A Jackson meeting was held in Lincolnton with D. M. Forney, Chairman, and Col. Michael Reinhardt, Secretary. On motion of J. P. Henderson, Major J. M. Brevard, Major D. M. Forney, Col. Michael Reinhardt, Jacob Forney and Larkin Stowe were appointed delegates to Congressional Convention. Peregrine Roberts, a Lincolnton lawyer, was district elector on the Jackson ticket.

July 24th. Advertisement. Dr. S. P. Simpson, Trustee, to satisfy payment of debts due David Ramsour and others, from Isaac Irwin, will sell on August 18th at public auction at Court House in Lincolnton, one negro woman, one cow and other property.

August 17th. H. W. Connor has been re-elected to Congress without opposition. Miles W. Abernethy was elected County Court Clerk and John D. Hoke, Superior Court Clerk.

Note: Lawson Henderson appointed Superior Court Clerk for life in 1808, was not a candidate, and when Hoke, who was elected demanded possession of the office, Henderson said it belonged to him. Then followed the famous suit of Hoke against Henderson, which resulted in the notable opinion of Chief Justice Ruffin in which he sustained the contention of Henderson that the office was his for life and therefore his property.

Dr. W. J. T. Miller (of Shelby) was married in 1833 to Elizabeth Fulenwider, daughter of Jacob Fulenwider.

September 28th. Peregrine Roberts, a Lincolnton lawyer, has issued proposals to publish a paper in that place to be called the *Lincoln Herald*.

Died in Lincolnton, October 9th, George McCullough, aged 70.

Note: He was father of Mrs. W. R. Clark, Mrs. Augustus P. James, Mrs. Propst, and Mrs. Harriet Bomar, the last named was postmaster in Lincolnton prior to 1868.

December. William Julius Alexander has been chosen solicitor for the 6th Judicial District by the Legislature.

Note: A brilliant lawyer, one time speaker of the House, father of Miss Mary Wood Alexander, who taught school in Lincolnton for many years, and grandfather of Chief Justice William Alexander Hoke.

1834

Franklin M. Reinhardt was married to Sarah Smith, daughter of David Smith, January 11, 1834.

Dr. Cyrus L. Hunter, January 18, 1834, married to Sophia Forney, daughter of General Peter Forney.

February 15th. Died at Georgetown, D. C., February 2nd, Rev. Lorenzo Dow, a well-known and eccentric itinerant preacher.

Rev. Allen Hamby was married in Lincolnton, February 26, 1834, to Barbara Schenck, daughter of Michael Schenck.

Married in Lincoln County, March 11, 1834, Mr. Simon Rhyne, four and one-half feet high and weighing 230 pounds, to Miss Nancy Lay.

Rev. Robert Johnston Miller, the pioneer Episcopal minister in Lincoln County, died at his home at Mary's Grove, in Burke (now Caldwell) County, May 13, 1834, aged 76 years.

June 28th. Thomas J. Holton, Editor of *The Charlotte Journal*, was married to Miss Rachel Jones by John Sloan, Esq., of Charlotte.

James H. White was married to Margaret Jenkins, July 3, 1834.

August 16th. Thomas N. Herndon, of Lincoln, was granted license by Supreme Court to practice law in County Court.

November 29th. Married, on November 20th, by Rev. Mr. Adams, John Graham to Miss Bridget Little.

James Madison Smith and Hettie Rudisill were married December 17, 1834.

Sheriff Logan H. Lowrance married to Margaret Hill, December 29, 1834.

General Peter Forney (son of Jacob Forney, the pioneer) was born in what is now Lincoln County, April 21, 1756. He attended local schools, served as volunteer in the Whig Army as a captain in the Revolutionary War, fought with Col. William

Graham in Rutherford in pursuit of troublesome Cherokee Indians, with Gen. Rutherford in various other contests, and in the skirmish against Tarleton at Torrence Tavern. Not only was he an aggressive soldier, but while away from home fighting for his country, suffered heavy loss by confiscation of all his supplies by Cornwallis, who encamped on the Forney lands. Peter Forney was in the march with Gen. Rutherford from Tuckaseege to Ramsour's Mill reaching the battleground two hours after the victory had been won by Col. Locke's troops. In 1783 he married to Nancy Abernethy and they reared a large family of sons and daughters, who along with their descendants, figured prominently in local and State history.

In 1787 Peter Forney with his brother, Abram Forney, Abram Earhardt and Turner Abernethy were the pioneers in the manufacture of iron in Lincoln County. Later they enlisted the interest of Gen. Joseph Graham and Capt. Alexander Brevard of Mecklenburg who moved to Lincoln and bought an interest in the iron business and from that time until about 1880 the manufacture of iron was the principal industry of the county, aside from agriculture.

After the war General Forney was commissioned General of the State Militia. He was a member of the House of Commons from 1794 to '97 (4 terms), State Senator, 1800-1802, and Councilor of State in 1811. In 1813 he was elected to the United States Congress over John Phifer of Cabarrus and served one term when he declined re-election and was succeeded by his son, Major Daniel M. Forney, who served from 1815 to 1819. He was a Jeffersonian Democrat and was Elector for Jefferson in 1804; for Madison in 1808; for Monroe in 1816, and for Jackson in 1824 and 1828. He died at his home (Mt. Welcome) in Lincoln County, February 1, 1834, full of years and honors. His body is buried in the private burying ground of the Forney family, located some three miles from the old Forney homestead. His tombstone bears the following inscription:

> "To the memory of General Peter Forney, who was born April 21, 1756, and died February 1, 1834. In public life the deceased acquitted himself with reputation as a useful and efficient member of Congress and as an Elector of the people of the United States. He carried out the Republican principle on which he voted through life by

voting successively for Jefferson, Madison, Monroe and General Jackson, and in all relations of private life he acquired the love and esteem of all who knew him."

1835

January 16th. William Williamson, of Lincoln, admitted to practice law in County Courts.

February 1st. Died, in Lincoln County, February 1st, William Price, aged 78 years, a soldier of the American Revolution.

Died at his home near Beatties Ford, April 10, 1835, James Connor, a patriot of the American Revolution, at the advanced age of 81. He was a native of Ireland and came to this country when a young man with his brothers, Henry Connor, Sr., and Captain Charles Connor. His body was buried at the Baker graveyard in Iredell County.

John W. Weber, of Iredell County, was married April 15, 1835, to Ann Lander, daughter of Rev. Samuel Lander, of Lincolnton.

The Constitutional Convention of 1835 was held in Raleigh, sitting from June 4, to July 11, 1835, (about 5 weeks) at a total cost of only $10,117.95. They practiced economy in those days. The delegates received a per diem of $1.50 and five cents a mile for travel expense to and from the convention. Lincoln County was ably represented by Bartlett Shipp and Henry Cansler. They voted with John Branch, William Gaston, Alfred Dockery, David L. Swain, Gov. Owen and others against the repeal of the law which up to that time granted suffrage to free blacks, but the majority voted for repeal. The vote stood 66 for and 61 against repeal.

Up to 1835 each county was entitled to a Senator and two Representatives in the House of Commons without regard to population. Cansler and Shipp voted for the change which provided that the Senate be composed of 50 members and the House of Commons, 120 members, distributed according to population. They voted to abolish the section which excluded Catholics, Jews and Quakers from holding office; for the election of the Governor biennially by popular vote, and members of the General Assembly every two years instead of the old custom of electing them annually.

THE ANNALS OF LINCOLN COUNTY 111

Prior to 1835 the Governor was elected annually by the Legislature. The Legislature was also elected anually prior to 1835.

They both voted to retain borough representation in the House of Commons.

They divided on the resolution which required the Legislature to elect Judges, Solicitors and other State officers by a viva voce vote rather than by roll call or ballot. Cansler supported and Shipp opposed this measure (see "Debates in Convention of 1835," pages 81-162-181-340-357 and 331). The Lincoln delegates were progressives in their day.

Daniel Hoke, for many years a popular and influential citizen of Lincoln County, was a son of John and Sabina Swope Hoke, born in Pennsylvania in 1773 and came to Lincoln County with his widowed mother and his brothers about 1797. He was a Captain in the War of 1812 of the company detached from 2nd Regiment of Lincoln County Militia. Also a member of House of Commons from Lincoln for seven terms, 1809 to 1813 and 1815-16 and Senator from 1829 to 1833, making a total of twelve terms in which he served in the General Assembly. In 1835 he migrated to Alabama with many other Lincoln people who went to that new state.

His wife was Barbara Ramsour and among his children were John D. Hoke, one time elected Clerk Superior Court in Lincoln County but in a legal contest with Lawson Henderson failed to get possession of the office. One daughter, Sarah, married to Jacob, son of General Peter Forney on March 5, 1817, and among their children, born in Lincolnton, were Wm. H. Forney, a Confederate Brigadier General and John H. Forney, a Major General of the Confederate Army.

Jacob Forney and family moved to Alabama with Daniel Hoke and some of the Forney relatives about 1836.

At the 20th of May celebration in Charlotte speeches were made by Gov. Swain and Senator Mangum and in response to a toast, Gen. Joseph Graham stated that he was present sixty years before and witnessed the adoption and signing of the Mecklenburg Declaration of Independence. ("Salisbury Western Carolinian," June 20, 1835.)

July 24th. At the July 4th celebration in Lincolnton, J. P. Henderson delivered the annual address. Col. John Hoke presided, assisted by Jacob Forney. Voluntary toasts were offered by Capt. Abram Forney, Daniel Seagle, Capt. J. T. Alexander, John Wilfong, Daniel Hoke, John Motz, J. P. Henderson, William Slade, E. H. Bissell, Jacob A. Ramsour, George W. Motz, Capt. John B. Harry, James Holsclaw, John Killian, James A. Johnston, Robert H. Burton, A. J. Forney, O. W. Holland, Alfred Graham, Thomas N. Herndon, William Williamson, Miles W. Abernethy, Daniel Hoke, Jr., John D. Hoke, Elcanah L. Shuford, Franklin H. Hoke and Andrew Motz.

November 20th. Alfred Graham, son of Gen. Joseph Graham, died November 16th at the home of his brother, John D. Graham, in Lincoln County, aged 32.

The Legislature in December, 1834, elected Romulus M. Saunders Superior Court Judge, over William Julius Alexander.

1836

General John Moore, son of William Moore was born in 1759 in what was later Lincoln, now Gaston County. His parents were Scotch-Irish. William had four sons, James, William, John and Alexander, all loyal patriots during the period of the Revolution. He was one of the guard at Tuckaseege, watching the movements of Cornwallis after his entrance into Lincoln County. Later he served as Commissary to the Army.

His first wife was a sister of Governor Adair, of Kentucky. His second wife was Mary Scott, widow of James Scott and daughter of Robert Alexander.

He represented Lincoln County in the House of Commons seventeen (17) terms and was Speaker of the House in 1806. He was a member from Lincoln of the Convention at Hillsboro in 1788 and of the Convention at Fayetteville in 1789.

About 1812 Governor Hawkins appointed General John Moore, James Welborn of Wilkes, and John Steele of Rowan to meet a like Committee from South Carolina to settle the boundary line between North and South Carolina. He died in 1836, and his body was buried in Goshen graveyard near Belmont.

(Dr. C. L. Hunter in his Sketches emphasized the fact that Gen. John Moore was in no wise related to Col. John Moore who led the Tories at the battle of Ramsour's Mill.)

General Joseph Graham was born in Pennsylvania in 1759. When but 7 years old he came to North Carolina with his mother who was a widow with five children and they settled near Charlotte. He was educated at Queens Museum in Charlotte and was an apt scholar. All through life he read good books and was a man of rare intelligence.

In his early years he heard much of British oppression and was present when only sixteen years old at the meeting in Charlotte on May 20, 1775, when the patriots of Mecklenburg declared themselves independent of British rule. He was an enthusiastic patriot and volunteered as a soldier in May, 1778, in the 4th Regiment of North Carolina troops under Col. Alexander Lytle. Later in that year he was with Gen. Rutherford in South Carolina. He was in command of the Whig forces at the Battle of Charlotte, September 26, 1780, and resisted the march of Tarleton's cavalry and infantry for four miles on Salisbury road. In this struggle he was wounded nine times; six were sabre wounds and three from rifle balls. He was then but twenty-one years old and led a brave company in a hard fought struggle. He was with General Davidson later and marched toward Wilmington and made a successful attack on a body of Tories near McFall Mill commanded by the Tory, Colonel McNeill. In this engagement, with 136 troops, he vanquished 600 Tories. During the war he served as Sergeant, Adjutant, Captain and Major, and was in command in fifteen engagements during the War of the Revolution and proved his courage, wisdom and military skill in such degree that he finally retired with the high respect and admiration of those familiar with his valiant service.

After the war he married to Isabella, daughter of Major John Davidson and reared a family of twelve children, among whom were James Graham, a lawyer of ability and for 7 terms Congressman from the Rutherford district; Gov. William A. Graham, who became one of the great men of North Carolina and John D. Graham of Lincoln County. He was chosen as the first Sheriff of Mecklenburg County and later represented that county in the State Senate from 1788 to 1794 (7 terms). Gen. Graham was a delegate from Mecklenburg to both Conventions of 1788 and 1789. In 1814 he was Councilor of State and in the same year was by Gov. Hawkins commissioned Colonel of North Carolina volunteers to suppress the Creek Indians in Alabama and arrived upon the scene of conflict about the time Gen. Jackson had won the victory at the Battle of Horse Shoe. After the war he was commissioned General of State Militia. In 1789 Gen. Graham moved to Lincoln County where he engaged in the manufacture of iron in which he was successful and was one of the influential citizens of the county until his death, on November 12, 1836. His body rests in Macpelah graveyard. General Graham was a devout Christian and an officer in the Presbyterian Church for many years.

Among the children of General Joseph Graham were:

1. John D. Graham, who married, June 13, 1815, to Betsy, daughter of Captain Charles Connor. He succeeded his father as an iron manufacturer and continued the business until his death in 1847. He was an elder in Unity Presbyterian Church, a member of the Committee to select location for the original buildings at Davidson College and to contract for and superintend the construction of same, and was also one of the incorporating Trustees of Davidson College.

2. James Graham, bachelor. (See 1851.)

3. Dr. George Franklin Graham married in 1825 to Martha A. Harris, only child of Charles Harris and Martha Ann Epps (formerly widow of Capt. Charles Connor). The only child by this marriage was Ann Eliza Harris, who married to Col. William Johnston of Charlotte.

4. Violet married Dr. Moses W. Alexander of Mecklenburg. Among their children was Capt. Sydenham B. Alexander, a soldier of the Civil War, pioneer advocate of road improvement in the State; State Senator five terms from Mecklenburg and member of Congress from 1891 to 1895.

5. Mary married Rev. Robert Hall Morrison. (See 1889.)

6. Governor William A. Graham married Susannah Washington of Newbern, June 8, 1836. (See 1875.)

For full details see "Life of Gen. Joseph Graham," by Major William A. Graham.

(A detailed sketch of his life may be found in Wheeler's "History" and Hunter's "Sketches.")

Governor Hutchins Gordon Burton (a cousin of Judge Robert H. and Alfred M. Burton, distinguished Lincoln citizens) was born in Granville County, North Carolina. Represented Mecklenburg County in the Legislature of 1809 and 1810 and in 1810 was elected Attorney General of the State.

He later moved to Halifax County, North Carolina. In 1817 he represented Halifax town in the House of Commons; was Congressman from Halifax district, 1819-1824; Governor of the State, 1824-27. Early in 1836 he drove from Halifax to visit his kinsfolk, the Burtons of Beatties Ford, en route was taken suddenly ill in Iredell County where he died, April 21, 1836, at the home of Henry T. Sloan and his body was carried to Unity graveyard near Beatties Ford and buried there in the Burton plot.

An interesting story connected with the death of Governor Burton was told by the late Capt. William H. Day of Halifax who was related to the Joyner family into which Mrs. Burton married after the death of Gov. Burton.

Mrs. Burton told Capt. Day that she was at her home in Halifax County walking with her children, when she saw, or thought she saw, her husband, the Governor, alight from his horse and walk into the house. She called the children to hurry for there is your father going into the house. They rushed in but Gov. Burton was not there. Later she learned that he had died on that same day and hour, in far away Iredell County as he was journeying toward Beatties Ford.

In his autobiography, David Crockett says he was born in 1786, Lincoln County. He was a son of John Crockett, a member of the Lincoln County Militia during the period of the Revolution. David was a rare product of the pioneer period who with courage undaunted sought adventure in the wilds of Tennessee. He was a hunter unafraid with a personality that appealed to the multitude of his time and they sent him to Congress from Tennessee. The story goes that after the election he went to Nashville and met there the political leaders. James K. Polk said to him: "Mr. Crockett, I think there will be an entire and radical change in our financial system at the next session of Congress." Crockett, not knowing what all that meant, replied: "I think it quite likely, Sir." After two terms he was defeated for re-election and then bitterly disappointed, went further West to Arkansas and then to Texas where he found congenial spirits whom he joined to fight for Texas independence; was one of the brave men at the Alamo who fought to the death when Santa Anna with 6,000 Mexicans stormed the fort and killed the 180 Texans including Crockett the famous pioneer and wit, on that March day in 1836. This terrible slaughter so enraged the Texans that with the slogan, "Remember the Alamo," they soon won a complete victory at San Jacinto, captured Santa Anna and organized the Texas Republic with Sam Houston as President late in the same year.

"The Trustees of the Female Academy met at Jacob Ramsour's, January 8, 1836. Present: Jacob Ramsour, Vardry McBee, Carlos Leonard, Peregrine Roberts, Michael Hoke and Jacob A. Ramsour, with Jacob Ramsour in the chair. B. S. Johnson was elected Trustee to fill the vacancy caused by the resignation of Jacob Ramsour.

"It was agreed by the Trustees that Miss Amelia Thompson have charge of the Academy for the next season; that the Secretary apprise her of this, and learn from her whether she would wish to teach longer than the next session. Adjourned.

JACOB A. RAMSOUR, Sec'y."

Advertisement: For Sale, tanyard and colored tanner at a bargain. Concord, January 21, 1836. Paul Barringer.

April 1st. Dry Pond post office has been established in Lincoln County with John F. Lowe, postmaster. (Now Denver.)

April 1st. Van Buren meeting in Lincolnton. John Wilfong, Chairman, M. W. Abernethy, Andrew Motz, James Quinn and Marcus L. Hoke, Secretaries. Henry Cansler presented the following which was unanimously adopted:

RESOLVED: That we will support for the next Governor of North Carolina, Richard Dobbs Spaight, a Republican of the old school, and a gentleman whose whole political course is without spot or blemish.

John Wilfong, a soldier of the Revolution, was nominated for Elector on the Van Buren ticket.

May 13th. The members of the Bar assembled at Rutherfordton hearing of the death of Governor H. G. Burton, passed appropriate resolutions of respect.

Married in Rowan County, May 26, 1836, Allen Alexander of Lincolnton to Adelaide, daughter of Moses Graham of Rowan.

In Newbern on 8th of June, William A. Graham was married to Susan, daughter of John Washington, of Newbern.

The 4th of July celebration of 1836 as reported in *Raleigh Standard* of 1836, follows:

THE ANNALS OF LINCOLN COUNTY 117

The address was delivered by L. E. Thompson and the Declaration of Independence was read by J. A. Wallace. After the public exercises about sixty persons attended the banquet, forty-eight of whom were for Van Buren and twelve for Hugh Lawson White. There were twelve Revolutionary soldiers seated at the table, headed by John Wilfong, the Van Buren elector. Peter Eddleman, Abram Forney, Robinson Goodwin, Joseph Morris and Frederick Lineberger were other Revolutionary soldiers present who responded to toasts. Others present who made brief speeches were M. W. Abernethy, Marcus L. Hoke, L. E. Thompson, J. E. Wallace, Capt. James Holsclaw, Col. Daniel Seagle, Maj. John Michael, Turner Abernethy, W. W. Monday, Daniel F. Ramsour, Benjamin Morris, Moses Martin, Jacob A. Ramsour, Willard Boyden, Lewis P. Rodrick, Lawson H. Kistler, Capt. William Slade, A. H. Porter, Maj. John B. Harry, John M. Butts, Felix M. Abernethy, B. M. Edney, John F. Hoke, J. J. Summey, Franklin A. Hoke, Jonas Rudisill, Ephraim Mauney, John Tingen, A. Robinson, E. A. Hooper and Edmund Osborne.

It was a non-partisan meeting, but the toasts for Van Buren, the Democratic presidential candidate, and for Hugh Lawson White, of Tennessee, who opposed Van Buren and got the electoral votes of Tennessee and Georgia, had strong partisan flavor. Toasts were drunk to Henry W. Connor, the Congressman, and to James Pinckney Henderson, who was at the time doing valiant service with Sam Houston for Texas Independence.

Died recently, David Abernethy, a merchant on Mountain Creek, Lincoln County.

August 19, 1836. *The Lincoln Transcript*, a new paper published in Lincolnton, says: "Lincoln County has one Cotton factory with 12 looms and 1,280 spindles, four furnaces, nine forges, ore banks without number and of very best and richest quality, twenty-five merchant mills making best quality of flour, a host of common grist and saw mills, limestone formations near Kings Mountain and gold in many places. Lincoln is an important section and will be one of the most desirable spots on earth if the contemplated railroads shall come this way. Lincolnton is remarkable for the number and skill of its mechanics and general intelligence of its citizens."

August 26th. Who will go to Texas?

Major John B. Harry, of Lincolnton, has been authorized by me with consent of Major Gen. Hunt and agents in Western Counties of North Carolina to name and enroll volunteer emigrants to Texas and will conduct such as may wish to emigrate to that Republic about October 1st next, at the expense of the Republic of Texas.

(Signed) J. PINCKNEY HENDERSON,
Brig. Gen. of the Texas Army.

October 1836. Railroad meeting was held in Salisbury, Bartlett Shipp, Chairman, and James R. Dodge, Secretary. Delegates were present from Anson, Ashe, Brunswick, Burke, Chatham, Cumberland, Cabarrus, Davidson, Iredell, Lincoln, Mecklenburg, Montgomery, New Hanover, Orange, Rowan, Rutherford, Surry, Wake and Wilkes.

Lincoln Transcript.
Volume 1, Number 25.

Published by Andrew R. Porter & Co.,
Subscription rate, $2.00 a year, paid in advance,
Not paid in advance, $2.50 a year.

Advertisements:

Lincolnton Female Academy—Miss Margaret Smith to have charge. Vardry McBee, D. Reinhardt, Carlos Leonard, B. S. Johnson, P. G. Roberts, Michael Hoke, J. A. Ramsour, Trustees.

Thomas Williamson advertises likely negroes for sale.

Giles Pearson—Grist and Saw Mill.

James Martin advertises house with four-acre square.

L. Montague appears to be the only poet who broke into print, the title of his work being "The Sailor's Bride." It is impossible to determine whether he was a Lincoln County resident, however.

1837

Three of those who emigrated with Major John B. Harry to Texas died on the way:

William Castles, of Charlotte,
William Gaston, of Lincoln,
Peter Mull, of Burke.

John D. Graham and Miles W. Abernethy, administrators of the estate of the late Gen. Joseph Graham advertise personal property, including forty-four negroes, for sale.

Robert Frederick, son of Michael Hoke, born May 27, 1837. Later became Major General in the Confederate Army.

W. W. Munday was married to Lucinda Shelton May 15, 1837.

Miles W. Abernethy, son of John D. and Susan Maria (Forney) Abernethy, was a prominent citizen of Lincoln County; member of the House of Commons in 1831 and 1832; Clerk of the County Court 1833 to 1837. He then moved to Alabama and was there member of the State Senate for several terms. He was married to Ann Hoke, June 17, 1835.

In Lincolnton, on August 18, 1837, there was a disagreement between Logan Henderson and Marcus Hoke, two impetuous young men and scions of prominent families. Finally they met in combat. The wound that Hoke received resulted in his death three days later. It was all deplorable and neighbors and friends were alienated, but time is the healer of all wounds so that today the bitterness engendered is forgotten. Perhaps no reference should be made to the regrettable conflict but this brief statement is a part of the history of the last century.

Joseph Graham, aged 40, and son of the late General Joseph Graham, died in Memphis, September 18th.

1838

In Lincolnton, on January 10, 1838, by Rev. A. L. Watts, Mr. Caleb Phifer, of Concord, was married to Miss Mary Adeline, daughter of David Ramsour, of Lincolnton.

John Wilfong, a soldier of the Revolution, aged 76, was, on June 18, 1838, on his way alone to the Springs some fourteen miles distant from his home. His horse was found tied to a tree and his dead body in the woods nearby. He was supposed to have taken sick and lain down to rest by the way.

Thomas Dews, Jr., a brilliant young lawyer, who moved from Lincolnton to Rutherfordton to practice law, died in Rutherfordton, August 2, 1838, aged 30 years. He graduated from the University in the class with Gov. Graham and shared class honors with him when only 16 years old.

Married in Lincoln County, September 6, 1838, by Rev. Adam Miller, James Abernethy to Mary Rankin and John Abernethy to Jane Rankin. (All Whigs.)

Married in Philadelphia, November 8, 1838, Col. John H. Wheeler, the superintendent of the Charlotte Mint, to Ellen, daughter of Thomas Sully, the famous portrait painter.

Note: Later Col. Wheeler moved to Beatties Ford and was a member of the House of Commons from Lincoln in 1852.

1839

Married, in Washington, April 9, 1839, by the Rev. Henry Slicer, Hon. Henry W. Connor, member of Congress from this district, to Mrs. Lucy Ann Coleman, daughter of the late Governor Hawkins of North Carolina.

John F. Phifer, of Concord, was married June 8, 1839, to Elizabeth Ramsour, daughter of David Ramsour, of Lincolnton.

October 3, 1839. Lincoln County is opposed to the free school law proposed by the Legislature. The Democrats claim it their privilege not to vote on the law, but for the legislators, and that it was a Whig trick to shift an uncertain issue from the Legislature to the people; that the districts should be laid off so that children can walk to school and according to the numbers to be benefitted; that the law enacted was particularly unjust to the east and harder still on the sparsely settled west.

Note: It seems that the Legislature was afraid to pass a school law, without submitting it to the people for approval. Any county that wanted to pay for what was a poor apology for a school could vote as much tax as it was willing to pay or do without the school. Lincoln citizens were slow to vote the tax and rejected it by a huge majority.

For Sale: Will sell at auction 7 or 8 likely young negroes; a new set of Cast Mill Irons and one milch cow. P. C. Caldwell, Administrator. October 5, 1839.

At 2 o'clock Sunday morning, December 1st, 1839, in Lincolnton, fire broke out in the work shop of B. Jetton and Sons, and spread, destroying the hotel of Mrs. Schenck and the two buildings occupied by Gen. Daniel Seagle as well as the Jetton and Ramsour stores and all buildings behind same in that block.

A portion of Ramsour's goods were saved but little or nothing belonging to others escaped the fire. The loss amounts to $25,000.00.

From *The Western Whig Banner* — June 27, 1839. H. W. Guion, Editor:

The Fourth of July will be celebrated in this place. The oration will be delivered by William Lander, Esq. The Committee of Arrangements for the occasion are Henry Cansler, Esq., J. T. Alexander, Esq., Capt. Thomas R. Shuford, F. A. Hoke and Paul Kistler. The citizens of the county generally, and surviving Revolutionary soldiers particularly, are invited to attend.

Caleb Miller requests us to announce him as a candidate for the office of sheriff of this county.

Bartlett Shipp, Esq., requests us to inform the citizens of Lincoln County that he is a candidate for a seat in the Senate of the next General Assembly.

Advertisement: Shady Grove Female School to be opened first Monday of next April. Mrs. McCutchan. Prices according to subjects pursued—$6.00, $8.00 and $10.00 per session of five months. Drawing and painting $5.00 extra per session. Board and Washing $7.00 per month. Lights extra. Music teacher will be procured if class can be organized. Mrs. J. S. McCutchan, Shady Grove, Lincoln Co., N. C.

CHAPTER XII

1840-1849

January 9, 1840. The *Lincoln Republican* has passed from Mr. Thompson into the hands of Robert Williamson, Jr.

The census takers in 1840 for Lincoln County are David Seagle and Moses T. Abernethy.

Col. John H. Wheeler, the first superintendent of the Charlotte Mint and a Democrat was appointed to this position by President Van Buren. Naturally he wanted to beautify the grounds and when he went to Philadelphia to get married in November, 1838, he placed an order with Landreth, florist and seedman, for shrubbery and flowers amounting to $218.25.

He bought 50 horse chestnuts at $1.00 each, and 50 Ailanthus trees for $1.00 each, and various and sundry shrubs and flowers, making the bill total $218.25.

The Charlotte Journal of June 18, 1840, carries a three-column criticism of this outlay of the public funds all copied from the Washington letter to the *Raleigh Register*, a Whig newspaper. A part of the correspondence reads as follows:

"Some might fear, perhaps, lest amidst these occupations of taste, these arduous labors of 'patriotism,' the proper duties of the mint should be neglected by the superintendent. But happily it requires little time or skill to superintend all the coinage done at Charlotte; and he must be a clever and ingenuous man indeed, clever and ingenuous beyond the little Colonel, who can contrive to leave much undone, where there is but little to do.

"I subjoin a copy of the 'Flower Bill,' which I think ought to be submitted to the people of North Carolina—the items of expenditure which I have referred to, both at the Mint and the White House, you may rely on as being accurately stated."

Then follows the itemized bill which is marked paid by B. Landreth & Company, on November 7, 1838.

In the old days of Whigs and Democrats there were small politicians as well as in these times, as is shown by the partisan Whig correspondent. This is all written because Col. Wheeler later became a citizen of Lincoln, active in public life. But specially do I want to say something about the 50 Ailanthus trees he bought in Philadelphia and planted on the Mint grounds. Of course the people far and wide wanted sprouts to plant in their front yards. Col. Wheeler was no doubt beguiled by the dealer to buy 50 Ailanthus trees, little thinking that this rare South American specimen, like sin, is a marvelous missionary which was to become a nuisance in nearly every town in the Carolinas, for it is no less than what is commonly called the copal tree which flourishes in the back lots of Lincolnton near the stables and pig stys—that offensively odoriferous tree that we can't get rid of, for when you uproot it here, it breaks out yonder, and the wind blows the missionary seed wherever it willeth. When I see copal trees in Lincolnton, Morganton, Taylorsville, Charlotte, everywhere, I think of Col. Wheeler and the curse he planted in North Carolina soil, little dreaming that he was scattering a pest which the generations since have been unable to eradicate. Ailanthus — Copal. How offensive the odor — how rapid the growth! How difficult to eradicate!

Col. John H. Wheeler, when his term as superintendent of the Mint expired, bought the Judge Burton property at Beatties Ford and lived there for about ten years, during which time he wrote *Wheeler's History of North Carolina*. He served as State Treasurer from 1843 to 1845 and is credited to Lincoln County in the North Carolina Manual of 1913. He also was in the House of Commons from Lincoln in 1852-53.

The Whig Convention was held in Lincolnton, January 22, 1840. Andrew Hoyle, Chairman, and Dr. D. W. Schenck, Secretary. Robert H. Burton stated that we meet to elect delegates to a Convention in Charlotte on Wednesday of Superior Court to select a district elector. The delegates chosen were Alexander McCorkle, William Oats, John Coulter, J. T. and R. M. Alexander and Jonas Bost.

March 26, 1840. Vardry McBee has resigned the Presidency of the Louisville, Cincinnati and Charlotte Railroad.

Col. Henry Fulenwider, of Lincoln, was nominated on April 18, elector for Van Buren, against David Ramsour, the Whig elector.

Cephas Quickel was married to Sarah Killian, May 16, 1840.

July 2, 1840. William M. Shipp, Albert M. Shipp, William Johnston and Charles Connor Graham, all of Lincoln, and Tod R. Caldwell of Burke, graduated from the State University.

July 2, 1840. Mr. Stanly, Whig Congressman from this state, on the floor of the House severely criticized Col. Wheeler for extravagance in buying shrubbery for the Charlotte Mint grounds. He also charged him with spending $225.00 for carpets, rugs and table covers; $71.50 for chairs; and further for buying a clock for the Mint office.

Dr. Elam Caldwell was married August 19, 1840, to Elizabeth Motz, daughter of John Motz.

A new county to be called Graham, from part of Lincoln, Iredell and Mecklenburg is proposed.

Jacob Forney, Jr., eldest son of Jacob Forney the pioneer, was a patriotic citizen and a gallant soldier of the Revolution. Soon after that war he settled in Burke County where he purchased a large body of land. He married to Mary Corpening of Burke and they had eleven children, one of whom died young. The others—seven sons and three daughters, all married and their descendants are numerous and substantial citizens of Lincoln, Catawba, Burke and Rutherford Counties.

His tombstone in a private cemetery on the old homestead bears the inscription:

"Sacred to the memory of Jacob Forney, born
November 6th, 1754, died November 7th, 1840,
aged eighty-six years and one day."

1841

January 14th. Albert C. Williamson, of Lincoln, has been granted license to practice law.

"The Board of Trustees of Lincolnton Female Academy, met at C. Leonard's February 5, 1841. Present: C. C. Henderson, C. Leonard, Dr. S. P. Simpson, J. R. Dodge and H. W. Guion. Tuition rates of the Female Academy were fixed. Resolved, that the Trustees procure the services of some competent lady as instructress of the Academy, and for such services bind the Corporation to pay not more than Five Hundred ($500.00) Dollars for the first year. It was further resolved that James R. Dodge and C. C. Henderson write to their respective friends at the North, to point out and name persons competent and willing to serve under the terms proposed.

H. W. GUION, Sec'y."

March 4th. A new post office called Cottage Home has been established in Lincoln County with Rev. R. H. Morrison as postmaster.

Cleaveland County was created in 1841 from parts of Lincoln and Rutherford Counties. At the end of the original bill signed by R. B. Gilliam and A. Joyner, President of the Senate and Speaker of the House, respectively, it is stated that the act has been "Read three times and ratified in General Assembly, this the 11th day of January 1841." "The name of Cleaveland" is given to the county and after the boundary lines are given a Committee was named to designate "some point in the said County of Cleaveland not more than four miles from Thomas Wilson's Mineral Springs, which shall be the County seat of said County." The Committee was composed of Judge Robert H. Burton, Alexander McCorkle, Henry Cansler, and Eli Hoyle, of Lincoln County, together with Ed Bryant, Achilles Durham, John McDowell, Samuel Andrews and David Gray, from Rutherford County, and they selected the land where the City of Shelby now stands, named for Gen. Isaac Shelby.

Cleaveland County was named for Col. Benjamin Cleaveland, of Wilkes, who was one of the gallant officers in the Battle of Kings Mountain. His name was Cleaveland—not Cleveland. When Grover Cleveland was elected President they had the Legislature to change the spelling of the County name from Cleaveland to Cleveland.

Davidson College Commencement address was delivered by Gen. John Gray Bynum. Richard E. Sherrill, of Lincoln, was valedictorian. He became a useful Presbyterian preacher for many years in Tennessee and Texas. Dr. James G. Ramsay, of Rowan, was one of the graduates.

Married at Beatties Ford, by Rev. Mr. Forbes, October 6, 1841, Eli Hoyle to Miss Elizabeth Burton, daughter of Alfred M. Burton.

Miss Jane E. Johnston, aged 18, and daughter of Dr. William Johnston, of Lincoln, died in Greensboro, October 24, 1841.

Green W. Caldwell, defeated Daniel M. Barringer, Whig, for Congress, by 800 majority.

Married by Rev. J. H. Crawford, in Lincolnton, November 17, 1841, Leonard E. Thompson, attorney-at-law, to Miss Harriet L., daughter of Jacob Ramsour.

Rev. Paul F. Kistler, a native of Lincolnton and a preacher of the South Carolina Conference, on December 16, 1841, was married to Miss Mary Wingard, of Lexington, S. C.

1842

William T. Shipp was married February 7, 1842, to Harriet, daughter of Robert Johnston.

March 2nd, 1842. Col. John Hoke conveyed to E. M. Forbes, Jeremiah W. Murphy, T. N. Herndon, Michael Hoke, L. E. Thompson and Haywood W. Guion, Trustees of St. Luke's Episcopal church, the lot on which the church stands.

Rev. Jesse R. Peterson and Mary Detter were married March 11, 1842.

Judge Robert Henderson Burton, son of Col. Robert Burton, of Granville County, was born in 1781; educated at the University of North Carolina and came to Lincoln County; was there admitted to the bar and became distinguished as a lawyer with a large and lucrative practice. The Legislature of 1818 elected him Judge of the Superior Court and after one year on the bench he resigned and resumed the practice of law. In 1830 the Legislature elected him State Treasurer, which office he declined. He was married May 11, 1813, to Mary Fulenwider, daughter of Col. John Fulenwider and settled on a plantation at Beatties Ford. They reared a family of 11 children, but only four of them married. One daughter, Frances, married to Col. Michael Hoke, a brilliant Lincolnton lawyer. Eliza married to Rev. J. M. H. Adams of the Presbyterian church. Augustus W. Burton, an able lawyer, married to Julia L. Olmstead. Henry W. Burton was a well-known citizen of Lincoln and married Mrs. Sarah (Hoyle) Keenan.

Judge Burton died at Beatties Ford, April 26, 1842, and the body was buried at Unity Church graveyard. Soon after his death at a meeting of the Lincolnton bar a Committee composed of Robert Williamson, Bartlett Shipp and Haywood W. Guion was appointed to prepare suitable resolutions of respect and transmit a copy of same to the family of Judge Burton. Judge Osborne who was present paid eloquent tribute to the deceased. He was a noble gentleman and ranked high among his legal compeers, including such men as William Julius Alexander, James W. Osborne, Haywood W. Guion, Michael Hoke, Robert

Williamson, Bartlett Shipp, James R. Dodge and his brother, Alfred M. Burton.

A meeting was held at Hoffman & Rhyne's Store, June 4, 1842, (in what is now Gaston County) to consider the question of dividing the County of Lincoln. The Committee on resolutions was composed of Henry Fulenwider, James H. White, Whiten Stowe, F. D. Hoffman, J. Webster and J. D. Rankin. After an earnest speech by James H. White it was resolved not to support any man for a seat in the Legislature who is not an open advocate of an equal division of the County. The delegates appointed to a County Convention to be held in Lincolnton on Tuesday of court were J. D. Rankin, Samuel Johnston, Leroy Stowe, Col. Richard Rankin, Daniel Rhyne, William Hanks and M. H. Rhyne.

William Preston Bynum graduated from Davidson College in August, 1842, and "Our Country" was the subject of his graduating speech.

Among those licensed to practice law by Supreme Court in 1842 were the following who became distinguished men: S. H. Walkup, Duncan K. McRea, Atlas J. Dargan, R. S. Donnell, John Baxter, Lewis P. Olds, father of the late Fred A. Olds, and William Johnston, the last named of Lincoln County.

Fayetteville market report, August, 1842: Beef, 3 to 6 cents; butter, 12½ cents; brandy, 38 to 40 cents per gallon; whiskey, 28 to 30 cents; green hides, 4 to 5 cents; dry hides, 12 to 14 cents; wool, 15 to 20 cents; cotton, 7 to 8 cents; bacon, 6 to 7 cents.

Mail Route schedule between Charlotte and Lincolnton is as follows: Leaves Charlotte Monday and Thursday at 4 P.M., and arrives at Lincolnton at 12 o'clock midnight. Leaves Lincolnton Sunday and Wednesday at 8 A.M., and arrives at Charlotte at 3 P.M.

Bill for new County of Catawba passed the House of Commons 64 to 48 December, 1842. Also passed the Senate. Division line near to Lincolnton and if Court House should be moved will greatly injure the town.

By authority of the General Assembly of 1842: "Be it known in pursuance of Act of General Assembly of the State of North Carolina, entitled, 'An act to lay off and establish a county by the name of Catawba' and an act supplemental to said act, a Court of Pleas and Quarter Sessions shall be opened and held for said county of Catawba at the home of Matthias Barringer on the third day of March, 1843," and on that day the following Magistrates met at the home of Matthias Barringer, near the present town of Newton: Frederick Hoke, Jesse Gant, Archibald Ray, Electius Connor, William Harmon, Henry Cline, John Yount, Ephraim Yount, Jonas Bost, John Killian, Absalom Brown, Geo. P. Shuford, Joshua Wilson, Peter Warlick, Peter Stamey, Major Hull, Thos. Ward, Alexander Ward, Nathaniel Edwards, John P. Shuford, Jacob Helderman, Wesley Munday, William Long, Lyman Woodford and Thomas Hampton. The 25 magistrates organized by choosing Frederick Hoke temporary chairman; Henry Cline, clerk; and Isaac Howe, sheriff.

The following additional magistrates were sworn in: Ambrose Lutz, Geo. P. Wilkey, Philip Burns, Joseph Fisher, Timothy Moser, William Abernethy, Joseph Lowrance, Nathaniel Wilson, Thos. I. Hamilton, Eli P. Shuford, Eli Deal, Jackson Whitener and Franklin Reinhardt. The following officers were then elected by ballot: Sheriff, Andrew H. Shuford; Trustee, Joseph Wilson; Solicitor, Wm. M. Shipp; Surveyor, Joshua Wilson; Clerk, Joseph A. Reinhardt; Register, E. P. Coulter; Processioner, Eli P. Shuford; Coroner, Wm. L. Mahaffey; Entry Taker, Henry Cline.

Select Court: Jonas Bost, chairman; Geo. P. Shuford, Joshua Wilson, Henry Cline and John Williams. Salary of Select Court, $1.50 per day. Various orders were passed and the Court adjourned to meet on June second at Newton.

The death, February 23, 1842, of David Ramsour, son of Jacob, son of Diedrich, the pioneer, removed a prominent citizen and enterprising Lincolnton merchant. His father, Jacob Ramsour, married Annie Carpenter, and operated the Ramsour mill at the time of the Battle of Ramsour's Mill. David was born August 4, 1775, nearly five years before that battle.

He married Sarah, daughter of John Wilfong, a Revolutionary patriot, July 12, 1805. He was one of the first Trustees of Pleasant Retreat Academy.

Among his children were:

Jacob A. Ramsour (See 1880) ; J. T. Ramsour; Annie, who married Henry Fulenwider, June 7, 1829; Cynthia, married Eli Hoyle, January 5, 1830; Adeline, married Caleb Phifer, January 10, 1838; Carolyn Elizabeth, married John F. Phifer, June 5, 1839.

1843

William M. Shipp was licensed to practice law January, 1843.

Married by Rev. E. M. Forbes, near Lincolnton, January 3, 1843, Dr. J. M. Happoldt, of Charlotte, to Sarah A., daughter of Robert Williamson. (The Lincoln Lithia Inn property was then known as the Robert Williamson place.)

Rev. George W. Welker, of the Reformed Curch, was married to Abagail Mason, April 6, 1843.

In 1843 The Lincoln Paper Mill, operated by G. and D. Mosteller, added Book Bindery and Blank Book Department where Ledgers, Cash Books and County Record Books were made.

Col. Lawson A. Mason was married to Catherine Lineberger on September 28, 1843.

Alexander McCorkle was a delegate to the Whig Convention.

Married in Lincolnton, May 6, 1843, by B. S. Johnson, Esq., William R. Edwards to Sarah A. Detter.

Hugh C. Hamilton, a Beatties Ford merchant, was married to Susan L. Massie by Rev. R. H. Morrison, November, 1843.

Major Lawson Henderson, (son of James Henderson, the pioneer) born March 22, 1774, died November 21, 1843; was a native of Lincoln County and filled a large place in the history of the County during the period of his active life.

He was Sheriff of the County from 1796 to 1801. When the sessions of the Superior Court of the Morgan district of which Lincoln was a part were all held in Morganton, it was a British custom handed down from Colonial times for one of the Sheriffs to escort the Judge from his hotel to the court room. On the day that Sheriff Henderson was expected to perform that duty he failed to, so the Judge entered the court room alone and called the Sheriff of Lincoln to explain why he had not complied with the custom. Henderson replied briefly that there was no law requiring it, and from that day the custom was abandoned. He was Clerk of the County Court from October, 1804 to April, 1807. When the Legislature changed the law by providing that sessions of the Superior Court be held in each county he was appointed in 1807 Clerk of the Superior Court for the term of his life.

When, in 1832, the Legislature made the office elective, John D. Hoke was elected Clerk, but Henderson, who was not a candidate, refused to vacate the office on the ground that it was his property for life. Hoke entered suit for it and lost when the Supreme Court in a decision written by Judge Ruffin sustained Henderson's claim to the office. Later, in 1837, he resigned.

Lawson Henderson possessed superior mental gifts, was a fine judge of law and his counsel was sought by many people. He was a very influential citizen and very popular as evidenced by the multitude of people in the county who were named for him. He married to Elizabeth Caruth, July 20, 1798, and reared a large family among whom were Chas. C. and James Pinckney. He died Nov. 21, 1843, aged 70 years, and his body was buried in the old White Church cemetery in Lincolnton.

An old autograph album which belonged to Miss Ann E. Henderson (1825-1901) contains the following, written by the paralytic hand of her grandfather, Major Lawson Henderson, bearing date 1839: "Nothing so becomes the maiden character as modest stillness and humility." (Signed) "L. H."

Among the children of Major Lawson Henderson were:

Wallace Alexander (1799-1823). Died at the house of Dr. L. Les Dalley in Havana, Cuba, April 24, 1823, Dr. Wallace Alexander Henderson. He was the eldest son of Major Henderson, When ten years old he commenced reading the Latin language with Rev. John Robinson of Cabarrus County; and finished reading Latin and Greek languages with Rev. John M. Wilson of Mecklenburg. From thence he was removed to Greeneville College in Tennessee where he obtained a diploma at the age of nineteen. Shortly after leaving college he returned to Lincoln and commenced the study of physics with Dr. William McLean; which he continued afterwards with Dr. McKenzie of Charlotte. After finishing his course he went to the city of New York to attend medical lectures, where, in the winter of 1821-1822, from the severity of that climate he contracted pulmonary consumption (*Western Carolinian*, June 17, 1823).

John Caruth (1801-1833) married Nancy Riley Gaffney, of Spartanburg District, S. C., in 1828.

Charles Cotesworth (1803-1869) a Lincolnton merchant and influential citizen, married Barbara Glen Bryden, of New York, December 7, 1824. (See 1869.)

Lawson Franklin (1805-1858) married Ann Dunavant of Chesterville, S. C.

James Pinckney (1808-1858) married in Saint George's Chapel, London, October 10, 1839, to Frances Cox of Philadelphia. (See 1858.)

Hugh Lawson, born 1812, and died on board the Brig Orson, James Chase, Master, on his passage from St. Croix to Savannah, January 20, 1837, twelve days before the boat arrived at Savannah.

George William (1814-1850) married Amanda M. Moore, September, 1835, in Spartanburg District, S. C.

Mary Graham (1815-1877) married Thos. N. Herndon, a Lincolnton lawyer. She died in New Orleans.

Logan Barry (1818-1844) died in Marshall, Texas. Bachelor.

Walter Caruth (1820-1850) died in Canton, Miss. Bachelor.

Wallace Alexander Irwin (1827-1851) died in Canton, Miss. Bachelor.

The *Lincoln Courier* (T. J. Eccles, Editor) of December 16, 1843, stated that of three large gold pieces found in Gibson Branch mine, three miles from town, operated by Cansler and Johnson, one weighed 192, one 153, and one 107 penny weight, carat said to be fine and worth 98½ cents.

Advertisement: In *Lincoln Courier*, December 16, 1843: Lincoln Academy (Pleasant Retreat) Jeremiah W. Murphy, A.M.

Classics, $15.00.
Astronomy and English, $8.00.
Spelling, reading and writing, $5.00 per term.

Students prepared for admission into any class of University of North Carolina.

Advertisements also appear of John A. Jetton, maker of saddles and harness; tailoring by D. P. B. Moorman, next door to Schenck's apothecary store; and of C. C. Henderson, John Hoke and Jacob A. Ramsour, who were the leading merchants.

Col. Absalom Sherrill, of Lincoln, was married December 20, 1843 to Sarah McAlpine, of Anson.

Samuel N. Stowe (son of Larkin Stowe) was married to Margaret Holland in 1843.

1844

G. D. Mosteller, proprietor of the Lincoln Paper Mills, supplied paper to the *Charlotte Journal* during 1844.

May 10, 1844. The *Charlotte Journal* carried at its masthead the name of Michael Hoke for Governor.

Later Michael Hoke was nominated for Governor by the Democrats in 1844 and defeated by only 3,000 votes in the August election by William A. Graham, both natives of Lincoln County.

Col. John Hoke was born in Pennsylvania and came with the family to Lincolnton about 1797. He married to Barbara Quickel, daughter of Michael Quickel, the pioneer, January 9, 1808, reared a large family and was the ancestor of a long line of distinguished men. He was a merchant in Lincolnton and one of the owners of the cotton factory built by James Bivens, Michael Schenck and himself at the Laboratory in 1819, and which was destroyed by fire in 1863. His residence was the present brick building now called Inverness Inn. Col. Hoke was a member of the German Reformed Church and an honored and useful citizen. He died June 9, 1844, aged 67, and the body was deposited in the Hoke vault in the Old White Church cemetery.

Their children were:

David married Nancy Bivins; Michael married Frances Burton; Marcus married Harriet Smith; Sarah married Dr. Andrew B. Crook; Colonel John F. married Catherine Alexander; Nancy married Col. L. D. Childs; Colonel William J. married Georgiana T. Sumner; Francis married Catherine Baker. (See 1844, 1888, 1912, 1925 and 1931.)

Col. Michael Hoke, son of Col. John Hoke, was born in Lincolnton in 1810. On May 8, 1833, married by Rev. R. J. Miller to Frances, daughter of Judge Robert H. Burton; was admitted to the bar in July, 1832, and soon took high rank in the legal profession; represented Lincoln in the House of Commons for five terms, 1834-35-36-38 and 40, during which time he made a brilliant record and a state-wide reputation. In 1844, when only 34 years old, he was the Democratic candidate for Governor against William A. Graham (also a native of Lincoln), the Whig candidate, who won the election by about 3,000 votes.

Col. Hoke, exhausted by the strain of the state-wide canvass, died of bilious fever at Charlotte, September 9, 1844, and his body was buried in the Old White Church cemetery in Lincolnton.

In his brief life he became an eminent citizen. He was the father of Gen. Robt. F. Hoke of the Confederate Army, Marcus Hoke, Dr. George M. Hoke, and Mary Brent Hoke who married Professor H. H. Smith, (parents of Governor Hoke Smith of Georgia).

Rev. W. I. Langdon was married, December 17, 1844, to Margaret Lander, daughter of Rev. Samuel Lander, of Lincolnton.

Jacob Shuford (February 12, 1770 to April 1844), son of Martin Shuford and grandson of the pioneer John Shuford, married in 1789 Margaret Hoyle (June 28, 1769 to June 20, 1840).

Their children were:

1. Elizabeth, born September 3, 1790, married John Smyer.

2. John J., born 1792, married Wilfong and Catherine Corpening.

3. Martin P., born 1794, married Rhoda Lowrance.

4. Abel, born October 11, 1796, married Nancy Perkins.

5. Eve, born June 26, 1799, married Jonas Ramsour.

6. Fanny born February 15, 1801, married Henry Cansler.

7. Eli, born April 4, 1803, married Evaline Collins.

8. Jacob H., born February 23, 1805, married Catherine Baker.

9. Elkanah, born August 10, 1807, married Emmaline Martin.

10. Andrew, born February 24, 1810, married Elvira Collins.

11. Susan, born June 12, 1813, married Lawson Reinhardt.

Martin P. Shuford represented Rutherford County in State Senate 4 terms, 1825-6-7- and 8.

His children were:

1. Mortimer, German Reformed preacher, married Lucinda C. Sohn, preached mostly in Virginia and Maryland, died November 7, 1883.
2. Margaret, married Theodore Houston.
3. Catherine, married John Carpenter.
4. Jacob L., Methodist preacher 50 years, married Roxanna Fulenwider.
5. Susan, married Nichols.
6. Eli P., married Rosanna J. Lee.
7. James Monroe, married Elizabeth Rabb.

Among other descendants of John Shuford, the pioneer, were:

1. David Shuford, sheriff of Lincoln County from 1801 to 1803 and State Senator for six terms: 1806, 1812, 1813, 1815, 1816 and 1820. He died in 1832.
2. Martin Shuford, sheriff of Lincoln from 1813 to 1816.
3. Andrew H. Shuford was in the House of Commons from Lincoln in 1848.
4. Abel A. Shuford represented Catawba in the Legislature of 1885 and was prominent in Hickory as a banker and manufacturer. He was a son of Jacob Shuford, Jr., son of Jacob and Margaret Hoyle Shuford.
5. George A. Shuford, an Asheville lawyer, and descendant of John Shuford, the pioneer, was Superior Court Judge of Asheville district from 1892 to 1895.
6. Alonzo Craige Shuford of Catawba County, son of George P., son of David, son of John Shuford, the pioneer, represented his district in the United States Congress from March, 1895, to March, 1899.

He was born in Catawba County, March, 1858, graduated at Catawba College, married Nov. 22, 1882, to Willie Ellen, daughter of Lieutenant Thomas L. Lowe and died at home of his daughter, Mrs. C. E. McIntosh, in Chapel Hill, N. C., February 8, 1932.

1845

Joseph M. Graham, brother of Gov. William A. Graham, was married in Newbern, March 12, 1845, to Mary Washington, daughter of John Washington. The bride is a sister of the wife of Gov. Graham.

Died May 21, 1845, at Mineral Springs, Catawba County, the Rev. Solomon S. Middlekauff, in his 28th year. The deceased, a native of Maryland was educated for the ministry at Marshall College, Penn. He came to North Carolina in the summer of 1842 and in July of that year was ordained a minister of the German Reformed church and was pastor of four congregations in Lincoln and Catawba Counties. His body rests in the White Church graveyard in Lincolnton.

Married in Lincoln County, May 28, 1845, by Rev. Samuel Lander, John E. Hoke to Nancy J., daughter of Elijah Sullivan, all of Lincoln County.

Democratic Congressional Convention held at Tavern of A. D. Kerr, of Iredell County, May 31, 1845.

Major Henry W. Connor was elected Chairman, with William S. McCoy of Rowan, James Young of Cabarrus, Josiah Stewart of Union, William M. Matthews of Mecklenburg and Col. John H. Wheeler of Lincoln, as Vice-Chairmen. J. F. A. Miller of Iredell, and A. W. Burton of Lincoln, were Secretaries.

Charles Fisher, of Rowan was nominated for Congress by a unanimous vote. The delegates from Lincoln were Henry W. Connor, Laban Wilson, Dr. H. M. Pritchard, Thomas Ward, John Abernethy, Absalom Sherrill, Elihu Lockman, A. H. Shuford, John H. Wheeler, L. A. Shuford, Dr. L. W. Coleman, W. W. Munday, Thomas Little, Calvin Wilfong, Jacob Plonk, L. B. Gaston, H. N. Gaston, John G. Lewis and A. W. Burton.

In the White Church graveyard are buried three members of the Hauss family and the inscriptions on the tombs are:

1. John Hauss, died August 2, 1845, age 48.
2. Peter Hauss, died in 1856, age 70.
3. John Hauss, died June 26, 1887, age 81.

Col. Robert Williamson was born in Pennsylvania, came to Lincoln County when a young man and established himself as a lawyer who ranked high among the able advocates who practiced in the Lincoln courts in his day. He represented the County in the House of Commons in 1818 and 1819, and in the Senate in 1821 and 1822, and was distinguished as one who exercised high influence in this section of the State.

He married to Elizabeth, daughter of Capt. John Reid, November 22, 1806, and reared a large family, nine of whom were sons.

Robert Williamson, Jr., and William Williamson were Lincolnton lawyers. Robert, Jr., was Clerk of the County Court from 1845 to 1853, and Clerk of the Superior Court for several years from 1853, while William was a reputable lawyer, who died in Lincolnton May 20, 1856, of dropsy, aged 45.

Albert settled in Charlotte where he practiced law. Thomas and Joseph were also lawyers. Dr. Dallas Williamson was a physician, Rufus R., a merchant, while James and John were farmers.

Col. Robert Williamson owned the Lincoln Lithia Inn property and lived there for many years until his death in July 1845.

Two of his great grandsons, Rev. Walter M. Walsh and Rev. Clyde J. Walsh, reared in Charlotte, are now Presbyterian ministers in Virginia.

Hugh Williamson (1735-1819) born in Pennsylvania, came to Chowan County, North Carolina and rendered brilliant service to the State, served with William Blount and Richard Dobbs Spaight in the Convention which formulated the Constitution of the United States and one of the signers of that immortal document, was an uncle of Col. Robert Williamson.

At a meeting of the Lincoln bar, of which Judge Richmond M. Pearson was made Chairman, and William Lander, Secretary, appropriate resolutions were passed in which high tribute was paid to Col. Robert Williamson who died in July, 1845.

John H. Wheeler, Burton Craige, Andrew H. Shuford, Henry Whitener and H. W. Robinson, Commissioners, advertise for bids for the building of court house and jail in Newton.

Lincolnton in 1845, as reported in *Lincoln Courier*, September 13, 1845. Editor, T. J. Eccles:

County Solicitor, William Lander; Superior Court Clerk, F. A. Hoke; Equity, William Williamson; County Court Clerk, Robert Williamson; Sheriff, Benj. Morris; Deputy Sheriff, Paul Kistler; Register, W. J. Wilson; Deputy, C. C. Henderson; Surveyor, Isaac Holland; Lawyers, Haywood W. Guion, L. E. Thompson, William Lander, V. A. McBee and William Williamson; Physicians, S. P. Simpson, D. W. Schenck, Elam Caldwell, Z. Butt, and A. Ramsour; Merchants, W. J. Hoke, B. S. Johnson, Jacob A. Ramsour, C. C. Henderson, J. Ramsour & Son and Johnson & Reed; Academies, Male—Benjamin Sumner, Female—Misses M. E. and J. F. Rodgers under charge of Mr. Sumner; Hotels, Mrs. Motz, William Slade, A. McLean and B. S. Johnson;

Grocers, G. Presnell, J. B. Rouche, W. R. Edwards and L. Rothrock; Watchmaker, Charles Schmidt; Saddle & Harness Makers, J. Taylor Alexander, J. A. Jetton & Co., B. M. & F. J. Jetton; Printer, T. J. Eccles, Editor *Courier;* Book Binder, F. A. Hoke; Painter, H. S. Hicks; Coach Factories, Samuel Lander, Abner McCoy, S. P. Simpson, Isaac Erwin, A. & R. Garner; Blacksmiths, Jacob Rush, M. Jacobs, Allen DeLane, J. Bisaner, J. W. Paysour; Cabinet Maker, Thomas Dews & Son; Carpenters, Daniel Shuford, James Triplett, A. Houser, Isaac Houser and John Houser; Tin Plate Worker & Coppersmith, Thomas R. Shuford; Shoe Makers, John Huggins, John A. Parker; Tanners, Paul Kistler, J. Ramsour; Hatters, John Cline, John Butts; Paper Factory, G. & R. Mosteller (4 miles South); Cotton Factory, John Hoke (2 miles South); Lime Kiln, Daniel Shuford (9 miles South); Iron Manufactories, High Shoals, H. W. Burton, Graham's Furnace, John D. Graham; Tailors, Daily & Seagle, Alexander & Moore, D. Hoover.

Whig Convention in Lincolnton, September, 1845, Alexander McCorkle, Chairman, and V. A. McBee, Secretary. Delegates appointed to State Convention were Robert Brevard, H. W. Guion, W. M. Shipp, M. L. McCorkle, Robert Perkins and V. A. McBee.

Democratic County Convention in Lincolnton, 1845

December 5, 1845, Isaac Holland, Chairman, Robert Williamson and James Quinn, Secretaries. John F. Hoke offered and spoke in favor of resolution approving State Convention in Raleigh on January 8th, 1846. Delegates appointed to this Convention were Samuel Venable, William Williamson, John F. Hoke, L. Gaston, Samuel N. Stowe, Henry Cansler, James Ferguson, Thomas Williamson, Philip Sandifer, E. Rhyne, T. J. Eccles, John Roberts, James H. White, O. W. Holland, Richard Rankin, Valentine Derr, Leroy Stowe, J. W. Reid, A. Love, Robert Baker, William Lander, John Webster, John G. Lewis, James Quinn, John Falls, David Abernethy, W. W. McGinnis, Major Hoffman, H. W. Gaston, William Ferguson, Joseph Holland and Larkin Stowe. Charles Fisher, of Rowan, was endorsed for Governor.

1846

John Hayes married to Catherine, daughter of Col. James Johnston, October 1, 1803, and lived near Toole's Ford on the

Catawba River. Dr. C. L. Hunter says, "He was a worthy Christian citizen, long a subject of patient suffering from disease and died peacefully April 13, 1846, aged 74 years."

He reared five daughters and two sons, one of whom, Dr. William J. Hayes, settled in Mecklenburg.

John Burton Hoke, 11-year old son of the late Michael Hoke, was shot and killed when he and a young Fulenwider boy, his kinsman, were playing with a gun.

Married by Rev. Mr. McDaniel in Lincoln County, March 6, 1846, Amos Morris to Mary E., daughter of William Davenport.

Ambrose Costner was on March 18, 1846, married to Malinda Quickel, daughter of Michael Quickel.

Married by Rev. J. Stacy, in Cheraw, S. C., April 23, 1846, the Rev. Albert M. Shipp to Mary Jane Gillespie. (Dr. Albert M. Shipp was a great preacher and educator who went out from Lincoln County. Was in his time President of Greensboro College, Professor at the University of North Carolina, President of Wofford College and later Professor in Vanderbilt University and a man of rare scholarship.)

Gaston County was organized, and lines of Lincoln to the north changed to present boundaries.

The people of Mountain Creek and Dry Pond section of Lincoln, dissatisfied because they are so far from the county seat, want the County boundaries changed. Evidently they were displeased because that territory had been transferred to Catawba County. Stirring resolutions were passed at the meeting which had Alexander McCorkle for chairman and Isaac Lowe for secretary.

Died in Lincoln County on August 2, 1846, William Sidney, and on the 12th, Robert Henry, infant sons of Dr. Sidney X. and Mrs. Harriet Connor Johnston.

William Preston Bynum was married December 2, to Miss A. E. Shipp, daughter of Bartlett Shipp.

The mysterious personage, Peter S. Ney, who taught school at one time near Beatties Ford, in Lincoln County, claimed to be Napoleon's Marshal, but the history says Marshal Ney was condemned to death for high treason by the Bourbon government after the defeat of Napoleon at Waterloo and shot in the garden of the Luxembourg in Paris, December 7, 1815—a cruel act of revenge. Many who knew Peter S. Ney as a teacher in Lincoln,

Iredell, Rowan and Davie Counties firmly believed he was the French Marshal. The story goes that the French guards used blank cartridges and when they fired Ney fell, apparently dead, was spirited away and came to Charleston and then to this State.

Mr. Vardry A. McBee said: "I was a pupil of Ney in 1834. No pupil, however large, would for a moment think of disobeying his slightest command. The great influence he exerted over the community was of a wholesome and elevating character."

Mr. Wallace M. Reinhardt said: "I went to school to Peter S. Ney in 1838, when he taught in Iredell. All his pupils, from the greatest to the least were afraid of him, and any one of them would have shed blood for him. He was very strict with his scholars and required absolute obedience and good lessons."

Theodorus H. Cobb said: "I have heard Chief Justice Pearson frequently speak of Peter S. Ney. He had a high opinion of his character and ability and was firmly convinced that he was Marshal Ney."

Many of his students believed that he was the French Marshal, while others did not. Dr. James G. Ramsay of Rowan, said "I knew P. S. Ney. It seems more difficult to say who he was than to believe he was Marshal Ney."

He died at the home of Mr. Osborne G. Foard in Rowan County, November 15, 1846, and the body was buried at Third Creek Presbyterian church in that County. Mr. Foard knew Ney intimately and firmly believed he was Marshal Ney. The question of his identity is debatable, but many believe he was the French Marshal.

1847

Railroad meeting in Lincolnton, March 3, 1847, Bartlett Shipp, Chairman, and Andrew Motz and T. J. Eccles, Secretaries. A railroad to Columbia or Camden was considered. The delegates appointed to a Railroad Convention to be held in Charlotte, April 27, were John F. Hoke, William Johnston, L. E. Thompson, Andrew Motz, Henry Cansler, B. H. Sumner, F. A. Hoke, L. D. Childs, John H. Wheeler, Dr. William McLean, C. C. Henderson, Dr. S. X. Johnston, Ephraim Brevard, Issac Lowe, W. W. Munday, John Coulter, Dr. C. L. Hunter, H. W. Guion, John F. Phifer and Michael Quickel.

Married, September, 1847, by Rev. R. H. Morrison, Dr. W. J. Hayes of Lincoln, to Isabella, daughter of Dr. M. W. Alexander, of Mecklenburg.

Advertisement: Bids are asked for building brick church at Brevard and Graham graveyard (Machpelah). The church to be 44 by 28 feet, with stone foundation 3 feet above ground and fifteen (15) feet from sills to plate. Three doors and ten windows, all to be completed in neat and workmanlike manner. October 20, 1847. Charles C. Graham, E. A. Brevard, William Johnston, C. L. Hunter, David Dellinger, building committee.

Joseph C. Cobb and Margaret Butts, daughter of John Butts, were married in Lincolnton, October 28, 1847.

Advertisement: The subscriber is now prepared with comfortable hack to convey passengers to or from Charlotte, on reasonable terms. His residence is near the east end of the town of Lincolnton. James Wells.

Charles Connor Graham has qualified as Executor of the Will of his father, John D. Graham.

Married near Charlotte, by Rev. Cyrus Johnson, November 2, 1847, Dr. Henry M. Pritchard, of Lincoln, to Sarah E., daughter of Maj. Benj. Morrow.

Major Daniel M. Forney, born in Lincoln County, May, 1784, oldest son of Gen. Peter Forney, was educated at local schools and at the State University.

When at the University he formed a warm friendship for Henry Y. Webb, Robert H. and Alfred M. Burton, his classmates, who came to Lincoln with him to be guests in the Forney home. Henry Y. Webb married to Eliza, sister of Major Forney, and the two Burtons married two sisters, Mary and Elizabeth Fulenwider, daughters of Col. John Fulenwider, and all became notable citizens of the County.

Major Forney married to Harriet Brevard, daughter of Capt. Alexander Brevard and built a handsome brick home which now stands on the original Forney estate, the finest private home then in this section of the State and the admiration now of all who visit it. He held local offices and engaged in agricultural pursuits. Clerk of County Court, July 7, 1807, to May 22, 1812. Was a Major in the War of 1812; member of Congress 1815-1818, succeeding his father; appointed in 1820 by President Monroe to treat with the Creek Indians; Senator from Lincoln 4 terms, 1823-26; served as Councilor of State 1829-30; moved to Lowndes County, Ala., in 1834, where he continued in agricultural pursuits, and died there October 15, 1847.

Robert F. Cope furnishes the following item concerning the first county court held in Gaston County:

The First County Court in Gaston

The following is a partial record of the first court held in Gaston County:

"Court of Pleas and Quarter Sessions, February Term, One Thousand Eight Hundred and Forty-seven. State of North Carolina, Gaston County. In conformity to the 7th section of an act supplemental to an act passed by the last General Assembly of the State of North Carolina entitled 'An Act to Lay Off and Establish a New County by the Name of Gaston and to Annex a Part of Catawba County to the County of Lincoln,' the following justices (being a majority of the whole number residing within the territory so laid off and erected into a county by the name of Gaston) met at the house of Jesse Holland in said county on the third Monday in February, A. D. 1847, viz: Alfred Abernethy, Isaac Holland, Andrew Love, John Webster, James Ferguson, R. M. Alexander, Abram Mauney, Thos. F. McGill, Robert Johnston, John Oates, Sr., William J. Wilson, John McGinnis, Andrew Hoyle, Major Whitesides, Jacob Plonk, J. G. Hand, John Falls, Andrew B. Cox, John G. Lewis, A. W. Davenport, Milton A. Smith, who, after organizing, proceeded to business by administering the usual oaths of office to the following justices, appointed for said county, viz: Christian Eaker, John R. Cates, Richard Rankin, Alexander Wear, and James M. Hannah, whose commissions are filed, after which the aforesaid justices, together with the new ones just qualified, proceeded to the election of Clerk of the Court of Pleas and Quarter Sessions for the said county and, a ballot being held, John H. Roberts having received a majority of the whole number of votes cast, was declared duly elected Clerk of the said court; whereupon he gave the several bonds required by law with the following sureties, viz: John D. Rankin, Lee A. Moore, Robert Johnston, Benjamin Smith and Christian Eaker, which bonds were approved by the court, the whole of the above named justices being present. The said John H. Roberts then took the usual oaths of office and entered upon the discharge of his duties."

Benjamin Morris was elected Sheriff; Richard Rankin, County Trustee; Samuel L. Caldwell, Solicitor; W. F. Holland, Surveyor; James M. Hannah, Entry Taker; and Jacob Plonk, Processioner.

The court then proceeded to the election of a special court, and prominent men were elected as justices.

Monday evening court adjourned to Tuesday morning at 10 o'clock. A number of other worthy citizens were elected to other offices of less importance.

In 1848 the first county court house was constructed, which was a temporary structure of wood, it being used until a brick one was built. In the year 1868, fire destroyed all but the brick walls, which served in the construction of the third building which is still standing in the town of Dallas, Gaston's first county seat.

At the Fall term, 1847, Judge Richmond M. Pearson appointed Felix M. Abernethy Clerk and Master of Equity for Gaston County and his bond was signed by S. N. Stowe, Daniel Hoffman, Robert Johnston, W. Stowe, John Webster and James H. White.

James Quinn was appointed Clerk of the Superior Court and his bond was signed by S. N. Stowe, Benjamin Morris and James H. White. The bond of Benjamin Morris, the Sheriff, was signed by A. W. Davenport, A. W. Abernethy, J. D. Rankin and Larkin Stowe. James Ferguson was elected Register of Deeds.

1848

February, 1848. Elms & Withers, merchants of Beatties Ford, are successors to the firm of H. H. Helper & Co.

Meeting of stockholders of High Shoals Iron Works called by Andrew Hoyle, President of the Company.

Married at Greenwood, Catawba County, at the residence of Major Henry W. Connor, by Rev. Jacob Hill, March 30, 1848, Mr. John W. Morrow of Mecklenburg to Miss Mary Ann Nuttall of Granville County.

Married by Rev. Samuel Lander, May 24, 1848, Uriah Cloyd of Caldwell County, to Rosannah Moore of Gaston.

Married in Iredell County, by Rev. C. H. Pritchard, August 9, 1848, Dr. J. H. Ward of Lincoln to Ann, daughter of Jacob Lemley.

The *Charlotte Journal* of September 6, 1848, contained a fine tribute paid to Benj. Theodore Rankin, aged 21, who died in Lincolnton, August 25, 1848. The young man was a son of Col. Richard Rankin.

THE ANNALS OF LINCOLN COUNTY 143

Paul Kistler, a valued citizen and churchman, died in Lincolnton in 1848, aged 66. He was the father of Lawson H. Kistler, Rev. P. F. Kistler, Mrs. Jacob Hill, Mrs. Richard Rozzell, and Mrs. Joseph Finger. Rev. C. E. Rozzelle is a great grandson.

Married by Rev. Mr. Anderson, November 8, 1848, Maj. D. H. Hill, 4th regiment U. S. Artillery, to Isabella, daughter of Rev. R. H. Morrison, of Lincoln.

James C. Jenkins was married to Barbara Schenck, daughter of Dr. David W. Schenck, December 20, 1848.

Daniel Coleman, of Cabarrus, was elected solicitor of the 7th Judicial District by the Legislature, succeeding Hamilton C. Jones.

1849

Carolina Republican—February 6, 1849. J. M. Newsom, Editor.

Justices of the Peace for Lincoln County: B. S. Johnson, Jasper Stowe, David Seagle, Franklin M. Reinhardt, David Dellinger, William J. Hoke, Ambrose Costner, A. P. Cansler, F. J. Jetton, David Williams, Cephas Quickel, Robert Blackburn and Elisha Saunders.

February 20, 1849. Jacob B. Reel was married to Miss Margaret M. Helderman by Rev. J. R. Peterson.

Died, John Skelly of this County, in the 28th year of his age.

February 27, 1849. Strangers meeting in our village must now be favorably impressed with the citizens of Lincolnton. Mr. Daniel Shuford in compliance with the wishes of the proper authorities has planted trees in tastefully arranged order all over the public square. They are well protected and we hope they may grow vigorously not only to shade promenading lovers, but for our tired friends when they seek our market.

February 27, 1849. It is proposed to hold a public meeting in Lincolnton to adopt measures to construct a plank road from this place to Charlotte to intersect railroad at Charlotte.

Soldiers in Mexican War

Lincoln Progress, September 13, 1873, copied from *Wilmington Journal*.

Part of W. J. Clarke Company I, 12th Regiment, U. S. Infantry, in Mexican War, recruited in Lincoln, Gaston, Catawba and Cleveland Counties.

James Marcus Bandy, 23, Catawba, died of measles on ship going to war, July 15, 1847.
Eli Bell, 19, Gaston.
William D. S. Bowen, 22 (Va.).
Thomas L. Burganer, 25, Catawba, dead.
James Compton, 21, S. C., dead.
J. Q. Carpenter, 19, Lincoln, killed at Seven Pines, 1862.
Peter Carpenter, Lincoln, 34, died in New Orleans.
Laban M. Cline, 18, Catawba, died at Puebla, Mex.
Turner Cody, 22, Lincoln.
George W. Dyson, 27, Burke.
Michael Eaker, 19, Gaston, died soon after war.
Thomas F. Elliott, 28, Cleveland, died at Vera Cruz.
Abel M. Fry, 25, Catawba, dead.
George A. Gentle, 22, Davie, killed at Cerro Gordo, Mex.
Noah Hallman, 21, Lincoln.
Penal Hearn, 29, Gaston.
Robert F. Henderson, 21, Gaston.
Philo Hoke, 18, Lincoln.
Thomas Hull, 19, Lincoln.
Newton Jackson, 18, died at Jalapa.
David Jarrett, 35, Cleveland, killed at Cerro Gordo.
Benj. Justice, 23, Cleveland, wounded at National Bridge, Mex.
William Kirksey, 20, Catawba, wounded at National Bridge, Mex.
Christopher Love, 22, Cleveland.
James I. Love, 19, Cleveland, wounded at National Bridge, Mex. The examining surgeon said he was the finest looking man in the army.
James Martin, 22, Catawba.
Lawson Mauney, 20, Lincoln.
David M. C. Nowlin, 21, Cleveland, dead.
Thomas D. Nowlin, 18, Cleveland, dead.
Thomas J. Ramsey, 19, Cleveland, dead.
Richard Henry Riddick, 21, Lincoln, was later Col. 34th N. C. Regiment in Civil War and killed in Virginia in 1863.
Moses Runnels, 23, Gaston.
Joseph T. Rudisill, 31, Gaston, died in Mexico.
James S. Sims, 19, Catawba, dead.
Henry Stamey, 22, Lincoln killed at National Bridge, Mex.
Fred A. Stauffer (Switzerland), 42, served under Bonaparte.
Andrew Summey, 21, Gaston, killed in Virginia, 1864.
Absalom Taylor, Lincoln, 20.
Henry Tevepaugh, 35, Lincoln, died at Jalapa, Sept. 26, 1847. Musician.
William F. Wacaster, 21, Lincoln.
Christopher Wells, 26, Gaston, died at Perote, Mex.
David Wells, 24, Gaston.
David S. Wells, 22, Gaston.
Benj. E. White, 26, Gaston, died of disease contracted in Mexico.
Joseph F. Williamson, 24, Lincoln.
The above enlisted by Lt. John F. Hoke, who was later a captain in the Mexican War.

Lincolnton Female Academy: J. P. Lindsay, Principal; Misses Julia and Maria St. John, Assistants. February, 1849.

March 13, 1849. Obituary: Mr. Michael Schenck, born in Lancaster County, Penn., February 15, 1771, came to Lincolnton about 1789 and since then a resident. 78 years of age and oldest inhabitant of Lincolnton when he died March 6, 1849. His disease was hydrothorax. He was a member of the Methodist church. He built and conducted the first cotton mill south of the Potomac River.

Carolina Republican, April 10, 1849. J. N. Newsom, Editor. Benj. White, 28, a brave patriotic soldier in Mexican War, died at home of his brother, James H. White, in Gaston County, last week.

The *Carolina Republican*, ardent supporter of Green W. Caldwell, for Congress says: "When Caldwell was a Cass Elector in 1848, not a single sentence discreditable to General Taylor, the Whig candidate, escaped his lips. Can liberal Whigs forget this or refuse to reward him for it?"

A public meeting is called at court house in Lincolnton, on Tuesday, of April court, to consider some of the acts passed by the last Legislature, viz: The Revenue Bill and the Internal Improvement System. His Honor, Judge John W. Ellis, Burton Craige, John H. Wheeler, John F. Hoke, H. W. Guion, William Lander, J. W. Osborne, H. C. Jones, Green W. Caldwell, William Julius Alexander and others, friendly or opposed to the measures, are invited to attend along with Hon. Henry W. Connor, Senator, and Representatives James H. White, Samuel N. Stowe, Franklin D. Reinhardt and Andrew H. Shuford. (April, 1849.)

Advertisements: Lincoln Cotton Mills. Cotton yarns, cloth, batting, candle wicks, bell cords, carpet chain, machine ropes, bell ropes. We manufacture machine irons and edge tools and Lincoln Factory axes. The store carries a full stock of general merchandise. L. D. Childs & Co. This factory and store located at Laboratory Mill.

Advertisements: Hoke and Michael, General Merchants, have a full supply of fall and winter goods.

Fall and winter fashions. Moore & Cobb. Still continue to carry on the Tailoring business.

Having just returned from Baltimore, Philadelphia and New York with ample supply of dry goods and wearing apparel, together with fancy merchandise, take pleasure in exhibiting their stock, the best and cheapest the market affords. Call and see. Ramsour & Jenkins. April, 1849.

Having taken contract for carrying the mail between these points I will operate a stage line from Lincolnton to Yorkville at a low rate of fare. Leave Lincolnton 8 A.M. Tuesday and Thursday; Return to Lincolnton 6 P.M. Wednesday and Friday. James Wells, Lincolnton, N. C.

May 11, 1849. Dallas Academy — Rev. J. H. Wagner, Principal.

July 6, 1849. Robert Williamson, Jr., is a candidate for re-election to the office of Clerk of the County Court.

Major Abram Forney, youngest son of Jacob Forney, Sr., was a gallant soldier of the Revolution and in many campaigns proved his courage and patriotism, in that long fought contest. He was in the front ranks at Ramsour's Mill and Kings Mountain.

He married Rachel Gabriel of Lincoln County. They had two sons, Abram E. Forney who lived in Lincoln to a ripe old age, and John W. Forney who died young.

Major Forney died July 22, 1849, in the 91st year of his age.

August 24, 1849. Died at Canton, Miss., July 28, 1849, at the residence of her son, Dr. Franklin Henderson, Mrs. Elizabeth Henderson, relict of Maj. Lawson Henderson, a native of Lincoln County, aged 66 years.

V. A. McBee was re-elected Clerk Superior Court, and Robert Williamson, of the County Court.

Nov. 23, 1849. Rev. Dr. Albert M. Shipp has been elected Professor in State University to fill vacancy caused by the resignation of Rev. William M. Greene.

Joseph P. Caldwell, Whig, was elected to Congress in 1849, from this district, the boundaries of which had been changed by the Whig Legislature, giving the Whigs such a majority that the Democrats offered no opposition. At Shuford's box (not far from the present Monbo) the Democrats all for a joke voted for a Mr. Mull, a Democrat of that precinct who was not equal to the office. Late in the afternoon Cyrus Peed, a sturdy Democrat, came to the polls when one of the young men gave him a Mull ticket for Congress and Mr. Peed said: "Boys, I think that is carrying the joke too far."

CHAPTER XIII

1850-1859

Died at Greenwood, in Catawba County, on February 10, 1850, Mrs. Lucy Hawkins Connor, wife of Major Henry W. Connor.

Carolina Republican, March 29, 1850:
"J. T. Alexander, Jacob A. Ramsour, Henry Cansler, William Lander, and Dr. David W. Schenck, Trustees of Lincolnton Male Academy, announce that Silas C. Lindsly, A.M., has been secured as Principal.
"Rates of tuition range from $5.00 to $15.00 per session."

A Convention held in Lincolnton in June, 1850, favoring a Plank Road from Lincolnton to Charlotte was organized by electing C. C. Henderson Chairman, and W. H. Michal and V. A. McBee Secretaries.

A Committee was appointed to co-operate with others to carry out the enterprise as follows: Henry Cansler, C. C. Graham, Solomon Rudisill, F. M. Reinhardt, Cephas Quickel, L. D. Childs, Dr. Z. Butt, Maj. A. A. McLean, B. S. Johnson, F. A. Hoke, Peter Summey, William Lander, L. E. Thompson, H. W. Guion, Thomas R. Shuford, Jasper Stowe, Dr. S. X. Johnston, Dr. C. L. Hunter, Dr. W. B. McLean and Isaac Lowe.

Hon. David S. Reid, in a letter to William Lander accepts the nomination as a candidate for Governor on the Democratic ticket at the coming August election.

Married at Brackettown, Burke County, October 30, 1850, by Rev. Mr. Parker, Captain John F. Hoke to Miss Catherine Alexander, daughter of Col. William Julius Alexander.

James Mullen, of Ironton township, was married to Emily Lowe, December 28, 1850.

Michael Quickel, Jr. (1781-1850), son of Michael Quickel, the pioneer, married Elizabeth Hoke.

Among their children were:
Cephas, born 1819, married Sarah Killian.
Catherine Malinda (1827-1903) married Ambrose Costner.

1851

Andrew Motz, of the firm of Motz, Barrett & Company, proprietors of Ivy Shoal Cotton Mill, on South Fork River at Clark's Creek, was drowned in Clark's Creek on the night of March 7, 1851. He either fell or was pushed off the bridge which was without rails. He was 34 years old. A reward of $100.00 was offered for the body. The body was found March 30, and the report of the jury was, "That Andrew Motz on the night of the 7th of March, 1851, about the hour of 8 o'clock left the house near the factory of Motz, Barrett & Co., on his way homeward by way of the bridge at mill of Capt. Slade, the night being dark and stormy; and that by cause unknown to this jury he got into the water at or near this bridge and met his death by drowning.

(Signed) W. H. Michal, Coroner."

The body was found one mile below Clark's Creek by Houser and Price.

Resolutions of regret and sympathy were passed by the Court January 28, 1851, on account of the death of John R. Stamey, Sheriff of Lincoln County.

The Western Plank Road was incorporated January 28, 1851, and legislative authority given to open subscription books in Newton under direction of Jonas Bost, Andrew H. Shuford and M. L. McCorkle; in Lincolnton under direction of C. C. Henderson, Jacob A. Ramsour, William Slade, Haywood W. Guion and L. E. Thompson, and in Charlotte under the direction of W. R. Myers, William Johnston, Henry B. Williams, Braley Oates, Charles T. Alexander and Benjamin Morrow. Shares $50.00 each. Subscription limited to $200,000.00. Estimated cost per mile, $1,500.00, and 160,000 feet of lumber per mile. Toll to be four cents per mile.

Rozzelle Ferry toll bridge authorized, with William W. Elms, Dr. S. X. Johnston, Richard Rozzelle, John W. Caldwell and Robert H. Brevard as incorporators. (Private Laws 1851, page 681.)

Mountain Lodge No. 19, Independent Order Odd Fellows, in town of Lincolnton, William Lander, William J. Hoke, T. J. Eccles, William Williamson, Andrew Motz, Alexander Ramsour and William H. Michal, body politic. Incorporated. (Private Laws 1851, page 638.)

Advertisement: Laurel Hill Factory, established 1851 by Andrew Motz and E. S. Barrett, Motz, Barrett & Co., Yarns Nos. 3 to 60 carpet chain, candlewick turns, ropes, batting. Lincolnton, N. C.

Note: This mill occupied the present site of the Elm Grove Cotton Mill, Lincolnton.

I. O. O. F. Mountain Lodge No. 19. William J. Hoke, N. G.; William R. Edwards, V. G.; J. M. Shuford, Secretary; William Ramsour, Treasurer. January 4, 1851.

Lincoln Courier. Died in this county at residence of her husband, near the brick church, May 2, 1851, Mrs. Abagail Welker, wife of Rev. G. W. Welker, of the German Reformed church.

Since the arrival of new goods the store of Ramsour & Jenkins is a regular bee hive. Call and see before the best bargains are disposed of, for they are going fast. (*Courier*, 1851.)

Last week Mrs. Jacob A. Ramsour and Mrs. John F. Phifer sent to our family some of the finest strawberries we ever saw. They were considerably longer than partridge eggs, not less than three inches in diameter, and delicious. (*Courier*, 1851.)

Governor Reid has appointed Henry Cansler of Lincoln, Charles McDowell of Rutherford, and Mark Coleman of Macon, Commissioners to value the Cherokee Indian lands.

Andrew J. Cansler announces that he is agent in Catawba, Lincoln, Gaston and Cleveland for *Wheeler's History of North Carolina*, just from the press. This valuable book of reference was written at Beatties Ford by Col. John H. Wheeler, who was for some years before and after 1851 a citizen of Lincoln and represented the County in the House of Commons in 1852.

May, 1851—Plank Road Notice. Subscription books for Charlotte and Lincolnton and Newton are open and can be seen at store of H. B. and L. S. Williams in Charlotte, William R. Myers, William Johnson, H. B. Williams, Braley Oates, C. T. Alexander, Benjamin Morrow.

George Mosteller, in May, 1851, advertised foolscap, letter, wrapping and envelope paper. Connected with the paper mill is a book bindery. Blank books of all kinds on hand.

Thomas Dews, Sr., died in Lincolnton, August 20, 1851, aged 71. He was born in the Guernsey Islands and came to Lincolnton about 1810, and conducted a cabinet shop. His son, Thomas Dews, Jr., who died in 1838, was then 30 years old. (See 1838.)

Lincoln Courier, 1851. Advertisement: Catawba College, Newton, N. C., H. H. Smith, President; M. Fry and J. C. Clapp, Tutors.

Lincolnton Division No. 45. Sons of Temperance. Officers: John P. Anthony, W. R. Clark, H. W. Abernethy, A. P. Cansler, Andrew Roseman, James H. Oates, Abner McCoy, M. L. Killian, Jacob Williams, F. J. Jetton and S. M. Alexander.

Philip S. White, the great temperance orator, was in Lincolnton, April 17, 1857, and spoke to multitudes and spoke also under the arbor at Rock Spring Camp Ground to a great assembly.

Legislative Acts of 1851 Pertaining to Lincoln County

1. Incorporation of Rock Spring Camp Ground. Thomas Ward, Robert Abernethy, Isaac Lowe, Isaac O. Robinson, Thomas Beatty, James Washington Lowe and Henry Asbury, Trustees of the property, 40 acres, conveyed by Joseph M. Munday in fee to Freeman Shelton, Richard Proctor and James Bivens and their successors in office, by deed dated August 7, 1830, for the use of the Methodist Church. Self-perpetuating Board of Trustees. (Private Laws of 1851, page 629.)

James Graham, eldest son of Gen. Joseph Graham, was born January 7, 1793, graduated from the State University in 1814, studied law and was admitted to the bar in 1818, and settled in Rutherfordton to practice law. He represented Rutherford County in the House of Commons in 1822-24-28 and 29, was elected to Congress for four terms, 1835 to 1843; defeated for re-election but was again elected to Congress as a Whig in 1846 after which he was not a candidate. He was a lawyer of splendid gifts and had a lucrative practice.

He died a bachelor in Rutherfordton Sept. 25, 1851, and the body was buried in the family plot at Machpelah in Lincoln County.

Married by Rev. R. H. Lafferty, October 19, 1851, Dr. E. O. Elliott, to Miss Martha McRee, all of Mecklenburg.

(Dr. Elliott for many years owned and operated the Catawba Springs near Hickory, N. C., and was grandfather of Esley O.

Anderson of Charlotte, and now an officer in the First National Bank of Lincolnton, 1934.)

Hon. W. W. Avery, of Burke, and Samuel Fleming (both attorneys) had a disagreement and altercation at Marion Court, resulting in the death of Fleming, in November, 1851.

Mary, wife of William Slade, died December 2, 1851, aged 51.

Lincoln Lodge No. 137, A. F. & A. M. Signers of petition for dispensation: A. W. Burton, Wm. Jenks, Thos. J. Eccles, E. S. Barrett, Jasper Stowe, Thad W. Bradburn and Samuel Lander, Jr. Dispensation granted June 16, 1851. Alonzo T. Jenkins, Grand Master, appointed A. W. Burton, Master; Wm. Jenks, Senior Warden; Thos. J. Eccles, Junior Warden. First meeting of Lincoln Lodge No. 137 held June 20, 1851. A. W. Burton, Master, appointed J. T. Alexander, Secretary.

MASTERS OF THE LODGE

A. W. Burton, June, 1851, to January, 1852.
William Lander, January, 1852, to December, 1853.
J. T. Alexander, December, 1853, to December, 1855.
M. King, December, 1855, to December, 1856.
William J. Hoke, December, 1856, to December, 1857.
Thomas Darling, December, 1857, to December, 1859.
J. T. Alexander, December, 1859, to December, 1860.
C. J. Hammerskold, December, 1860, to December, 1861.
William Tiddy, December, 1861, to December, 1863.
Samuel Lander, December, 1863, to December, 1865.
William Tiddy, December, 1865, to December, 1866.
David Schenck, December, 1866, to December, 1867.
H. W. Burton, December, 1867, to December, 1868.
Dr. J. A. Sherrill, December, 1868, to December, 1870.
William Tiddy, December, 1870, to December, 1871.
H. H. Smith, December, 1871, to December, 1872.
S. P. Sherrill, December, 1872, to June, 1874.
William Tiddy, June, 1874, to June, 1878.
T. H. Cobb, June, 1878, to June, 1881.
Dr. J. M. Lawing, June, 1881, to June, 1883.
B. C. Cobb, June, 1883, to June, 1886.
T. H. Cobb, June, 1886, to June, 1888.
H. W. Burton, June, 1888, to June, 1892.
A. Nixon, June, 1892, to June, 1899.
J. E. Love, June, 1899, to June, 1901.
R. S. Reinhardt, June, 1901, to June, 1902.
A. Nixon, June, 1902, to June, 1904.
C. E. Childs, June, 1904, to June, 1905.
A. Nixon, June, 1905, to June, 1907.

152   THE ANNALS OF LINCOLN COUNTY

C. R. Simmons, June, 1907, to June, 1910.
J. S. Armstrong, June, 1910, to June, 1916.
T. C. Abernethy, June, 1916, to June, 1917.
Dr. I. R. Self, June, 1917, to June, 1920.
Harry Page, June, 1920, to June, 1922.
K. B. Nixon, June, 1922, to June, 1923.
D. A. Yoder, June, 1923, to June, 1924.
C. C. Crowell, June, 1924, to June, 1926.
E. L. Rudisill, June, 1926, to June, 1928.
Jas. A. Shuford, June, 1928, to June, 1930.
H. G. Crowell, June, 1930, to June, 1931.
Dr. W. G. Bandy, June, 1931, to January, 1933.
E. L. Rudisill, January, 1933, to January, 1934.
J. R. Nixon, January, 1934—.

SECRETARIES OF THE LODGE

J. T. Alexander, June, 1851, to January, 1852.
William J. Hoke, January, 1852, to December, 1852.
Thos. R. Shuford, December, 1852, to December, 1855.
J. T. Alexander, December, 1855, to December, 1856.
Dr. J. M. Richardson, December, 1856, to December, 1858.
William J. Hoke, December, 1858, to December, 1861.
T. W. Robinson, December, 1861, to December, 1862.
J. T. Alexander, December, 1862, to December, 1863.
W. H. Alexander, December, 1863, to December, 1864.
William Tiddy, December, 1864, to December, 1865.
A. S. Haynes, December, 1865, to December, 1866.
William J. Hoke, December, 1866, to December, 1867.
Peter A. Summey, December, 1867, to December, 1868.
W. H. Alexander, December, 1868, to December, 1869.
Dr. J. M. Lawing, December, 1869, to December, 1872.
B. H. Sumner, December, 1872, to June, 1874.
Dr. J. M. Lawing, June, 1874, to June, 1881.
A. S. Haynes, June, 1881, to June, 1883.
Dr. W. W. Noland, June, 1883, to June, 1884.
S. P. Sherrill, June, 1884, to June, 1891.
R. S. Reinhardt, June, 1891, to June, 1893.
B. C. Wood, June, 1893, to June, 1894.
R. E. Costner, June, 1894, to June, 1895.
C. E. Childs, June, 1895, to June, 1896.
S. P. Sherrill, June, 1896, to June, 1897.
J. C. Tipton, June, 1897, to June, 1900.
W. M. Sherrill, June, 1900, to June, 1903.
R. L. Wyckoff, June, 1903, to June, 1905.
H. A. Self, June, 1905, to June, 1907.
W. A. Fair, June, 1907, to June, 1908.
W. Latta Massey, June, 1908, to June, 1910.
R. L. Wyckoff, June, 1910, to June, 1911.

THE ANNALS OF LINCOLN COUNTY

C. D. Thompson, June, 1911, to June, 1914.
W. L. Mustain, June, 1914, to June, 1916.
Herbert Miller, June, 1916, to June, 1918.
E. W. Joyner, June, 1918, to June, 1919.
T. C. Abernethy, June, 1919, to June, 1921.
Herbert Miller, June, 1921, to June, 1922.
Summey Alexander, June, 1922, to June, 1926.
D. A. Yoder, June, 1926—.

The above list of Lodge officers was supplied by Summey Alexander, Sr. Date of Charter of Lincoln Lodge, December 4, 1851.

Mountain Lodge No. 19, Independent Order of Odd Fellows, in the Town of Lincolnton, was incorporated in 1851 (See Private Laws 1851, Page 638) with William Lander, William J. Hoke, T. J. Eccles, William Williamson, Andrew Motz, Alexander Ramsour, and W. H. Michal, body politic.

On January 4, 1851, William J. Hoke was elected Noble Grand; William R. Edwards, Vice-Grand; J. M. Shuford, Secretary; and William Ramsour, Treasurer.

The Lodge was organized early in the year 1849, and the following were among the Charter members: Alexander Ramsour, William Ramsour, William J. Hoke, William Williamson, Andrew Motz, W. R. Edwards, Jasper Stowe, William Lander, Augustus McLean, Wallace H. Alexander, Augustus W. Burton, J. M. Shuford and W. H. Michal.

In March, 1850, Abner McCoy and L. E. Thompson deeded land in block 10, East Main Street, thirty (30) by forty (40) feet to Alexander Ramsour, Andrew Motz, Jasper Stowe and A. W. Burton, Trustees for Mountain Lodge No. 19, I. O. O. F., for seventy-five dollars. A two-story frame building was erected, covering the entire lot. On February 12, 1853, Mrs. Harriet Bomar and Jacob A. Ramsour, for twenty-four dollars ($24), deeded a strip of land 8 feet front running full length to the street in rear, which was used as an alley, where the members hitched their horses when attending Lodge meetings.

The building was used by the various fraternal organizations of the town until it was sold. On the Lodge site, now owned by Dr. J. R. Gamble and Dr. J. F. Gamble, is the Reeves Hospital, operated by these physicians.

About 1898 the Lodge disbanded and the charter was cancelled. On October 8, 1900, it was re-organized under the same name and number, with the records of the old Lodge. The charter members of the new Lodge were: John C. Tipton, A. M. Wingate, J. E. Love, W. R. Edwards, Thomas Wells, L. S. Fox, T. N. Hale, Rev. A. E. Wiley, Fred L. Hoffman, Levi Gheen, W. F. Willetts, S. W. McKee, H. S. Hyman, Blair Jenkins, D. A. Yoder, Austin F. Wood, W. W. Motz, Chas. E. Childs, Dr. J. E. Pressly, J. H. Lineberger, A. E. Helton, Karl L. Lawing, Elcanah Ramsour, F. E. McLean, and Ed Setzer.

On March 1, 1930, the Grigg Building on Main Street was destroyed by fire and all the Lodge records and furnishings on the top floor were lost. The officers of the Lodge at the present time are:

Harry Hartman, Noble Grand.
Grover McGee, Vice-Grand.
J. D. Mitchum, Recording Secretary.
Frank Rhyne, Financial Secretary.
N. P. Williams, Treasurer.
E. L. Rudisill, N. P. Williams and T. H. Thompson, Trustees.

1852

Died, near Lenoir, January 23, 1852, Mrs. Susan Mott, consort of Rev. T. S. W. Mott, of the Protestant Episcopal church, aged 38 years. Rev. Mr. Mott was one time Rector of St. Luke's church, Lincolnton. He died about 1870 and his body rests in St. Luke's graveyard.

February 7, 1852. Plank road meeting was held at Rozzelle Ferry. Henry Cansler, Chairman and Dr. C. L. Hunter, Secretary.

The Committee on proxies consisting of Gen. J. A. Young, Dr. S. X. Johnston and C. C. Henderson reported that 474 shares were represented in person or by proxy. It was ordered that the road from the center of Charlotte to Rozzelle Ferry be located as surveyed. L. E. Thompson advertised for bids for bridge at Rozzelle Ferry. Specifications to be seen at Braley Oates, R. A. Rozzelle's and V. A. McBee's. Also bid for grading plank road from Charlotte to Rozzelle Ferry and from the river to Lincolnton. This road was completed to Lincolnton in 1853.

Married, in Charlotte, by Rev. Cyrus Johnson, May 13, 1852, John Sloan of Greensboro, to Eliza P. Graham, daughter of the late John D. Graham.

Motz Hotel built and owned by John Motz, completed in 1852, was the leading hotel in Western Carolina. (Now the North State Hotel, 1934.)

Died, June 8, 1852, in Lincoln County, Mrs. Adalaide M. Cansler, wife of Col. A. P. Cansler and daughter of George Conley, of Caldwell County.

At a meeting of the Justices of the Peace, Lincoln County, in July 1852, it was decided that a new court house be built in Lincolnton and H. W. Guion, L. E. Thompson, C. C. Henderson, Jacob Ramsour, George Mosteller, Maxwell Warlick and B. S. Johnson were appointed commissioners to secure plans and let the contract for building it. The contract was let to Jacob Ramsour, Maxwell Warlick and Caleb Miller. The corner stone was laid with Masonic ceremonies in August, 1853, when an address was delivered by William Lander, and the building was completed about 1855. Haywood W. Guion drew the plans for the building.

August, 1852. Advertisement in *Charlotte Journal*. Schedule Charlotte and South Carolina Railroad: Leave Columbia 7:15 A.M.; Arrive at Fort Mill 11:10 P. M.

Stages run from the head of the road to Charlotte. From Charlotte a line of stages to Salisbury and Raleigh. We hope by October 1st to be delivering freight in Charlotte.

August 4, 1852. Nathaniel Wilson, a prominent citizen, an active supporter of the bill for the division of the County and a Democratic candidate for re-election to the Legislature at the August election, was killed by a son-in-law named Wilson England, who cut him in the bowels and he died instantly. Wilson lived in Catawba but after the county division the three counties voted together for legislators until after 1852, as old Lincoln had four representatives in the House of Commons. His death occurred on the eve of the election and the result was J. A. Caldwell was elected as the fourth representative along with William Lander, John H. Wheeler and Henderson Sherrill.

Gen. Winfield Scott has been nominated by the Whig Convention for the Presidency and Gov. William A. Graham (a native of Lincoln) for Vice-President.

David S. Reid, Democrat, defeated John Kerr, Whig, for Governor on the free suffrage issue. Until then only those who owned 50 acres of land could vote for candidates for the State Senate.

C. C. Henderson & Son and Jacob Ramsour & Son, of Lincolnton, both advertise leather for sale.

The Lincolnton Chapter of Royal Arch Masons was organized August 14, 1852, by M. E. Comp. Myers, Deputy Grand High Priest, assisted by Comp. Luke Blackmer of Salisbury, Robert H. Lewis of Milton, and H. W. Hudson of Rittenhouse Chapter of Connecticut. The following officers were elected: Comp. James A. Caldwell, High Priest; E. S. Barrett, King; J. T. Alexander, Scribe; Augustus W. Burton, Captain of the Host; Lawson P. Henderson, Principle Sojourner; Martin D. Phifer, Royal Arch Captain; Dr. William Sloan, Master 1st Veil; Samuel Lander, Master 2nd Veil; Jacob Q. Carpenter, Master 3rd Veil; John A. Jetton, Janitor.

Advertisement of Laurel Hill Tannery operated by Jacob Ramsour & Son. (1852.)

Lincoln Courier. Lincolnton Female Academy, Rev. C. H. Albert, Principal; C. C. Henderson, Chairman; B. S. Johnson, Secretary Board of Trustees. December 1852.

Governor Reid on December 9, 1852, advertised, offering a reward of $300.00 for Wilson England, late of Catawba County, who stands charged with the murder of one Nathaniel Wilson of said county.

Judge M. L. McCorkle, with the vision of a seer, proposed that a college be built in Newton and it soon bore fruit, for the German Reformed church set about to establish Catawba College. With the "Loretz Beneficiary Fund" and land donated by Reuben Setzer the college was established December 17, 1852, and the first board of trustees was composed of Joshua Clapp, Philo Hedrick, George Setzer, M. L. McCorkle and J. H. Cranford.

The first president was C. H. Albert. Later H. H. Smith, a Bowdoin College graduate, from New Hampshire, was president. Among those who served later were Dr. J. C. Clapp, (from 1861 to 1900), and Chas. H. Mebane. Dr. Samuel Lander, for a while, and Major S. M. Finger were members of the faculty. The school did a wonderful work for this section. It was moved to Salisbury in 1922.

1853

"We are glad to learn that our personal friend, William Lander, of Lincolnton, has been elected Solicitor for this Judicial district. He will make a bold, fearless and efficient prosecuting officer." January 1853. *(Charlotte Journal.)*

Hosea Hildreth Smith was married to Mary Brent Hoke, daughter of the late Michael Hoke, in the Episcopal Church, in Lincolnton, on May 19, 1853, by Rev. T. S. W. Mott, Rector of that church.

Married, by Rev. Mr. Little, in Gaston County, October 30, 1853, Miss J. H. C. Jenkins, daughter of Hugh Jenkins, to D. H. Byerly, of Charlotte. (She was a sister of the late Mr. J. C. Jenkins, of Lincolnton.)

Advertisement: John Reep offers 3c reward and no thanks for delivery of Elijah Sane, an indented apprentice between 16 and 17 years old, who ran away from me, December 19, 1853.

Rev. Samuel Lander, Jr., was married to Laura McPherson, in Lincolnton, December 20, 1853, by Rev. Samuel Lander, father of the groom.

Motz Hotel, Lincolnton, Thomas R. Shuford, Proprietor.

1854

Jacob Shuford died January 18, 1854, aged 45.

Eli H. Fulenwider was married in Lincolnton, February 28, 1854, to Martha Lander, daughter of Rev. Samuel Lander. The officiating minister was Rev. William I. Langdon.

Jacob Rush died April 13, 1854, aged 56.

George P. Langford, of Lincoln County, murdered his wife, September 10, 1852, was convicted of the crime and sentenced to death. William Lander was the State's Attorney, who examined 150 witnesses, made no memorandum of evidence but argued the case before the jury for a full day without notes. Haywood W. Guion, an able lawyer, was counsel for the defendant, who appealed to Supreme Court for a new trial. The Supreme Court in its opinion rendered by Judge Nash sustained the ruling of Judge Caldwell, the trial Judge. Langford confessed the crime on the scaffold immediately before he paid the death penalty in 1854.

Dr. William Johnston, a prominent physician and son of the Revolutionary patriot, James Johnston, died September 30, 1854, aged 64 years, and the burial was at Machpelah.

Caroline Guion, daughter of Mr. Haywood W. Guion, died in Lincolnton, September 4, 1854. She died in the Episcopal faith and the burial was in the church yard across from the Guion home on North Cedar Street.

Railroad meeting in Lincolnton, October 19, 1854. Gen. Daniel Seagle, Chairman; B. S. Guion, Secretary. After L. E. Thompson explained the object of the meeting the chair appointed C. C. Henderson, John F. Hoke, W. B. Withers, Richard A. Burch, Robert Brevard, Caleb Miller, Dr. William McLean, James A. Caldwell, James Johnston, B. S. Guion, Jacob Ramsour, L. E. Thompson, Henry Cansler, B. H. Sumner, H. W. Guion, B. S. Johnson, V. A. McBee, W. J. Hoke, Dr. Elam Caldwell and R. R. Templeton delegates to General Internal Improvement Convention in Salisbury, November 2nd.

November 11, 1854, B. S. Guion and J. F. Hoke advertised for sale the saw mill three miles east of Lincolnton, on Plank Road, together with 18 mules and wagons.

Robert Johnston, son of Col. James Johnston, married April 21, 1807, to Mary Reid, daughter of Capt. John Reid. They reared a family of twelve children, among whom were Dr. Sidney X. Johnston, Col. William Johnston, Rufus M. Johnston and John Reid Johnston. Robert Johnston died May 23, 1854, aged 76 years.

Dr. William Johnston, youngest son of Col. James Johnston, was a physician and a successful business man, engaged for many years in the manufacture of iron in Lincoln County. Member of the House of Commons from Lincoln, 1820.

He was married to Nancy, daughter of Gen. Peter Forney, October 3, 1820, and reared a large family. His daughter, Annie, married Dr. Joseph W. Calloway, of Rutherford. She died in 1928 in Alabama, aged 101 years. Five of his sons, Capt. James F., Gen. Robert D., Capt. William A., Capt. Joseph F., and Midshipman Bartlett Shipp Johnston, all were soldiers of the Confederacy. Several of these were distinguished men.

Dr. Johnston died September 30, 1854, aged 64 years, and was buried at Machpelah.

William Rankin was born in Pennsylvania, January 10, 1761. He came to Tryon, afterwards Lincoln County, when a young man. He married to Mary Moore, sister of Gen. John Moore. In the days of the Revolution he proved to be a brave patriot and served his country well in field and camp. He was a useful citizen and died in 1854 at the ripe age of 93. His son, Col. Richard Rankin, was for long years a fine citizen and represented Lincoln County in the Legislature of 1844 and 1850, and Gaston in 1856.

Rufus Reid, son of Capt. John Reid of Catawba Springs, died at his home in Iredell County in 1854 in his 66th year. He represented Iredell in the House of Commons for two terms, 1844 and 1846, and was a progressive citizen of that county.

1855

The Wilmington, Charlotte and Rutherford Railroad, Incorporated 1855, has opened books for subscriptions in Lincolnton with Henry Cansler, J. F. Hoke, L. D. Childs, J. T. Alexander and B. S. Johnson, Soliciting Committee.

Robert Nixon and Milly Womack were married by R. H. Abernethy, Justice of Peace, on April 24th, 1855. They were parents of the late Alfred Nixon, of Lincolnton.

May 7, 1855. Subscriptions for stock of the Wilmington, Charlotte and Rutherford Railroad have been secured as follows: from Rutherford, $30,000; Shelby, $40,000; Lincolnton, $105,000; Dallas, $50,000; Beals Old Field, $30,000; Hopewell, $50,000.

Robert Williamson, Jr., has been chosen Clerk of Superior Court for Lincoln County.

Samuel N. Stowe candidate for Congress on the Know Nothing, or American Party ticket, was defeated by Burton Craige of Salisbury.

1856

William Williamson, for many years a reputable lawyer of Lincolnton, died May 20, 1856, of dropsy, aged 45. He was a son of the late Robert Williamson who resided in Lincoln and was well known as a lawyer in Western Carolina. William Lander, in a tribute paid to him, said: "Few men possessed so many ennobling qualities of head and heart. He was kind, charitable, generous to a fault, and was remarkable for his amiability and courtliness. He left many relatives and friends and died without an enemy."

Birth at sea, October 1, 1856, on board steamer Roanoke at 9 P.M. off Barnegat, West by South, the lady of J. Wilkes, Esq., of Charlotte, was delivered of a girl named Isabelle Roanoke, in honor of the steamer on which she was born. *(Charlotte Journal.)*

Haywood W. Guion, of Lincolnton, has been elected President of Wilmington, Charlotte and Rutherford Railroad.

1857

Copy of a letter which the author received from Mr. George M. Lore, of Concord, N. C., bearing date, January 4, 1926, and which will be interesting to many people:

"About 1856 or 1857, I was a boy nine or ten years old and was in Lincolnton, N. C., with my father. About 12 o'clock a friend of my father, Charles Cotesworth Henderson, called to us to go with him to dinner. After dinner Mr. Henderson went out but soon returned with something wrapped in paper, and then said: 'Mr. Lore, I went to New Orleans on business a few weeks ago and got through with the business quicker than I expected, and as I had not seen my brother, Pinckney, for fifteen years decided to take a stage and go to Austin, Texas, to visit him. When I reached Austin, about 11 o'clock in the morning, I went to the hotel and prepared to meet my brother. Coming down into the lobby I inquired where I might find Governor Henderson. Some gentleman spoke up and said Governor Henderson was in the Senate Chamber addressing the Senate on some matter. So I went to the door and the door-keeper gave me a direct look and said, 'you must be a brother of the Governor,' I told him I was but that my brother had not seen me for fifteen years and would not know me. He took me down the aisle and gave me an end seat. As I sat down I noticed my brother halt in his talk and give a look in my direction, and in a few words told the Senate he would finish what he had to say later. He picked up his hat and when he got to me caught me by the ear and led me out saying, 'Even a Henderson can't get lost in Texas.' This incident caused me to remember all that followed.

"Mr. Henderson said, on opening the package, 'Mr. Lore, Brother Pinckney gave me five heads of what he called sorghum seed and further said, 'we are making a fine quality of molasses out of it, take it home and see if you can grow it in the Old North State, we got it here a few years ago from some Island and find it a valuable plant.' Now, Mr. Lore, I can't look after my farming interests very close and I am going to give you three heads and ask you to give it a fair trial, which task was gladly accepted by my father, who planted it in good ground and had nearly an acre of as good cane as you ever saw grow. When it was ripe the molasses making started and a great many people from all over the State, and other States, got seed to plant the next year, and from this started the cultivation of this valuable plant all over the South. When the war came on a few years later it was a great boon to the South, as sugar was not obtained except in Louisiana.

"I am almost sure this was the first seed of this plant that came east of the Mississippi River, and Charles Cotesworth Henderson and his brother Pinckney were alike responsible for its being brought here."

G. M. LORE.

Note: It is hardly probable that this was the first sorghum seed ever planted in Lincoln, but an improved quality of seed; for the people in the early days used sorghum for sugar.

Col. William Julius Alexander, a brilliant orator and lawyer, died in Lincolnton, Sunday, February 15, 1857.

Dr. James W. Calloway, a native of Rutherford, but for some years a physician in East Lincoln, died May 15, 1857, aged 72 years. His wife was Ann Johnston, daughter of Dr. William Johnston.

Married by Rev. Dr. Drury Lacy, July 16, 1857, Major T. J. Jackson, Professor in Military Academy at Lexington, Virginia, to Mary Anna, daughter of Rev. R. H. Morrison.

S. P. Sherrill was married December 8, 1857, to Sarah C. Lander, daughter of Rev. Samuel Lander, of Lincolnton. The officiating minister was Rev. John W. Kelly.

Died, December 23, 1857, Mrs. Catherine Hoke, wife of Col. John F. Hoke, and daughter of the late Col. William Julius Alexander.

Andrew Hoyle, the third son of Peter Hoyle, the pioneer, married to Catherine, daughter of Major George Wilfong, a soldier of the Revolution.

He was known as the rich Hoyle and lived at Hoylesville, three miles east of Dallas. When he died in 1857 he left large landed property, stores and slaves. It is said that his personal property converted into cash amounted to $200,000.00, the largest single estate ever left in Gaston County prior to the Civil War. He had fine business qualities and wide influence. He was Senator from Lincoln three terms: 1807-1809.

1. His son, Eli Hoyle, married first to Cynthia Ramsour, and their children were Mrs. Thomas Grier, Mrs. Henry W. Burton, Mrs. E. S. Barrett and Laban A. Hoyle. Eli Hoyle's second marriage was to Elizabeth, daughter of Alfred M. Burton of Beatties Ford. By this marriage there was one son, Alfred E. Hoyle, who died in defense of his country in Battle of Seven Pines, May 31, 1862, aged 18 years.

2. One daughter by his first marriage, Mary, married to Jacob Fulenwider and their children were:

(1) Roxanna, who married Rev. Jacob Shuford.
(2) Sarah, who married Monroe Forney.
(3) Elizabeth, who married Dr. W. J. T. Miller.
(4) Eli H., who married Martha Lander.

Larkin Stowe (Aug. 23, 1788—June 12, 1857), son of James Stowe, one of the early settlers in Lincoln County, figured prominently in public affairs for many years, and was a highly respected and influential citizen. He represented Lincoln in the Commons in 1842 and in the Senate 1844 and 1846, and was Councilor of State in 1854. He married Susan Spratt Neal and had four sons, all of whom became leaders in both business and public life. Among them were Col. Jasper Stowe (1821-1902), a great-hearted gentleman and immensely popular. He, with his brother, E. B. Stowe (1823-1904), established a cotton factory on the South Fork River in lower Gaston County in the early 1850's and operated it successfully until the Civil War, when fortune turned. After the war it was taken over by Thos. H. Gaither, and operated by him for some years until it was abandoned. Jasper Stowe was Senator from Lincoln in 1860 and from Gaston in 1881.

Samuel N. Stowe (1822-1894) was in the House of Commons from Lincoln in 1848 and 1850, but in 1854 he ran on the

Know Nothing ticket for Congress against Burton Craige and was defeated. Later he moved to Texas.

Col. Wm. A. Stowe represented Gaston in the House in 1872 and 1874.

Dr. William Sloan, who married Elizabeth, daughter of Col. Larkin Stowe, for many years practiced medicine in Dallas; was the delegate from Gaston to the Constitutional Convention of 1865; State Treasurer in 1865; and later was President of the Wilmington, Charlotte and Rutherford Railroad. He died in Charlotte about 1885.

1858

General James Pinckney Henderson was born in Lincolnton, March 31, 1808, son of Major Lawson Henderson and Elizabeth (Caruth) Henderson; was educated at Pleasant Retreat Academy in Lincolnton; studied law and admitted to the bar in 1829 and at once gave promise of a brilliant career, for he was an eloquent speaker and soon took high rank in legal circles. In 1835, he moved to Canton, Miss., and there established himself in the law, but in 1836 when the Texas revolution broke out "he heeded the call of the wild," organized a company of troops for service in behalf of Texas freedom, went with his company to Austin, was there commissioned as Brigadier General; returned to the United States, called for volunteers and among those secured were a goodly number of Lincoln men, who, under command of John B. Harry, went to Texas, but arrived after the victory at San Jacinto and the establishment of the Republic of Texas.

President Sam Houston appointed Henderson to the important post of Attorney General in his cabinet in 1836 and after a year made him Secretary of State.

In 1838 he was appointed Minister to France and England and after protracted diplomatic effort on his part France recognized the Texas Republic as an independent nation.

When in Paris, he met Mr. John Cox and family of Philadelphia, and fell in love with the daughter, Frances, an accomplished young woman, and they were married in St. George's Chapel, London, October 29, 1839.

Returning from France he was sent to Washington in 1844 to represent Texas and perfected the terms for the admission of Texas into the union in 1845. He was one of the prominent members of the Texas Constitutional Convention of 1845; was elected as the first Governor of Texas in 1846 and while Governor volunteered as a soldier and served as Major General in the Mexican War with such distinction that Congress presented him with a sword for gallantry. When the war closed he resumed his duties as Governor but refused to accept the salary for the time he spent in military service.

When his term as Governor expired he declined re-election and resumed the practice of law. Upon the death of Senator Rusk in 1857 he was appointed to fill that vacancy and served as Senator from Texas until he died in Washington, June 4, 1858, and his body was buried in the Congressional Cemetery. In 1932 the remains were removed by the State of Texas to Austin for final interment in the State which he had served with honor and distinction. He had two daughters: 1. Julia married a Mr. Adams and had one son, Pinckney Henderson Adams, and one daughter, Julia, who married Arthur H. Geisler of Oklahoma City, American Minister to Guatemala during the Coolidge administration. Mrs. Geisler died in Guatemala, February 14, 1925, and was buried in Oklahoma City, March 14, following. 2. The other daughter, Frances, married Baron Von Preuschen of Austria and their descendants live at Allenstieg, Austria.

General Henderson was classed along with Gen. Sam Houston and William B. Ochiltree as one of the three greatest citizens who have figured in Texas history.

Died, in Concord, June 27, 1858, Mrs. Eugenia Barringer, wife of Rufus Barringer and daughter of Rev. R. H. Morrison.

August 24, 1858. Bids are advertised for to build a brick Methodist church in Lincolnton, 42 by 54 feet in size, with tower 64 feet high. All to be completed by December 1, 1859.

SAMUEL LANDER,
JOHN E. BOGER,
H. W. ABERNETHY,
J. C. JENKINS,
W. H. MICHAL,
Committee.

Married by Rev. E. W. Thompson in Union, S. C., September 15, 1858, Eli H. Fulenwider, of Shelby and Mrs. Mary C. McConnell.

At a meeting of the stockholders of W. C. & R. Railway, H. W. Guion was elected President, V. A. McBee, Treasurer of Western Division and C. C. Henderson, Director.

John D. Shaw was married November 3, 1858, to Margaret B. Henderson, daughter of C. C. Henderson, by Rev. R. N. Davis.

Died in Lincoln County, near Catawba River, December 9, 1858, Thomas Williamson, aged 85.

Died in Lincolnton, December 21, 1858, Robert Williamson, Jr., Clerk of Superior Court, aged 45.

Advertisement: Charlotte Hotel, J. B. Kerr, Proprietor. The house has been thoroughly furnished throughout and in every part of it creature comforts are abundant and tangible, especially in the dining room where the "inner man is renewed day by day." Table board $8.00 per month, with room and fire, $12.50 per month. Connected with this hotel are stables affording room for 100 horses.

1859

Died in Gaston County, January 19, 1859, Hugh Jenkins, aged 71, father of J. C. Jenkins, of Lincolnton.

Mecklenburg Bonds offered for sale by H. W. Guion, President W. C. & R. Railroad.

Advertisement: North Carolina Military Institute, Charlotte, N. C., Major D. H. Hill, Superintendent, Expense, $300.00 per year.

Executors Sale, at Hoylesville, Gaston County, March 17, 1859, 9 negroes, 1 good wagon, horses, mules, cattle, household goods, etc. W. P. Bynum, Thomas Grier, Executors of Estate of Andrew Hoyle, deceased.

Married in Lincolnton, August 25, 1859, at the residence of Jacob A. Ramsour, the bride's father, David Schenck to Miss Sallie Ramsour, of Lincolnton.

Died in Shelby, August 24, 1859, Rev. William I. Langdon, President of High Point Seminary. The body was buried in the Methodist graveyard in Lincolnton.

Alfred M. Burton, a son of Col. Robert Burton was born in Granville County in 1785. He was educated at the State University, settled in Lincoln County, and was admitted to the bar in 1807.

On June 1, 1811, he married Elizabeth, daughter of Col. John Fulenwider, and lived at Beatties Ford. His brother, Judge Robert H. Burton, married a sister of Mrs. Alfred Burton. Mr. Burton was a lawyer and had a good practice, which, together with his large landed interests, took all of his time. He ranked high as a lawyer among the many men of mark in the profession, among whom, during his fifty years in the practice, were included James Graham, Robert Williamson, Robert H. Burton, Bartlett Shipp, Michael Hoke, James R. Dodge, W. P. Bynum, William Lander, Wm. Julius Alexander and others. He was an old fashioned Southern gentleman, courtly in bearing, honorable to a high degree, dignified, charitable and influential. He never sought public office "choosing rather to obey than to execute the law."

He reared a large family among whom were Mrs. Sarah V. Young, Mrs. Eli Hoyle, Mrs. Connor and Miss Fannie Burton. The late Alfred Burton Young, a prominent citizen of Concord, was his grandson and Burton H. Smith of Charlotte, a great grandson.

He died in 1859 and his body rests in the family plot in the Unity Church Cemetery.

CHAPTER XIV

1860-1869

Dr. Eli Crowell was married to Miss M. B. Lowrance, April 10, 1860, by Rev. A. J. Fox.

Married by Rev. R. N. Davis, in Lincolnton, April 18, 1860, Mr. William Tiddy, to Pattie P., daughter of Dr. J. C. Rudisill.

June 1, 1860. Died in Lincoln County last week, Charles W. Hammerskold, aged 52 years.

Amendments to the Charter of Lincolnton, 1860: That the Commissioners shall have power to levy and cause to be collected in the manner prescribed by the Charter, the following taxes:

1. Public billiard tables not exceeding $25.00.
2. On every bowling alley, whether called 9 or 10 pin alley, $15.00.
3. On all lectures for reward, unless for charitable purpose, $5.00.
4. On all artists or picture takers, not exceeding $10.00.
5. On all riding or pleasure vehicles of value of $50.00, or upward, tax of $1.00.
6. On all gold watches, except those worn by ladies, $1.00.
7. On all silver watches, $0.50.
8. On all pianos, except those used in schools, $1.00.
9. On all pistols, $1.00.
10. On all dirks, bowie knives or sword canes if worn about the person, $2.00.
11. On all itinerant traders, not residents, 5 per cent on all sales.
12. On every pack of playing cards sold, $0.20.
13. Livery stables, not over $10.00.
14. All non-residents engaged in putting up lightning rods, $10.00.

No person shall sell spirituous liquors in quantities less than a quart, but by vote of the people license may be granted to sell same by small measure.

Harland Bone, alias Edward Icem, was born in Jackson County, Georgia, about 1830. In 1859, he murdered James Cornelius, a prominent citizen of Lincoln County who lived on the

Catawba River a few miles north of Beatties Ford. Bone was convicted at Dallas, sentenced to death, and later paid the death penalty at Dallas, May 25, 1860.

Married, in Dallas, November 29, 1860, Dr. William Sloan to Miss E. E., daughter of Larkin Stowe.

After a heated presidential campaign with four candidates for the Presidency, namely, Douglas, Northern Democrat; Breckinridge, Southern Democrat; John Bell, American; and Abraham Lincoln, Republican, the last named was elected to the Presidency in November, 1860, and the South fearful of the effect in the slave states was greatly alarmed. South Carolina seceded from the Union, December 17, 1860, and the country was on the verge of war.

At a meeting held in Lincolnton, December 1, 1860, with C. C. Henderson, Chairman, and A. Costner and V. A. McBee, Secretaries, serious consideration was given to the war situation and the attitude that should be taken. William Lander offered a resolution endorsing the message of Governor Ellis and demanding perfect equality in the Union. After speeches by John Coulter, Henry Cansler and V. A. McBee the resolutions were adopted.

Schedules on W. C. & R. Railroad: Trains leave Charlotte at 9 A.M.; Arrive at Brevard (now Stanley) at 10:30. Hacks to Lincolnton. V. A. McBee, Master of Transportation.

The Wilmington, Charlotte & Rutherford Railroad was completed to Lincolnton late in the year 1860, and the first train to arrive was welcomed by a vast multitude enthusiastic because Lincolnton was at last by rail opened to the outside world.

Mr. T. J. Holton, publisher of the *N. C. Whig*, died in Charlotte in January, 1861. He had been publisher since 1830 of the *Charlotte Journal*, later called the *Charlotte Jeffersonian* and last called the *North Carolina Whig*. (For several years after his death his wife was editor and publisher of the paper.)

Married, May 1, 1861, the Rev. R. Z. Johnston, to Miss Kittie M. Caldwell, daughter of R. B. Caldwell.

The war began at Charleston, S. C., when Fort Sumter fell on April 13, 1861.

Alphonso C. Avery, of Morganton, was married February 7, 1861, to Susan Morrison, daughter of Rev. Dr. R. H. Morrison, of Lincoln County, by Rev. J. L. Kirkpatrick.

1861

The Southern Stars, a Lincolnton Military Company, was organized April 22, 1861, and in less than two months took part in the first battle of the Civil War at Bethel. April 25th, when they started to the war was a sad day to those they left behind. Before they departed a beautiful flag was presented by Rev. Samuel Lander in the name of the ladies of the town, and accepted in appropriate words by Sergeant L. J. Hoyle. Prayers were offered by Rev. L. M. Berry (Baptist), Rev. C. T. Bland (Episcopal), Rev. R. N. Davis (Presbyterian) and Rev. G. W. Ivey (Methodist). Then the soldiers, followed by a large company of friends, marched to the depot and were off for war and engaged in the first battle of Bethel.

The 97 men composing the Company were:

William J. Hoke, Captain
W. M. Reinhardt, 1st Lieutenant
Robert F. Hoke, 2nd Lieutenant
Edward E. Sumner, 3rd Lieutenant
W. R. Edwards, Sergeant
A. S. Haynes, Sergeant
E. W. Stubbs, Sergeant

L. J. Hoyle, Sergeant
John F. Speck, Sergeant
Thomas J. Cansler, Corporal
David A. Coon, Corporal
L. A. Dellinger, Corporal
William A. Summerow, Corporal
A. A. Ramsour, Ensign

Dr. J. M. Abernethy, Surgeon

William Adams
Hiram W. Abernethy
James L. Alexander
J. A. Arnes
M. A. Bland
T. J. Ballard
James Ballard
Perry Boyd
R. E. Brown
John Brookhead
James C. Conley
James Cody
Jesse Cody
John E. Close
Peter Dellinger
Jacob Dellinger
Lafayette Earney
Eric Erson
B. F. Grigg
Ephraim Garrison
John Gathon
H. M. Goodson
G. M. Hoke
M. M. Hines
H. S. Hines
J. Hoke
Marcus Henry

A. M. Houser
A. J. Hand
W. H. Howell
J. A. Hawkins
J. P. Hawkins
John Hayes
Thos. Hope
A. J. Houser
J. W. Houser
R. W. Hargrove
A. L. Haynes
F. Holbrook
O. L. Jackson
W. H. Jetton
Samuel Lander, III
C. L. Leonard
J. Leatherman
C. L. Lines
John Lyons
William Martin
A. J. Mooney
Henry W. Morton
J. F. Millsaps
James Nichols
A. J. Pardue
J. G. Rudisill
J. Pendergrass
J. W. Pettus

J. F. Reinhardt
J. W. Reinhardt
O. A. Ramsour
W. G. Ramseur
W. R. Raglan
J. Roney
W. S. Rush
W. M. Rodgers
John G. Stamey
W. H. Shuford
G. W. Shuford
M. H. Smith
J. I. Smith
W. A. Smith
J. O. Sullivan
Allen R. Stowe
J. E. Sumner
Robert Stroupe
Nelson Sherrill
W. A. Sherrill
William White
J. D. Wells
Angus Wingate
Murchison Wingate
Adolphus Wacaster
R. M. Warlick
W. A. Williams

Robert F. Hoke became a Major General; William J. Hoke was promoted to Colonel; Eric Erson became Lieutenant Colonel; A. S. Haynes,

W. R. Edwards, John F. Speck, L. A. Dellinger and B. F. Grigg became Captains, and L. J. Hoyle, D. A. Coon, O. A. Ramsour and W. A. Summerow, Lieutenants.

About the same time the Beatties Ford Riflemen was organized at Beatties Ford with the following members in part:

A. H. Houston, Captain
W. P. Bynum, 1st Lieutenant

Robt. D. Johnston, 2nd Lieutenant
R. B. B. Houston, 3rd Lieutenant

Thomas Asbury	Robert Hager	Mark Munday
Mark Ballard	Henry Howard	Josiah Munday
Monroe Ballard	James F. Johnston	James McCall
Clem Blythe	William Johnston	Joseph Nance
William Burch	James H. Johnston	Mark Nance
James Burch	Adolphus King	T. H. Proctor
Henry Connor	James King	Pink Rendleman
John Caldwell	Jacob Killian	John Ragan
George Dellinger	John Killian	William Ruddock
Henry Fulenwider	William Lockman	Erastus Rodgers
Monroe Gabriel	L. A. Lockman	Daniel Reinhardt
Albert Gabriel	Eli Lockman	Thomas Shelton
Charles Gattis	Alfred Little	Spencer Shelton
Frank Goodson	Hugh Little	Albert Shelton
Albert Goodson	James Little, Sr.	S. L. Thompson
Alfred Hoyle	Robert Little, Jr.	John Thompson
William Hunter	Connor Little	William Torrence
Stanhope Hunter	Jacob Lineberger	Needham Wingate
Andrew Hall	Jacob Long	John Washam
Thomas Hall	Isaac Lynch	John White
Green Hager	James Moore	Ansolem Withers
Sidney Hager	William Munday	

There were in all eighty-two men in the company.

At Garysburg, in June, 1861, the company was re-organized with Robert D. Johnston, Captain; William Johnston, 1st Lieutenant; J. F. Goodson, 2nd Lieutenant; and William Hunter, 3rd Lieutenant. Lieutenant W. P. Bynum was the only married man in the company and was commissioned May 8, 1861, Lieutenant Colonel and promoted to Colonel September 17, 1862. He resigned in December, 1862, to accept the office of State Solicitor for the Lincolnton District.

The Southern Stars and Beatties Ford Rifles were but two of the nine companies that went into the Confederate Army from Lincoln County. The seven other companies were commanded as follows:

1. George W. Seagle, Captain; Thomas J. Seagle, 1st Lieutenant; Lee Johnson, 2nd Lieutenant; Sidney A. Shuford, Jr., 3rd Lieutenant; Augustus P. James, 1st Sergeant.

2. John F. Hill, Captain; James F. Seagle, 1st Lieutenant; Henry Rhodes, 2nd Lieutenant.

3. A. S. Haynes, Captain; D. A. Coon, 1st Lieutenant; L. J. Hoyle, 2nd Lieutenant; O. A. Ramsour, 3rd Lieutenant.

4. Eric Erson, Captain; Wm. A. Summerow, 1st Lieutenant; L. A. Dellinger, 2nd Lieutenant; A. R. Nisbet, 1st Sergeant.

5. Joseph B. Shelton, Captain; James M. Kincaid, 1st Lieutenant; Daniel Wells, 2nd Lieutenant; Henry Wells, Jr., 3rd Lieutenant; Wm. D. Thompson, 1st Sergeant.

6. John F. Speck, Captain; John H. Boyd, 1st Lieutenant; Philip Carpenter, 2nd Lieutenant; J. Q. Carpenter, 3rd Lieutenant; Thos. J. Cansler, 1st Sergeant.

7. Peter Z. Baxter, Captain; George L. Phifer, 1st Lieutenant; James T. Adams, 2nd Lieutenant; T. W. Lindsay, 3rd Lieutenant.

Among the Lincoln men who were in high command were Major Gen. Stephen Dodson Ramseur, Major Gen. Robert F. Hoke and Brig. Gen. Robert D. Johnston, all Lincoln soldiers, besides Major Gen. John H. Forney and Brig. Gen. Wm. H. Forney, natives of Lincoln County but volunteers from Alabama. Lincoln County had a population in 1860 of 8,195—when we deduct 2,196 negroes, we have left 5,999 white men, women and children in the county. With less than 6,000 white population the County furnished from start to finish 1,311 soldiers to the Confederate Army. That record is hard to beat. They were patriots, fighting for what they thought was right.

Legislative Acts of 1861 Pertaining to Lincoln County

Incorporation of Balls Creek Camp Ground with George S. Hooper, Henry Cline, Elias Smoyer, Henderson Sherrill and John F. Paine as Trustees (with power to fill vacancies) of the property given for the use of the Methodist Church. (Private Laws 1861, page 39.)

The Lincoln Copper and Gold Mining Company with Henry Cansler, John F. Hoke, William J. Hoke, Francis Hoke and Daniel Seagle, constitute a body corporate and politic by the above name. (Private Laws 1861, page 91.)

Salem Camp Ground was established with 4 acres (situated 4 miles south of Lincolnton) for the use of the Baptist Church, with Bartlett Stroupe, William Garrison, and Thomas R. Shuford, Trustees, with power to fill vacancies. (Private Laws 1861, page 41.)

The Constitutional Convention met in Raleigh and the Secession Ordinance was adopted unanimously, May 20, 1861. North Carolina was the last one of the Colonies to adopt the Federal Constitution and came into the Union too late to take part in the first election of Washington to the Presidency. She was also the last of the Southern States to secede, but being sandwiched between Virginia and South Carolina, both of which had withdrawn, the delegates decided there was nothing else to do. William Lander was the delegate from Lincoln, but later when elected to the Confederate Congress he resigned and David Schenck was chosen as Convention delegate to succeed Lander.

June 18, 1861. "Mr. William Tiddy, Sr., leaves for the seat of war Thursday night and will cheerfully take any small packages, letters, etc.; parents and friends will do well to look to this chance."

"For Congress—William Lander, of Lincoln." *N. C. Whig*, Oct. 15, 1861.

Dr. David Warlick Schenck, for many years a physician in Lincolnton, and father of Judge David Schenck, died in Lincolnton, December 20, 1861.

Notice: I will sell for cash at public square in Charlotte, January 1, 1862, two likely negroes: a man, 55, and a woman 34. Maxwell Warlick. (December 24, 1861.)

1862

At a political meeting held in Charlotte, March 8, 1862, with John Walker, Chairman, and L. S. Williams, Secretary, speeches were made by James W. Osborne, David M. Lee, A. C. Williamson and others.

The Resolutions Committee was composed of J. W. Osborne, W. J. Yates, William Johnston, J. H. Wilson, Dr. J. M. Miller, W. M. Matthews, James H. Davis, Dr. J. M. Ross, J. S. Davis, J. M. Potts and J. M. Hutchison.

Col. William Johnston was endorsed for Governor and was later nominated as the war candidate for that office but was

THE ANNALS OF LINCOLN COUNTY 173

defeated at the polls by Col. Zebulon B. Vance, who distinguished himself later as the War Governor of the State.

John T. Butler, the Charlotte jeweler, advertises that he will pay the highest cash price for 500 ounces of gold.

V. A. McBee, Master of Transportation, advertises railroad schedules from Charlotte to Lincolnton, 1862.

Dr. E. L. Dusenberry, a Lincolnton physician, died April 25, 1862, in his 38th year.

Captain Sidney A. Shuford, Co. B, 23rd N. C. Regiment, C. S. A., killed in Battle of Seven Pines, May 31, 1862, aged 25 years.

Winchester Pegram was a leading citizen, born in Lincoln County, June 23, 1799. He married in 1818 to Mary, daughter of Jacob Stowe, and died in Dallas, Nov. 28, 1862. He was a good man, a merchant, kept hotel in Dallas and reared a family of splendid sons and daughters, among whom were Miles P., long time a Charlotte banker, W. W., E. L., Theodore and Frank Pegram.

Mary married H. N. Ward and Violet married first to W. F. Holland and second to Jacob Froneberger of Dallas.

Jacob Ramsour died December 30, 1862. He was a grandson of Diedrich Ramsour the pioneer (see page 42).

He was born in 1788, married to Barbara Summey, September 10, 1811. She died September 14, 1865, according to the tombstone record in Old White Church graveyard. He was a Lincolnton merchant for many years, a large landowner, a useful citizen, a friend of education and trustee for some years of the Lincolnton Academy.

He reared a large family as follows:

1. Eliza S. (1812-1871) married..............Phifer, no children.

2. Daniel F. (1814-.........) migrated to Texas.

3. Harriet E. (1816-1872) married Leonard E. Thompson, lawyer.

4. William (1818-1900) married Martha A. Ramsour.

5. Alexander (1821-.........), physician, married Miss Thompson, sister of Leonard A. Thompson. Their daughter, Alice, married Dr. John M. Richardson.

6. Mary A. E. (1823-.........) married Rev. S. S. Middlekauff, September 12, 1843. He was a minister of the German Reformed church.

7. Alfred A. (1827-.........) did not return from the Civil War.

8. Myra A. (1831-1911) married to Benjamin H. Sumner.

9. Edmund G. (1835-1885) married Miss Burgin.

These were good people and their descendants lived well and exercised fine influence.

1863

Captain B. F. Grigg, on furlough from war, was married January 1, 1863, to Mary McCoy, daughter of Abner McCoy. Rev. R. N. Davis officiated.

Monroe Seagle wrote from camp that David A. Coon had been killed in battle, but it was later discovered that he had been wounded.

Rev. Samuel Lander, Jr., in 1863 established a school called the Lincolnton Seminary, in the present North State Hotel building.

Hua Little, a respected citizen of the Beatties Ford section was murdered by two of his slaves on February 25, 1863. They were tried and convicted of the crime and publicly hanged in the same year at the plantation where the crime was committed.

General Thomas Jonathan (Stonewall) Jackson (Jan. 21, 1824-May 10, 1863) was severely wounded by the fire of his own men May 2, and died of pneumonia at Guiney's Station, south of Fredericksburg, May 10, 1863. He graduated from West Point Military Academy in 1846. In the Mexican War he was commended by Gen. Scott and was a Brevet Major. He resigned his commission in U. S. Army in 1861 and joined the Confederate Army. He was ordered to Richmond, April 21, 1861, and when his name was presented for a Commission a member of the Convention asked: "Who is this Major Jackson?" He was a devout Christian, rigid in observance of the Sabbath, would not mail a letter that would be in transit on Sunday, and prayed much the night before a battle. He was absolutely loyal to Lee and said he would follow him blindfolded. When he died Lee said: "I know not how to replace him."

Four Notable Marriages in Lincoln.

A historian has said of him: "The Army of Northern Virginia was never the same after Jackson died, and though Lee conducted in 1864 some most brilliant maneuvers he did not find another lieutenant who so well understood him, or could execute his orders with such powerful co-ordinated hammer strokes of attack. In any list of the half dozen greatest American soldiers, Jackson is included by virtually all critics, though his career of field service in the Confederate Army was limited to hardly more than two years and his opportunities for independent command were few and brief."

While the world admires the brilliant record of this brave soldier, Lincoln County folks feel closer to him because six years before his death he married to Mary Anna Morrison, a Lincoln County lady.

His record is known to all the world. His body was buried in Lexington, Va., where he had been instructor in the Virginia Military Institute prior to the war.

1864

Vardry McBee, for many years a leading citizen of Lincolnton, where he became wealthy as a saddle maker and merchant, and who served for twenty-one years (1812-1833) as Clerk of the County Court, died in Greenville, S. C., January 23rd, 1864.

Vardry McBee was born June 19, 1775, in Spartanburg District, S. C. His parents came from Virginia to the upper part of South Carolina; though Quakers, they took an active part in the Revolution. Vardry McBee was taken from school at the age of twelve, and for six years worked on the Limestone Farm, assisting in the manufacture of lime. In 1794 he went to Lincolnton to learn the trade of saddler under his brother-in-law, Joseph Morris. In 1800 he went to Charleston to seek his fortune but did not find it and promptly returned to Lincolnton. He then, in the same year, accompanied his parents to Kentucky. The next Spring he removed to middle Tennessee where he established a saddlery. Then, at the request of James Campbell of Charleston, he returned to Lincolnton and opened a store in partnership with Mr. Campbell. In 1804 he was married to Jane Alexander, daughter of Colonel Elias Alexander of Rutherford County. In 1805 he discontinued his mercantile business and invested in a farm, and a house and lot in Lincolnton. As a farmer he was highly successful. In 1812 he became Clerk of the

County Court, which office he held for twenty-one years. While Clerk he continued his business as a saddler. In 1815 he bought, from Colonel Lemuel J. Allston, some thousands of acres of land in and around Greenville, S. C. In 1817 he built a flour mill there, and in 1829 built another. Later, about seven miles below Greenville on the Reedy River, he built a flour mill, a paper mill, a cotton factory, and a wool factory, thus engaging in the manufacture of flour, news print, wrapping paper, writing paper, cotton and woolen yarns and cloth. In 1833 he was a delegate to the Internal Improvement Convention at Raleigh, in which he took a prominent part. In 1836 he removed from Lincolnton to Greenville. There he was elected President of the Agricultural Society and was more than once awarded prizes for the best managed farm in the district. He subscribed liberally to the Louisville and Cincinnati Railroad, of which he became President. When the Greenville and Columbia Railroad project was on the point of failure he saved it by subscribing a total of $50,000. In 1847, while in the North in search of information about railroads, he subscribed to the Seaboard and Roanoke Railroad. He gave liberally towards the establishment of an academy for boys and girls in Greenville. He made generous donations for sites of the Episcopal, Methodist, Presbyterian, and Baptist churches in Greenville. His ventures, farms, factories, and railroads, on the whole proved successful and made him a wealthy and influential man. Physically he was a small man, with a mild and pleasing expression of face. He was crippled when a young man by being thrown from his horse, but at age seventy-seven he was active and vigorous, able to ride daily fifty miles. He adhered to a high standard of morality, and was always strictly temperate. As is well known, he and his descendants have been benefactors of both North and South Carolina.

Children of Vardry McBee and his wife, Jane Alexander:

1. Joseph Gallishaw McBee: died young.

2. Malinda Penelope McBee: born October 15, 1807; died (unmarried) January 2, 1891.

3. Silas Leroy McBee: died at age of 18; probably born 1808; attended Pleasant Retreat Academy and University of North Carolina; year of death not known but probably ca. 1826.

THE ANNALS OF LINCOLN COUNTY 177

4. Luther Martin McBee: born January 19, 1809; died November 28, 1851; married Susan B. McCall, born December 5, 1815; died December 23, 1894. (Five children.)

5. Hannah Echols McBee: probably born ca. 1813, died young.

6. Martha (Patsy) Adeline McBee: born May 1, 1816; died September 26, 1870; married Tench Coxe Carson, born January 12, 1810; died April 27, 1861. (Four children.)

7. Vardry Alexander McBee: born April 7, 1818; died February 17, 1904; married Mary Elizabeth Sumner, born January 11, 1829; died July 6, 1907. (Nine children.)

8. William Pinkney McBee: born August 7, 1820; died October 6, 1860. (Named for William Pinkney, prominent Maryland lawyer and statesman.) Married Harriet Ford Butler, born February 13, 1823; died March 14, 1904. (Four children.)

9. Alexander McBee: born May 22, 1822; died August 14, 1897; married Henrietta R. (D'Oyley) Thurston, a widow, born April 2, 1833; died November 8, 1893.

Vardry McBee and his wife, Jane Alexander, and their children—Malinda Penelope McBee; Luther Martin McBee and his wife; Martha Adeline (McBee) Carson and her husband; William Pinkney McBee and his wife; and Alexander McBee and his wife—are buried in the churchyard of Christ Church, Greenville, South Carolina. Silas Leroy McBee, who died at the age of 18, is buried in the Lutheran Cemetery in Lincolnton. Joseph Gallishaw McBee and Hannah Echols McBee also are probably buried there as at the time of their deaths their parents appear to have been living in Lincolnton. Vardry Alexander McBee and his wife, Mary Elizabeth Sumner, are buried in the churchyard of St. Luke's Church with the life of which they were closely associated throughout their earthly pilgrimage.

William Wilson Broadfoot, of Fayetteville, a youth of fifteen years, visiting in Lincolnton, was accidentally killed near the Cansler Spring, April 16, 1864. He, with a number of other boys, was out hunting. He hid himself, secure as he thought, behind a huge oak tree and told one of the Burton boys to shoot. Young Burton was slow to obey and Broadfoot peeped around the side of the tree to see what caused the delay at the very second Burton pulled his trigger. Broadfoot was shot in the head and killed. It was a deplorable accident which brought sorrow to the friends and community. The body of Broadfoot was buried in the Episcopal graveyard.

Mrs. R. H. Morrison, wife of Rev. Dr. R. H. Morrison, of Cottage Home, died April 16, 1864, aged 64 years. She was a daughter of General Joseph Graham.

Chas. T. Bland, Jr., son of Rev. Chas. T. Bland, the Rector of St. Luke's Church in Lincolnton, died May 15, 1864, and his body rests in the churchyard.

Peter Summey, an old and respected citizen, died September 17, 1864.

Samuel Lander (1793-1864) came with his family from Ireland to America, landing at Boston in 1818. By easy stages they came southward, arriving in Salisbury about 1824 and there he took out naturalization papers. Their home in Salisbury was destroyed by a fire in which they lost heavily. About 1826 they moved to Lincolnton where he established himself as a coach maker and was successful in building up a business of considerable proportions. In the old country the family were members of the Church of England, but soon after they came to Lincolnton they joined the Methodist Church and became active in it. Mr. Lander had rare native intellect, was a local preacher of ability, and exercised for long years a godly influence. He gave his children the best school advantages. Six of his descendants were Methodist ministers.

He died at his home in Lincolnton, December 17, 1864, aged 71 years and his grave is in the Methodist cemetery.

His children were:

Ann, married John W. Weber. (See 1926.)

William, married Sarah Connor of Cokesbury, S. C. (See 1868.)

Margaret, married Rev. William F. Langdon.

Eliza, never married.

George, died in childhood.

Samuel, married Laura McPherson. (See 1904.)

Sarah Catherine, married S. P. Sherrill.

Martha, married Eli H. Fulenwider of Shelby.

Greene W. Caldwell was born in Lincoln County, near Belmont, on April 13, 1806; was educated at local schools and graduated from medical department of University of Pennsylvania in 1831; assistant surgeon in U. S. Army, 1832. Later studied law and was admitted to the bar, settled in Charlotte where he was successful as a practitioner. Member of the House of Commons from Mecklenburg, 1836 to 1841. In 1841 he was elected to Congress over Daniel M. Barringer and served until 1843; was not a candidate for re-election. Superintendent of Charlotte Mint, 1844; Captain of Infantry in Mexican War; State Senator, 1850; unsuccessful candidate for Congress in 1850. He died in Charlotte, July 10, 1864, and his body was buried there.

Gen. Stephen Dodson Ramseur, son of Jacob A. and Lucy (Dodson) Ramseur, was born in Lincolnton, May 31, 1837. He was prepared for college at Lincolnton Academy, then became student at Davidson College. There, encouraged and aided by Gen. D. H. Hill he was appointed by Burton Craige to West Point Military Academy and was graduated in 1860. Was assigned to military duty as Lieutenant in Light Infantry but resigned in April, 1861, to join the Confederate Army. He was soon a Captain and then promoted in turn to Major and Colonel. Wounded at Malvern Hill, July 1, 1862, he was disabled for some time. While convalescing he received his commission as Brigadier General, but fearing that promotion was coming too fast, was disinclined to accept it, but his friends prevailed on him not to put it aside. The late Judge W. P. Bynum who was a Colonel spoke in Lincolnton after the death of Gen. Ramseur as follows:

"Assigned to a command in which I served I knew him well. He succeeded the lamented Gen. Anderson, an officer of great ability and well skilled in the art of war, commanding the love and confidence of his men. Gen. Ramseur came to the Brigade a stranger from another branch of the service, but he at once disarmed criticism by his high professional attainments and amiability of character, inspiring his men by his own enthusiastic nature with those lofty martial qualities which distinguished the Southern soldier."

An historian wrote:

"At Chancellorsville the military tactics of Ramseur were so noteworthy that Gen. Stonewall Jackson and Gen. A. P. Hill who watched his advance, thanked him on the field for the matchless conduct of his men, and Gen. Lee on June 4, 1863, in a letter to Gov. Vance, commended in highest terms the glorious record made by Gen. Ramseur in that battle. He was with Gen. Lee at Gettysburg where he distinguished himself for gallantry as he led his brigade, being among the first to enter the captured town. In October he was granted a leave of absence and went to Milton, N. C., where on October 27, 1863, he was married to Miss Ellen Richmond, after which he soon returned to his Brigade.

"Gen. Ramseur's military tactics shone most brilliantly at Spottsylvania Courthouse, May 12, 1864, when for twenty hours without ceasing his brigade fought to re-establish their lines, his men, willing to follow him in the jaws of death, fought through the terrible conflict to a glorious victory. For his distinguished service in this struggle he was sent for by Gen. Lee, who, in person, commended him for his gallantry and that of his men in what he considered one of the most notable battles in history, and in recognition of the brilliant record made there he was commissioned as Major General and assigned to the command of Early's former division."

On September 19, at Winchester, he bore the brunt of the conflict, holding back Sheridan's army for many hours until other divisions came to his relief and the enemy began to fall back.

Just a month after this battle he was mortally wounded at Cedar Creek and captured by the enemy. He was taken to the Federal hospital where his surgeon and the Federal surgeons did all possible to save his life, but he died October 19, 1864, and his last words were: "Tell Gen. Hoke that I die a Christian, and have done my duty." The day before that battle he heard of the birth of his daughter, little dreaming that in another day he would be in Eternity. Early said of him: "Gen. Ramseur fell into the hands of the enemy mortally wounded, and in him not only my command but the country suffered a great loss. He was a most gallant and energetic officer, whom no disaster appalled, but his courage and energy seemed to gain new strength in the midst of confusion and disorder. He fell at his post fighting like a lion at bay and his native state has reason to be proud of his memory."

Col. James T. Morehead of Greensboro in speaking of his courageous bearing in battle said: "Gen. Ramseur was the only man I ever saw fight like it was represented in pictures." He always led his men, sword in hand; he never said, "go forward," but, "come with me." No braver soldier ever

Top left: Gen. Robert F. Hoke (1837-1912). See 1912.
Top right: Gen. Stephen Dodson Ramseur (1837-1864). See 1864.
Center left: Gen. John H. Forney (1829-1902). See 1861.
Center right: Gen. Robt. D. Johnston (1837-1919). See 1919.
Lower left: Lieut. William Ewen Shipp (1861-1898). See 1898.
Lower right: Captain Rufus Z. Johnston (1874-   ) U. S. Navy. See 1908.

led a charge. He was a chivalrous gentleman, a brave and gallant soldier, and an humble, faithful Christian. His body was brought to Lincolnton and interred in the Episcopal graveyard. Thirty-six years later his wife died and her body was buried by the side of his grave.

In the hall of history in Raleigh is a portrait of Gen. Ramseur, the gift of his daughter, Miss Mary Dodson Ramseur. The presentation speech was delivered by Judge Walter Clark.

In 1919, near Winchester, Va., there was unveiled and dedicated to the memory of Gen. Ramseur a handsome monument, located at the entrance of Shenandoah Valley highway to Belle Grove where his death occurred.

His daughter, Mary Dodson Ramseur, died February, 1935, in Davidson, N. C., and her body rests by the side of her parents' graves in Lincolnton. She never married.

1865

In March, 1865, immediately before the surrender, foodstuff sold in Confederate money as follows: Bacon, $7.50 a pound; corn, $30.00 a bushel; potatoes, $30.00 a bushel; salt, $70 a bushel; eggs, $5.00 a dozen; flour, $500.00 a barrel; molasses, $25.00 a gallon. Many people wore clothes patched in many colors; hats were made of wheat straw; and when leather was very scarce some even wore wooden shoes. That was the most terrible depression ever known in America, but the people by slow degrees worked their way out of it.

The great Civil War which had been waged for four long years came to an end when Lee surrendered at Appomattox, April 9, 1865.

President Lincoln was assassinated at Ford's Theatre, in Washington, April 14, 1865, and died the following day.

It was about April 20, 1865, that a conquering army marched into Lincolnton from Newton. It was the Federal Cavalry Brigade of Gen. John C. Palmer, composed of some five thousand troops. When I saw that long procession of "blue coats" ride down the streets in front of our home, not knowing what it all meant, I was filled with fear and amazement. Why did all that host come to feed upon a people who had no bread to spare? Had not Lee and Grant at Appomattox made full settlement and brought peace to the Nation?

General Palmer found quarters for himself and staff at the home of Col. John F. Phifer, a leading citizen, who lived then in the house now occupied by Mr. J. A. Abernethy, on West Main Street. (This General Palmer in 1896 was the candidate of sound money Democrats for President against William Jennings Bryan.)

I have never heard of any shocking brutalities committed by these troops in Lincolnton, but some of them came by night and seized my little white pony and led it away. My uncle, Dr. Samuel Lander, at the time was principal of a girls' school in the present North State Hotel, diagonally across the street from the military headquarters, (Col. Phifer's) and it was said because he was a Mason that he had influence with Gen. Palmer, who was also a Mason, thus protecting the community from the cruelty and robbery of the irresponsible soldiers. Let that be as it may, General Palmer, at the request of Dr. Lander, had my pony returned to our stable.

As a five-year-old child, watching as the invading army entered the village, little did I dream that some heartless soldier in that group had the day before, in Newton, for no provocation, shot and killed a brave Confederate Lieutenant, Charles T. Connor, who had for four years been a gallant soldier of the South. It was a brutal and cowardly act. That young Lieutenant, killed April 17, 1865, left a little three-year-old girl, who grew to womanhood and in 1884 became my wife and still abides with me. (1936.)

It was a conquering army which came to Lincolnton in April, 1865. But one day later in that same month of April I saw a part of a defeated army, a long line of men, poorly clad, march up the streets in Lincolnton from the old depot. Some were halt and lame, and some with one arm or one eye. Four years before, these brave men with high hopes went forth to reap the glories and the victories of war. They had braved many battles and left many of their comrades slain on bloody lelds. They came home discouraged by defeat and found the country impoverished by the long and fruitless struggle.

It was springtime—the world looked new with its fresh foliage and flowers, but coming home with downcast hopes these men saw no poetry or sentiment in nature. They were weary and hungry, returning to find welcome and to look again upon the faces of those they loved, and to discover the changes which anxiety and hardship had wrought upon the mothers and wives. They found the fields laid waste, the garners empty, the farm tools and stock exhausted and no crops planted. In desperation they went to work and built a mighty state upon the ruins of the old.

The morning these Confederate soldiers were to return, my aunt gathered all the roses in the garden and as these brave men in defeat walked by I handed out roses to them, little realizing the tender sentiment expressed in the deed. What a contrast there was in April, 1865, in the coming of a conquering and of a defeated army!

It was a long and bloody war. The personal experiences of the soldiers in camp and battle would fill many books. The great multitudes slain in battle and by disease and the painful experiences of untold thousands who suffered by hunger and wounds can never be estimated. But the worst was not that endured by soldiers diseased or dying far from home. The mothers and wives at home suffered more by constant suspense and fear, by day and by night, as they anxiously looked for news from the front, and when the letters came they were almost afraid to read them lest the tidings might reveal the worst. Mothers with broken hearts heard that sons were slain and that others were in hospitals of pain; while wives likewise constantly feared that husbands whom they loved more than life might be gone forever. Terrible is war to those at the front and to those back home. Think of the poor widows and orphan children, made so by the brutal horrors of war. Many of the soldiers came back maimed in body, with health undermined, to face poverty and want. The after effects of war too often strangle the public conscience and leave only a wrecked morality that it takes many years of effort to rebuild. It was markedly so after the Civil War. It has been terribly so ever since the World War; and it will be a long time yet before America will climb back to the moral standards she fell from after 1914.

To understand the conditions our fathers faced in 1861, we must look from their angle fully to appreciate the problems which they attempted to solve. Slavery had for nearly two hundred years been rooted in Southern soil. It represented vast millions in property, permeated every Southern commercial interest, and completely molded Southern thought and sentiment. A great system, accepted without question through long generations could not be uprooted without terrific struggle. That conflict was faced bravely by our fathers. Let us not forget their heroic self-denial and devotion to principle. The courage they manifested should inspire us in our day to perform our tasks with a measure of devotion and sacrifice akin to that which they put forth in their day.

Seventy years had passed since the close of the great Civil War. Nearly all who took part in that bloody struggle have died. The wondrous changes wrought since peace was made were never dreamed of by the patriotic leaders of that period. The wide breach has been healed. A mighty Nation has been built upon the ruins of the past and sectional feeling has almost faded away.

When the war closed the State had to be reorganized. A Convention to prepare a new Constitution was assembled in 1865 and Col. W. P. Bynum (later Judge Bynum) was the delegate elected to represent Lincoln County.

1866

Benjamin Sumner, for many years an educator in Lincolnton, died April 3, 1866.

Dr. W. S. Jenkins, by request, wrote the following sketch of his great grandfather:

Benjamin Sumner, classical scholar, legislator, and educator, son of Jethro Sumner and Elizabeth Turner, was born in Gates County, North Carolina, February 12th, 1801. His father, a descendant of the third generation from John Sumner who came from England to Nansemond County, Virginia, about 1650, was a Colonel in the militia, Sheriff and Clerk of Court of Gates County. Colonel Jethro was a first cousin of Brigadier General Jethro, the first Grand Master of the Order of the Cincinnati in North Carolina.

At the University of North Carolina (1818-1822) Benjamin Sumner became the devoted pupil of Dr. William Hooper,

Professor of Ancient and Modern Languages, and from this association he formed a life-long devotion to classical studies. In after years Dr. Hooper wrote that Sumner "was distinguished while at college for his superior scholarship and good conduct." At Chapel Hill he also came under the influence of President Joseph Caldwell, and the eminent scientist, Dr. Elisha Mitchell, whom he impressed as being "highly successful in the prosecution of his studies in all the different branches of learning." The University records show that he roomed in number six Old South with his cousin, Thomas J. Sumner. He took an active part in the work of the Philanthropic Literary Society, being selected as one of the commencement orators in his Junior year. At the commencement of 1822 he was graduated with highest honors and delivered the class salutatory in Latin.

On December 16th, 1824, Benjamin Sumner and Sarah Duke Hunt, daughter of Dr. Thomas Hunt and Elizabeth Duke, were married in Oxford, North Carolina. She was descended on her father's side from Memucan Hunt, a prominent figure in early North Carolina politics, and on her mother's side, from William Duke who came to Virginia in 1720 to live with his relative, Colonel William Byrd of Westover. To Sarah and Benjamin Sumner were born ten children.

Following graduation, Benjamin Sumner at once began his career as a teacher of young men preparatory to their entering college. Five years later, at the commencement of 1827, in recognition of the excellent work that he was doing, the University awarded him the honorary Master of Arts degree. He represented Person County in the House of Commons during the sessions of the General Assembly 1831-1833. The legislative journal shows that he was placed on the select committee on education and that he took a prominent part in the discussions dealing with the "Literary Fund and the Common Schools."

In 1833, at his retired home place, Arcadia, sixteen miles west of Oxford, in Person County, he established a seminary to prepare young men for admission to college. For this undertaking, Dr. Mitchell pronounced him "eminently qualified by his natural talents and disposition, his habits and acquirements." Under his personal supervision the course of studies embraced "the English, Latin and Greek Languages, Ancient and Modern Geography, Mathematics, Natural and Moral Philosophy, Rhetoric and Logic." Sessions were continued at Arcadia Academy until 1840, when the Sumner family moved to Oxford.

In 1844 Benjamin Sumner was invited by the trustees to come to Lincolnton and assume supervision of the "male and female academies." He accepted the offer and served in this capacity for a period of ten years. At Lincolnton he endeavored to maintain in the academies high standards of scholarship and to provide instruction of the classical character that had been offered at Arcadia. In the Female Academy he was aided in the teaching of the languages by his daughter, Mary Elizabeth, who later married Vardry A. McBee. In the Male Academy, his son, Thomas Jethro, who was graduated with honors from the University in 1845, assisted in the teaching of mathematics. By 1848 his reputation as principal of classical academies had become such that he was one of three teachers considered by the trustees of the University to fill the chair of languages left vacant by the resignation of Dr. John DeBernier Hooper.

While in Lincolnton the Sumner family lived on East Main Street in the house now occupied by Mr. Sherwood Childs. Traditional Episcopalians, the Sumners took a leading part in the work of St. Luke's parish. Benjamin Sumner was for years Senior Warden, and, being a talented musician, he directed the music of the church. The first window given to St. Luke's church is a memorial to Benjamin Sumner and his wife, Sarah Duke Hunt. Its subject is St. Luke, and like the other beautiful windows in this church, with one exception, is the work of an English artist—Booth of London.

About 1855 Benjamin Sumner and his wife moved to their plantation near Salisbury, in Rowan County, where he died, April 3, 1866. She died in Lincolnton at the residence of her daughter, Georgiana T. Hoke, November 6, 1875. They are both buried in what is called "The Old English Cemetery" across the street from St. Luke's church, Salisbury.

Their children were:

1. Thomas J. Sumner (1825-1890) graduated from University of North Carolina in 1845; skilled in mathematics, he was a tutor at the University for a while; assisted his father

Top left: James Graham (1793-1851). See 1851.
Top right: William H. Forney (1823-1894). See 1894.
Center: Henry W. Connor (1793-1866). See 1866.
Lower left: William Lander (1817-1868). See 1868.
Lower right: Chas. A. Jonas (1876-   ). See 1928.

at Pleasant Retreat Academy in Lincolnton; active civil engineer in construction of North Carolina Railroad; superintendent of N. C. Railroad during Civil War, rendering valuable service, keeping the line of supplies open to General Lee. After the war he lived in Rowan where he had extensive landed interests and served for many years as County Commissioner of Rowan. He was a bachelor.

2. Benjamin Hunt (1827-1897) married Myra H., daughter of Jacob Ramsour. (See 1897.)

3. Mary Elizabeth (1827-1907) married Vardry A. McBee. (See 1904.)

4. Georgiana T. (1831-1903) married Col. William J. Hoke. (See 1870.)

5. Julian (1833-1901) married Jennie Loftin and lived in Thomasville. One daughter, Daisy Hunt, married John W. Lambeth of Thomasville and their son, J. Walter Lambeth, Jr., was State Senator in 1921; Mayor of Thomasville, 1925-29; Congressman from 8th N. C. District since 1931.

6. Edward Everett (1836-1884) married Bettie Shannonhouse. Lieutenant in Civil War. After war Superintendent Chester and Lenoir Railway. They had three children:

Benjamin H., for many years conductor on Southern Railway. He died in 1936.

Eva, one time Lincolnton postmistress, married H. E. C. Bryant, the well-known news writer. They live in Washington, D. C.

Sarah is engaged in Y. W. C. A. work.

7. Laura (1838-1892).

8. Ellen (1841-1912) married Charles Hampton McKenzie of Rowan.

9. Charles Wadsworth, born 1843, married Nancy Wiseman.

Major Henry W. Connor, son of Capt. Charles and Ann (Epps) Connor, was born near Amelia Courthouse in Prince George County, Va., August 5, 1793, moved with his parents to Mecklenburg County, N. C., about 1800, was educated at University of South Carolina and graduated in 1810. He was commissioned by Gov. Hawkins as Major and served on the staff of

Gen. Joseph Graham on the expedition against the Creek Indians in Alabama in 1814. He then settled in Lincoln County where he had large landed interests.

He represented the Lincoln district in the United States Congress for twenty years, from 1821 to 1841, when he declined to serve longer; was elected as one of the Councilors of State in 1842 and Senator from Lincoln in 1848.

The following excerpts from the address made by Major Connor in his campaign for re-election to Congress in 1839 show how the smoldering fires of anti-slavery sentiment were beginning to blaze in the North. Referring to it he said:

"Abolitionism, when I last addressed you seemed to be confined to a few fanatics only, and so absurd seemed their views and pretensions that serious apprehension could not reasonably be entertained, but such has been their rapid growth in a short time, that in several of the states they hold the balance of power in politics, and abolitionism has, therefore, become a political question with the avowed object of striking at the rights and property of the South, and there is reason to believe they will not be particular as to the mode of carrying out their plans, whether peacefully, or by wading through blood of men, women and children.

"The desks of abolition members (especially John Quincy Adams and Slade) are loaded with thousands of anti-slavery petitions which have been presented within the last two years, asking Congress to interfere with your rights and property. This heartless and unjustifiable policy must and will be met by the South at the proper time with manly determination to protect and defend our rights and privileges at all hazards.

"In Congress all that can be done has been done by resolutions which declare: 'that every petition, resolution or proposition touching or relating in any way to slavery be laid upon the table without debate or reference to any committee.' This is strong and indicates the feeling of the majority in Congress. I would myself prefer they should not be received at all but the scruples of many in regard to the right of petition have prevented such action."

On April 9, 1839, he was married in Washington to Mrs. Lucy (Hawkins) Coleman, a daughter of Gov. William Hawkins. The children were Chas. T. Connor, a Confederate Lieutenant, who was killed by Federal soldiers in Newton at the close of the Civil War in 1865; Ann Connor, who married J. M. Ivy of South Carolina, and Henry W. Connor, Jr., who died in Baltimore in 1873.

The elder son, Chas. T. Connor, married Mary, daughter of Hiram Sherrill, by whom he had three children, T. F. Connor, who now (1935) lives at Terrell, N. C., Luetta, who married Wm. L. Sherrill, and Charlie, who married Dr. W. B. Ramsay.

Major Connor was a handsome man of distinguished bearing and engaging manners. Col. John F. Hoke said he was the most popular man who ever lived in Lincoln County and a Democrat of the Nathaniel Macon type.

The late F. Brevard McDowell in *The Broad Axe and the Forge*, referring to Major Connor, wrote: "On one occasion two Whig farmers who had a business engagement found the Congressman sitting on his porch in shirt sleeves mending harness. His cordial manner and urgent invitation to dinner made his quondam opposers his warmest friends and when it was asserted on the hustings that Connor was an aristocrat and owner of one hundred slaves, the harness incident was effectively cited to prove that he was a plain man and a champion of the people."

He died at Beatties Ford, January 6, 1866, and the interment was in the family plot in Rehoboth Methodist church cemetery at Terrell on the Lincolnton-Mooresville highway.

Benjamin Withers was murdered near Beatties Ford in 1866 by a man named Owens, who was tried and convicted of first degree murder at Dallas Court and hanged in 1867. The attorneys for the defense were Zebulon B. Vance, William Lander and David Schenck, and the prosecuting attorneys were W. P. Bynum, the Solicitor, and Judge James W. Osborne.

The last speech Mr. Lander ever made before a jury was his defense of Owens.

William T. Thompson, a Lincolnton youth only 11 years old, was drowned June 11, 1866.

Mrs. Catherine Shipp, wife of Judge W. M. Shipp, died June 28, 1866, aged 41 years.

Dr. George M. Hoke, a young Lincolnton physician and son of the late Hon. Michael Hoke, died November 1, 1866.

James M. Bandy, 18 years of age, was married to Martha Leonard, November 4, 1866, by D. A. Haines, J. P.

Henderson Sherrill (1807-1866), a man of uncommon force and influence in Lincoln County for many years, was a son of Jeptha and Elizabeth (McCorkle) Sherrill. He lived near the present town of Catawba, had large landed interests and slaves, was active in politics and as a Democrat was representative in the House of Commons from Lincoln in 1850 and 1852, and from 1854 to 1858 from Catawba County.

He married Mahala Long, July 19, 1832, and reared a large family. Three of his sons, John, James H., and Walter L. Sherrill, were substantial citizens and lived in Catawba. Dr. Coite L. Sherrill, a skilled surgeon of Statesville, and the late Oscar Sherrill, prominent in Catawba County affairs, until his death in 1934, were his grandsons.

James Taylor Alexander (Feb. 20, 1794-March 14, 1866) was for many years a prominent citizen of Lincolnton and for a long period a Magistrate in Lincoln County, one of the charter members of the Lincolnton Masonic Lodge (No. 137) and a Ruling Elder in the Presbyterian church. His wife was Harriet Clark, of Greenville, S. C., who died April 13, 1869, aged 75 years.

Mr. Alexander was a harness maker by trade and followed that business to the end of his life. For a while his brother-in-law, Vardry McBee, was his partner in the business.

Among his children were:

(1) Wallace Henderson Alexander (Feb. 4, 1824-June 1, 1872), who married Mary Royal Robinson of Caswell County, who lived 24 years after the death of her husband. Their daughter, Ella, married to Chas. H. Motz.

(2) Elias James Alexander (May 2, 1829-October, 1865) married Barbara L., daughter of Peter Summey. She died in 1895, aged 62 years. Summey Alexander, is a son of this couple. He is now an elderly man and fine citizen of Lincolnton (1935).

This Alexander family has an interesting background. Elias Alexander I. lived in Maryland and died there in 1747. His wife was Anna Taylor, who died in Mecklenburg in 1800. Elias Alexander II., a son of this couple, was born in Maryland in 1746. He came to Mecklenburg County, North Carolina, with other Alexanders and settled in the Sugar Creek settlement a few miles north of Charlotte. He later moved to Rutherford County, was a valiant soldier of the Revolution and fought at Kings Mountain and Guilford Court House. His wife, Agnes Alexander, died in 1826, and Col. Elias Alexander died in Rutherford County, May 13, 1818. His eleven children were:

(1) Francis Alexander (1778-1852) was county surveyor for Rutherford County, 1797 to 1845. His daughter, Jane McBee, married Francis S. Coxe, of Philadelphia, April 24, 1823. They were the parents of the late Col. Frank Coxe, of Asheville.

Margaret Rebecca, another daughter of Francis Alexander, married to Rev. Campbell Smith, of the South Carolina Methodist Conference and among their children were the late Dr. Thos. C. Smith, of Asheville, the late Joseph C. Smith, of Shelby, and Stephen O. Smith and Mrs. W. C. Abernethy who now live (1935) in Gastonia. Ross Alexander, Jr., son of Francis Alexander, married Charlotte Hill, and the late J. F. Alexander, prominent lumberman and textile manufacturer of Forest City, and A. C. Alexander, now of Georgia, were sons of this couple.

(2) Major Ross Alexander, Sr., son of Elias Alexander II., was thrown from a mule and killed July 4, 1849. The inscription on a granite marker near Hazelhurst Farm, three miles south of Forest City, bears the inscription: "In memory of Ross Alexander, born February 29, 178.... (chipped off.) He was thrown from a mule against an oak tree on this spot and killed July 6, 1849. He was district surveyor for many years. He left a wife and six children. Erected by E. Ross Doggett, a grandson."

(3) Anna, daughter of Elias Alexander II., married to Stephen Camp.

(4) Jane, daughter of Elias Alexander II., married to Vardry McBee, and they were the ancestors of all the McBee family of Lincolnton.

(5) Margaret, daughter of Elias Alexander II., married to Col. David Reinhardt.

(6) Patsy Blanton, daughter of Elias Alexander II., married Jacob Fisher.

(7) William, son of Elias Alexander II., died in 1821, as evidenced by his will which was executed September 4,

1821, and probated in October, 1821, witnessed by his brothers, Elias III. and James Taylor Alexander.

(8) Elias III., son of Elias Alexander II., was prominent in Rutherford and was Senator from that county in 1823. He was living in Greenville, S. C., in 1875.

(9) James Taylor Alexander, another son of Elias II., has already been referred to.

(10) and (11) Two other sons, Thomas and Alston Alexander, died young.

Col. Alexander had deep convictions and was an uncompromising Revolutionary Whig, with a fine sense of humor. His great grandson, the late Col. Frank Coxe, of Asheville, records the story that Col. Alexander was once invited to Bush Doggett's for breakfast and when he arrived he found the lady of the house in very fine humor, which he knew was a very uncommon thing, but as he was to breakfast with them she could not be otherwise, so at the table he was asked to say Grace and he responded as follows:

"God be praised when woman's pleased
For 'tis but now and then.
We will eat our diet in peace and quiet,
In the name of God.—Amen."

The Alexanders were not friendly to William Green because of his record as a Tory, but Clarence Griffin, the Rutherford County historian, says "Green had been forced by circumstances beyond his control to accept a commission as Major in Ferguson's Army and commanded a company of Loyalists at Kings Mountain.

Despite this fact he later was so popular that he was chosen State Senator for Rutherford for fifteen terms, but finally Elias Alexander laid plans for his defeat as evidenced by the following story:

In Schenck's *History of North Carolina*, 1780-81, page 151, is the following:

I find in the *North State* (a Greensboro newspaper) the following anecdote of Elias Alexander which is worth preserving for its humor and to illustrate the feeling that continued after the war was over:

"Elias Alexander, of Rutherford County, was an old Revolutionary Whig, who fought at Kings Mountain, and years afterward, with twenty-seven British and Tory buckshot in his body. Old Major Green, of the same county, was a Tory, and was in the Battle of Kings Mountain on the Tory side. After the war Green was several times elected to the State Senate from Rutherford County, and seemed invincible. In 1823 Alexander determined to have Green beaten and brought out his son as a candidate against him.

"Green became apprehensive of defeat and concluded that something must be done. He fell upon the idea of joining the Baptist church, and in carrying out the project was immersed in the French Broad River. Alexander, somewhat discouraged at this turn but nothing daunted, went to witness the ceremony. Leaning against an old tree on the bank of the river within speaking distance of the scene, he silently and doubtingly watched the process of regeneration.

"Everybody expected some kind of a declaration from him before the crowd dispersed. Just as Green was raised out of the water, wet as a rat and gasping for breath, Alexander, who was very tall and towered above the bystanders, slowly raised his hand and pointed at him, at the same time saying in a loud and measured tone:

'There stands old Major Green, now neat and clean,
Though formerly a Tory,
The darndest rascal that ever was seen,
Now on his way to glory.'

"This furnished a campaign song and worked an overwhelming defeat of Green at the polls."

The following in memory of Col. Elias Alexander, was written by Hon. Joseph McDowell Carson:

"Thou that hither may'st chance to wander
Here lies the dust of Elias Alexander,
For independence in that fearful strife
He pledged his all, his honor and his life.

The great boon obtained, would have no less,
Retiring, dwelt in a wilderness;
The waste of war, by diligence retrieved
And greatly independent lived.

Calm as a Franklin or great Socrates,
Marked out his grave mid these lofty trees;
Green be their leaves, may they ever bloom
And wave their freshness o'er the patriot's tomb.
That independence he thought so dear
Oh! guard his heritage and his name revere."

Green River, Rutherford County, N. C.

Other Alexanders who figured prominently in the early history of Lincoln County, though not closely related to those of Rutherford, were:

Wallace Alexander, Senator from Lincoln for four terms, 1796-7-8-9; lived in Lincolnton and married Ann Dobson, daughter of Captain Dobson who was killed in the Battle of Romsour's Mill and buried there. They had two children:

(1) Lawson Henderson Alexander, who married his cousin, Jane, daughter of McK. Alexander.

(2) Sarah Caroline, who married her cousin, Nathaniel, a son of McK. Alexander.

Wallace Alexander had a brother, William, who was the father of the brilliant lawyer, William Julius Alexander (grandfather of Judge William Alexander Hoke). (See 1905.)

He was also closely related to Nathaniel Alexander, who represented Lincoln in the House of Commons in 1792 and 1793.

1867
LINCOLNTON IN 1867

County Officers

County Attorney, L. E. Thompson; Clerk County Court, W. R. Clark; Clerk Superior Court, S. P. Sherrill; Clerk and Master in Equity, W. J. Hoke; Chairman of County Court, Henry Cansler; Coroner, John F. Speck; Register, Peter A. Summey; Treas. Wardens and Treas. Public Buildings, R. H. Abernethy; Wardens of the Poor, William Tiddy, Abner McCoy, John Asbury, James Seagle and Philip W. Carpenter; Sheriff, L. H. Lowrance; Deputy and Jailer, John P. Anthony; Deputy Sheriffs, Stanly Baites, John McIntosh and Daniel Goodson; Surveyor, John B. Smith; Standard Keeper, S. W. Stubbs; Trustee, W. H. Michal.

Town Officials

Mayor, V. A. McBee; Town Clerk, W. J. Hoke; Constable, Henry W. Morton; Treasurer, John P. Anthony; Sexton, Jacob Bisaner; Commissioners, C. C. Henderson, Dr. Elam Caldwell, B. H. Sumner, P. A. Summey, S. P. Sherrill, A. A. McLean, William Lander, Dr. M. L. Brown.

Schools

Pleasant Retreat, Rev. W. R. Wetmore; Lincolnton Seminary (Female Department) Mrs. T. W. Brevard, in North State Hotel;

THE ANNALS OF LINCOLN COUNTY 195

(Male Department) Judge T. W. Brevard; Female Seminary, Miss Mary Wood Alexander; Episcopal Parochial School, Miss Kate Heidick; Colored School, N. W. Hill.

Ministers

Lutheran, Rev. Dr. A. J. Fox and Rev. Luther Fox; Presbyterian, Dr. R. H. Morrison, Rev. R. N. Davis and Rev. J. S. Barr; Episcopal, Rev. W. R. Wetmore; Baptist, Rev. L. M. Berry; Methodist, Rev. John Finger, Rev. John Watts, Rev. Henry Asbury; German Reformed, Jeremiah Ingold; Northern Methodists, Rev. T. H. Postelle, Rev. S. Matton, Rev. John Ballard, Rev. J. A. Huggins, Rev. John T. Miller; Methodist Protestant, Rev. Parson Naylor. Colored: Isaac Cansler, Baptist; George McLean and Anderson Hoke, Methodist.

Lawyers

W. P. Bynum, Alex F. Brevard, B. S. Guion, John F. Hoke, A. B. Howard, William Lander, Samuel Lander, Jr., V. A. McBee, W. M. Shipp, David Schenck, Bartlett Shipp, L. E. Thompson and T. W. Brevard.

Merchants

R. H. Abernethy, J. L. Alexander, Lawing & Means, Druggists, Borders & Homesley, E. Childs, J. C. Cobb, A. S. Haynes, C. C. Henderson, J. C. Jenkins, W. H. Michal, Stowe & Leecraft, S. P. Sherill, J. F. Speck, of Lincolnton, Culp & Caldwell, and Ivey & Goodson, Beatties Ford, J. M. Kidd, Dry Pond, D. A. Lowe, Lowesville.

Wood Carving: O. B. Jenks; Pottery: Daniel Hartsog, Seagle & Goodman; Cotton Factory: Phifer & Allison; Chair Factory: J. H. Marsh; Paper Mills: Wiswall & Tiddy, Grady Banister & Co.; Iron Works: J. W. Derr, J. M. Smith, Samuel R. Oats, Shipp & Reinhardt (F. M.), A. F. & R. A. Brevard & Alex Goodson; Hatters: William Cline; Carriage Shops: Abner McCoy & J. L. Wilkey; Cabinet Shops: Warren Gheen and A. P. James; Blacksmiths: John Detter, J. Bisaner, Alfred Slade (colored).

Carpenters: E. H. Cauble, H. W. Abernethy, Thomas Wells.

Shoemakers: Harrison Wilson, Elcanah Hartzoag, William Hinson, Alex Schenck (colored).

Photographers: J. B. Martin.

Tanneries: H. F. Ramsour, H. E. and E. F. Ramsour, Daniel Finger, D. F. Beam, L. H. Hill, C. C. Henderson, D. A. Lowe, R. E. Burch.

Gold Mines owned by J. F. Hoke, W. J. Hoke, Daniel Seagle, Henry Cansler, B. S. Johnson, Dr. Pollock, Lewis Keener, Joseph Stone, Lawson Keener, C. Beal and Elizabeth Buxton.

Flour and Corn Mills: Green Abernethy, Thomas Bess, Grady Banister & Co., J. M. D. Bollinger, A. F. and R. A. Brevard, Henry Cansler, Mary A. Beam, David Crouse, D. Dellinger, J. W. Derr, T. J. Ramsour, Michael Finger, Joseph Houser, J. F. Reinhardt, G. W. Hull, Dr. C. L. Hunter, J. H. Killian, F. M. Reinhardt, J. M. Smith, Maxwell Warlick.

Hotels: B. S. Johnson, L. H. Kistler.

Physicians: J. M. Abernethy, M. L. Brown, L. D. Black, E. A. Brevard, Elam Caldwell, Eli Crowell, J. M. Lawing, T. H. Means, W. B. McLean, J. M. Richardson, J. C. Rudisill, W. A. Thompson, G. W. Wacaser.

Lincolnton Postmistress: Mrs. Harriet E. Bomar.
Killians Mills Postmaster: Ulysses Alexander.
North Brook Postmaster: O. B. Jenks.
U. S. Gauger and Brander: Allen Alexander.
Express Agent: W. H. Alexander.
Rail Road: B. S. Guion, Supt.; V. A. McBee, Treas.; J. G. Justice, Agent; A. S. Haynes, Agent at Iron Station.

Rev. Samuel Lander, who had been principal of the Lincolnton Seminary and pastor of the Methodist church for several years, was elected President of Davenport College in Lenoir, in 1867.

1868

Prior to 1868, we had no penitentiary and criminals were publicly flogged at the whipping post for minor crimes; branded with hot iron for horse stealing, robbery or murder in the second degree and hanged for capital crimes. I never saw one flogged at the whipping post but have seen multitudes rushing to the old jail to see a poor fellow publicly receive 40 stripes save one. It was in 1926 that Mr. F. A. Propst of Indiana, visited Lincolnton and in a reminiscent mood told how things were in 1867 before he went West some 55 years before. He said that everything about Lincolnton now looked new as compared with the

THE ANNALS OF LINCOLN COUNTY 197

long ago, except the old jail, which looked the same, save that the whipping post had been removed. He said that he and his brother, John Propst came from Newton to witness the public flogging of a negro, under the direction of the law, in 1867. The changes made in our organic law in 1868 abolished imprisonment for debt, public flogging and branding with a hot iron, and established instead the State prison for felons.

A Constitutional Convention was held in the spring of 1868, and the new Constitution was adopted by vote of the people. J. H. King was the delegate from Lincoln. In April, W. W. Holden was elected Governor. In the November election General U. S. Grant carried the State over Horatio Seymour for the Presidency.

In 1868 the old County Court system was abolished and County Commissioners were provided to attend to the County business. The first Board elected in 1868 was composed of J. H. Marsh, Chairman, J. H. King, James Mullen, O. B. Jenks and Henry Rhodes.

When Sheriff L. H. Lowrance died in September, 1868, the Commissioners elected J. H. King Sheriff, and R. N. Hager was appointed Commissioner to succeed Sheriff King.

Lawson H. Kistler, son of Paul Kistler, a substantial citizen, died September 22, 1868, aged 50.

On December 25, 1868, Mr. and Mrs. David A. Coon, received a fine Christmas present in the person of a baby boy, whom they named Charles Lee Coon. They little dreamed that he would in the coming years grow into an educator and author of note. He is one of the finest products of Lincoln County.

The daily wage for a common laborer in 1868 was fifty cents and board. If the worker preferred to prepare his own meals the employer would furnish him with the following diet per week: one peck meal, 4 pounds bacon and one quart molasses. One who boarded himself received seventy-five cents per day. Ordinary wages per month were about ten dollars and board.

William Lander, eldest son of Rev. Samuel and Eliza Ann (Miller) Lander was born in County Tipperary, Ireland, May 8, 1817; came with his parents to America in 1818 and to Lincolnton about 1826. He was educated at the Lincolnton Academy and at Cokesbury College, S. C.; read law under Col. James R.

Dodge, then of Lincolnton, and was admitted to the bar in 1839. He was soon elected County solicitor, distinguished himself at the start as a prosecutor and built up a large law practice. He was a member of the House of Commons in 1852; in 1853 was elected State Solicitor and held that office until 1862, when he resigned, having been elected to the Confederate Congress.

He was the spokesman of the North Carolina delegation to the Democratic National Convention at Baltimore in 1860, and when it appeared that the demands of the South were imperilled, he said:

> "Mr. Chairman: Painful as the duty is, yet nevertheless it is my duty as one of the representatives from the good State of North Carolina, call her Rip Van Winkle if you will, to say that a very large majority of our delegation is compelled to retire permanently from this convention on account as we conceive of the unjust course that has been pursued toward some of our fellow citizens of the South. The South has heretofore relied upon the Northern Democracy to give us the rights which are justly due us, but the vote today has satisfied the majority of the North Carolina delegation that these rights are now refused, and this being the case, we can no longer remain in this convention."

Most of the Southern delegates, with those from California and Oregon, withdrew from the convention, joined by Caleb Cushing, the Chairman, and B. F. Butler, both of Massachusetts, and nominated Breckinridge for President, and this party split made possible the election of Lincoln.

Two weeks before the Presidential election of 1860, according to the Charlotte Democrat, Zebulon Vance, the young lion of the mountains, and Mr. Lander met in Newton in joint discussion of the issues of those troublous times. Vance supported Bell and Everett and opened the discussion with a two-hour speech, in which his points were clinched with anecdotes. He stood for the Union and assailed the Democrats for their rebellious spirit. He eulogized Jackson for his stand against nullification and pleased his Whig friends with his powerful argument.

When Mr. Lander arose to reply he was greeted with prolonged applause, and then in most withering style he exposed the weakness of the Bell party, the inconsistency of Mr. Bell on the Nebraska bill, and his anti-Southern record; and the subterfuge on which he relied for a platform was held up in contempt to his audience. He gravely depicted the crises of the country and deprecated the use of ridicule and comedy at a time like this, when men should be seriously considering the safety of their homes and firesides. He told his fellow Democrats "to beware of Whigs who praised dead Democrats." He did not think the election of Lincoln would in itself be cause of secession, but it was impossible to foresee the conditions which might surround that event, and held himself ready to cast his lot with North Carolina, whatever it might be.

The debate was a contest of giants. The Whigs were satisfied with the argument of their great champion, while the Democrats, who were largely in the majority, thought that Lander won the day.

In 1861 Mr. Lander was the delegate from Lincoln to the Constitutional Convention and signed the Secession Ordinance. Dr. Kemp P. Battle, writing of the record of the Lincoln delegate to that convention, said:

"I belonged to the Graham-Badger party, while Mr. Lander was classed with the original Secessionists, but I regarded him as a very able, honorable, courteous, high-minded man, and he was considered one of the best members of that very able body."

He resigned before the Convention finally adjourned, when he was elected to Congress and David Schenck succeeded him as the convention delegate from Lincoln County.

He was a constant student, delved deep into the law and into classical literature, history, poetry, science and philosophy; was a Shakespearian scholar and a diligent student of the Bible. He could scan a book at one sitting, gather all the salient points, never forget a date or an incident, and possessed the rare faculty of commanding any fact stored in memory just when he needed it. His verbal memory was wonderful and made him ready and accurate in quotation in his extemporaneous speaking.

As State Solicitor in the noted Langford murder trial, he examined 150 witnesses, made no note of testimony, but in an all day speech to the jury marshalled every particle of the salient evidence and convicted the criminal, who on the scaffold said that Mr. Lander in his speech before the jury had described in his imagination the scene and circumstances of the murder as vividly and accurately as if he had been present and witnessed the deed.

His former law partner, the late Judge David Schenck said:

"I have traveled all over North Carolina and listened to all her great lawyers and orators and never heard one who was the equal of William Lander before a jury."

On another occasion Judge Schenck said:

"He was a brilliant, impetuous, chivalrous and noble gentleman, who passed by the stately honors of the judgeship that he might enjoy the more splendid triumphs of the forum, and whose brilliant eloquence found congenial fellowship amid the fiery spirits of the Confederate Congress."

William J. Yates, Editor of the *Charlotte Democrat*, in reporting the speech of Mr. Lander in Charlotte during the Congressional campaign of 1864 stated:

"Though we have not taken and may not take an active part in the present canvass, we will say that as an honest and conscientious public man William Lander has no superior. Unimpeachable in his private and public life, industrious and energetic, he merits the confidence of the people. Less than this we could not say—more is unnecessary."

He was a friend of Education and Trustee of the State University from 1859 to 1867.

On his 22nd birthday, May 8, 1839, he married Sarah Connor, daughter of Dr. Francis Connor of Cokesbury, S. C., and they reared a large family, among whom were Samuel Lander III., who married Alice Jenkins, Agnes, who married Dr. J. M. Lawing, Frank, who married Lou Templeton, all of Lincolnton; and Ella, who married Dr. LeGree Connor of South Carolina.

Mr. Lander died Jan. 8, 1868, and was buried in the family plot in the Methodist graveyard in Lincolnton.

1869

There was a total eclipse of the sun in August, 1869, visible in Lincolnton. It was dark for two hours.

The first District Conference of the Methodist church ever held in Lincolnton met in August, 1869. Bishop Doggett was present and preached a great sermon.

Rev. Thomas S. W. Mott died in Catawba County, August 30, 1869, and the body was buried in St. Luke's (Episcopal) graveyard, in Lincolnton. He was twice Rector of Saint Luke's Church. He was born at Preston, Nova Scotia, July 28, 1800.

He was the father of Dr. J. J. Mott, Dr. Walter B. Mott and Dr. Henry Y. Mott, all of whom lived and died in Iredell County.

In September, 1869, Prof. Hosea Hildreth Smith, one time Professor of Modern Languages at the University, and Rev. W. R. Wetmore, the Episcopal minister, opened a school of high grade in the Male Academy. They were both fine teachers and drew students from several states. This school was conducted for several years and many who were students there became distinguished.

Franklin M. Reinhardt, son of Christian Reinhardt, Jr., and Mary (Forney) Reinhardt, was an enterprising citizen. He and his kinsman Bartlett Shipp, for long years manufactured iron at the Reinhardt furnace. He married Sarah, daughter of David Smith and reared a large family. Among his children were J. F., called "Jack" Reinhardt, J. Ed., Forney, Ephraim and Robert S. Reinhardt, all of whom were influential men. One daughter, Mary, married M. T. Boyd, and they were the grandparents of Miss Maude Mullen of the *Lincoln Times*. F. M. Reinhardt died June 12, 1869, aged 62.

Bartlett Shipp was the first of the name to live in Lincoln County. He was born in Stokes County, March 8, 1786, son of Thomas and Hannah Joyce Shipp. His father, a soldier of the Revolution, was at Yorktown with Washington in 1781.

Joseph Wilson, a distinguished son of Stokes, came to Charlotte to practice law and young Shipp came with Wilson, read law under him and was a tutor at the same time in the Wilson family. Prior to this, Bartlett Shipp was a soldier of the War of 1812.

Mr. Wilson was for long years the State Solicitor and was a vigorous prosecutor of counterfeiters and other law breakers, some of whom threatened him with violence. Riding over a lonely road on the way to court one day Shipp asked Wilson to swap hats with him, fearing the white hat worn by Wilson might be too good a target for a sharpshooter. He made the suggestion to protect Mr. Wilson. When Wilson intimated that it would be a risk for the young man, Mr. Shipp, who was afraid of no man, replied: "I reckon he would look under the hat before shooting."

Mr. Shipp made a visit to Lincoln County and to the home of Gen. Peter Forney. There he met Susan Forney, to whom he was married on Dec. 15, 1818, by Rev. Robert Johnston Miller. Soon thereafter he bought the home of his brother-in-law, Jacob Forney, and lived on that plantation until 1869, when the family moved to Lincolnton.

He possessed superior intellect, was well educated and a profound student of the law and for many years had a large and lucrative practice in all the counties from Mecklenburg to the mountains. He was a logical and convincing speaker and had a wide reputation as a trial lawyer. He possessed keen wit and was brilliant in repartee.

He was interested in the Iron business with Franklin M. Reinhardt at what was Reinhardt's furnace and also at High Shoals with the Fulenwiders, Hoyles and Burtons.

He represented the County in the House of Commons in 1824, 1826 and 1828-30 (5 terms) and in the Senate in 1834; he and Henry Cansler were the delegates from Lincoln to the Constitutional Convention of 1835.

When 83 years old he died in Lincolnton, May 26, 1869, and the body was interred in the Episcopal graveyard.

His children were: 1. Judge William M. Shipp; 2. Eliza, who married to Judge W. P. Bynum; 3. Susan, who married to Capt. V. Q. Johnson, for many years Superintendent of the Carolina Central Railroad, now a part of the Seaboard system.

At four o'clock on Tuesday morning, Aug. 24, 1869, Robert B. Babington was born at Rehoboth Furnace about seven miles east of Lincolnton, where his father, Elisha B. Babington and his grandfather, Benjamin B. Babington, were employed during the Civil War and until about 1871 or 1872.

His mother was Isabella Haynes, born March 26, 1850, daughter of Robert G. Haynes (born 1806) and Elizabeth (Carpenter) Haynes (born 1808). She had five brothers in the Civil War, three of whom were killed in action. The other two were John Haynes and Captain Albert Sidney Haynes, one time sheriff of Lincoln County.

Robert Babington attended country schools and when seventeen years old studied telegraphy and worked at Mount Holly as operator for the Seaboard Railway.

His first wife was Buenavista Biggerstaff. His second wife, who still survives, and to whom he married in 1898, was Hattie

McLurd, of Stanley. Since 1899 he had been the manager of the Gastonia Telephone Company and active in many Gastonia enterprises. He, with the late Col. C. B. Armstrong, erected the Armington Hotel in Gastonia. He was a progressive, public-spirited citizen, an enthusiastic Mason and a devout Methodist, serving for more than thirty years as an official of Main Street church in Gastonia. He was much beloved, fond of little children, and gave more of his thought and time for the past twenty-five years to the betterment of unfortunate and crippled children than to anything else. His greatest accomplishment in life was not business success, but philanthropic service in behalf of distressed children. He told me that he had a vision or dream one night in March, 1909, of a hospital for crippled and deformed children, and the next day resolved to labor steadily for the fulfillment of that dream. Year after year he came to the Methodist Conference and saw to it that a resolution was passed urging the establishment of an Orthopedic Hospital for deformed children in North Carolina. Likewise he attended the State meetings of other denominations, Synods and Conventions, and secured approval of the idea from the Baptists, Lutherans, Episcopalians, Presbyterians, and others. Favorable sentiment was thus slowly developing. For eight years he attended sessions of the Legislature and begged the representatives to make an appropriation for the hospital for the deformed children of the state. The Committees gave him only brief time to plead his cause and sent him away, because, they said, there was no available money for the project. Year after year he returned in the spirit of Dorothea L. Dix (the mother of hospitals for the insane of America) who spent the winter of 1848 in Raleigh, pleading for a hospital for the insane of the State, before representatives inclined to place economy before mercy, but who, despite discouraging conditions, finally succeeded in the accomplishment of the noble purpose. So Robert B. Babington, with the need of poor helpless children heavy on his heart, finally overcame the opposition, and the Legislature of 1917 appropriated the first small sum of $40,000, on condition that some town would donate a like amount. Back to his home in Gastonia he hastened and succeeded in raising the additional $40,000, and then donated the land upon which the hospital was located, now known as Babington Heights.

The institution, with sixty beds, was opened in July, 1921, and steadily the work has grown until now the bed capacity is one hundred and sixty. The building and grounds are now valued at about $500,000, and during the fourteen years since it was established the hospital has returned to their several communities thirty-five hundred children cured of their infirmities and fitted for the tasks of life. They came there deformed and suffering, without much hope of cure, but they went away with bodies restored and with lofty ambition to make the most of life. When the trustees first organized, very properly Mr. Babington was made President of the Board and continued such until his death.

He was the friend of all men and I appreciated his friendship. For years past when we met I greeted him with the question, "Is your monument still growing?" It was a monument to his faith, and prayers and labors. He gave the best of his life to the building of that monument, never dreaming that any one really so regarded it.

Almost suddenly on November 28, 1935, this good man was mortally stricken and all who knew him mourned. A great multitude attended the funeral and his body was laid to rest under the shadow of the great monument which he builded. Through the decades and centuries let us hope this monument may continue to grow in size and in service and stand as a sentinel over the grave of its builder. A life spent so unselfishly for human betterment will not be forgotten, but memories of his service will be treasured gratefully by the thousands of crippled children who have reaped the benefits of his labors, and by the thousands unborn, who will be the inheritors of his sacrifice. The whole state mourns the loss of this noble benefactor and the people of his native county are doubly proud of his splendid record, because in the early dawn of an August day in 1869 he first looked out upon the world from a Lincoln County cradle. As his mother then beheld him with hopeful pride she hardly dreamed that some day he would be a Good Samaritan, bringing comfort and strength to helpless childhood.

He left the world better than he found it.

The Memorial marker to his grave in front of the North Carolina Orthopedic Hospital in Gastonia, N. C., bears the inscription:

"Robert B. Babington, August 24, 1869-Nov. 28, 1935. The ,North Carolina Orthopedic Hospital is his monument. Its need was revealed to him by God. Wherefore he was not disobedient to the heavenly vision. His zeal and perseverance made it a reality."

CHAPTER XV

1870-1879

The Federal Census Taker for Lincoln County in 1870 was Captain B. F. Grigg.

C. C. Henderson, son of Major Lawson Henderson, was born at the family homestead two miles west of Lincolnton, educated in local schools, and was a lifelong citizen of the town. He was at one time perhaps the principal merchant in Western Carolina and owned a large tannery, the product of which was manufactured into shoes and harness. His business judgment was far-seeing.

In the 1850's he bought about 20,000 acres of Texas land at 15 cents per acre, and this brought a large profit to his descendants. He was a large contractor in the construction of the railroad from Columbia to Charlotte which was the first railroad to enter that town. He was public-spirited and one of the active promoters of the old plank road from Charlotte to Lincolnton and a large subscriber to stock in the old W. C. and R. Railroad.

He reared a large family and among his descendants were Theodorus H. Cobb, Chas C. Cobb and John D. Shaw, 2nd and 3rd, and Angus Clifton Shaw, all of whom were lawyers of ability.

He died in Lincolnton, June 25, 1870, aged 69. His body sleeps in Old White Church graveyard.

The children of C. C. Henderson were:

Annie E., who never married.

Lawson P., married Willie Caldwell of Burke.

Barbara M., married (1) B. Y. Cobb, (2) S. P. Sherrill.

Margaret B., married Major John D. Shaw.

Theodora, married Robert Sowers.

Mary Helen, married Laban A. Hoyle.

Frances E., married George L. Davis.

Chas. C., who went West, never married.

Top: View of Court House from West Main Street, 1870.
Center: View of Court House from South Aspen Street, 1910.
Lower: View of new Court House from East Main Street, 1930.

Judge William M. Shipp was elected Attorney General of the State in the August election, over Samuel F. Phillips.

Major Henry W. Burton married to Mrs. Sarah (Hoyle) Keenan, October 5, 1870. It is said that he courted her before she first married to Martin Phifer; courted her again after Phifer died, but she married Mr. Keenan; and when Keenan died, still faithful, he courted and married her at last in 1870.

General Robert E. Lee died at Lexington, Virginia, October 12, 1870.

The Northern Methodist Conference was held in the Court House. Bishop Matthew Simpson, a great pulpit orator, presided. He was a guest in the home of Mr. J. C. Jenkins, a prominent member of the Lincolnton Methodist Church, and the Bishop preached to a capacity congregation in the Methodist Church on Sunday.

Col. John F. Hoke was present and heard the sermon. The next day my father asked Col. Hoke what he thought of the sermon, and he replied: "Sherrill, that was preaching, for it moved me and it takes preaching to do that."

Zebulon B. Vance was elected United States Senator to succeed Joseph C. Abbott, but was ineligible because his political disabilities had not been removed. Then Gen. M. W. Ransom was elected and took his seat in the Senate, March 4, and served four terms until March 4, 1895.

Henry Cansler was one of the most useful and influential citizens of Lincoln County in his day.

His grandfather was Philip W. Cansler, the pioneer, a man of rare sense, business judgment and frugality. Philip's wife was Barbara Rudisill and they were the ancestors of all the Canslers of this section. (See 1804.)

Philip Cansler, son of the pioneer, married to Mary Quickel, June 12, 1790, and died about 1840, aged 71.

Henry Cansler, the son of Philip and Mary Quickel Cansler, married to Fanny, daughter of Jacob and Margaret Hoyle Shuford, June 13, 1822, and they reared a large family, all of whom have died.

Henry Cansler was a large landowner and slaveholder, prominent in the public life of the County. He was Sheriff of the County, 1826-1829; Clerk of the County Court from 1837 to 1844; County Surveyor, and Chairman of the County Court. He represented Lincoln in the House of Commons for (1831 to 1836) six terms, and a 7th term in 1854, when he made a brilliant canvass against Know Nothingism. He was also a delegate from Lincoln to the Constitutional Convention of 1835, along with Bartlett Shipp. He possessed a clear and penetrating mind, was able in debate and a speaker of uncommon force and conviction.

I remember seeing him as an old feeble man, riding horseback down the street, seemingly 80 years of age, about 1870, and think he died that year, sixty-five years ago. His body is buried in the Cansler graveyard not far from the old Cansler home which is now occupied by W. E. Grigg. His tombstone is broken, the inscription illegible, and it seems difficult to secure the date of his birth or death. In his palmy days he was a mighty man and his record deserves prominent place in the history of the County. Not many Lincoln people to-day are familiar with the history of this notable citizen.

Children of Henry Cansler were:

1. Adolphus P., legislator from Lincoln, 1856, born April 29, 1823, married Adelaide M. Conley, moved to Mississippi.

2. Alex. Jacob, born May 26, 1825, married Mary A. Marshall of Wilkes County. He was a Baptist minister and moved to Arkansas late in life and died there in 1872.

3. William H., born July 26, 1827, married Mary J. Morrow of Missouri.

4. Abel T., born October 22, 1829, married Nancy McNeely of Iredell County, moved to Texas and died there in 1879.

5. George W., born October 29, 1831, married Jane E. Long of Catawba, died 1896.

6. John P., born February 4, 1834, married Kate Murphy of McDowell County, October 24, 1854. Their son, Edwin T. Cansler, is one of the great lawyers of North Carolina, an extraordinary trial lawyer and advocate before a jury. When a young man he began the practice of law in Charlotte as the junior partner of the law firm of Burwell, Walker and Cansler. (Burwell and Walker were both later Associate Justices of the State

Supreme Court.) Mr. Cansler has never sought public office, having concentrated all his time upon his large law practice.

7. Barbara, born July 13, 1836, married H. Fite of Gaston County in 1861, died May 6, 1896.

8. Fanny J., born November 30, 1838, married Dr. L. N. Durham, May 30, 1859. They lived in Asheville, N. C.

9. Daniel, born October 4, 1841, died February 18, 1853.

10. Thomas J., born August 13, 1843, died February 7, 1863, in hospital in Richmond, Va., a soldier in Civil War.

11. Adelaide, born September 19, 1845, married William Cobb and moved to Jackson County, N. C.

Col. William J. Hoke died suddenly in Columbia, S. C., in 1870. He went into the Civil War as Captain of the Southern Stars and was promoted to the rank of Colonel. His wife was Georgiana T., daughter of Benjamin Sumner, the teacher. (See 1866.)

Their children were:

Michael; Thos. H., married Annie Michal; Mary, married George L. Bartlett; Georgiana, married R. H. Templeton; Lollie, married Rev. John Deaton, a Lutheran minister; Nancy, married Dr. Alex Ramsour; and Virginia, never married.

In 1870 the saloons were wide open in Lincolnton. On Saturdays the street behavior of drunken men made it necessary for the women to keep indoors. The police were defied by those who cared not for law. I have seen drunken men on mule back ride down the streets, pistol in hand, shooting and cursing. Temperance reform has made great progress since then.

The cows and hogs had right of way on the streets. No one questioned the old custom of free range for cattle.

When the farmers came to market and brought produce to sell or feed for the horses, it was not uncommon to see Mr. J. C. Cobb's black spotted cow or some other cow, with front feet in the wagon feasting upon what it could find, but when the farmer discovered what was taking place, he was in no mood to go to prayer meeting. Then Peter Summey's old black sow let the people know she had rights of her own, and most of those are now dead who saw that sow make for a young limb of the law, who ran up the old court house steps for safety, and seeing the sow "fast following after," took refuge in the upper court room. In those days there were hitching racks for horses with all day rights, and no policeman dared arrest for overtime parking.

1871

In the stormy days of Reconstruction from 1869 to 1871, a secret semi-political organization called the Ku-Klux-Klan operated in several Southern States and was strong in this part of our State. It was claimed by those in sympathy with it that its purpose was to punish those the courts did not or could not reach, and that it was not responsible for many acts of cruelty perpetrated by non-members in the name of the Klan. A terrible situation had arisen and the State seemed unequal to the task of preserving order so that the Federal Government through its courts took matters in hand and the Klan was suppressed.

Federal troops were stationed at various points to maintain order and a company of cavalry was sent to Lincolnton late in 1871. The North State Hotel was the barracks of Company C, 7th Cavalry, until late in 1872, when it was transferred to Charlotte. The Commander of this troop was Col. V. K. Hart, son-in-law of Senator Oliver P. Morton, of Indiana, who was the War Governor of that State. His grandson, Dr. V. K. Hart, is now (1934) a physician in Charlotte. Other officers were Lieut. James Calhoun, a handsome man and a fine horseman, related to the South Carolina Calhouns, and Lieut. Harrington. The orderly sergeant was named Edwin Bobo.

About 1875 these troops were transferred to the West and all but two of this Company were killed in the Custer massacre in the Black Hills of Dakota, by the Indians led by Sitting Bull, Chief of the Sioux Tribe, in 1876. Sergeant Bobo and every other member of his company were killed in that massacre except two men, one of whom was Daniel A. Kanipe, probably of Lincoln County, who, in about a year after that bloody battle, married to the widow of Sergeant Bobo. She was a daughter of Capt. William Wykoff, of Catawba County, a Confederate veteran, and she died May 25, 1934, in McDowell County, where she had lived for many years after the conflict. One son by the second marriage is J. Ed Kanipe, for some years a Federal Prohibition Officer in Western Carolina and stationed in Charlotte.

Rev. Robert N. Davis, after having served as pastor of the Presbyterian church in Lincolnton from 1850 to 1871, died April 24, 1871, and his body was buried in front of the old Presbyterian church on West Water Street; later when the church was sold and a new church built, the body was moved and now rests under the present church building on West Main Street.

Mrs. W. D. Lee, wife of Rev. Dr. W. D. Lee, pastor of the Methodist Church, died in Lincolnton, May 29, 1871.

Dr. Lee was father of Rev. William B. Lee, Methodist missionary in Brazil; Hon. T. Bailey Lee, Chief Justice of the Idaho Supreme Court; and Miss Bertha M. Lee, who was for many years teacher of German in the State Normal College at Greensboro, N. C.

At an election held in August, 1871, for or against a Constitutional Convention, Alfred J. Morrison was the Lincoln delegate elected over B. F. Grigg, the anti-convention candidate, but as the convention was defeated, he did not serve.

The Legislature brought impeachment charges against W. W. Holden, the Governor, and they were sustained by the required two-thirds majority and Lt. Governor Tod R. Caldwell, of Burke, succeeded to the Governorship.

From 1869 to 1872 Lincolnton was fortunate to have Prof. Hosea Hildreth Smith and Rev. W. R. Wetmore as co-principals of the Lincolnton Male Academy.

Prof. Smith, (See 1869) came to Newton from New Hampshire, was the first President of Catawba College and married in Lincolnton, May 19, 1853, to Mary Brent Hoke, daughter of the late Michael and Frances Burton Hoke. Later he served as a member of the University faculty at Chapel Hill until that institution was closed during the Civil War. He was a bright belles-lettres scholar and a teacher of rare accomplishments.

Dr. Wetmore was an alumnus of the State University and for a time a tutor in mathematics there. He then read law but abandoned it to become an Episcopal minister. In 1864 he became Rector of St. Luke's Episcopal Church in Lincolnton and continued in that relation for forty years until his death in March, 1904. He was a prodigy in mathematics and along with his church work was a busy teacher for many years. Mr. Wetmore, by his daily walk as a teacher in and out of the class room and as a churchman, exerted a fine influence for all the forty years he lived in Lincolnton. He stood for high educational and religious standards and will be long remembered as a noble gentleman, a patriotic citizen and a saintly minister. (See 1904.)

The school flourished under their management. Patronage came from neighboring counties and distant states. As I recall the boys of that early period, there were W. E. Beggs and Robert Bratton from Mississippi; Sandy Childs, Jr., and W. T. Spratt from South Carolina; Wm. D. P. King of Washington City; A. G. Smith, Stephen Smith, Walter Smith and Robert S. Wetmore of Alabama; Ed H. Bratton and W. A. Potts of Charlotte; Wm. W. Mott of Statesville; Charles W. Broadfoot and Lucien H. Holmes of Fayetteville; John C. Rankin and Robert Rutledge of Gaston.

Among the local students were John L. Cobb, Theodorus H. Cobb, Thomas Lee Cobb, Dr. Henry A. Costner, Robert S. Edwards, Capt. Charles E. Childs, Edward T. Childs, Michael Hoke, Thomas H. Hoke, William Alexander Hoke, James B. Heim, Frank Lander, John, Charles and Benjamin Motz, Carroll and Benjamin Leecraft, Dr. Sumner McBee, Silas McBee, Vardry McBee, William Pagenstacher, Forney Reinhardt, Robert S. Reinhardt, Thomas J. Ramsour, John and Charles Stubbs, Dodson R. Schenck, Hoke Smith, Burton Smith, Jacob, Charles and Jethro Sumner, William L. Sherrill, Charles Wilkes, James Jenkins, Edward Wilkes, Dr. J. M. Templeton, Alfred Thompson, David S. Jenkins.

It would be interesting to follow up the history of all these in their varied fields of endeavor.

Professor Smith was a good musician and the rule each day at the closing hour was to have a lesson in music. The old "Carmina Sacra," popular in those days, contained the old, familiar church hymns, and was used. The teacher, with tuning fork, marked time as he led the singing. The only song of lighter vein was the brief couplet:

> "Go to Jane Glover
> And tell her I love her,
> And by the light of the moon
> I will come to her."

Professor Smith was also an elocutionist and every Friday the boys had to declaim. *Comstock's Elocution* contained many patriotic speeches and classic poems, and the boys were taught intonation, emphasis, gesture and proper position on the platform. Alex Hoke got eloquent when he recited Tennyson's *Charge of the Light Brigade.* Addison G. Smith with dignity recited Scott's "Not far advanced was morning day, when Marmion did his troop array." Hoke Smith's favorite speech was "At midnight in his guarded tent, The Turk was dreaming of the hour, When Greece her knee in suppliance bent, Should tremble at his power." Silas McBee was a graceful speaker and once got the prize for oratory, while in another contest Theodorus H. Cobb won the prize, a handsome copy of Milton's poems.

As I recall the class roll of sixty-five years ago, nearly all have passed from the scene of action. Addison G. Smith, Vardry McBee, Edward T. Childs and the writer, I believe are the few still living. That was a great school. Out of it came some wonderfully brilliant men who never went to college but were educated, cultured and distinguished. Theodorus H. Cobb, William Alexander Hoke, Hoke Smith and Addison G. Smith were all great lawyers, and Silas McBee was a great layman of the Episcopal Church for many years, editor of *The Churchman,* a general organ of that denomination in America. Dr. Sumner McBee, Dr. J. M. Templeton, Capt. Charles E. Childs, Dr. H. A. Costner and others of that group proved to be worthy and notable products of Lincoln County.

1872

Rev. Dr. Needham B. Cobb, came to Lincolnton as pastor of the Baptist Church. His son Collier Cobb, then about ten years old, edited and published a little paper called the *Home Journal,* thus giving early promise of future usefulness. He was for many years Professor of Geology at our State University, and died November 28, 1934. (See 1934.)

The Legislature chosen in August assembled in November. The political disabilities of Governor Vance had been removed and the Democratic caucus nominated him for the United States Senate to succeed John Pool, Republican. There was a small but influential Democratic faction that supported A. S. Merrimon, who had been defeated for Governor in the August election by Gov. Tod R. Caldwell, Republican. This faction refused to abide by the action of the caucus and voted for Merrimon. Vance failed to receive the required majority. A deadlock followed, but it was finally broken when the Republicans threw their strength to Merrimon and he was elected and served from 1873 to 1879, when Vance finally was made Senator and served until his death in 1894.

Rev. R. Z. Johnston, accepted the call to the pastorate of the Lincolnton Presbyterian Church early in 1872.

Wallace H. Alexander, (son of J. Taylor Alexander), a well-known and prominent citizen of Lincolnton, died June 1, 1872, in his 48th year.

Rev. J. S. Barr, a Presbyterian minister, died at his home in Lincoln in 1872, aged 46 years.

It was a brilliant campaign waged between William Shipp Bynum, Republican, and Alfred J. Morrison, Democrat, for the Legislature in 1872. Morrison was elected, as the Democrats were in the majority, but he resigned in the middle of his term to pursue his studies preparatory to entering the Presbyterian ministry. Two years later Mr. Bynum abandoned the law to enter the ministry of the Episcopal church.

In the August election of 1872, Tod R. Caldwell was re-elected Governor, defeating Augustus S. Merrimon by 1,800 votes.

In November, Grant defeated Greeley for the Presidency, and carried North Carolina by 25,000 majority. William S. Bynum was the Grant elector from the 6th district.

William Alexander Hoke was granted license to practice law by the Supreme Court, on his 21st birthday, October 25, 1872.

1873

When the *Lincoln Courier*, edited by E. H. Britton, suspended publication about 1867, Lincoln County was without a newspaper until April, 1873, when the *Lincoln Progress* was established by Monroe Seagle and James H. Smith.

The South was doubly unfortunate when the financial panic of 1873 struck the country for we had, for full ten years before, passed through a terrible period of depression, during and after the Civil War, and the 1873 panic continued for almost six years, until the resumption of specie payments September 1, 1879. Money was scarce; there were but two banks in the State west of Charlotte; and living was so high that the family budget was hard to balance; but the people, forced to self-denial, generally lived on what they got and avoided debt as much as possible.

Phifer's Cotton Factory, Marsh's Chair Factory, Tiddy's Paper Mills, and Derr's Iron Furnace had small payrolls which added little to the buying power of the people. The only other sources of income were the limited cotton crop and the surplus flour ground at our local mills.

At that time there was not a mile of railroad west of Cherryville and Morganton, not a bath tub in this part of the State. Turner Bynum, a colored man, carried daily in one sack from the train to the post office all the mail that came to Lincolnton, and hardly a dozen daily papers came to this post office. Charles Roseman, the colored drayman, with one mule moved all the freight which came into and went out of town. One engine pulled all the traffic and freight from Charlotte to Cherryville and two engines drew the trains (one each way daily) from Salisbury to Morganton. We had slow transportation; the young men on Sunday afternoons took their sweethearts for a walk to Cansler's Spring and drank water out of the iron ladle which was securely chained to the overshadowing oak, and never dreamed of disease germs which the world was ignorant of in those days.

But the women were brave and self-denying. They inspired the men with courage to endure. The people were honest and industrious, intelligent and law abiding. They thought high thoughts while they lived the simple life. It was a long time until the inventor dreamed of telephones, electric lights, radios and aeroplanes. There were no paved streets or great public school buildings, but the homes were lighted by kerosene lamps and sometimes by tallow candles. The people were self-dependent and fought their way to a better day.

From *Progress,* May 17, 1873: Monroe Seagle, James H. Smith, proprietors.

Town Government: Dr. Robert J. Brevard, Mayor; Commissioners: Sumner McBee, William Thompson, F. A. Tobey, C. S. Rozzelle, Dr. H. A. Costner, W. J. Crowson, D. R. Hoover and George L. Bartlett; Clerk and Treasurer: James Jenkins; Marshal: Capt. M. I. Eudy.

County Government: Clerk Superior Court: S. P. Sherrill; Sheriff: J. A. Robinson; Register of Deeds: P. A. Summey; Treasurer: James C. Jenkins; Surveyor: D. D. Beam; Coroner: Peter S. Beal; Commissioners: W. A. Thompson, B. H. Sumner,

I. R. Self, L. S. Camp, Dr. C. L. Hunter; Magistrates: A. G. Harrell, M. L. Loftin, Robert Nixon, A. F. Barnett, Henry Houser, H. E. Ramsour, W. A. Thompson, J. A. Davis, B. F. Grigg, A. Alexander, J. L. Wilkey, J. G. Justice, Melchi Rhodes, Edward Beatty.

Lincolnton Markets: Saturday, May 17, 1873: Cotton, 10 to 16; corn, bu. 60; eggs, doz. 12½¢ to 15; hams (N. C.) 12½¢ to 15; liquor, N. C. corn, 1.50 to 2.00; apple brandy, 1.75.

2,700 Bar Rooms to be closed when the prohibitory liquor law goes into effect in Massachusetts.

The *Progress*, May 31, 1873: Regular services at Episcopal churches at and near Lincolnton, Rev. W. R. Wetmore, minister.

Advertisement: Wanted—A young gentleman, aged 23 years, of good moral habits, with black hair, black eyes, fair complected, 5 feet, 10 inches high, in moderate circumstances, wishes to correspond with a young lady of 18 summers, with bright blue eyes, light hair and medium height, with a view to matrimony. Address, Latta, Lincolnton, N. C.

Advertisement: John D. Shaw, Attorney-at-Law; J. F. Hoke, Attorney-at-Law; Dr. H. A. Costner, Dentist.

Kistler House, Lincolnton, N. C. A beautiful view of the mountains can be had from an observatory on top of the Hotel Building. Mrs. L. H. Kistler, Proprietress.

Henderson House, South side of Public Square. In my yard is an alum well, not inferior to the celebrated alum springs of Virginia. Robert Sowers, Prop.

M. I. Eudy, Groceries and Confections; E. K. Evans, Tinware and Stones; Wilkey & Brothers, Carriages and Wagon Makers; Eben Childs, Groceries, Dry Goods, Shoes; Warren Gheen, Furniture, Coffins made on Short Notice; J. W. Bean, Harness, Saddlery, Bridles; E. W. Stubbs & Co., Machinery of all kinds, Established 1852; J. C. Cobb, General Merchandise; John G. Justice, General Merchandise, Notions, Sugar, Piques, Muslins.

Rev. V. A. Sharpe, Books: Bibles, Methodist Hymn Books, Stevens' *History of Methodism, Wesley's Sermons, Life of John Kitto, D.D.*

Hildebrand & Cobb, Groceries and Confections; J. Logan McLean with E. W. Stubbs & Co., Machinery.

John A. Huggins, M. W. Robinson, R. A. Yoder, W. I. Hull, J. M. Bandy, Frank J. Hoke, W. F. Reep, George A. Hauss and

Scott Graham (colored) were, on July 12, 1873, granted certificates to teach in the public schools of the County. Rev. W. R. Wetmore, Rev. R. Z. Johnston and Dr. J. M. Lawing were the Board of Examiners.

J. M. Bandy later served as Professor of Mathematics in Trinity College, later Duke University.

R. A. Yoder became a Lutheran and W. I. Hull, a Methodist minister.

Upon the death of Judge Nathaniel Boyden, of the State Supreme Court, Gov. Caldwell, in November, 1873, appointed Col. W. P. Bynum, the State Solicitor, to fill the vacancy, and Judge Bynum served as a member of that Court until January 1, 1879.

Governor Caldwell tendered the appointment of Solicitor to William S. Bynum, but he declined it. Then the Governor appointed Joseph L. Carson, of Rutherfordton, to fill out the term as Solicitor.

At a special election held to choose a successor to A. J. Morrison, resigned, Ambrose Costner was elected to the Legislature. (The Legislature met annually until 1876.)

1874

In 1874 the first telegraph line to Lincolnton was completed.

The bill to charter Rock Spring Seminary was ratified by the Legislature January 30, 1874, with J. W. Puett, J. A. Kids, F. W. Howard, J. B. Shelton and Thomas Thompson, as Trustees.

The Legislature passed an act to secure better drainage of Clark's and Maiden Creeks, with L. E. Thompson, Emanuel Poovey, Michael Finger and William McCaslin, of Lincoln, and John Killian, Joseph H. Bost, Caleb Rhodes, Robert P. Reinhardt, Welborn Boyd and H. A. Forney, of Catawba County, to devise and perfect plans for draining said creeks.

W. S. Bynum delivered the literary address at the close of Rock Spring Seminary in June, 1874.

Governor Caldwell died in July, 1874, and his body was buried in Morganton.

David Schenck defeated Judge G. W. Logan for Judge in August, by 2,200 majority. W. J. Montgomery was chosen Solicitor over J. L. Carson.

From 1861 to 1874 the Republican party was in absolute control of the Federal Government. Grant, in 1872, overwhelmingly defeated Greeley, but the panic of 1873 with its train of distress brought about in the Congressional election of 1874 a change of sentiment so great as to give the Democrats a good working majority in the lower House of Congress, and heartened them for the presidential contest of 1876.

Rev. Henry Asbury died at his home in Lincoln County, October 1, 1874, aged 75 years. He was a useful local preacher of the Methodist church and son of Rev. Daniel Asbury, the pioneer Methodist preacher west of the Catawba River. Henry Asbury reared a large family and exercised a fine religious influence for many years. Some years before his death he had a premonition that his death would be violent, and so it was, for as he was asleep in front of the fire he awoke to find his clothes in flames and he was burned to death.

The Rock Springs Masonic Lodge, No. 341, was organized in December, 1874. The charter members were Dr. J. A. Sherrill, Isaac E. Paine, J. W. A. Paine, A. E. King, Dr. J. D. Munday, David Cherry, David W. Shelton, M. Bynum, N. A. Wingate, Osborne W. Asbury, T. S. Shelton, J. T. Morrison, A. L. Cherry, Sidney V. Goodson, Marcus W. Sherrill, H. Cornelius, H. Hager and D. Robert Smith (18).

Those who served as Master and Secretary of the Lodge, each serving until his successor was chosen, are:

Masters	Secretaries
Dr. J. A. Sherrill, Dec. 30, 1874	Dr. J. D. Munday, Dec. 30, 1874
J. W. A. Paine, Jan. 1, 1875	T. H. Proctor, Dec. 27, 1878
Dr. J. A. Sherrill, Nov. 25, 1876	A. L. Shuford, Dec. 27, 1879
W. A. Day, Dec. 27, 1878	R. A. Smith, Dec. 27, 1880
J. W. A. Paine, Dec. 27, 1881	W. A. Day, Dec. 27, 1881
Alfred Nixon, Nov. 18, 1882	J. W. A. Paine, Nov. 18, 1882
J. W. A. Paine, Dec. 27, 1883	T. H. Proctor, Dec. 27, 1883
J. F. Brower, Dec. 29, 1885	J. F. Brower, Dec. 27, 1886
Dr. J. A. Sherrill, Dec. 27, 1886	T. H. Proctor, Dec. 27, 1887
A. L. Cherry, Dec. 27, 1887	A. L. Cherry, Dec. 27, 1891
Dr. J. A. Sherrill, Dec. 27, 1890	D. H. Drum, Dec. 27, 1893
A. L. Cherry, Dec. 27, 1893	A. L. Cherry, Dec. 27, 1895
Dr. J. A. Sherrill, Dec. 27, 1895	J. W. Little, Dec. 27, 1898
A. L. Cherry, Dec. 27, 1898	B. A. York, Dec. 27, 1903
Dr. H. N. Abernethy, Dec. 27, 1900	A. L. Cherry, Dec. 27, 1906
J. W. Little, June 13, 1908	J. O. Munday, June 13, 1908
Dr. H. N. Abernethy, June 10, 1911	C. B. Armstrong, June 11, 1911
J. W. Little, June 26, 1915	J. W. Little, June 14, 1913
R. E. Proctor, June 22, 1918	Jesse McConnell, June 26, 1915
C. B. Armstrong, June 7, 1919	Dr. C. L. McCaul, June 16, 1917
J. W. Little, June 23, 1923	J. W. Little, June 22, 1918
W. E. King, June 7, 1924	C. B. Armstrong, June 23, 1923
W. A. Poole, June 6, 1925	R. W. Smith, June 6, 1925
Clyde Smith, June 14, 1930	W. E. King, July 18, 1927
C. B. Armstrong, March 19, 1934	

1875

Hon. Burton Craige, son of David Craige, a patriot of the Revolution, was born in Rowan County, March 13, 1811, prepared for college by Rev. James Otis Freeman, and graduated from the State University in the class with Dr. Sidney X. Johnston, of Lincoln, in 1829.

He studied law and began to practice in Salisbury. Represented the county in House of Commons in 1832 and 1834. He married to Elizabeth, daughter of Col. James Erwin, of Burke. Later he moved to a plantation in Lincoln County on the Catawba River, in what is now Catawba County, and practiced in the courts of Rowan, Iredell, Mecklenburg, Catawba, Lincoln, Burke, and other counties. He had a brilliant mind, attractive manners which won to him many friends, and was a giant physically, measuring six and one-half feet in height. He was a powerful jury lawyer and popular with the people. It has been said that often the jury would return a verdict for "Uncle Burt" as he was familiarly called, rather than for his client. He was a stranger to fear and once when some man of diminutive stature challenged the six and one-half foot lawyer for a duel he accepted the challenge on condition that the contest should be with swords in water six feet deep. Of course that settled the difficulty.

He was one of the Committee designated to organize the new County of Catawba which was created in 1842. Later he returned to Salisbury and was elected to Congress in 1854-56-58 and 1860. He resigned in 1861 and cast his lot with the South, and as a member of the Constitutional Convention of 1861 was the able leader of the Secession party. He was a distinguished lawyer and statesman in his day and died December 30, 1875, in Concord at the home of his son-in-law, Alfred B. Young. The body was buried in Salisbury.

His son, Kerr Craige, was an able lawyer, who represented Rowan in the Legislature, was nominated for Congress in 1884, but declined the honor when he was sure of election. He served as Collector of Internal Revenue, 1886-89, and was Assistant Postmaster General during Cleveland's administration. His two sons, Burton and Kerr Craige, are the third generation of lawyers in the family. For more than one hundred years the Craiges have practiced law in Salisbury and these younger men measure up to the high standards of their ancestors as to legal ability and lofty character.

At the August election Caleb Motz was chosen delegate to the Constitutional Convention which met in Raleigh in September.

Lorenzo Ferrier, a Frenchman, for many years a citizen of Lincolnton, and who had been a soldier in the French Army under Napoleon, died August 16, 1875, aged 96 years. He was a bachelor and somewhat eccentric, but educated and warmhearted. Parts of his will are expressed in classic language. His faith in the future life was clearly manifested in the will, in which is found the following: "I am also in hope to see and embrace my kind friends, Michael Hoke, William Lander and other good and honest friends with whom I hope to enjoy an eternal felicity."

In August, 1875, I rode into Shelby on the first passenger train that rolled into that town and the whole country seemed to be there to welcome it.

William Rufus Clark, Clerk of the County from 1857 to 1865 and from 1866 to 1868, died in Lincolnton, August 22, 1875, aged 60.

William A. Graham, son of Gen. Joseph Graham, was born in Lincoln County, September 5, 1804; was prepared for college in local schools and graduated from the State University in 1824, studied law and was admitted to the bar in 1825 and settled in Hillsboro. Married, June 8, 1836, to Susan Washington of Newbern. Represented Hillsboro in House of Commons, 1833, 1834 and 1835, and Orange County in 1836-38 and 1840. Speaker of the House in 1838 and 1840. Elected as a Whig to United States Senate and served from November 25, 1840, to March 3, 1843, filling the vacancy caused by the death of Col. Robert Strange. Was Governor of North Carolina 1845-1849. Declined appointment as Minister to Spain in 1849. Secretary of the Navy in the Fillmore Cabinet, 1850-53. It was during his administration that Commodore Perry, by treaty with Japan, opened the hermit nation which has since developed into a great world power. Gov. Graham was the Whig candidate for Vice-President in 1852; member of the State Senate 1854, 1862 and 1865; Confederate States Senate in 1866 but his credentials were never presented; one of the Trustees of Peabody Fund from 1867 to 1875; arbiter

Top left: Gov. J. P. Henderson (1808-1858). See 1858.
Top right: Gov. J. F. Johnston (1843-1913). See 1913.
Center: Gov. W. A. Graham (1804-1875). See 1875.
Lower left: Senator W. L. Hill (1873-   ). See 1936.
Lower right: Gov. Hoke Smith (1855-1931). See 1931.

selected by Virginia to study the boundary dispute with Maryland; was elected from Orange County as delegate to Constitutional Convention in August, 1875, but died August 11th of that year at Saratoga Springs, N. Y., before the convention assembled. His body was buried at Hillsboro.

Gov. Graham was a distinguished citizen and exercised through his long life a fine influence in that state which he honored and which honored him as its Legislator, Governor and U. S. Senator, and served the nation with distinction as Secretary of the Navy.

Conservative, dignified and wise he proved to be a leader who could be trusted for any task and proved well his fitness by measuring always to the highest expectations of the people. His sons, John W. Graham, Augustus W. Graham, James A. Graham and William A. Graham, all figured prominently in the public life of North Carolina. Dr. Joseph Graham was a skilled surgeon and Dr. Geo. W. Graham, an eye and ear specialist, both of Charlotte. One daughter married to Judge Walter Clark and among their children are David Clark of Charlotte, W. A. Graham Clark of Washington and Thorne Clark of Lincolnton.

1876

Rev. Alfred James Morrison (Oct. 1, 1849-July 6, 1876), youngest son of Rev. Dr. R. H. Morrison, was a brilliant young man, who resigned his seat in the Legislature in 1873 to enter the Presbyterian ministry, with every promise of a very useful career as a preacher of righteousness, but died in triumph after three years of ministerial service. His body rests by the side of his ancestors in Machpelah graveyard. His tombstone carries no dates. He married on February 24, 1875 to Portia Lee Atkinson. They had one son, Alfred James Morrison, LL.D., born July 11, 1876 (only five days after his father died). He never married but died January 22, 1923.

In January, 1876, license to practice law was granted to Theodorus H. Cobb.

Rev. William S. Bynum was ordained Deacon by Bishop Lyman in St. Luke's Episcopal Church in Lincolnton, March 12, 1876.

Dr. M. L. Brown, for many years a Lincolnton physician and one time Legislator from Lincoln County, died July 22, 1876, aged 41 years.

Rock Spring Seminary Commencement at Denver, May, 1876, as reported in *Lincoln Progress:*

Prof. D. Matt Thompson, Principal.
Annual Sermon, by Rev. Dr. D. R. Bruton.
Annual Address, by Dr. Braxton Craven, President of Trinity College.

RECITATIONS BY YOUNG LADIES:
Early Piety, Emma L. Kelly (Mrs. Durant Howard).
Improve Your Time, Lizzie Howard.
Live Within Your Means, Iola J. Robinson (Mrs. Alfred Nixon).
Hard Times, Dora H. Davenport (Mrs. C. E. Hutchison).
Love Begins at Home, Luetta Connor (Mrs. W. L. Sherrill).
Good Society, Ella Howard (Mrs. William Munday).
100 Years Ago, Zetta Munday (Mrs. Frank Smith).
Refinement a National Benefit, Sallie Asbury (Mrs. Duke).
Cramming, Mary Paine Puett (Mrs. A. W. Andrews).

SPEECHES:
Old Fashioned Total Abstinence, Henry A. Howard.
Boys on the Farm, James W. Shelton.
Necessity of Industry, T. M. Davis.
What Shall I Do for a Living, R. Kelly Davenport.
Voice of the Dead, L. M. Smith.
The Uses of the Ocean, Luther E. Finger.
Auction Extraordinary, Alex. M. Shelton.
Humbug Patriotism, James C. Loftin.
Moral Power of Woman, R. Eugene Lineberger.
John Ploughman's Talks to the Idle, Charles L. McCall.
Independence Bell, J. Allen King.
My Rhyme, Master Tommie M. Shelton.
Mental Improvement, Adolphus R. Rudisill.
Try is the Song, T. F. Connor.
Choice Books Good Company, L. F. Black.
The Magic Wires, J. M. Roberts.
Universal Education, John H. Rutledge.
Standards of Human Greatness, J. W. Kelly.
Young America, Sidney J. Whitener.
Agriculture, Adolphus W. Clark.

Music by Catawba Brass Band.

Visitors: Rev. J. T. Harris and Mr. J. C. Jenkins, of Lincolnton.

Denver Merchants: W. C. Proctor, J. C. Puett, J. M. Kids. Dr. Charles S. Rozzelle, Physician.

The heavy rains in June, 1876, did much damage to the wheat crop, a great deal of it sprouting in the shock.

September 16, 1876. Judge Thomas Settle (Republican) and Governor Z. B. Vance (Democrat), candidates for Governor, spoke in Lincolnton. Two of the handsomest men in the State as well as two of the greatest. It was a battle of giants in a hotly fought canvass. Vance was elected in November by 13,000 majority over Settle.

Christmas, 1876, was ushered in with a terrible snowstorm, followed on January 1st by another heavy snow. It snowed now and then until late in March, with a great wheat crop following in 1877.

Captain John Guion Justice, a prominent citizen and merchant, died December 22, 1876, after a brief illness. He was a gallant soldier in the Civil War and lost a limb in battle. He was born in Newbern, October 8, 1844. Married Jennie, daughter of V. A. McBee. She died in New York, December 12, 1881. Their daughter, Elizabeth, married W. B. Grimes of Raleigh. Captain Justice was shot in the stomach in battle but in three weeks was back in the ranks. Later he lost a leg in another charge. He was a warm-hearted nobleman and held in high regard by all who knew him.

1877

Major Augustus W. Burton, son of Judge Robert H. Burton, was born at Beatties Ford, August 29, 1815, and died in Lincolnton, February 15, 1877. He was Mayor of Lincolnton at the time of his death.

He was a graduate of the State University and was admitted to the bar, January 29, 1849. His license was signed by Chief Justice Ruffin and associate Justice Frederick Nash and Richmond M. Pearson.

On April 25, 1849, he was married to Julia L. Olmstead, sister of Rev. Dr. A. F. Olmstead, one time Rector of St. Luke's Episcopal church in Lincolnton. They settled in Shelby where Mr. Burton was successful in the practice of law until 1861 when he volunteered as a soldier of the Civil War and went to the front as Captain of the Cleveland Guards in April, 1861. He was promoted to Major in 2nd N. C. Regiment and his commission was signed by Gov. Ellis, May 14, 1861. After two years active service he was transferred to the commissary department and stationed in Charlotte until the war closed in 1865. In 1866 he went North on a business trip and lived in New York for four years when, broken in health, he returned South and made his home in Lincolnton until his death in 1877. From the time he was admitted to the bar until 1861 he was an influential citizen of Shelby, represented Cleveland in the House of Commons in 1852, was elected State Solicitor for the Western District by the Legislature in 1853, and served in that position with distinction until 1858. He was State Senator from Cleveland in 1860.

He had two sons. Frank O. Burton, born in 1851, went to Dakota, where he engaged in the cattle business and died at Custer, June 21, 1898. The other son, Robert H. Burton, born in 1853, entered the Episcopal ministry and served various churches in Connecticut until his death in 1933.

On November 23rd, 1877, the heavy rains raised the waters of Clark's Creek and the South Fork River out of banks, and that night Harrison Grice went from Phifer's Factory down to the Creek crossing with Jacob Sumner and Michael Hoke to row them across in the canoe. The current was so strong that they were all carried down to the river, where the boat capsized and Grice disappeared in the flood. Sumner and Hoke held on to the boat in mid-stream until it reached the bend of the river, north of the Seaboard bridge, when the boat drifted toward the shore. Hoke caught to an overhanging limb, climbed to the body of the tree, but, surrounded by deep water, sat there till 2 o'clock the next day when he was rescued by a boatman who approached from the west side of the stream. When Hoke was safe in the tree, Sumner in desperation grabbed a sapling which he clung to for an hour, when he cried back to Hoke, "Mike, I can't hold on any longer," and sank. It was several days before his body was found and two weeks later the body of Grice was found lodged under a fish trap near the Seaboard bridge. It was a tragedy which stirred the whole community.

The Presidential election of 1876 was claimed by both parties and at one time it was feared that there might be a bloody contest to decide whether Hayes or Tilden should be President. From the November election until late in February, 1877, feeling ran high. Congress arranged for a peaceful settlement by creating an Electoral Commission composed of five Justices of the

Supreme Court, five Senators and five Representatives to decide the questions involved. The Senate was Republican and the House Democratic, so there were ten Congressmen on the Commission, equally divided politically. On each issue the Commission voted 8 for Hayes and 7 for Tilden, with the result that Hayes was given 185 and Tilden 184 electoral votes and Hayes was in March inaugurated as the 19th President of the United States.

Judge Theodorus W. Brevard, a notable son of Lincoln County, moved to Alabama in 1833 to practice law, and there served as Judge of the County Court. In 1847 he moved to Florida and from 1855 to 1860 was Comptroller of State. He was further honored by his adopted State when the County of Brevard was named for him.

His wife, Carolina Mays, was a cultured lady of South Carolina. After the Civil War they returned to Lincolnton, where, in 1868-1870, they conducted a boarding school in the present North State Hotel building. Mrs. Brevard taught the girls, while Judge Brevard had a class of boys who were day scholars.

Judge Brevard died in 1877, aged 73 years. Mrs. Brevard died in 1892, aged 81 years, and their bodies rest side by side in Machpelah graveyard. They had two sons who were skilled physicians, Dr. Ephraim A. Brevard, who was thrown from his horse and killed in 1871, aged 32 years, and Dr. Robert J. Brevard, who practiced his profession in Charlotte where he served four years as Mayor and died in 1906, aged 56 years.

Another son, Theodorus W. Brevard, Jr., born in Alabama, married to Mary Call, daughter of Governor R. K. Call, of Florida. He served in the Florida Legislature in 1858 and later served as Adjutant General of the State. He was Colonel of the 11th Florida Regiment in the Civil War, and March 22, 1865 was commissioned Brigadier General, but the war closed before the commission reached him. He served in Florida Legislature during the reconstruction period and died in Tallahassee in 1882.

His daughter, Caroline Mays Brevard (1860-1920) named for her grandmother Brevard, was a woman of rare culture, a teacher in the Florida Women's College and author of a history of Florida (2 volumes), covering the period from 1793 to 1900, a work which gives her a permanent place in Florida history.

James L. Wilkey and L. T. Wilkey were for nearly two generations useful Lincolnton citizens. They were natives of Rutherford County who came here when young men and married two good Lincoln girls and reared a lot of fine children.

J. L. Wilkey was a magistrate for some years and his brother, L. T. Wilkey, served as County Treasurer for eight years, from 1886 to 1894. They were skilled mechanics and conducted a business in the western part of town where they made wagons and did general repair work, employing several extra men and blacksmiths.

It was sometime in 1877 when the sound of the hammer was heard in their shop at night and it all seemed a mystery. Spiritualism had been much discussed in the town and some people were excited over it. The hammer striking the anvil at Wilkey's Shop, breaking the midnight silence of a quiet community was attributed to a spirit—good or evil. Night after night multitudes of the town folks went up to the shop and heard first hand the clear but mysterious noise. Delegations would go inside with lanterns to discover if possible the cause but never found the explanation. It was the talk of the town and the excitement ran high. At last one of the shopmen told Jake Bisaner as a secret that they had placed an anvil under a box with a hammer on a pivot above. This hammer was connected with the outside by a cord so that one could sit on the ground outside in the dark and by pulling the cord cause the hammer to strike the anvil at will. The story was so good that Jake Bisaner could not keep the secret and the excitement subsided when he told it.

1878

Saloons were voted out of Lincolnton in 1878.

The question of no fence law was agitated. Up to this time cattle and hogs had free range and field crops had to be fenced in. A lawful fence was "horse high, bull strong, and hog tight."

In the earlier days farmers with free range for hogs and cattle found it better to fence in crops, but since rail timber had become scarce and field crops of more value, the sentiment grew for the no-fence law, though the proposed change was bitterly opposed by many people.

The Southern Stars Military Company, with Silas McBee, Captain, Michael Hoke and B. F. Seagle, Lieutenants, and

Charles E. Childs, Orderly Sergeant, attended the State Fair at Raleigh in October, 1878.

In the November election W. N. H. Smith, Thomas S. Ashe and John H. Dillard were elected Judges of the Supreme Court, without opposition. Their terms began January 1, 1879.

J. R. Hawkins, bridge builder on Carolina Central Railroad, was killed April 6, 1878, at a railway crossing in Charlotte, when the crank-car upon which he was travelling collided with a train where two railway tracks crossed. He and Captain K. S. Finch were on the crank-car going to Lincolnton to spend the week-end and he was killed before they got out of Charlotte. Captain Finch escaped unhurt.

Jacob Bisaner, Sr., died in Lincolnton, July 8, 1878, aged 79 years. He was a mechanic and a good citizen. In an article published in the *Lincoln Progress* at the time of his death Judge David Schenck paid high tribute to him. On the afternoon when he was buried an angry storm swept over the town, followed by a glorious sunset. Judge Schenck in picturesque language used the storm as an illustration of his earthly trials, and the sunset as the peaceful end of a life well spent.

1879

Governor Zebulon B. Vance was elected to the United States Senate by the Legislature which met in January, succeeding Augustus S. Merrimon, and his term began March 4th. Lt. Gov. Thomas J. Jarvis succeeded Vance as Governor.

David Summerow, an old and highly respected citizen of the Lowesville section, died June 23, 1879. His son, W. A. Summerow, volunteered as a soldier of the Confederacy and died in Petersburg, Virginia, in 1862.

In August, 1879, a revival meeting was held in the Old White Church, by the Baptist pastor, Rev. A. L. Stough, assisted by Rev. F. M. Jordan, a militant preacher of force and zeal. The other congregations co-operated and large crowds attended. The Baptists were few in number then but that meeting gave impetus and growth to the denomination, which has increased with the growth of the town until today they have a large membership and a handsome, well-located church.

Robert A. Brevard, son of Capt. Alex Brevard the pioneer, and a life-long citizen of the County, died at his home east of

Lincolnton, August 17, 1879, aged 80 years, and his body was buried at Machpelah. He, for many years, was engaged in the iron industry in the County. Among his sons was Capt. Alexander F. Brevard, a lawyer by profession, who died October 22, 1909, aged 84 years.

In September, William L. Sherrill, when nineteen years old, established in Dallas the first drug store ever operated in Gaston County.

John B. Hoyle, the 15-year-old son of Laban A. Hoyle, while hunting was killed October 18, 1879, by the accidental discharge of his gun.

Theodorus H. Cobb was married to Miss Ellen V. Johnson, daughter of Captain V. Q. Johnson, in November, 1879.

CHAPTER XVI

1880-1889

James R. Dodge, a lawyer of note, lived in Lincolnton from 1834 to 1845. He was born in New York State, October 27, 1795. In the War of 1812 he was first aide to his father, General Dodge, at Sackett Harbor. In 1817 he settled in Petersburg, Va., where he met with financial failure in 1819. In 1820 he went to Raleigh, N. C., with a letter of introduction to Chief Justice Ruffin, who befriended him. He was licensed to practice law and lived for a while in Stokes County where he married Susan Williams, May 24, 1826.

In 1834 he was elected State Solicitor for the Lincoln District, which position he held for some years. He was a member of the Lincolnton School Board, 1838-1841. About 1846 he met with financial misfortune in Lincolnton. There was no homestead exemption in those days and all his property was sold for debt. Mr. Dodge was a nephew of Washington Irving, the author, who presented him with a full set of his literary works. These books, sold for debt, were bought by William Lander, his friend, who gave them back to Mr. Dodge.

He lived in Lincolnton at the old B. H. Sumner residence on East Main Street, and it was there his daughter, Annie Dodge, was born. She later married to Chalmers L. Glenn, of Rockingham County, and became the mother of Governor Robert B. Glenn.

From May, 1847, to 1858 Mr. Dodge was Clerk of the Supreme Court (Morganton). Prior to that time he was for about twelve years a clerk in the Legislature. Mr. Dodge possessed rare literary gifts and was a lawyer distinguished in his day. He died at the home of his daughter, Mrs. Chalmers L. Glenn, in Rockingham County, North Carolina, February 24, 1880. He was a life-long member of the Episcopal church.

From the *Denver Seminary Gazette* of May 20, 1880, published by J. B. Ivey, now one of the leading merchants of the State, the following news notes are found:

The Denver Seminary Commencement Marshals elected are: M. F. Jones, Gaston, Chief; A. P. Cannon, W. F. Farrar, H. M.

Eddleman and W. V. Rutledge, of Gastonia, L. C. Holler, of Mecklenburg, and J. P. Benton, of Rockingham, Assistants. Col. W. W. Flemming of Marion will deliver the literary address.

Prof. D. Matt Thompson was principal of the school and among the students were R. K. Davenport, Augustus Proctor, Chas. L. McCall, Eugene Lineberger, O. F. Howard, Furman Kids, J. B. Ivey, George F. and Eugene C. Ivey, the marshals above, and the following young ladies: Misses Doris and Eunice Davenport, Mollie and Soule Puett, Etta Munday, Julia Johnson, Ella Howard, Dora Cannon and Lula Cannon.

At the tournament at River Bend, March 18, 1880, R. K. Davenport, the successful knight, crowned Miss Mamie Sherrill, of Sherrill's Ford, the Queen of Love and Beauty; William Henderson crowned Miss Etta Haynes, of Newton, first maid of honor; Edgar Henderson crowned Miss Eunice Davenport second maid of honor, and George Davenport crowned Miss Springs third maid of honor.

The leading merchants were: T. F. Stacy, T. H. Proctor, John A. Kids and Lowe and Munday. Dr. Chas S. Rozzelle was the local physician.

Charles C. Cobb graduated from the State University in June, 1880, the first Lincoln man to complete the course there since the institution was reopened in 1875. Among his classmates were Gov. Chas. B. Aycock, Gov. Locke Craig and Judge A. L. Coble.

Mr. James C. Jenkins long a leading citizen, merchant and churchman, died August 9, 1880. He was County Treasurer from 1872 until his death. His wife was Barbara, daughter of the late Dr. David W. Schenck. Mr. Jenkins was for long years an active official in the Lincolnton Methodist church. Among his children were Susan, who married to S. H. Hopkins; Alice, married Samuel Lander III.; Bessie, married Burgin Ramseur; Addie, married Dr. W. A. Presley, of Rock Hill, South Carolina; Blair, married Mary Sumner; Hugh, married Christie Waddell. All the children are dead (1935) except Mrs. Ramseur and Mrs. Presley.

The children of Blair Jenkins are James C. Jenkins, prominent insurance man of Charlotte; Dr. William S. Jenkins, professor of Political Science in the University of North Carolina;

Lieutenant Hugh Jenkins in the Naval Air Service as Instructor at air base at Pensacola, Fla.; and Blair Jenkins in telephone service in Raleigh, N. C.

On October 7, 1880, a great crowd assembled at the Kings Mountain battle ground for the Centennial celebration of the glorious victory for human freedom won there a hundred years before. Senator John W. Daniel, of Virginia, delivered the principal address.

At the November election Garfield was elected President and Thomas J. Jarvis was re-elected Governor over Judge Ralph P. Buxton by 6,000 majority.

Dr. James Abernethy (1807-1880) came of good Revolutionary stock and was related to most of the Abernethys of this section. He was a son of John Abernethy (1774-1826) and a grandson of Miles Abernethy (1750-1812). Dr. Abernethy was born in Lincoln (now Gaston) County, was a physician who had a large practice in the Mount Holly and River Bend section of Gaston County and an influential and worthy citizen.

He married to Mary Rankin and among his numerous children were:

1. Washington Clay Abernethy, for some years Sheriff of Gaston County. He married to Mattie Smith.

2. Theodore R. Abernethy, for many years a pharmacist in Newton, where he married to Janie Campbell.

3. James Alonzo Abernethy, a prominent textile manufacturer, of Lincolnton, who married to Sarah, daughter of Moses H. Rhyne of Gaston County.

Jacob A. Ramseur, leading citizen and long time prominent Lincolnton merchant was born January 1, 1808, and died in 1880.

He married to Lucy Mayfield Dodson in 1833.

Among their children were:

1. Sarah Wilfong, who married Judge David Schenck (See 1902).

2. Stephen Dodson (the Confederate General. See 1863), married Ellen Richmond.

3. Charles, moved to Texas and died there.

4. Fannie Dodson, married John Minter of Laurens, South Carolina.

Their son, Rev. William Ramseur Minter, born at Sedalia, S. C., July 9, 1873, graduated from Davidson College in 1892. Received the degree of Doctor of Divinity from the same College in 1913. He was ordained into the ministry of the Presbyterian church in 1897. Married Harriet Marie Smith of Glenn Spring, S. C., December 21, 1898. Pastor at Shelby and Rutherfordton until 1905; Principal Westminster School, 1905-1907; Pastor Lincolnton Presbyterian Church, 1907-1915; Pastor First Presbyterian Church, Austin, Texas, since 1915. One daughter, Josephine, married former United States Senator, Nathaniel B. Dial, lawyer of Washington, D. C., and Laurens, S. C.

5. Addie, married Calvin E. Grier, a Charlotte lawyer. They had three children, Mrs. T. S. Shaw of New Orleans, Miss Sadie Grier of Charlotte and Mrs. J. W. Barineau, of Lincolnton.

6. Harvey, married Mary Badham. They lived in Birmingham, Ala.

1881

On January 23, 1881, the Indian Creek trestle, four miles west of Lincolnton, on the Carolina Central Railroad, gave way as the combined passenger and freight train coming east started across. Everything but the engine fell in and caught fire from the stoves in passenger cars. John Bloom, mail agent, S. W. Goodson, Insurance Agent, and Harry Smith, a New York shoe drummer, together with Jim Warlick and Bill McKenzie, colored brakemen, all unable to escape from the car, were burned to death. Harry Johnson, the conductor, thrown to the ground, was dazed but not killed. The engine had reached the east side of the trestle when the crash came and the engineer, John Hall, threw the throttle wide open and jerked the engine loose from the front car and hurried with the engine to town for relief, which arrived there too late to render any help. This terrible accident carried gloom to this whole section of the State.

The opposition to the common custom of a free range for cattle and hogs had grown rapidly for several years and townships voted for no-fence law in various counties, which is indicated by the legislative acts passed in its favor.

THE ANNALS OF LINCOLN COUNTY 233

The Legislative Acts of 1881, page 91, provides that Indian Creek shall be a lawful fence from the Gaston County line to its forks near or above George Beam's in Lincoln County.

Also, the same year, on page 140, Commissioners of Lincoln, Catawba, Cleveland, Gaston and Iredell, were empowered to condemn land twenty feet in width to build fences around townships or counties.

Alfred Nixon graduated from the University of North Carolina in June, 1881.

The summer of 1881 was the driest season known in North Carolina since 1845.

The Legislature submitted to the people for rejection or adoption a law providing for a restricted sale of liquor, but it was defeated by 120,000 majority in August.

Dr. Cyrus Lee Hunter (1807-1881), son of Rev. Humphrey Hunter, the pioneer Presbyterian preacher west of the Catawba River, was a notable citizen of Lincoln County. He had a scientific turn of mind, was a skilled physician, a devout churchman and an ardent patriot. He took great interest in the Revolutionary history of Western North Carolina. He was the author of *Hunter's Sketches*, a valuable book which preserves the earlier history of this section, and we owe to Dr. Hunter a debt of gratitude for accuracy and care in the preparation of that volume which was, on his part, a labor of love and not for pecuniary profit. Dr. Hunter died at his home near Cottage Home, December 15, 1881, loved and respected by all who knew him.

President Garfield was shot in the Washington City Railway station at 9 o'clock A.M., July 2nd, as he was starting to the commencement at Williams College, his alma mater. He lingered for ten weeks and died at Elberon, N. J., September 19th.

Judge David Schenck resigned the judgeship and Gov. Jarvis appointed Judge William M. Shipp to succeed him.

The Chester and Lenoir Railroad was completed to Lincolnton late in 1881.

Benjamin S. Johnson, one of the oldest and most prominent citizens and proprietor of Johnson's Hotel, died in 1881.

Jonas W. Derr died at his home in Ironton township in 1881. He was the largest landowner in the County. He was an enterprising and frugal man, who took good care of his money, and, believing that land was the safest investment, made it his rule to buy all the land adjoining his, so far as he was able to pay the cash. He had for many years engaged in the manufacture of iron on account of the abundance of a good quality of iron ore in his community, and was the last of a long line of enterprising men who had for many decades engaged in iron production in Lincoln County. A prominent Methodist steward once approached Mr. Derr, who was not a church member, with request for a contribution for the pastor of the neighboring Methodist church. Mr. Derr cheerfully agreed to help, and the steward said, "I will be glad to hand to the preacher any amount you may give." Then Mr. Derr said, "I will hand it to him myself, the next time I see him, and then I will know he gets it." He was a bachelor and wealthy.

1882

Rev. William Shipp Bynum was ordained priest in Saint Luke's Episcopal church in Lincolnton by Bishop Lyman on March 5, 1882.

At 8 o'clock in the morning of July 26, 1882, in the Lincolnton Methodist church, Samuel Lander, III, was married to Alice, daughter of James C. Jenkins.

Dr. W. L. Crouse was elected to the Legislature, Capt. A. S. Haynes, Sheriff, and Alfred Nixon, Surveyor, at the November election.

After an aggressive campaign Judge Risden Tyler Bennett, of Anson, was elected Congressman for the State at large, defeating Col. Oliver H. Dockery by only 250 votes. During the campaign they met in joint debate in Lincolnton; both were popular speakers and well matched. Judge Bennett spoke first and witheringly denounced the Internal Revenue law, which was not popular, and said, "If you elect me to Congress I will see that the infamous law is repealed." In that statement he gave opportunity for his adroit opponent to get the advantage, and when Dockery arose to reply he said:

"North Carolina for some years has been ably represented in the United States Senate by Gen. Matt W. Ransom and Zebulon B. Vance, who through long service are influential members of that distinguished body, and have repeatedly, by argument and diplomacy, done all they could to repeal the Internal Revenue law and failed utterly, but despite that fact, Judge Bennett tells you that if he is elected he will have that law repealed.

"I imagine that, if he should get to Washington, the Congress will be nervously awaiting his arrival, and when he enters the door of the House the Speaker will announce in stentorian voice: 'Let the House arise for Risden Tyler Bennett from North Carolina has just entered the hall and is coming down the aisle to take the oath, and will at once make ready to have the Internal Revenue law repealed.' "

Col. Dockery knew that reason is helpless in the presence of ridicule.

Col. John Hill Wheeler (1806-1882) was a notable citizen who rendered valuable service to the state as the author of *Wheeler's History of North Carolina*, editor of the *North Carolina Manual of 1874*, of the *Autobiography of Col. David Fanning*, and as author of *Reminiscenses of Distinguished North Carolinians*. These books preserve much valuable State history.

Col. Wheeler was born in Murfreesboro, N. C.; prepared for college by Rev. James Otis Freeman, and graduated from Columbia College, District of Columbia in 1826; admitted to the bar in 1827; same year represented Hertford County in House of Commons and served for four years until 1831; appointed first Superintendent of the Charlotte mint in 1837 and served until 1841; was nominated for the Commons by the Democrats of Mecklenburg in 1842, but declined the honor because he planned to move to Lincoln County. He was elected State Treasurer that year. Later moved to Beatties Ford, where he wrote the History of the State and in 1852 was elected to the Commons from Lincoln. From 1854 to 1857 he was United States Minister to Nicaragua. His later years were spent in Washington where he was engaged in literary work.

He married first to Mary, daughter of Rev. G. B. Brown, of Washington; second marriage was to Ellen, daughter of Thomas Sully, the noted sculptor, of Philadelphia. Col. Wheeler died in Washington, December 7, 1882. (See also 1840.)

1883

Charles C. Cobb was granted license and located in Shelby to practice law.

Henry W. Morton died in 1883. He came to Lincolnton before the Civil War, whence, no one knows. He volunteered as a soldier and went out with the Southern Stars in April, 1861, and came back at the close of the war; was Express Agent, Town Marshal and a Clerk in the store of Borders & Justice and later in the stores of John G. Justice and Silas McBee. He was an intelligent and agreeable man who had his weaknesses, but the people had full confidence in his integrity. He never referred to his early life and after thirty years' residence in the town died leaving no testimony of his origin. His life was a mystery and he kept the secret well.

To fill the vacancy caused by the resignation of Sheriff A. S. Haynes, the County Commissioners elected Alfred Nixon Sheriff, which office he held until 1890, when he declined to be a candidate for re-election.

By this time the no-fence law sentiment had become so popular that the greater part of Lincoln and the counties adjoining had adopted it. Like all innovations it first met with bitter opposition from tenant farmers who wanted free range for hogs and cattle, while at the same time the tenant had to split rails and keep up fences to protect his crops from destruction by roving cattle.

Warren Gheen, a respected and useful citizen, died March 16, 1883, in his 70th year. Mr. Gheen was a skilled cabinet maker and in the earlier days before we had railroads to bring in machine made furniture, Mr. Gheen and his helpers made by hand much of the old furniture in use in this section. Coffins in those days were never imported, but made to order whenever there was a death, and Mr. Gheen did a large business in coffins, aside from furniture.

Haywood W. Guion, of Newbern, N. C., graduated from our State University in 1835, after which he read law and in the late 1830's came to Lincolnton, a well-furnished young lawyer, became a notable citizen of the County and by 1839 was editor of the *Western Whig Banner*. He was in 1841 a member of the local school board and was successful in the practice of law, but never held political position. He was counsel for Langford, who, in 1854, was tried for the murder of his wife. He made a strong argument before the jury, but Langford was convicted and confessed the crime on the scaffold.

Mr. Guion possessed superior literary accomplishments and the *Comet*, a novel from his pen, was highly regarded by literary critics.

After the Civil War he moved to Charlotte where clients flocked to him. As counsel for the Atlanta and Charlotte Railway about 1873 in a law suit of importance, it is said he received a $10,000.00 fee, unusually large in that day, or in this day for that matter.

His wife was Ellen, daughter of the late Governor Owen.

Mr. Guion died in Charlotte in October, 1883, and his will was probated in Mecklenburg County, November 16, 1883. His wife was executrix of the will and the sole beneficiary. He was a life-long member of the Episcopal church.

The following tribute to Hon. James H. White appeared in the *Gastonia Gazette* of November 16, 1883:

The reaper, Death, day by day snatches from our midst some friend. One by one the old landmarks take their last steps on the march to Eternity. The subject of this sketch was born in Derry County, Ireland, in May, 1802, and died at his residence in Gaston County, N. C., November 1st, 1883, in the 82nd year of his age.

When but 16 years of age he emigrated to America, landed at Charleston, S. C., and located in Gaston (then Lincoln County, N. C.), and settled down as a farmer.

He always took great interest in public affairs, was elected to the House of Commons in 1842-'44-'46 and '48, was chosen State Senator in 1850, to the House from Gaston in 1854 and 1860, and again to the Senate in 1862, making a total service of sixteen years in the General Assembly. He once told the writer that the proudest act of his public life was securing the charter of the Dallas & Kings Mountain Railroad (now the C. & L. R. R.). At that time there was throughout the State bitter opposition to the granting of charters to any railroads leading out of the State, but he fought hard in the Assembly for the passage of the bill granting this charter and was successful, and to him more than to anyone else are we indebted for our narrow gauge railroad, binding as it does the hills of North Carolina with the lowlands of the Palmetto State.

Mr. White was always a true Democrat of the Calhoun school. While not a fine orator, he was a positive and forceful speaker, admired more for his depth of argument than for eloquence. He was a bold and aggressive advocate of what he thought was right, yet frank and generous to his opponents. He was also an ardent lover of individual liberty and personal rights, and at a recent election in which he thought a just privilege was being trampled upon, he remarked as he cast his ballot, "I was born in a land of tyranny, but I want to die in a land of liberty." He has taken but little interest in politics since the late war, but his name will stand prominent in the history of this section of the State.

Personally Mr. White possessed that warm-hearted generous disposition characteristic of every true son of Erin. He was a great admirer of Burns' poetry and was consequently a lover of the grand and beautiful in Nature.

An affectionate husband and loving father, a steadfast friend and generous foe, loved by his friends and admired by all, he well ever be kindly remembered. He died in the Presbyterian faith, and a nobler, manlier soul never winged its flight heavenward.

> "Green be the turf above thee,
> Friend of other days;
> None knew thee but to love thee,
> None named thee but to praise."

Dallas, N. C., November, 1883.   William L. Sherrill.

Mr. White was active in the movement for the creation of the County of Gaston, which was established in 1846. He married to Margaret Jenkins, July 3, 1834, and reared a large family. One son, John B. White, was Clerk of the Superior Court in Gaston from 1878 to 1890, and represented Gaston in the Legislature of 1893. The body of Mr. White rests in the Jenkins family graveyard, a few miles west of Dallas. There is no tombstone because it was his request that no marker be placed over his grave.

1884

In January, 1884, Charles C. Cobb and John Morehead Avery, of Morganton, went to Dallas, Texas. They were partners in the practice of law there for nearly forty years.

William L. Sherrill was married in Mooresville, N. C., May 21, 1884, to Miss Luetta Connor, daughter of the late Charles T. Connor of Catawba County.

Rev. Alfred J. Fox, M.D., D.D. (Sept. 6, 1817-June 10, 1884), was a native of Chatham County; entered the gospel ministry in connection with the Tennessee Synod of the Lutheran church in 1837 and preached for some years in Tennessee and Alabama. Finally, in 1854, he settled in Lincoln County, where he served as pastor of Salem, Daniel and Trinity churches for thirty years until his death in 1884. His early educational advantages were poor, but with a strong mind, combined with great diligence and perseverance, he became a ripe scholar and a preacher of great usefulness. He was also a medical doctor, successful in his practice, but his ministerial work was given first place.

He had a strong physical constitution and at one time, when in Alabama, he was the pastor of nine congregations, as well as a busy medical practitioner. Like the Lord, whom he served, he was a healer, teacher and preacher.

Dr. Fox was an attractive and instructive preacher, ready in speech, logical in argument, full of courage and zeal, and his ministry was fruitful and his influence lasting for good. On April 5, 1842, he married to Lydia Bost, of Cabarrus County, and of the seven children, three were physicians: (1) Dr. Albert C. Fox, practiced medicine in Waynesboro, Va., and later in Lincolnton; (2) Dr. J. Frank Fox, also was a Lincolnton physician, and (3) Dr. Claude B. Fox, established a hospital in Tennessee where he distinguished himself as a physician.

Two other sons became Lutheran ministers: Rev. Luther A. Fox, D.D., was for many years Professor of Philosophy in Roanoke College, Salem, Virginia, and Rev. Junius B. Fox, D.D., was a prominent minister, who served as pastor of churches in both Tennessee and South Carolina. Rev. R. A. Smith, Ph.D., a great grandson of Dr. A. J. Fox, is a minister of the Western North Carolina (Methodist) Conference.

Rev. Dr. Alfred J. Fox was buried at Salem church, which he served as pastor for thirty years.

Miss Mary Wood Alexander, daughter of the late William Julius Alexander, a woman of rare culture, died at her home in Lincolnton, September 23, 1884, aged 56 years. Everybody spoke of her as Miss Mary Wood and she was appreciated and loved by all who knew her. She founded Mary Wood School, for girls, about 1855, and taught for nearly thirty years until her death in 1884. She was a thorough teacher who wrought a refining influence upon the student body. The patronage was more than local, for multitudes came from far and near to secure the quality of instruction she imparted. The wide influence she exerted can never be estimated, and when she passed to her reward sorrow came to the hearts of all her old pupils and friends.

Mrs. Elizabeth Ramsour Phifer, wife of Col. John F. Phifer, died in 1884, aged 75 years. (See 1886.)

Capt. William R. Edwards, who served the County as Register of Deeds from 1874 to 1884, retired after making a creditable record for ten years and was succeeded by Henry E. Ramsour.

In November, Grover Cleveland, Governor of New York, defeated Blaine for the presidency—the first Democrat to occupy that position since James Buchanan went out of office March 4, 1861.

Dr. Tyre York, of Wilkes, was defeated for Governor by Gen. Alfred M. Scales.

1885

David Cherry, a prominent citizen of East Lincoln, died this year.

Edmund G. Ramsour, a Lincolnton merchant, died February 20, 1885, aged 50 years.

Gen. U. S. Grant died in New York in August, 1885, of cancer of the throat. Much of the second volume of his *Memoirs* was written that year. Despite the pain he labored on, and had the satisfaction of completing that historical work a very short time before he died.

Dr. Sidney X. Johnston, a son of Robert Johnston, was a skilled physician and practiced medicine in East Lincoln and Gaston Counties, and lived on his plantation near Lowesville. When Gaston County was erected in 1846 his home was in the new county. The only political position he ever held was delegate from Gaston to the convention of 1861 when he signed the Secession ordinance. He was an officer in Unity Presbyterian church for many years. He married to Harriet, daughter of Henry Connor, Sr., on Sept. 9, 1835, and they had two daughters, Mrs. J. A. Woodcock, and Miss Jane Johnston (See 1854), who never married. Dr. Johnston died July 21, 1885.

Gen. Daniel Seagle was from early manhood a useful and patriotic citizen of Lincoln County where he was born January 28, 1796. He was for a long time a Lincolnton merchant, until 1844 when he and J. F. Dailey conducted a tailoring business for several years. He then bought the farm in Howard's Creek where he spent the remainder of his life. He married first to Catherine Hoover, who died three weeks later of typhoid fever. His second marriage was to Mary Elizabeth Bollinger, and they had six daughters and nine sons. One daughter, Catherine, married to Eli A. Warlick, and another, Sarah Ann, married to F. J. Jetton.

All the sons were named for noble men: Thomas Jefferson, George Washington, James Madison, Andrew Jackson, Monroe, Martin Van Buren, Nathaniel Macon, Dallas Polk and Benjamin Franklin. They were all fine citizens and all Confederate soldiers. It was a great disappointment to Gen. Seagle that he (65 years old) could not go to the war with his sons. Thomas J. Seagle rose to rank of Major, and George W. organized a company of which he was the Captain. He and his brother, Dallas Polk, were wounded, and Martin Van Buren was killed in action at Chancellorsville, May 3, 1863. Daniel Seagle was a General of State Militia for many years until 1865.

He learned to read German before English as his father was a native of Germany. He was a devout Lutheran and all his children were baptized in that faith. He died Nov. 6, 1885, loved and respected by all the people. All the children have died except Benjamin Franklin, now 86 years old (1935) who dwells in Hickory, honored and respected as one whose life has been spent in useful service.

B. F. Seagle, Jr., a grandson of Gen. Daniel Seagle has furnished the following interesting facts about the pioneer, John Seagle and some of the Seagle connection:

"Pioneer John Seagle emigrated from Wurttemberg, Germany, as a young man and settled in Lincoln County. He fought in the Revolutionary War on the American side with Shelby and Sevier in the Battle of Kings Mountain, October 7, 1780, in the defeat of Ferguson.

"John Seagle first married Barbara Clay, who was born in Lincoln County and a close relative of Caleb Clay, then prominent in Burke County. From this union were born two children, General Daniel Seagle, and Susan Seagle, who married David Shell.

"John Seagle by his second wife had four sons and two daughters: David, who married a Miss Finger; John, married Barbara Sides; Jacob, first married a Miss Duckworth, and second, Miss Claywell, mother of Jacob Seagle of Lenoir; Henry, who settled in Tennessee; Betsy, married George Coon; and Sarah, married Solomon Yoder.

"John Seagle was the pioneer of the Seagle family in this section and is buried in the old Daniel's churchyard in Lincoln County."

James Logan McLean, for many years a Lincolnton citizen and official, was born in Lincoln (now Gaston) County in 1837. He married about 1861 to Margaret Ann Smith of Dallas. Soon after his marriage the Civil War began and he volunteered as a private in Company B, 13th North Carolina Regiment, Scales Brigade, and was among those paroled at Appomattox Courthouse, April 12, 1865. The historian states that this "regiment was in every battle in which Stonewall Jackson's Corps was engaged." The record further states "that at 2 o'clock P.M., April 12, 1865, in view of all Federal Brigades standing at present arms, the 13th Regiment of North Carolina troops stacked its full quota of muskets, thus helping to make up a greater total from North Carolina than from the remainder of General Lee's army." Logan McLean was one of that noble group.

Mr. McLean moved to Lincolnton soon after the Civil War, and was a citizen of the town to the end of his life. He was a genial gentleman. He wrote a splendid hand, was a capable accountant, and for some years rendered good service as assistant to the Clerk of Superior Court, in which position he became familiar with the law, was a good judge of law, a Magistrate for many years, and Mayor of Lincolnton for the years 1882 and 1883. His last illness was aggravated by a breast wound received in the Civil War and he died April 12, 1885, just twenty years to the day after his regiment surrendered at Appomattox.

His children were:

1. J. Thomas McLean, who for many years operated a marble yard and who served as Mayor of Lincolnton in 1903 and 1904. He died in 1922.

2. Mattie McLean, who died single about 1887. She and her parents were buried in the old Methodist church graveyard in Lincolnton.

3. Carrie L. McLean, who graduated from Chowan College, Murfreesboro, N. C.; taught school for one year; went to Charlotte in 1894, and held a position in a business office there for many years; studied law and was admitted to the bar in 1918, and has practiced law in Charlotte since 1921. She represented Mecklenburg in the Legislature of 1927, one of the few women of the State who have served in that capacity. She made a good record as a law maker and is a capable and successful lawyer. She is now, and has been since 1916 Public Administrator for Mecklenburg County.

4. Mary L. McLean, married in 1903 to James H. Taylor of Wilmington. He died in 1931. Mrs. Taylor and her only daughter, Carrie McLean Taylor, now (1935) live in Burlington, N. C.

The Lincolnton High School Commencement was held May 28, 1885, under the direction of Prof. D. Matt Thompson, the principal. The marshals were Frank Alexander, Chief, assisted by J. N. Hauss, W. A. Eudy, R. E. Harrill and J. F. Phifer. Rev. P. R. Law, of Monroe, preached the sermon and Thomas Dixon, Jr., of Shelby, delivered the literary address. Students who took part in the exercises which followed were: J. N. Hauss, Irva Reinhardt, Betty Wilkey, William Eudy, Lula Detter,

Robert Harrill, Ella Summerow, Moulton Phifer, Lucy Cauble, Jennie Johnston, Jennie Noland, Sallie Nixon, Ada Costner, Sallie Odell, Aubrey Motz, Holland Thompson, Frank Alexander, Connie Lawing and Carrie Motz.

1886

Late in 1886, Theodorus H. Cobb, a prominent Lincolnton lawyer, moved to Asheville, a growing city, where he continued to practice law. (See 1905.)

Albertus D. Childs, a member of the well-known Childs family, died in Lincolnton in 1886, aged 76.

Robert Caldwell Johnston (eldest son of Rev. R. Z. Johnston, the pastor of the Lincolnton Presbyterian Church), was instantly killed in a cyclone in Parson, Pennsylvania, in November, 1886. He was a fine boy, only 17 years old, and his untimely death cast a cloud of sorrow over the community.

David A. Jenkins, son of Aaron Jenkins, was born in Lincoln (now Gaston) County, April 5, 1822, and became a prominent citizen of the State. He was successful in all his business ventures and commanded the confidence of the people.

He represented Gaston County in the Legislature of 1865 and 1866; was elected State Treasurer in 1868 on the Republican ticket and re-elected for a second term in 1872, and served until 1877; settled in Gastonia and lived in retirement until his death, September 10, 1886.

In the Reconstruction days when corruption was rampant he stood as a stone wall against even the appearance of fraud, and so won the respect of the people without regard to party, that they called him "Honest Dave" Jenkins, believing that no ill gotten gain had ever soiled his hands.

He married Lodema Holland, daughter of Jesse Holland of Gaston, and among their children were: Mary, who married John H. Craig; Elmira, married Dr. W. H. Hoffman; Martha, married L. M. Hoffman, late of Dallas, lawyer, banker and historian; Aaron D., married Claudia, daughter of the Rev. Dr. Thomas H. Pritchard, of the Baptist church; Wm. W., married Nannie Mangum of Wake County, Postmaster in Charlotte for some years; James C., married Susie Scruggs of Atlanta—he became a Federal Judge in the Philippine Islands; David H., a textile manufacturer, married Bettie Conrad; Laban L., the youngest son, established the First National Bank in Gastonia and grew to be a capitalist and had interest in many Gaston County cotton mills.

Dr. John M. Richardson, a popular Lincolnton physician, died in 1886, aged 53 years. He was the only son of Rev. J. J. Richardson, of the South Carolina Methodist Conference, and his wife, Catherine Schenck, daughter of Michael and Barbara (Warlick) Schenck, of Lincolnton. When Dr. Richardson was very young his father died and he was reared in Lincolnton in the home of his grandfather Schenck. He became a physician and practiced medicine in his home town and community to the end of his life. He married December 21, 1858, to Alice, daughter of Dr. Alex Ramsour; one of their daughters, Mary Richardson, married to Rev. Chas. L. Hoffman, an Episcopal minister. Other children were Leonard, Malvina, Lila and Julia (who married Dr. H. K. Dillard of Philadelphia). Dr. Richardson was an active member of and a lay leader in the Episcopal church, and a much loved physician whose death brought sorrow to many people.

Col. John F. Phifer (1810-1886), a native of Cabarrus, married June 5, 1839 to Elizabeth, daughter of David Ramsour, a Lincolnton merchant. He had farmed on Coddle Creek, west of Concord, for a while and later was a planter in Lowndes County, Alabama, until 1842 when he settled in Lincolnton. He had extensive landed interests and many slaves. Before the Civil War he and his kinsman, Col. R. W. Allison of Concord bought the Ivy Shoals Cotton Mill, now Elm Grove Mills, which they operated under the management of Col. Phifer until his death. He was regarded in his day, in Lincolnton, as a very rich man— one of the few business men in that community who carried a bank balance and was always glad to accommodate those who wanted to exchange cash for checks. It was common in his day when referring to some wealthy person to hear the expression, "He is almost as rich as Col. Phifer." In politics he was an old line Whig and opposed to the Civil War, but when war began he stood loyal to the Confederate government and all but one of his sons died in military service.

In 1865 when the conquering army invaded this section a brigade of Federal Cavalry under command of Gen. John C. Palmer, entered Lincolnton and General Palmer made his headquarters in the home of Col. Phifer, whose courtliness and diplomacy no doubt influenced Palmer to restrain his troops to such effect that the minimum of pilfering was perpetrated while they were here.

1. His son, Capt. George L. Phifer, the only son who lived after the Civil War, was active with his father in managing the cotton mill. He married a daughter of the late Col. Moulton Avery of Burke and reared a large family.

2. His only daughter, Mary Wilfong Phifer, born December 25, 1856, was a beautiful and charming young woman, loved by all who knew her. She married to Stephen Smith, of Livingston, Alabama, in 1880, and died February 3, 1936, at the home of her son, Phifer Smith, in Mentone, Alabama, and was buried in Livingston, Alabama.

Col. Phifer was a son of George Phifer (1782-1819) and grandson of Martin Phifer, Jr. (1756-1837), who married Elizabeth, daughter of Gen. Matthew Locke, of Rowan. He was a Presbyterian in faith, a loyal churchman, and a patriotic citizen, a public-spirited and genial gentleman, held in high esteem by all the people. He was the tender-hearted friend of every distressed man, white or black, and won the frindship of the poor by being a friend to those less fortunate than himself. When he died the people mourned.

Mr. Abner McCoy, one of the oldest and most highly respected citizens of Lincolnton, died in 1886, in his 82nd year. He was a devout good man, an officer of the Presbyterian church.

I was awakened at 9 o'clock P.M., August 31, 1886, when my house shook violently, the dishes rattled and the noise made by brick falling upon the roof of a house across the street proved it to be an earthquake. Great damage was done in Charleston, S. C.; it was plainly felt in the Carolinas and shook our great mountains. Many people throughout the land were filled with consternation, thinking the end of the world was at hand.

Rev. M. V. Sherrill, preaching at the time at Rock Spring Camp Ground was concluding a sermon on the final judgment, when all at once the earth trembled, the old arbor shook and the congregation felt that it would not be long until time would be no more, and the altar was soon crowded with penitents pleading for mercy. In the memory of living man that earthquake shook this part of the country with greater force than any ever before and the event made a deep and lasting impression upon many people.

1887

Mrs. Susan Jenkins Hopkins, second wife of S. Harris Hopkins, and daughter of James C. Jenkins of Lincolnton, died March 5, 1887. She was a good woman, who before her marriage taught this writer in the Sunday School when he was a very small boy, and through the long years since he has remembered her with grateful appreciation.

Two military companies, the Southern Stars of Lincolnton, and the Hornets Nest Riflemen of Charlotte, fought together at Bethel in the first battle of the Civil War, June 10, 1861. The two companies with ranks filled by younger men who did not fight in the Civil War met in Lincolnton, June 10, 1887, to celebrate the anniversary of that memorable contest. At this later date Charles E. Childs was the Captain, J. E. Love and R. S. Edwards, Lieutenants, and Thomas H. Hoke, Orderly Sergeant, of the Southern Stars. Captain Thomas R. Robertson was Captain of the Charlotte Company, and Heriot Clarkson (then a young man, and now a Justice of our Supreme Court) was 1st Lieutenant. Beverly C. Cobb delivered the address of welcome to the visitors and Col. John F. Hoke made the principal speech of the day. George E. Frick, Editor of the *Shelby New Era*, and Col. John C. Tipton also spoke. It was a great day in Lincolnton, sad because of the memories it revived, but glad as the people looked hopefully into a future full of promise.

Captain V. Q. Johnson, a soldier of the Confederacy, came to Lincolnton after the Civil War and became Assistant Superintendent of the Carolina Central Railway, being in control of that road west of Charlotte. Later when the gap between Wilmington and Charlotte was built he was made superintendent of the whole line and continued in that position until the road was taken over by the Seaboard system. He possessed rare executive and business ability. His eldest daughter, Ellen, married to

Theodorus H. Cobb, one of the leading lawyers of Western Carolina. Some years after the death of his first wife Captain Johnson married to Miss Susan Forney Shipp, daughter of the late Hon. Bartlett Shipp. He died October 15, 1887, after a sudden heart attack. His body is buried in the Episcopal graveyard.

A new day, commercially, dawned upon Lincolnton this year. Prior to 1854, when Charlotte got the advantage as a railroad centre, Lincolnton, next to Salisbury was the most important town in Western Carolina. Charlotte people shopped in Lincolnton but the railroads after 1854 gave Charlotte the advantage. It became the cotton market for East Lincoln and the town of Lincolnton lost business accordingly, and from then through the Civil War and on to 1886 its population and its business hardly held its own. It had the support of that fine farming community north and west of the town, but the eastern section traded largely with Denver, Beatties Ford and Charlotte. East Lincoln folks rarely came to Lincolnton except on legal and court business.

After the Civil War many moved away and others lost heart, while the few called rich were too conservative to risk money in public or manufacturing enterprises. In 1880 Lincolnton had less than 800 inhabitants, its manufactures were insignificant and the exports brought small returns from the outside world.

But in 1887, Daniel E. Rhyne and J. A. Abernethy came up from Gaston County, bought the Laboratory property for its water power, and built and operated there the Laboratory Cotton Mills. It proved a profitable investment. They then built the Daniel and Wampum Mills in Lincolnton. The water power at the old Lincoln Paper Mill and Long Shoals sites on the South Fork were utilized for cotton mills built by W. A. Mauney, of Kings Mountain, and others. Then came Edgar Love and John M. Rhodes, who built mills in Lincolnton. All these attracted other industries, labor found employment, pay rolls grew and Lincolnton became an industrial center with a population now of 5,000 with several thousand more in the suburban communities of Goodsonville, and Saxony Mills. This wonderful growth in population and business began with the coming of Daniel E. Rhyne and J. A. Abernethy in 1887.

THE ANNALS OF LINCOLN COUNTY 249

The Rev. Dr. Albert M. Shipp was born in Stokes County, January 15, 1819, son of John and Elizabeth (Oglesby) Shipp. His father died when Dr. Shipp was very small and the widow with two sons moved to Lincoln County to be near her brother-in-law Bartlett Shipp. Albert and his cousin, William M. Shipp, were prepared for college in local schools and graduated from the State University in 1840. Both were bright scholars and shared first honors when they graduated.

Mrs. John Shipp was a devout Methodist and took special pains to rear her sons Albert M. and William T. Shipp, in the fear of God. Albert was converted and joined the church at Rock Springs Camp Meeting in August, 1834, and his life motto was "Seek ye first the Kingdom of God and his righteousness." Upon his graduation he gave himself to the Christian ministry, was, at Lincolnton in December, 1840, licensed to preach and a month later was admitted into the South Carolina Conference. Was ordained deacon by Bishop Andrew in February, 1843, and Elder by Bishop Soule in December, 1844. He served as pastor in Cokesbury, Charleston, Santee, Cheraw, and Fayetteville, and as Presiding Elder of the Lincolnton District until 1848. He was then elected President of Greensboro College and served in that capacity for two years. Was Professor of History at the University from 1849 to 1859; President of Wofford College 1859 to 1875; Professor of Exegetical Theology in Vanderbilt University 1876 to 1886, when on account of ill health he retired. In 1887 his physician advised him for a change to go to Cleveland Springs and there, attended by skilled physicians without benefit, he died June 27, 1887 and his body was buried near Cheraw, S. C. Dr. Shipp was a mighty man in his day; a wise leader in the church; a delegate to every General Conference from 1850 to 1886; member of the Centenary Conference in Baltimore in 1884; author of a comprehensive History of Methodism in South Carolina. The honorary degree of Doctor of Divinity was conferred on him by Randolph-Macon College in 1859 and Doctor of Laws by the University of North Carolina in 1883. His versatility is shown by the fact that he taught history at the University of North Carolina, mental and moral science at Wofford, and Exegetical Theology at Vanderbilt. One of his old Wofford students remembered him as a spare-built man, stoop-shouldered and clean shaven, a master of pure English and oratory, and, while a strict disciplinarian, loved by the student body.

Dr. William Martin in *Southern Christian Advocate*, December 15, 1887, paid to Dr. Shipp this high tribute: "He was a close student all his life and a scholar of high order. He was a noble gentleman, generous in deed, pure in life, courtly in bearing, considerate of the weak, and chivalrous to women. As a preacher he occupied a place in the front rank of theologians; his pulpit efforts were marked with clearness of conception, systematic in arrangement, powerful in thought, vigorous in expression, and always instructive and impressive."

At the session of the S. C. Conference at Morganton in 1867, he preached a sermon of overwhelming power and eloquence from John 12:48, which brought a shout from Dr. Chas. Betts.

He was married in Cheraw, S. C., April 23, 1846 to Miss Mary Gillespie and among their children were:

1. John Wilds Shipp, who died in 1888. He, like his father, was an educator, and professor of Languages in Bellevue College at Caledonia Mission.

2. Samuel W. G. Shipp of Florence, S. C., one of the most learned lawyers of South Carolina, a judge of the Superior Court for many years. He is a man of wide culture and ranks high among the lawyers of his state.

3. Harriet Elizabeth Shipp, married John M. Webb, one of the founders of the celebrated Webb School, located at Bell Buckle, Tenn. Their son, Albert Micajah Webb is a professor of French at Duke University.

4. Mary Wade Shipp, married Rev. Samuel G. Saunders, a Methodist minister of Texas. Their son, Shipp Saunders, teaches Greek and Latin at the University of North Carolina (1935).

5. Sarah W., who died in 1882 at Cheraw, S. C., when about 18 years old.

6. Susan V. Shipp, who now lives in Durham, N. C.

7. Albert W. Shipp, who died recently (1937) in Nashville, Tenn., where he was a merchant for many years.

8. J. Thornwell Shipp, a graduate of Vanderbilt University, a Civil Engineer now residing at Chattanooga, Tenn.

Dr. Albert M. Shipp was one of the great men who went out from Lincoln County and his descendants honor the name.

Top left: Rev. Dr. Albert M. Shipp (1819-1887). See 1887.
Top right: Rev. Dr. R. L. Abernethy (1822-1894). See 1894.
Center: Rev. Dr. Robt. H. Morrison (1798-1889). See 1889.
Lower left: Rev. Dr. Alfred J. Fox (1817-1884). See 1884.
Lower right: Rev. P. F. W. Stamey (1849-1890). See 1890.

1888

Col. John F. Hoke was a lawyer of first rate ability. He was a graduate of the State University and was admitted to the bar and practiced in Lincoln and adjoining counties until his death. He was born in Lincolnton, May 30, 1820, and died suddenly, October 27, 1888, while sitting on his porch watching a political procession pass. His parents were Col. John Hoke and wife, Barbara (Quickel) Hoke.

He was a notable citizen and for many years influential in county politics. At the outbreak of the Mexican War in 1846 he volunteered for service, was commissioned Captain and took part in several hotly contested battles.

Was State Senator in 1850, '52 and '54, and a member of the House of Commons in 1860 and 1865.

He resigned his seat in the House in 1861 to accept the office of Adjutant General, resigned that office when commissioned Colonel by Gov. Ellis, and was active as a soldier until the close of the Civil War.

Col. Hoke was married to Catherine, daughter of Col. William Julius Alexander, October 30, 1850. They had three children: Judge William Alexander Hoke, Sallie Badger and Nancy Childs Hoke, cultured and brilliant women. Mrs. Hoke died December 23, 1857.

Dr. Chas. S. Rozzelle, Republican, was defeated for the Legislature by W. A. Hoke in the November election.

Benjamin Harrison, Republican, defeated Grover Cleveland for President, and Daniel G. Fowle, Democrat, was elected governor over Oliver H. Dockery, Republican.

1889

Rev. Dr. Robert Hall Morrison filled a high niche in the history of the Presbyterian Church in North Carolina. He was born in Rocky River Section of Cabarrus County, September 8, 1798, and died in Lincoln County, May 13, 1889. He graduated from the State University, when 19 years old, in the class with Gov. Wm. D. Moseley, of Florida, Bishop William M. Greene, of the Episcopal church, Hamilton C. Jones of Rowan, and James K. Polk, who divided honors with him. He took a course at Princeton Theological Seminary; was ordained to the ministry in 1820 by Concord Presbytery; was pastor of Providence church in Mecklenburg County two years; served the Fayetteville church five years; then Sugar Creek and while there organized the First Presbyterian church in Charlotte with 38 members. He was active in the founding of Davidson College of which he was the first President. He helped raise $30,000 for the school, which was a heavy task in those days. After three years at Davidson he resigned on account of ill health in 1840 and moved to his farm in Lincoln County. For thirty years he was Pastor of Unity Presbyterian church, and during that period he organized Castanea Grove and Machpelah churches and served as pastor of these congregations along with Unity.

Dr. Morrison rendered valued service in promoting the religious and educational growth of this section. He was consecrated to his task, and a pulpit orator of superior gifts. His messages were full of instruction and delivered with an earnestness which aroused the conscience and quickened the spiritual life of the people.

On April 27, 1824, he married Mary, daughter of General Joseph Graham of Lincoln County and they reared twelve children. The daughters:

1. Isabella married Gen. D. H. Hill.
2. Mary Anna married Gen. T. J. (Stonewall) Jackson.
3. Eugenia married Gen. Rufus Barringer.
4. Susan married Judge A. C. Avery.
5. Harriet married James P. Irwin.
6. Laura married Col. John E. Brown.

The sons:

1. William M. was a Major in the Confederate Army.
2. Joseph G. was aide to Stonewall Jackson (See 1906).
3. Dr. Robert H. Morrison, Jr., was on the staff of General D. H. Hill. (See 1922.)
4. Alfred J. Morrison became a Presbyterian minister and served churches in Franklin, N. C., and Selma, Ala., until his death in 1876. (See 1876.)

Notable among his grandsons were Dr. Paul B. Barringer, a skilled physician and educator; Dr. Randolph W. Hill, Chairman of the State Board of Health of California, died in Los Angeles, California; Joseph Morrison Hill, one time Chief Justice of the Arkansas Supreme Court; Dr. D. H. Hill, Jr., President of State College, Raleigh, until his death; Isaac Erwin Avery, a brilliant newspaper writer and one time in Consular service in China; Alphonso C. Avery, Jr., a successful lawyer; Col. R. H. Morrison; Rev. Edmund Brown; Joseph Graham Morrison, Jr., the County Farm Agent of Lincoln County, whose son, Joseph Graham Morrison, III, is now a Presbyterian minister (1936); and Major T. J. Jackson Christian of the U. S. Army.

CHAPTER XVII

1890-1899

In July, Governor Holt appointed Col. Matthew Locke McCorkle Judge to fill the vacancy caused by the death of Judge Shipp.

Joseph H. King, a leading citizen and merchant of the Beatties Ford section died of typhoid fever in July, 1890. He was the delegate from Lincoln to the Constitutional Convention of 1868, and in the same year was elected Sheriff of the County, by the Commissioners to fill the vacancy caused by the death of Sheriff Logan H. Lowrance, and served in that office until September, 1872, when he was defeated by J. A. Robinson.

William Marcus Shipp was a learned lawyer with the judicial mind which weighed every phase of a legal problem and came to a just conclusion. He had poise and wisdom, the qualities which made him a great judge and few of his decisions were reversed by the Supreme Court.

Lawyers regarded him as one of great ability. He was born in Lincoln County, November 9, 1819, the son of Bartlett Shipp (an able lawyer) and Susan (Forney) Shipp. He graduated from the State University in the class of 1840 and received highest honors as did his cousin, Rev. Dr. Albert M. Shipp, who delivered the valedictory, Judge Shipp delivering the salutatory address (in Latin). He was admitted to the bar in 1842 and settled in Rutherfordton to practice law. He represented Rutherford County in the House of Commons in 1854. When Judge John Baxter moved to Tennessee about 1857 Judge Shipp bought the Baxter home in Hendersonville, moved there and built up a good practice. He was the delegate from Henderson to the Convention of 1861 and signed the Ordinance of Secession. He volunteered for service in the Civil War, was made Captain of a Hendersonville company, and was the only married man in it.

He was the Senator from Henderson County in 1862; was elected Judge of the Lincoln district in 1863 and served until 1868, when he was defeated at the polls by George W. Logan. He then settled in Charlotte as a lawyer. In 1870 he defeated Samuel F. Phillips for Attorney General and distinguished himself by the able manner in which, as Chairman of the Shipp Commission, he conducted the investigation of the Swepson-Littlefield frauds of 1868 and '69. He was in 1872 defeated for re-election to the Attorney Generalship, and practiced law in Charlotte until 1881 when Governor Jarvis appointed him Judge of Superior Court for the old 9th district to fill the vacancy caused by the resignation of Judge David Schenck. He held that position until his death June 28, 1890.

Dr. Jerome Dowd gave the following high estimate of Judge Shipp as a man and lawyer:

"Judge Shipp was one of the best informed lawyers in the State. He had a markedly legal mind, reasoned closely, and as a jurist was eminent. He had no superior on the bench. He was fond of history and the literature of our language, especially the standard works. He was interesting and lively in conversation and had much wit and humor."

He inherited quickness at repartee and lively wit from his father. Many of his humorous sayings are remembered by lawyers over the State.

He married Catherine, daughter of Hon. John A. Cameron, of Fayetteville, January 21, 1851, and they had four children:

1. Anna, who married Dr. Sumner McBee.

2. Catherine, who never married but became a distinguished educator.

3. William Ewen Shipp, the brave Lieutenant, who was killed in the Spanish-American War. He married Margaret Busbee of Raleigh.

4. Bartlett, a bright lawyer, married Prue Crouse of Lincolnton. He died in Hendersonville in 1914.

Mrs. Shipp died in 1866. Judge Shipp's second marriage was to Margaret Iredell of Raleigh, daughter of Gov. Iredell, and their daughter, Mary Preston Shipp, lives in Raleigh.

Leonard E. Thompson, who for many years practiced law in Lincolnton, and was prominent in County affairs, died about 1890, aged 95 years. He came to Lincolnton from New Jersey in the early 1830's with his sisters, one of whom, Miss Amelia Thompson, was for some years principal of the old Lincolnton

Female Academy. Mr. Thompson was a man of education, a civil engineer as well as a lawyer and a citizen of character and influence. He was an Episcopalian.

Lincoln Courier—February 7, 1890. J. M. Roberts, Editor.

A special meeting of the stockholders of Lincoln Lithia Water Company will be held in Lincolnton February 20, 1890, for the election of a Board of Directors to serve for the ensuing year and for such other business as may be brought before the meeting.

January 31, 1890. W. H. Lacey, Secretary.

Church Directory

Presbyterian: Rev. R. Z. Johnston, Pastor—Preaching at Iron Station, 2nd Sunday, 3 P.M. Preaching at Paper Mill Academy, 4th Sunday, 3 P.M.
Methodist: Rev. M. H. Hoyle, Pastor.
German Reformed: Rev. J. L. Murphy, Pastor.
Lutheran: Rev. J. C. Rudisill, Pastor.
Lutheran: Rev. M. L. Little, Pastor.

The County Commissioners: J. A. Robinson, Chairman; P. A. Reep, W. M. Hull, L. B. Camp and J. W. A. Paine met Monday, February 3, 1890, and transacted routine business. The following were drawn for jury service for spring term of Superior Court: J. L. Reinhardt, Levi Kaylor, Harrison Cauble, J. B. Abernethy, J. A. Johnson, H. A. Gilland, J. M. Rendleman, George W. Cauble, Thomas Stamey, A. S. Coon, E. T. Childs, Jesse Reep, W. S. Kids, E. P. Cloniger, A. P. Rudisill, Aaron Goodson, R. B. Sullivan, C. L. P. Heavner, J. L. Shrum, G. F. Helderman, Pink Monday, Thomas Ballard, J. Brotherton, Rankin Cherry, R. S. Edwards, Daniel Keener, Jacob Miller, Z. B. Cauble, Andrew Sain, W. P. Huss, J. J. Sullivan, H. W. Burton, J. E. Keever, Nat Hager, John M. Motz, Clingman Wood.

D. Matt Thompson, principal of Lincolnton Seminary, advertises for students.

The Lowesville School is open for male and female pupils, with Rev. R. W. Boyd as Principal.

Rev. Paul Franklin Winfield Stamey was born May 6, 1849, a son of Rev. Alexander and Belzorah Stamey. His father was a Baptist minister. His grandfather, Daniel Stamey, with two brothers, John and Peter, came from Pennsylvania in 1787, and settled in Burke County near the Lincoln line. John R. Stamey, the sheriff of Lincoln County, who died in 1851, was a member of this clan.

In 1864 a lad in his teens he was converted at Palm Tree Methodist church, Lincoln County, in a meeting conducted by his Baptist father, and then joined the Methodist church and became an active member. He was educated at Rutherford College where he came under the influence of the great teacher, Dr. R. L. Abernethy; was licensed to preach and in 1873 was admitted into the North Carolina Conference and served in the order mentioned, the following charges: Dallas, Morganton, Newton, Iredell, Mooresville and Albemarle Circuits, Reidsville Station; in 1889 was appointed Presiding Elder of the Trinity District; on July 4, 1890, died of typhoid fever.

He was loved by all who knew him, for he had a warm magnetic nature, was deeply spiritual, always drew large congregations, and was wonderfully successful as an evangelistic preacher. During a ministry of seventeen years he added some 2,500 members to the church.

Rev. E. H. Davis, who wrote his obituary, said:

"Among his brethren of the Conference he was regarded as a remarkable and unusually successful winner of souls. If there was any other object of legitimate endeavor before a gospel minister, any side track of pleasurable pursuit outside of this, he did not know it.

"He was a man of one work and of one way of doing it, and that way, 'constant, unremitting, faithful use of the Word'; and success, as he understood the word, as applicable to himself and his work, crowned his efforts.

"A true preacher packs his sentences with the gospel, rather than with logic, and transcends ordinary pulpit speakers, not in the beauty of his periods, but in the multitude of his converts. Take this estimate of true preaching and lay beside it the life and labors of P. F. W. Stamey and say if he has not received the 'well done' of Him whom he loved to serve."

He married in early life to Miss Harriet F. Wyant of Catawba County.

1891

Rev. M. L. Little, a prominent minister of the Lutheran church, pastor of Daniels Church, 1882-83, President of Gaston College, which he founded in 1883, was killed in a railway accident three miles south of Newton on Chester and Lenoir Railway, February 16, 1891.

Mr. Little went to Dallas in 1882 as principal of the Dallas Academy. Soon thereafter he enlisted the interest of prominent Lutherans, Jonas Hoffman, Henry Setzer, John L. Rhyne, Miles A. Rhyne, J. S. Mauney, W. A. Mauney, John M. Rhodes, Moses H. Rhyne, A. P. Rhyne, Ambrose Costner, David Mauney, L. L. Suggs, and others, who contributed $10,000 for the establishment of Gaston College in Dallas. He secured Rev. Dr. L. A. Bikle, Dr. L. L. Lohr and J. M. Roberts (later editor of *Lincoln Courier*) as teachers, and the school prospered until its buildings were destroyed by fire about 1915.

Rev. Mr. Little was an able minister, who undertook, at a time when money was hard to raise, to launch and carry to a successful finish a campaign for higher education in Gaston County. A useful man he was, and North Carolina lost a fine citizen when he met with a tragic death.

1892

Grover Cleveland defeated Benjamin Harrison for President in the November election. Elias Carr was elected Governor, defeating Judge D. M. Furches, the Republican candidate.

Rev. Marcus W. Boyles was born in Lincoln County, October 29, 1842, and died in Lexington, N. C. January 15, 1892. He was brought up on a farm, reared in obscurity and with limited educational advantages. His people were religious, his grandfather, John Boyles, a local Methodist preacher. From childhood the solid foundation of a Christian character was laid under the restraint and helpful influence of godly parents, and in 1860 he joined the Methodist church.

On July 9, 1861, when eighteen years old, he entered the Confederate Army as a soldier in the First Regiment of North Carolina Volunteers and served faithfully until the close of the war. He was married to Susan A. Wood, of Lincoln County, March 14, 1866, and among their children were: Augustus C.,

Franklin C., Joseph H., Marcus M., Pitman A., and a daughter, Mrs. Blanche Carr Sterne, of Greensboro. He felt the call to the Christian ministry early in 1870, and, determined to prepare himself for that work, attended Rutherford College under the instruction of Dr. R. L. Abernethy. In June, 1873, he was licensed to preach at Palm Tree church (South Fork Circuit), was admitted into the North Carolina Conference in November following, and served as pastor of six several charges, covering eighteen years until his death early in 1892.

He was a good man, faithful to duty, and successful in his ministry in every charge to which he was assigned. His son Frank C. Boyles was for many years a Greensboro bank officer and is an active official of the church in that city.

1893

Financial panics come about every twenty years, 1817, 1837, 1857 were panic years. After the Civil War the panic came in 1873, ahead of time, and then in 1893 the people were again in financial distress. Farm products were low and there was general depression in all branches of trade, which continued for about four years, during which time the people found the way back to a better day by hard work and rigid economy.

Dr. Sumner McBee, of Lincolnton, son of Mr. Vardry A. McBee, a fine physician and lovable man, died in September, after a lingering illness.

Miss Nannie Childs Hoke, younger daughter of Col. John F. Hoke, was a woman of fine intellect and rare culture, as was also her sister, Miss Sallie Badger Hoke. They were charming women who made friends of all they met and their father had good right to be proud of them. Miss Nannie was postmistress in Lincolnton from 1885 until her death in 1893.

On December 23, 1893, the old historic White Church, which was nearly as old as the town and the first church built in Lincolnton, was destroyed by fire. It is said that every congregation now in Lincolnton used the old church to worship in, until each denomination built a church of its own. It was built first of logs prior to 1788, was later enlarged, weatherboarded, ceiled and painted white. It then ceased to be called the Dutch Meeting

House, and was known as the Old White Church. Rev. John Gottfried Arndt, the first Lutheran minister in Lincolnton, was buried under the old church.

In the early 1870's Bishop John J. Moore of the African Zion Methodist Church, came to Lincolnton and lived here for several years. His color was coal black and his head was not large, but he possessed superior intellect, was a Hebrew and Greek scholar, and a preacher of wonderful pulpit power. His history is interesting.

He was born free in Berkeley County, Virginia, now West Virginia, about 1804, but his mother, with her two children, were kidnaped and carried into slavery, from which they finally escaped. One of the children, John, the subject of this sketch, was later bound to a Pennsylvania farmer, who, after the boy had reached majority, continued for several years to profit by his labor, until a friendly Quaker interposed in John's behalf and had him released.

In 1833 he joined a Methodist church in Harrisburg, Penn. Later he felt the call, and in 1834 was licensed to preach. From 1836, for three years, under private teachers, he not only studied the English branches, but also Latin, Greek and Hebrew and became one of the greatest preachers of his race. In 1839 he united with the Philadelphia Conference and served various congregations. As early as 1852 he planted churches in San Francisco, San Jose, Napa and other points in California.

In 1868 he was elected Bishop and in this larger field of opportunity he became widely known. The writer has heard him preach on several occasions sermons of rare force and eloquence, for he was not only a fine Bible scholar but knew how "in the simple language of the poor" to illuminate a text and then with overpowering spiritual fervor grip and hold the attention of both cultured and ignorant people. Few of this generation remember that more than sixty years ago this humble and godly man lived in Lincolnton during the period when he had oversight of the various Conferences of his church in this section of the South.

He died in 1893 at the advanced age of 89 years.

Benjamin S. Guion, for many years a citizen of Lincolnton, died in Charlotte, November 9, 1893, aged 68 years.

Benjamin S. Guion (1825-1893) married Catherine C. Caldwell (1846-1930) in Lincolnton, October 26, 1864. She was the daughter of Dr. Pinckney C. Caldwell a distinguished citizen of Charlotte. The Rev. W. R. Wetmore, Rector of St. Luke's church was the officiating minister.

Mr. Guion was born in Newbern, graduated from the State University in 1848 in class with Judge Victor C. Barringer, Gen. L. D. Pender, Col. O. H. Dockery, Judge O. P. Meares, Seaton Gales and others. He then studied law and was admitted to the bar. He was for many years a citizen of Lincolnton, was a skilled civil engineer and superintended the construction of the Seaboard Railroad from Shelby to Rutherfordton. Later he moved to Charlotte and died there. He was a brother of the late Haywood W. Guion, a distinguished lawyer.

His children were:

Katie, who married Dr. J. W. Babcock, a skilled physician, for many years Superintendent of the State Hospital in Columbia, S. C.; Effie, who married Dr. J. P. McCombs of Charlotte and now lives in New York with her daughter, Dr. Anne Parks McCombs, who is a physician there; Alice, who married S. J. Vason; Laura, who married A. C. Haskell of Columbia; Louis, who married Elizabeth Guignard, lives in South Carolina and is District Vice-President and Director of the Federal Farm Loan Bank; Mary Wood, who married S. D. Newton; Benjamin S., who married Claudia Cashwell, lives in Gastonia and is Vice-President and Secretary of the A. H. Guion Contracting Company; Vivian Q., who married Louise Daniel; Connie M. Guion, M. D., a New York medical practitioner; Alex H., who married Anne, daughter of the late John D. B. McLean of Gastonia, is President and Treasurer of the A. H. Guion Co., General Contractors of Charlotte; Ridie Justice, who is a teacher in Massachusetts; Josephine Wilson, who married O. O. Wood and lives in Berkeley, California.

1894

General William H. Forney, was born in Lincolnton Nov. 11, 1823, son of Jacob, and Sarah (Hoke) Forney. When eleven years old he went with his family to Alabama. Was educated at the University of Alabama; served as Lieutenant in the Mexican War; member of the Alabama Legislature 1859-60; volunteered for service in the Civil War, was commissioned Captain, was promoted several times for gallantry and came home from the war with the rank of Brigadier General; Member of the Alabama Senate, 1865-66; Member of Congress 1875 to 1893, when on account of ill health he declined a renomination; died at Jacksonville, Ala., Jan. 16, 1894.

The County officers whose terms expired in December, 1894, were John K. Cline, Sheriff; Chas. E. Childs, Clerk Superior Court; B. C. Wood, Register of Deeds; John C. Quickel, Treasurer; O. C. Thompson, Surveyor; J. B. Heim, Coroner; and R. M. Roseman, A. L. Cherry, P. A. Reep, J. Ed Reinhardt and W. M. Hull, County Commissioners.

At the election held in November the Fusion ticket was elected, with Chas. H. Rhodes for Sheriff; G. A. Barkley, Clerk Superior Court; J. F. Killian, Register of Deeds; and D. L. Yount, Treasurer.

J. W. A. Paine, an enterprising citizen of the Lowesville section, and State Senator in 1891, died in 1894.

The Farmers Alliance, which had been organized for several years, finally got into politics, and as cotton was selling for less than $25.00 a bale, the blame was laid, as usual, upon the party in power, though Mr. Cleveland, the President, was in no wise responsible for it. The Populist Party was organized, a great many farmers affiliated with it, formed an alliance with the Republicans, carried the State by an overwhelming majority and elected Marion Butler, a Populist, and Jeter C. Pritchard, a Republican, to the United States Senate. Lincoln County was carried by this fusion of Populists and Republicans.

Dr. John M. Lawing, a native of Mecklenburg, graduated from the State University in 1857, then attended lectures at Jefferson Medical College in Philadelphia and secured his degree as a medical doctor.

When the Civil War began he served as hospital steward and later as a surgeon. In 1866 he came to Lincolnton and established a drug store and in connection with it began the practice of medicine. He was both a skilled physician and a skilled pharmacist and continued in the practice until his death in 1894.

He married Agnes, daughter of the late William Lander. They had three children:
1. Connor, who married Stephen Herndon.
2. Lander.
3. Karl L., who after his father's death took over the drug business and managed it with splendid success for forty years until he died in 1934.

Col. Wm. H. Michal (1821-1894) was for almost a lifetime a Lincolnton merchant. He knew how to buy goods and how to sell them, for he was a fine salesman with rare business judgment and succeeded in all his financial ventures. He was not only a good business man but a loyal churchman, a Presbyterian elder, and a citizen of high standing. The home of Col. Michal was a center of hospitality where friends far and near were graciously entertained.

There were four children: (1) Sarah, who was an invalid; (2) Annie, who married Thomas H. Hoke; (3) Catherine; (4) Robert.

Mrs. Hoke was the only one of the four who married. She was an accomplished musician and for many years organist at the Presbyterian church. On account of her musical talent she generally directed the music at Lincolnton marriages and funerals. Her daughter, Katherine, married John Hall of Wilmington and their son, Rev. Frank Hall, is a promising minister of the Presbyterian Church, now serving as pastor in Morehead City, North Carolina.

Robert Laban Abernethy, President and founder of Rutherford College, died November 28, 1894. He was born in Lincoln County in 1822, of good Revolutionary stock, son of Turner and Fannie (Whitener) Abernethy and grandson of Robert Abernethy, one of the patriotic delegates from Tryon County to the Halifax Convention of 1776. At the period of his birth the family was hampered by various reverses, but the son, Robert, a precocious youth, without books, teacher, school, leisure, or even health, had a thirst for knowledge which inspired him to make every sacrifice to satisfy that thirst. Despite arduous farm labors he found intervals to collect text books, and so eager was he for learning that he once walked across two counties to get a copy of Pike's Arithmetic and an English Grammar. After a day of hard work on the farm, instead of sleeping he studied by the firelight and was literally a self-educated man.

When twelve years old he joined Wesley Chapel (Methodist) in the western part of the County, and his father and mother joined at the same time in 1834. When he reached his majority he was licensed as a local preacher and for several years assisted in meetings at old Wesley Camp Ground and other points. He joined the South Carolina Conference and was ordained deacon November 5, 1854, and was pastor in York, S. C., and later Burke circuit, North Carolina, which included Burke County and the country to Blue Ridge Mountains. When preaching in this territory he taught old fashioned grammar schools and later established Rutherford College. He was a flaming evangelist and in the three years of his early ministry thousands were moved by his eloquent appeals and great multitudes added to the church.

But his zeal was greater than his strength and he was forced to give up the active ministry for the work of a teacher. He came to the class room well equipped as a linguist, historian, mathematician and psychologist, and withal a great personality. His students loved him and he was a mighty inspiration to many pupils who had little faith in their capacity.

He was the soul of generosity, with a heart full of the milk of human kindness, and the friend of all men. He was willing to take the coat from his back to relieve distress, or to divide his last loaf with a hungry man. Many times his last dollar has gone to meet the wants of a needy soul, and too often the sharper preyed upon his generous nature. He gave liberally to various charitable calls when it was a struggle to maintain his large family. He was an enemy of the liquor traffic and once, when a blockader sold whiskey to his students, he had him indicted and convicted, and then out of sympathy paid the fine for the poor culprit to keep him out of jail.

The far reaching influence of his educational work can never be known. No boy was ever turned away from his school on account of poverty. In fact more than two thousand poor boys have been educated by him and fully one thousand of these were converted to Christ through his teaching and influence and many became useful ministers of the gospel. Though self-educated he became a great scholar, a great teacher, and a great preacher.

He had a commanding presence, a magnetic nature, a fervent spirit, a logical mind with a brilliant imagination, which illuminated the truth and made it plain to the most unlettered, and at the same time held in firm grip the interest of the most cultured, which made him a preacher of great power.

In 1869 he received his Master's degree from Trinity College, and in 1880 the degree of Doctor of Divinity from Alfred University.

On February 11, 1847, he married to Mary A. Hayes of Caldwell County, a woman of rare native gifts, who was a faithful helpmeet. Among their children were:

1. Rev. John T. Abernethy, a brilliant preacher and member of the North Carolina (Methodist) Conference. In the early 1890's when Sam Jones, the Evangelist, holding a meeting in Wilmington, was disabled for several days, Mr. Abernethy preached for that time with great force and acceptability. He had several sons of more than ordinary talent. Hon. Chas. L. Abernethy, of Newbern, a good lawyer, was solicitor of his district for several terms, and Congressman from the Newbern district for twelve years. Two other sons were physicians. Dr. Claude Abernethy was a prominent Raleigh physician and Dr. Eric Abernethy was the University physician at Chapel Hill until his death in 1933.

2. Rev. L. Berge Abernethy, now a prominent member of the Western North Carolina Conference (Methodist) and one time President of Weaver College. He is a prodigy in Mathematics and could fill well the chair of Mathematics in any school in the country. His daughter, Ethel Abernethy, Ph.D. (University of Chicago), for some years has filled the Chair of Psychology in Queens-Chicora College of Charlotte, N. C. Another daughter, Irene Abernethy, has been a capable teacher and is now a skilled accountant in the office of the Duke Power Co., in Charlotte. His son, John Abernethy, like his father, is brilliant in Mathematics.

3. Rev. William E. Abernethy, a brilliant orator, one time a college professor and Methodist minister, then a Baptist minister, now deceased.

4. Arthur T. Abernethy, a gifted speaker and author of many books.

Dr. Jerome Dowd, in *Piedmont North Carolinians*, said:

The force of its own merit makes its way.

Dr. R. L. Abernethy is a striking instance of a self-made man. He was born poor, and had not even good health with which to fight the battle of life, but he bravely faced the world and with many manly strokes overcame every barrier until he won a high position among the educators of the State.

He possessed the rare but admirable faculty of inspiring his pupils with a laudable ambition. His mental powers were strong and he dared say what he thought. Many a poor boy has knocked at the door of his college and received a free education.

Governor Vance once said, "I believe that Dr. Abernethy has done more good than any other North Carolinian, living or dead."

Dr. J. T. Bagwell, one of his former pupils, pays the great teacher the beautiful tribute which follows:

I would uncover my head and unsandal my feet as I write the name of Dr. R. L. Abernethy, whose history challenges the admiration of angels and men.

Poor, yet making many rich; sorrowful, yet always rejoicing; struggling against adversity; bearing almost intolerable burdens; giving out his life's blood drop by drop, for the vitalization of others; performing more unrequited labor than almost any man of his generation, and yet possessing amid it all a cheerful optimistic spirit, with a mind as free from sordid ambition and lust for place or power as a little child; his hopes for improving facilities, for more efficient and extended work were always baffled; performing herculean labors to the last hours, then dying with his mind surcharged with broad plans and lofty aims, he finished a life for idyllic embalmment to be sung to children yet unborn.

If it be true that he lives the greatest who lives in the largest number of the lives of his countrymen, surely Dr. Abernethy was a great man. As such true history should write him.

Maxwell Warlick, for many years one of the most substantial men of the County, died May 5, 1894, at the advanced age of ninety years, and left to his children the rich heritage of a good name. He came of good German stock. The Warlick name has

THE ANNALS OF LINCOLN COUNTY 267

for six generations stood for industry, frugality and high integrity. He was a great grandson of Daniel Warlick, the pioneer, whose land grants bear dates, 1750 and 1751. He never had political ambition, but took an active interest in public affairs. He served as Magistrate and as a member of the County Court, and was one of the contractors who built the old Court House in the 1850's, which was torn away in 1922 to make room for the present handsome structure.

Mr. Warlick was married to Catherine Coulter, August 7, 1837 and their nine children were:

John C., who married Mary Lutz.
Eliza Jane married John F. Roberts.
Barbara married Frank Low.
David C. married Mary Rhodes.
Henry D. married Betty Wharton.
Margaret married John T. Hoover.
Anna married A. B. Dorsey.
Sallie married Martin Hovis.
Jacob R. married Emma Wharton.

The pioneer, Daniel Warlick, I, was one of the early settlers in the County and three of his sons were:

1. Nicholas Warlick, who, with his brother, Phillip, and Israel Sain, was killed in the Battle of Ramsour's Mill, all three being buried in one grave. Nicholas had a son, Daniel, III, who was the father of Maxwell Warlick.

2. Daniel Warlick, II, had a daughter named Barbara, who, on May 11, 1801, married to Michael Schenck, the pioneer who came in the early days from Pennsylvania and settled in Lincolnton where he established the first cotton factory south of the Potomac River. Their sons, Henry and Dr. David Warlick Schenck, were prominent in their day.

Henry was the father of Maj. H. F. Schenck, late of Cleveland County, and grandfather of John F. Schenck, of Shelby.

Dr. David Warlick Schenck lived in Lincolnton and was the father of the late Judge David Schenck (1833-1902) and grandfather of Judge Michael Schenck, now (1935) a justice of the North Carolina Supreme Court.

3. Lewis Warlick, the youngest son of Daniel Warlick, the pioneer, married Mary Hoyle, and Solomon (one of his sons) married, August 15, 1817, to Barbara, sister of Maxwell Warlick. Among their children were:

(a) Lewis Franklin Warlick, who married first to Sarah Balina Robinson whose daughter, Anne, married to Rev. J. N. Payne, of Burke, and they were the parents of Dr. Bruce Ryburn Payne, President of Peabody Teachers College, Nashville, Tenn., until his death, April 21, 1937.

(b) Eli A. Warlick, another son of Solomon and Barbara Warlick, was for several years a teacher in Catawba College, and later a Newton merchant until his death. His first wife was Catherine, daughter of Gen. Daniel Seagle. They had three sons:

George A. Warlick, a prominent business man of Newton.

William M., one time editor of the *Lincolnton News* and later went to Texas where he died.

Thomas, who become a lawyer. He married Mattie Wilson, of Catawba County. Judge Wilson Warlick is their son.

1895

Caleb Motz, son of John and Catherine Loretz Motz, of Lincoln County, and for many years an influential citizen, died February 20, 1895, aged 69 years. He was a progressive farmer and active in county politics, and the delegate from Lincoln to the Constitutional Convention of 1875. He married Emmaline Almira Carson of Marion, October 26, 1858. Their children were:

Matilda Ellen, died December 5, 1863.

John Carson, unmarried.

William Wilson, married first, Mary Helen Sherrill, of Lincolnton; second, Edna Easterday, of Jefferson, Maryland.

Samuel Cochrane, died July 11, 1891.

Aubrey, married Mary Catherine Stribling of Roswell, Georgia.

Guy, died June 24, 1872.

Caroline Matilda, married John Yancey, Jr., of Marion, N. C.

Alda McDowell, married Joseph L. C. Bird, of Marion.

Elizabeth Hampton, married William E. Grigg, of Lincolnton.

Enoch Marvin, died May 29, 1878.

Caleb Carson, married Katherine Eloise Armistead, of Nashville, Tenn.

Frederick Victor, married Annie Belle Gattis, of Durham, N. C.

Joseph C. Cobb, a native of Lincolnton, from small beginnings grew into a leading citizen and successful merchant, and for many years commanded the patronage of the people. Mr. Cobb was a modest man, true to high principle and honest dealing. He died September 16, 1895, aged 75 years. He married to Margaret, daughter of John and Elizabeth (Mauney) Butts, of Lincolnton. They had two sons, Beverly C., and John L. Cobb. The elder son, Beverly C. Cobb, was a lawyer, who practiced at the Lincoln bar for nearly thirty years, until his death, September 16, 1900. He represented the County in the Legislature in 1877 and 1879.

Robert Johnston Shipp, son of the late William T. Shipp, one time a Lincolnton lawyer, died at his home in Newton, August 14, 1895. He married Mrs. Houston of Newton and left two sons: Robert J., and William T. Shipp, both prominent citizens of Newton.

Lincoln Courier—January 4, 1895—F. S. Starrett, Editor.

Mrs. Sarah Shuford Ramsour, died December 31, 1895. The funeral was held at the Presbyterian church of which she was one of the oldest members. She was the wife of the late Henry F. Ramsour and had lived at Lincoln Paper Mill since the Civil War.

Public School Directory

Rev. R. Z. Johnston, Chairman Board of Education, with S. V. Goodson and I. R. Self as members.

Alfred Nixon, Superintendent of County Schools.

Quarterly meetings for examination of those desiring to teach.

Lincolnton Officers

Mayor, S. W. McKee; Secretary and Treasurer, H. E. Ramsour; Constable, John P. Bean.

Commissioners: P. J. Pate, Blair Jenkins, H. A. Kistler, J. Thomas McLean, Dr. T. F. Costner, J. C. Quickel, H. S. Robinson, B. C. Wood.

1896

Dr. R. B. Killian is now (1934) the oldest physician in Lincoln County. When practicing medicine in Alexander County away back fifty-eight years ago, he was called on January 17, 1876 to see a sixteen-year-old boy, named Ransom Sharpe, near Hiddenite, who was suffering desperate pain, and found that his appendix should be removed. There was no X-ray in those days but he, then and there, showed his surgical skill by taking out the appendix. The boy got well and grew to be an old man Dr. Killian had the honor of being the first physician in the state to perform such an operation. Dr. Killian died June 7 1935. (See 1935.)

In June, 1896, William J. Bryan captured the Democratic National Convention with his "cross of gold" speech and was nominated for the presidency on the 16 to 1 silver platform while William McKinley was the Republican candidate on a gold standard platform. It was a hotly contested battle and McKinley carried the election in November.

In North Carolina, the Populists fused with the Democrats and supported Bryan, but on State issues fused with the Republicans with the result that the State cast its electoral vote for Bryan, but the Republican-Populist combine elected the State ticket, the Legislature and all the Congressional candidates, except Thomas Settle, Jr., who was defeated by W. W. Kitchin, Democrat.

The Fusion candidates for county offices were elected in Lincoln, but J. F. Reinhardt, Democrat, defeated Captain E. W. Ward, Republican, for the Legislature, by only four votes.

The Finger family has generally been noted for honesty, frugality and good citizenship. Peter Finger, the pioneer, came to Lincoln County from Pennsylvania in the pioneer days.

Among his children were:

1. John, married Katie, daughter of Philip W. Cansler, the pioneer.

2. Daniel married Elizabeth Hildebrand and of their sons: (1) Peter married Catherine Warlick and, (2) Michael married Rachel Warlick (sisters of Maxwell), and (3) Daniel married Sarah Finger (parents of Major S. M. Finger).

3. Joseph married Nancy, daughter of Paul Kistler.

4. Henry married Polly, daughter of Jacob Killian.

5. Mary married Solomon Rudisill.

Major Sidney M. Finger was born in Lincoln County in 1837 and died in Newton, December 25th, 1896. He attended Catawba College at Newton when Prof. H. H. Smith was President of that institution; graduated from Bowdoin College in 1859 and then for many years taught in Catawba College.

He was elected State Senator from the Lincoln-Catawba district in 1876 and 1880 and was State Superintendent of Public Instruction from 1884 to 1892. Most of his life was spent in educational work which continued during the period of his service as Senator and as a State officer superintending the public education system of the State. His training and experience as a teacher prepared him well for this last position in which he served with credit and ability.

He was a good man and a life-long member of the German Reformed church. He married Miss Sarah Hoyle Rhyne of Gaston County.

Col. William Johnston, late of Charlotte, was a notable citizen who did much for the material development of the state. He graduated from the University in the class of 1840 with William M. Shipp, Albert M. Shipp, and Charles Connor Graham, of Lincoln, Tod R. Caldwell, of Burke, and Calvin H. Wiley, the first Superintendent of Public Instruction in the State. He then attended the famous law school of Judge Richmond M. Pearson, at Richmond Hill and graduated in the first class of the long line of law students, who received instructions from that able jurist.

He then settled in Charlotte in 1842 to practice law; was president of the Charlotte and Taylorsville plank road and in 1846 (when but 29 years old) was elected President of the Charlotte and South Carolina Railroad (from Charlotte to Columbia) which was completed about 1853. Then in 1859 he was also elected President of the Atlantic, Tennessee and Ohio Railroad, which was completed to Statesville in 1861 and work on it was then suspended on account of the Civil War.

Col. Johnston and Judge James W. Osborne were the delegates from Mecklenburg to the Convention of 1861 and voted for the Secession Ordinance. When he saw thirteen Charlotte Jews volunteer for military service he had no trouble in persuading the convention to repeal the provision which prohibited Jews from holding office in North Carolina.

Governor Ellis recognized the fine judgment and business ability of Col. Johnston by appointing him Commissary General with the rank of Colonel. He resigned his seat in the Convention to accept this position and served with satisfaction until September 16, 1863 when he resigned to give his full time to the management of the railroads of which he was still President.

In 1862 he was the candidate of the War party for Governor, but was defeated at the polls by Zebulon B. Vance. In 1864 President Davis tendered him the appointment of Commissary General of the Confederate States, but he declined the position, thinking he could render better service to the Government by giving his full time to the railroads of which he was President. In 1865 Federal troops destroyed sixty miles of the railroad track between Columbia and Charlotte, but by 1866 Col. Johnston had it fully rebuilt and in the same year began work on the extension of the road to Augusta. His railroad duties commanded his time so completely that he was forced to abandon his law practice. He was a public spirited and progressive citizen, one of the founders of the Commercial National Bank of Charlotte in 1873 and served as Mayor of Charlotte for seven years between 1875 and 1887. As a public speaker he was persuasive and logical, though not of the style that enthused the multitude, but he possessed mental gifts, which qualified him for any position.

He was born in Lincoln County in 1817, son of Robert and Mary (Reid) Johnston. (See 1854). It is said that when Robert Johnston asked Captain John Reid for his daughter in marriage that Captain Reid said: "You can make the money and Mary will take care of it." This indicates where Col. Johnston got some of his fine business ability.

On March 16, 1846 he married to Anne Eliza, daughter of Dr. Geo. F. and Martha A. Graham. They had two sons, Frank G., and Wm. R. Johnston, and two daughters: Julia, who married Col. A. B. Andrews, of Raleigh, and Cora, who became the wife of Col. Thos. R. Robertson. Among the grandchildren are William Johnston Andrews, A. B. Andrews, Jr., Graham H. Andrews, and John H. Andrews of Raleigh, and Maj. W. R. Robertson and Miss Julia Robertson, of Charlotte.

On May 20, 1896, he died in Charlotte, where, for fortyfour years he had been a useful and honored citizen. He was distinguished in appearance and looked the patrician. He was cultivated in mind, polished in manners, dignified and courtly in bearing, always faultlessly dressed and commanded the high respect and confidence of the people.

1897

Benjamin H. Sumner died in Lincolnton, June 10, 1897, aged 70 years. He was postmaster for 10 years, from 1855 until 1865 and one time chairman of the board of County Commissioners. He was a son of Benjamin Sumner, the distinguished teacher, frequently referred to in these Annals. Mr. Sumner was for many years a useful and highly respected citizen of Lincolnton. He served as Captain in the Commissary Department during the Civil War. He was an active member of the Episcopal Church, serving as vestryman and warden for many years. He married Myra A. Ramsour, daughter of Jacob Ramsour, June 8, 1852. Their children who grew to maturity were:

Jacob, who was drowned in 1877.

Charles McBee, who married Margaret Stokes McKenzie.

Thomas Jethro, not married.

Mary Elizabeth, who married Blair Jenkins.

William Hoke, who married Mary Bynum.

The Legislature re-elected Jeter C. Pritchard to the Senate for the full term, beginning March 4th.

Col. Seth W. Stubbs was a useful citizen of Lincolnton for many years. In early life he came here from Massachusetts. He was a great mechanic; he knew all about machinery, could make a clock and made a good one for the County, placed it in the tower of the courthouse about 1856 and kept it in accurate running order as long as he lived. The old town clock was standard time for Lincoln County for many years before the telegraph line was built and until the old courthouse was torn down in 1922. He knew all about metals and knew how to build a locomotive. He established the Stubbs Machine Shop and Foundry and made machines of all kinds for the people, far and wide, and in the foundry manufactured kitchen ware, pots and ovens, molasses mills and other castings. When Col. Stubbs grew old, the business was turned over to his son, Elbridge W. Stubbs, who inherited his father's mechanical skill, and operated the business as long as he lived. All the Stubbs family are now dead or moved away, but the valuable service rendered by Col. Stubbs should not be forgotten for he deserves the gratitude of the people for training a long line of efficient machinists who have served well our county and section.

Capt. Edward W. Ward, of the United States Army was born in Greenburg, Kentucky, September 15, 1843, son of Gen. W. T. Ward, who volunteered as a Union soldier in 1861, and Captain Ward, a youth of eighteen years, went to war with his father, and after the surrender continued in active military service until he retired in 1879. He married first to a daughter of the late Governor Tod R. Caldwell, and his second wife, was Bettie Lee, daughter of S. P. Sherrill, of Lincolnton.

Captain Ward was a resident of Lincolnton from 1882 until his death December 13, 1897. He took much interest in public affairs. Was Mayor of Lincolnton, 1887 and 1888. Was Republican candidate for Congress in 1888 and defeated by Col. W. H. H. Cowles, and defeated for the Legislature in 1896 by J. F. Reinhardt, by only four votes. He was a widely informed man, an attractive public speaker, and an active member of the Methodist church.

1898

Cuba had been under the tyrannical rule of Spain for 200 years, and the Cubans were now in revolt. To protect American interests the Maine (U. S. Warship) was anchored in Havana harbor, when on the night of February 5, 1898 the Maine was blown to pieces by dynamite and 266 seamen killed. A wave of indignation swept over the United States and War against Spain was declared by Congress April 9th. The Army was organized and great excitement prevailed throughout the country. Spain was defeated and Cuba was freed.

Major Henry W. Burton died at his home in Lincolnton, May 9, 1898, in his 77th year.

THE ANNALS OF LINCOLN COUNTY 275

After a terrifically hot campaign the Democrats carried the State in the November election and the Legislature was largely Democratic.

Alfred Nixon was elected Clerk of Superior Court in November.

The first bank established in Lincoln County was a private institution called the Bank of Lincolnton, with $10,000.00 capital and was opened for business by Capt. B. F. Grigg on February 10, 1898, and the holders of the stock were Judge W. A. Hoke, Capt. B. F. Grigg and his son, William E. Grigg. This private bank continued in business with B. F. Grigg as President and W. E. Grigg, Cashier, for ten years, until 1908 when the management organized the County National Bank with Ambrose Costner, President; R. S. Reinhardt, Vice-President; W. E. Grigg, Cashier. These, with Capt. B. F. Grigg, J. M. Rhodes, A. L. Quickel and Capt. C. C. Wrenshall, were the Directors, and the capital was increased from time to time until it reached $50,-000.00. Upon the death of Mr. Costner in 1911, Captain B. F. Grigg was made President, which position he held until his death in 1915, when he was succeeded by his son, W. E. Grigg.

J. A. Robinson, born in 1832, was a soldier in the Civil War, married December 17, 1865 to Nancy Rhodes; elected sheriff of Lincoln County in August 1872 and for eight years held the office, until 1880, when he was defeated by Capt. A. S. Haynes. He was a good sheriff, showed no favors, making every man meet tax bills as promptly as possible. Later he served as County Commissioner. He died November 15, 1898. His body was buried at Daniels church. He left four sons. The eldest, Robert, went to Texas when a young man and died there. Charles and Henry S. Robinson were sturdy men and active in business in Lincolnton for many years. David W. Robinson was a lawyer and partner for a while of Judge Hoke. About 1900 he moved to Columbia, S. C., and became one of the ablest lawyers in that state. He died in 1935.

William Ewen Shipp, eldest son of Judge William M. and Catherine (Cameron) Shipp, was born in Asheville, August 23, 1861. He attended the Lincolnton Academy about 1875 and

1876 when Rev. W. R. Wetmore was the principal and was a classmate there of this writer. Later he attended the Carolina Military Institute in Charlotte until 1879 when he entered the United States Military Academy at West Point, from which he graduated in 1883, received his commission as a Lieutenant and was a soldier until his death July 1, 1898. He was a handsome man, above the average height, of soldierly bearing, courageous spirit and lofty ideals, combined with a high quality of loyalty to friends and country. He had superior intellect, with promise of a brilliant career and would have developed into a great soldier but for his untimely death.

When he received his commission in 1883 he was assigned to the 10th Regiment of Cavalry at Fort Davis, Texas. (He never served in any other regiment). Later his regiment was transferred to Fort Apache, Arizona. In 1885, Major Gen. Crook in his report of operations during this period against hostile Apaches and Sonoras mentions Lt. Shipp, 10th Cavalry ... who commanded companies or expeditions of Indian scouts in Mexico for bearing uncomplainingly the almost incredible fatigues and privations, as well as the dangers incident to their privations. After which he was appointed Inspector of State troops with headquarters in Raleigh. There he met and later married to Margaret, daughter of the Hon. Fabius H. Busbee. His next assignment was that of Commandant of Cadets at the Davis Military School, Winston-Salem, N. C. There his two sons, William Ewen Shipp, Jr., and Fabius Busbee Shipp were born.

In 1896 he returned to his regiment at Fort Assiniboine, Montana. Serving there at the same time were Lieutenant W. H. Smith, his roommate and his classmate at West Point, and Lieutenant John J. Pershing, (later General Pershing) who had been one class behind them at West Point. When war was declared with Spain in 1898 all three went to Cuba. At the battle of Santiago July 1, 1898 Lieut. Shipp was killed as he was leading his troops in the charge. Not far away, after the battle, the dead body of his friend and comrade, Lieut. W. H. Smith, was found.

In March, 1899, the body of Lieutenant Shipp was brought to Lincolnton and buried in Saint Luke's Episcopal graveyard, by the side of the grave of his mother.

General Leonard Wood paid high tribute to the soldier in a letter written to a member of the Shipp family under date, April 9, 1924, as follows: "I had succeeded to command of the Brigade on the night of June 30, consequent to the illness of General Young, and early on the morning of July 1 we were ready to move out to the front and did so. The 10th Cavalry was in my Brigade (the 2nd Cavalry Brigade) and formed the left of the line; the other regiments of the Brigade were the First Regular Cavalry and the First Volunteer Cavalry, commonly known as the Rough Riders. The Rough Riders were on the extreme right; then came the First Regular Cavalry and then the Tenth Regular Cavalry—two squadrons of each regiment.

"I lost quite early in the action, Major Morton Henry, who had been shot through the thigh. Shortly afterwards, Mills, who had gone out to join Col. Roosevelt, was shot through the head, although we did not know this for some time. All brigade staff officers who were present in the action, and practically all the brigade non-commissioned staff officers were either killed or wounded. Lieut. Shipp was the only staff officer left available to transmit orders to the troops in line. I sent him along the Brigade with orders to notify the troops to be ready to advance; to carry the order from one end of the line to the other; and on reaching the extreme right, having transmitted the order to hold themselves in readiness, to return and give to each organization as he passed it, the order to advance on a general objective, which included Kettle Hill and other sectors of the enemy's line. He delivered his orders to the troops to prepare for an advance and on his return passed the word along to move forward on our prescribed objective. When he came to his own troop he joined it on the advance and both he and his friend, Lieut. Smith, were killed within a few yards of each other on the slope of Kettle Hill. He rendered most gallant and able service during the short time we were together. I had known him for many years before the war and always had a high opinion of him as a man and officer. It can be said of him that he fought right and he died right— an American soldier in the discharge of his duty. General McCoy recalls very well Lieut. Shipp's delivery of the order to advance and remembers distinctly his advancing with his troops, waving the big Stetson hat which he wore at that time. That was the last time he saw Lieutenant Shipp alive."

His elder son, William E. Shipp, Jr., born, November 9, 1894, attended Woodberry Forest School (Virginia) and in 1912 was appointed Cadet at U. S. Military Academy, West Point, by Senator Overman. He graduated in 1916 and was commissioned 2nd Lieutenant in June; 1st Lieutenant, July 1916, and Captain, July 1917. He served in the 12th Cavalry at Columbus, New Mexico, as troop, squadron and regimental Commander until 1918; instructor in French at West Point, 1918; after this he rendered valiant service overseas in the great war. Later after 1930 he was military attache at the American Embassy in Rome, with the rank of Major. He was later military attache at the American Legation at Riga, Latvia. He is now stationed at Fort Riley, Kansas.

Lieut. Shipp's younger son, Fabius Busbee Shipp, born April 23, 1896, was prepared for college at Raleigh High School, then attended the State University to the end of his Junior year when he joined the American forces in the World War. Commissioned 2nd Lieut. of Cavalry, June 16, 1917; promoted to 1st Lieut. same date, and Captain (temporary), August 5, 1917. Transferred to 5th Cavalry, March, 1919, at Columbus, New Mexico and served on border and with American forces in Germany and Belgium from May, 1919, to June, 1922, much of the time as Embarkation officer at Antwerp. He was promoted to rank of Captain in Cavalry, June, 1920, and joined 10th Cavalry, his father's old regiment, at Fort Huachuca, Arizona, and served there until his death by accident on the polo field, November 6, 1925. His aunt, the late Miss Kate Shipp, in a letter to the writer, with tender affection said of him: "He was brave to a fault, handsome in person, brilliant in mind, gentle, considerate, loving, devoted to his home ties, he was cut off in the flower of his youth. His mother and brother brought his body back to the home church, and there, with military honors, he was laid to rest by the side of the grave of his noble father in Saint Luke's graveyard in Lincolnton."

The Rev. William Shipp Bynum, only son of Judge William Preston Bynum (1820-1909) and Ann Eliza (Shipp) Bynum, was born in Lincoln County, February 9, 1848, and died October 21, 1898. While attending Col. Tew's school in Hillsboro, when only twelve years old, he was preparing to enter the Confederate Army and the record shows that he enlisted for active service September 25, 1862, and was 4th Sergeant in Company K, 42nd Regiment, Captain Sydenham B. Alexander's Company. He was for a while held as a prisoner by the Federals at Point Lookout,

Md., where his health was seriously impaired, for there is no doubt the exposure in camp and in prison caused his early physical breakdown. He was admitted to the bar in 1870, and practiced law in Lincolnton until 1874, when he gave it up to enter the ministry of the Episcopal church.

He was ordained deacon by Bishop Lyman in Saint Barnabas Church in Greensboro, March 12, 1876, and priest by the same Bishop in Saint Luke's Church in Lincolnton, March 5, 1882. He served as rector of churches in Greensboro, Winston-Salem, Calvary at Fletcher, and as Evangelist at large in the Diocese of North Carolina until 1888, when his health gave way, and then with great reluctance he retired from active service.

He had brilliant intellect and was a polished, fervent and attractive speaker. His language was classic, his earnest delivery gripping, and the people heard him gladly. He was completely consecrated to his holy task, was loved by the people in all the fields of his active ministry and his faithful work was fruitful and permanent. The Sermon on the Mount was his high standard for the Christian life. He once told the writer that every man should take Christ for a model and strive to live as near as possible to that lofty ideal.

His mother possessed remarkable intellect, combined with deep piety and doubtless it was through her influence and training that the son became a clergyman. He was a ripe scholar and a cultured gentleman, who exercised a saintly influence wherever he labored.

The high tribute paid to Mr. Bynum by Bishop Cheshire at the Diocesan Convention of 1899 follows:

"I shall ask indulgence for the introduction of another name in this place, a name not on our clergy list since 1895, but one whose whole ministry was associated with this Diocese.

"October 21, 1898, the Rev. William Shipp Bynum, of Lincolnton, in the jurisdiction of Asheville, fell on sleep. He was ordained deacon by Bishop Lyman, March 12, 1876, and ordained Priest six years later, and until his health failed in 1888 was most faithful and zealous in the work of his holy calling. He submitted with great reluctance to the advice of his physicians that he should cease from work, and once endeavored to take up the burden which he no longer had the strength to bear. In 1895 at my request he undertook the charge of two Missions, but after a brief servce was obliged to give up the attempt. After that he had no charge and was able to perform no regular service. His whole ministry was spent in this Diocese.

"Mr. Bynum was a very remarkable man in both spiritual and intellectual gifts. In many respects he seemed to me the most brilliant man who has entered the ranks of the ministry in this Diocese within my day, and one who gave the greatest promise of fruitfulness in his ministry; and until the failure of his bodily health he fulfilled that promise.

"His service was not long in any of the few places where he labored but in all he left an impression upon the people, which will not soon be effaced. In 1882 he acted as Evangelist and traveled through many portions of the Diocese, then embracing the whole state. Wherever he went he attracted large congregations by his earnest and eloquent preaching, and deeply impressed the people by the ardor and enthusiasm of his character. He was indifferent to ease, personal comfort and advantage for himself, but unstintedly generous to others and solicitous of the welfare and advantage of his friends. The church commanded all that he possessed, whether of strength or worldly means, and he never turned his face from any poor man. It was my privilege at one time to enjoy his confidence and affection and opportunities of frequent personal intercourse. I have never known a man of nobler qualities or of a more attractive personality.

"I wish to place on record in the proceedings of our Convention this evidence of my regard and expression of my sorrow, for the loss to the church, of a life which promised so much and which, until touched by the hand of disease, so nobly fulfilled its promise. He rests in peace where no evil can touch him."

Mr. Bynum married in Hillsboro, December 8, 1870, to Mary Louisa, daughter of the Rev. Dr. M. A. Curtis, rector of the Episcopal church in Hillsboro and who many years before was rector of Saint Luke's church in Lincolnton. Mrs. Bynum died June 30, 1929, over thirty years after the death of her husband.

They had eight children:

1. William Preston died in 1891, when a student at the State University and in his memory his grandfather Bynum, whose name he bore, presented to the University the present Gymnasium building. Dr. Richard H. Lewis in accepting the generous gift referred in high terms to the young student, who was of the class of 1893, but lived to complete only two years of his course. The Dean of the University spoke of him as an exceptionally brilliant student, of fine, manly qualities and lovely character, and added, "I have been teaching for thirty-two years and have known many

THE ANNALS OF LINCOLN COUNTY 281

fine young students, but young Bynum's name always comes first to my mind when I think of them."

2. Mary deRosset, married William Hoke Sumner, of Lincolnton. They now live in Asheville.

3. Eliza Shipp married B. A. Justice of Rutherfordton. She lives in Rockville, Maryland.

4. Katherine Fullerton died in 1886.

5. Minna (Barbara) married Dr. Archibald Henderson, Professor of Mathematics at State University and author of many books and historical sketches. They live at Chapel Hill.

6. Curtis Ashley married Florence Helen Boyd, of Appleton, Wisconsin, on July 10, 1907. He was prepared for college at Horner Military School and graduated from State University in 1903; received degree of J.D., University of Chicago, 1907; admitted to the bar, 1914; served as Captain and Adjutant 321st Regiment, U. S. Infantry in World War; graduated at Army General Staff College, Langres, France, 1918; decorated German Red Cross, 1933. He rendered valued service to Lincoln County as compiler of *Marriage Bonds of Tryon and Lincoln Counties, 1769 to 1868*, which he published at his own expense, and he deserves the gratitude of our people for this splendid and unselfish service. He lives in Asheville and is an attorney in that city.

7. Bartlett Shipp died in 1894.

8. Susan Allan (Suzanne) lives in Charlotte.

1899

When the Legislature met in January, an amendment to the Constitution requiring an educational qualification for suffrage was passed and submitted to the people for ratification or rejection at an election to be held in August, 1900.

Judge M. L. McCorkle was born on Mountain Creek, Lincoln County, in 1817 (now Catawba County), graduated from Davidson College in 1838, studied law at Pearson Law School, was licensed to practice and settled in Newton, was married November 10, 1850, to Martha Ann Wilfong; was Clerk of Superior Court for Catawba County, 1848-50; Captain and promoted to Colonel in the Civil War; State Senator 1865-66; member of the Constitutional Convention of 1875; appointed Judge of Superior Court in June, 1890, by Governor Holt to succeed Judge Shipp, deceased. Judge McCorkle died in Newton, July 11, 1899, in his 80th year. Of lofty character, he commanded the high respect of his countrymen.

The children of Judge McCorkle were:

Catherine, who died aged 5 years.

Frank W., when a medical student died in Baltimore about 1876.

Henry W., died Tyler, Texas, married Emma Bell Hickle.

George married Annie N. Sorber.

Dr. J. Macon, died about 1897, married Matt Ransom.

Mary Locke married Eugene Simons.

Anna, died about 1897, married Jerome Dowd.

Alberta married (1) Charley Ingram, (2) William Boylan.

Lieut. Col. Charles M., died about 1932, married Mae Newland.

The death of Ephraim H. Cauble, which occurred October 27, 1899, removed a useful citizen. Mr. Cauble was 70 years old. He and Mr. Thomas Wells were, for many years co-partners under the firm name of Cauble & Wells, Contractors and Builders, and many of the old homes in Lincolnton were constructed by them. Mr. Cauble had a reputation for rapid work. It was said that he could drive twice as many nails in a day as the average workman. He was an active member of the Baptist church.

Lincoln Journal—March 24, 1899—John C. Tipton, Editor.

Bridges Badly Damaged

There was a tremendous rainfall Saturday night. I. R. Self reports $500.00 damage to his land. Dams of Howard's Creek Milling Co., on Leonard's Fork and of Bess Roller Mill at Orleans were washed away. Hoover's bridge on Howard's Creek, Weaver's bridge on Mill Creek and Rock Dam bridge greatly damaged.

The body of Lieutenant William E. Shipp was laid to rest in Saint Luke's churchyard (Episcopal). He was a brave and gallant soldier of the Spanish American War and a Christian gentleman.

A monument placed in front of the Charlotte post office bears the following inscription:

"Amongst a grove the very straightest plant."
William Ewen Shipp
1st Lieutenant—10th Cavalry
U. S. Army
Born August 23, 1861
Killed at San Juan, Battle of Santiago
July 1, 1898.

CHAPTER XVIII

1900-1909

In August the amendment to the State Constitution restricting the right of suffrage to those who could stand the educational test was adopted by a large majority.

Charles B. Aycock was elected Governor at the August election, to succeed Daniel L. Russell.

Beverly C. Cobb, for thirty years a Lincolnton lawyer, and legislator from Lincoln in 1877 and 1879, died September 25, 1900, aged 52 years.

In November William McKinley was re-elected to the Presidency, defeating William Jennings Bryan, for the second time.

William Ramsour, a well-known citizen of the County, died December 23, 1900, in his 72nd year.

Eben Childs, an old and respected citizen and merchant of Lincolnton, died in 1900, in his 88th year. He was a native of New York, came South with his brothers, L. D. and A. D. Childs, and settled in Mitchell County. About 1864 he moved to Lincolnton where he engaged in the mercantile business until his death. He was the father of the late Capt. Charles E. Childs, and Edward T. Childs.

1901

On January 16, 1901, Rev. Hiram Rhodes Revels, in his 79th year, had a stroke at Aberdeen, Mississippi, and died, while addressing a colored Methodist Conference, which was in session there at the time. It is interesting to know that many, many years earlier he was a citizen of Lincolnton.

He was a quadroon, born Fayetteville, N. C., September 1, 1822, of free negro parents. When a young man he came to Lincolnton in the early 1840's; was a barber and also sold cakes, candies and other confections in a small building on the present North State Hotel lot, between the hotel and Water street, facing the Court Square. In the 1840's Rhodes Revels could be seen on Lincoln County muster days selling ginger cakes and locust beer to the multitudes that gathered to witness the militia drills. I have often heard my mother say that she bought cakes at his store when she was a little girl. Late in the 1840's he went West and was educated at the Friends' College at Liberty, Indiana. Later he became a minister of the African Methodist church and a leader among the negroes of Ohio, Indiana, Illinois and Missouri. Naturally he was opposed to slavery and during the Civil War his influence was used to induce negroes to enlist in the Federal army, and when the war ended he followed the Union troops to Mississippi and there became a religious leader among the negroes. He hesitated to enter politics, but while pastor of a Methodist church in Natchez in 1869, was elected to the Mississippi State Senate from Adams County, and was elected by that body to the United States Senate in 1869 as a Republican, to the seat vacated by Jefferson Davis at the beginning of the Civil War. He served in the Senate from February, 1870, until March 4, 1871. He was the first negro who ever was a member of that body and the only one, except Blanche K. Bruce, who later (1875-1881) was a Senator from Mississippi.

In 1873 Revels was Secretary of State in Mississippi for a short time, and in the same year was made President of Alcorn University, the State College for negroes, but Dr. J. G. deRoulhac Hamilton in *Dictionary of American Biography* (1935) says: "In 1874 Governor Ames for political reasons dismissed him from Alcorn University and he returned to ministerial work . . . In 1875 he was active in behalf of the Democratic party in the State campaign, which led to the overthrow of the carpet bag government and defended his course in a strong letter to President Grant, and printed in the *Jackson Daily Times*, November 10, 1875, in which he said that all good men had combined to defeat the Republicans. In 1876 he was again made president of Alcorn University and did much to restore the confidence of the negroes in it. In June of the same year he became Editor of the *Southwestern Christian Advocate*."

This paper was the organ of the colored membership of the Methodist Episcopal church (Northern) which Revels transferred to from the African Methodist church. Revels had intellect and character and was said to be a preacher of rare gifts and exercised a fine influence among his people in those troublous times.

He had Indian blood in his veins for the late Hamilton McMillan, of Robeson County, stated in North Carolina Booklet of January, 1911, that "the Croatan tribe of Robeson County contributed Hiram Rhodes Revels to the United States Senate." But this extraordinary and interesting man, who became notable as a minister, educator and United States Senator, was some ninety years ago a barber in Lincolnton, who sold cakes and candies to supplement his meagre income, for it seemed that no wider field of service would ever open up to him, though doubtless at the same time he was longing for education and an opportunity. At any rate he decided to go to Indiana and study there in a Quaker school and became a Christian minister and a leader of his race.

From *Lincoln Courier*, September 13, 1845.

R. H. REVELS, *Barber*
Respectfully

Informs the public, that he has recommenced his old business on the Court Square and having received excellent tools direct from Philadelphia he is prepared to shave as cleanly, and cut the Hair to suit the physiognomy equal to any in his line of business. As due attention will be given, and charges moderate, he solicits the public patronage.

VALUABLE PROPERTY FOR SALE

Which the subscriber desires to sell privately, consisting of the following articles, viz:
One Cupboard, and its contents
China Cups and Saucers.
Plates, Spoons, etc., all of the finest kind.
One Clock, Two Candle Stands.
One Falling Leaf Table, of the best kind of Walnut.
Two Small Tables.
One Clothes Press, very fine.
Several Bedsteads, of the finest kind.
One fine Milch Cow.
Together with many other articles too tedious to mention.

Any person wishing to purchase would do well to call on the subscriber, as bargains will be given, for things will be sold low for cash.

R. H. REVELS.

September 19, 1845.

Dr. W. S. Jenkins writes:

"My father told me of the occasion when Rhodes Revels on returning to Mississippi at the end of his short term in the Senate (1871) stopped in Lincolnton. He had known my grandmother, Mrs. J. C. Jenkins, and paid her a visit. My father and the other children were brought in to see him."

Many model citizens have dwelt in Lincolnton, but none better than John E. Boger. No man could charge him with any evil design for truly he strove "to do justly, and to love mercy, and walk humbly." He was of few words, but busy in performance of worthy deeds. He had not worldly ambition but men looked up to him as a model to measure by. He spent most of his days in Lincolnton. Was happily married to Miss Mary Ann Ramseur, December 5, 1848, and she was a worthy helpmeet. He was first a jeweler and later associated with his brother-in-law, Col. W. H. Michal, in mercantile trade and was known for his just dealings. The present Methodist parsonage was a gift to the church from him many years ago. He was a devout Christian, an office bearer in his church and a generous contributor to all worthy calls. He passed to his reward in 1901 and left no heirs. Few people living here today knew this good man, who left the splendid record of a noble life.

The Legislature, which met in January, elected F. M. Simmons United States Senator to succeed Marion Butler.

President McKinley was assassinated in Buffalo, N. Y., where he was attending the Buffalo Exposition, in September, 1901. He died September 6, and Theodore Roosevelt succeeded to the Presidency.

Miss Ann E. Henderson, eldest daughter of the late Charles C. Henderson, was remarkable for memory and wide information. She was a natural historian, who knew almost every family in the County and was familiar with the history of many notable people throughout the country. Judge Schenck once said that when she died a wealth of local history would be buried. Had she put into permanent form her first hand knowledge of the County and its people, she would have rendered a service of inestimable value. She died April, 1901, aged 76 years.

James H. Marsh, an Englishman, came to Lincolnton prior to the Civil War and established a small chair factory at the Laboratory. He was a workman, who never turned out shoddy work. Recently I saw in a home in Avery County chairs he made fifty years ago and they were as solid and good as when they first came from the shop. Mr. Marsh was one time Chairman of Board of County Commissioners and Postmaster in Lincolnton from 1870 to 1885. He was an old man in 1901 when he died of cancer.

Robert Alexander Cobb, son of James and Fannie (Helton) Cobb, was born near Lincolnton, October 1, 1839, and took to newspaper work in early life. At the beginning of the Civil War he enlisted and was commissioned as Lieutenant in Company F, 23rd North Carolina Regiment, which was attached to Hoke's Brigade. Later he was transferred to the Commissary Department. He married Matilda, daughter of John Z. Falls, of Cleveland County, July 27, 1862. After the war he was a merchant in Newton for a while but moved to Morganton in 1868 and became editor of the *Blue Ridge Blade* and later of the *Morganton Star*, which he sold to the *Morganton Herald* in 1890. He was prominent in politics as a Republican, was Postmaster in Morganton, and Revenue Collector, and elected State Librarian in 1898, but lost that office when the Supreme Court in 1899 reversed the famous decision of Chief Justice Ruffin in the case of Hoke against Henderson. During his last years he was a merchant in Morganton. He was a Methodist in faith and died March 26, 1901.

Theodore G. Cobb, late of Morganton, and son of R. A. Cobb, was born in Newton, May 9, 1867, and began his active life in the printing office of his father in Morganton when only thirteen years old. Later, with his father, founded the *Morganton Star*. From 1890 to 1897, he was foreman on *Morganton Herald*, but in the latter year went into the business of job printing. In 1897 he founded the *Morganton News*, a Democratic weekly, and in November, 1901, he bought the *Morganton Herald*, merged it with the *News* and called it the *News-Herald*, a weekly paper, Democratic in politics, which he owned and edited until his death in 1916.

In 1907 and 1908 he was Historian for the North Carolina Press Association. Prominent in politics and commanding the confidence of the party leaders he served as a Clerk in the State Legislature from 1903 to 1907, when he was advanced to the position of Chief Clerk of the House and served as such for five sessions until 1916.

In 1887 Mr. Cobb married Ella, daughter of Robert N. and Margaret (Conley) Kincaid, of Burke County. He was a public-spirited and progressive citizen and was a leader in the movement for a better road system and improved school facilities for the whole state. He was a member of the Knights of Pythias, Independent Order of Odd Fellows and the Junior Order of United American Mechanics, of which he was State Councilor. A consistent member of the Methodist church, he died in the faith July 5, 1916.

Miss Beatrice Cobb, eldest daughter of Theodore G. Cobb, and granddaughter of R. A. Cobb, is one of the most prominent women in North Carolina newspaper circles. She was graduated from Asheville Teachers' College in the Class of 1909, and taught in the city schools of Hickory and Morganton until the death of her father in 1916, when she became owner and editor of the *Morganton News-Herald*. In 1933 the paper was changed from a weekly to a semi-weekly. She has been Secretary of the State Press Association since 1921; served as member of the Board of Trustees of the North Carolina School for the Blind, 1927-1933; delegate to Democratic National Conventions of 1928 and 1932, and in 1934 elected member of the Democratic National Committee as Committeewoman for North Carolina.

1902

David Schenck was the only son of Dr. David Warlick Schenck (1809-1861) who was son of Michael Schenck, III, who married Barbara, daughter of Daniel Warlick, II, son of Daniel Warlick, the pioneer. These forbears were of fine German stock. The Warlicks have from the time of the first settlers of that name been sturdy and splendid citizens, and Michael Schenck, III, who came to Lincolnton from Pennsylvania, late in the eighteenth century, it is said stopped at the cross roads and asked the way to Lincolnton and when informed that he was then in the very heart of the village pitched his tent, built the first weatherboarded house erected there and became one of the influential citizens of the County. Later he established at McDaniel's Spring, about two miles east of the village, the first cotton mill operated south of the Potomac River. He joined the Methodist church after coming South and was one of the charter members of the Lincolnton congregation, which was organized about 1824. His son, Dr. David Warlick Schenck, married to Susan R. Bevens, November 8, 1832, and David Schenck, the subject of this sketch, their son, was born in Lincolnton, March 24, 1835, educated at the Lincolnton Academy, a school of high grade, read law under Haywood W. Guion, after which he attended the famous Pearson law school, was licensed to practice law in County Court in 1856, and in the Superior Court in 1857. He then located in Dallas as a lawyer and was soon made County Solicitor for Gaston. On August 25, 1859, he married Sallie Wilfong, daughter of Jacob A. Ramsour, a prominent Lincolnton merchant.

In 1860 he returned from Dallas to Lincolnton and became the law partner of William Lander. When war was declared in 1861 he volunteered for service, was commissioned as Captain in Commissary General Department, North Carolina Troops, May 21, 1861, and resigned September 20, 1861, when elected delegate from Lincoln to the Constitutional Convention of 1861 to succeed William Lander, who vacated his Convention seat when elected to the Confederate Congress.

Mr. Schenck soon took high rank in that Convention of very able men and made a state-wide reputation as a ready and able debater. He continued a member of the law firm of Lander and Schenck until the death of Mr. Lander in 1868 and developed into one of the great trial lawyers of the state. He was a powerful advocate before a jury and had a large practice in Lincoln, Gaston, Cleveland and Catawba Counties. In August, 1874, he was elected Judge of the Superior Court for the 9th Judicial District, then composed of the Counties of Cabarrus, Mecklenburg, Gaston, Lincoln, Cleveland, Rutherford and Polk. After the rotation plan was established in 1876 he held courts throughout the state and was regarded as a lawyer and judge of brilliant mind and clear intellect. In 1881 he resigned the judgeship to accept the position of General Counsel for the Richmond and Danville Railroad and changed his residence from Lincolnton to Greensboro. In 1882 he was by Governor Jarvis appointed Associate Justice of the Supreme Court to fill the vacancy caused by the death of Judge John H. Dillard, but declined the honor, and continued as Counsel for the Railroad for about fifteen years, when he resigned on account of failing health. Judge Schenck was a great citizen and was honored with the degree of Doctor of Laws, conferred by the State University in 1880.

One who knew him well has said:
"As a lawyer where the varied demands call for strength, fertility, resource and generalship are greatest, he found his greatest opportunity. The practice of law was his profession and pride; history was a passion and a pastime."

He was the author of *Railroad Law in North Carolina* as well as the historical work, *North Carolina, 1780-81*. He loved Lincoln County, was proud of its history and in his earlier days wrote many interesting historical sketches for the local press. He died in Greensboro, August 26, 1902.

While Judge Schenck will be remembered as an able judge and a brilliant advocate, he will also be remembered as a patriot and historian, who, in a labor of love, was the author of *North Carolina, 1780-81*, in which he resurrected much almost forgotten history and put it in permanent form in that volume, and then did more than any other man to arouse public interest, and placed many markers on the grounds where the battle of Guilford Courthouse was fought. From his introduction to that great historical volume I quote:

"A visit to the battlefield in the autumn of 1886 suggested the idea of the formation of the Guilford Battleground Company, which was incorporated by the Legislature of North Carolina, March 7, 1887. (The Incorporators were J. W. Scott, Juilus A. Gray, Dr. D. W. C. Benbow, Thomas B. Keogh and David Schenck.)

"The Author was elected President of that Company and in the examination of the different histories of the Battle of Guilford Courthouse by Lee, Johnson and some other writers of less reputation, he became convinced that a great injustice had been done to the Militia of North Carolina in regard to their conduct on that occasion. Further research confirmed this opinion and led to the conviction that the injustice done to North Carolina was not confined to the events occurring in this battle, but that the state had been robbed of the honor due her for repelling the British invasion in 1780-81; that the credit of her noble deeds had been ascribed to others; that the citizenship of her heroes had been claimed by other states, and that the truth in regard to these stirring events had either intentionally or by gross negligence, been greatly and wrongfully perverted to the injury of her good name. The Author therefore, as a dutiful son of North Carolina, determined to write this book in defense of his native state and in vindication of the honor and patriotism of her people."

At the memorable reunion or convention of North Carolinians held at the Guilford Courthouse battleground in 1903 Gen. Matt W. Ransom, who presided at that notable meeting said:

"I ask this great audience to resolve that its thanks are eminently due to the late Hon. David Schenck for his patriotic, diligent and successful labors in presenting the true history of the battle and in demonstrating and proving the faithfulness and bravery of North Carolina on this field."

The following was then adopted: "Resolved that this Convention puts upon record its profound conviction of the inestimable service which the late Hon. David Schenck has rendered to historical truth in vindicating and establishing by incontrovertible and unanswerable argument, that the soldiers of North Carolina did their whole duty in the battle of Guilford Courthouse, and that we will cherish all gratitude and honor to the memory of this devoted patriot."

The children of David and Sarah Wilfong Schenck were:

1. Dodson R. Schenck, physician in Rutherford County, who died in 1934.

2. Weldon E. Schenck, commercial traveler. One of his sons, Rev. Lewis J. Schenck, is a Presbyterian minister and Professor of Bible in Davidson College.

3. Lucy, married John L. Cobb. She died in early womanhood.

4. Rebecca lives in Greensboro, and taught for a number of years in the State Normal College, now the Woman's College of the State University, and in Saint Mary's School in Raleigh. She is a cultured woman and a teacher of superior gifts.

5. David, Jr., was a lawyer of great promise and died in his 30th year. A great lawyer said of him: "He possessed one of the most brilliant of minds and while others by hard study, arrived at conclusions, he seemed to grasp the point of a legal problem instinctively."

6. John R. who lived in Greensboro and died early.

7. J. Simpson is in the insurance business in Fayetteville.

8. Michael Schenck—(*Who's Who in America* says of

him) : He was born in Lincolnton, December 11, 1876. Student at State University 1893-95 and in Law department 1902 and 1903. Married Rose Few of Hendersonville. Admitted to the bar in 1903, practiced law in Greensboro until 1905, when he moved to Hendersonville. Was Mayor of that city 1907-09. Solicitor 18th district 1913-1918; resigned to enter the Army in which he was Major Judge Advocates Department, 1918-1919; was re-elected Solicitor but declined the office. Judge Superior Court from November 10, 1924, to 1934, when he was appointed by Governor Ehringhaus a Justice of the Supreme Court to succeed Justice W. J. Adams, deceased.

9. Paul W. Schenck (according to *Who's Who in America*) was born in Lincolnton, January 7, 1882. Was a student at State University; married Margaret McClung Alexander (daughter of Dr. Eben Alexander, Greek scholar and diplomat) of Chapel Hill, June 16, 1909; engaged in 1901 in insurance business in Greensboro; in 1911 he organized and was made President and Manager of Carolina Insurance Agency Co.; succeeded his father as President of the Guilford Battleground Company. His work there was recognized by the Federal government in the erection of two arches costing $5,000 each and a monument to General Nathaniel Greene costing $30,000.

Rev. M. V. Sherrill, aged 65, a prominent retired minister of the Methodist church, died at his home in Denver in November, 1902, after a protracted illness. He was the father of the late Rev. C. F. Sherrill, of the Methodist Conference, and of John B. Sherrill, founder and editor until his death in 1934 of the *Concord Tribune*.

Dr. W. L. Crouse, son of David Crouse, was born on his father's farm near the village of Crouse in 1852. After the Civil War he took a medical course and practiced his profession in Lincoln County where he made a good reputation as a physician. He represented Lincoln in the lower house of the Legislature for three terms, 1883-85 and 1893, and the Senate in 1887. In later life he engaged in the cotton mill business with good success, and died in 1902, aged 50 years.

Dr. Crouse married June 4, 1873, Miss Mattie Anna Stowe, daughter of Stephen Decatur and Margaret (Abernethy) Stowe. Their chilrden were: Prue, who married Bartlett Shipp; Minerva, who married John Malcus Merritt; Sallie Bright, who married Charles N. Wrenshall; David Stowe, not married (1936).

William Tiddy was an Englishman, at one time a worker in stone and also sold tombstones. Early after the Civil War he formed a co-partnership with A. C. Wiswall (who came from Massachusetts) and engaged in the manufacture of paper at the Lincoln and Long Shoals Mills. Later with his brother, Richard Tiddy, under the trade name of W. & R. Tiddy, got control of those mills and operated them until the business was abandoned about 1890 on account of the wood pulp paper competition in the North. He was a Presbyterian elder and a member of the Masonic fraternity.

He first married Martha, daughter of Dr. J. C. Rudisill, and his second marriage was to Lucy Mayfield, daughter of Jacob A. Ramsour. He had no children.

1903

The First National Bank of Lincolnton was organized and opened for business on January 15, 1903, with the following officers: J. A. Abernethy, President, Charles E. Childs, Vice-President, Claude Ramsour, Cashier. These with Dr. T. F. Costner, Edgar Love, H. S. Robinson and J. H. Ramsour, constituted the Board of Directors.

Lee S. Overman was elected Senator in Congress in January by the Legislature to succeed Jeter C. Pritchard, whose term expired on March 4th.

1904

Rev. Dr. Samuel Lander, educator and Methodist minister, was born in Lincolnton, January 30, 1833, son of Rev. Samuel and Eliza Ann (Miller) Lander. He was given a prophet's name and he walked a prophet's road. Eminent preparation for life was his good fortune and eminent service was the return he rendered. He was nurtured in a Christian home and an intellectual atmosphere. When but six years old, under the great teacher, Jeremiah W. Murphy, he studied Latin and Greek and at twenty was an honor graduate of

Top left: Rev. Dr. Samuel Lander (1833-1904). See 1904.
Top right: Rev. Dr. R. Z. Johnston (1834-1908). See 1908.
Center: Rev. Dr. W. R. Wetmore (1834-1904). See 1904.
Lower left: Rev. Dr. R. A. Yoder (1853-1911). See 1911.
Lower right: Rev. William S. Bynum (1848-1898). See 1898.

Randolph-Macon College. He studied law but gave it up for the work of a teacher and minister. His first service as a teacher was with Hosea Hildreth Smith at Catawba College in Newton. The next year he taught at Olin Academy; in 1855 he was adjunct Professor of Language at his Alma Mater, where he took an A.M. course; back to Olin Academy for a year and then called to Greensboro College to teach mathematics. In 1859, when 26 years old he was made President of High Point Normal School. From 1863 to 1867, principal of Lincolnton Female Seminary. In 1861 he was licensed as a local preacher of the Methodist Church and admitted into the South Carolina Conference in 1864. His appointments then were: 1865, Lincolnton Seminary; 1866, and 1867, Lincolnton Station; 1868-69 and 70, Davenport Female College; 1871, Spartanburg Female College; 1872, Williamston Circuit; 1873 and to his death July 14, 1904, President of Williamston Female College. In addition to his college work he was pastor of Williamston Station, 1877-78 and 79, and of Williamston Circuit in 1885 and 1889.

The gifts of Dr. Lander as a teacher were so conspicuous and the demand for his service so great, that he was given but little opportunity in the regular pastorate. He had, however, marked success when he was a pastor. In a six-weeks' meeting in his native town of Lincolnton in 1867 great multitudes were quickened in spiritual life and fully one hundred were added to the churches of the town, but for the most part his school was his charge and his pupils his congregation. He often longed for the pastorate, but realized that to teach the young was truest preaching and to care for the young women of the South was a great opportunity for the highest gifts of any man. He was conscientious and thorough as a teacher and magnified in his school work the prime importance of moral and religious training. The long procession of young women, who for fifty years came under his influence as a teacher appreciated his good work and carried through life affectionate regard for him.

The building equipment of Williamston by 1904 was not sufficient to meet the needs of the school. The people of Greenwood made a generous offer for its removal to that city, which was accepted. In September 1904 the college was opened for students there and the name changed to Lander College.

Dr. Lander died a few weeks before the opening at Greenwood. He was a great teacher and came to his own in the class room. During the Civil War when the South was blockaded and books could not be secured from the outside he prepared a work on Mathematics called, "Lander's Common School Arithmetic," which was for some years a text book in North Carolina schools. He was master of seven languages and when the honorary degree of Doctor of Divinity was conferred on him and he was ignorant of the Hebrew language he learned it so well that later he was able to read the Old Testament in that language.

He was a preacher of superior gifts—a teaching preacher. His pulpit ministrations were full of instruction for his hearers. His spirit of humility was a source of power, as it always is with preachers and with laymen as well. A capable critic returning from church after hearing Mr. Lander preach said, "When the former pastor preached his whole demeanor suggested his self-importance, but Mr. Lander tries to hide behind the cross and seems to feel that he has nothing to do but to be a voice, a mouthpiece for the Master." That was indeed his spirit; he never sought preferment for he wore the beautiful garment of humility. He knew that honest work was righteousness and God would take knowledge of it. He was too busy at his task to think of the applause of men.

His gentility, his pure life, his guileless nature, his sturdy adherence to principle, his thorough and honest performance of duty—all these together with his faith, which was the foundation of all the rest, appealed to and affected the conduct of his pupils, and they carried back to their homes and through their lives those larger conceptions of duty and service which they learned from him.

Dr. W. P. Few, President of Duke University, said: "So far as I know the old Williamston Female College, under the guidance of Dr. Samuel Lander, was a pioneer among Southern colleges for women in the handling of solid intellectual wares. The battle for plain, straight-forward honesty in education has not been completely won, and the man who started the fight in a part of the field where it was most urgently needed, should be remembered with gratitude."

Dr. Thomas N. Ivey said: "No history of American education, no catalogue of high American exploits, no record of American success built on the self-sacrifice of God-filled hearts can be complete without the name of Samuel Lander, the Evangel of Christ, and a Christian educator."

Bishop H. M. DuBose said: "These commonwealths have had great men in the civic and political spheres. Which of them has added a more enduring element to the forces that are to expand and preserve their lives than Samuel Lander, who educated so many of their sons and daughters, and who, dying, left behind him so substantial a contribution to Christian culture?"

Bishop John C. Kilgo said: "Dr. Lander knew how to make education a saving force; he knew how to reach and bring out those energies of mind and spirit which make for real progress; he rightly distinguished between the frivolous and vital qualities of mind and character. By fidelity to his belief he has sent out into this Commonwealth a young womanhood whose distinct traits are seriousness, sincerity and womanly integrity. He has founded an institution which has a clear and definite mission to young women."

North Carolina has furnished to the Church and State many who have distinguished themselves in peace and war, but when final results are measured only a few have rendered to humankind a service so far-reaching and uplifting as that of this modest, but truly great man, who, to the end of his days, was busy, in season and out of season, striving to prepare young women of the land for larger life and nobler service.

On December 20, 1853, he married Laura Ann, daughter of Rev. Angus McPherson and among their children were:

Dr. John M. Lander, for more than forty years a missionary to Brazil, and died there in the midst of his labors.

Martha, who married Judge George E. Prince, a notable lawyer and jurist of Anderson, South Carolina.

Dr. Wm. Tertius Lander and Dr. Frank Lander, both of Williamston, S. C., where they are practicing physicians, skilled in their profession.

Kathleen, who married Dr. John O. Wilson, an able Methodist minister and educator, who succeeded Dr. Lander as President of Lander College, for twenty years until his death in 1924.

Malcolm M. Lander, who was in the government postal service for forty years, until his death in 1934.

Ernest M. Lander and Angus M. Lander, who have held responsible positions in textile companies and are still active in business.

The sons and daughters are all college-bred and cultured people.

Vardry Alexander McBee, fourth son of Vardry McBee and his wife, Jane Alexander, was born in Lincolnton in the old family residence (which stood where the present Methodist Church is located) on April 17, 1818. He died on February 17, 1904, in the same house in which he had lived all his days. He had a bright mind, was a good student, had the best school advantages, was educated at Pleasant Retreat Academy in Lincolnton of which his father was one of the founders, and at the University of North Carolina from which he graduated in 1841 in the class with his friend Col. John F. Hoke. Although licensed as a lawyer, Mr. McBee was never active in the practice; he was three times Clerk of Superior Court, covering in all a period of 14 years; and represented the County in the Legislature in 1861. He was a public-spirited and progressive citizen. He subscribed liberally to all movements for the public welfare; he was active in the construction of the old plank road from Charlotte to Lincolnton; in the building of the old Wilmington, Charlotte and Rutherford Railroad of which he was treasurer and master of transportation, and later took a prominent part in organizing the Chester and Lenoir Railroad of which he was a director for many years.

He owned a large plantation several miles from Lincolnton and prided himself in raising blooded stock, fine horses, cattle, hogs and even dogs and encouraged the people of his native town to do likewise. He kept a good saddle horse and was a graceful rider and delighted in this exercise until far advanced in years. He wore a beard, spotlessly white, and never had a razor on his face.

He lived a leisurely life, was a student all his days, never forgot the classics of his youth and could read Latin in his old age as fluently as English, and always kept abreast of the times.

On December 16, 1847, Vardry Alexander McBee and Mary Elizabeth Sumner were united in holy matrimony in Old St. Luke's Church by the then Rector, the Rev. Joseph C. Huske. She was born in Granville County, January 11, 1829, the daughter of Benjamin Sumner and of his wife, Sarah Duke Hunt. She had come with her family to Lincolnton about 1845 when her father became the principal of the two Lincolnton academies. He and his oldest son, Thomas J. Sumner, taught in the Male Academy and his daughter was one of the teachers in the Female Academy.

Mr. and Mrs. McBee had ten children, to some of whom reference has already been made. All were Episcopalians and very loyal to their church. When the Bishop of the Diocese came to Lincolnton on his annual visitations he was always a guest in the McBee home.

None of the name now live in Lincolnton.

The daughters of Mr. and Mrs. McBee were:

1. Jane, who married (1) Capt. John G. Justice; (2) Beverly C. Cobb.

By the first marriage she had one child:

I. Elizabeth Justice, who married William Grimes of Raleigh. Children: (a) William; (b) Jane, who married Mason Thomas of Charlotte.

2. Sarah (Sally), who married James T. Williams of Greenville, S. C. She died July 18, 1907; he, August 6, 1936. Both are buried in Lincolnton. Children (not in order of age):

I. James T. Williams, Jr., of Washington, D. C. See full sketch in *Who's Who in America*.

II. Vardry McBee Williams of Orlando, Fla.

III. Silas Williams of Chattanooga.

IV. Mary Elizabeth Williams of Greenville, S. C.

V. Sumner McBee Williams (Lt. Col. U. S. A., died March 29, 1935) married Elizabeth Beattie. Children:

(a) Kathryn; (b) Anne Marshall; (c) Elizabeth Cleveland; (d) Sumner McBee, Jr.

VI. Sarah McBee, who married Lt. D. L. Ryan U. S. N. Children:

(a) D. L. Ryan, Jr.; (b) Sally McBee Ryan; (c) Elizabeth Sexton Ryan.

3. Mary, who married Judge William Alexander Hoke (See 1925). One child:

I. Mary, married E. R. Slaughter of the University of Va.

4. Anne, who married Rt. Rev. William A. Guerry, Bishop of South Carolina. Children:

I. Dr. Alexander Guerry, President University of Chattanooga.

II. Rev. Sumner Guerry of Charleston, S. C.

III. Rev. Moultrie Guerry, Chaplain University of South, Sewanee, Tenn.

IV. Rev. Edward Brailsford Guerry of Tappahannock, Va.

V. Anne, who married James Perry of Columbia.

5. Martha Turner, who married William E. Mikell, Dean of Law School, University of Pa. Children:

I. William E. Mikell, Jr., of University of Pa. Law School.

II. Thomas Price Mikell of Philadelphia.

III. Mary, who married Rev. Dr. Oliver J. Hart of Washington, D. C.

The sons of Mr. and Mrs. McBee were:

6. Dr. Sumner McBee (died 1893), married Anna Cameron Shipp. They had no children.

7. Silas McBee (died September 3, 1924), married (1) Mary Estelle Sutton of Mississippi. Children:

I. Emma Estelle McBee of Ashley Hall, Charleston.

II. Dr. Mary Vardrine McBee, Principal of Ashley Hall.

III. Silas McBee, Jr., of New York.

Silas McBee, Sr., married (2) Louise J. Post of Great Neck, N. Y.

8. Vardry McBee (died May 20, 1937), married Annie Joyce Gwyn.

9. Thomas McBee (December 10, 1866-April 29, 1908), married Sudie Avery of Morganton. Children:

I. Elizabeth, who married Capus Waynick of Raleigh.

II. Avery McBee of Baltimore.

III. Silas McBee of High Point.

Prof. B. P. Caldwell was chosen School Superintendent for Lincolnton and a graded school system was established. Four years later in 1908 ,the first class of thirteen students graduated from the Lincolnton High School. In 1907 the cornerstone was laid for the grammar school building. E. D. Johnson was made Superintendent in 1919 and four additional school buildings were erected.

Prof. W. M. Pickens, the present Superintendent, was elected and the enrollment of the City Schools is now 1,274 whites and 186 colored. In 1904 the school property of Lincolnton was valued at $25,000, while now (1933) it is $350,000.

In November Judge W. A. Hoke was elected Justice of the Supreme Court of the State.

Theodore Roosevelt was elected President for the full term, beginning March 4, 1905.

Rev. Dr. William Robards Wetmore as an educator and as a rector of St. Luke's Episcopal Church, made a great contribution to religious and educational life in Lincoln County and to regions beyond. His influence still abides in the life work of many of his parishioners and the students who were taught by him. He was a cultured man, who consecrated his life to his high calling and used all of his time to the end of his days in useful service for others.

He was born in Raleigh (on the corner where the Supreme Court building now stands and within ten feet of where the Chief Justice presides over that court) November 23, 1834, son of Ichabod Wetmore, born in Middleton, Connecticut, March 14, 1792, died October 7, 1857, who was then Cashier of the North Carolina State Bank, and his mother, Elizabeth Ann (Badger) Wetmore, a sister of that great North Carolinian, Judge George E. Badger. So Mr. Wetmore was brought up in an intellectual atmosphere. The bank was moved from Raleigh to Fayetteville in the early 1840's and Mr. Wetmore received his primary education there at the Donaldson Academy. He then entered as a student at the State University, from which he graduated with the A.B. degree in 1854. In

1856 he received the A.M. degree from the same institution. While Assistant Professor of Mathematics there he studied law and was admitted to the bar in 1858, when he moved to Livingston, Alabama, where he practiced law with his brother, Col. Thomas B. Wetmore.

Responding to the call to the ministry, he abandoned the law, attended the General Theological Seminary in New York, from which he graduated early in 1861; was ordained deacon in Trinity Church, Mobile, Alabama by Bishop William M. Green, June 25, 1861, and then entered upon his ministerial career in Newbern, N. C., as assistant to the rector, Dr. Watson, later Bishop of the Eastern Carolina Diocese. While connected with this church in Civil War times the town was captured by Federal troops and the Commander ordered Mr. Wetmore to conduct a service on Sunday for his troops, which he agreed to do, but with the clear understanding that the prayer authorized by the church, would be for the President of the Confederate States and not for the President of the United States. This so angered the General that he ordered the arrest of the minister, but in a few hours he was released and finally had his way by using the prayer for the President of the Confederacy.

He was later, for a brief time, a chaplain in the Confederate Army with the rank of captain, but in the latter half of 1862 he came to Lincolnton as rector of Saint Luke's church and in it was ordained priest by Bishop Thomas Atkinson, September 21, 1862, and from that time to the end of his life he was a notable citizen of Lincolnton. During the period covered by the War and the years following he had a meagre salary and had to supplement it by teaching, for which he was well equipped, and the long line of students, who through the years came under his tuition, would all testify of the thoroughness of his work and of his high moral influence. As a teacher he came in contact with all types of people, whom he impressed as one of firm faith, decided convictions, broad charity and accurate scholarship.

Reference has already been made to his work as a teacher, but it bears repeating for he was distinguished as a linguist and mathematician. He could read Latin or Greek as fluently as English, and no knotty problem in mathematics was hard for him to solve. He was a disciplinarian who ruled by kindness and rarely by coercion. He knew how to impart knowledge. His students believed in him and he inspired them with lofty purpose. Many of them became notable as ministers, teachers, physicians, lawyers, jurists, statesmen, industrialists, and planters.

The two-teacher school in the Lincolnton Male Academy, conducted by Dr. Wetmore and Professor H. H. Smith, during the years following the Civil War, was not excelled by any Academy in the country. Dr. Wetmore was a practical teacher, who took the students out into the fields and forests to give them practical lessons in surveying. He was a great civil engineer and had he given his life to it would have been distinguished in that field.

But he was first of all a minister, who magnified his calling. He was enthusiastic in his ministerial work and his energy was amazing, for he seemed never to tire, but constant at his task, going through storm or cold to minister to the sick or distressed. He was deeply interested in the poor and neglected and through his tactful interest brought many of these into the fold. He established mission chapels in many communities, where church facilities were poor, and thus reached many who needed the blessings of the gospel.

Among the mission churches which he built were Saint Paul, three miles north of Lincolnton, Saint Stephen, a mile west of town, Saint John at High Shoals, and Saint Cyprian in Lincolnton for the colored communicants, besides churches in Gastonia and other points. He helped with his own hands to build some of these churches. He painted the altar panels of St. Paul's. The present Saint Luke's church in Lincolnton was practically rebuilt during his rectorship in 1886, when the corner stone was laid. The belfry and spire of the old church were retained in the new building. He preached many times at nearby points, Beatties Ford, Dallas, Gastonia, Shelby and Hickory by special appointment.

No day was too cold for him to brave the elements to meet his appointments. On one dismal sleety day he started on horseback to High Shoals to preach. After riding a mile or more over a slick and icy road, fearing for the safety of himself and his horse, he stabled the animal at a farmhouse and then walked some five miles over the treacherous icy way and preached as he had started out to do. He was a great walker and cared nought for distance. Once he walked ten miles to Cherryville to preach Sunday night. The boys all gathered next morning at the Male Academy for school and when some one said Mr. Wetmore was in Cherryville we all were happy in the prospect of a holiday, but at 9 o'clock were sorely disappointed as Mr. Wetmore walked in from Cherryville exactly on time to open school. He had a fine sense of humor. He told me with great interest of an experience he had, as he was walking from Stanley to visit the Johnston family that lived some six miles further on. When he reached the creek a few miles from Stanley he found the stream swollen, with the water two feet over the bridge. Just at the right moment a colored man, who proved to be a Baptist preacher, approached. A bargain was made. Mr. Wetmore got on the back of the colored preacher and rode across, paying twenty-five cents for transportation.

He married in 1861 to Mary Bingham, of Mocksville, N. C., and they had eight children, five of whom died early. Three sons grew to manhood:

1. Lemuel Bingham Wetmore, born December 2, 1865, was educated by his father and at Horner's Military Academy in Hillsboro; read law under Judge D. M. Furches, of Statesville and was admitted to the bar in September, 1889, and was a Lincolnton lawyer for nearly thirty years, until his death, May 21, 1918. He had a brilliant mind, was well versed in the law, and was successful, both as a counsellor and advocate. He never held public office but confined himself to his profession for which he was so well equipped. His first marriage was to Miss Nellie Jarrett, daughter of Frank Jarrett, of Newton. Later he married to Clara, daughter of the late Frank C. and Lou (Templeton) Lander, of Lincolnton.

2. Thomas Cogdell Wetmore, born August 23, 1869, was educated and well prepared by his father for the Episcopal ministry and upon his ordination he was assigned by Bishop Horner to Calvary Church, near Fletcher, but he preached at several nearby missions. Here he married, on his birthday, 1893, Susan Allan, an accomplished lady and niece of Mrs. Theodore B. Lyman, and it was their dream to establish a

church in that section. To find the money to build it was their problem, but with faith they sought and found it and established in 1900 Christ's School, located about twelve miles from Asheville. It prospered and through faith and sacrifice the property now consists of twenty-eight (28) buildings valued at $200,000. The value of the work done there among the 100 boys who annually attend cannot be estimated. Before it was completed this consecrated young man died August 3, 1906, but his splendid work will continue to bear abundant fruit.

The workman died but God carried on the work.

3. Silas McBee Wetmore, born February 18, 1877, is a successful lawyer in Florence, S. C. He married Katherine Dale, daughter of Dr. J. Y. Dale, of LaMont, Pennsylvania, December 18, 1907. Their son William Robards Wetmore was born May 10, 1909.

Rev. Dr. Wetmore was a great good man. Sixty and more years ago when he was my teacher I loved him and as the years have drifted by my regard for him developed into a warm affection. His labor was always effective and he left the world better than he found it.

He died March 24, 1904 and his body rests in the graveyard of Saint Luke's church in Lincolnton, under the shadow of the church which he had faithfully served for more than forty years.

1905

Theodore Roosevelt was inaugurated President for a second term on March 4, 1905.

Since the early days when Michael Quickel, the pioneer, settled in Lincoln County, the Quickel name has figured prominently in the religious and public life of this section, and the Quickels were closely related to the Canslers and Hokes, many of whom are descendants of the pioneer Quickel.

Cephas Quickel, a splendid citizen, son of Michael Quickel, Jr., was born February 14, 1819, married Sarah Killian, May 16, 1840. Among their children were Levi H., who married Alice Robinson; John C. married Josephine Crouse; Catherine married George Cansler; Caroline married Samuel D. Burgin.

John C. Quickel, son of Cephas Quickel, was a sturdy and dependable citizen, who in later life was a Lincolnton merchant and treasurer of the County, held in high respect by the people. He married to Josephine Crouse, of Lincoln County, and among their children are Dr. Thomas C. Quickel, a physician of high standing, who has for many years practiced his profession in Gastonia, and Judge Augustus L. Quickel, a Lincolnton lawyer of ability, who was one time mayor of the city and served several years as secretary to Congressman E. Y. Webb (now Federal Judge for this district). Judge Quickel also represented Lincoln County in the State Legislature for three terms, 1903, 1911, 1921 and 1923. He also for several years served as an Emergency Judge of the Superior Court, by appointment from Governor Gardner.

Theodorus Henderson Cobb died at his home in Asheville, August 20, 1905. He was born in Lincolnton, August 20, 1854, son of B. Y. and Barbara (Henderson) Cobb (See 1913); was educated in Caswell County schools and at the Lincolnton Academy. He read law under the direction of Major John D. Shaw, attended the Pearson Law School, licensed by Supreme Court to practice law in January, 1876, and then as the law partner of Major Shaw began to practice in Lincolnton and adjoining counties. He loved the law, was a diligent student and well grounded in the basic principles of jurisprudence. He was a wise legal counsellor as well as an able advocate before a jury, and from the start a successful practitioner. He was judicially minded, never cared for public office, spent all of his active life in the practice of law and would have made a great judge.

He distinguished himself as counsel for the Seaboard Railway in 1886 when he won the suit against Rutherford County for the delivery of bonds, voted by the people prior to the Civil War, to be issued to the Wilmington, Charlotte and Rutherford Railroad when completed to Rutherfordton. In another hotly contested suit brought in Buncombe County about 1902 he represented the Hilliard estate in which a large amount was involved. He alone was counsel for the defense, while six able lawyers represented the plaintiffs. He won in the two jury trials and in two appeals before the Supreme Court. In 1886 he moved to Asheville where he found a wider field of opportunity and remained there until his death.

Mr. James G. Merrimon, of Asheville, said:

"I formed a partnership with Mr. Cobb, which lasted for six years, and I never had a closer, warmer friend, and he treated me like a son, for he was my elder in years. He was one of the most attractive men I have known. He was exceedingly generous, popular with the people and popular with his brethren of the bar, although he made no particular effort to make friends. He despised anything like trickery and chicanery and had great courage and high professional ideals. He had a very keen, penetrating and analytical mind and was one of the cleanest, most logical and forceful speakers we had at the Asheville bar. He was the kind of lawyer who would have made a great judge, because of his learning, his patience, his sweetness of character, his love of humanity and his intense desire to see justice and right prevail. Too much cannot be said of the kind disposition and intellectual characteristics of Mr. Cobb."

Judge Burwell of Charlotte paid him the following tribute:

"The announcement of the death of Theodorus H. Cobb has brought sorrow to many who knew and admired that brilliant lawyer, and knew and loved that kindly man and citizen. He was a native of Lincoln County and, when licensed to practice law in 1876, he selected that and adjoining counties as the field for his professional labors, and, for ten years, in all the exacting duties of a busy lawyer's life, he displayed such ability, both in Council Chamber and in forum, as to win the confidence of the people and the esteem of his brethren, who recognized not only the skill of the practitioner, but also the lovable spirit of the gentleman. In the year 1886 he sought a wider scope and became a citizen of the City of Asheville and a member of the distinguished bar of that county. It is a sufficient tribute to his professional ability to say, that, removed from those associates who had known the boy and hence loved the young man, he soon took place in that honorable company to which his talents entitled him, and which his generous associates most willingly accorded him."

His body was buried in Riverside Cemetery in Asheville.

1906

John Barnett Smith, a useful and intelligent citizen, died at his home in Ironton township on February 2, 1906, aged 79 years. He was a farmer, a devout member of the Lutheran church and a grandson of the Rev. John Gottfried Arndt, the pioneer Lutheran minister.

Captain Joseph Graham Morrison, a popular citizen, who represented the County in the Legislature of 1881, died at home near Lowesville, April 11, 1906, aged 64 years. He was a son of Rev. Dr. R. H. Morrison (See 1889). He married Elizabeth Davis of Salisbury in 1862.

Their children were:

Mary Graham married Rev. Chas. E. Raynal of the Presbyterian church.

Louise married Frank E. Lloyd of Salisbury.

Alston married Allison L. Badger, granddaughter of Judge George E. Badger.

Col. Robert Hall Morrison married Portia L. Owen. They live in Charlotte.

Anna Jackson married Ronald B. Wilson of Raleigh.

Joseph G., Jr., married Pearl, daughter of the late Colonel Junius P. Gardner of Shelby. He is a valuable citizen and Farm Agent for Lincoln County.

Col. R. H. Morrison rendered valiant service on the Mexican border in 1916; was Captain Machine Gun Co. of the 30th Division in World War, and now holds the rank of Lieut. Colonel in the United States Army Reserves.

Dr. Robert J. Brevard, one time Lincolnton physician, and later Mayor of the City of Charlotte, died in that city, August 11, 1906, aged 57 years. He was a son of the late Judge Theodorus W. and Caroline Mays Brevard.

In May, 1906, Thos. A. Edison drove into Lincolnton and registered at the North State Hotel, with his son, Charles Edison, and his son-in-law, John Miller, all of Orange, N. J. Mr. Edison was seeking for cobalt. They spent ten days in Lincolnton where they found rich ore, but in such small quantity that it was not profitable to work it. Later he mined cobalt on a small scale in Jackson County. The visit of Mr. Edison to the town was an event long talked about. Mr. M. C. Padgett was proprietor of the hotel at the time.

1907

Patrick Mullen came from Ireland to this country when a young man and settled in the Ore Bank section in the eastern part of the County. He married Mary Keever on December 27,

1824, and lived in the County for the remainder of his life, and died when he was 103 years of age.

His only son James Mullen, was born September 18, 1831. Like most successful men he was born poor, learned lessons in self-denial, developed the frugal habit, spent less than he earned, accumulated a little money and went into the mercantile business in the Ore Bank community and developed into a successful merchant and farmer and a public-spirited and popular citizen.

In politics he was a Republican but always tolerant toward those who differed with him. He served as County Commissioner and stood for economy in public spending, and was for some years a Justice of the Peace.

Some twenty years before his death he had a paralytic stroke and never walked afterwards, but despite this physical disability, he never gave up, for seated in a chair he directed his mercantile business and rode in his buggy to oversee and give direction to his large landed and other interests, as in other days. From small beginnings he prospered and amassed a good estate, consisting of valuable personal property and about two thousand acres of land. That shrewd man of affairs, Jonas W. Derr, who amassed a large fortune, recognized the high character and fine business judgment of Mr. Mullen by selecting him to act as the executor of his will.

James Mullen married Emily Lowe, December 28, 1850, and they had twelve children, five of whom died early. Those who grew to maturity were William C., Jonas W., John P., George S., and S. L. Mullen, Mary, who married J. L. Gryder, and Lucy, who married S. L. Bolinger. Only Mrs. Gryder and S. L. Mullen are now living (1935). They were all sensible, sturdy, substantial people of character and influence in the county. John P. Mullen, the third son, was Postmaster in Lincolnton in 1893, and a grandson, Clyde G. Mullen, was Postmaster there in 1923.

Jonas W. Mullen was a prominent citizen of Charlotte for some years and Postmaster in that city from 1897 to 1903. His latter days were spent in Lincolnton. He married Virginia Shipp Boyd, daughter of Marcus and Mary Reinhardt Boyd (See 1869), and their children are Charles G., Maude R., Ellie Reid, who married William S. Baskerville, Josephine, who married Thornton M. Epperson, Paul J., John M., Earl, Elizabeth and Edwin F. Mullen. Mr. Mullen died June 24, 1926.

James Mullen was a Baptist in faith and when he died, April 4, 1907, his body was buried at Amity Baptist church in Lincoln County on land he had donated to the church. Mrs. Mullen died July 20, 1908.

Wallace M. Reinhardt died June 17, 1907, aged about 84 years. He married to Frances Johnson, daughter of B. S. Johnson, October 13, 1845. Was Clerk of Superior Court from 1874 to 1880. A very kindly man who was held in high regard by all who knew him. He was a son of Michael Reinhardt and grandson of Christian Reinhardt, the pioneer, and lived for many years in the ancestral home near the Ramsour Battleground, on the road leading to the old Ramsour Mill site.

Col. Lawson A. Mason, State Senator in 1868-69, died at Dallas, September 6, 1907, in his 87th year.

Charles A. Jonas, a young Lincolnton lawyer, was appointed Postmaster in 1907, and served until 1910, when he resigned.

Rev. Chas. T. Bland, Rector of St. Luke's Episcopal church in 1861 and for several years prior thereto, died April 25, 1907, and his body was buried in St. Luke's churchyard.

The Lincoln Hospital was built in 1906 and 1907, and opened for patients, March 11, 1907. This institution was started by Dr. Lester A. Crowell and Dr. R. W. Petrie, and the bed capacity of the original building was twelve. Dr. Petrie remained with the hospital about two years. The Lincoln Hospital has been enlarged four times. The last and largest addition was made in 1925. The death of Dr. Gordon Bryan Crowell, son of Dr. L. A. Crowell, occurred during the construction of this building, which is called the Gordon Crowell Memorial Building. The hospital has had a nurses' training school since its establishment. The bed capacity is now forty and the value of the property is estimated at about $150,000. The present medical corps is:

1. Dr. Lester A. Crowell, graduate of Baltimore Medical College in 1892.

2. Dr. William F. Elliott, graduate of Medico-Chirurgical College of Philadelphia in 1916.

3. Dr. Abner M. Cornwell, graduate of George Washington Medical School in 1927.

4. Dr. Lester A. Crowell, Jr., graduate of Tulane University School of Medicine in 1930.

The nursing staff consists of the Superintendent of Nurses, the Superintendent of the operating room and fourteen undergraduate nurses. The nurses are housed in the nurses' home near the hospital. The first patient to enter the hospital was A. J. Bagley and more than a thousand since have gone there for surgical treatment.

Dr. Lester A. Crowell is a son of the late Dr. Eli Crowell, who was a prominent Lincoln County physician and a State Senator in 1870 and 1871, and his wife, Mary Beatrice (Lowrance) Crowell, daughter of the late Sheriff Logan H. Lowrance, who died in 1868.

Dr. Eli Crowell was a native of Union County, North Carolina, and a son of Michael Crowell, of that county.

Dr. L. A. Crowell was born October 17, 1867 near Reepsville, Lincoln County, attended county schools until 1886 when he entered high school at Dallas, North Carolina. He entered Baltimore Medical College (now a part of the University of Maryland) in the fall of 1889. The following spring he returned to Lincoln County where he practiced and read medicine under his father, Dr. Eli Crowell (as was then the custom) until the fall of 1891, when he returned to Baltimore for the second course of lectures and received his degree of Medical Doctor in April, 1892. He then practiced medicine in Lincoln County near the home of his father, and later moved to Lincolnton.

He is a member of the Lincoln County Medical Society, of which he has been both Secretary and President; member of the Catawba Valley Medical Society, of which he was the first president; the North Carolina Medical Society, of which he was president in 1930; the Tri-State Society of the Carolinas and Virginia; the American Medical Society; the Southeastern Surgical Congress and the American College of Surgeons. He is a director of the Western Hospital for the Insane of North Carolina at Morganton.

Dr. Crowell has a wide reputation as a Surgeon and stands high in medical circles. He was married September 12, 1894,

to Mary Jane, daughter of the late M. F. Hull, of Catawba County. The children are:
1. Dr. Gordon Bryan Crowell, a bright and promising young physician, who died May 9, 1926.
2. Mary Beatrice, who married to Thomas C. Abernethy.
3. Georgia Corinne, who married J. W. Schenck, of Shelby.
4. Dr. Lester Avant Crowell, Jr.
5. Frank Hull Crowell.

Ural L. Hoffman, a bright Lincoln boy, graduated with honors from Trinity College, (now Duke University) in the class of 1907. Then he served for a while on the news staff of the *Charlotte Observer;* went west and became prominent in newspaper work on the Pacific Coast. He was for a while an Instructor in Journalism at Tacoma, Washington, and author of a textbook for newsmen, entitled *See, Know and Tell-Well,* and also wrote the *Handbook for News Writers.*

He has made a good record.

John R. Detter, a lifelong citizen of Lincolnton, died December 27, 1907. He was a good man and a skilled worker in iron, who ran a blacksmith shop on East Main street for many years. He did honest work, served his day and generation well and lived eight more years than the allotted three score years and ten.

1908

Nearly all good and great men had forebears strong in faith and character. Such was the case with Rev. Robert Zenas Johnston, who sprang from sturdy God-fearing pioneer stock. His pioneer ancestor, Robert Johnston, came with his family from Pennsylvania about 1750 and settled on Third Creek, Rowan County, North Carolina. His son, William Johnston (1735-1798) married Elizabeth Dickey, and their son, Robert Johnston (1777-1800) married Eleanor Gillespie, then their son, Robert D. Johnston (1803-1863) married Alice Graham (daughter of James Graham, 1758-1834) and they were the parents of Rev. R. Z. Johnston. All of these ancestors were Scotch-Irish Presbyterians on both sides of the house and all old enough, during the period of the Revolution, were active in the struggle for American freedom. All four of his Johnston forebears are buried side by side in the old Third Creek Presbyterian churchyard in Rowan.

Mr. Johnston was born in Rowan, December 14, 1834. He joined the church of his fathers in early youth, graduated from Davidson College in 1858 and from Columbia Theological Seminary in 1861. In the same year he was licensed to preach by the Concord Presbytery, ordained elder and installed pastor of Providence and Sharon churches in Mecklenburg County.

He married to Miss Catherine Caldwell, of Chester County, South Carolina, May 15, 1861. She was an elect lady, gentle, cultured and consecrated, and proved a genuine helpmeet and inspiration to her husband in his work as a Christian minister, until her death September 29, 1901.

After eleven years of fruitful service at Providence and Sharon, Mr. Johnston accepted the call to the Lincolnton Presbyterian church and there labored faithfully and effectively until he died April 24, 1908. He entered upon his life work well prepared in head and heart, was a preacher of superior gifts and loved by his people as evidenced by the fact that he had but two pastorates in a ministry which covered forty-seven years. He went to the pulpit with a prepared message, which he delivered with fervor and tenderness, exhorting his people to holy living, and pleading with sinners to choose the better life. His work for a considerable period was not confined to the local church, but he preached at Long Shoals, Iron Station, Stanley, Mount Holly, Dallas, Shelby and other points, until self-supporting churches were established at most of them.

He possessed a warm, magnetic nature and made friends of all he met, for he was interested in people, rich or poor, cultured or ignorant, young or old, black or white, good or bad, and they all had confidence in him. He was a busy pastor, walked into every door of opportunity and ministered tenderly to the sick and sorrowing, doing all he could to give comfort and hope to troubled hearts. His long residence in the county acquainted him with most of the people and while he was a loyal churchman he had the broad catholic spirit, which made him a brother to all men. He co-operated heartily with his brethren of other churches, in every movement for social uplift and human betterment. He was deeply interested in public education and served several terms as county superintendent of schools; was chairman of the Board of Education and Trustee of the Lincolnton Academy. His family life was beautiful and the sons and daughters have led lives of such usefulness as to reflect high honor upon their parents.

When he died many high tributes were paid to him:

The Lincolnton Ministerial Association:

"The good this co-laborer in Christ has done in his public and private ministry is beyond reckoning. For many years he served faithfully and zealously the church of his conviction, and the great number of whom he was pastor sufficiently testify to the fervor of his devotion to the Master's cause.

"Beyond and above his ministry to his own church Mr. Johnston was the friend and shepherd of all kinds and conditions of men, without respect to their church affiliations. He was an apostle to those who were friendless and to all wandering ones."

Raleigh News and Observer:

"The death of Rev. R. Z Johnston of Lincolnton removes one of the best of the old-fashioned, big-brained Presbyterian preachers to whom North Carolina owes a big debt. He was a Confederate soldier, and after the surrender he was a faithful soldier of the Cross. North Carolina had no worthier leader in patriotism and righteousness."

The Lincoln Times:

"Mr. Johnston in the councils of his church received every honor his brethren could bestow. He took a lively interest in education and did much for the public schools ... He was a trustee of Davidson College and contributor to the secular and religious press ... He was a loyal Presbyterian and lovingly discharged all the duties of pastor, but his friends and friendships were not bounded by denominational lines ... The great work he performed was not less due to the excellent qualities and personality of the man, than to his ability as a preacher. Gentle, affable, sympathetic, cheerful, he was loved and honored and his passing leaves a great void."

THE ANNALS OF LINCOLN COUNTY 315

The children of Rev. R. Z. and Catherine Caldwell Johnston were:

1. Lida W., who married James A. Lore, of Lincolnton, April 23, 1888.

2. Nettie W., married Rev. John C. McMullen, August 30, 1883. She died suddenly on the train as she and her husband were journeying to Kentucky, November 23, 1893. Three of her children served as missionaries to China: Rev. Robert Johnston McMullen, D.D., Ph.D., has been active there in mission work since 1910 and is now connected with Hangchow College in Hangchow, China; his sister, Mrs. Kittie McMullen Farrior, is with her husband and family, stationed in Chinkiang, China since 1912; another sister, Miss Nettie McMullen, also served as a missionary in China for fifteen years, when, because of ill health, was forced to retire.

3. Kate C. married Daniel G. Crawford of Chester, S. C., August 30, 1887. She died June 1, 1893, from a stroke of lightning.

4. Bessie D. married Dr. John W. Saine, of Lincolnton, December 23, 1896.

5. Robert Caldwell, killed in a cyclone storm in Pennsylvania, November 18, 1886, aged 17 years.

6. Jennie S. Johnston, married Augustus M. Hoke, November 17, 1900. She died March 29, 1906.

7. Captain Rufus Z. Johnston, U. S. Navy, born June 7, 1874. Attended Lincolnton schools; entered United States Naval Academy (Annapolis, Md.), September, 1891, graduated from same, June 7, 1895. Won the gold medal for marksmanship. Was Ensign and served as secretary on staff of Captain C. E. Clark, Commander of the Oregon, which rounded Cape Horn in 1898, on the memorable voyage to Santiago during the Spanish American War, and took part in the Battle of Santiago; thence to the Philippines and the Boxer uprising in China; served as executive officer on the U. S. Ship New Hampshire in 1914 in the attack on Vera Cruz, Mexico. Rear Admiral Fletcher, in reporting the Vera Cruz attack, said: "In the second day's fighting Lieut. Staton and Lieut. Commander Johnston, Regimental Adjutant, were eminent and conspicuous in their conduct. They exhibited courage and skill in leading the Twenty-second and in the final occupation of the city."

For this action he was awarded the Congressional Medal of Honor. He did service at Naval Training Station during the first nine months of the World War. Intensive training of boys for service was required. He was then placed in command of United States Cruiser Minneapolis for convoy duty, made ten trips overseas, was seriously injured on last trip and placed in hospital upon return to America, where he received two years' medical treatment. He is now restored to health and was retired with rank of Captain in 1932 at the age of 58 years. He married Eunice Pegram, June 2, 1903. He resides at Newport, Rhode Island.

8. Mary Knox Johnston, married Robert S. Abernethy, June 6, 1905. They live in Winter Haven, Florida.

9. Joseph B. Johnston, born March 2, 1881, married Annie Lee Davidson, January 29, 1907. Was prepared for college in Lincolnton schools and graduated from Davidson College in the class of 1901 with distinction in Chemistry and Mathematics. After spending several years with a Steel Company in Atlanta he returned to Lincolnton in 1910, and established himself in the Ice and Fuel business. About 1920 he was elected County Commissioner and during his term in that office the new county courthouse was built. He was also an active member of the City School Board and the present High School building was constructed during that period. He was elected by the Presbyterian Synod of North Carolina late in 1921 to the office of Superintendent of the Barium Springs Orphans Home and assumed control in February, 1922, and still holds that position. He has fine executive ability and has succeeded wonderfully in that very important position.

In May, 1908, the people of North Carolina, by a decided vote, adopted the prohibition law which is still in force. (1934.)

The first class to graduate from the Lincolnton High School (established in 1904) was composed of the following, who finished the course and received certificates of graduation, May 8, 1908:

1. Katherine Crawford, now living in Jacksonville, Florida.
2. Mary Dellinger (Mrs. Victor Fair).
3. Eva James, Assistant Postmaster of Lincolnton.
4. Margaret Cobb, New York.

5. Ethel Long, Clerk in Lincolnton Post Office.
6. Annie McKee (Mrs. L. Cash Nixon).
7. Leitha Self, (Mrs. Bess) California.
8. Wade Hampton Childs, lawyer and one time State Senator, Lincolnton.
9. John Mason Pressly, physician at Belmont, N. C.
10. Carson Motz, died in Maryland in 1931.
11. Samuel C. Dellinger, professor in University of Arkansas.
12. Macon Epps, printer, Newton, N. C.
13. John C. Ramseur. salesman, Lincolnton.

The Board of Commissioners of Lincoln County for two terms, from December, 1904, to December, 1908, was composed of Thomas F. Cline, J. Ed Reinhardt, W. T. Carpenter and in addition to these, J. Allen King and Junius Blanton for the first term. The two last named were succeeded by David Cherry and Cephas Beam for the second term.

Thomas F. Cline, a successful farmer with fine business judgment and who knew how to get a hundred per cent value for every dollar spent, was made chairman. That was before heavy taxes were laid for improved roads, modern school buildings, longer school terms and better paid teachers, and the County was managed at minimum cost. During that period the annual County expense was less than $40,000, the tax rate 89 cents and at the end of four years they left a surplus of $11,000 in cash and uncollected solvent taxes, with absolutely no debt. The board worked together in complete harmony and the public interests were directed as economically as were their personal affairs.

To Mr. Cline, the chairman, was committed the oversight of all public works and he gave personal attention to the urgent demands arising between the monthly sessions of the Board. This required much of his time, but with an eye single to economy he was careful to save every cent possible for the county and to this day he is justly proud of the fine record made by the County Board during the period he served as its chairman.

1909

Rev. James Allen Arndt, pastor of the Lutheran church in Newton, died in that town, June 30, 1909. He was a great grandson of Rev. John Gottfried Arndt, the pioneer Lutheran preacher.

Captain Alexander F. Brevard, son of the late Robert A. Brevard, and grandson of Captain Alexander Brevard, the pioneer, was born at the Brevard homestead in Lincoln County, October 3, 1825, and died at the same place October 22, 1909. He was a lawyer by profession and owned a large estate in Ironton township. He never held political position and never married.

He was the last of his line and his body was buried in the family plot at Machpelah.

Judge William Preston Bynum was born June 16th, 1820 in Stokes County, North Carolina. His parents were Hampton Bynum (1783-1861) and Mary Coleman Martin (1785-1855), daughter of John Martin of Stokes County. His father's parents were Gray Bynum (1737-1814) and Margaret Hampton (1742-1800), daughter of Anthony Hampton, of Surry County, later of South Carolina. The families of Bynum, Martin, Hampton, Shipp and Cox, from which Judge Bynum was descended, were Virginians who came to North Carolina before the Revolution, took active part in that War, and afterwards had an active part in shaping the development of their State.

Judge Bynum graduated with first distinction from Davidson College August 4, 1842. He read law under Judge R. M. Pearson and first settled in Rutherfordton as a lawyer. On December 2, 1846 he was married to Anna Eliza Shipp, daughter of Hon. Bartlett Shipp, and located in Lincolnton. He was a Whig in politics and an ardent Union man, opposed to the Civil War, but when war was declared he volunteered and was elected Lieutenant of the Beatties Ford Rifles, the only married man in the company. He was commissioned Lieut. Colonel by Gov. Ellis, ranking from May 2, 1861, and Colonel by Governor Vance, ranking from September 17, 1862. The State Legislature on December 12, 1862, elected him State Solicitor for the Lincolnton District, which position he held for eleven years, when Governor Caldwell on November 21, 1873 appointed him Justice of the Supreme Court to fill the vacancy caused by the death of Judge Nathaniel Boyden. He served with distinction in that court until his term expired January 1, 1879. He was the delegate from Lincoln to the Constitutional Convention of 1865 and represented the Lincoln district in the State Senate in 1865.

He was in 1868 re-elected Solicitor without opposition and actively supported Gen. Grant, the Republican candidate for President that year.

When he retired from the Supreme Court bench he resumed the practice of law in Charlotte and died in that city December 30, 1909, aged 89 years. He was a great lawyer, an able prosecuting officer and one of the greatest Judges who ever sat upon our Supreme bench. His written decisions rank among the greatest ever rendered by that court. He was a great citizen, a great patriot and would have been great in any age. He was a communicant of the Episcopal church. The Chapel at the Thompson Orphanage in Charlotte and the Episcopal church near the State Normal College in Greensboro were built at his expense.

The only son of Judge Bynum was the Rev. William Shipp Bynum of the Episcopal church, to whom reference has already been made, and who was a cultured gentleman, consecrated to his holy task, but in his latter days on account of ill health lived in retirement, and his only daughter was Mary Preston Bynum (1849-1875).

The following is a worthy tribute to Judge Bynum by Capt. William H. Day, who presented the Bynum portrait to the Supreme Court, February 19, 1898, nearly twelve years before the death of the Judge. Mr. Day said:

"Had Judge Bynum lived during the period of the Revolution he would have been one of the few who shaped and molded government.

"Living in these days of banalities, he by his life gives expression to the highest anticipation of the fathers.

"Strong, virile, earnest in his manliness, is his power. These great attributes will leave upon coming generations the impress of this man. Judge Bynum is too original and sincere to be an imitator. He stands for himself, sometimes isolated, but always erect. He was courageous enough in 1865 to wring himself away from the baneful prejudices of 1861, a strength vouchsafed to but few men of those titanic days.

"In her army, in her legislative halls, upon her bench he has served North Carolina well. Called to this court in 1873, he at once commanded the respect, and then the admiration of the legal profession, and through it, that of our entire people. His dissenting opinion in the State against Blalock rang out upon our profession like a tocsin in the dark; its clear tone aroused them to a full appreciation of their rights. So true was its vibrant ring, the next succeeding Legislature unanimously enacted it to be the law. In the State against Turpin his clear sympathetic reasoning exorcised from our State the last ghost of common law brutality.

"In his opinion in State against the Richmond and Danville Railway, with the keen foresight of a genuine seer he foretold the result upon our liberties, of the aggregation of corporate power. He said:

"'The rapid multiplication of these bodies, their resources and far-reaching ambition, their ubiquity and vast combinations, all moved and directed by concentrated power and talent constitute them a distinct and almost independent overshadowing power in our government and in fact the great social and political problem of the age. Whether they shall control governments or whether governments shall control them are questions that are forcing themselves upon public attention and fast assuming practical importance. They should and will be maintained in the exercise of all their essential and legitimate powers, as necessary and useful institutions of modern civilization. But if, in addition to the dangerous power of transferring all their property and franchises to anybody, anywhere, it should also be held that their corporate powers are such contracts as puts them beyond the reach of all legislative check or control, then the problem will have been solved.

"'But government, in my opinion, will have abdicated its sovereignty, heretofore supposed inalienable, and society will be left without protection against chartered irresponsibility.'

"When these words were uttered many called them wild. A few called them wise. Today every thinking man shudders to know that these truths fell upon deaf ears. Had this timely warning been his only life's work, it would not be flattery to say his services to the State had been great.

"His opinion contained in our Reports from Volume 70 to 79, rank him easily by the side of the greatest judges who have ever adorned your bench, and who have helped to make Anglo-Saxon law synonymous with human liberty.

"Judge Bynum is the best misunderstood man in North Carolina. He will not be fully appreciated until we have lost him, and he shall have joined the silent majority. Then—not until then—will the unostentatious charity of his life be known—a charity as broad and genial as the casing air."

THE ANNALS OF LINCOLN COUNTY 321

After his death the Mecklenburg Bar Association adopted resolutions of respect which contained the following:

"So fearlessly and so faithfully did he act under all the trying circumstances covering the Civil War and the years following, that after the adoption of the Constitution of 1868, he was supported by both parties for State Solicitor and in the political campaign of 1868 he gave his support to the National Republican Party and asserted that the interest of the South as well as the interests of the whole country would be best conserved by the election of Gen. Grant. He was appointed Justice of the Supreme Court in November, 1873, and served until January, 1879 after which he took rank as the most eminent member of the Charlotte Bar and enjoyed as was his desert, an extensive and lucrative practice."

Judge Frank I. Osborne in brilliant style eulogized Judge Bynum, speaking in part as follows:

"He was of antique and Roman mold, stern in appearance, sometimes cool in manner and difficult of approach, always checking familiarity, but beneath the rugged appearance, as we find the pearl beneath the billows of the ocean, and as the nugget of gold in the heart of the mountain, there was that priceless jewel the golden heart. He had a mind instinct with the principles of the legal profession, and the finest constructive intellect with which I have come in contact in the practice of the law. He was always strongest for the plaintiff and was the ablest solicitor of this generation. He once changed the opinion of an entire jury.

"After the Civil War he was promoted to the bench and carried there his elegant style of speech, which flowed in a pellucid stream, with no flowers on the banks, to a logical conclusion, but he carried something more than that, something brighter and better—humanity and mercy."

Hesitating to invade the holy of holies, of that surpassing relation between man and his God, known as religion, he quoted the Judge as saying:

"The teachings of our holy religion must and should be received by faith."

Then Osborne continued:

"That great and constructive intellect admitted its limitations. He could not construct a satisfactory religion for himself, but like a little child must fall back into the arms of that faith which is the gift of God.

"His was a great name, a lofty spirit, a splendid intellect. These two names, Preston and Hampton, the one his own, the other that of his father, tell to Americans and especially to Southerners who and what were his forebears. He came from a family of great lawyers. His brother, Gen. John Gray Bynum, had a bright, but not a deeper intellect and two nephews won distinction. But it is not from any glory which he may have inherited from his ancestors, it is not from any reflected light from any of his collateral relatives that the lustre of William Preston Bynum shines."

The late Col. William S. Pearson, of Morganton, in a brief sketch referring to Judge Bynum on the bench, said:

"There is a clearness and precision in his written opinions that make them models. Many of them are notable. In his construction of contracts all of his opinions breathed the spirit of the olden time when it was considered disgraceful not to pay a debt. In Belo against Commissioners, he announced with emphasis as a proper principle of public action the wise doctrine of 'pay as you go' which won for him high praise and by it he impressed himself largely on the policy of the State.

"In Brown against Turner he rose above party when the question involved was whether the public printer was an officer or contractor, holding it to be a contractor while the minority of the court held that it was an office to be filled by the Governor.

"His decision in Wittkowsky against Wasson (71 N. C.) contains a noble tribute to the value and sphere of the jury."

Pearson said further:

"North Carolina is indebted to Judge Bynum for saving its credit. That the greatest authority upon municipal bonds in the United States said in the argument of the Wilkes bond case in the Supreme Court of the United States that the opinion written by Bynum in the case of Belo against Commissioners (76 N. C. Reports) concerning the law upon municipal bonds was never excelled by any Justice of any court in the United States. Indeed, after the Stanly bond case was decided against the bond holders it was upon the strength of this opinion that the action of the lower court was reversed and a new hearing was granted. The principles laid down in the opinion were decisive in both cases."

In this opinion Judge Bynum said:

"No check against our indebtedness is so effectual as that you must pay as you go, but this is utterly disregarded in the legislation which authorizes the issue of bonds payable at a remote future period. As soon as the sting of taxation is felt, the self-burdened people cast about for relief, and after some hesitating scruples, plunge into repudiation or other methods involving the sacrifice of public faith, with its dismal trail of evils. No refuge for repudiation can be found in the legal tribunals of the Country."

Pearson then continues:

"So important did the counsel for the plaintiffs in the Supreme Court of the United States in the Wilkes bond case regard this opinion, that the entire record and opinion both were printed in the briefs filed in that court."

Judge Bynum was one of the last of his generation and for some years before his death lived in retirement in Charlotte. Mr. I. E. Avery in *Idle Comments* refers to the old gentleman beautifully in the classic prose poem which follows:

"The last of the Romans says but few words to any man and he is seen oftenest as he bends his whited head and waters his roses. He has finished with the long fray; has seen all there is to see in life and now in the evening he leaves the haunts of men, and leans heavily over the smallest rosebud that blossoms in that tangled hedge. He is the most striking figure that comes on these streets and he walks alone and unheeding, save when he is stopped now and then by one who would ask a kindness. He who has seen all his generation pass into the dust has found solitude without courting it, but since it has come, he takes it as a philosopher unafraid, clear-eyed, strong, straight, not stooping except where the roses grow.

"If he has always cared for flowers, that is not known. He has been in the great tumultuous struggles and has done his part therein. Maybe he had no time for flowers then but he loves them now. They keep the last of the Romans from being too severe and he is very human and approachable as he, the distinguished jurist and gentleman, stands by the rose bush, still touched with the glories of the dying sun."

CHAPTER XIX

1910-1919

Rev. Dr. J. C. Clapp, a leading minister of the German Reformed church, and an educator of high rank, having been President and Professor of Catawba College, died in Newton in 1910.

Wade Hampton Motz, son of John and Catherine Loretz Motz, a lifelong citizen of Lincolnton, and for many years prominent in business, died July 14, 1910, in his 83rd year. He married Jane, daughter of B. S. Johnson. Their children were John M. who never married; Jennie, who married E. T. Childs; Charles H., who married Ella, daughter of Wallace H. Alexander; Catherine, who married Captain Chas. E. Childs; Benjamin J., who married and lived in Elberton, Georgia; Margaret; and Caldwell.

Capt. C. C. Wrenshall, a Captain in the Confederate Army, a skilled engineer and an honored Lincolnton citizen for many years, died in Lincolnton in 1910, aged 75 years.

1911

This section suffered more on account of the dry weather this summer than at any time since the dry period of 1881.

Rev. Dr. R. A. Yoder died suddenly in Lincolnton, in 1911, in his 58th year. He was a pastor of the Lutheran church from 1905 until his death. He came of good German stock and was a descendant of Conrad Yoder, one of the early pioneers. When a young man he was a school teacher until he entered the ministry of the Lutheran church. He was the chairman of the local school board at the time of his death.

He was the youngest of a family of twelve children, Dr. Yoder, the son of Solomon Yoder and Sarah-Seagle Yoder, was born in Lincoln County August 16, 1853. His mother was a sister of General Daniel Seagle. He was brought up in an environment distinctively religious. His forebears were most excellent people, frugal, industrious, and God-fearing. He belonged to a long-lived race, although himself cut down in the midst of his best years. Almost all lived to be quite old. He had a brother who died in his 93rd year. This brother had a twin sister who died in her 96th year. They were recognized as the oldest twins in the state. He attended the common schools of the community. Later on he entered North Carolina College at Mt. Pleasant where he graduated in 1877. Having the office of the ministry in view he was a student for two years in the Lutheran Theological Seminary at Philadelphia. In 1879 he was ordained to the office of the gospel ministry in the chapel of Concordia College, Conover. He became President of Concordia College in 1888, and when the college was removed to Hickory he held the same position till 1901. He was President of the United Synod of the South, 1892-1896, and Treasurer of the Tennessee Synod from 1894 until his death in 1911.

In addition to his work as an educator, he was quite active as a pastor. During his 32 years of pastoral work he served the following congregations: St. James, Concordia, Ebenezer, Grace, Salem, St. Andrews, Mt. Olive, Sardis, Beth Eden, Mt. Calvary (Maiden), Emmanuel (Lincolnton). He died very suddenly at the latter place, Tuesday morning, May 16, 1911. His mortal remains were taken to Daniel's the next day, the place of his childhood and youth, and interred by the side of of his parents.

On May the 9th, 1878, he was married to Miss Rosa Fisher of Salisbury. They had six children, two sons and four daughters:

R. A., Jr., Columbia, S. C., a wholesale merchant.

Dr. Paul E., Supt. Forsyth Tubercular Hospital, Winston-Salem.

Lela, wife of Rev. John Hall, U. S. Army Chaplain, stationed at Indianapolis, Indiana.

Blanche, wife of Rev. B. L. Stroup, Colburn, Indiana.

Margaretta, wife of Dr. Robert E. Rhyne, Gastonia.

Dr. Yoder's gifts were varied, his talents were many, a historian, a theologian, an executive, a mathematician, a surveyor, an architect and above all, a strong and able minister of the gospel of Christ.

In Catawba County, near to the Lincoln line in the neighborhood of Henry post office, James Marcus Bandy was born on January 8, 1848, son of Wesley and Martha (Lynn) Bandy. He came of substantial Dutch and Scotch-Irish stock. His mother's people came from Ireland and she possessed rare native intellect. The local school facilities were not good so that the boy in his early years had poor school advantages.

When but thirteen years old he went as a drummer boy with the local military company into the great Civil War. He was brave in battle and his courage on the field won for him a Lieutenancy in his Company. When the war closed he was acting Captain as the last gun fired from his company, at Bentonsville.

As a seventeen-year-old lad he returned home from the war in April, 1865. A year later he was married to Martha Leonard, in Lincoln County. She was a daughter of Elcanah Leonard (who was killed in the Civil War) and his wife, Emma Leonard, who was a devout member of Palm Tree Methodist church in North Brook township. Young Bandy was not afraid to work and with the same quality of courage shown in battle, went forth to make a living for his little family.

While he had little education he had a brilliant mind and an ambition to make the most of life. When twenty-one years old, he was digging stumps in a new ground. Suddenly he dropped his pick and said to his uncle who was helping him: "I am worth more to the world than digging stumps, so I will take my wife and the two children to the home of her mother, and go to Rutherford College to school." He went to school a while and then taught to get money to go back to school. In 1873 he taught a free school in Lincoln County. In 1878 he taught at Black Rock Academy (now Belwood) in Cleveland; in 1880-81 he was a teacher in Shelby High School, and later filled the chair of mathematics in Kings Mountain Military Academy until 1884.

In the spring of 1884 he secured a Trinity College catalogue in the hope of entering that institution. After careful examination of the course of study he decided that he could at once stand the examination for the full four years. He asked for that privilege and it was finally granted. He went there, stood the examination on the full course, graduated with the class of 1884; received his diploma, and a medal for fine scholarship. The faculty was so impressed with Mr. Bandy that he was at once tendered the chair of mathematics, which he filled with distinction until 1894, when he resigned.

He developed into a ripe scholar, was fond of history and classical literature, was a master of mathematics and could have filled with credit the chair of mathematics in any university. He loved the great out-of-doors and the singing of the birds. He was a fine violinist and the soldiers in the great war marched into battle in step to the music of this drummer boy.

When he left Trinity he settled in Greensboro where he was for some years the City Engineer. Later he was employed by the Page Brothers to build the railroad from Asheboro to Aberdeen and then by the Dukes to build the road from Durham to Duke.

He fought a good fight. He proved his courage in the stormy days of the Civil War when he won laurels which he treasured through life. But it took greater courage to face the trials and overcome the obstacles after the bloody struggle. He fought against ignorance and conquered and became a notable and cultured man, a blessing to his fellows and an honor to his family and his State. A Lutheran in faith, he was steadfast to the end. He died in Greensboro, August 23, 1911, and a great company assembled in West Market Street church for the funeral. He was intimately related to Lincoln County and deserves a place in this record. This story should be an inspiration to every boy who feels unable to conquer difficulty in order to make a man of himself.

Ambrose Costner, an honored product of Lincoln County, came of good Revolutionary and Lutheran stock and was a patriotic and Christian citizen. He was a son of Jacob Costner (who married Anna Rudisill) son of Michael Costner, son of Thomas Costner (a Revolutionary soldier pensioned March 4, 1831), son of Adam Costner, the pioneer.

Ambrose Costner was educated at the Lincolnton Academy, a school of high grade, and he married March 18, 1846, to Catherine Malinda Quickel and lived on the South Fork River, four miles north of Lincolnton. He was an extensive farmer and owned the Costner Flour Mill, which in its day turned out a fine quality of flour.

He was a modest, wise and dignified gentleman of the old school, and commanded the high respect of his fellow citizens. He was not a place seeker, but the people chose him for many positions of responsibility, and he always measured up to their high expectations. In his day he served as Magistrate, Chairman of the County Court, represented Lincoln five terms in the Legislature, four terms, 1858, 1862, 1864 and 1873, in the House, and 1883 in the Senate, was President of the County National Bank from its organization until his death in 1911. When Gaston College was established in Dallas under the auspices of the Lutheran Church he was one of the largest contributors to the movement.

While not physically able to enlist as a soldier in the Civil War he furnished the uniforms for the soldiers of Captain George W. Seagle's company. He died June 5, 1911, full of years and honors.

Mr. L. M. Hoffman, in his valued historical book, entitled "Our Kin," paid high tribute to him as follows:

"Ambrose Costner was one of nature's noblemen—a most lovable man of born dignity, without the slightest suggestion of egotism, a straightforward, candid man, whose voice and bearing compelled confidence. He was a gentleman of fine intelligence, temper and judgment. He held many places of honor and public trust and always with the utmost fidelity to duty and credit to himself. Most of his life was spent on his farm near Lincolnton, but after the death of his wife he spent his remaining days in Lincolnton.

"The Lord gave him neither poverty nor great riches, but an abundance of comfort and he always found means to lend a helping hand to others in need and to materially assist in all the charitable work of his community. He was one of the founders of Gaston Female College, and without ostentation or intolerance he was a staunch supporter of his church and all its enterprises—the church of his fathers—the Lutheran church to which he was devotedly attached. He died in 1911, aged about 86 years and is buried beside his wife in Salem churchyard in Lincoln county."

Among the children of Mr. and Mrs. Costner were:

1. William A. Costner, married, 1st, to Sarah Frazier; 2nd, to Mrs. Emma Killian. Dr. George Costner, a Lincolnton physician, is his son.

2. Dr. Henry A. Costner (dentist) married Lizzie Kirk. He practiced his profession in Chicago where he died.

3. Martha, married Abel P. Rhyne, the cotton manufacturer, of Mt. Holly.

4. Dr. Thos. F. Costner, married Dora Gatewood. He is now practicing medicine in Lumberton. (Died there in December, 1936.)

5. Robert E. Costner (lawyer) married Mamie Parker. He lives in Mt. Holly.

6. James A. Costner, married Gertrude Dewstoe. For many years he was in the banking business in Mt. Holly and lives there now (1936).

1912

Col. D. A. Lowe, died in May, 1912, at a ripe old age. He was born and lived in East Lincoln all his days. He was a successful merchant and farmer at Lowesville, and prominent in county affairs, having served many years as Magistrate and represented Lincoln in the State Senate in 1899.

Gen. Robert F. Hoke, with a brilliant record as a soldier, came home from the war in 1865 to be a private citizen and never capitalized the honors of military life for political promotion.

He was born in Lincolnton, May 27, 1837, son of Michael and Frances (Burton) Hoke. His father was a brilliant lawyer and orator and Democratic candidate for Governor in 1844.

Gen. Hoke was educated at Lincolnton Academy and at Kentucky Military Institute. He entered the Confederate Army as Second Lieutenant of Southern Stars in April, 1861; was soon promoted to rank of Major and then to Lieut. Col. of 33rd N. C. Regiment and rendered valiant service in many campaigns. In 1862 he was commissioned Colonel of the 21st N. C. Regiment and in January, 1863, was made Brig. General for gallant service at Fredericksburg. Through the winter of 1862-63 he was with Gen. Lee and was wounded at Chancellorsville. In the fall of 1863 he was in command in Western Carolina in the effort to suppress desertion and outlawry and early in 1864 went to extreme Eastern Carolina to check through military force serious disloyal movements and so brilliantly succeeded that in April, 1864, he was on the battlefield made Major General by President Davis himself. He aided in overcoming Butler near Richmond and distinguished himself in the struggle against Grant at Cold Harbor. Then back to North Carolina, his troops bore the brunt of the fight at Bentonville and surrendered with Johnston on April 26, 1865. His soldiers loved him and his final words to them were:

"You are paroled prisoners—not slaves; the love of liberty which led you in the contest burns now as brightly in your hearts as ever; cherish it, nourish it and associate it with the history of the past. Transmit it to your children. Teach them the rights of freemen and teach them to maintain them. Teach them too that the proudest day in all your proud career is that on which you enlisted as Southern Soldiers."

Capt. Samuel A. Ashe said: "Hoke was Lee's best General and the most distinguished soldier in North Carolina."

When he returned to private pursuits he refused all political honors. He did with reluctance accept the appointment from Governor Vance as State Director of the North Carolina Railroad and held that position for a few years.

Soon after his return from the war he hitched his war horse to the plow and made a crop. The story goes that one hot day in summer as he was ploughing a man passing by called to him saying: "Ain't you Gen. Hoke?" The General stopped his horse and replied, "Yes." The man then asked: "Ain't that thar the horse you rode in the army?" And he replied that it was. The stranger looked at him for a moment in deep emotion, and in vigorous language expressed his amazement and then bending over and hiding his face in his arms rode silently away.

The first work that Gen. Hoke did after the war was to raise a crop. Well does this writer remember that great, big, black horse that Gen. Hoke rode home from the war. Later when he was employed in washing gold in the mountains, a Court of Inquiry was ordered to investigate the execution of Federal soldiers near Newbern in 1864. His mother advised him to leave the country for fear effort would be made to implicate him, but he told her he had done no wrong, and went to Raleigh where the court was in session. From there he went to Washington to see Gen. Grant who told him that he knew all about the execution of the men at Kinston and that Gen.

Hoke had nothing to fear, that his parole protected him, and Grant said further: "If anyone molests you, let me know." That was the end of the matter so far as Gen. Hoke was concerned.

On January 7, 1869, he married Lydia VanWyck and they had six children, one of whom, Dr. Michael Hoke, is now (1935) a distinguished Orthopaedic Surgeon in Atlanta, Ga.

Gen. Hoke for a while operated the Cranberry Iron Works and was also President of the N. C. Home Insurance Company in Raleigh, where he lived for many years. On July 3, 1912, he died in Raleigh and was buried with military honors from the Church of the Good Shepherd (Episcopal) of which he was a member.

The older citizens well remember George L. Bartlett, a modest and good man. He clerked for his uncle, Col. W. H. Michal for many years. His hearing was defective and on August 2, 1912, as he was crossing the railroad track at Mount Holly, he was killed by a passing train.

The Progressive element of the Republican party rejected the action of the National Convention which renominated President Taft, and supported Theodore Roosevelt as the Progressive candidate. This split the Republican party and resulted in the election of Woodrow Wilson for the Presidency in November, just as the Democratic split in 1860 gave the Presidency to Lincoln.

David A. Barkley, Esq., says that "In Lincoln County there lived a Dutch farmer very precise. His daughter was dropping corn in season and the father followed to cover. The girl was not doing her duty in the eyes of the father, so he hit upon the idea of dropping at exact distances. With a rope he bandaged in the bottom of the girl's skirt (present hobble skirt way), and as the girl jumped, every time a grain of corn dropped same distance apart. Thus originated the hobble skirt long before the style was adopted in Paris."

"'Twas the idea of the Dutch,
The hobble of which we hear so much,
North Carolina deserves the glory,
According to Mr. Barclay's story."
—*Charlotte Chronicle*, 1912.

1913

Samuel Pinckney Sherrill (February 21, 1834—January 27, 1913), was born in Lincoln County, son of Lawson L. and Elizabeth (Wilkinson) Sherrill. His first business, late in his teens, was to clerk in the store of H. C. Hamilton at Beatties Ford. He came to Lincolnton about 1855, and engaged in the mercantile business for many years. In December, 1857, he married to Sarah Catherine, daughter of Rev. Samuel Lander, Senior. In 1861 he was appointed Clerk of Superior Court by Judge Saunders, to fill the vacancy caused by the resignation of V. A. McBee. In 1865 and in 1868 he was elected for full terms and served as Clerk from 1861 to 1874.

His official relation with courts and lawyers gave him fine legal training for a layman, and served him to good purpose later on when he, as a Magistrate, for many years had to pass on many intricate points of law. Appeals from his court were often taken and his judgments were generally sustained by the Superior Court, and never reversed by the Supreme Court. He was a lifelong Methodist and for many years a church official and an active member of the Masonic fraternity.

There were two children by his marriage to Sarah Lander:

1. William Lander Sherrill, who married Luetta Connor.

2. Bettie Lee Sherrill, who married Capt. E. W. Ward.

The second marriage of Mr. Sherrill was to Mrs. Barbara Henderson Cobb (daughter of the late Chas. C. Henderson See 1869), widow of Bartlett Y. Cobb, of Caswell County. She had three sons by her first marriage, Theodorus Henderson, Charles Cotesworth and Thomas Lee Cobb, all of whom are now dead. By the second marriage there was a daughter, Mary Helen Sherrill, who married to W. W. Motz in 1888. She died in October, 1907.

The writer is now (1935) the only living member of the large family.

Thomas Lee Cobb died, September 26, 1876, of typhoid fever when only fifteen years of age.

Theodorus Henderson Cobb married to Ellen V., daughter of Captain V. Q. Johnson in November, 1879. He died in Asheville, August 29, 1905, and she died in Los Angeles, California, March 26, 1933. (See 1905.)

Charles Cotesworth Cobb was married in August, 1927, to Nancy, eldest daughter of Henry and Sallie Glenn (Shaw) Fairley. He died in April, 1930. (See 1930.)

John T. ("Jack") DeLane and his brother, Francis H. DeLane, learned the printing business under E. H. Brittain, Editor of the *Lincoln Courier*, prior to 1868, when that publication was suspended. Afterward the DeLane boys went to Tennessee and found employment as type setters with the *Whig* when the brilliant and erratic parson, Gov. W. G. Brownlow was the editor of that sparkling sheet. They saved some money in Knoxville, returned to Lincolnton about 1875, bought the *Lincoln Progress* from Monroe Seagle, and managed the paper successfully for some years. Jack DeLane died in 1913, aged 65 years.

Major John D. Shaw died at his home in Rockingham, October 9, 1913, in his 80th year. He graduated from the State University in 1854. Rev. Dr. W. R. Wetmore (Episcopalian) and Rev. Dr. Needham B. Cobb (Baptist), ministers who are remembered in Lincolnton, graduated in the same class.

Mr. Shaw then attended Pearson's Law School, was licensed to practice law, and on November 3, 1858, was married to Margaret, daughter of the late C. C. Henderson, of Lincolnton.

He was a Major in the Confederate Army. Immediately after the Civil War he located in Marshall, Texas, and became the law partner of the brilliant Judge William B. Ochiltree. He came back to North Carolina and settled in Lincolnton in 1868 where he practiced law until 1879, when he removed to his native County of Richmond, and built up a large practice and was active up to the time of his death. He never held public office but was a learned lawyer.

Major Shaw as a speaker was pointed and forceful. He possessed rare reasoning powers and a strong analytical mind. It was his good rule to go into court well prepared, for he studied the issues from both angles, anticipated the arguments of opposing counsel and was ready to meet them. In the noted trial of the State against Fuller for the murder of Parker,

Major Shaw was one of the counsel for the defendant. Dr. McDuffie, a witness for the defendant, testified that Fuller had been seriously injured in the encounter with Parker. Jones, the leading counsel for the state, in cross examination of Dr. McDuffie, ridiculed the Doctor for saying he used a cold water application to relieve the irritation. Jones was by no means a tidy man and when he chewed tobacco expectorated so freely that his beard and shirt were besmeared. Major Shaw in reply said: "It is plain to see that Jones is afraid of cold water—in or out."

Major Shaw distinguished himself as an able trial lawyer when he represented McDougle, of Cumberland County, charged with the murder of his uncle, in which the evidence was altogether circumstantial. It was a hotly contested trial but he cleared his client.

He had two sons who became successful lawyers. John D. Shaw, Jr., a University graduate (who married to Miss Bettie Thomas, of Laurinburg), was the leading lawyer in Scotland County; he died, September 15, 1905, in his 42nd year. Another son, A. C. Shaw, died in Portland, Oregon, in 1933, aged 67 years; he practiced law with his father in Rockingham, 1888-93; then he became an attorney in the General Land Office in Washington, D. C., where he remained until 1910, when he went to Oregon and become famous there as a title lawyer. His eldest daughter, Sallie Glenn, married Henry Fairley, of Scotland County; Mr. Fairley died about 1925, and Mrs. Fairley and family now live in Charlotte. Miss Easdale Shaw, the second daughter, for many years an active worker in the Daughters of the King, now (1934) is a Trustee of the Stonewall Jackson Training School and also of the Women's Department of the University of North Carolina. John D. Shaw, III, son of John D. Shaw, Jr., is a practicing attorney in Charlotte and represented Mecklenburg County in the Legislature of 1927.

Joseph Forney Johnston, son of Dr. William and Nancy (Forney) Johnston, was born in Lincoln County, March 23, 1843. Attended Catawba College (See 1854) at Newton, Charlotte Military Institute at Charlotte under General D. H. Hill and Wetumpka Military School in Alabama. On April 21, 1861, enlisted as a private Confederate soldier in Com-

Top left: Vardry McBee (1775-1864). See 1864.
Top right: Major W. A. Graham (1839-1923). See 1923.
Center: Colonel William Johnston (1817-1896). See 1896.
Lower left: J. F. Reinhardt (1844-1913). See 1913.
Lower right: Ambrose Costner (1825-1911). See 1911.

pany I—18th Alabama Regiment, promoted to 1st Sergeant and then to 1st Lieutenant. Was wounded at Chickamauga. Was with Bragg at Perryville. Transferred to Army of Virginia and made aide on staff of his brother, Gen. Robert D. Johnston and later Captain. He was wounded four times during his service. Studied law under his kinsman, General William H. Forney and in 1866 was admitted to the bar. Practiced law in Selma, Ala., for 18 years until 1884, when he moved to Birmingham. Was there President of Alabama National Bank until 1904. Governor of Alabama, 1896-1900. Was elected U. S. Senator in 1907 to fill vacancy caused by death of Senator Pettus and in same year was elected to fill the full term beginning March 4, 1909, and served until his death in Washington, August 8, 1913. He was buried in Birmingham. He was a successful lawyer, an able advocate, had fine business qualifications, was a popular Governor and ranked high in the Senate. He had a fine sense of humor, was a fine story teller, good at impromptu speech, a diligent student of the Bible and a devout Episcopalian.

His old soldiers loved him and always called him Captain. He was a progressive business leader and had a great part in the industrial development of his adopted state.

He married to Theresa Hooper of Alabama, a descendant of William Hooper of North Carolina, who was a signer of the Declaration of Independence. He left one son, Forney Johnston, a brilliant lawyer of Birmingham.

John Franklin ("Jack") Reinhardt was for many years a popular and influential citizen of the county. He was as brave as Julius Caesar, with highest quality of moral courage combined with a warm-hearted personality, and was liked by all classes, both white and black, and when he was a candidate many negroes were his staunch supporters, even if he was a Democrat. He was a stranger to fear and when a venturesome youth in his teens volunteered as a soldier in the Civil War. No braver soldier ever faced a foe.

He was a son of Franklin M. Reinhardt (See 1869.) He was married first on May 1, 1871, to Leckie, daughter of James Madison Smith, and second to Miss Allie Abernethy on September 16, 1909. After the Civil War, he, for a while, operated the old Rehoboth Iron Furnace and bought the old Bartlett Shipp plantation in East Lincoln and lived there until his death in 1913. He represented Lincoln County in the Legislature (lower house), 1895, 1899 and 1901, and was Senator in 1902, 1906 and 1910.

When a candidate for the House in 1898 it was rumored that the Legislature would attempt to restrict the right of suffrage to those only who could stand the educational test, the purpose being to deprive the ignorant negroes of suffrage rights. The race question was a tense issue in the campaign, though the suffrage question was not raised. A goodly number of negroes were for Mr. Reinhardt and when they counselled with him about suffrage he frankly told them he would oppose the restriction of it. When the Legislature met in January, 1899, the Democrats almost to a man were for the educational test, but "Jack" Reinhardt, whose word was his bond, stood square to his promise, running the risk of being discounted for not being "regular." A weak-kneed politician under pressure would have forgotten the promise and gone with the crowd, but Reinhardt saved his self-respect by being true to his word, with the result that he made friends by so doing, as was proved in four later contests in which his majorities steadily increased. The people believed in him and stood by him, for they could depend upon him always.

All of his children were by the first marriage, five sons, J. M., W. B., J. F., R. R., and W. H. Reinhardt, and three daughters, Hettie, Edna and Louise Reinhardt. Hettie made a wonderfully fine record as a nurse overseas during the great war; Edna has been a teacher for some years in the Black Mountain schools; and Louise has been both a nurse and welfare worker.

Mr. Reinhardt was a great citizen and his sudden death under the surgeon's knife, June 9, 1913, at the age of 69, was a great shock to his multitude of friends. He was a Mason and a Presbyterian. The body was buried at New Hope Methodist Church in East Lincoln.

1914

The greatest war of all history began almost suddenly in August, 1914, and nearly all the world was drawn into it and it continued until November 11, 1918, at the cost of the lives of half of the young men of nearly all the countries involved, and all lands suffered terrible demoralization after four years of human slaughter, leaving the world in a state of moral degeneracy and financial bankruptcy. It will require many long years to recover from it all. When the war broke out in August, 1914, the average American little thought we would ever be drawn into it.

Bartlett Shipp, son of the late Judge W. M. Shipp, was born in 1865. His mother died in 1866 when he was about one year old. He attended the school of Miss Mary Wood Alexander in Lincolnton and prepared for college at the Military Academy in Charlotte, graduated there, and then entered the University of North Carolina and graduated in 1883; studied law under Col. G. N. Folk in Lenoir and was admitted to the bar in 1885. For a while he worked in the law office of Judge W. P. Bynum, of Charlotte, later formed a co-partnership with Judge W. P. Bynum, the younger, in Greensboro. From there he went to the State of Washington, where he practiced law for some years, but returning to North Carolina, settled in Lincolnton where he married Prue Crouse, daughter of Dr. W. L. Crouse. Later he moved to Hendersonville, where he practiced law until his death in February, 1914, aged fifty years.

He was a handsome man, had a brilliant mind, was a great student and a most companionable and entertaining conversationalist. His wit was sparkling and he was a fine story teller.

His son, Cameron Shipp, a bright newpaper writer, now connected with the *Charlotte News*, gives promise of a brilliant literary career.

Joseph Pearson Caldwell, the brilliant editor of the *Charlotte Observer*, died in October, 1914. He was the son of the late Hon. Joseph P. Caldwell, of Iredell, who represented his district in Congress from 1849 to 1853, and a nephew of Dr. Elam Caldwell, of Lincolnton.

Chas. A. Jonas was elected in November to the State Senate from the Lincoln-Catawba district and re-elected in 1916.

1915

Mrs. Thomas Jonathan Jackson, widow of the distinguished Confederate General, "Stonewall" Jackson, was a native of Lincoln County and daughter of the late Rev. Dr. R. H. Morrison. She was born July 21, 1831, married July 16, 1857, to Major T. J. Jackson, then an instructor in the Virginia Military Institute, at Lexington, Virginia. He was mortally wounded, May 10, 1863. Mrs. Jackson lived in Charlotte after the Civil War and died there, April 8, 1915, at the advanced age of 84 years. Her death brought sorrow to a wide circle of friends and admirers all over the South.

Capt. B. F. Grigg died, April 9, 1915, in his 80th year. He was born in Lincoln (now Cleveland) County. He came to Lincolnton when a young man, volunteered as a private in the Southern Stars in 1861, fought at Bethel; came home on furlough and married to Mary, daughter of Mr. A. McCoy, January 1, 1863. He returned to camp, and for valiant service came home a Captain in 1865. He was the census taker for Lincoln County in 1870, and acting postmaster in the early 1880's.

He possessed a strong mind, fine business judgment and high integrity. For many years he was a successful merchant and in 1898 organized the first bank ever established in the County. As stated, he was a brave Confederate soldier, and died on the fiftieth anniversary of the surrender of Lee at Appomattox.

1916

Woodrow Wilson is re-elected President over Charles Evans Hughes, the Republican candidate.

When the World War broke out in July, 1914, America was on the verge of a financial panic. Cotton was bringing only $20.00 a bale and all other farm products were correspondingly low, and industry in all lines was running on short time, but when the flame of war broke out in Europe, the demand for American products was so great that cotton brought nearly $200.00 per bale. Wheat advanced to $3.00 a bushel and business was so rushed that the fields, furnaces and factories were strained to supply the heavy foreign demand. Every precaution had been taken to maintain our neutrality, but the foreign relations, especially with Germany, became more and more strained and many of our people were impatient to enter the conflict against Germany, but President Wilson was slow to take a step so uncertain and perilous until the sinking of the Lusitania by the German submarine.

1917

We kept out of the World War for 33 months, until America entered April 6, 1917, after the steamer Lusitania was sunk by German submarines a short while before. It seems that all had been done that could be done to keep America out of the World War, for our national policy had been for neutrality, but we sold supplies to England, France and Italy, but very little to Germany, because Germany had no ships to come after the goods. So her attitude became vicious and by her submarines many vessels carrying supplies to her enemies were destroyed at sea, among them the British liner, Lusitania, which went down, carrying hundreds of American passengers. This tragedy aroused the indignation of our people, and on April 6, 1917, America entered the war on the side with Britain, France and Italy. Training camps were at once established in many parts of the Republic and four million American boys, the flower of our youth, were called to the colors, went to camps for training, and two million of them crossed the sea and bravely fought to make the world safe for democracy.

Isaac R. Self (1842-1917) was a fine citizen, a devout Christian, and progressive farmer. He lived about six miles west of Lincolnton. On November 3, 1865, he married to Mary Young and among their children were:

1. Hilary Augustus (deceased) married, 1st, to Laura Baxter, of Lincoln County; 2nd, to Bertie Howard, of Catawba County. He served as Register of Deeds for ten years, from 1898 to 1908.

2. Susan Etta, married J. J. Hovis, of Gaston County (both deceased).

3. Ila Rebecca, married 1st to Dr. Philip Holcomb, of Boonville, N. C.; 2nd to Wesley Holcomb, of Boonville.

4. Mary Lula, married to Dr. E. A. Houser, of Lincoln County.

5. Dr. Lester L., married Mattie Peeler, of Cleveland County. He is an active practitioner of medicine at Cherryville.

6. Rev. Marvin Y., married Lucy Harrell, of Sunbury, N. C. He is an active minister of the Methodist Church, now stationed in Durham, N. C.

7. Dr. Isaac Ruffin, married Isabel Tobey, of Lincolnton. He has for many years been a leading dentist in Lincolnton.

8. Alda Malinda, married Alonzo C. Hoyle, of Cleveland County.

Dr. W. W. Noland, one of the oldest and best known citizens of the County died at his home at Crouse, September 18, 1917, aged 84 years.

He was for many years a Lincolnton dentist, an officer in the Presbyterian church and a member of the Masonic fraternity.

The following items taken from scattered issues of the *Lincoln Times* of dates indicated give some interesting details of the record made by Lincoln County in the World War:

Off For Columbia

"Off for the training camp at Columbia. Off for the rifles, the smoke and the trenches. On for the drill, the march, the thunder of the brass throated guns.

"On September 18th the first contingent was ticketed for the army camp at Columbia, S. C. Five fine, virile specimens of Lincoln's manhood, fresh from the corn and cotton fields answered the call to duty.

"Messrs. Melvin L. Sipe, George Clifton Warlick, William C. Talent, Jacob Emanuel Miller and Fred Ray Kiser left on the afternoon train for the training camp where they will soon be prepared to take part in training the boys that will follow after them.

"While many of their friends saw them off with sad hearts, gladness crept in as they thought of the splendid manhood that was going to the front to represent us as a patriotic people."

September, 1917

"In accordance with the proclamation of the Governor of North Carolina, Lincolnton was hostess Saturday to her quota of drafted men, who are to become soldiers in the National Army. She also had as her special guests, the Confederate veterans of this County. The weather was ideal and crowds came from all parts of the County to pay honor to the boys who are soon to be called into the service of their country, as well as to the boys who once wore the gray. In honor of the occasion all the business houses and a number of residences were decorated with the national colors.

"Governor Thomas W. Bickett was the orator of the day. From a stand erected in the northwest corner of the court square he spoke for more than an hour, delivering one of the ablest and most patriotic speeches that Lincolnton citizens have been privileged to hear since the declaration of war. He said in part: 'The draft law is the very essence of Americanism. It embodies the principles of equal rights and justice to all, with special privileges to none; it treats every man precisely alike and under it every man is compelled to do his duty. Unless a man is willing to carry his part of the public responsibility in this emergency he is not a good American citizen. I sympathize very deeply with the men who will have to face danger and death on the firing line. I also sympathize with the men and women whose loved ones are going away, but the man who is to be pitied above all these is the able-bodied young man with no sacred obligations to keep him at home, and who yet is willing to skulk in the background while others do their part in this dark hour of the world's history."

September 18, 1917

"This list, from the date of its posting at the office of the Local Board, constitutes notice to those whose names are listed hereon, that they have been selected for military service, and charges them with an obligation to watch the bulletin board of the Local Board and to hold themselves in readiness to report for military duty at the office of the Local Board at date to be specified in a later notice to be posted at that office.

"Date of posting this notice at office of this Local Board September 14th, 1917.

"H. E. Reid, Chair.; Chas. A. Jonas, Sec'y.

"Office of District Board for Western District of N. C., Statesville, N. C., September 13, 1917.

"The following list of men, called for military service by the Local Board for County of Lincoln, have been duly passed upon by the proper Local and District Board and are hereby certified as selected for military service and not exempted or discharged: Everett Edgar Heavener, Melvin L. Sipe, Wade Smith, Alvin Loyd Huss, James Bellenger, Benjamin F. Miller, Charlie T. Keener, Cyrus Houser, William McKinley Schrum, George Clifton Warlick, James Marion Laney, William C. Tallent, Murphy W. Campbell, Arthur Bailey, Samuel L. Blalock, Roy Jonas, Jacob Emanuel Miller, Thomas Crowder, Odus Clyde Carpenter, Austin Bond Pool, Augustus Andrew Abernethy, John Henry B. Reinhardt, Memory Everett Heavner, Robert B. Finger, McLean Asbury Howard, James Mosteller, Beecher M. Smith, Franklin Iron Hull, Abram Willis, Samuel A. Hovis, Joseph McCaul, Gerard Stamey, Fred Ray Kiser, Charlie C. Leonard, Robert Summitt, Lee Oliver Holsclaw, Julius Collins Elmore, Kelly Boston Sain, William Emery King, Richard Caswell Williams, Beverly Ingle, Hugh Bynum Hoke, Thomas Davis Bass, Thomas Finger, George Ulysses Black, Earl McNairy Schrum, Walter Herbert Boring, William Sylvanus Morrison, Earlie Ernest Abernethy, Edward Yarborough, Roy Lee Beam, Miller Rhyne, James Fred Eury, Bidwell Loftin, Flay Houser, Sidney C. Garrison, Clarence Parker, Espy B. Link, Horace Boyd Blanton, Burgin Sidney Kistler, David Weldon Ramseur, Charles C. Lingerfelt, Robert Ray Womack, Harvey R. Duckworth, William Arthur Mullen, William Lee Ward, Robert N. Wingate, Leon C. Canthurs, James Alonzo Houk.

The District Board for Western District of N. C.

W. B. Gibson, Chairman.

S. H. Halloway, Secretary.

"The following named men are hereby ordered to report at the office of this Local Board for military duty and for transportation to a mobilization camp.

"The time they must report is 3:30 P.M., on September 18, 1917.

"Important Notice! From the hour and date above named, the men herein shall be in the military service of the United States and subject to military law. Failure or unpunctuality in reporting are serious military offenses. Wilful failure to report with intention to evade military service constitutes desertion, which is a capital offense in time of war.

THE ANNALS OF LINCOLN COUNTY 343

"The posting of this list in the office of the Local Board constitutes notice to each of the persons named herein that they are ordered to report at the hour, date, and place named, and that from that hour they are in the military service of the United States.

"Local Board for County of Lincoln, N. C.
H. E. Reid, Chairman,
Chas. A. Jonas, Secretary.

"Date of posting September 14, 1917.

"Wade Smith, Charlie T. Keener, Wm. McKinley Schrum, Murphy H. Campbell, Samuel L. Blalock, Roy Jonas, Thomas Crowder, Odus Clyde Carpenter, Austin Boyd Pool, Augustus Andrew Abernethy, John Henry B. Reinhardt, Memory Everett Heavner, Benjamin F. Miller, James Mosteller, Abram Willis, Joseph McCaul, Gerard Stamey, Julius Collins Elmore, Kelly Boston Sain, William Eurey King, Richard C. Williams, Hugh Bynum Hoke, Thomas David Bass, Wm. Sylvanus Morrison, Earlie Ernest Abernethy, Roy Lee Beam, Miller Rhyne, James Fred Eury, Bidwell Loftin, Flay Houser, Clarence Parker, Horace Boyd Blanton, David Weldon Ramseur, Harvey R. Duckworth, Robert N. Wingate, Leon C. Canthurs, James Alonzo Houk."

October 2, 1917

"Twenty-one More Boys to Leave Wednesday.

"Twenty-one white boys are to report here today for army service. They will leave October 10th on the afternoon train for Camp Jackson.

"The colored men who have been called to report in a few days will go later, as official orders have not been received yet by the local board, giving the date of their departure.

"Following are the names of the boys who will go tomorrow:

"Ernest Edgar Heavner, Alvin Loyd Huss, James Ballinger, Cyrus Houser, Arthur Bailey, Robert B. Finger, Beecher M. Smith, Franklin Leon Hull, Samuel A. Hovis, Charles C. Leonard, Robert Summitt, Lee Oliver Holsclaw, Thomas Finger, George Ulysses Black, Earl McNairy Schrum, Walter H. Boring, Edward Yarborough, Burgin Sidney Kistler, Charles C. Lingerfelt, William Arthur Mullen, William Lee Ward."

October 18, 1917

"Seven More Boys To Leave.

"Next Thursday will witness the leaving of seven more of Lincoln County's drafted boys who will be encamped at Columbia, S. C. This will be the fourth increment of this County's quota that has been ordered out for service. They have been notified to report here Wednesday, ready to leave Thursday on the C. & N. W. train for Camp Jackson.

"The names of the boys that will leave Thursday are: Louis Edgar Schrum, Julius P. Digh, Wade H. Boyd, Willie Crouse, William F. Howard, Lee Burgin Williams, Zeb Lee Jenks."

October 23, 1917

"List of Persons Called Into The Service of the United States.

"Not Exempted or Discharged.

"District Board, County of Lincoln, N. C., hereby certifies to District Board for Western North Carolina the following list of the names and addresses of persons who have been duly and legally called for the military service of the United States, and who have not been exempted or discharged: Thomas Rozzell King, Stanley; Benjamin Scronce, Stanley; Martin Luther Abernethy, Iron Station; Thomas Eaker, Lincolnton; William T. McCoy, Lincolnton; Durant Hartsell Little, Sherrill's Ford; Clyde Workman, Cherryville; Henry Kistler Keever, Alexis; Lawrence Nantz, Alexis; John Blair Hallman, Lincolnton; Wm. Guy Robinson, Reepsville; Ben Grigg, Lincolnton; George Smith, Lincolnton; Lander Means Burton (col.), Lincolnton; John Nixon (col.), Alexis; Henry Nixon (col.), Stanley; Millard P. Womack, Iron Station."

Colored Women's Exhibit

"Thank People of Lincolnton.

"The colored women wish to thank their white friends, Mrs. W. A. Hoke, of Raleigh, the postmaster, and merchants of Lincolnton who so willingly gave prizes for their exhibit of canned products, given under the instructions of Mrs. Winn and they wish to thank Mrs. Winn for the most valuable instruction she gave them. There were no second prizes given except red ribbons."

Lizzie Lander took 8 prizes; Mary Reinhardt, 3; Annie Childs, 2; Rilla Hoke, 1; Fannie Weldon, 1; Anna Edwards, 1; and Beatrice Friday, 1 prize.

Lincoln County Home Guard

The Lincoln County Council of Defense has appointed the following as members of the Lincoln County Home Guard:

Lincolnton Township:
  D. A. Yoder; substitute, S. W. McLean.
  Dr. I. R. Self; substitute, J. M. Smith.
  J. Thomas McLean; substitute, J. Oscar Shuford.
  Burt Barlow; substitute, Jas. S. Armstrong.
  Harry Page; substitute, M. A. Putnam.

Ironton Township:
  Robert F. Goodson; substitute, G. A. Howard.
  W. L. Finger; substitute, D. W. Dellinger.
  D. O. Long; substitute, McLain Mundy.
  W. J. Wingate; substitute, O. A. Keever.
  Ola Hill; substitute, J. M. Shuford.

Catawba Springs Township:
  John Reinhardt; substitute, Graham Morrison.
  Roscoe Kincaid; substitute, H. C. Cashion.
  Ira H. Howard; substitute, Oscar Long.
  Frank Brotherton; substitute, Boon Sherrill.
  William Little; substitute, Robert Mundy.

Howard's Creek Township:
  J. M. Jetton; substitute, William Hoover.
  T. M. Hoover; substitute, James A. Sain.
  A. J. Heavner; substitute, D. C. Killian.
  Milton Rudisill; substitute, Martin B. Aderholdt.
  Sidney Beatty; substitute, E. C. Sullivan.

North Brook Township:
  H. W. Wooley; substitute, John P. Beam.
  James Sain; substitute, Osto Hull.
  T. P. Jenks; substitute, Planer Hoyle.
  Ed. Bess; substitute, William Wehunt.
  George L. Beam; substitute, J. F. Beam.

The following gentlemen compose the Soldiers' Business Aid Committee: R. J. Mauser, Chairman, W. E. Grigg, M. H. Cline, W. H. Sigmon, J. E. Reinhardt, Dr. R. B. Killian, C. W. Beam.

Lincoln County Council of Defense

R. S. Reinhardt, Chairman, J. W. Mullen, L. B. Wetmore, Robert F. Goodson, Dr. H. N. Abernethy, Dr. W. C. Kiser, David J. Beam.

The above named have been commissioned by the Governor as members of the Lincoln County Council of Defense and have appointed a committee of 25 in each township to co-operate with them as follows:

Lincolnton Township: L. B. Wetmore, Chairman, J. T. Perkins, J. F. Mullen, J. P. Lore, Rev. Z. Paris, J. Ed. Kale, E. C. Baker, Dr. J. S. Wise, R. L. Wycoff, Dr. W. S. Wilson, R. H. W. Barker, Rev. C. C. Wheeler, B. C. Wood, R. H. Dellinger, R. M. Michal, Rev. Enoch Hite, R. M. Roseman, Doras Cloniger, Rev. W. H. McNairy, Julius A. Suttle, W. L. Mustian, R. L. Sigmon, A. Nixon, H. A. Kistler, W. C. Mullen, Henry Smith.

Ironton Township: Robert F. Goodson, Chairman, Fred Keever, R. M. Beal, M. A. Lawing, Bud Loftin, James Abernethy, Tull Lynch, Roy S. Keener, J. E. Cronland, Mott Reel, I. B. Grier, Rev. W. B. McClure, Samuel Keever, Ed Bradshaw, E. J. Rhyne, G. W. Brown, W. A. Goodson, W. L. Garrison, John Self, Mark Armstrong, C. P. Miller, J. E. Reinhardt, D. A. Troutman, J. E. Mullen, James Boyd, George M. Michael.

Catawba Springs Township: Dr. H. N. Abernethy, Chairman, P. A. Thompson, J. A. King, Lee Killian, Lyman Brotherton, Boone Sherrill, Louis Howard, Alonzo Whitener, A. A. Keever, Luther Sigmon, R. L. McCorkle, J. H. Scronce, Alfred Abernethy, Graham Morrison, Roscoe Kincaid, Sid Hinkle, Johnnie Nixon, Harvey Luckey, Sid Nixon, Will Luckey, Ollie Proctor, David Cherry, Wiley Sifford, D. C. Wilkinson, Alonzo Pool, James Hager.

Howard's Creek Township: Dr. W. C. Kiser, Chairman, Dr. L. L. Lohr, Dr. R. B. Killian, Charles Yoder, Perry Sigmon, William Wise, John Bangle, T. M. Lutz, John B. Reep, L. E. Houser, P. M. Houser, George Wise, Marcus Hoyle, George Baxter, Capt. I. R. Self, T. A. Warlick, J. R. Warlick, E. I. Mosteller, P. W. Ramseur, C. A. Leonard, J. R. Goins, S. E. Lutz, Lawrence Leonard, Rev. D. L. Miller, John E. Heafner, Dr. C. H. Hoover.

THE ANNALS OF LINCOLN COUNTY 347

North Brook Township: David J. Beam, Chairman, (Henry), C. W. Beam, A. F. Craft, John Baxter, J. P. Beam, H. F. Royster, Cephas Beam, Z. M. Dellinger, W. C. Childers, T. M. Bess, Wilson Dellinger, Pressley Brown, C. D. Dellinger, R. A. Tillman, John Stamey, J. M. Beam, J. C. Willis, W. L. Baker, W. T. Cansler, T. P. Jenks, J. F. Leatherman, B. C. Hoyle, Samuel Talent, George L. Beam, James Sain, Jesse Wright.

At the Gaston County Fair held at Gastonia, October 9-13, Lincoln County won all the sweepstakes (five loving cups) offered by the Fair Association. Lincoln County competed with Cleveland and Gaston Counties. Loving cups were offered to the county having the best exhibits for the following:

A loving cup was offered for the county having the best individual exhibit. Lincoln County won, having 515 jars and glasses in this exhibit. Out of this number 18 jars competed and Lincoln County was awarded 13 sweepstakes.

A loving cup was offered for the county having the best display. Lincoln County had five displays and four prizes were awarded—1st prize, Janie Brown, Iron Station, $10.00; 2nd prize, Suley Brown, Iron Station, $7.50; 3rd prize, Elizabeth Coon, Daniels, $5.00; 4th prize, Nettie Willis, Henry, $2.50. The display winning first place then competed against the best displays in the other two counties and again Lincoln County won.

A loving cup was offered to the county having the best Community Fair exhibit and Lincoln County won again.

A loving cup was offered to the county having the best ten ear exhibit of corn. Lincoln County won again.

A loving cup was offered for the county having the best single ear exhibit of corn. And again Lincoln County won.

After the prizes were awarded at the Gaston County Fair the Home Demonstration Agent selected forty of the best jars and shipped them to Raleigh to the State Fair. This was a difficult task, owing to the fact that Lincoln County had about 1,500 fancy jars. The judge, the Assistant State Agent, Miss Jamison, said it was difficult work and that Lincoln County had the best products she had ever seen. The Home Demonstration Club at North Brook received almost a perfect mark on canning at the State Fair. Lincoln County won first prize, having the best exhibit at the State Fair. A prize was offered for the 3rd or 4th or 5th or

6th year county having the best general exhibit. First prize was given to Lincoln County, but our Agent notified the judge that Lincoln was only a second year county and was not eligible. So a special prize was given for the best exhibit.

The Seaboard Air Line Railway Company asked the State Agent to purchase for them an exhibit for their New York office to be used as a window display. Since Lincoln County had the best exhibit, she purchased from them. Those whose jars were selected will receive fancy prices for their products.

An exhibit is also wanted for the Department of Agriculture at Washington and Lincoln County will be represented there again.

Individual Prizes Offered at State Fair

Best jar of beans, Mary Mosteller, Reepsville. This jar will be placed in a glass case in the dining room of the Governor's Mansion. He said he would rather have canning club products than fancy china.

Best jar of soup mixture, Ethel Long.

Best exhibit of canned vegetables or fruits, Janie Brown, Iron Station.

Names of some of Lincoln County folks whose products will be shown in New York:

Mrs. Essie Beam, Miss Nellie Beam, Miss Florence Beam, Mrs. C. O. Childers, Mrs. Ethel Childers, all of Cherryville; Miss Ilese Kiser of Reepsville; Mrs. J. F. Reinhardt and Miss Virginia McConnell of Stanley; Miss May Dorsey, Mrs. George Rinck, Mrs. G. W. Rinck, Miss Mary Wise, Mrs. M. L. Yoder and Lizzie Lander of Lincolnton.

Buy a Liberty Bond Today

J. W. Mullen, Secretary.   R. S. Reinhardt, Chairman.

Lincoln County Council National Defense.

Dr. H. N. Abernethy, Catawba Springs; R. F. Goodson, Ironton; L. B. Wetmore, Lincolnton; Dr. W. C. Kiser, Howard's Creek; D. J. Beam, North Brook. Com. National Defense.

September, 1917.

1918

World War and Other Items Taken From "The Lincoln Times" Issue of June 2, 1918

Nine-tenths at War

"The population of the world is given, in round figures as one billion, six hundred millions. Today the people of the world are divided into three portions, two of them at war and one neutral. Of the 1,600,000,000, only 120,000,000—less than one-tenth —are at peace. The other nine-tenths are at war, and are in one of two camps, that of the Central Empire or that of the Entente Allies. In the camp of the Central Empires are 160,000,000 people; in the camp of the Entente Allies are around 1,320,-000,000. This means that the Allied people of the world outnumber those of the Central Empires about eight to one."

June 11, 1918

"The county commissioners met in regular session on Monday of last week with all present. Besides the regular routine, the following business was transacted:

"Mr. G. A. Royster was elected by the board to superintend the County Home for the next year. His compensation will be $8.50 for each inmate per month.

"The levy of the tax for the coming year, 1918, was fixed as follows:

For State purposes as levied by the General Assembly	23 2-3 cents
For Pensions	4 cents
For Schools	20 cents
Poll Tax	$1.43
State Pensions	12 cents
For Schools	38 cents
For County Maintenance of Poor	$1.50

"Jurors for the next term of court which convenes July 15th were drawn as follows: E. L. Rash, C. D. L. McGinnis, J. F. Cashion, A. L. Mauney, J. A. Leonhardt, J. A. Smyre, A. C. Dellinger, Forney Link, George P. Arney, Webb Hager, Thomas B. Saine, John Noles, D. Claud Hines, J. C. Beam, C. H. Holdsclaw, Robert Jonas, W. M. Rodgers, George Gilbert, A. F. Scronce, E. M. Hallman, J. H. Lucky, J. O. Allen, G. T. Wise, Lewis S. Ballard, M. A. Lawing, J. W. Little, P. C. Whitesides, A. A. Summey, T. L. Center, W. C. Asbury, B. W. Saine, N. J. Bland, Coon Reinhardt, L. L. Houser, G. P. Rhyne, J. Lester Little."

All alien registrants who are entitled to register in this county both male and female are hereby notified to call on Postmaster John K. Cline for registration which opens on July 17th. For further information call on me or write.

John K. Cline, Registrar,
Lincolnton, N. C.

LIST OF WORLD WAR REGISTRANTS, JUNE 5, 1918

Clarence Abernethy
Edgar Hanks Abernethy
Wm. Sidney Abernethy
Clyde Auton
Noah Beal
William Bryan
Wm. Fred Douglas Bess (Col.)
Craige Burton Bost
Wilbur Summerow Bost
Francis Edgar Byers
Abbey Winslow Bynum
Claude Franklin Bynum
John Wesley Canipe
Roy Sidney Carpenter
Wm. Russell Carswell
Ira Franklin Cline
Burgin Cloninger
Raymond Ernest Cook
Douglas Alexander Craig
Joseph Conrad Crooks
Zeb Crowell
Fred Davis
David Cowles Dellinger
Fay W. Dellinger
Louis Bryan Dellinger
Jennings Bryan Dellinger
Jennings Bryan Edwards
John Hubert Eury
John Clinton Falls
John Alexander Fisher
Reuben Lila Ford
Russell Forest Foster
Augustus Garrison
Gaston D. Gilbert
Marshall Emanuel Gilbert
John Robert Gardner
Frank Goodson
Pinkney Goodson
Orion St. Leon Goodson
Kearney Roosevelt Graham (Col.)
Harold Edgar Grigg
Deck Hager
Edgar Lee Heavner
Ernest Sidney Heavner
Marcus Audie Helms
Wesley Helms
Henry Jefferson Hill
Earl Preston Hoke
Claudis Hugh Holly
Calvin Earl Hoover
Cleatus Houser
Ed Alexander Howell
Arthur Raymond Hoyle
Stowe William Hoyle
John Albert Hoyle
Thomas Russell Hoyle
John Hudson
Marvin Ray Hall
Tillman Bryan Hall
John James Hullett
Caley Pinkney Huss
Noah Carse Huss
Jacob Craig Johnson
James Jones
Sinclair Davidson Killian
Lyman Kiser
William Samuel Lander
Lester Lawing
William Lewis Lawing
Daniel C. Leatherman
Zeb Leatherman
Martin Luther Ledford
Raymond Lenhardt
Robert Carl Leonard
Zirkle Carr Leonard
Robert P. Sylvanus Lineberger (Col.)
William Perry Little
James V. Lore
Horace Ernest McAlister
Eugene McLain (Col.)
Dennis Lee McNeely
Pink Moses Martin
Zenis Eddie Martin
Clarence Mauney
Edgar Moore
Lester Morrison (Col.)
Wm. Austin Morrison (Col.)
Geo. Warston Mosteller
Whitt Sherman Mullen
Thos. Wilson Munday
Wm. Russell Munday
Martin Zebulon Miller
Wm. Eugene Nash (Col.)
Leroy Parker
Calvin Winchester Pegram
Carl Hovis Plonk
Will Poovey
Isaiah Irson Putnam

Edmund George Ramseur
William Ramsaur (Col.)
Pank Carl Rendleman (Col.)
Presley Ramsey
Austin Moore Reynolds
Paul Rhodes
Gerry Lee Rhyne
William Kilgo Rogers
John A. Robinson
Jake Ross (Col.)
Vance Christian Ross
John Corlie Rudisill
Ira McKinley Sain
Solomon Scronce
Adolphus Hugh Scronce
Clarence Self
Chas. Floyd Shaw
Wm. McKinley Sherrill
Burgin Lee Shrum
S. B. Shuford
Thomas Shuford
Earl Franklin Sigmon
Thos. Lee Sigmon
Robert Albert Smith
Roscoe Marshall Smith (Col.)
Thomas Walter Smith
John Earl Tillman
John Herman White
Early Raydes Whitener
Jesse Clayton Willis
Reid Alfred Wilson
Henry Kiser Wood
Verge Woodford

Large Crowd Hears Judge Pritchard
June 18, 1918

"Saturday afternoon, June 15, 1918, the courthouse was filled to its capacity to hear Judge J. C. Pritchard, of Asheville, who came down to speak in the interest of the War Saving Stamp drive which begins Monday and closes June 28th. Mr. Pritchard spoke for about one hour and made one of the strongest and most interesting talks the people of Lincolnton have had the privilege to listen to in all the campaigns here for war funds.

"Judge Pritchard spoke at some length on the needs of our Government to win this war and the dangers confronting us as a nation if we should fail to respond to many calls that are coming to us in these strenuous days of war and sadness. He made mention of some of the ways in which our American boys stood ahead of any nation in the world. He gave a number of illustrations showing how we, as American people, by working together, will do great things in winning the war, and that speedily the victory will be ours. Many times he was cheered for the way he encouraged all to stand together as patriots in every line of work possible to help the Government to care for and equip our army as fast as it could be done.

"The Judge said while war was an awful thing, he expected to see our boys win the war and return home a better developed set of men than when they left."

"County Food Administrator R. S. Reinhardt and Secretary J. W. Mullen returned yesterday from Raleigh where they attended a State meeting of the Food Administrators. They report several changes to take place July 1st in the use of flour, sugar and other products that go to help win the war.

"Mr. Reinhardt says that the ruling on the food situation will be given out later for publication. It is understood that all fountains using sugar which did not make their reports and applications before June 10th will have to close up that part of their business at once."

June 28, 1918

"A number of prominent speakers will address the people at a number of places in the county tonight. This is the closing round in the big National War Saving Stamp Drive.

"The colored people are invited to attend each of these meetings as the time was short and a special arrangement could not be made for them except in Lincolnton, which will be tonight at the Colored Masonic Hall at 9 o'clock.

"The list of speakers to go to the school houses throughout the County Friday night, June 28th, 1918, at half past eight o'clock, except for the courthouse, Lincolnton:

"North Brook Township—C. A. Jonas, C. L. Eaker, Dr. L. L. Lohr, W. A. Hull and W. D. Baxter, Prof. M. S. Beam, G. Lee Heavner and Capt. C. E. Childs, M. T. Leatherman and J. J. Hull, Ben Sain, D. C. Upton, F. J. Leatherman, Ed Bess, W. F. Boyles and J. G. Stamey.

"Howard's Creek Township—Rev. Mr. Miller, Dr. W. C. Kiser, H. A. Jonas, Guy Rinck, Luther Carpenter, W. L. Smarr, Rev. W. H. McNairy, L. O. Keever, R. L. Sigmon, Rev. O. W. Aderholdt, Rev. D. P. Waters, M. H. Hoyle, A. B. Heavner, V. V. Aderholdt, H. H. Heafner, L. Berge Beam.

"Lincolnton Township—Dr. W. S. Wilson, E. W. Joyner, D. H. Mauney, Rev. W. W. Rimmer, C. S. Little, J. T. Perkins, W. N. Williams, Edgar Love, A. M. Hoke, Edgar Heavner, G. L. Clendenin, John K. Cline, J. O. Allen, D. C. Williams, R. S. Reinhardt, Jos. B. Johnston.

"Ironton Township—Rev. W. B. McClure, Mrs. Florence R. Winn, Rev. C. E. Bently, R. C. Goode, D. A. Troutman, J. E. Reinhardt, J. W. Mullen, R. J. Mauser, Sheriff A. P. Willis, G. B. Goodson, W. C. Asbury, L. A. Abernethy, Rev. O. T. Fortenberry, C. L. Goodson, Rev. H. B. Chronister, H. F. Hovis, J. R. Bradshaw.

"Catawba Springs Township—Rev. W. B. Shinn, W. H. Sigmon, Kemp B. Nixon, Robert F. Graham, E. C. McIntosh, C. M. Henkel, Rev. J. A. Sharpe, J. Graham Morrison, John E. Reinhardt, W. H. Childs, Percival Hall, F. A. Slate, Dr. C. L. McCall."

Lemuel B. Wetmore, a bright and genial gentleman and a lawyer of first rate ability, died May 21, 1918, aged 53 years. He was generous and wholehearted and left many friends to mourn their loss, when he died. He was a son of the late Rev. Dr. W. R. Wetmore, the Episcopal clergyman and educator. (See 1904.)

Henry S. Dellinger, one of the older and highly esteemed citizens of the County, died in Atlanta, Georgia, May 27, 1918, aged 82 years, and the body was brought home and buried in the family graveyard in Ironton Township. He was married three times. His second wife was a daughter of the late James H. Marsh. He left two sons, Chester Dellinger, at whose home he died in Atlanta, and Marsh Dellinger, of Monroe, N. C. Mr. Dellinger was a Confederate veteran of Company F, 9th North Carolina regiment.

David Milo Wright, son of Mr. and Mrs. J. A. J. Wright, of Lincolnton, was the first Lincoln County man to lose his life in the World War. He was killed in action in France, May 29, 1918, and was only twenty years old when he met his tragic death. The body reached New York from France, March 20, 1921, and was brought home for burial. He had fine character, enlisted for the war in 1917 and in two months sailed for France, where a year later he gave his life for his country.

November 11, 1918, the terrible World War came to an end and peace was declared. The whole world was overwhelmed with joy because the great tragedy was over and the anxiety and fear which had filled the heart of mankind for four long weary years was lifted.

1919

Mrs. Agnes (Lander) Lawing, daughter of the late Hon. William Lander and widow of the late Dr. John M. Lawing, on Sunday, October 23, 1917, had the misfortune to fall and break hip bone, from which she suffered much for nearly fifteen months, until she died January 5, 1919, aged 73 years. She was born in Lincolnton in the old family residence in which she spent her life and died. Mrs. Lawing possessed superior intellect and was loved by all who knew her.

Theodore Roosevelt, the 25th President of the United States, died January 6, 1919, aged 61 years. He had been in declining health but his condition was not considered serious. His last words, spoken to a servant at bed time, were "Put out the lights" and when morning came he was found dead in bed.

Gen. Robert D. Johnston, son of Dr. William Johnston and Nancy (Forney) Johnston (See 1854), was born in 1837 at Mt. Welcome, the home of his grandfather, Gen. Peter Forney, in Lincoln County. He graduated from the State University in 1858. When the Civil War broke out in 1861 he volunteered as a private and enlisted in the Beatties Ford Rifles; was elected Lieutenant. In May, 1862, he was made Lieutenant Colonel in the 23rd N. C. Regiment. He was wounded at Seven Pines and at Spottsylvania, and at Gettysburg was promoted to rank of Brigadier General. He participated in all the battles of the Army of Northern Virginia and was wounded for the 5th time at Hares Hill near Petersburg and paroled at Charlotte in 1865. His wife was Miss Lizzie Johnston Evans, a granddaughter of Gov. Morehead. He practiced law in Charlotte with unusual success as a partner of the late Col. Hamilton C. Jones until 1877, when he moved to Birmingham, Ala., where through his law practice, banking interest and mining promotions he took a leading part in the growth and development of Birmingham. He was at one time Register of the Federal Land Bank Office in Birmingham and he and Mrs. Johnston were largely responsible for the establishment near Birmingham of the State Industrial School for Boys.

He died at the home of his son, Evans Johnston, in Winchester, Va., Feb. 1, 1919, aged 82 years, and was buried in the Confederate cemetery there.

As a soldier, lawyer, banker and industrial leader, he distinguished himself by his courage, legal ability and wise business judgment.

Mrs. Addie (Ramseur) Grier, daughter of the late Jacob A. Ramseur, died March 17, 1919, aged 68 years. She married to Calvin E. Grier, a brilliant Charlotte lawyer, in 1878. He died about 1888. The funeral service for Mrs. Grier was conducted from the home of her daughter, Mrs. J. W. Barineau, of Lincolnton, and the body was buried in Saint Luke's Episcopal graveyard in the plot near the grave of her brother, Gen. Stephen Dodson Ramseur, the gallant Confederate commander, who was mortally wounded in battle in 1863.

Miles O. Sherrill (1841-1919), a native of Lincoln, became a citizen of Catawba when that County was created. He was a soldier of the Civil War and lost a limb in that struggle. Was Clerk of Superior Court of Catawba, 1868-1882; Representative from Catawba in the House, 1883; Senator, 1885 and 1893; State Librarian, 1898 to 1918, when he retired on account of feeble health. He died April 9, 1919. He was a patriotic citizen and a devout churchman, one of the few active in politics who always placed Christian duty first.

One daughter, Dr. Mary Sherrill, is Professor of Chemistry in Mt. Holyoke College.

Col. Clarence O. Sherrill of the Army was Aide to President Coolidge, but resigned in 1927 to accept the office of manager of the City of Cincinnati in which position he became nationally prominent as an organizer and economical administrator. After five years service he resigned to enter commercial life.

Dr. J. Garland Sherrill, another son, is a physician and surgeon in Louisville, Kentucky.

A grandson, Sidney Sherrill Alderman, is a brilliant lawyer and now General Solicitor of the Southern Railway with offices in Washington (1935).

David A. Coon, a good farmer and splendid citizen, died April 10, 1919, aged 86 years. He went to the war in 1861 as a Sergeant in the Southern Stars and was later given a commission as Lieutenant. He was once wounded and Monroe Seagle wrote home that he was killed, but it proved to be a mistake. In 1870 he was elected Sheriff over Sheriff J. H. King, but did not serve as the courts ruled that the law provided that the old Sheriff would hold on until 1872.

He reared a large family, one of whom, Charles L. Coon, became a great teacher and educational leader in North Carolina and author of a valuable history of education in the State. Miss

Betty Coon, now a teacher in Lincolnton, and Mrs. T. H. Cansler are his daughters.

Frontis H. Anthony was a Lincolnton boy, much beloved, who gave promise of great usefulness as a minister of Christ. He was well prepared for his life work; was ordained a Priest of the Episcopal Church, May 15, 1918, and became Rector of the Church at Valle Crucis in Watauga County. His labors there were brief for he became a victim of the influenza epidemic and died almost at the beginning of his task at Valle Crucis on January 5, 1919, when hardly thirty years old. His life was beautiful and its end triumphant.

During the pastorate of Rev. D. M. Litaker, the Methodist church building, corner of Main and Academy Streets, was erected in 1919. A Building Committee of nine men was chosen and from these an active committee composed of Chas. A. Jonas, chairman, E. C. Baker, Plato Miller and R. C. Goode, together with the pastor, directed the work of building at a cost of about $55,000.00. In October, 1923, the church was dedicated after a sermon preached by Bishop Collins Denny.

The first Methodist church erected in Lincolnton about 1828 was a wooden building and located on South Aspen street. In 1857 the brick structure which still stands in front of the Methodist graveyard was built, so that the present handsome church is the third building the Methodists of Lincolnton have worshipped in.

The following paragraphs are copied from the souvenir program, *Welcome Home Day to Our War Heroes*, published by John M. and Paul J. Mullen, World War veterans, July 1, 1919:

In September, 1917, with the National Guard units in federal service and training for overseas duty, with the local draft boards sending to camp men from every community and with the number that had volunteered at the declaration of war, the number of young men left, that could be called upon for any emergency had reached its minimum.

Following the proclamation of the governor in September creating the North Carolina Reserve Militia, a call went out through the Council of Defense to the counties, assigning each a quota and calling on Lincoln County to furnish twenty-eight men to form a part of the 33rd N. C. R. M. of Hickory. On November 3, 1917, these men mustered at the Courthouse and were sworn into service. Harry Page, of Lincolnton, a Spanish-American War veteran, being elected First Lieutenant.

Being dissatisfied with its small part and with many patriotic men of the town and county anxious to serve, but unable to leave home, by order of the Adjutant General in August, 1918, Co. 63, Inf. N. C. R. M., with a full membership of sixty-four men, was organized with First Lieutenant Harry Page being made Captain; J. W. Barineau, First Lieutenant, and Dr. I. R. Self, Second Lieutenant.

Unable to secure a state or national fund for the purchase of uniforms and equipment, Lincolnton and Lincoln County, together with its citizens, gave approximately $1,400.00 for this worthy cause.

Faithfully throughout the period of the war and at the present time Co. 63 meets every Wednesday night for drill in order to keep themselves in readiness for any emergency that might arise and for any service that they may render to the state and government until the re-organization of the National Guard.

Troop A—Lincoln's Own—Its Organization, Growth and Service on the Mexican Border and in France.

Troop A, 30th Military Police, 30th Division, U. S. A., "Lincoln County's Own," will forever be synonymous with such names as Ypres, Voormezelle, The Hindenburg Line, Bellicourt and others, for at these places Troop A upheld the traditions of their forefathers in the World War.

Realizing the necessity of a local military company and the advantages to be had by the young men of the county in receiving military training, Troop A, N. C. N. G., was organized in February, 1912, by W. A. Fair—now Lieut. Colonel in the United States Army—with himself as Captain; J. O. Shuford, First Lieutenant and R. S. Reinhardt, Jr., Second Lieutenant.

At its organization every member was from Lincoln County and it remained so until the troop was called to the Mexican border, at which time its ranks were filled with men from the adjoining counties.

From the time of its organization until the spring of 1916, Troop A, with the exception of several changes in the officers and men, carried out the routine prescribed by the state for National Guard organizations, attending its weekly drills and the summer encampments given as a recreation for the men and for a better insight into the molding of a successful military machine.

In the spring of 1916 with war raging in Europe and the rights of America being trampled upon, the war department, realizing the power of the National Guard units, ordered Troop A to Fort Oglethorpe, Ga., for training with the 11th Cavalry. After two weeks of intensive training the boys returned better prepared to take up the service for country that was to be theirs when the Mexican trouble broke in the spring of 1916.

With our border states exposed to lawless Mexicans, with lives being lost and property being destroyed Troop A, then N. C. N. G., with W. A. Fair as Captain; C. H. Hinson, First Lieutenant; and B. C. Lineberger, Second Lieutenant, was ordered to entrain on June 20th, 1916, for mobilization at Morehead City for duty along the border. Amid the waving of flags, and the tears of mothers, sisters and sweethearts, Lincoln County men again took up the fight for the principles of right. Arriving at El Paso, Texas, September 28, 1916, Troop A saw active duty until March 14, 1917, when they entrained for Lincolnton. They reached home March 21, 1917.

At this time, with the war clouds hovering over America and the coming break with Germany that seemed inevitable, Troop A stood ready for any further service that our country might need. With the declaration of war, April 6, 1917, and with the broadcast order of the war department for all National Guard units to hold themselves in readiness for foreign service, the boys of Troop A were ready to carry on.

With orders for mobilization came notice of the promotion of Captain Fair to Major of the First Squadron, First North Carolina Cavalry, of which Troop A was a part. With this change Lieut. C. H. Hinson became Captain; Second Lieut. W. B. Abernethy was made First Lieut.; and Sergeant Arthur F. Lackey was made Second Lieut. With these officers in command Troop A entrained for Camp Sevier, S. C., August, 1917. The company retained the same officers throughout the war and until it was mustered out at Camp Jackson, April 14, 1919.

Upon arrival at Camp Sevier Troop A was shifted from the First Squadron, N. C. Cavalry to the 105th Military Police—later

30th M. P., forming Company A, and with the same officers in command; Major Fair being made Provost Marshal of the 30th Division.

Acting in the arduous capacity of military police during the training of the 30th Division at Greenville, Troop A landed at Le Havre, France, with the Division on the 28th day of May, 1918, in the same capacity.

Though not being a combatant unit in the true sense of the word, the military police of the present war must receive every credit, for it was their duty during the action of the division to keep the lines of communication open, direct traffic, supply the front line with food and ammunition, arrest stragglers and take care of prisoners. Troop A alone handled while in France over 3,000 German prisoners. It received its baptism of fire and though in active service at all times the troop did not lose a Lincoln County man. Its unselfishness to duty and country will forever link it with the history of Lincoln County.

Troop A's greatest distinction is that as a part of the famous 30th division, it began on September 29, 1918, the assault on the Hindenburg Line, breaking through impregnable networks of forts, which resulted in the signing of the armistice the following November, bringing to a close the most terrible war in the history of man.

The Work of the Red Cross in Lincoln County During the War

"To the Southern Stars Chapter of the United Daughters of the Confederacy is given credit for the beginning of the Red Cross work in Lincoln County. In the spring of 1917, just after the declaration of war the President of this organization—at that time Mrs. J. W. Saine—called a mass meeting to discuss plans for the formation of an Auxiliary or a Chapter. This meeting was held April 20th and resulted in the organization of an Auxiliary with Mrs. L. A. Crowell, Chairman; J. W. Mullen, Vice-Chairman; and Mrs. T. B. Smith, Secretary.

"Interest grew rapidly and after two months it was deemed advisable to suspend the Auxiliary and form a Chapter. This was done June 27, 1917. Officers were elected as follows: J. W. Mullen, President; Mrs. W. W. Motz, Vice-President; Mrs. H. E. Reid, Secretary; and M. H. Cline, Treasurer. The Chapter began its existence with 200 members and no better illustration could be given of its remarkable growth than to say that at the present time it has 2,040 members including 11 Auxiliaries together with 550 active Junior members.

"During the war a Work Room was fitted up in Memorial Hall which the Daughters of the Confederacy so generously offered for this purpose. Mrs. J. S. Wise, Chairman of the Work Room Committee, kept the room open one afternoon in each week and had general supervision of all work done.

"Some idea of the task accomplished by the noble women of Lincoln County may be gathered from the list of supplies given below that were made and sent out for overseas shipment; 129 sweaters, 214 pairs of socks, 13 helmets, 28 mufflers, 15 wristlets, 99 pajama suits, 372 hospital shirts, 180 operating gowns, 284 handkerchiefs, 408 towels, 44 wash cloths, 84 napkins, 34 slings, 280 property bags; a total of 2,184 pieces. This does not include the hundreds of articles of comfort furnished our own boys.

"In addition to war work the Red Cross Chapter has been active in civilian relief work. During the influenza epidemic in the fall of 1918 it established an emergency hospital in the graded school building in Lincolnton where 75 patients were cared for and many more were supplied in their homes with food and medical attention.

"At the present time a Home Service Section in charge of Mrs. Ola Hines Heafner is being maintained in the Reinhardt Building. Mrs. Heafner is prepared to render valuable aid to the returned soldiers in recovering allowances, allotments, etc.

"All credit is due the women of this County for it was through their untiring efforts that Lincoln Chapter reached a maximum degree of efficiency during the war and the men who went out from Lincoln County went with the knowledge that everything possible for their comfort and protection was being done by the people at home."

The following persons from Lincoln County are veterans of the World War, though this roll is not absolutely complete:

Hal Abernethey, W. B. Abernethy, Summey Alexander, Jr., E. A. Ballard, R. L. Beam, Troy Boring, Summey Bynum, Ed Bolton, Leroy Boyles, Oscar Blackburn, J. M. Barnes, L. Clyde Beam, T. C. Bolick, Dr. B. M. Bradford, W. B. Beam, Marshal Black, O. E. Ballard, R. E. Beatty, M. L. Baker, L. F. Blanton, S. M. Cashion, C. E. Cloninger, T. F. Corriher, R. W. Carter, W. L. Collins, Noah Cline, Ira Cline, Dr. W. V. Costner, Dr. A. M. Cornwell, Odus Carpenter, A. B. Cochrane, F. S. Childs, C. C.

Crowell, Lee F. Cline, H. Grady Crowell, M. L. Cash, Van D. Chapman, Rev. T. D. Cranford, R. C. Carswell, James B. Case, W. A. Dennis, Judd Elmore, Thomas Eaker, John W. Evans, Rev. H. L. Fesperman, W. A. Fair, Boyce Faries, Reuben Ford, Victor N. Fair, Claude F. Frye, C. L. Fisher, L. A. Glenn, E. P. Heavner, R. Carl Hoover, Hugh B. Hoke, Charles Houser, Haywood Hull, Stowe Hoyle, Russell Hastings, John L. Herndon, T. B. Hord, M. C. Hoover, B. E. Houser, B. L. Heavner, Bryan Hull, C. Flay Houser, B. H. Hamell, Geo. W. Hine, William Hoffman, R. Burgin Hauss, Claude A. Holly, Hugh Holly, W. F. Hoyle, Hal Hoyle, Ed. L. Heavner, Boston Huss, C. H. Hinson, Ernest B. Hoyle, W. C. Helms, F. D. Helms, M. E. Heavner, Jeff Hill, Roy C. Hoyle, R. W. Hubbard, A. J. Jeffries, Z. V. Johnson, Z. L. Jenks, Ed W. James, B. S. Kistler, W. H. Kiser, H. A. Kuhn, C. E. Kiger, Reid D. Koon, J. Clyde Arrowood, Dock Bivens, Fred Kiser, Harvey Kistler, Bruce Lander, W. S. Lander, P. E. Lutz, Robert Leonard, J. E. Leonard, A. S. Lineberger, L. B. Lilly, C. L. Leonard, R. C. Leonard, L. L. Lohr, Zene Martin, Mason Miller, R. S. Miller, Herbert Miller, David Mosteller, Paul J. Mullen, W. P. Miller, Lenoir A. Mosteller, W. E. Mauney, R. S. McLean, William McCoy, Joe McCaul, L. F. Plonk, W. K. Rogers, L. R. Rhyne, Chas. C. Randall, H. B. Ramseur, J. Loy Rhyne, Ellis Rhyne, Miller Rhyne, R. S. Reinhardt, Dorsey Rhyne, Paul Rhodes, H. W. Rudisill, Frank Reinhardt, B. E. Reynolds, Dr. R. R. Reinhardt, A. H. Scronce, E. F. Sigman, Merman Smith, M. S. Roseman, Guy Robinson, Gerard Stamey, Coy. L. Stamey, R. V. Smyre, L. I. Smith, Earl A. Stroup, R. W. Smith, Grover Summey, Craig Seagle, John R. Schrum, M. L. Sipe, F. E. Sain, R. U. Shuford, Dr. S. H. Steelman, Geo. Whitfield Tobey, W. M. Van Dresser, R. C. Williams, Claude I. Warlick, V. E. Yount, M. P. Womack, H. E. Wilson, J. L. Wise, Lander Wood, B. H. Wood, J. Ernest Wood, M. B. Winstead, Lewis Womack, Lee Willis, R. C. Workman, D. W. Barker, T. L. Handsell, M. H. Hauk, M. L. Dellinger, Russell Poole, W. C. Tallent, S. D. Howard, J. A. Abernethy, Jr., Pat Goodson, C. W. Churchill, W. R. Carswell, Clarence Hoover, J. T. McLean, Lewis Moore, Martin E. McGinnis, C. D. Keever, R. D. Newton, F. R. Navey, Marvin Propst, Wiley M. Pickens, W. E. Love, L. E. Rudisill, G. S. Sain, Dennis Hoover, M. G. Plonk, R. S. Mullen. Effort is being made to perfect the roll. The names of those who were killed are referred to elsewhere.

CHAPTER XX

1920-1929

Edgar Love met with a tragic death October 8, 1920, when he was struck by a railroad train and killed instantly as he was driving his motor car across the railway track on the way to Charlotte. He was a progressive and valued citizen who came from Gastonia to Lincolnton in 1899 to join with his uncle, D. E. Rhyne, in building the Daniel Cotton Mill, the first cotton mill to manufacture combed yarn. Later he established the Saxony and other Cotton Mills in Lincolnton.

He was more than a manufacturer. He was a community builder who was willing to be taxed for needed improvements, for better school facilities, for paved streets, for the city water and light system and for modern school buildings. As Mayor of the city and as chairman of the school board, he led in a hard fought struggle for the installation of these indispensable modern requirements. There were many good conservative citizens who were opposed to these progressive measures but today all are agreed that the rejection of them would have been a grave mistake.

He represented the County in the Legislature for two terms (1917 and 1919) and fathered the bill which required the County Commissioners to build the present handsome County Courthouse. Mr. Love was an affable and popular man whose death came as a shock to his many friends. He was only 51 years old when the final call came so suddenly. His work seemed unfinished, but what he accomplished will abide.

The Federal census report of 1920 gives to Lincolnton 3,390 inhabitants, while Lincoln County has 17,862 inhabitants, Denver has 243, Crouse, 209, and Iron Station, 223 inhabitants.

The Lutheran Church on South Aspen street is the most beautiful church building in the County. It was completed in 1920 at a cost of $65,000.00. The Building Committee consisted of D. A. Yoder, Chairman, J. M. Rhodes, D. P. Rhodes, J. T. Lore, T. H. Cansler, D. C. Leonard, D. H. Mauney and the pastor, the Rev. W. J. Roof. H. A. Kistler had charge of the construction work. The architectural plan is perfect and the structure is the admiration of all who look upon it. The chimes were contributed by Mrs. Charles H. Rhodes in memory of her late husband who was a staunch and loyal member of that congregation. The parsonage built about five years later at a cost of $15,000.00 is the comfortable home of the pastor.

1921

Early in January David C. Warlick, a veteran of the Civil War, presented to the Memorial Hall a framed picture entitled, "The Death Bed Scene of General Robert E. Lee." The presentation speech was made by Alfred Nixon.

The body of Private Ralph Davis, a soldier of the Great World War, arrived from overseas January 20, 1921, and was buried at Bess Chapel.

Frederick L. Hoffman, a fine citizen and devout Christian, and a loyal member and official of the Methodist Church, died in April, 1921. He was active in the business life of Lincolnton and head of the office force at Elm Grove Cotton Mill.

The bond issue for $200,000.00 for new school buildings and other school improvements was voted for and carried by a good majority at an election held in Lincolnton, April 7, 1921, though the election was the quietest ever held in the town.

The body of Private Bidwell Loftin, Lincoln County's second loss on the field of battle during the World War, was buried in April, 1921, in Pisgah Methodist graveyard in Lincoln County.

John M. Rhodes (August 29, 1849-April 20, 1921), son of Caleb Rhodes (1818-1896), was an active and influential churchman and business man in Lincolnton for some fifteen years prior to his death. When he married to Margaret Aderholdt in December, 1870, he settled on a farm in Gaston County; was Register of Deeds for four years, ending in December, 1882; engaged in the textile business in Gaston for a while; later formed a co-partnership with George B. Hiss, cotton manufacturer, and established the Rhodhiss Mills. Severing connection with that company in 1906, he came to Lincolnton, built the Rhodes Mill, which he operated until his death, after which his son, D. P. Rhodes, took charge of the business and succeeded well with the enterprise.

Mr. Rhodes not only possessed fine business capacity, but was just as active as a member of the Lutheran Church. He was a moving spirit in organizing the Gaston College in Dallas in 1883, and a trustee of Lenoir (now Lenoir-Rhyne) College, located in Hickory.

His wife was Margaret Aderholdt, and among their children were: (1) David Polycarp Rhodes, a leading citizen of Lincoln County, a devout member of the Lutheran Church, an active and successful textile manufacturer and for six years a member of the County Board of Commissioners. His sudden death, January 21, 1936, brought sorrow to many friends throughout this section of the state. He was 65 years old. (2) Lillie May Rhodes, married Rev. J. L. Cromer, a Lutheran minister, and their son, Rev. Voigt R. Cromer, was pastor of the Lincolnton Lutheran church for some years until December, 1935, when he resigned to accept the call to the First Lutheran Church of Concord. (3) Violet Almetta Rhodes, married to Dr. John B. Wright, a distinguished physician, of Raleigh. (4) Mabel Rosalie Rhodes, married Rev. W. J. Stirewalt of the Lutheran church. (5) Georgia Agnes Rhodes, married to Michael C. Quickel. (6) Ada, married to Geo. D. Huss. They live in Wachula, Florida. (7) C. J. Rhodes, married first, to Ida Plonk; second, to Fulla Torrence.

Mr. Rhodes married the second time to Nina, daughter of G. Edward and Katie (Rhodes) Crowell, of Lincolnton.

The Rhodes family, prominent in Lincoln County since the pioneer, Frederick Rhodes, settled on Hoyle's Creek about 1750.

His children:

1. Peter, who married Betsy Pack, December 27, 1785. Of his descendants, some went to Alabama and Arkansas and some are still in this section.

2. Susan, married Thomas Linkhorn (Lincoln), April 22, 1808.

3. Mary, married Daniel Best, December 16, 1794.

Susan and Mary, with their husbands, moved to Missouri.

4. Titus.

5. Jacob, married Sarah Weathers, August 12, 1782.

6. Henry (Lutheran minister), born Sept. 2, 1753; married Clary Hire, of Maryland. He settled in Lincoln County. His children were:

Elizabeth, born June 27, 1790, married Rev. Jacob Hoyle.

Solomon, born July 27, 1792, married a Miss Godfrey of Alabama.

Rudolph, born August 24, 1795, married Mary Carpenter.

Henry Rhodes, Jr., born December 29, 1799, married Catherine Carpenter.

Catherine, born April 29, 1802, married Andrew Leonard.

Mary, born November 28, 1803, married Rev. Philip Ramsour.

Henry Rhodes, Jr., above, son of Rev. Henry Rhodes (Lutheran minister), who married Catherine Carpenter, had the following children:

E. Titus Rhodes, born March 30, 1830, married Barbara Brittain in Alabama and lived there twenty years, then returned to Lincoln. Among the children were:

Charles H. Rhodes, who married Effie Heavner. He was sheriff of Lincoln County, 1894-1898, and from then until his death was a leading business man and churchman of Lincolnton. (See 1931.)

Carrie Rhodes, married Lemuel Shuford.

Mamie Rhodes, married Charles Yoder.

Jacob Henry Rhodes, born July 23, 1833 (son of Henry Rhodes, Jr.), married Nancy Hoke. Their children were Ella, who married Dr. R. B. Killian; George P., married Mary Seagle; Katie, married G. Ed Crowell, of Lincolnton; Robert, married Mary Killian.

The daughters of G. Ed and Katie (Rhodes) Crowell were: Maude, married Harvey A. Jonas; Nina, married John M. Rhodes (2nd wife), and later, W. Edgar Flack; Mae, married Hoke Quickel.

The other children of Henry Rhodes, Jr., were Mary, who married David Warlick, son of Maxwell Warlick; and Nancy, who married Sheriff J. A. Robinson.

7. Christian Rhodes, I, son of Frederick Rhodes, the pioneer, married Sophia Shetley, April 11, 1791. He, with wife and nine of their children, went to Missouri. He died there April 4, 1839, in his 79th year.

His son, Christian Rhodes, II, remained in North Carolina and married Madalene Rhyne. They had nine children: Caleb Rhodes, married Myra Hoffman; John, died single at 22, Lutheran minister; Mary married Caleb J. Lineberger, the cotton manufacturer; Melchi, married Caroline Killian; Catherine, married Eli Pasour, of Dallas; Sophia and Annie died single; Elizabeth, married Frank W. Thompson; Lucinda, married Jacob Carpenter.

E. Grant Pasour, son of Eli and Catherine (Rhodes) Pasour, was Postmaster at Gastonia for a four-year term.

Rev. L. D. Thompson, a prominent minister of the Western North Carolina (Methodist) Conference, and Howard R. Thompson, an influential citizen of Gaston County, now serving his tenth year as Register of Deeds in that County are grandsons of F. W. and Elizabeth (Rhodes) Thompson.

Caleb Rhodes (1818-1896), son of Christian Rhodes, was married first to Myra Hoffman (1822-1871) on August 27, 1840. There were ten children, among whom were:

1. Sarah Jane Rhodes, married to Dr. J. F. Smyer, January 15, 1879.

2. Dora Emily Rhodes, married to Daniel Elias Sigmon on February 15, 1881. Two of their sons, Rev. Paul Cromer Sigmon (1892-1932) and Rev. Robert Bruce Sigmon, were Lutheran ministers. Dr. William Sigmon is a dentist and Jesse Caleb Sigmon is a Newton lawyer, one time Judge of Recorder's Court for Catawba County and State Senator in 1929.

3. Christian William Rhodes, married to Elizabeth E. Mauney, December 28, 1893.

4. John Melancthon Rhodes. (See above.)

Caleb Rhodes married second time to Hester Ann Heedick and they had six children.

Caleb Rhodes was a frugal, intelligent, public-spirited citizen. He lived in Gaston for some twenty-five years after his first marriage, until 1867, when he and his brother, Melchi Rhodes, sold the Rhodes gold mine tract, (the original home of their father) near Hoylesville, to Dr. William Alexander and William Richards for $20,000 in gold. He then bought a big plantation about six miles south of Newton and lived there until his death in 1895. He was a devout Lutheran and his body was buried at Salem Church in Lincoln County.

Melchi Rhodes (1827-1892), son of Christian Rhodes, II, had in him the urge for adventure, for before he reached his majority he joined a gold seeking group of young men to go to far away California to find fortune in gold mining, and after a six months' voyage, via Cape Horn, they reached San Francisco and he got a job paying $25.00 a day as overseer of the waterway used for washing gold. Within three years he returned home, choosing the perils by land rather than the perilous sea voyage in a sail boat. Each of the party brought three broncho ponies, one to ride, one to carry food and another to carry baggage and bedding, for there were no hotels on the way, and after six months he arrived at home with his cash, all in $20.00 gold coins, carried in a buckskin belt.

He then for a while taught school in Gaston. One day a pupil was called forward for punishment and when ordered to remove his coat the boy refused to obey, whereupon the teacher undertook to take it off, but finding no shirt under the coat, sent the boy to his seat saying, "that is punishment enough."

Mr. Rhodes married to Carolina Killian, April 3, 1855 (See 1935), and settled on the plantation near Salem Church in Lincoln County. In 1861 he enlisted as a Confederate soldier and when peace finally came he returned home, cast down because his fortune, invested in Confederate bonds, was absolutely lost. Like many another Southern soldier, with a brave heart he determined to solve his problem by hard work and economy and amassed a good estate. He was a Lutheran in faith, loyal to his church and a generous giver to every worthy cause.

His three children were: Cecelia Elizabeth, who married September 17, 1905, to John G. Little; Oliver P. Rhodes, who married Sarah Alice, daughter of Jonas Hoffman, of Dallas, November 16, 1881; and Edward R. Rhodes, who married Bessie Irene Heedick, February 27, 1920.

Oliver P. Rhodes settled in Dallas in 1878 and engaged in mercantile business and farming. He is a fine citizen and a loyal member of the Lutheran Church. He had seven children and gave to each of them a college education or its equivalent. His son, Clarence K. Rhodes, and daughter, Caroline Rhodes, graduated from Lenoir Rhyne College in 1910. Clarence became a Lutheran minister and has served as pastor of congregations in North and South Carolina and Virginia. Caroline married to Rev. Carl H. Deal, a Methodist minister, and they went as missionaries to Korea and labored in that mission field for eighteen years. They now live in Salisbury, N. C. Dora C. Rhodes, another daughter of Oliver P. Rhodes, graduated from Lenoir Rhyne College and received the medal for public speaking, and has been a high school principal for some years.

Prof. E. D. Johnson, superintendent of the Lincolnton city schools since 1919, resigned to take effect at the close of the term in May, and Prof. Wiley M. Pickens, of Salisbury, was elected to succeed him.

1922

The Baptist Church was organized in Lincolnton in 1859. Rev. L. M. Berry was the pastor of a small congregation and services were held in the Old White Church. In 1873 when Rev. Dr. N. B. Cobb was the pastor, a lot was bought on Water street from B. C. Cobb for $250. A Building Committee composed of E. Childs, J. L. and L. T. Wilkey, submitted plans for a building and the church was not erected until 1884.

In 1919 this property was sold to Edgar Love for $16,000, and the lot corner of Main and Cedar streets bought for $6,200, and the present handsome church was completed in 1922, at a cost of $40,000, and the small congregation of 1859 has grown to be a large and influential body of Christians.

Dr. Robert Hall Morrison, a skilled physician, and son of the Rev. Dr. R. H. Morrison (See 1889), the Presbyterian divine, who established Davidson College, was born at the Morrison home in East Lincoln in 1843. He was a soldier of the Civil War, after which he graduated in medicine and practiced for a while in California; returned to North Carolina where he married Lucy, daughter of the late Rufus Reid, of Iredell County, and then settled in Shelby, where for thirty or more years he had a lucrative medical practice. In 1922 he died at the Reid homestead in Iredell County, where his only son, Dr. Reid Morrison, now lives.

1923

Major William A. Graham (son of the late Governor William A. Graham) State Commissioner of Agriculture, died in Raleigh, December 23, 1923, and the body was buried at Machpelah in Lincoln County. Major Graham was born in Hillsboro, December 26, 1839. He was educated at private schools; the University of North Carolina, 1856-1859, and Princeton from which he received the A.B. degree in 1860.

In the Civil War he was Captain of Company K, 2nd N. C. Cavalry, and Major and Assistant Adjutant General of North Carolina State Troops.

He was a Baptist in faith, served as Moderator of the South Fork Association, and was for thirty years Chairman of the Executive Committee of that Association. He also served as President of the North Carolina Baptist State Convention.

He was active in the councils of the Democratic party. Represented Lincoln County in the lower house of the Legislature in 1905, and was the Senator from this district in 1874-75 and 1878-79. He served as a member of the State Board of Agriculture from 1899 to 1908, when he was elected Commissioner of Agriculture and continued in that office until his death in 1923.

He was a student of State and Church history and was the author of several valuable historical books, among them, *General Joseph Graham and his Revolutionary Papers, The History of South Fork Baptist Association, The Life and Service of General William L. Davidson, Battle of Ramsour's Mill, History of Second Regiment N. C. Cavalry and North Carolina Adjutant General's Department, 1861-1865.*

Major Graham was married to Miss Julia Robertson Lane, of Amelia County, Virginia, on June 8, 1864, and they lived in Lincoln County for the remainder of their lives. They reared eleven children, one of whom, William A. Graham, III, upon the death of Major Graham, was appointed by Governor Morrison to succeed his father as Commissioner of Agriculture. He has held the office by re-election since 1924 to the end of 1936.

Their children were:

Florence Lane, died unmarried in 1900.

Susan Washington, married Casper Walke of Richmond, Va.

Julia Evalin, married S. W. Huff of New York.

William Alexander, III, unmarried; State Senator, 1923; State Commissioner of Agriculture, 1923 to end of 1936.

Elizabeth Hill, married James P. Parker.

Martha and Sophia, twins, died early.

Caroline Brevard, married J. S. Wahab.

Alice Caldwell, married Montague G. Clark of Georgia.

Ellen Wales, married J. S. Calvert, for many years and still in the United States Consular Service.

Joseph, married Elizabeth Fitzsimmons of Charlotte.

Edgar Love, Representative from Lincoln County, introduced the bill which was passed by the Legislature of 1919 directing the Commissioners of Lincoln County to erect a new courthouse and the plans were adopted and contract let in January, 1920, for the handsome building now in use. The old courthouse completed in 1855 was vacated in May, 1921, and torn down. The present building was completed in June, 1923, and the first court held in it convened July 16, 1923, with Judge James L. Webb presiding. Alfred Nixon, the clerk, had prepared an interesting history of the courts and court buildings of the past which was read by his son, Joseph R. Nixon, followed with an appropriate address by Associate Justice of the Supreme Court, William Alexander Hoke.

1924

Lincolnton lost her oldest citizen when Mrs. Amanda Calvert Finch passed to her reward on June 19, 1924, in her 95th year. She was the widow of George Finch. The family came here from Virginia after the Civil War and have figured prominently in the social and religious life of the town ever since. Mrs. Finch was a staunch Baptist and very active as a church worker, but withal a Christian whose sympathies extended beyond her own communion. She had many friends because she was friendly.

William Alexander Hoke, Associate Justice of Supreme Court, was on June 2, 1924, appointed Chief Justice of that court by Governor Morrison, to fill the vacancy caused by the death of Judge Walter Clark.

Dr. Silas McBee, son of V. A. McBee, was born in Lincolnton, November 14, 1853, was educated at the Lincolnton Academy and the University of the South where he was graduated in 1876, and then was Trustee of his Alma Mater for 27 years.

He was a courtly gentleman, a fine scholar, a loyal Episcopalian, and one of the most prominent laymen of his church in America. For sixteen years, from 1896 to 1912, he was the Editor of *The Churchman*, the general organ of the Episcopal church in the United States, until he resigned in 1912 in order to found and edit *The Constructive Quarterly* in New York, of which he was editor from 1912 to 1923, when his health gave way. In 1919 the University of the South conferred upon her distinguished son the honorary degree of Doctor of Civil Law. Dr. McBee was recognized as an authority on church architecture. The present St. Luke's Episcopal Church in Lincolnton was built according to his plans and under his supervision; its altar and reredos carved by his own hands and all of its beautiful stained glass windows with one exception the work of the incomparable Booth of London in consultation with his devoted friend the architect. The churches in Waynesboro, N. C., and Florence, S. C., Walsh Memorial Hall at the University of the South, the memorial altar and reredos in St. James Church, Wilmington, over the burial place of Bishop Atkinson, also bear witness to the talents of Mr. McBee as an architect. His aid was also "generously and patriotically given" in formulating the plans for the bronze of Zebulon Baird Vance in Statuary Hall in the United States Capitol. Dr. McBee was also consulting architect with Ralph Adams Cram in perfecting the plans for the Cathedral at Manila and upon invitation of Bishop Satterlee of the Diocese of Washington delivered a series of lectures in favor of the construction of a Gothic cathedral in the Federal City, now well under way. He died in Charleston, S. C., September 3, 1924, and the body was buried September 5 in the University Cemetery in Sewanee, Tenn.

The following editorial appeared in *The Churchman*, published in New York City, September 13, 1924:

"In the death of Silas McBee the Christian forces of this world have lost one of the most ardent advocates of Christian unity. During the years when Dr. McBee was editor of *The Churchman*, and subsequently of the *Constructive Quarterly*, he laid foundations of good will between the various Communions that have helped to intensify that longing for re-union now so widespread, and pointed out avenues to fellowship the following of which has resulted in stimulating more intelligent efforts toward the end he sought.

* * * *

"We know of no other layman whose purpose has been more clarified and undeviating or whose work has been more constructive toward the realization of the Kingdom of God than that of Silas McBee."

Silas McBee married on June 21, 1877, to Mary Estelle Sutton, of Mississippi. She died in Lincolnton, June 24, 1891. Their children were Miss Emma Estelle McBee, a member of the faculty of Ashley Hall, Charleston, S. C.; Dr. Mary Vardrine McBee, a native of Lincolnton and founder and principal of Ashley Hall; and Silas McBee, Jr., a graduate of the University of the South and of the Harvard Law School, who served overseas in the Great War with the rank of Major and now commands a Regiment in the organized Reserves with headquarters in New York City.

Later Mr. McBee married Miss Louise J. Post of Great Neck, N. Y. She survived him for only a few years.

Cephas A. Jonas, father of Hon. Charles A. Jonas, of this city, died at his home in the Reepsville section of the County, in November, 1924, aged 77 years.

Alfred Nixon, to whom the County owes a debt which it can never pay for the valuable and accurate historical data of Lincoln County, which he discovered and preserved, died March 26, 1924, aged 67 years.

He was born near Beatties Ford, May 26, 1856, son of Robert and Milley (Womack) Nixon, and the descendant of William and Elizabeth Nixon, the pioneers, who came from Charlotte County, Virginia, in 1780 and settled near Beatties Ford. When a youth he attended Rock Springs Seminary with Prof. D. Matt Thompson, as his teacher, and later entered the State University from which he graduated in 1881 in the class with J. Y. Joyner, Dr. Chas. D. McIver, John Morehead Avery, Judge Wm. J. Adams and J. D. Murphy. Then for a while he taught school, was elected County Surveyor in 1882; and in 1883 was elected Sheriff to succeed A. S. Haynes, who resigned; was re-elected Sheriff in 1884, and served until 1890, when he declined to run again; consented to hold the office again from 1891-1892. For some years he was Superintendent of County Schools. In 1898 he was elected Clerk of the Superior Court and held that position for 26 years, until his death in 1924.

He was a Presbyterian in faith, a bright Mason and from young manhood was a valued and highly esteemed citizen. He was a modest and lovable man, true in every relation he sustained to society, the friend of all men, and died without an enemy. The concise history of the County published in the *North Carolina Booklet* in 1910 is a valuable literary and historical product from his pen. He did much research work and his name will be a household word in Lincoln in the generations to come.

His wife before her marriage was Miss Iola Robinson, a descendant on her mother's side of Rev. Daniel Asbury, the pioneer Methodist preacher. Among their children are Kemp B. Nixon, a Lincolnton lawyer, who has represented the Lincoln district in the State Senate two terms, 1931 and 1935, and Joseph R. Nixon, a teacher, now serving as Superintendent of the Schools and Historian for Lincoln County.

1925

Robert S. Reinhardt, son of Franklin M. Reinhardt (See 1869), born January 1, 1858, married to Laura Pegram, daughter of Edward L. Pegram, of Gaston County, February 13, 1879, and died September 11, 1925. He traced his ancestry back to Jacob Forney, Christian Reinhardt and the noted Lutheran preacher, Rev. John Gottfried Arndt, all pioneers and notable men in their time. "Bob" Reinhardt as he was familiarly called was first a merchant at Iron Station, where for ten years or more he conducted a successful business. In 1889 he moved to Lincolnton where he and Stephen Smith bought the Ivy Shoal Cotton Mills which had for many years been operated by Col. John F. Phifer in co-partnership with his kinsman, Col. R. W. Allison, of Concord. The business was conducted by Mr. Reinhardt until his death in 1925 and after that by his son, Stephen Reinhardt, as the Elm Grove Cotton Mill.

He was one of the organizers of the Southern Cotton Spinners' Association in 1897, and when merged in 1904 with the American Cotton Manufacturers' Association was unanimously elected president of it.

He was a public-spirited citizen, identified with many progressive movements, a safe business man who amassed a good fortune. He was a big-hearted man and the friend of all men, generous, hospitable, popular and patriotic. There was never any friction or misunderstanding between him and his employees for he was fair, reasonable and sympathetic. When he died the State lost a fine citizen whose passage was mourned by many friends. He was active in the Masonic fraternity and a Presbyterian in faith. His daughter, Lena Reinhardt, who married to George A. Brown, is an accomplished lady, a patriotic and active member of the Daughters of the American Revolution and anxious to preserve every scrap of Lincoln County history.

Fabius Busbee Shipp (son of the late Lt. William E. Shipp and wife, Margaret Busbee Shipp), Captain 10th Cavalry, United States Army, was accidentally killed in military camp in Arizona, when thrown from his horse in a polo game, November 6, 1925. He was a fine gentleman, a brave soldier in the World War and gave promise of a brilliant career. His body rests in the family plot in St. Luke's (Episcopal) graveyard in Lincolnton. (See 1898.)

Dr. Albert C. Fox, son of the late Rev. Dr. A. J. Fox, died in Lincolnton, April 9, 1925, after a lingering illness. He had been a practicing physician for many years.

Professor D. Matt Thompson, after more than fifty years as an educational leader, and teacher of first rank, died June 30, 1925. The service which he unselfishly rendered was of incalculable value to this section of the state.

He was a born teacher and made teaching his life work; was well equipped for his task, always thorough in his work; inspired his pupils to lofty endeavor and exercised a fine moral influence over the student body. He was born in Randolph County, June 5, 1844; was a Confederate soldier; married to Miss Mary Elizabeth Rice, of Randolph County. He moved from Randolph to Denver, Lincoln County, in 1873, became principal of Denver Seminary, drew students from the surrounding counties and from other States, and the influence which went out from that institution has enriched the life and character of the homes that furnished students for the school.

The free school system of North Carolina being at that time in its infancy and, in a degree, inefficient, students from Denver Seminary were in demand as teachers, and eligible for entrance into colleges of high grade. After eleven years of faithful work at Denver Professor Thompson became principal of Piedmont Seminary in Lincolnton and was from 1898 to 1899 Superintendent of Lincoln County Schools, which he conducted on the same high plane for seven years, making eighteen years that he taught in Lincoln County. Among his students were those who became useful as lawyers, physicians, ministers, teachers, authors, college professors, public officers and industrial and agricultural leaders.

In 1891 he accepted the superintendency of the Statesville Graded School just established in that city, organized the school, assembled a corps of high grade teachers, including Miss Angie Caldwell and J. N. Hauss, who went with him from Lincolnton, and gradually brought the school to rank among the best of its type in the state. He was most successful as an administrator and always strove for work of enduring quality. After twenty-nine years of splendid service in Statesville he was on November 20, 1920, seriously injured in Statesville by an automobile, which struck him as he was crossing the street. As a result of this accident he was completely disabled and lingered in a helpless condition until his death, June 30, 1925.

He was an active member and official of the Methodist Church from early life until his death. His body was buried in Statesville.

The three sons, Holland, Walter and Dorman Thompson, all developed into men of character, usefulness and distinction.

1. Holland Thompson, the eldest son of D. Matt and Lucy (Rice) Thompson, was born in Randolph County, July 30, 1873. He was prepared for college by his father and graduated from the State University in the class of 1895 with Ph.B. degree; A.M., Columbia University, 1900; Ph.D., 1906 (same university); Principal Concord (N. C.) Graded School, 1895 to 1899; Fellow of Columbia University, 1899-1900; Tutor of History, 1901-1902; Instructor in History, 1902-1906. He has been for some years and is now (1935) Professor of History in the College of the City of New York; Lecturer in History, Columbia University, 1923-24. The university honored him with degree of Doctor of Laws in 1935. Author of many books including *From Cotton Field to Cotton Mill*, 1906; *History of Our Land*, 1911; *Prisons of the Civil War*, 1911; *The United States*, 1916; *The New South*, 1919; *The Age of Inventions*, 1921.

He was a contributor to the *Encyclopedia Brittanica* and *Dictionary of American Biography*. He married Isabel Aitkin, of New York, in July, 1905. Dr. Thompson is a ripe scholar and a teacher and regarded in literary circles among the eminent authors and teachers of this generation.

2. Walter Thompson was born in Denver, Lincoln County, January 26, 1876. He was prepared for college by his father, graduated from the State University, was superintendent of the Concord Graded School for several years until elected Superintendent of South Greensboro Graded School, in 1898 was made Superintendent of the Stonewall Jackson Training School, which position he filled with great acceptability until December, 1912, when he was made Superintendent of the Children's Home (the Methodist Orphanage) located in Winston-Salem, which position he held for nearly nine years, until his death September 21, 1921. He married Miss Emily Gregory of Greensboro, who died in January, 1936. He had fine preparation in both home and school training and possessed fine executive ability.

3. Dorman Thompson was born in Denver, Lincoln County, November 11, 1878. Like his brothers he got his educational training in his father's school and at the State University. He chose the profession of law, was a very successful young lawyer in Statesville and gave promise of a brilliant career. He possessed high character and was popular with the people. Was State Senator from Iredell for three terms, 1913, 1915 and 1919, and made a fine record as a lawmaker. He was a prominent churchman and Methodist layman. He was teacher of a large class of men in Broad Street Church, Statesville, often a delegate to the Annual, and once delegate to the General Conference. He married Miss Stella Morrison, of Statesville, who died in 1921. He was widely known and much loved and when he died, October 2, 1923, the Church lost a valued member and the State lost a notable citizen.

William Alexander Hoke, son of Col. John F. and Catherine (Alexander) Hoke (See 1888) was born in Lincolnton, October 21, 1851. His father was a son of Col. John and Barbara (Quickel) Hoke, and was a lawyer of first ability. His mother was a daughter of Col. William Julius Alexander, and a granddaughter of Joseph Wilson, both of whom were brilliant lawyers and orators. (See 1866.)

Alex Hoke, as he was familiarly called, was educated at the Lincolnton Male Academy, finished there when Rev. Dr. W. R. Wetmore and Prof. H. H. Smith were the teachers. He was an apt scholar and early gave promise of the distinction to which he later attained.

After completing the academic course he attended Pearson's Law School, was admitted to the bar on his twenty-first birthday and settled in Shelby where he practiced law for about eight years, when he returned to Lincolnton and formed a co-partnership with his father, which continued until the death of his father in 1888. He was a good lawyer, a logical and attractive speaker and enjoyed an extensive practice. Col. Hamilton C. Jones, referring to the brilliant legal ancestry of Judge Hoke, said: "He would have had less excuse for not being a great lawyer than any man of my acquaintance."

He held only one political position, that of representative from Lincoln County in the Legislature of 1889, but in that one session he displayed such qualities of leadership and such wide

Top left: Judge William M. Shipp (1819-1890). See 1890.
Top right: Judge David Schenck (1835-1902). See 1902.
Center: Judge Wm. Preston Bynum (1820-1909). See 1909.
Lower left: Judge Wm. Alexander Hoke (1851-1925). See 1925.
Lower right: Judge M. L. McCorkle (1817-1899). See 1899.

knowledge of law that he took first rank in that body. In 1890 he was elected Judge of the Superior Court for the Lincoln district and served in that capacity for fourteen years, until January, 1905; he was elected a Justice of the Supreme Court in November, 1904, and continued in that office until June 2, 1924, when by appointment of Governor Morrison he was made Chief Justice of that court to fill the vacancy caused by the death of Chief Justice Walter Clark, but resigned on account of ill health on March 3, 1925, after having served on the bench since January, 1891.

He married Mary, daughter of V. A. McBee, of Lincolnton, December 16, 1897, it being the fiftieth anniversary of the marriage of her parents. Their daughter, Mary Hoke, married Edward Slaughter and lives in Charlottesville, Virginia.

Judge Hoke was a courtly gentleman, cordial in manner and popular with the people. His brethren of the bar held him in high respect because of his lofty character, legal learning and judicial poise. He was a life-long member of the Episcopal Church and for many years an office bearer in Saint Luke's Church in Lincolnton.

On July 4, 1902, he was admitted into membership of the Society of Cincinnati as the representative of his great grandfather, Lieutenant William Lee Alexander, of the Fourth North Carolina Continental Infantry, who was an original member of this Society.

He was justly proud of the honor conferred when he was appointed Chairman of the Commission to provide a suitable statue of Senator Zebulon B. Vance to be placed in the Hall of Fame in Washington, and in his brilliant presentation speech, June 22, 1916, in Washington, when the statue was unveiled, he referred to Governor Vance, as follows:

> "As a man amongst us who pre-eminently filled the requirements of the Act of Congress dedicating this Hall to the great and good men of the Nation . . . an illustrious citizen, distinguished for civic and military virtues, Vance, was indeed, my countrymen, a great leader of his people in war and peace; great in intellect, great in character, and achievement, great in breadth and quality of his sympathy. His people followed him with unfaltering trust for more than thirty of the most eventful years in their history and were not disappointed. They admired and loved him for his integrity and his courage, for his wisdom and strength, his genius, his matchless eloquence and far-seeing vision, for

his loyal-hearted, unchanging devotion, at all times and under all circumstances, as he was given light to see it. His hold upon the affections of the people of North Carolina endures and grows stronger with time, and we are deeply gratified to have you with us here today, in paying this tribute to his memory."

He was a patient in Rex Hospital, Raleigh, when he died September 13, 1925. Sitting on a chair talking to his physician about the high day of his life when he had the privilege of taking part in the honor paid to his friend, Senator Vance, his heart failed and he died suddenly, as did his father and also his grandfather Hoke. His body was taken to Lincolnton and buried in the family plot in Saint Luke's graveyard under the shadow of the church of which he had been a lifelong member, and among those he had known and loved.

When the degree of Doctor of Laws was conferred upon him by the State University in June, 1909, Dean Smith said: "Judge Hoke has exemplified and exhibited in every position that he has filled, those qualities of head and heart which North Carolinians love to honor. Of strong convictions, he has the faculty of putting himself in others' places, so that prejudice is disarmed and justice is tempered with understanding. His ingrained honesty, his judicial poise, his wide charity of hand and thought and his sense of stewardship as man and as citizen commend him as peculiarly worthy of the distinction which we today confer upon him."

He was also honored by Davidson College, which conferred upon him the same degree.

Excerpts from the interesting address of Hamilton C. Jones, Jr., of Charlotte, who presented the portrait of Judge Hoke to the Supreme Court follow:

"Judge Hoke fully met the requirements of a good judge according to the statement made by Rufus Choate in the Massachusetts Constitutional Convention of 1853: 'In the first place he should be profoundly learned in all the learning of the law, and he must know how to use that learning. In the next place he must be a man, not merely upright and well intentioned—this of course—but a man who will not respect persons in judgment, and finally he must possess the perfect confidence of the community, that he bear not the sword in vain' . . . for fourteen years he held the exalted position of Superior Court Judge with rare ability, impartiality and learning. Inflexible honesty, mastery of law, love of justice and loftiness of character moulded this outstanding nisi prius judge as the idol of the people . . . His Supreme Court decisions, characterized by accuracy and facility of expression, cut to the heart of the subject with an elucidation and clearness which leave no vestige of doubt as to the principle of law which he is enunciating."

Mr. Thomas C. Guthrie, an able Charlotte lawyer, commenting on the character and legal learning of Judge Hoke, said:

"As a Superior Court Judge he was a model in temperament, learning and character. He lent to his Court the dignity of a Mansfield, the learning of a Blackstone and the character of a Hale. His continual striving was not only to administer even and equal justice to all, but to make litigants feel that they were being fairly and justly treated. He presided over his Court with great dignity and composure. He would not tolerate quarreling among lawyers, or confusion or wrangling in presenting arguments, either to the court or jury. He would permit only one lawyer to speak at a time, and required every one else to be seated while the speaker presented his argument . . . He had an innate sense of justice and gave all lawyers and suitors a square deal. He had great respect for authority and precedent but was not slavishly led into the perpetuation of wrong or injustice when technicalities conflicted with equity and good conscience. No man emerged from his Court, either as winner or loser, who did not feel that his case had been disposed of by a just and righteous Judge, even though he might not agree with the decision . . . Judge Hoke sat upon the Supreme Court bench from January, 1905 to June, 1924, as Associate Justice, and upon the death of Chief Justice Clark, was appointed Chief Justice, and presided over the Court until March, 1925, when he resigned his office on account of ill health, having served in this high court for more than twenty years . . . His opinions are innumerable upon general questions of civil law, relating to contracts, wills, conveyances, notes and controversies arising between individuals and corporations in this busy and complicated civilization in which we live, but in the abundance of his writings it is impossible in limited space to make adequate and satisfactory selections. His many opinions are recorded in the Supreme Court Reports from the 137th to the 189th volume inclusive . . . Before taking leave of him as a Judge, attention should be called to his attitude in criminal cases. He loved justice and fairness, and while he had no false sentiment or sympathy toward criminals he wanted them not only to have, but to believe they were getting a square deal from the Court . . . Judge Hoke was always alert to protect the legal rights of a prisoner accused of crime in all proper cases, but he was also in favor of holding criminals to a strict accountability for their misdeeds, and no case of his can be found where he yielded to sentiment or sympathy at the expense of the public good."

Chief Justice Stacy in a tribute to Judge Hoke related the following interesting story:

"A negro was brought into his Court, charged with a capital assault upon a white woman. There was much excitement in the community over the occurrence. The crime had been committed the day before. The defendant lodged a motion for a continuance upon the ground that he had not had time to summon his witnesses or to get ready for the trial. It was suggested that a lynching would probably take place if the case were not tried at that term of Court. To this the Judge promptly replied: 'If there is to be any violence it is better for the prisoner to be lynched by the mob than to be mobbed by the Court.'"

Judge Stacy, closing his tribute to Judge Hoke, said:

"So long as the establishment of justice shall remain the end of all government, and so long as men everywhere shall continue to seek the right, he will ever live with the deathless dead, for in the temple of the law, he hath builded for himself a monument more lasting than marble, and more enduring than bronze. His epitaph is written in his own hand and will be found in the North Carolina reports."

1926

The County Commissioners advertised for bids until March 1, 1926, for the purchase of $275,000.00 of County Road Bonds. The bonds to mature as follows:

$20,000.00 annually for the years 1945-6-7 and 9.
$45,000.00 in March, 1953.
$75,000.00 in March, 1955.
$75,000.00 in March, 1956.

Rev. Dr. Samuel A. Weber, aged 88 years, died in Charleston, S. C., in June, 1926. He was a grandson of the late Rev. Samuel Lander, Sr., and a preacher of rare gifts and a polished and scholarly writer and author. He was a minister of the Methodist Church in South Carolina for 64 years, and widely known in Southern religious circles.

He had two sons, Dr. William Lander Weber, a college professor until his death in 1911, and Rev. Dr. John Langdon Weber, a brilliant orator, preacher and author, who served as pastor in Tennessee and Kentucky cities, and died in March, 1923.

Jonas W. Mullen, a native of Lincoln County, and for some years postmaster in Charlotte, died June 24, 1926, in a New York hospital. His body was brought to Lincolnton for burial.

Portraits of the late Sidney J. Whitener and W. W. Brooks, who had been teachers in the Denver High School, were presented to that institution at the Commencement in May, 1926, at Denver.

Dr. Gordon B. Crowell (1895-1926), a young and popular physician, associated with his father, Dr. Lester A. Crowell, in the practice of medicine and in the management of the Lincoln Hospital, died May 9, 1926, his death bringing sorrow to a wide circle of friends. He was born and reared in Lincolnton, graduated from the City High School and the State University, took his medical course at the University of Pennsylvania and settled in his home town as a physician and surgeon. He married Frances Geitner, of Hickory, and their daughter was four years old when he died. He loved his profession, was successful in the practice and gave high promise of a brilliant career in his life work, but stricken down too soon, he died when only 31 years old. (See 1907.)

In 1926 there were 3,910 automobiles in Lincoln County, or one car for every 4.6 inhabitants, averaging one car for each family. Estimating the average car to cost only $450.00 the people of the County had $1,759,500.00 invested in automobiles.

Lincoln as a farming county was well advertised in the *Manufacturers Record* of August 12, by the Seaboard Railway. The advertisement in that great industrial publication follows:

"Lincoln has long been noted as a wheat producing county. As far back as 1781 Cornwallis stopped his army at Ramsour's Mill to secure flour. The United States Department of Agriculture maintains a wheat experiment plot located five miles from Lincolnton, the county seat. From this test valuable information is secured.

"Lincoln County produces tobacco of good quality besides corn and other grains.

"This County has lately sprung into prominence because of its wide interest in the raising of poultry. This new industry is returning thousands of dollars in cash to the farmers each year and adds greatly to the prosperity of the County."

Joseph Edgar Reinhardt, son of Franklin M. and Sarah (Smith) Reinhardt (See 1869), was descended on both sides from sturdy and prominent pioneer stock, and was scrupulously honest and dependable, frugal and industrious, making a valuable and influential citizen. He lived near the old Rehoboth furnace and was a large landholder, busy looking after his extensive farm interests, but found time for other commercial activities. In 1889 he, with his brother, Robert S. Reinhardt, and other friends, purchased the old Phifer factory, changed the name to Elm Grove Cotton Mills, and operated it for thirty-six years, he being vice-president of the company.

He had fine business judgment and served as County Commissioner for about ten years, and his frugal habit and clear insight made him a valuable member of that Board.

He married to Miss Fannie Wilson, of Catawba County, on December 16, 1873, and they lived happily together for fifty-three years, until he died, October 3, 1926, aged 75 years. Their living children are J. Ed Reinhardt, Jr., now a resident of Catawba County, Mrs. S. J. Smyer, of Newton, Mrs. W. L. Puckett, Mrs. J. H. Newton and A. Forney Reinhardt, the popular sheriff of Lincoln County from 1928 to 1936. Mr. Reinhardt was a ruling elder of the Ironton Presbyterian Church, from which his funeral was held, and the service at the grave was conducted by his brethren of the Masonic fraternity.

He was held in high esteem and when he died the County lost a valued and honorable citizen.

1927

Charles Lee Coon, son of David A. and Frances (Hovis) Coon, was born in Lincoln County, December 25, 1868. His father, a splendid citizen, a Lieutenant in the Civil War, was wounded nine times at Gettysburg while leading his Company in Pettigrew's Brigade.

Charles L. Coon attended the local schools and began to teach when eighteen years old, graduated from Conover College in 1887 and entered upon his teaching career.

He was Principal first of Denver Academy, in Lincoln County, 1889-91; taught in Conover College, 1891-96; Principal of Lincolnton Schools, 1896-97; taught in Charlotte Schools, 1897-99; Superintendent Salisbury Schools, 1899-1903; Secretary of the Bureau of the Southern Educational Board, Knoxville, Tenn., succeeding P. P. Claxton, 1903-04; Chief Clerk in the office of the Superintendent of Public Instruction in 1907, until chosen Superintendent of Wilson City Schools; since 1913 was also Superintendent of Wilson County Schools, which position he held until his death, December 27, 1927.

After much research work he issued in two volumes, in 1908, *The Beginning of Public Education in North Carolina*. In 1915 he issued in one volume *North Carolina Schools and Academies, 1790-1840*. These volumes were published by the North Carolina Historical Commission, and in them are assembled a wealth of documentary history of the growth of public education in the State.

In the preparation of these volumes Mr. Coon rendered to the State a service of inestimable value. But his life work was teaching and he was a progressive teacher who did more than any other man to improve rural schools in North Carolina. In fact he led in the fight to drive the one-room school house out of the State and give the rural population graded school facilties as good as in the city schools.

He possessed superior literary gifts and Joseph P. Caldwell pressed him into service as a contributor to the *Charlotte Observer*, and he wrote regularly under the nom de plume of "Teacher." He reported the brilliant and original address of Walter H. Page on "The Forgotten Man," to which Mr. Caldwell referred editorially as follows:

> "It has been many a day since the *Observer* printed anything better than the contribution of "Teacher," reviewing the recent Greensboro speech of Mr. Walter H. Page and his critics. It would be well if that speech and this review of it were framed and hung in every home in the State."

His style was cogent, forceful, pungent, brilliant. He always hewed to the line without compromise. He was too honest and frank to flatter. He had no patience with double-mindedness. He stood for truth as he saw it and wore no man's collar. He once said:

> *"No organization shall be my master;*
> *No necessity of bread shall seal my lips;*
> *No hope of preferment shall ever make*
> *Me say what I do not believe is the truth."*

His courage was manifest when he established the *Lincoln Democrat* to advocate the cause of sound money and to fight the free silver movement of 1896. He lost money by it but it introduced him to the newspaper world.

He championed an unpopular cause and aroused the opposition of the politicians when in 1897 he canvassed Lincoln County for a special school tax levy. The time was not then ripe for progress and they called him a socialist, but he got the better in the argument even if for the time the cause met defeat.

He was willing for others to get the glory for much that he did for education, for he was always too busy at his great task to seek publicity. When he died the State lost a great citizen and a great teacher. In the resolutions of respect passed by the Wilson County teachers after his death we find the following:

> "Many will praise Mr. Coon as pioneer organizer, able executive, keen analyst, facile writer, courageous moralist, and fearless leader, but those who knew him intimately realize that he would prefer to be remembered for what in all these capacities he truly was—a great interpreter of life—a great teacher."

He came of good German stock and appreciated the sturdy, frugal, conservative and religious German character. It was his purpose to write a history of the contribution the German population has made to the State. What a pity he was called hence before he accomplished that task. He was a distinguished product of Lincoln County and we should be proud of the great work he did for education in the State. He married to Carrie Louise Sparger, of Mount Airy, October 21, 1903, and she was a teacher of high grade. They had three children: Frances Elizabeth, Mary Moore and Charles Lee, Jr.

The industrial statistics of Lincoln County for 1927, according to the report of the State Department of Conservation and Development, show that in the 32 manufacturing industries of the County, 1,794 wage workers are employed; the total wages paid was $1,225,327.00, the cost of material, fuel and power was $3,367,776.00, and the total value of goods produced, $5,425,726.00.

Included in the above were 15 textile industries, that gave employment to 1,613 wage workers, to whom $1,074,389.00 was paid in wages; the cost of raw material, fuel and power was $2,989,146.00 and the value of goods produced, $4,723,552.00. Of farm products the report shows:

No. Acres Cultivated	Amt. Produced	Value
Cotton, 28,623	13,653 bales (according to gin reports)	$1,311,736.00
Corn, 20,540	455,880 bushels	388,617.00
Wheat, 11,267	123,937 bushels	178,469.00
Oats, 3,115	59,185 bushels	42,021.00
Hay, 3,251	2,581 bales or loads	62,305.00
Horses and Mules—Number 3,228		418,636.00
Cattle, number 4,514		213,061.00
Hogs, number 4,314		50,474.00

James Nixon, aged 84, died at Denver in 1927, and the body was buried at Unity graveyard. He was a soldier of the Civil War in the Confederate Army.

Charles C. Cobb, of Dallas, Texas, was married in Asheville, N. C., August 15, 1927, to Miss Nancy Fairley, daughter of Mr. and Mrs. Henry Fairley, of Rockingham, N. C. (See 1913.)

Bartlett Shipp Johnston, son of Dr. William Johnston, of Lincoln County, was born at the old Forney homestead in Lincoln. He left school when sixteen years old to enter the Confederate Navy; was in the war on the Carolina coast, and at the battle of Sailors Creek, April 6, 1865, was captured and held as a prisoner on Johnson's Island, and pardoned at the close of the war.

He then settled in Baltimore where he actively engaged in business for the remainder of his life. He married to Caroline Brooks, of Baltimore, and died at the home of his daughter, Mrs. Gibson, near that city, June 25, 1927. He came of noted Lincoln County stock, and was a splendid and influential man.

At a memorial service held in Lincolnton, June 2, 1927, for Lincoln County war dead, under the auspices of the American Legion, Judge L. E. Rudisill presided and Congressman A. L. Bulwinkle delivered the address.

Mrs. John Rees placed the wreath for the soldiers of the Revolution; J. M. Reinhardt, for the Civil War dead; Harry Page for the Spanish American; and Fitzhugh Hoyle for the World War dead.

Judge Rudisill then read a list of World War soldiers, who died during the war or since peace was declared, as follows:

1. Private Meade Ewing, son of J. B. Ewing, of Ironton township, died at Vancouver, Washington, March 6, 1918.
2. Private David Milo Wright, son of J. A. J. Wright, Lincolnton, Route 1, killed in action in France, May 29, 1918. Lincoln County's first loss on the field of battle.
3. Private Freeman Henkle, son of S. C. Henkle, of Lowesville, killed in action in France. Date undetermined.
4. Private Thomas Garland, son of Stephen Garland, Long Shoals, died of disease in France. Date undetermined.
5. Private Paul Cornwell, son of J. H. Cornwell, served overseas. Date of death unknown.
6. Private Clyde Workman, son of W. P. Workman, deceased. Died in camp. Date unknown.
7. Private Bidwell Loftin, son of O. C. Loftin, Long Shoals, killed in action in Belgium, August 10, 1918. Member Company M, 120th Infantry, 30th Division.
8. Private Jesse Craven Wingate, son of W. J. Wingate, died of pneumonia in France, October 1, 1918. Member 31st Division.
9. Private Morris Summey, son of J. M. E. Summey, Ironton township, died of disease at Camp Hancock, Georgia, October 16, 1918.
10. Private Ralph Davis, died in action in France, 1918.
11. Private Furman Martin, son of W. P. Martin, Lincolnton, died at Knotty Ash Camp Hospital, England, November 22, 1918.
12. Lieutenant John Bethea Mallard, son of John Mallard, deceased, died December 20, 1920.
13. Private Grady Bess, died in 1922.
14. Captain John R. Cornwell, son of the late Thomas Cornwell, drowned August 11, 1922. Served overseas.
15. Lieutenant Arthur Lackey, son of J. M. Lackey, deceased, shot while on duty with police force at Greenville, S. C., and died March 4, 1925.
16. Captain Fabius Busbee Shipp, died November 6, 1925, at Fort Huachuca, from injuries received in polo game. He was a son of Lieutenant William E. Shipp, U. S. A., killed in action in Spanish American War.
17. Dr. Gordon B. Crowell, son of Dr. Lester A. Crowell, of Lincolnton, died May 9, 1926. He served in Medical Corps overseas in World War.

THE ANNALS OF LINCOLN COUNTY 387

18. Private Alonzo G. Mauney, died at Oteen hospital, December, 1926.

19. Private John Crooks, son of H. J. Crooks, died in hospital in New York, in 1924.

20. Private Albert E. Shuford, died February 28, 1919.

21. Private Charles Carpenter (colored) son of Alexander Carpenter, of Lincolnton, died of disease in Camp Dix, N. J., November 25, 1918.

22. Private Robert Finger (colored) served overseas in World War. Died April, 1926.

1928

Herbert Hoover was elected President by a great majority in the Electoral College over Alfred E. Smith.

Bishop W. A. Guerry, of the Diocese of South Carolina, was related to Lincolnton by his marriage to Miss Annie McBee, daughter of V. A. McBee, on November 27, 1889. He was born in Clarendon County, S. C., July 7, 1861, was educated at the University of the South at Sewanee, Tenn., where he received the A.M. degree in 1884, and the B.D. degree in 1891; was prominent in the counsels of the Episcopal Church, served in various fields as rector and as college professor until 1908, when he was made Bishop of S. C., which honored position he held until his tragic death on June 9, 1928, when he was shot down by a demented priest who took his own life after mortally wounding the good Bishop.

In August, 1928, near the old Dutch Meeting House, close by Machpelah Presbyterian church in Catawba Springs township, a boulder was erected in honor of Jacob Forney, the pioneer, and his wife, Maria Bergner, bearing the following inscription:

"In memory of Jacob Forney, French Huguenot and pioneer, born in Alsace in 1721, died in North Carolina, 1806, and his wife, Maria Bergner."

Many of their descendants were present. The principal address was delivered by Judge Wilson Warlick, of Newton. Others who spoke were Curtis Bynum, of Asheville, Miss Kate C. Shipp, of Lincolnton; E. J. Forney and Dr. E. L. Stamey, of Greensboro.

An organization of the descendants was then effected and Miss Kate C. Shipp was elected president; Mrs. J. Ed Reinhardt, 1st vice-president; Mrs. Susan Wilfong, 2nd vice-president; Mrs. George A. Brown, secretary-treasurer; Curtis Bynum, historian.

Miss Angie Caldwell, daughter of the late Dr. Elam Caldwell, a gentle woman, a cultured teacher, who gave her life to teaching, died in 1928, aged 81 years. She died beloved by all who knew her and left an impress for good upon the many young people who came under her influence in and out of the classroom. The value of such a life can not be estimated. It is an unending influence.

Charles A. Jonas, of Lincolnton, was elected to Congress from the ninth district in November, 1928, over A. L. Bulwinkle, by about 3,043 majority, the first Lincoln man to represent the district in the United States Congress since 1841, when Major H. W. Connor retired after twenty years of service.

Mr. Jonas, a native of Lincoln County, was born August 14, 1876, near Reepsville, the section of the County which produced many other notable men, such as Dr. R. L. Abernethy, Prof. J. M. Bandy, Dr. Chas. L. Coon, Judge A. L. Quickel, Dr. L. A. Crowell, and others. His grandfather, Daniel Jonas, a substantial citizen of that section, was a soldier of the Confederacy, killed in action, and whose fortune was swept away leaving his family in the post war period in poor financial condition.

His father, Cephas A. Jonas (who married Martha Scronce, daughter of Conrad Scronce) on account of the desolation following that war, was like most of the people of that trying period, forced to struggle for existence, but self-reliant and industrious, he rented land and it was in his tenant farm house that his son, Chas. A. Jonas, was born. By hard work and rigid economy he finally saved money to buy a farm of his own, but the income from it was sufficient only to support a growing family, and however anxious he was to educate his children, he had no surplus money with which to make that important investment.

Young Charlie had a bright mind and was encouraged by his father to make a real man of himself. He first attended the short term Laurel Hill public school in winter months. In 1896-97, for two years, he literally worked his way at Ridge

Academy, conducted at Henry, in Howard's Creek township, by Rev. Jacob Wessinger, the pastor of Trinity and Cedar Grove Lutheran churches, after which, for two more years, he attended Fallston Institute, in Cleveland County, when S. C. Thompson, of Burlington, was principal, assisted by Miss Sallie Wilson, a Lincoln County girl, who later married William Newton, of Shelby. She was an inspiration to the young student and kindled the spark of ambition in his soul.

At the end of the two years his teacher advised him to go to the State University and when he arrived there in September, 1899, he had but forty dollars, but he had faith and determination, and worked his way through, doing all kinds of honest work to meet his expenses, and at the same time made good grades and completed the full four-year College course in only three years. At one time during his last year he was discouraged for lack of funds, for he had but two dollars to his name. Prof. W. D. Toy encouraged him to stay and offered to give him fifty dollars to help out, but young Jonas, poor as he was, and as much as he appreciated the interest and generosity of the good professor, could not sacrifice his self-respect and accept a free gift, but finally did receive the money as a loan, for which he gave his note, and paid it back out of the first money he made after he left College.

He was an apt scholar from the time he entered High School to the end of his college course. When only a Freshman in the University he won the Dialectic Society Debaters medal and in his Junior year, the Inter-Society medal as the best debater of the four representatives from the two Societies.

It is good fortune for a boy to be born poor and these struggles in the early life of a courageous young man are emphasized to show that adverse conditions can be conquered, and that it is not ill fortune to be born without money if one has character, faith, and a lofty purpose, for

> *"Human strength and human greatness*
> *Come not from life's sunny side,*
> *Heroes must be more than driftwood*
> *Floating on a waveless tide."*

In June, 1902, he graduated with honor from the University in the class with Marvin Stacy, later dean and acting president of the University, Dr. Chas. E. Maddry, famous Baptist divine, Ivey Lewis, dean of the University of Virginia, and others who achieved distinction in various fields of activity. In August following he married Miss Rosa Petrie, an alumna of Lenoir College, and during the four years following they taught in Winston city schools, Mount Holly and Dallas, in the order mentioned. He organized and served as Superintendent of Graded Schools in both Mount Holly and Dallas until 1906. During the four years he studied law, spending the summers at the University Law School, was admitted to the bar in 1906 and settled in Lincolnton. His prospects were discouraging at the start, for clients were few and fees small, but in time he prospered. From 1907 to 1910 he was Postmaster in Lincolnton, when he resigned to give full time to his growing law business.

From 1915 to 1918 (two terms) he was State Senator from the Lincoln-Catawba district; for several years he was Attorney for the City of Lincolnton; Assistant United States Attorney from 1921 to 1925, when he resigned; member of the Board of Trustees of the State University since 1917; North Carolina member of the Republican National Committee since 1927; member from Lincoln in State House of Representatives, 1927 and 1935; member of Congress from ninth district, 1929 to 1931; United States District Attorney, 1931-32, a recess appointment made by President Hoover. In all of these positions he served with credit and acceptability. He took high rank in Congress for a new member and rendered good service for the district, and against opposition secured the large appropriation required to build the extensive addition to the Charlotte post office.

He is a public-spirited and patriotic citizen of rare mental ability and moral courage—one of the notable men of North Carolina. He ranks high as a lawyer, is a wise legal counselor, an able advocate before the jury and commands an extensive and lucrative law practice. He is a logical, forceful and persuasive speaker and sometimes extraordinarily compelling in argument. He made many speeches favoring the 18th Amendment to the Federal Constitution in 1933, and a notable Charlotte lawyer said the speech Mr. Jonas made in Mecklenburg was the ablest prohibition address he had ever heard.

Like most men who have succeeded in the highest sense Mr. Jonas had a good ancestral background. His forebears were industrious, honest and spiritual-minded people. The Jonas, Lohr, Killian, Hanks, and Scronce families all stood high as sturdy, honest, patriotic and religious folks and he inherited the splendid traits of this German lineage. He is an active official member of the Methodist church in Lincolnton, has frequently been a delegate to the Annual Conference and was a lay delegate to the last General Conference held in May, 1934, in Jackson, Miss. The General Conference is the law-making body of the Methodist church.

He has three children:

1. Celeste, a graduate of the Woman's College of North Carolina (Greensboro), was a teacher prior to her marriage to L. T. Gibson, a banker of Gibson, N. C.

2. Charles Raper, who made a fine record as a University student and was honored with the position of President of the Student Body, and was one of the Inter-Collegiate debaters. He was admitted to the bar in June, 1928, is a good lawyer and partner of his father in Lincolnton. He married Annie Elliott Lee, daughter of the late Dr. R. E. Lee, who was a Lincolnton physician.

3. Donald, who also graduated at the State University and made a good record there. He holds the position of sales manager for the Johnston chain of cotton mills, with offices in Charlotte. He married Annie, daughter of the late Sheriff A. P. Willis, of Lincolnton.

It is an interesting fact that when the great leader of the Reformation, Martin Luther, died in February, 1546, Dr. Justus Jonas, who was one of his faithful disciples at Wittenberg, delivered the funeral oration. This Justus Jonas cannot be connected with the Jonas and Wittenberg families that came to this section about 1760, except that they were Germans and strong in the Lutheran faith.

The pioneer, Simon Jonas, with his family, together with the Wittenberg family, settled on Lyles Creek, near the present town of Conover before 1761, for the record shows that Simon Jonas in 1761 received a grant for 500 acres of land from Lord Granville, and by 1794 had secured a boundary of about 1,000 acres on Lyles Creek.

From Manuscript Records in office of Secretary of State (See *Colonial Records*, Vol. 9—Pages 91-92) is found the petition for a new county west of the Catawba River, signed by Simon Jonas, William Wittenberg, Joseph Wittenberg, John Connally, Joshua Perkins, John Dobson, Adam, Samuel and Ute Sherrill, and many others, which indicates that in 1762, soon after Simon Jonas and the Wittenbergs settled on Lyles Creek, they were active supporters of the forward movement in the community.

This Simon Jonas had, among other children, a son, John Jonas, who married Nancy Dobson; one daughter, who married William Wittenberg, and another who married into the Killian family. Another son of Simon Jonas, according to J. Y. Killian, the historian of the Killian family, married Mary, daughter of Andreas Killian, and they had a son, John Jonas, Jr., called "Little John Jonas" (to distinguish him from other Johns in the Jonas family). Some of the Jonas tribe moved West and settled in Kentucky, and the tradition is that one of these froze to death as the party was crossing the mountain at a point now known as Jonas Ridge, about 30 miles north of Morganton.

John Jonas, Jr. (Little John) did not go with that party but moved over to Indian Creek in Lincoln County, and there, in 1810, met and married Euphronia Lohr, or Lore, daughter of Valentine Lohr, a patriot soldier of the Revolution, who had but recently arrived from Pennsylvania and settled in the Reepsville or Trinity community, and was the ancestor of the numerous Lohr families of this section. John Jonas, Jr., and his wife, Euphronia Lohr, are the ancestors of all the Jonas tribe now living in this section.

Their children were:

1. Daniel Jonas, who married, February 20, 1849, Adeline, daughter of Richard Hanks.

2. John; 3. Abel, who married Catherine Sain, February 15, 1838.

4. Andrew; 5. Katie, who married Henry Shitle, November 15, 1836.

6. Rebecca, who married Adam Canipe; 7. Amy, who married Marcus Roderick, April 10, 1847.

8. Henry, who married Elizabeth Bangle, January 31, 1839.

Daniel Jonas, the eldest son of John, Jr., had six children, among whom was Cephas A. Jonas, who married Martha, daughter of Conrad Scronce, a large landowner, Confederate veteran and Lutheran of the Daniels Church community.

The children of Cephas A. Jonas were:

1. Alice, married Pinckney Workman, of Catawba. She died in 1906.

2. Chas. A., married Rosa Petrie, daughter of Michael and Eliza (Yoder) Petrie.

3. Henry, married Mamie, daughter of Chas. A. Leonard, of Reepsville.

4. Robert, married Alice, daughter of Luther Bangle, of West Lincoln.

5. Harvey A., prominent Lincolnton lawyer and one time Judge of the Recorder's Court, married Maude, daughter of Edward Crowell and granddaughter of the late Dr. Eli Crowell.

6. Lucy, married John Harding, of Mocksville, N. C.

7. Perry, married Minnie, daughter of P. A. Reep, for whom Reepsville was named.

8. Effie, married Zeb Saine, son of the late Jacob Saine.

9. Kate, married Dennis Hoover, son of Tom Hoover and grandson of Edney Hoover of the Reepsville community.

1929

When the Great War closed with the signing of the Armistice on the night of November 11, 1918, wild joy was heard in every nook and corner of the civilized world. During the four years of brutal slaughter the blood of ten million men from all the nations had flowed down in the same furrows to enrich the soil of Belgium and France at the cost of anguish and distress of millions of mothers and orphans of all lands. Now that hostilities had ceased all peoples rejoiced in the groundless hope that the "War to end wars" had brought permanent peace, not realizing that a peaceful world can never be established by force.

The hatreds engendered by that war are still alive and the nations of Europe, filled with jealousy and suspicion are prepared at the least provocation to renew the struggle for greed and territorial expansion. War means not only the development of human hate, the destruction of human life and the loss of the accumulated wealth created through generations of toil and sacrifice, but moral bankruptcy, for the heaviest penalties that have followed every war are lower moral ideals and degenerate conceptions of life and duty. In Europe the flower of the young manhood was destroyed and the freedom of opportunity for which they struggled is now in many countries only a memory.

When hostilities ceased America was richer materially than ever before, because the Great War created a market for American produce from field and factory far beyond our capacity to supply, and at prices greater than we had ever known. Wealth was rapidly created in all commercial lines; wages for labor had increased more than fourfold; the standard of living for the average man was higher than that of 15th Century Kings. Money was cheap, credit was boundless and there was developed a quality of extravagance and prodigal waste, which naturally tended to inflate pride, weaken faith and cause the moral thermometer to fall to a low degree.

There was great joy when the war ended, but we forgot that whatever men or nations sow, that shall they also reap. When America entered the Great War in April, 1917, our young men to the number of 4,000,000 were called to the colors and half of these saw service across the sea, where the bodies of thousands of these brave lads lie buried in unknown graves and under foreign skies. Millions more, who were not conscripted, were attracted from the farms, found employment in the cities and industrial communities, but when peace was declared very few of these returned to farm life.

The world markets were ours when the battle raged, but were lost when peace came, and it was then that our financial troubles began. Europe was bankrupted on account of losses incurred in the war and had no money to pay for our surplus goods, nor to repay the billions borrowed from our Government during the war. Even then the powerful momentum of our prosperity could not be stopped in a day, and we kept on living at a fast rate, and instead of paying debts when money was easy we pyramided debt with greater debt. The people, led to believe that the Federal Reserve System (great as it is) was a permanent panacea against hard times, lived like the rich fool who thought the chief end of life was to "eat, drink and be merry," forgetful of the scriptural truth that "man shall not live by bread alone." Farms and factories continued to produce even when the demand was on the wane, until forced to reduce the output and close the shops. Then wages for the workman stopped with the result that distress and want became general throughout the county.

In October, 1929, the crash came, banks closed, fortunes melted away and dire calamity stalked abroad. If this was our greatest panic—greater than the financial misfortunes of 1873 and 1893 and the years following—it is on account of the drift of population from the farms to industrial centers after the Great War began.

THE ANNALS OF LINCOLN COUNTY

The farmer generally has some corn in the crib, a pig in the pen, cows, chickens and garden truck, and can get along in some fashion in spite of panic, but when wage workers in the cities are idle, the pay stops and they are dependent, unless they have in prosperous times laid aside a part of their earnings for the rainy day.

It will be a long time before the financial crash of 1929, and the trying years following, are forgotten, but it all came as naturally as that harvest follows sowing.

The Sesquicentennial of the organization of Lincoln County was celebrated in Lincolnton in October, 1929. A large crowd was present at the Home-Coming, and Hoke Smith, of Georgia, delivered the address.

At Sherrill's Ford on August 2, 1929, a huge boulder was unveiled which bears the following inscription:

"This Boulder Commemorates the Crossing of the Catawba River by Adam Sherrill, the Pioneer, with his eight sons and others in 1747, at the ford which bears his name. Erected by his descendants, August 2, 1929."

The address was delivered by William L. Sherrill.

Henry Barkley came from Pennsylvania in the early days and settled in Rowan County. His son, Robert Barkley, came to Lincoln County from Rowan about 1780 and settled on Little Mountain Creek, about two miles from the present town of Denver, and he was the ancestor of all of the Barkley name in this section.

He was a patriot of the Revolution and fought at Ramsour's Mill, Cowan's Ford and Kings Mountain. His wife was Eleanor Cathey to whom he married about 1775, and among their children were:

1. Henry Barkley, II, born August 20, 1777. He married Mary Cawthorn and they had seven children. He was a soldier in the War of 1812, and died July 18, 1869.
2. Archibald C. Barkley.
3. Mary Barkley.
4. Avis Barkley.
5. James Barkley.

The Robert Barkley Historical Association was organized at the Barkley reunion held at Rock Springs Campground on July

28, 1926. Later a handsome monument was placed in Unity Presbyterian graveyard and unveiled with appropriate ceremony July 31, 1929.

The stone bears the following inscription:

> ROBERT BARKLEY
> PIONEER
> SOLDIER OF THE REVOLUTION
> AND HIS WIFE
> ELEANOR CATHEY
> ERECTED BY HIS DESCENDANTS
> 1929

On the occasion of the unveiling, Congressman Chas. A. Jonas, an honorary member of the Association, delivered an interesting speech, following the business session. In the afternoon Senator A. W. Barkley, of Kentucky, arrived from Washington, was introduced by Mr. Jonas and in an address traced his ancestry back to Robert Barkley, the pioneer. His speech was on the Barkley family history; he said a Barkley was a Chief Lieutenant of William the Conqueror, and that former Vice-President Adlai E. Stevenson, was closely related to the Barkley family.

For one hundred and fifty years the Barkley family has been prominent in the history of Lincoln County. They have been sturdy, law abiding, religious and patriotic citizens from the time Robert Barkley came to the County in the early days.

The Federal Census reports give the cotton statistics for Lincoln County from 1839 to 1929, as follows: In 1839 Lincoln County, which then embraced the Counties of Lincoln, Gaston, Catawba and a part of Cleveland, produced 1,479,396 pounds of lint cotton, which was equal to nearly 2,959 bales.

Prior to the next census the County was divided, which explains the reduced production which in 1849 was only 506 bales. In 1859 it dropped to 367 bales, and in 1869, to 242 bales. In 1879 the production grew to 2,945 bales; in 1889 the census reported 3,584 bales; 1899, it grew to 5,124 bales; in 1909 the increase was to 6,446 bales; in 1919 the report was 8,333 bales; in 1929, the largest ever reported, 22,971 bales.

According to gin reports published in the *Charlotte Observer* of March 24, 1935, the production in 1933 was 15,727, and in 1934 it dropped to 13,985 bales.

Burton Craige Wood, born in Lincoln County, June 25, 1853, was educated at Rutherford College, married November 2, 1876, to Mary E. Hill (1854-1884), a daughter of Captain John F. Hill, who served in the Civil War in Company E, 34th N. C. Regiment. His second marriage was to Miss Emma Hudson, of Catawba County, who died in 1928.

Mr. Wood, a popular citizen, was Register of Deeds for Lincoln County from 1888 to 1894; was again elected to the same office in 1914 and served until 1920, when on account of ill health he declined to serve longer.

During the last illness of Alfred Nixon he acted as Deputy Clerk of the Superior Court and after the death of Mr. Nixon, until a new clerk was appointed.

Mr. Wood was an active member of the Methodist church and when he died, May 17, 1929, his body was buried in the family plot at Zion Methodist church, west of Lincolnton.

His son, A. F. Wood, has for many years been connected with the Newton Post Office.

CHAPTER XXI

1930-1936

Charles C. Cobb (See 1913) was a Lincolnton man, who went to Texas and succeeded both professionally and materially. He was born March 15, 1859, educated in local schools and at the State University from which he graduated in June, 1880, in the class with Gov. Charles B. Aycock, Gov. Locke Craig and Judge A. L. Coble; then for two years he took the law course at the Dick and Dillard Law School in Greensboro, was licensed as a lawyer in January, 1883, for a year practiced law in Shelby and in January, 1884, went to Dallas, Texas, where he and John Morehead Avery from Morganton, N. C., were law partners for forty years.

They were good lawyers and built up a large general practice. He made a good reputation as a land title lawyer; was also a good business man with wise judgment and amassed a large estate, which demanded so much of his time that he abandoned the practice of law to attend to his private affairs.

On August 15, 1927, he married Nancy, daughter of Henry and Sallie Glenn (Shaw) Fairley, of Rockingham, N. C. As age advanced his health gave way and he died in Dallas, Texas, April 7, 1930, and the body was buried in Riverside Cemetery in Asheville, N. C.

The Gamble Clinic, Inc., was established in June, 1930, by Doctors J. F. and J. R. Gamble. The first patient was Elizabeth Asbury, daughter of Van and Lona Asbury. (Acute appendicitis operation.)

This hospital was re-organized under the Duke Endowment April 1, 1933. It is now incorporated as Reeves Hospital, a non-profit institution operated by a Board of Trustees, with Dr. J. R. Gamble as Superintendent. The Reeves Hospital, Inc., rents the building from the Gamble Clinic, Inc., in which the stock is held mainly by Dr. J. R. Gamble.

An addition was made to the building in 1934, making it a twenty-five-bed hospital. It is well equipped with an up-to-date X-ray machine and Laboratory. The Operating Room and sterilizing equipment are among the most modern in the State.

The active medical staff is composed of Dr. T. C. Bost, of Charlotte, Surgeon in Chief; Dr. J. R. Gamble, Supt., and Resident Surgeon; Dr. W. V. Costner, Dr. W. G. Bandy, Dr. J. F. Gamble, associate staff.

Mrs. John A. Seagle, of Lincoln, is known as the lady who makes the old fashioned wool coverlets and she finds demand for her product over the State and in many other States. In 1930 she was 77 years old but began to make these bedspreads in her seventeenth year. During the 60 years past she has woven many thousands of them. In 1929 she made and sold seventy-seven of these beautiful spreads. In the olden days nearly every family possessed woven wool bedspreads, but in the latter days weaving has become almost a lost art, but Mrs. Seagle in 1930 could not supply the demand for her bedspreads.

The Sesquicentennial of the Battle of Ramsour's Mill was celebrated in Lincolnton, June 20, 1930, with an interesting program. Hon. Chas. A. Jonas delivered the principal address, which was preceded with a five-minute speech by William L. Sherrill, who briefly covered the prominent facts in the life of Col. Francis Locke, the Commander of the Whig forces in that battle. Among others taking part in the program were Miss Kate Shipp, Mrs. George A. Brown and Judge Wilson Warlick. Perhaps the largest crowd ever assembled in Lincolnton attended.

Immediately following the addresses a stone commemorating the battle was unveiled on the north side of the public square and the inscription thereon follows:

"Half a mile north from here was fought the Battle of Ramsour's Mill, between the Whigs and the Tories, June 20, 1780.

"Col. Francis Locke commanded the Whig Army.
"This tablet is placed by the Jacob Forney Chapter D. A. R., June 20, 1930."

The descendants of Jacob Plonk, a Revolutionary hero, gathered on Tuesday, July 15, 1930, at the old Plonk homestead, three miles from Lincolnton, to celebrate the 78th birthday of Joseph Plonk, a descendant of the pioneer, Jacob Plonk.

At the same time the Jacob Forney Chapter, of the Daughters of the American Revolution, unveiled a marker at the grave of Jacob Plonk with appropriate ceremonies. The marker, a handsome bronze tablet, was given by Calvin Plonk, of Hickory. Jacob Plonk, with his brother, Peter, came to America from

Germany, before the Revolution and settled in this section and both married into the Kiser family.

The land on which Jacob Plonk settled was granted him by King George III., shortly after they reached America. The tract has never been out of the possession of the family and is now owned by P. C. Chapman, a descendant of the pioneer.

Many friends and relatives gathered for the ceremonies and the picnic dinner and addresses were delivered by Judge A. L. Quickel and Kemp B. Nixon.

Rev. James C. Postelle of the Methodist church lived in Lincolnton during his early life; son of the late Rev. James H. Postelle, one time of the South Carolina Conference; grandson of Rev. John Postelle, another South Carolina minister; and great grandson of Captain John Postelle who was in Francis Marion's Brigade in the War of the Revolution. The mother of Mr. Postelle was Cornelia (Wilson) Postelle, a niece of Joseph Wilson, the brilliant lawyer and State Solicitor of the old Salisbury district from 1823 to 1833. Mr. Postelle was an active minister from 1886 until his retirement from active service.

He was born in York, S. C., October 21, 1854, married to Miss Martha Frances Cook of Surry County, N. C., in 1889, served as pastor in many churches in Tennessee and Western Carolina for more than forty years and died in Lenoir, N. C., June 23, 1930.

Population of Lincoln County from 1790 to 1930. Official figures from Federal Census Bureau:

1790—Whites, 8,384; Slaves, 935—Total 9,319
1800—Whites, 11,119; Slaves, 1,523; Free blacks, 18—Total 12,660
1810—Whites, 13,862; Slaves, 2,489; Free blacks, 8—Total 16,359
1820—Whites, 14,791; Slaves, 3,329; Free blacks, 27—Total 18,147
1830—Whites, 17,506; Slaves 4,882; Free blacks, 67—Total 22,455
1840—Whites, 19,658; Slaves, 5,386; Free blacks, 116—Total 25,160

At that time Lincoln had more population than any other county in the State.

Between the years 1840 and 1850 Catawba and Gaston Counties were created and the Census figures from and including 1850 give the population of the present County of Lincoln:

1850—Whites, 5,655; Slaves, 2,055; Free blacks, 36—Total 7,746
1860—Whites, 5,999; Slaves, 2,115; Free blacks, 81—Total 8,195
1870—Whites, 6,814; Colored, 2,759—Total 9,573

1880—Whites, 8,180; Colored, 2,881—Total..11,061
1890—Whites, 10,028; Colored, 2,558—Total..12,586
1900—Whites, 12,537; Colored, 2,961—Total..15,498
1910—Whites, 14,335; Colored, 2,797—Total..17,132
1920—Whites, 15,630; Colored, 2,231—Total..17,862
                                                                  Includes 1 Mexican
1930—Whites, 19,550; Colored, 3,321—Total..22,872
                                                                  Includes 1 Chinaman

The 1930 population by townships is as follows: Lincolnton township, 8,789, of which 3,781 are in the incorporated city of Lincolnton; North Brook, 4,042; Howard's Creek, 3,730; Ironton, 3,524; Catawba Springs, 2,787. Total, 22,872. Number of farms in the county, 2,449.

1931

Huke Smith, of Atlanta, Georgia, died at his home in that city, November 27, 1931. He was born, September 2, 1855, in Newton, where his father, Hosea Hildreth Smith, was President of Catawba College. He was a student at the Lincolnton Academy, 1869-1871, when his father taught here, moved to Atlanta in 1872, married in 1883 to Birdie, daughter of Gen. T. R. R. Cobb, of Georgia; married 2nd time, 1924, Mazie Crawford. He was admitted to the bar in 1873, and practiced law for 31 years; Proprietor of the *Atlanta Journal*, 1887-1896; Secretary of the Interior in Cleveland's cabinet, 1893-96, when he resigned to support Bryan for the Presidency. Governor of Georgia two terms, 1907-09 and 1911-13, and Senator in Congress ten years, from 1911 to 1921. His mother was a daughter of Michael Hoke (1810-1844), a distinguished son of Lincoln County. (See 1844, 1853, 1871, 1912.)

John K. Cline, an active and influential citizen of Lincolnton, served the County as Sheriff for twelve years (1892-94 and 1898-1908), and was the Lincolnton postmaster from March 11, 1914, to January 10, 1923. He died in 1931, aged 75 years.

Charles H. Rhodes died in his 65th year in 1931. He served the County as Sheriff from 1894 to 1898, after which he engaged in business in Lincolnton until his death. He was a model citizen and a loyal churchman of the Lutheran faith. (See 1921.)

Blair Jenkins, son of the late James C. and Barbara (Schenck) Jenkins, died in Lincolnton suddenly January 14,

1931, aged 68 years. His father was a Lincolnton merchant from about 1850 until his death in 1880, and two sons, Blair and Hugh, took the business over as partners and conducted a high class dry goods store for many years following.

Blair Jenkins was an enterprising and public-spirited citizen, a loyal member of Saint Luke's Episcopal Church, in which he served for some years as Senior Warden. He had a genial disposition, was familiar with Lincoln County history and withal was a lovable man and devoted to his friends. He married first to Sallie Hunt McKenzie, of Rowan. Second, to Mary, daughter of the late B. H. Sumner; they had four sons: James, who is a prominent insurance man of Charlotte; Blair, Jr., who holds a responsible position with the Bell Telephone Co., in Raleigh; William S., Professor of Political Science in our State University, and Hugh B., now in Government Air Service in Pensacola, Florida.

The following authentic and interesting story relating to the well-known Lutz family was furnished by Rev. W. A. Lutz, a prominent minister of the Lutheran Church. Dr. Lutz is now retired from active work and lives in Salisbury.

"Brief History of the Lutz Family in North Carolina.

"Two brothers, George and Jacob Lutz, who came to America on an English ship in 1752, first settled in Berks County, Pennsylvania, and in 1756 came to North Carolina. George Lutz bought 200 acres of land on Jacob's Fork, about a mile south of Grace Church in what was later Tryon, and later still, Lincoln County. It is now known as the Daniel Lutz farm.

"Jacob Lutz bought a farm of 200 acres on Bett's branch, a tributary of Clark's Creek, two miles west of Newton, afterwards known as the Miles Thornberg home. This home was built in 1775 of hewed logs, and stood until it was torn down a few years ago.

"George Lutz came to North Carolina with five small sons, (1) Jacob (who was my grandfather); (2) Daniel; (3) George; (4) Ephraim; (5) David. Some years later David moved to Indiana; George moved to the Valley of Virginia; Ephraim went back to Pennsylvania and later moved to Kentucky. My grandfather, Jacob Lutz, had three sons and five daughters. He gave a home to each one of his children. Daniel built a home eight miles west of Lincolnton and lived there. He was a charter member of Trinity Lutheran Church and had four sons and six daughters. The sons were Eli, Ambrose, Ephraim and Manlius.

"From these two, Jacob, who was my grandfather, and his son, Daniel Lutz, have sprung all the Lutz name in North Carolina. Jacob Lutz, Senior, the pioneer, sold his farm to my grandfather, Jacob Lutz (son of George Lutz, the pioneer) and bought 1,000 acres on Pinch Gut Creek and 6,000 acres on Clark's Creek. He and his wife and one son were buried in the Lutz graveyard near Maiden, N. C. All of his descendants moved to Jefferson County, Indiana, soon after Indiana was admitted as a State.

Signed, W. A. Lutz."

The facts above were furnished by Dr. Lutz in 1931.

1932

Franklin D. Roosevelt was in November elected to the Presidency by a record breaking majority over Herbert Hoover.

Charles E. Childs, son of the late Eben and Marietta Sheldon Childs, died at the age of 75. He was educated at the Lincolnton Academy and the Charlotte Military Academy. Engaged in mercantile business with his father, Eben Childs (See 1900), was Clerk of Superior Court from 1886 to 1894 when he was licensed to practice law. Was, as a lawyer, painstaking and accurate in the preparation of legal papers and a wise counsellor. He was successful in all his business ventures. He married first to Miss Eva Finch, who died early. His second marriage, August 28, 1884, was to Miss Katie Motz, daughter of Wade H. and Jane Johnson Motz, late of Lincolnton. Their children were: Chas. E. Childs, Jr., of New York, married Evelyn Lane, of N. Y.; Bessie, married Drayton Wolfe, of Charlotte (both deceased); Susie, married W. H. Truesdale; Wade Hampton, married Miriam Johnston of Atlanta; Fred Sherwood, married Maude Hall of Fayetteville, N. C.

Dr. James M. Templeton, a native of Lincolnton, died at his home in Cary, N. C., in 1932, in his 76th year. He was recognized as a skilled physician and was a prominent member of the State Medical Society. From his youth he was a strong advocate of temperance and when a boy in his teens was active in municipal campaigns in his support of the dry ticket, by writing temperance articles for the town paper and by public addresses in advocacy of the dry cause. He early aligned with the Prohibition party and was its candidate for Governor in 1896. Two of his sons, Alfred J. and James M. Templeton, Jr., are practicing attorneys in Raleigh.

At the old McCorkle graveyard, two miles north of Denver, a huge boulder was unveiled September 2, 1932, in memory of Major Francis McCorkle, a Revolutionary patriot, and his wife, "Betsy" Brandon, and bears the following inscription: "In memory of Major Francis McCorkle (1741-1802) a soldier of the American Revolution, who fought at Ramsour's Mill, Kings Mountain, and other battles. Here also rests the body of his second wife, Elizabeth Brandon (1761-1801), who shared his trials and triumphs. She was a daughter of Richard and Margaret Locke Brandon, of Rowan County. Erected by their descendants, 1932."

Some three hundred of their descendants were present and addresses were made by three of them: George McCorkle, of Washington, Judge Wilson Warlick, of Newton, and William L. Sherrill, of Charlotte.

Miss Kate C. Shipp, younger daughter of Judge William M. and Catherine (Cameron) Shipp, was born in Hendersonville, March 18, 1859, but the greater part of her life was spent in Lincolnton and Charlotte. She first attended the noted preparatory school conducted in Lincolnton by Miss Mary Wood Alexander, and later graduated from Saint Mary's School in Raleigh. She then for a while taught in the Raleigh City Schools and later at Saint Mary's (Raleigh), Charlotte City Schools, Charlotte Seminary and Presbyterian College (now Queen's) in the order named until 1900, when she and her sister, Mrs. Anna C. McBee, opened a private school in Lincolnton, called the Mary Wood School, in honor their former teacher, the late Miss Mary Wood Alexander. The school had a good patronage of both boarding and day pupils, but in 1904 it was closed for several years as Miss Shipp realized that to prepare girls for college she should herself have a College degree, so in 1904 she entered the Teachers College of Cambridge University, England, where, after two years' study a degree was conferred. Then upon her return home she taught again for a year at Saint Mary's.

With her varied experience as a teacher, combined with the benefits acquired at Cambridge, she was exceptionally well prepared to carry out her plan to found a high school for girls, where students could be prepared for entrance into colleges of highest grade. So in 1907 the celebrated Fassifern School was established in the northwestern part of Lincolnton on an elevated site overlooking the South Fork River, and on land secured from the late Robert S. Reinhardt.

There, for seven years, she and Mrs. McBee had every success and attracted pupils from many sections of this and other States. So great was the patronage that additional buildings were constructed and still there was not room.

About this time business men of Hendersonville offered liberal financial aid on condition that the school be removed to that town. This offer was accepted, larger equipment was provided and in 1914 Fassifern School was opened in Hendersonville, and it flourished wonderfully. In 1924 Mrs. McBee died and Miss Shipp, unwilling to continue by herself, sold her interest in the school to Rev. Joseph R. Sevier, who has conducted it since that time. Miss Shipp then returned to Lincolnton, the home of her childhood, to spend the remainder of her life among old friends and younger ones, who had been her students in Lincolnton. She was gladly welcomed back and the old students who held her in affectionate regard organized the Kate Shipp Alumni Association, and annual celebrations were held with their old teacher as the honored guest.

She was a lady of rare native intellect and high culture, with capacity to impart knowledge and to inspire students to reach up for lofty ideals. She knew well how to govern and control young people, and possessed rare discriminating judgment and withal that quality of business capacity, which helped her to carry on the school without financial loss.

A distinguished lawyer, who knew her well told me that she possessed such wonderful mental vigor and such qualities of leadership combined with fine judgment and general information as would have made her a great Governor of the State.

She was a Great Citizen and a patriot saturated with love for country, for State and for Lincoln County, conversant with general history, and did much to stimulate our county people, and especially the younger element, to learn and to preserve the splendid history made in peace and in war by the people of Lincoln County. She was proud of the brilliant record made by so many Lincoln people for nearly two hundred years in law, medicine, statecraft, education, agriculture, as soldiers and Christian ministers and in other fields of endeavor. She was active in every movement to perpetuate the history of Lincoln County. She led in the organization of the Jacob Forney Chapter of the Daughters of the American Revolution; was active in the 1929 homecoming in celebration of the sesquicentennial of the organization of Lincoln County, the celebration of the 150th anniversary of the Battle of Ramsour's Mill in 1930, when the tablet was unveiled on the Court Square to commemorate that battle, and the placing of the marker in East Lincoln in memory of Jacob Forney, the pioneer, and his wife, Maria Bergner.

She was a Great Teacher. She loved her calling for which she was so thoroughly qualified. It was an important part of the education of her students to associate with one so broadly cultured and who knew how to convey her knowledge to young people in such a way that they would remember it. Her instruction was mind quickening to such a point that pupils wanted to go to the bottom of a subject and know it thoroughly. Her warm magnetic nature drew the students very close to her, and it was thus easy for her to impress upon their young minds high moral ideals and intellectual aspirations. Her whole life was filled with unselfish service and her fine influence lives, not only in those she taught, but in all who knew and appreciated her fine qualities of mind and heart.

She was a Great Christian, with a great faith and in her last days endured affliction as a good soldier of Jesus Christ. On October 12, 1931, she fell and broke a hip bone and was never well afterward, suffering great pain until her release, November 12, 1932. She was a devout Episcopalian, loved her church, and was for many years an active and useful member. She had broad charity and a Christian spirit which reached out to all of every faith and order and to those without faith. When she died a great citizen, a great teacher and a great Christian entered into rest. The body was buried in the Shipp plot in St. Luke's graveyard in Lincolnton.

Walter Ney Keener graduated from Wake Forest College (in the literary department) in 1902 and finished in law at the same school in 1903. He then engaged in the practice of law and in newspaper work in Lincolnton for several years and represented Lincoln County in the Legislature of 1907. Later he was city editor of the *Raleigh Times* until 1912, after which he was on the editorial staff of the *Durham Sun, Charlotte Chronicle, High Point Enterprise* and *Wilmington Dispatch* in the order named, until September, 1918, when he became editor of the *Durham Herald,* and continued in that relation until his death in 1932.

From 1929 to 1932 he was the editor of both the *Herald* and the *Sun.*

He was born in Lincoln County, August 2, 1880, son of Elijah W. Keener, died in Durham, November 26, 1932, and his body was buried there.

The Durham Sun of November 29, 1932, pays the following high tribute to Mr. Keener: "A great editor has written his thirty. Many are called to the newspaper field. A few actually attain that thirty-third degree of the profession, the mark of the true journalist. Walter Keener was one of the few. His writing was lucid and bold, not lacking in sinew or stiletto, yet free of untoward malice or injustice. He was not distracted by the rattling of the rabble, nor blinded by camouflage, nor was he unmindful of the contentions of the other side. Temperate in all his characteristics and inherently modest, he diligently and confidently pursued the clear cut tenor of his chosen way. He was a loyal and considerate friend, an entertaining conversationalist and never narrow or overbearing."

Mr. Keener was a man of superior gifts, an editor of discriminating judgment, who exercised a fine influence and was an honored son of Lincoln County.

1933

Industrial statistics for 1933 as published by S. H. Hobbs, Dept. of Rural Social Economics, State University *News Letter,* April 17, 1933, Lincoln County:

Number of Industrial Establishments	16
Number of Wage Earners	1,409
Wages Paid	$1,719,200
Cost of Material, Fuel and Power	1,719,377
Value of Products for 1929	5,707,554
Value of Products for 1933	2,800,412
Decline in Production	2,907,142

The following figures are found in the report of the State Superintendent of Public Instruction for the scholastic year, 1932-33.

The School Population of Lincoln County is:

	White	Colored	Total
Rural	5,375	978	6,353
Lincolnton	1,431	216	1,647
	6,806	1,194	8,000

School Attendance:

	White	Colored	Total
Rural	3,819	802	4,621
Lincolnton	1,274	186	1,460
	5,093	988	6,081

White Teachers, not including principals—Rural, 111; Lincolnton, 35; Total, 146.

Value of Taxable Property—Rural, $10,413,258; Lincolnton, $4,400,000; Total, $14,813,258.

Value of School Property—Rural, $231,165; Lincolnton, $273,300; Total, $504,465.

Cost of Maintenance—Rural, $135,111; Lincolnton, $44,106; Total, $179,217.

Transportation cost for the year on 33 Busses, $17,761.

There are fifteen brick and three wooden school buildings for white people and sixteen wooden buildings for blacks. There are ten one-room school buildings in the County.

When Daniel E. Rhyne died February 25, 1933, Lincoln County lost a citizen who accomplished as much for the material advancement of the County as any other one citizen.

When he came to Lincolnton in 1887 the only manufacturers were Phifer's Factory and Tiddy's Paper Mill and the pay rolls were very small. He and his brother-in-law, J. A. Abernethy were the modern pioneers in industrial progress, in Lincoln, and to those men who led in the movement for textile growth we owe much for the business development of Lincolnton and the increase of the population of the County, from about 11,000 in 1887, to about 23,000 in 1930. Of course, there were other mill operators like R. S. Reinhardt, Edgar Love, John M. Rhodes, W. A. Mauney and others who also established industries which attracted new people who came to find employment, but Rhyne and Abernethy were very prominent in this business development.

Mr. Rhyne was a generous contributor to the building of the handsome Lutheran church on South Aspen street, and his princely gifts to Lenoir-Rhyne College place him among the notable patrons of education in North Carolina.

He was born near Mount Holly, February 8, 1852, son of Moses H. Rhyne. Like most boys in teen age after the Civil War, he was deprived of good school advantages, but despite that handicap he was well educated in the school of practical experience and was wonderfully successful in all his business ventures. He was a bachelor 81 years old when he died.

At a reunion of the Rhyne family held at the old Rhyne homestead between Dallas and Stanley in August, 1934, an interesting sketch of Jacob Rhyne, the pioneer, and some of his descendants, was read by Mrs. T. H. Hoover, as follows:

"Jacob Rhyne was the pioneer of our family in this section of the County, coming from the Palatinate, a section of Germany on the upper Rhine River. Like most of our German ancestors he came first to England, and there he shipped to America, landing in Philadelphia. He settled for a short time in York County, Pennsylvania, and then came South, making his home in what is now Gaston County, on Hoyle's Creek. It is thought that he married in Germany before sailing for America. His wife was Elizabeth Wills.

"Jacob Rhyne was a Lutheran, as are most of his descendants to this day. He attended the Dutch Lutheran Church, which was probably the first Lutheran Church established in this section. A tradition has it that he gave to this church over thirty acres of land for its location and it is also remembered in his will. He died in 1794 or 1795. If his grave is marked at all it is by a rough hewn and unlettered stone, and no one can point to the definite place where he and his wife rest.

"His original will is still preserved in the office of the Clerk of the Superior Court of Lincoln County. It is signed in German and any of his descendants may there see the signature of this, our worthy sire. On and in this will the name of Rhyne is spelled three ways. The body of the will, written supposedly by a lawyer, spells it Rine, the endorsement by the Clerk spells it Rhyne. However, the man who knew, spelled it in his native language Rein, and this means pure. Let all of us who are descendants of this pure ancestor strive in life to illustrate our name by purity of heart, thought and conduct.

"Jacob Rhyne, I, had a son, Jacob Rhyne, II, and he was born about 1740 to 1745 and died in 1825. His wife was Marie Elizabeth Best, daughter of Bastian Best and granddaughter of the pioneer, Peter Hoyle.

"Jacob Rhyne, II, had nine children, one of whom was Jonas Rhyne, born November 5, 1789. He married Annie Kiser in 1812 and settled near Reepsville in the present County of Lincoln. He died there December 24, 1858, and he and his wife are buried at Trinity Lutheran Church. Among his twelve children was our ancestor, Jacob K. Rhyne, and his twin sister, Peggy, who died single.

"Jacob K. Rhyne married Barbara Costner and lived for a short time in Lincoln County, near Reepsville, on the farm now owned by the widow of Cousin Elias Rhyne. He later moved to Gaston County, where we now hold our reunions.

"Jacob K. Rhyne had seven children. Three of them, Sarah, Ambrose and William, were born in Lincoln, while Frank, Mary, Ellis and Thomas were born in Gaston County. Tradition has it that Jacob K. Rhyne and his seven children never all at once sat at the table and ate together. This was due to his early death and to the further fact that at about the age of ten, his son returned to Lincoln County and made his home with several aunts who remained single.

"Jacob K. Rhyne's children are as follows:
"Sarah, married John C. Friday; Ambrose P. H., married Emmeline Costner; William H., married Sarah Jane Sain; Frank, married Hannah Pasour; Mary, married Lee A. Friday; Ellis, married Ella Brown, and Thomas married Lena Alexander and Beatrice Finger."

There were many other descendants of the pioneer, Jacob Rhyne, not included in the above sketch, among them Moses H. Rhyne, a substantial citizen of Gaston County, whose sons, Abel P. Rhyne, late of Mount Holly, and Daniel E. Rhyne, late of Lincolnton, were prosperous business men, who engaged largely in the cotton textile industry.

The Rhyne name stands for industry, frugality and good citizenship, and the numerous families of that name have done their full share in the development of this part of the State.

Rev. J. Frank Armstrong, pastor of the Rutherfordton Methodist Church, was killed in an automobile wreck near Raleigh, on June 15, 1933. He was born 56 years ago near Denver, Lincoln County, and his body was buried at Bethel, the church of his boyhood.

In 1933 chimes were installed in the tower of Lincolnton Lutheran Church by Mrs. Charles H. Rhodes, in memory of her husband, who died in 1931, the first and only chimes installed in the County.

1934

On June 20, 1934, one hundred and fifty-four years after the battle of Ramsour's Mill, the first monument to be placed on that once bloody field was unveiled. It is a handsome granite stone, erected in memory of three brave soldiers of the Tory army, Nicholas Warlick, his brother, Phillip Warlick, and Israel Sain. It was unveiled after appropriate remarks made by Judge Wilson Warlick (a kinsman of these brave men) and Hon. Charles A. Jonas.

The inscription on the stone follows:

"In memory of Nicholas Warlick, a loyal subject of the King, and Captain of Volunteers, who, with his brother, Philip Warlick, and Israel Sain, died in the battle of Ramsour's Mill here, and were buried in one grave, June 20, 1780. Erected by his descendants, J. M. Barnhardt, R. A. Ramsour, David, Henry and Jacob Warlick, 1934."

Beneath the tablet and embedded in the granite is a small slab which marked the grave. Carved on it are three hearts entwined, the initials N. W., P. W. and I. S., and the date, June 20, 1780.

Dr. Collier Cobb, Professor of Geology at our State University for more than forty years, was a great character, a great scholar and a great educator. He was born in Wayne County, North Carolina (son of the late Rev. Dr. Needham B. Cobb, an able minister of the Baptist Church), March 21, 1862. (See 1872.)

Collier Cobb was a precocious youth. When only ten years old, when his father was the pastor of the Baptist Church in Lincolnton, he edited and published a tiny paper called the *Home Journal,* and when fourteen he taught a school in Anson County. He was even then a skilled stenographer, who took down in shorthand the noted Vance and Settle political debates in 1876. Many a precocious youth has later met with an arrested development, but he had no such experience for his mind continued to grow to the end of his useful life. He was educated at Wake Forest, the University of North Carolina and Harvard University. At 18 he went to Chapel Hill to teach Greek and

Physical Geography and later taught in the schools of both Wilson and Waynesville. Then he entered Harvard and was a bright scholar, and paid his way there by working as a newspaper correspondent. During some of his vacation periods he worked as a telegraph operator and was at one time supply operator for the old Carolina Central Railroad.

He was a most versatile man, brilliant in many lines, an artist of superior skill, a scholar of varied gifts; he was thoroughly grounded in the classics, in the sciences, particularly in Geology which was his life study, a facile writer, contributor to various magazines and the author of many volumes, including *Where the Wind Does the Work, Human Habitations, Geography of North Carolina*, as well as various volumes relating to Geology. His great library of 10,000 volumes was one of the largest private libraries in the South.

With all his rich mental training and studious habits, he was immensely popular with the student body and University faculty, and in fact among all classes, for he never lost the common touch. He was jovial always, magnetic by nature, a fine story teller and carried a smile that was infectious. He was literally a world traveler—had visited all lands except Australia. He had eyes to see, ears to hear and a memory which never failed him, and could relate tales of China, Brazil, Russia, or South Africa as familiarly as stories from North Carolina. Many of his wise sayings were often quoted by faculty and students. One was: "We are all what we are, because we are where we are"; and another: "Each one of us is an omnibus on which all his ancestors ride."

He was a teacher of high rank and made a wonderful record for the forty-year period during which he served at the head of the Geological department at the University.

For two years prior to his death, which occurred November 28, 1934, his health was feeble, and in September, 1934, he was appointed with Dr. M. C. S. Noble and Dr. A. C. McIntosh, Kenan professor emeritus. Withal he never forgot the religious lessons taught by his good parents by the home fires in his early years. He was a Baptist in faith and for more than a score of years Superintendent of the Baptist Sunday School at Chapel Hill.

When he and I were small boys in Lincolnton we were close friends and that friendship continued through all the succeeding years. Because of his early association with Lincolnton, more than sixty years ago, this sketch is included in these ANNALS.

Laban Miles Hoffman died at his home in Dallas, Gaston County, on Sunday, February 25, 1934, at the advanced age of 88 years.

He was a lawyer, educator, manufacturer, banker, and historian, and for forty years served faithfully as Superintendent of the Lutheran Sunday School in Dallas.

He was a modest gentleman, the very soul of honor, unselfishly devoted to his people and to his country and served in many useful ways, not for personal profit, but for the common good. Gaston County and North Carolina lost a model citizen by the death of this splendid Christian man. His father was the late Jonas Hoffman, prominent Gaston man and his wife was Martha, daughter of the late Hon. David A. Jenkins, of Gaston County. (See 1886.)

Mr. Hoffman was the author of *Our Kin*, a large volume containing 585 pages, published in 1915. It contains valuable history of many families of this section of the State, beginning with the Hoffman and Jenkins families, but reaching out with genealogical accuracy, and including a very wide circle of the connections, and many of these were Lincoln County citizens, concerning whom he gives a wealth of interesting facts and family genealogies.

When Ed Lowe died at Lowesville, August 25, 1934, aged 78 years, East Lincoln lost one of its older citizens, and his body was buried at Hill Chapel graveyard near by. He was a son of the late John Washington Lowe, who served as sheriff of the County from 1848 to 1854. For many years Ed Lowe was a Lowesville merchant. The Lowe family has been prominent in the County ever since 1779 when the County was established.

David Schenck Lowe, of Belmont, who is familiar with the family and a grandson of Thomas Lowe, who was perhaps the earliest settler of the name, has furnished much of the material found in this sketch.

Thomas Lowe had a large family and died at an advanced age in 1829, according to the date on his gravestone. His will bears date, June 26, 1829, and provides landed property and one negro slave for each of the children, and to his son, Alexander, he added one black mare and a saddle.

There was a Methodist minister, the Rev. Isaac Lowe, who served as Presiding Elder in this section during the years 1791-1792 and 1793, who was probably a relative of the Lowe family of Lincoln County, for they have generally been Methodists and Isaac has been a family name among the Lowes. Mr. D. S. Lowe writes: "I can't find any record of the preacher, Isaac Lowe, but think he must have been a brother of my grandfather, Thomas Lowe."

According to the will referred to Thomas Lowe had seven sons and two daughters for these are all provided for in the will.

1. His eldest son, Isaac Lowe (1798-1880), married Nancy Kincaid, March 24, 1827.

2. Alexander Lowe, married Susanah Kincaid, February 17, 1824.

3. Greenbury Lowe, married Elvarna White, January 24, 1829.

4. Franklin Lowe, married Martha Monday, April 28, 1829.

5. John Washington Lowe, married Abigail Shelton, April 30, 1830.

6. Rufus Lowe, married Susanah Helderman, December 6, 1842.

7. There seems to be no record of marriage of the seventh son, Thomas Lowe.

Elizabeth, married Jesse Wingate, January 3, 1820, and Frances, the other daughter, married Henry Shelton, August 29, 1830. (These marriage dates are found in Bynum's "Marriage Bonds of Tryon and Lincoln Counties.")

Thomas Lowe's eldest son, Isaac Lowe, who married first to Nancy Kincaid, was, like his father, a large landowner, for the 1850 Census report shows that he then owned 2,994 acres of land besides personal property valued at more than $10,000. They had four children:

1. Col. D. A. Lowe (1825-1912), who married Margaret Melchor.

2. Jane C., married Rev. E. W. Thompson, a Methodist minister of the South Carolina Conference, December 28, 1858.
3. Martha, married Dr. Crider, a physician.
4. George, who died when ten years old.

Isaac Lowe's second marriage was to Mrs. Mary A. Cole in 1877. Their children were:

1. David Schenck Lowe, born 1878. Now a merchant of Belmont, N. C., who has furnished some of the facts connected with the family history.
2. Isaac McLean Lowe, who married a daughter of Jacob Long.

Col. D. A. Lowe (generally referred to as Col. "Aleck" Lowe) was a large landowner and for many years a Lowesville merchant. He was also prominent in county affairs, served for a long period as a Magistrate and was a member of the State Senate from Lincoln in 1899. His children were:

1. Laura, who married S. Houston Lowe, a Lowesville merchant for many years until his death in 1891.
2. Haywood, married Effie Akers. He died about 1925.
3. Sidney J. Lowe was a Charlotte business man and married a Miss McDowell of Mecklenburg County.
4. Ella, married Joseph C. Smith, a cotton manufacturer, late of Shelby.
5. Isaac C. Lowe, was for many years a Lowesville merchant and planter, and later invested in various textile companies and banks, succeeded in business and now stands high in financial circles. He married Mary Neal Mellon, and lives in Charlotte.

Col. D. A. Lowe's second marriage was to Miss Cora Henderson. By this marriage there was one child, Nancy.

John Washington Lowe (1810-1882) son of Thomas Lowe, who married Abigail Shelton had nine sons: Tullius, James, Ed, Milton, Meacom, William, George, Samuel D. and Sidney Houston. Of these Ed Lowe, who died in 1934, and Sidney Houston Lowe, who died in 1891, were Lowesville merchants.

William was a Denver merchant for many years.

Samuel D. Lowe entered the Confederate Army as a Lieutenant, August 15, 1861, was a gallant soldier, rapidly promoted in turn to the rank of Captain, Major, Lieutenant-

Colonel, until November 1, 1862, when he was commissioned Colonel. He was wounded at Gettysburg July 3, 1863. He was a merchant at Iron Station, 1870-1873; later moved to another state.

Concerning the other sons no accurate information has been secured. Doubtless some of them were soldiers of the Confederacy and were lost in military service.

Mary was the only daughter and she married Pinckney Monday, of Denver.

John Washington Lowe, the sheriff, lived and died near Denver.

The Lowes have generally been industrious, thrifty and progressive, and had the confidence and respect of the people. They cared little for public position and were so busy at gainful pursuits that they rarely sought office.

Karl Lander Lawing died after a brief illness in August, 1934. He was a lifelong citizen of Lincolnton. Was only 20 years old in 1894 when his father, Dr. John M. Lawing died, and immediately succeeded his father in the drug business, and for forty years was a druggist here. All who knew Karl Lawing loved him and his passing brought sorrow to a wide circle of friends.

1935

The Killian Family

The following is a history of the Killian family as related by J. Yates Killian, of Newton, N. C., at the first annual Killian reunion, held at Salem Lutheran and Reformed Church on August 22, 1935, and reported in *Lincoln Times* of August 25, 1935:

"On October 4, 1732, Andreas Killian landed in Philadelphia on the British ship 'Adventure.' His signature to the declaration of allegiance to the Colonial government, on a photostat copy of the page on which he signed his name, and the signature on a will made by Andreas Killian of Lincoln County, North Carolina, September 2, 1785, were made by the same person.

"Just what time Andreas Killian and his family crossed the Catawba River to the west side is not known, but the Colonial Council granted to John Killian 1,000 acres of land in Anson County on April 13, 1749, and on September 30, 1749, John Killian received another grant of 1,000 acres on

Killian Creek, south side of the Catawba River. Also on the same date, September 30, 1749, Andreas Killian received a grant of 1,850 acres on Killian Creek, and Leonard Killian, also on the same date, 1,200 acres of land on Killian Creek. Therefore it is evident that the Killians crossed to the south or west side of the Catawba River early in the year 1749, or before this year. We are of the opinion that the Sherrills, Henry Weidner, Simon Hass and the Killians came together to the east bank of the Catawba and crossed about the same time and moved in different directions to build their homes. Killian's Creek in Catawba County was named for the Killian family, on which stream this pioneer family lived until the latter part of the year 1754. For a few years when the Cherokee Indians began hostilities against the white settlers, and had some fighting with the Forneys, who, with the Hagers had entered land on Killian's Creek in 1752-53, Andreas Killian with his family moved back to the east side of the Catawba River.

"But in the year 1776 (June 26), Andreas Killian and his son, John, bought of Matias Beaver, several hundred acres of land on both sides of Clark's Creek, which is the land on the Newton-Hickory road, near Saint Paul's church, a few miles west of Newton, adjoining the Crowdertown land, but Leonard Killian continued to live on his Killian Creek land.

"Andreas Killian sold his land on Killian Creek to the Forneys and other settlers about the year 1765, the deeds being signed by him and his son, Andrew.

"Pioneer Andreas Killian probably was married twice as is evidenced in his will. His family consisted of twelve children, six boys and six girls. He made a will September 2, 1785 (which will was probated in 1788) in which he names the following children: Margaret, the oldest child, supposed to have been born about the year 1721, being eleven years old when the family came to America; she married Michael Price.

"Leonard, the oldest son, was born May 15, 1723; his wife's given name was Mary Margaret, but no record has been found of her maiden name. They had four children, or more; William, Mathias, Mary and Margaret. Leonard Killian died May 15, 1795, and was buried at Saint Paul's Church, near Newton.

"John, the third child of Andreas Killian, was born about the year 1726. He married Mrs. Elizabeth Zimmerman (Carpenter), who had a son, Michael, by her first husband. John and Elizabeth Killian's children were: a daughter, who married David Smith; Jacob, born April 8, 1760, married Rebecca Creasemore and settled on what is now the A. J.

Seagle farm near Salem Church in Lincoln County; Marellis, married Jacob Yount; John; Phillip; Mary (first married John Jonas, and had one child, John Jonas, Jr. Then she married Jacob Fey, a saddler, of Crowdertown, in 1791. Jacob Fey died in 1800, and Mary married Martin Suttlemyre in 1801. Mary Killian thus became the mother of all the Jonas clan in Lincoln and Catawba Counties, the mother of the entire Fey family in North Carolina and the mother of part of the large Suttlemyer family of this section of the State) ; Abraham; and Sarah, who married Jacob Deitz.

"Jean, the fourth child of Andreas Killian, married William Lewin (Lawing) of the Hager neighborhood.

"Crete, the fifth child of Andreas Killian, married probably a brother of pioneer William Hager, likely George Hager.

"Andrew, Jr., the sixth child of Andreas Killian, Sr., was rather a favorite of his father. They owned land together and Andreas, Sr., in his will included Andrew, Jr.'s, two sons, Andrew and David, in the division of his property. Andrew, Jr., built a mill on the waters of Liles Creek, on what is known as the Noah Rowe place.

"George was the seventh son of Andreas Killian, Sr.

"Bunia, the eighth child, married James Pritchett.

"Daniel, ninth child, is supposed to have been the oldest child of Andreas Killian's second wife, whose name was Mary, thought to have been a Miss Cline or a Miss Beaver.

"Samuel was the tenth child of Andreas Killian, Sr. He married Barbara, the youngest child of William Hager, who lived on Killian's Creek. Andreas, Sr., gave to these two sons, Daniel and Samuel, all the real estate and stipulated in his will that they were to provide for his wife (their mother) during the remainder of her life.

"Christiana, the eleventh child of Andreas, Sr., married John Barringer.

"Elizabeth, the twelfth child of Andreas, Sr., married Michael Hank. This Elizabeth was received into the Lutheran church, 'Catawber,' by the Rev. John Gottfried Arndt, June 19, 1776, and Michael Hank by the same Rev. Mr. Arndt into the South Fork Lutheran church (now Saint Paul's) in August, 1776.

"Jacob Killian, Jr., son of Jacob, son of John, son of Andreas Killian, the pioneer, married Catherine Carpenter (See 1902), and among their children were Caroline, who married Melchi Rhodes, and John, who married Ibby Wilkinson, and lived near Denver in Lincoln County.

"Andreas Killian died in the year 1788, at about the age of 85 years, and is supposed to be buried at Saint Paul's

Church. These pioneer Killians remembered the first commandment of the Bible given to man, 'Be fruitful and multiply.' Andreas had twelve children and his children were like unto him to the extent that their descendants can be found in every Southern State from Virginia to Arkansas.

"Following the address of J. Yates Killian, the clan was organized and the following officers elected: President, John Carpenter, of Maiden; Vice-President, Ramon Heafner, of Hickory; Secretary-Treasurer, J. Yates Killian, of Newton."

Dr. R. B. Killian, a general practitioner of medicine for nearly sixty years, mostly in Lincoln County, and one time representative from Lincoln in the State Legislature, died at his home on Howard's Creek, June 7, 1935, at a ripe old age.

He spent his life as a country doctor, busy at the high task of ministering to human sufferers, going day and night through cold and heat to alleviate the ills of the people and going without hope of fee or reward when they had not the means with which to pay. Such unselfish service is its own reward. (See also 1896.)

Mrs. Elizabeth (Davis) Morrison, daughter of the late D. A. Davis, of Salisbury, the pioneer banker of Western Carolina, and widow of the late Captain Joseph Graham Morrison, of Lincoln County, died at the home of her son, J. G. Morrison, the county farm agent, on December 24, 1935, aged eighty-nine years, and the funeral service and burial was at Machpelah on Christmas Day, where the body was interred by the side of the grave of her late husband, who died in 1907. Mrs. Morrison was a cultured and gentle woman, and had lived in Lincoln County since she married in early womanhood.

Robert M. Roseman, son of the late Andrew Roseman, died at his home in Lincolnton, February 4, 1935, lacking but three days of being eight-nine years old. He enlisted in the Southern Stars in April, 1861, in his seventeenth year, and when he died there were but two living veterans in the County, of the 1,300 Lincoln men, who served in the Civil War. He was a lifelong citizen of Lincolnton and for fifty years an official of the Lincolnton Presbyterian church.

David W. Robinson, son of the late sheriff J. A. Robinson and Nancy (Rhodes) Robinson, was born near Lincolnton in August, 1868. After his school days he studied law, was granted license in 1890 and practiced his profession in Lincolnton for ten years, when he moved to Columbia, S. C., and was a practicing lawyer there until his death, April 17, 1935. He possessed fine intellect, was judicially-minded, built up a lucrative practice and ranked as one of the most distinguished members of the South Carolina bar. He was not only a great lawyer but a great citizen, of whom his native county has right to be proud.

He married to Edith, daughter of William G. Childs, of Columbia, and among their children are David W. Robinson, Jr., and Miss Alice Robinson, who were trained by their father for the law and they are both Columbia lawyers now; Rev. William C. Robinson, a Presbyterian minister, a Professor in Columbia Theological Seminary, Decatur, Georgia; and Dr. Edith Robinson Schartz, who lives in Boston, Mass. They reared a fine family and trained them for capable service.

The number of teachers allotted for Lincoln County schools for the scholastic year 1935-1936 are:

For rural schools .... 126 teachers
For Lincolnton schools .... 44 teachers

Total .... 170 teachers

October 10, 1935, was a great day in Lincolnton. The whole population of the County seemed to be there and a great multitude from the regions beyond to celebrate the 150th anniversary of the establishment of the town of Lincolnton. Great preparation had been made for it. There was a grand street procession in which numerous floats portrayed interesting historical facts of a local nature in picturesque and impressive style.

While the streets were jammed with people all were in good humor and well behaved, which proved the high type of the citizenship of the County. More people were present that day than dwelt in the vast territory west of the Catawba River in 1785, and they all seemed to be filled with the spirit of the brave and adventurous ancestors of that earlier day, and proud to have a part in a celebration in honor of the patriots who laid the foundation of the State and made it possible for a great civilization to be built upon that foundation. J. Laban Lineberger was the Chief Marshal, and William A. Graham, III, Commissioner of Agriculture, the Master of Ceremonies. After the procession passed the reviewing stand which had been erected in front of the Methodist Church on Main Street various notable visitors were introduced and some of them made brief remarks, after which Governor Ehringhaus was presented and delivered an appropriate address.

It was an epochal day in the history of the County and the impressions made that day will linger long in the memory of those who were there.

We have in the century and a half since Lincolnton was established grown wonderfully in many ways and will continue to grow if, with faith, courage and patriotism such as they possessed, we go forth holding high the ideals of industry, frugality, education, love of country and love for God.

Lieut. Col. Sumner McBee Williams, U. S. Army, died suddenly late in April, 1935, at San Antonio, Texas, of a heart attack. He was acting Quarter Master of the 8th Corps and on the staff of Major General Johnson Hagood, and stationed at Fort Sam Houston.

He was a son of James T. and Sallie McBee Williams, of Greenville, S. C., and born in that city, August 23, 1885. The body was brought to Greenville for burial. He was a grandson of the late V. A. McBee, of Lincolnton. (See 1904.)

1936

James Alonzo Abernethy came from Mount Holly to Lincolnton in 1887 with Daniel E. Rhyne and they established the Laboratory Cotton Mill two miles south of Lincolnton on the South Fork River. They succeeded so well there that they built several other factories in and around Lincolnton that contributed much to the development of the community as an industrial center.

Mr. Abernethy, conservative by nature, but with rare judgment, succeeded well in nearly all his business undertakings and amassed a good fortune. He is now one of the older and highly respected citizens of the County, and has retired from active business. A Presbyterian in faith, he has been an active official and liberal contributor to the Church. He was born near Mount Holly, November 17, 1851, son of Dr. James and Mary Rankin Abernethy. When a young man he engaged in business there and on December 16, 1875 married Sarah Elizabeth, daughter of Moses H. Rhyne of that community. They had five children:

1. Lula, married J. Haywood Hull of Shelby.
2. Robert Sidney, married Mary Knox, daughter of the late Rev. Dr. R. Z. Johnston of Lincolnton.
3. John Daniel, married Grace DeBerry of Mount Gilead.
4. Mary Elizabeth, married Dr. George H. Costner of Lincolnton.
5. James Alonzo, Jr., married Edna Harris of Rutherfordton.

Mrs. Abernethy died November 14, 1931. The two daughters died: Mrs. Costner in 1917 and Mrs. Hull in 1936. The three sons are active business men; R. S. Abernethy in Winter Haven, Florida; and John D. and James A., Jr., in Lincolnton.

Pinckney A. Thompson, one of the oldest and most respected citizens of the County died at his home at Denver, January 2. He had been a merchant and farmer until too old for active duties and had served as County Commissioner for several terms. He was a son of the late John Thompson, and grandson of Bartholomew Thompson, a Revolutionary soldier, and also a great grandson of Francis McCorkle, another Revolutionary hero. He was a lifelong Methodist and for many years a church official.

D. P. Rhodes, a leading citizen, prominent in business circles, cotton manufacturer and member of the Board of County Commissioners, died at his home in Lincolnton, January 31, aged about 65 years. He was a son of the late John M. Rhodes and succeeded his father in the management of the Rhodes Mill. He was public-spirited and popular and a loyal and active member of the Lutheran Church. (See 1891.)

Mrs. Margaret Busbee Shipp, widow of the gallant Lieut. William E. Shipp (See 1898), who was killed in action in the Spanish American War, died in Rome, Italy, March 13, and the body was brought to Lincolnton and buried in the Shipp plot in Saint Luke's graveyard, April 19. She was born November 9, 1871, daughter of the late Fabius H. Busbee, a brilliant Raleigh lawyer, and possessed rare literary accomplishment, was a writer of pure English and contributed interesting articles to leading publications. For several years she taught in Fassifern School when Miss Kate C. Shipp was principal and had many friends in Lincolnton. Her son, Major W. E. Shipp, of the U. S. Army, who was military aide at the American Legation in Riga, Latvia, accompanied the body to Lincolnton. He is now stationed at Fort Riley, Kansas.

Adolphus P. Willis, a prominent citizen of Lincolnton, died March 21, 1936, having been seriously ill for several weeks prior to his death. He was born May 3, 1872, near Daniels Church and was a son of Robert H. and Sarah Coon Willis. He was a highly esteemed and useful man, Sheriff of the County from 1914 to 1918, and was a charter member and elder of Emanuel Reformed Church in Lincolnton since it was established in 1910.

Dr. Thomas C. Quickel died at his home in Gastonia, April 28, 1936, aged 60 years. He was a skilled physician, specialized on diseases of the eye, ear and throat in Gastonia for twenty-seven years, though he had been in feeble health for two years past. He was born six miles from Lincolnton, son of John C. and Josephine Crouse Quickel. He was born April 28, 1876, and died on his sixtieth birthday.

Dr. Quickel married, June 13, 1902, to Miss Addie Guy, who with two sons, Dr. John C. Quickel, of Gastonia, and Thomas C. Quickel, of Jamestown, N. Y., survive. Judge A. L. Quickel is a brother.

Dr. John C. Quickel, who has for some years practiced with his father, is a physician of superior gifts.

The death of this good man, a lifelong member of the Lutheran Church, is deplored by many friends. He came of good German stock and his people have long been prominent in Lincoln County and contributed many notable men to the County and State.

John Lindsay Hunter, Clerk of the Superior Court since 1930, died in Lincolnton, May 12, following a paralytic stroke. He was born in York County, South Carolina, but had been a Lincolnton citizen for thirty years and was a member of the Presbyterian Church. He was 54 years old when he died. To fill the vacancy caused by his death Judge Warlick, on May 14, appointed James A. Abernethy, Jr., Clerk of Superior Court.

Sunday, May 31, 1936, was a great day at Daniels Church for then the handsome monument purchased by the North Carolina Classis of the Reformed Church, to mark the grave of the Reverend Andrew Loretz, was presented and unveiled to take the place of the modest stone, which had for long years marked the resting place of this great man.

This sainted minister was born in Switzerland in 1761, organized Daniels congregation in 1786 and died March 31, 1812 (See 1812.)

A great multitude, including many of his descendants, was there to witness and take part in the interesting exercises of the day. The ministers on the program were Rev. Dr. O. B. Michael, the pastor, who presided; Rev. Dr. J. C. Leonard, who delivered the memorial address; Rev. Milton Whitener, who preached the morning sermon; Rev. J. A. Koons, Rev. C. W. Warlick, Rev. C. C. Wagoner, Rev. Carl Clapp, Rev. K. B. Schoffner, Rev. H. R. Carpenter, Rev. H. L. Fesperman, the chairman of the marker committee, who presented the monument in appropriate words, and Rev. W. H. Roof, of the Daniels Lutheran Church.

Laymen on the program were J. W. Warlick, Hugh Warlick, Farrell Warlick, H. D. Warlick, and K. A. Link.

The presentation of this handsome marker by the Classis was a beautiful expression of high respect for the patriotic and sainted pioneer, who, a wise leader in his day, laid the solid foundation for his church in this section of North Carolina.

He loved his people of the Daniel's section, where he lived for many years. In 1792 he bought about 2,000 acres of fertile land for which he paid fourteen pounds, North Carolina currency, and built a large brick home near the church, and there he died in 1812.

On the night of July 10, 1936, just forty days after the unveiling of the Loretz monument in Daniel's graveyard, the brick church building near by was struck by lightning and destroyed by the fire. A small part of the church furniture was saved, including a bronze tablet which was placed in the church in 1905 in memory of Mr. Loretz, by his granddaughter, Mrs. Caroline Motz Cochrane, of Boston, Mass.

This tablet bears the inscription:

"In memory of Rev. Andrew Loretz, born in Chur, Switzerland, 1761. Died in Lincoln County, North Carolina, March 31, 1812. I have finished my course, I have kept the faith."

This tablet was carried from the burning building by L. A. Yoder, who lived near by.

Plans are now being formulated to build a new church on this historic spot. The old church was built about 1894.

When the Daniels congregation was celebrating on May 31, 1936, the Methodists were gathered at McKendree Church on the Lincolnton-Newton highway, five miles north of Lincolnton to worship for the first time in the beautiful stone church which had just been completed through the sacrifice and devotion of the pastor, Rev. W. B. Shinn, and his faithful parishioners. It is constructed of native stone, is churchly in appearance and architectural design.

A large crowd was present for a full day. In the morning Joseph R. Nixon, spoke of the history and growth of the church, after which Rev. W. L. Hutchins, of Concord, preached a sermon appropriate to the occasion. In the afternoon brief talks were heard from Rev. C. H. Moser, Rev. J. B. McLarty, Dr. A. W. Plyler, E. M. Cole, the Conference Lay Leader, C. W. Kirby, the District Lay Leader and others.

More than one hundred years ago Rev. Samuel Lander, Sr., of Lincolnton, an active Methodist and local preacher, held frequent preaching services at this place with the result that a congregation was organized and a log church built, called McKendree, for the distinguished Bishop of that name. The early members were the Blackburns, Littles, Haynes, Carpenters, Shrums, and other families, names of whose descendants are still on the roll. Some fifty years after the church was established the old log meeting house was abandoned and a neat frame building erected on the same site, and now in 1936 the handsome stone structure takes the place of the frame building. In the graveyard rest the bodies of many of the older ones who had worshipped at this place. The membership of this congregation is now but 55 and the new church is an expression of their faith and self-denial.

Mrs. Mamie Phifer Smith, daughter of the late Col. John F. Phifer, and widow of Stephen Smith, late of Livingstone, Alabama, died at her Alabama home, February 2. She was born in Lincolnton, December 25, 1856. She was a beautiful, lovable and cultured woman and the news of her death brought sorrow to a wide circle of friends and relatives. (See 1886.)

Sixty-five young people graduated from the Lincolnton High School in May, 1936, as follows: Grady Abernethy, Annie Inez Abernethy, Enid Ethel Avery, Stephen Berkley Barineau,

Doris Adell Bandy, L. Berge Beam, Jr., Glenn Baker Beattie, Ethel Margaret Bradshaw, Pearl Bynum, Rose Elizabeth Campbell, Gladys Carpenter, Victor C. Cashion, Jr., Walter Boggs Cashion, La Vada Cauble, Margaret Jane Childs, Nancy Loretta Cloniger, William Lloyd Cornwell, Grace Elizabeth Costner, Alfred Nixon Costner, William Joseph Dellinger, Frances Pauline Ewing, Van Buren Ewing, Myrtle Pernell Finger, Barney Harry Fleeman, Florence Louise Funderburk, Joseph Wilson Gates, Margaret Elmina Glenn, Mary Louise Goodman, Gladys Goodson, Garland Goodson, Mildred Hardin, John Nelson Hauss, Jr., Glenn Heafner, Margaret Inez Heafner, David Calvin Heafner, Joseph B. Hinkle, Mary Ella Hoffman, Stella Camilla Hoyle, Thelma Jenkins, Bruce M. Jenkins, Harvey A. Jonas, Jr., Mabel Lucille Kendrick, Virginia Lineberger, J. R. Lineberger, Johnnie Rebecca Link, Brownie Lipe, John Munday Mauney, Conway McGee, Bettie Ernestine Modlin, Elizabeth Joyce Norman, Lorene Bennett Parker, Calvin Bynum Phillips, James Neely Porter, Jr., Lelia Cynthia Reinhardt, Dorothy Dean Reynolds, Ottileen Robinson, James Paul Rudisill, Jack Rudisill, Mary Self, Evan Shelton, Sue Smith, Joseph Fred Shuford, Virginia Stroupe, Edna Elsie Thomas, Gertrude Pauline Waters.

The three High Schools in Lincoln County, outside of the Town of Lincolnton, are North Brook, Rock Springs and Union High Schools. Those who in 1936 graduated from these follow:

North Brook High School: J. Harlan Heafner, principal; Orias Barnes, Evan Baxter, Heman Beam, Donald Bingham, C. M. Brown, Norris Childers, Wilford Dellinger, Blaine Devenny, Harvey Heavner, Hilliard Howell, Craig Hull, Boyce Huss, Willard Lackey, Tollie Mosteller, Kemp Wehunt, W. C. Willis, Hal Bess, C. V. Howell, Thelma Beam, Mozell Boyles, Inez Boyles, Mildred Cook, Hazel Davis, Hazel Eaker, Earlene Hoover, Hazel Huss, Annie Mae Lackey, Ella Mitchem, Edith Mull, Shirley Lackey, June Richmond, Marguerite Wehunt, Marine Wehunt, Susan Whisnant, Merle Woolley, Lucile Upton, Bryte Young.

Rock Springs High School: J. E. Ramsey, principal; Amos Armstrong, Jennings Ballard, Lewis Ballard, Wayne Ballard, Craig Barker, Horace Brotherton, Clem Canipe,

Harold Cherry, Rex Dellinger, Harlo Duckworth, George Hager, Russell Helderman, Charles Henkle, Thomas Huskins, Ernest Lawing, James Luckey, Colvert Nixon, Roy Nixon, Roy M. Nixon, Louie Reel, Hulick Scronce, Marvin Sherrill, Blair Wilkinson, Marshall Wilkinson, Naomi Black, Laura Ellen Canipe, Agnes Cherry, Bernice Cherry, Annie May Duckworth, Sue Goodson, Margaret Graham, Nancy Graham, Clie Hager, Ora Hager, Lois Jetton, Vivian Jones, Edith Lawing, Oma Long, Helen McIntosh, Aldean Morrison, Billie Munday, Lois Reel, Patsy Sifford, Ruth Smith, Willie Hoke.

Union High School: J. Frank Turner, principal; Ned Holly, Billie McSalls, Clyde Propst, Paul Quickel, Cary Smith, Thomas Seagle, Thomas Shuford, Ralph Scronce, DeWitt Sigmon, DeWitt Wise, Clyde Yoder, Edith Bass, John Beam, Mary Kathryn Beam, Mary Ella Blackburn, Viola Crawley, Lois Fortenberry, Naomi Guess, Faith Heavner, Joyce Heavner, Lela Helms, Dorothy Jonas, Helen Jonas, Nannie Leatherman, Louise Smith, Frances Smith, Edna Scronce, Lois Sain, Alda Wise, Frances Wyantt, Helen Yount, Pauline Yount.

One hundred and seventy-nine young people graduated from the High Schools of Lincoln County in 1936. This is history worth recording and one who may read this list of names thirty years hence will doubtless find some of whom the County may well feel proud.

Time has wrought great changes in the landscape of the territory east and northeast of Lincolnton in the past four decades, for at the beginning of the present century one could, after passing the eastern limit of Freedman drive through lonely forests for nine or ten miles to the Catawba line and pass but four farmhouses, and on the Buffalo Shoals road go further still and not see a house. That whole section was sparsely settled, but now much of the forest has been cleared and the roads lined with modern homes surrounded by good farms. Today, along the Lincolnton-Charlotte highway, from the Lincolnton city limits for several miles east, it is thickly built up with residences, with a business district in the heart of the community, good church buildings of various denominations, and a population twice as large as Lincolnton had in 1890. Soon after this wonderful growth began enterprising men of vision from Northern States decided that this Goodsonville community near the Seaboard Railway would be an ideal place to establish a cotton mill. The late H. W. Weidner, an experienced cotton mill executive, enlisted the interest of Robert C. Boger, a Philadelphia capitalist and manufacturer, with the result that the Boger-Crawford Company was in 1919 incorporated and a large mill established there to manufacture fine yarns, and the business grew so rapidly that additions to the mill were built, one in 1926 and another in 1930, at which time they operated 43,000 spindles. In May, 1936, work began on another enlargement, increasing the capacity to 63,000 spindles, to give employment to more than a thousand operators. This would mean a pay roll of about $14,000 a week when the mill is run on full time. When it was announced early this year that the Boger-Crawford Company contemplated this extensive enlargement, the people, as an expression of appreciation, proposed that the Goodsonville community be named Boger City in honor of Mr. Boger, who had done so much for the development of that section and the post office and Seaboard station were both, upon petition, changed to Boger City, effective July 1, 1936. The wilderness of 1890 "now blossoms as the rose" and the meager population of the former time has so multiplied that Boger City looks like a little city and has an industrious, progressive and contented citizenship.

The Boger-Crawford Co. specializes in fine combed cotton yarns, the finest quality that can be made and the demand for their product is equal to their capacity. The whole County is proud of the growth and progress of this company and of the high class citizenship of the Boger City community.

The North Carolina division of the American Legion at the annual meeting held in Asheville, July 26 to 28, 1936, paid high and deserved tribute to Captain Wiley M. Pickens when he was unanimously chosen Commander of the Division for the next year. Captain Pickens is a useful citizen of Lincolnton and has been superintendent of the Lincolnton City Schools since 1926.

James T. Williams, of Greenville, S. C., died August 7, aged 94 years. The body was brought to Lincolnton and buried in Saint Luke's graveyard. Mr. Williams had for many years been a hardware merchant in Greenville and later editor of a Greenville newspaper. He was a veteran of the Civil War and had served as Mayor of the City of Greenville. His wife who was Miss Sallie McBee, daughter of V. A. McBee, died some years ago.

William Luther Hill, born in Gainesville, Florida, October 17, 1873; attended private and public schools and the East Florida Seminary (now University of Florida) ; graduated from University of Florida, LL.B.; member Phi Kappa Phi honorary fraternity and of The Alumni Association, University of Florida; member of Methodist Episcopal Church, South; life member of Masonic bodies; engaged in banking, insurance, and practice of law; served as Secretary to United States Senator Duncan U. Fletcher of Florida from May, 1917, to June, 1936; Clerk to Senate Committee on Commerce, 1917-1921; Clerk to Senate Committee on Banking and Currency, 1933-1936; appointed United States Senator by Governor Dave Sholtz, to fill the vacancy caused by the death of Honorable Duncan U. Fletcher, and served as United States Senator from July 1, to November 3, 1936; declined to be a candidate for election to fill the unexpired term.

His parents were Lawson Logan Hill, born in Lincoln County and Louisiana Elizabeth Zetrouer Hill, born in Alachua County, Florida; his grandparents were Captain John Fletcher Hill and Frances (Carpenter) Hill, both of Lincoln County; and his great-grandparents were Rev. James Hill, a Methodist circuit rider and Precious (Stokes) Hill, both of whom died and were buried in Lincolnton.

He and his wife Mary Hoffman Hill are parents of two children: Robert Hoffman and William Logan.

Louis H. Hepp, Superintendent in charge of the property of the American Consolidated Tin Corporation located in Lincolnton, announced in September the discovery of rich strike of tin ore, assaying from two to fifteen per cent and he wired the New York office of the Company the following message:

> "Have drifted through tin-bearing reef from swamp shaft STOP Reef at hanging wall contact eight feet thick STOP Grab sample assayed better than $50.00 per ton complete sampling through eight feet averaged $25.00 per ton assays by John H. Banks Laboratories, New York STOP Have run drift parallel with reef 16 feet then crosscut reef

again assay of sampling full width of reef $46.00 per ton STOP Will continue parallel drift toward Carpenter shaft 1,000 feet north and quarry 2,200 feet north making cross cuts in reef every 20 feet STOP Rock formation found at quarry and Carpenter shaft is similiar to that found in reef at swamp shaft STOP Similar tin-bearing formation also found at Henry shaft 4,000 feet south of swamp shaft STOP Believe this same rock formation extends the 1 1-4 miles from quarry to Henry shaft STOP On top of tin reef at Condon but have not yet gotten water low enough to explore width of reef and sample."

On October 22 a portrait of Theodorus Henderson Cobb which was presented to Lincoln County by his children, Miss Ellen Cobb and Bartlett Cobb of Los Angeles, California, was unveiled in County Court room at the opening of the afternoon Court session.

The presentation speech was delivered by Judge A. L. Quickel, who, in appropriate words, spoke of the legal attainments of the brilliant lawyer, a native of Lincolnton, who practiced law in the County for many years before he moved to Asheville where he died in August, 1905.

Judge Alley presiding, in accepting the portrait, paid high tribute to Mr. Cobb and stated that when he was preparing himself for the legal profession he had found the pleadings filed by Mr. Cobb the most perfect he had ever read.

This is the first portrait of a lawyer ever placed upon the wall of the County Court room. Many brilliant lawyers have lived in the County and it would be most fitting for others to present portraits of some of these jurists to be placed along side that of Mr. Cobb in the Court room.

Dr. R. W. Petrie died suddenly in his office at Murphy, November 17, 1936.

He was born near Reepsville, May 5, 1876. Son of R. M. and Eliza (Yoder) Petrie. He located in Lincolnton in 1907 when he and Dr. L. A. Crowell opened the Crowell Hospital. Later he went to Charlotte and specialized on diseases of the eye, ear, nose and throat. He established a hospital in Murphy a few years later and was a skilled physician and surgeon.

His first marriage was to Eva, daughter of the late L. T. Wilkey of Lincolnton. His second marriage, in 1936, was to Miss Annie Rhyne.

Dr. Petrie was a Lutheran in faith, held in high regard and, the State lost a fine citizen when he died.

Summey Alexander, a highly respected citizen of Lincolnton, died November 23, 1936. He was born in Lincolnton, August 29, 1858, son of Elias J. and Barbara (Summey) Alexander. On February 10, 1884, he was married to Jennie Cauble, who died April 27, 1931. He was for some years connected with the Tiddy Paper Mills, and when that enterprise was abandoned, become general manager of the Long Shoals Cotton Mills. He served as a magistrate for several years and was thoroughly conversant with local history.

He was an active Mason and a faithful member of the Methodist church. He had a wide circle of friends who mourn their loss in the departure of this splendid man.

Dr. Thomas F. Costner, aged 78 years, son of the late Ambrose Costner, died at his home in Lumberton, December 28, 1936, and the body was brought to Lincolnton and buried at Hollybrook Cemetery on the following day. He was a native of this County, read medicine when a young man and practiced his profession for many years, first at Mount Holly, then in Lincolnton and Charlotte, until finally he located in Lumberton where he was a leading physician.

His wife, who was Miss Dora Gatewood of Wadesboro, died some years ago. Dr. Costner retired from active practice in 1934, and returned to Lincolnton to live among old friends and kindred, but later went back to Lumberton where he spent his last days.

Mrs. Louise Lander, daughter of Rufus B. and Frances McPherson Templeton, was married to Frank C. Lander, December 15, 1880. He died in 1902 and she, a much loved woman, died, December 21, 1936, aged 75 years.

She was the mother of eight children, all of whom survive. They were:

Clara, married Lemuel Bingham Wetmore, April 18, 1906.

Frank T., married Eunice Flow, September 15, 1915.

Sarah Connor, married John Laban Lineberger, November, 1935.

Nora McPherson, married M. Herbert Kuhn, June 16, 1915.

Samuel William, Rufus Jackson, Bruce Ramsay and John Lawing Lander are unmarried.

Recently Prof. J. N. Hauss found among some old papers in his home in Lincolnton a copy of Sons of Temperance program dated July 4, 1850, which was printed by the *Lincoln Courier*, then edited by Thomas J. Eccles, and on July 4, 1936, Prof. Hauss read it (Odes and all) at a meeting of the Women's Christian Temperance Union held in his home in Lincolnton on that day.

The old program follows:

FOURTH OF JULY PROGRAM, 1850
LINCOLN DIVISION, NO. 56

Morning

1—Prayer by the Chaplain, Rev. Colin Murchison.
2—Ode.
3—Presentation of a banner on the part of the ladies by William Lander, Esq.
4—Ode.
5—Address by Thomas J. Eccles, W. P.
6—Ode.
7—Address by Samuel P. Jones.
8—Ode.
9—Address by Alexander J. Cansler.
10—Ode.
Benediction.

Evening

1—Prayer by Chaplain.
2—Ode.
3—Address by Brother W. C. Clark.
4—Ode.
Benediction.

The Odes were temperance poems varying in length from one to four verses. For lack of space they are omitted.

The Lincoln Lithia Inn has had a good patronage this summer under the management of James A. Abernethy, Jr., who now owns the property. The Lincoln Lithia water has long been famed as a remedy for kidney troubles and was for many years shipped to all parts of the country, and for a time was on sale at the Raleigh drug store fountains. The analysis of this water shows grains to the gallon of

Sulphate of potash, 1.1350; sulphate of lime, .8900; chloride of soda, .9805; bicarbonate of soda, .1807; bicarbonate of iron, .1870; bicarbonate of lime, 5.1452; bicarbonate of magnesia, .5708; bicarbonate of lithia, 2.8118; silica, .5460; traces of phospate of soda and alum. Total solid matter to the gallon, 12.647 grains.

The spring was first developed by Major Henry W. Burton, who sold the property to Gen. Robert F. Hoke. After his death it passed into the hands of Daniel E. Rhyne and is now owned by James A. Abernethy, Jr., an enterprising man, who hopes to make it a resort for those who need the benefit of this healing water.

CHAPTER XXII

Something About the Colored Folks

The colored population of the County deserves proper recognition in these ANNALS, for they have been good, law abiding and industrious, contributing their part in the development of the County. In the old days prior to the Civil War they were capable helpers in the manufacture of iron and on farms as producers of cotton, wheat, corn and other crops.

Writing more from personal knowledge of Lincolnton from 1865 to 1880, many of them were useful as mechanics as well as in other lines of work. Alfred Linton was a skilled blacksmith; Caesar and Bob Henderson and Henry Kistler were tanners; Monroe Thompson, Alexander Schenck, Bill Schenck, Harry Pralow, Ned Cobb, Henry Huskey, and others were shoemakers; Jim Lander was trained in the Lander Coach Factory and knew much about that business, and his wife, Caroline, was a fine housekeeper of gracious manners and gentility. Ben McLean, Bob McBee, Caleb and Tench Lander were capable house carpenters. Caleb Lander has a grandson, who practices dentistry in Charlotte now. Ishmeal Roberts (born free) was for many years before and after the Civil War a capable brick mason and worker in stone; Richmond Scott was the colored merchant; Chas. Roseman was the village drayman and handled about all the freight to and from the old Carolina Central station; Ephraim Hoke was the town liveryman, kept good horses and carriages and rendered acceptable service, and John Connor was the only barber in town. Aunt Harriet Henderson was the finest baker in all the country and nearly all the Lincolnton folks depended on her to bake the Christmas and wedding cakes and she never failed to make the best. Aunt Mariah Slade was the community midwife and many were the times she went through cold and storm to minister to those in distress.

Many of these were devout Christians. The people had faith in the piety of Ben Mooney, Jeff Herndon, his son Sully Herndon (preacher), Ben McLean (preacher), Anderson Hoke (preacher), Isaac Cansler (preacher), Alex Schenck, class leader and director of the singing at the colored Methodist church. There were many others just as good but these are mentioned as outstanding leaders among them.

A large majority of the colored people in Lincolnton during this period were Methodists. Bishop J. J. Moore, a rare scholar and pulpit orator lived in Lincolnton from 1872 to 1877. In time a Baptist congregation was organized; and then a Presbyterian Church with Rev. C. A. Baker, a good man, now in Danville, Va., as pastor. Rev. Dr. Wetmore had a group of colored members in Saint Luke's Church and later a separate church was organized for them. These all served their generation well and almost all have completed their earthly pilgrimage, but many of their children have risen up to take their places.

CHAPTER XXIII

Industrial Growth in Lincoln County

1—Iron Manufacture

Among the first settlers in the County were farmers, skilled workers in iron and wood, blacksmiths, carpenters, tanners, weavers, tailors, millers, shoemakers and other tradesmen, and though they had to be farmers first, there were many skilled artisans, who manufactured leather, shoes, cotton and woolen cloth, farm tools, furniture, wagons and other absolute necessities. They were self-reliant and self-dependent. In 1789 when iron ore was first discovered in the County, Peter Forney, Abram Forney, Abram Earhardt and Turner Abernethy erected a forge at Big Ore Bank in Ironton township and were the pioneer manufacturers of iron in this section of the State. Later Peter Forney bought the interest of his partners and finally formed a new co-partnership with John Davidson, of Mecklenburg, Joseph Graham and Alexander Brevard, the last named being a skilled worker in iron. They erected Vesuvius and Mount Tirzah furnaces and became large producers of iron.

When Mr. Forney grew older he sold his interest to his partners and they continued the business under the trade name of Joseph Graham and Co. Mr. Forney, however, reserved Mount Welcome furnace, which he left to Dr. William Johnston, his son-in-law, who, with his sons, operated it successfully until 1860, when it was sold to Jonas W. Derr, who continued the business until his death in 1881.

J. Madison Smith bought Vesuvius furnace from the Grahams and operated it many years and sold the product during the Civil War to the Confederate government. After the death of Mr. Smith, his son-in-law, J. F. Reinhardt, continued the business until about 1880.

Alexander Brevard left Mount Tirzah to his son, Robert A. Brevard, and Rehoboth furnace to his son, Ephraim Brevard, who operated it until 1852, when he sold it to Bartlett Shipp and F. M. Reinhardt. After the Civil War it was taken over by Bartlett Shipp and J. F. (Jack) Reinhardt and they continued the business until the death of Mr. Shipp in 1869.

Turner Abernethy, one of the original group mentioned as a pioneer iron industrialist in Lincoln County in 1789, built Mount Carmel forge on Mountain Creek and in later years it was operated by Isaac E. Paine. James Madison Smith built and for many years operated the Rough and Ready forge on Mountain Creek and during the Civil War built Stonewall furnace on Anderson Creek and operated it successfully until his death in 1873. In addition to these John Fulenwider (a native of Switzerland) who lived in Rowan, and was known as a master iron worker, moved to Lincoln County and became one of its great and successful citizens. He first erected a forge on Maiden Creek, near the present town of Maiden in 1804, for some years manufactured iron there and then sold the property to A. F. and E. J. Brevard, and they later sold it to William Williams, who continued the business until 1880. John Fulenwider developed several other furnaces and was the founder of the High Shoals Iron Works, and one of the first to use charcoal in the process of manufacturing pig iron from iron ore. He did an extensive business at High Shoals and manufactured cannon balls there, under government contract, for use in the War of 1812, shipping the product to Charleston in flat boats. After his death the business was continued for some time by his descendants. After the Civil War it was bought by Admiral Charles Wilkes (U. S. Navy), and he carried on the business until about 1871, when it was abandoned as an iron producing enterprise.

The following excerpts from an article on "Iron-Making— A Forgotten Industry of North Carolina," by Lester J. Cappon, of the University of Virginia, which appeared in *The North Carolina Historical Review* of October, 1932, give interesting facts about iron manufacturing in Lincoln County:

"It was in Lincoln County that iron-making developed with most promise and fulfilled the dreams of its founders. Here within a decade after the act of 1788 ('to encourage the building of iron works in the State.') five families were engaged in the manufacture of iron, all of them inter-related and destined practically to control the industry of the North Carolina piedmont for three generations. A few miles east of Lincolnton, the county seat, was the "Big Ore Bank," which Peter Forney and three associates obtained in 1789 after a jury had examined the tract and found it unfit for cultivation. Forney soon purchased the interests of his partners and in the course of the next two years sold part to Major John Davidson and to Davidson's sons-in-law, Alexander Brevard and Joseph Graham, both officers in the Revolutionary army. The early years of the nineties saw activity in iron-making grow apace as Captain Brevard moved his family from Iredell County to Lincoln and built Mount Tirzah Forge on Leeper's Creek, while General Graham migrated from Mecklenburg County and established himself at Vesuvius Furnace, then building on land adjoining Brevard's. In 1795 they bought out the interest of Forney who continued to operate independently works of his own at Mt. Welcome, along with agricultural pursuits which went hand in hand with iron-making. Meanwhile these new industrialists had become acquainted with another who had acquired a valuable site for his works near High Shoals on the South Fork of the Catawba. This was John Fulenwider, for 15 years entry-taker of Lincoln County, a position which afforded him intimate knowledge of the most desirable lands, mineral and agricultural, in the district.

"So firmly was the manufacture of iron established here by these pioneers who learned the practice of furnace and forge by crude empirical methods that the industry persisted years after its best markets had disappeared in the ever-quickening current of economic change. The flourishing condition of this business during the early decades of the nineteenth century is to be credited partly to the fact that it was a sort of family affair in which the position of ironmaster won distinction worthy of being perpetuated. The association of Graham and Brevard came, as we have seen, through their common father-in-law, John Davidson; while through the sons of Peter Forney, the Brevards were related by marriage to the Fulenwiders. Something of that feeling of pride which prompted the old man to begin his will 'I, John Fulenwider, Iron Master of the County of Lincoln, State of North Carolina,' must have been instilled likewise in his sons and in Capt. Brevard's sons and grandsons, who continued some of the works even after the Civil War. The early years of prosperity, however, had a significant bearing upon contemporary economic conditions quite aside from the personal element.

"With the rapid extension of the plantation system through the upper Carolina piedmont after 1800, as a result of the increasing profitableness of cotton-growing, new lands for the cultivation of the staple were most desired. In Lincoln and neighboring counties the iron ore deposits were an added inducement to settlers, but the risks of iron-making were great and the returns uncertain, compared with those of cotton cultivation during this period of expanding markets. Nor did such conditions give rise to a manufacturing element in the modern sense of the term. An iron-master was for many decades essentially a planter himself, dividing his efforts between two phases of domestic industry with a versatility that seems amazing in the present age of specialization. The economic self-sufficiency of the southern plantation was always a relative matter, even on the frontier, and since plantations distant from the iron deposits also needed metal goods, the ambitious iron-master was awake to the opportunity of enlarging his sphere of business and building up trade with the outside world. In seeking distant customers, however, the upland industrialist was confronted by the tidewater merchant with his imported wares, and the age-old rivalry for intermediate markets ensued.

"How the remote piedmont iron-masters managed to compete with the well-established manufacturers and merchants of the coast may be gathered from the activity of the Brevards and Grahams who co-ordinated the management of the iron works with that of their agricultural interests. About the beginning of each year the furnace was blown in and kept in operation continuously until late spring or early summer, producing castings in the form of skillets, pots, pans, dog-irons and ovens, while the forge turned out tools and implements. Spring work in the fields and around the barns and cottages made iron 'suitable for implements of husbandry . . . most in demand.' Water power was greatest in the spring and more slaves were available to assist in iron-making at this time of the year than in the busy harvest season of cotton picking, baling and hauling.

"By establishing a good reputation for his metal Captain Brevard expanded this trade into South Carolina where, at Camden on the Catawba River, his brother Joseph, a prominent lawyer and judge, acted as his agent. Not only did Joseph Brevard store the iron wares pending a favorable market, and keep on the watch for customers, but he was also informed on prices in Charleston and elsewhere in order to send advance word to the Lincoln works on the trend of the market. He advised 'In the summer after the crop is laid by, there is little occasion for iron until the latter end of the year, when the land is again begun to be broke up, unless it is for Boat-building; and those people who are able to build Boats generally buy iron by the quantity in Charleston and bring it up in their Boats, the freight not standing them in anything. But if you could afford to undersell the Charleston price, you would find a ready sale for all you could spare.'

"Wares imported at Charleston from northern iron works and from abroad were shipped up the Catawba as far as Camden every spring to supply the plantations in the valley. Likewise the Brevards and Grahams transported their goods down the valley by road or river, to and beyond Camden, ever watchful to make the most of a dry season when the river was tardy in rising sufficiently to allow boats to ascend. Now roads were being projected into South Carolina, and the Lincoln works were not so far distant that wagons could not be successfully used in carrying their goods to Camden in less time than the four weeks which Charleston merchants had to allow to market their goods and return. The opportunity to sell in the local market in advance of outside competition was not to be overlooked at a time when reports of prices in the iron marts of the country were infrequently received.

"In addition to this business, the iron-masters were visited every year by traveling merchants who brought imported food and clothing, house furnishings and novelties, and news from foreign states and countries. Their goods, which added to the comforts of the plantation, were exchanged for iron and iron wares. In a country where hard money was scarce, payment was either made in kind or long postponed before cash was forthcoming. Bar iron was a medium of exchange in some regions, just as tobacco was in others, and an iron master of high repute could secure extended credit on his product.

"Slave labor of the plantation was used for most of the tasks about the iron works and the proprietor was kept informed as to the status of the slave market. In 1804 Joseph Brevard wrote to his brother that . . . 'the average price for young slaves was about 300 dollars. To pick them $350 was asked. I have been led to believe the average price will decrease to $250—or $200—but this last is said to be lower than the West India market. I am disposed to think that you may purchase northward negroes on better terms at present than Africans: but I believe they are not to be preferred' . . .

"The slaves were usually assigned to specific tasks, such as cutting wood for charcoal or hauling the ore to the furnace, and those of exceptional ability were trained for such skilled work as forging the metal. That these negroes were regarded as an integral part of the iron works is borne out in the sale of John Davidson's share of Mount Tirzah Forge and Vesuvius Furnace in 1804 to Joseph Graham and Alexander Brevard who received 12 slaves along with 'all the Cattle, Horses, Wagons, Smith Tools, Forge Hammers, Furnace Utensils . . .' Apparently the economy of this labor system was unchallenged at the time and a generation later when doubt was raised as to the profitableness of slave labor in manufacturing, Charles Fisher in the State Legislature retorted:

" '. . . It is to the interest of Northern manufacturers to hold these ideas, but that they should be entertained by well-informed persons acquainted with our black population is strange indeed. What branch of mechanics have we in our country in which we do not find negroes often distinguished for their skill and ingenuity? . . . One of the great advantages of black labor is that you can attach it permanently to the establishment by purchase.'

"Dr. Elisha Mitchell commended the iron masters of Lincoln County for the 'skill and judgment with which the business is conducted. The demand at present (1827) is no greater than this single County may supply: low priced European iron continues to exclude domestic manufacture from the market along the seaboard.'

"Lincoln County, as Mitchell predicted, maintained her leadership in iron production which, by the mid 'twenties, had earned a very creditable reputation. In 1823, according to General Graham, ten forges and four furnaces were making about 900 tons of bar valued at $6\frac{1}{4}$ cents per pound and 200 tons of castings at 5 cents. John Fulenwider, who died in 1826, bequeathed a handsome patrimony of plantations, iron works, slaves and stock on hand, worth more than $50,000 to his four sons, and when his old friend, Capt. Brevard, followed him four years later, he too entrusted his extensive estate including the iron works to his four sons.

"The cultural and religious interests of these hardy planters and industrial pioneers are reflected in the special mention which the one made of 'the small library, including books of a Religious, Scientific and amusing Description,' and the bequest of the other of $500, 'the interest of which is to go as it may be collected to the payment of Ministers of the Gospel for preaching Sermons at or near our family graveyard' . . .

"The Forneys and the Grahams likewise maintained an interest in the iron business, the latter being associated in part with Robert A. and Ephraim A. Brevard who assumed the major responsibility in their late father's business. Ore was always plentiful, but by the 'forties the problem of timber supply for charcoal was causing some concern, for both the Brevards and John D. Graham were competing for the acquisition of the 400-acre wooded tract of William Fulenwider who was forced to sell. The expense of operations at Vesuvius and Rehoboth furnaces, Mt. Tirzah and Spring Hill forges, however, had been reduced somewhat by the discovery of limestone near the works, whereas formerly it had been hauled twenty-five to thirty miles from the foot of Kings Mountain.

"Although iron-making in this region had resulted in considerable fortunes to a few individuals, its full potentialities were never realized. Closely allied to the plantation system as a subsidiary enterprise, it failed to reach out beyond the limited markets of the local area.

"By the mid-'fifties, of the original families engaged in iron-making in Lincoln County, only the Brevards continued their operations at Mt. Tirzah and Vesuvius, and at a new forge, the Jenny Lind, erected by the grandsons of old Capt. Brevard. The day of the individual iron-master was gradually waning in the face of large capitalized companies so typical of the growing industrial revolution, although more slowly in the South than in the North. In Gaston County, to the south of Lincoln, the High Shoals Manufacturing Company, with New York connections, renovated the old Fulenwider project at Columbia Furnace and erected a rolling-mill, but the venture was abandoned early in 1854."

2—Cotton Manufacture

The first cotton mill south of the Potomac River was built by Michael Schenck on the branch near the McDaniel Spring a mile and a half east of Lincolnton. The contract to build this mill was given to Absalom Warlick and Michael Beam, April 16, 1816. They were skilled workers in iron and made by hand most of the machinery, though a part of it was bought in Providence, R. I. (See 1816.)

It was a small mill and made cotton thread, which was in great demand, for knitting purposes, as the women in those days knit all the stockings and wove about all the cloth; and the business was conducted at good profit.

In 1818 Michael Schenck, John Hoke and Dr. James Bivens formed a co-partnership and built a larger cotton mill at the present Laboratory site on the South Fork River, two miles south of Lincolnton, with three thousand spindles. Axes and other tools were also made by this company. Later Col. Hoke bought the interest of Schenck and Bivens and continued the business until his death in 1844. Then it was taken over by Col. L. D. Childs, son-in-law of Col. Hoke, and operated by him until it was destroyed by fire in 1863. The capacity of this mill must have been reduced after it was first built, for the *Lincoln Transcript* of August 19, 1831, stated that Lincoln County had one cotton mill with twelve looms and 1,280 spindles.

Top left: Daniel E. Rhyne (1852-1933). See 1933.
Top right: James A. Abernethy (1851-   ). See 1887 and 1936.
Center left: John M. Rhodes (1849-1921). See 1921.
Center right: Robt. S. Reinhardt (1858-1925). See 1925.
Lower left: D. P. Rhodes (1871-1936). See 1936.
Lower right: Isaac C. Lowe (1867-   ). See 1934.

About 1850 Andrew Motz, E. S. Barrett and others built a cotton factory on the South Fork River immediately above its confluence with Clark's Creek. It was called Laurel Hill Cotton Factory and the firm name was E. S. Barrett and Co. About 1858 this property was bought by Col. John F. Phifer and Col. R. W. Allison (of Concord) and they operated it under the name of Ivy Shoal Cotton Mill until the death of Col. Phifer in 1884, when it was continued for a while by Geo. L. Phifer until it was taken over by R. S. Reinhardt, Stephen Smith and others and called Elm Grove Cotton Mill.

These three were the only cotton mills ever operated in Lincoln County until 1887 when Daniel E. Rhyne and J. A. Abernethy came from Mount Holly and built the present Laboratory Mill two miles south of Lincolnton. They operated it with profit and built another at the old Lincoln Paper Mill site a mile further down the river and later the Daniel and Wampum Mills in Lincolnton. Then John M. Rhodes built the Rhodes Mill, Edgar Love built Saxony Mill, J. L. Lineberger the Eureka, and in 1919 the Boger-Crawford, the large mill at Boger City, was built. Another mill was the Mariposa Mill near Lowesville, operated by Captain Joseph G. Morrison.

According to David Clark's Textile Year Book in 1933 the Lincoln County mills were:

Boger-Crawford Spinning Mill, R. C. Boger, president, A. P. Setzer, secretary, 30,352 spindles; Carter Mill, A. B. Carter, president, J. H. Clark, secretary, 12,096 spindles; Elm Grove Mill, R. S. Reinhardt, president, J. M. Reinhardt, secretary, 6,088 spindles; Eureka Mill, J. L. Lineberger, president, 1,306 spindles; Excell Mfg. Co., R. F. Craig, manager, 6,048 spindles; Indian Creek Mill, D. P. Rhodes, president, Paul Rhodes, secretary, 3,000 spindles; Laboratory Mill, W. W. Glenn, manager, F. H. Whitesides, secretary, 5,100 spindles; Lincoln Spinning Mill, C. W. Bagby, president, R. J. McGee, secretary, 14,074 spindles; Massapoag Mill Corp., David Clark, president, Thorne Clark, secretary, 5,600 spindles; Melvin Mill, W. W. Glenn, manager, W. E. Crenshaw, secretary, 7,004 spindles; Rhodes-Rhyne Mill, D. P. Rhodes, president, T. J. McNeely, secretary, 4,032 spindles, 128 looms; Rudisill Spinning Mill, A. A. Whitener, president, H. R. Whitener, secretary, 4,600 spindles; Textile Co. (Merco plant), W. R. Armstrong, Agt., W. E. Crenshaw, secretary, 5,760 spindles; Long Shoals Cotton Mill, C. N. Neisler, president, H. G. Whitesides, secretary, 14,160 spindles; Mariposa (Alba Twine), A. E. Woltz, president, A. J. Bumgarner, secretary, 3,300 spindles; Southside-Lincoln Mill, W. W. Glenn, manager, C. S. Little, secretary, 6,656 spindles; Total, 16 Mills, 129,176 Spindles, 128 Looms. When these mills were all running full time they employed about 2,200 operators and the weekly pay roll amounted to about $30,000.

Before and after the Civil War, O. B. Jenks operated a wool carding business in North Brook township. About 1880 B. H. Sumner and George L. Phifer established and operated a wool carding mill in Lincolnton for several years, but as sheep husbandry languished in this section, thus reducing the local wool supply, this enterprise was abandoned and a cotton mill was later built on the site of the Sumner and Phifer Woolen Mill.

3—Pottery

A letter dated May 14, 1928, and written by Mr. John Johnson, of Vale, contains interesting facts about the manufacture of pottery in Lincoln and Catawba Counties.

He says:

"I now being 87 years old, the first I remember about the pottery business in this section was when Moses Ritchie run a jug factory about 75 or 80 years ago, and he had three sons, Thomas, Henry and Joseph, who engaged in pottery after their father died, and one of these is running it extensively now.

"William Campbell also engaged in the same business for several years, but moved to Virginia after the Civil War and there continued the same work.

"My brother, Eli Johnson, and my cousins, Harvey M. and J. D. Johnson, all engaged in the pottery business. Eli Johnson moved his pottery to Virginia after the Civil War and there continued in the same work for many years, and Harvey M. and J. D. Johnson some years ago transferred to South Carolina where they were a year or so ago, still making pottery. All these and others operated in Catawba County.

"Turning to Lincoln County Daniel Seagle (not Gen. Seagle) was in the pottery business 75 years ago. A few years later Sylvanus Hartzoke owned a pottery in Lincoln County and then moved it to Catawba County and continued in the business until about five years ago. His father, Daniel Hartzoke was in the business many years before his son became a potter.

"Franklin Carpenter was a potter until his death about 65 years ago. Nelson S. Bass operated a pottery at one time and William Brackett is now running the Bass factory. J. M. Lynn and Samuel Propst are now in the business in Lincoln County near Catawba line. Jacob Propst, the father of Samuel, made it a lifetime business, but let this suffice for the present."

Continuing Mr. Johnson says:

"As to who first introduced it in this part of the country I am not able to say, but have heard it was handed down to the whites by the Indians. It is evident that the Indians manufactured pottery, for I have seen in my earlier life many specimens of the Indian product."

Others say the art of making pottery in this section was begun in the early days, first by Jacob Weaver, who brought it from Germany when he settled in what is now known as the Jugtown community, along the Lincoln-Catawba boundary line, northwest of Lincolnton, where he found a fine quality of pottery clay, and an abundance of wood, and that the business flourished and grew as it was taken over by succeeding generations of his descendants. Three brothers, E. A., S. W., and C. W. Hilton, some years ago moved their pottery from Jugtown out to the State Highway between Conover and Hickory and now carry on an extensive pottery business there, and they have a steady and growing demand for their product. This business has been profitable in the Jugtown section for several generations, and the product was delivered in wagons over long stretches of primitive roads to market long before paved roads were ever dreamed of.

4—Paper Mills

About 1832 George Mosteller established a paper mill at Long Shoals on the South Fork River, four miles south of Lincolnton and the business grew and another mill was erected at the Southside Cotton Mill site two miles above Long Shoals. Paper of good quality was made from cotton rags, writing paper as well as book, news and wrapping paper, which in the absence of other paper mills, found a wide and ready market. The firm name was later changed to G. and D. Mosteller when a book bindery was added and many of the Lincoln County record books in the Court House are the product of these mills. About 1857 the business was taken over by Samuel Gates and conducted by him until 1867, then for a brief period by Grady and Banister, until it came into possession of A. C. Wiswall, an experienced paper manufacturer from Massachusetts, and William Tiddy, under the firm name of Wiswall and Tiddy, who conducted it for some years. Then William and Richard Tiddy bought the property and operated the mills (adding a third mill which they built at Buffalo in Cleveland County) until about 1894, when they could no longer successfully compete with manufacturers of paper made from wood pulp in the North, so that the local business was abandoned.

During the period these mills were operated the merchants for fifty miles around bought old rags at three cents a pound, paying in goods, and sold them to the paper mills at the same figure for cash. The company maintained a long train of wagons, which delivered the rags to the mills to be converted into paper. When postal cards were first used about 1873, these mills, under contract, manufactured large quantities of postal card paper for the United States Government. Finally cotton mills were built on the Long Shoals and Lincoln paper mill sites.

5—Tanneries

In the early days when a beef was butchered the local tanner converted the hide into leather, taking one-half for toll and the owner had the local shoemaker to make shoes for the family out of the other half. In 1845 Paul Kistler, Jacob Ramsour and others were among many tanners in the County, and at that time and for many years following John A. Huggins, John A. Parker, Harrison Wilson, Elcanah Hartzoke and William Hinson were fine shoemakers. About 1867 and later the tanners were Henry E., Henry F., and E. F. Ramsour, D. F. Beam, L. H. Hill, D. A. Lowe, R. E. Burch, Daniel Finger, and others outside of Lincolnton. C. C. Henderson a Lincolnton merchant, bought hides and conducted an extensive tanning business, converting the leather into boots and shoes which he sold locally. When he died in 1869 S. P. Sherrill, a merchant, bought the Henderson tanyard and continued the business, converting the leather into shoes for the local market until 1875 when the tannery was abandoned. Later Woodcock and Cobb operated a Tannery about two miles south of Lincolnton and finally sold it to J. S. Martin and S. M. Asbury, who carried it on for several years until it was abandoned.

The changes of the years have been against the small-scale tannery and now the business is conducted by large companies in the mountain section of the State where tan bark is abundant.

6—Furniture

Early in the last century Thomas Dews from the Guernsey Island came to Lincolnton and lived on the site of the Baptist Church on East Main street and had a cabinet shop at the same place. He was father of the brilliant Thomas Dews, Jr., and also ancestor of Mrs. Mattie Anthony, of Lincolnton.

Many years after Mr. Dews died Warren Gheen came from Rowan County and engaged in the same business and Augustus P. James, before and after the Civil War, had a cabinet shop. All these were skilled workers in wood and supplied most of the furniture of high quality to the people of this section. They made all kinds of furniture and coffins and it was all hand work. At the time they went out of business the machine age had dawned and furniture was made on a large scale by machinery, much of it inferior in quality to that made by these local men. At the present time Lincolnton has two furniture factories—one extensive plant, the Ideal Chair Company, established in 1915 by Mark Zimtbaum, and furniture of high grade is sold by this firm to all parts of the country. The Cochrane Manufacturing Co., also makes fine show cases as well as other furniture.

7—Workers in Iron

Skilled workers in iron came to Lincoln early, as evidenced by the fact that Absalom Warlick and Michael Beam made much of the machinery for the Michael Schenck Cotton Mill in 1816. "Millwright" Jacob Ramsour was also a skilled worker in his day. Col. Seth W. Stubbs came from New England in the early days, and could make almost anything from a collar button to a steam engine. He made the town clock and placed it in the old courthouse tower to strike the hours with never failing regularity for sixty years, until the old building gave way for the present new courthouse. His son, Elbridge W. Stubbs, operated a machine shop for many years, until his death, and made engines, farm machinery, molasses mills and all kinds of kitchen ware in the foundry. The business was later taken over by J. Laban Lineberger and is now (1936) called Eureka Iron Works and operated by Harry Page.

8—Coach Makers

Samuel Lander came to Lincolnton about 1826 from Salisbury. He was an Irishman and a coach maker. Then there was not a railroad in the world. Carriages were in great demand and he soon established a reputation for honest workmanship, made coaches of high grade and found ready market for his product in all this section of the State and in upper South Carolina. He engaged in this business until his death in 1864. A few old people can yet remember the large building on East Main street in which coaches were manufactured and the sign in large letters, "Samuel Lander, Coachmaker." Abner McCoy, before the Civil War and after, and James L. and L. T. Wilkey from 1865 as long as they lived, built wagons and buggies, but not so extensively as before the railway came.

9—Corn and Flour Mills

From the early pioneer days grist mills were built in Lincoln. Ramsour's Mill was in operation on Clark's Creek in 1780 when the battle of Ramsour's Mill was fought. In 1845 there were many corn and flour mills in the County. In 1867 mills were operated by Green Abernethy, Thos. Bass, Grady, Banister and Co., J. D. M. Bollinger, A. F. and R. A. Brevard, Henry Cansler, Mary A. Beam, David Crouse, A. Dellinger, J. W. Derr, G. W. Hull, J. F. Reinhardt, Joseph Houser, Dr. Cyrus L. Hunter, F. M. Reinhardt, J. Madison Smith. Besides these, Theodore J. Ramsour, Michael Finger, J. H. Killian, Maxwell Warlick, John Rudisill continued in the business after 1867, along with Ambrose Costner, C. and W. H. Motz, Coulter, and others, all of whom operated mills and made flour of good grade and fully supplied all the local demands, until the modern roller mill superseded the old burr mill. Today in Lincolnton two modern roller flour mills are operated, one by B. J. Ramsour and Heim Hoover, and the other by Silas Carpenter, Walter Mullen and Levy Hallman. Lincoln County farmers are large wheat growers and these mills grind most of their product and are carried on successfully.

10—Miscellaneous

In 1845 and many years following Thomas R. Shuford was a tin and copper smith. John Butts and John Cline were hat makers until the railroad brought other styles from the North.

Tobey and Hoke and John Warlick manufactured brooms. Gold mining in Lincoln was profitable at one time. As late as 1867 mines were operated by John F. Hoke, Wm. J. Hoke, Daniel Seagle, Henry Cansler, B. S. Johnson, Dr. Pollock, Lewis and Lawson W. Keener, and Christopher Beal. Lawson W. Keener also operated a lime kiln at his farm some nine miles northeast of Lincolnton and supplied the local demand for lime used in iron manufacture and for tanning and building purposes.

CHAPTER XXIV

The Progress of Education

The early pioneers were better schooled than were their children for several generations after, because these first settlers could write legibly, while many of their children could not sign their names. The reason was that the people of those times, struggling hard for bread, had problems to solve which came before books. They had the Bible, but other books were rare and as literary taste was neglected the art of reading was lost and it took several generations to rediscover it.

Judge Archibald D. Murphey said that in 1794 there were not more than three schools in the State in which the rudiments of a classical education could be acquired. In 1810 in an early settled eastern county not over one-third of the women could read and very probably it was no better in Lincoln County.

Governor Burton said that in 1826 primary education was harder to secure than in 1776. In 1838 in many large families neither parents nor children knew the alphabet and there was general indifference to education.

The State in 1789 chartered a University with no provision for a free school system to feed it. It was fifty years later before the Legislature had the courage to enact the first law authorizing one free school for every six square miles of inhabited territory, with a tax levy of twenty dollars for each district and forty dollars added from the State Literary fund, where school houses had capacity for fifty scholars, but this law was not effective except in counties that accepted it by popular vote. Lincoln County rejected it by majority vote and never had a free school until the State-wide law was adopted in 1853.

It was an age of individualism. The taxpayer said it was unjust to tax a man to educate the children of other men. They rejected the truth that the strong should bear the infirmities of the weak. Provincialism waged a long and bitter fight against free schools, but right finally conquered. Even then for thirty years, because of short school terms and the lack of trained teachers, the public school service was defective and those especially interested in better education patronized subscription schools.

Top left: Prof. D. Matt Thompson (1844-1925). See 1925.
Top right: Major S. M. Finger (1837-1896). See 1896.
Center: Miss Kate C. Shipp (1859-1932). See 1932.
Lower left: Dr. Chas. L. Coon (1868-1927). See 1927.
Lower right: Prof. James M. Bandy (1848-1911). See 1911.

THE ANNALS OF LINCOLN COUNTY 451

There were many reasons why the sentiment for public schools grew so slowly.

Money was very scarce and farm products very low so that the average man had a hard time to make ends meet. The plainest living was a necessity and the people demanded most rigid economy in the expending of public funds. In 1835 it cost the small sum of $87,000 to maintain the State Government and $40,000 of this was for the Legislative branch. The cost of the Constitutional Convention of 1835, which sat for five weeks, was only $11,000 and the members served for a dollar and a half per day.

In 1833 the tax income of Lincoln County was $756.93 from land tax and $947.71 from poll tax receipts. There was no road, school or pauper tax and most of the County expense was for court and jail costs. Schools would have required more tax and the people then, as now, dreaded taxes.

The whole environment of the average man made him indifferent and often positively opposed to schools. In most homes there were no books. Newspapers were so rare that in 1810 there were only 10 newspapers published in the State and those had very limited circulations. In 1800 there were sixty-eight post offices in the whole State and letter postage was twenty-five cents, payable on delivery. The first mail stage from Salisbury to Lincolnton was established in 1826 and at that time there was not a railroad or telegraph line in the world and not a good turnpike in North Carolina.

It was late in 1860 when the first railway train ran into Lincolnton and not until 1874 was the telegraph office established at the Seaboard station.

There were some who believed in education, at least for their own children. Long before the free school system was established a body of extraordinary men were the trustees of a school of high grade in Lincolnton, which was chartered in 1813 as Pleasant Retreat Academy. These trustees were Rev. Philip Henkel (Lutheran preacher), Rev. Humphrey Hunter (pioneer Presbyterian preacher), Major Lawson Henderson, Gen. Joseph Graham, Gen. Peter Forney, Col. John Hoke, Col. John Fulenwider, Col. Robert Williamson, Martin Shuford, Daniel Shuford, J. Reinhardt, Daniel Reinhardt, Vardry McBee, Henry Y. Webb, George Caruth, Dr. William McLean, Judge Robert H. Burton,

David Ramsour, Capt. John Reid, Peter Hoyle and Daniel Hoke. In 1819 the number of trustees was reduced from twenty-one to five men, who were Judge Robert H. Burton, Lawson Henderson, John Hoke, David Ramsour and Robert Williamson.

Recognizing the equal importance of female education the Lincolnton Female Academy was chartered December 21, 1821, with James Bivens, Vardry McBee, Daniel Hoke, Rev. James Hill, John Mushat, Joseph E. Bell and Joseph Morris as trustees.

The complete list of teachers in the two schools is not available but John Mushat, a Reformed preacher, graduate of Yale University, classical scholar and great teacher, was the principal of the Pleasant Retreat Academy, 1822 to 1825. Some of his students at that time were Robert, Rufus, William and Jacob Williamson, sons of Col. Robert Williamson, Hugh L., Chas C. and James Pinckney Henderson, sons of Major Lawson Henderson, William Davidson, Theodorus W. Brevard, Thomas Dews, Henry Fulenwider, Dr. Sidney X. and James Johnston, Samuel and James Connor.

Among other principals of Pleasant Retreat Academy in irregular order were Dr. S. P. Simpson (after 1825), Nathaniel M. Smith, John Dickey, Thomas Dews, George W. Morrow (1834), Jeremiah W. Murphy, Benjamin Sumner, Samuel C. Lindly (1850), and later Rev. Robert N. Davis, Rev. Jeremiah Ingold and others down to the period of the Civil War. One of the essential requirements for teaching was moral and religious character. It was said that John Dickey was a man of deep piety and always opened the school with prayer, but he was not an exception to the rule observed in that day, for all schools were opened with prayer and the Bible was used as a text book.

Among many students who attended this celebrated school for the forty years prior to the Civil War, besides those above mentioned were Dr. Cyrus L. Hunter, Richard T. Brumby, William and Samuel Lander, Michael Hoke, John F. Hoke, Vardry A. McBee, William M. Shipp, Albert M. Shipp, William Johnston, David Schenck, Robert D. Johnston, Robert F. Hoke, Stephen Dodson Ramseur, Ambrose Costner, Cephas Quickel, Henry Cansler, Henry F. Schenck, Lemuel J. Hoyle, William R. Myers, Joseph W. Alexander, and others, who became distinguished in many fields of endeavor.

Among the text books used during that period were *Webster's Blue Back Speller, Walker's Dictionary, The New Testament, The Columbian Orator, The Childs, The Shorter* and *Blair's Catechism, Pike's Arithmetic, Murray's Grammar, Bonnycastle's Algebra, Latin Grammar, Virgil* and *Cicero, Greek Grammar and Testament, Xenophon's Cyropaedia, Watt's Logic* and *Blair's Lectures.*

Among those who taught in the Male Academy, who deserve special mention, were Benjamin Sumner and Jeremiah W. Murphy. Benjamin Sumner came to Lincolnton from Person County in 1845, had charge of both the Male and Female Academies and was assisted by his son, Thomas J. Sumner, and his daughter, Mary Elizabeth, who became the wife of Vardry A. McBee. As a member of the Legislature from Person (1831-32), Mr. Sumner took a prominent part in the enactment of legislation for the promotion of education and was a teacher of rare gifts. Dr. Elisha Mitchell, Professor of Chemistry and Geology at the State University, wrote, July 31, 1833, of Mr. Sumner, as follows:

"Mr. Benjamin Sumner of Person County, N. C., a graduate some years since (1822) of the University of North Carolina, was pronounced by the faculty the first scholar in the class of which he was a member, having been highly successful in the prosecution of his studies in all the different branches of learning. He is believed by me to be eminently qualified by his natural talents and disposition, his habits and acquirements, for the business (the instruction of youth) in which he is at this time engaged."

Mr. Sumner had charge of the Lincolnton schools until about 1850, when he moved to Rowan County. Thomas J. Sumner, his son, who was a good scholar, also settled in Rowan and was for many years a prominent citizen of that county; he was a bachelor.

Jeremiah W. Murphy was an Irishman and Episcopalian and first came to Lincolnton to visit Rev. Samuel Lander and family, Mrs. Murphy being a sister of Mrs. Lander. He had three sons, who were Episcopal clergymen: William, Reginald Heber and Joseph W. Murphy, all of whom served churches in Maryland, though Joseph W. Murphy was for some years Rector of the Episcopal Church in Hillsboro, N. C. Mr. Murphy, the teacher, was a ripe scholar and a good instructor, who advertised that he prepared students to enter any class in the State University (*Lincoln Courier*). He had but one rule in his school, said to be about twelve inches long which was vigorously applied to the palm of the hand of every unruly student.

During the latter years of the Civil War Rev. W. R. Wetmore taught in this Academy and from about 1869 to 1872 he was associated there with Professor Hosea Hildreth Smith, and the school had a high reputation. Later Mr. Wetmore continued to teach there until about 1877. Among those who attended the school during that period were Hoke Smith, W. A. Hoke, Silas and Sumner McBee, Addison G. Smith and Stephen Smith, Theodorus H. Cobb, Chas. E. Childs, Henry A. Costner, James M. Templeton, William W. Mott, John C. Rankin, Forney and R. S. Reinhardt. One of the old students, Addison G. Smith, a distinguished lawyer in Birmingham, Alabama, in a letter dated July 11, 1927, said: "I loved the old town and most of the people in it and I have never yet gotten over that feeling, though many, many years have passed since my school days there. I have been back several times to see the town and the friends I left behind me. The last time I was very much saddened because I found that so many of my old friends had died, and I stayed only one day, when I first intended to stay several days. I often think of the following families and remember them with a great deal of pleasure: the Phifer, Brevard, Cobb, Smith (H. H.), Rev. Mr. Wetmore, Maj. Burton, Col. W. J. Hoke, Col. J. F. Hoke, Reinhardt, Lusk, Rudisill, Alexander, Bynum, McBee, Lander, Lawing, Schenck, Sherrill, Sumner, Abernethy, Michal, Jenkins, Shaw, Childs, Caldwell, Johnson, Woodcock, Motz, and other families. They were all fine people and no town had better."

Later the teachers at the Academy in the order mentioned were: R. S. Arrowood, Prof. Mebane, W. H. Bass, Rev. J. W. Jenkins, George W. Hahn and probably others, until about 1885 when Professor D. Matt Thompson took charge of the Lincolnton schools and taught in the old Female Academy (then called Piedmont Seminary). In 1908 the Pleasant Retreat Academy was transferred to the Daughters of the Confederacy and converted into a Memorial Hall, where many historical relics are preserved. A part of the building is used as a public library.

The old Female Academy was established in 1821 but the full list of the teachers is not available. Among them were Miss Lucretia Matthews, 1825; Miss Mariah Allyn, 1826 to 1832; Miss

Amelia Thompson, 1836 to 1841; and from 1841 for several years Miss Abigail Mason, of Pennsylvania.

The wisdom of the people, who in the early part of the nineteenth century established first class schools in Lincolnton resulted in the development of a highly intelligent citizenship and made Lincolnton a center of culture and refinement.

The Mary Wood School for girls and small boys was established in Lincolnton prior to the Civil War by Miss Mary Wood Alexander, daughter of the brilliant lawyer and orator, William Julius Alexander, and she drew patrons at home and abroad and continued to teach until her death in 1884. She was a gentlewoman and accomplished teacher and exercised a very fine influence over all her pupils.

Rev. Samuel Lander, Jr., during the Civil War and until the close of 1867 conducted a boarding school for girls in the present North State Hotel and it was called the Lincolnton Seminary. Upon his selection for the Presidency of Davenport College (Lenoir) he was succeeded in Lincolnton by Mrs. Caroline Mays Brevard, who continued the school until about 1871.

The Fassifern School was established in Lincolnton in 1907 by Miss Kate C. Shipp and many students came from various points, besides a large local patronage, and under the capable management of Miss Shipp work of superior merit was done here. The demand for larger equipment was met by enterprising business men of Hendersonville on condition that the school be moved to that city and there a much larger student body found accommodation and the school was recognized among the best of its kind in the State. Miss Shipp finally sold the property in Hendersonville to Rev. Joseph R. Sevier, under whose management it has continued to prosper. Fassifern will always be a monument to the rare genius and sacrifice of Miss Shipp, who founded and built it into an institution of high grade.

Other schools conducted in Lincoln County were taught at Beatties Ford in 1823 and 1824 by Nathaniel M. Smith and advertised by Robert Johnston, Henry Connor and John Hayes, who were patrons.

In 1825 a school was advertised by Robert Abernethy, Alfred M. and Robert H. Burton to be taught by M. O'Reilly at Beatties Ford. Peter S. Ney taught at Catawba Springs from 1841 to 1843. Patrick J. Sparrow, Thomas Sparrow, Robert G.

Allison, of Iredell County and Prof. Dewey from the North taught at Beatties Ford at different times in the early days.

Patrick J. Sparrow in 1827 taught at Buffalo Academy, 17 miles southwest of Lincolnton, according to an advertisement published by Lawson Henderson and David Kiddoe. According to an advertisement in *Raleigh Register* in 1829 Richard T. Brumby taught a school near Buffalo Shoals and limited the patronage to those whom he could accommodate in buildings adjoining his home. He also advertised for a limited number of law students.

L. A. H. Wilkinson was the founder of Rock Spring Seminary, located at Denver. He cut the logs, built the house, hired a teacher to assist him and started the school about 1871. In 1873 Prof. D. Matt Thompson took charge and conducted the school until about 1884 when he moved to Lincolnton. Following Professor Thompson at Denver were James F. Brower, for about five years; Charles L. Coon, for several years more; then Leon Cash, Sidney J. Whitener, and W. M. Brooks, in the order named.

Some years later the Denver Academy was established there and public schools have been conducted for some years. It is now a State high school with J. E. Ramsey, principal. Besides it there are two other State high schools in the County, besides the Lincolnton High School. They are the North Brook and Union Schools in the western part of the County, with J. Harlan Heafner, principal of North Brook, and J. Frank Turner, principal of Union High School.

For about four years from 1894 Rev. D. M. Litaker pastor of the Lowesville group of the Methodist churches, taught school at Lowesville and following him Rev. R. W. Boyd, of the Presbyterian Church taught there. George W. Hahn, for some years before he taught in Lincolnton, conducted a successful school in the Reepsville section. At the present time Lincoln County schools rank high and at the close of the 1935-36 scholastic year 179 young people graduated from the high schools of the County.

The Lincolnton City Schools since 1884, when Prof. D. Matt Thompson was made superintendent, have steadily grown in attendance and efficiency. He served until 1890, when he went to Gainesville, Florida, for a year and during his absence Mrs. Thompson carried on the school. After Prof. Thompson went to Statesville, Prof. Wm. E. Mikell, now Dean of the Law School of the University of Pennsylvania, was principal of the Academy in 1892 and 1893, when he was succeeded by Prof. Dick. Prof. Linney, of Taylorsville, taught for a while. Chas. L. Coon was superintendent in 1896-97. Then came Horace Flack, who was succeeded by B. P. Caldwell who remained until 1912. Those who served since were Prof. Blythe, John James, Michael S. Beam, E. Y. Joyner, E. D. Johnson, until 1926, when W. M. Pickens was made superintendent and is now (1936) still serving in that capacity.

The High School was established in 1904 and the class of that year graduated in 1908. In 1936 the graduating class numbered 65 young men and women.

The superintendents of the County Schools since D. Matt Thompson's terms were Rev. R. Z. Johnston, J. E. Hoover, J. N. Hauss (three months in 1899), G. T. Heafner, S. C. Garrison, L. Berge Beam, 1915 to 1927; J. N. Hauss, 1927 to 1931; Joseph R. Nixon since 1931.

The battle against ignorance has been long and hard but slowly and steadily the people have sought the light and finally found a brighter day. The struggle began in 1813 when forward looking men had Pleasant Retreat Academy chartered and a school of high grade established in Lincolnton for boys. Then nine years later came the Female Academy for girls. Those who patronized these schools had to pay for it. Many were indifferent and others too poor to pay tuition, but sentiment was slowly growing for general education until the public school system was finally established. Though not of a high grade at the start the leaven was working until at last we have a first class free school system. In 1936 we had 179 young people graduated from the Lincoln County high schools. It was a long way from 1813 to 1936 when we had more students to complete the high school course than was the total school attendance in the County in 1813. Before 1813 we had practically no school houses in the County, but now the school property is valued at more than $500,000. There are 8,000 school children and the cost of maintaining schools annually is about $180,000.

Lincoln County has made valuable contribution to education in this and other states by raising great teachers, such as Rev. Albert M. Shipp, Rev. Dr. R. H. Morrison, Rev. Dr. Samuel Lander, Rev. Dr. Robert L. Abernethy, Prof. J. M. Bandy, Dr. Charles L. Coon, D. Matt Thompson, Miss Mary Wood Alexander, Miss Kate C. Shipp and Rev. Dr. W. R. Wetmore, of all of whom prominent mention has already been made; besides these we should mention Rev. Dr. Patrick J. Sparrow, one time professor in Davidson College and later President of Hampden-Sydney College in Virginia, and Major Sidney M. Finger, for many years Professor in Catawba College (Newton) and State Superintendent of Public Instruction (1884-1892).

Prof. E. J. Forney, son of Major H. A. Forney, son of A. E. Forney, son of Abram Forney, the Revolutionary patriot, son of Jacob Forney, the pioneer, has filled the Chair of Commercial Education (since 1893) 43 years in the State Normal College in Greensboro, giving instruction and inspiration to thousands of young women during that long period of splendid service. Many who have come under his influence and tuition have said of him: "Two people above all others, I owe most grateful thanks: first, my mother who taught me earliest lessons and Mr. Forney, who gave me a new mental life and helped to make me an independent woman."

Dr. Samuel C. Dellinger came of good German stock, born near Iron Station, January 14, 1892, son of Robert Hoke and Laura (Loftin) Dellinger. He graduated from Lincolnton High School in 1908 and graduated with honors from Duke University in 1915; received A.M. degree from Columbia University and Degree in Zoology in 1917; professor of Zoology, Hendrix College, for a while and now (1936) fills the Chair of Zoology in University of Arkansas.

Mention should be made of Miss Angie Caldwell and Miss Bettie Coon, who for many years rendered extraordinary service as teachers in graded schools.

Miss Vardrine McBee, born in Lincolnton, September 24, 1879, daughter of Silas and Mary (Sutton) McBee; A.B., Smith College, 1906; A.M., Columbia University, 1908; Litt. D., Converse College; founded Ashley Hall private school in Charleston, S. C., in 1909, and has conducted it since.

John N. Hauss was born near Lincolnton in 1869, son of Andrew and Mary (Ramsey) Hauss. Attended the local community school and in 1886 entered Piedmont Seminary conducted by D. Matt Thompson in Lincolnton. In 1891 he went with Professor Thompson to Statesville where he taught in graded school three years, when, in 1894, he entered Peabody College for Teachers, in Nashville, Tenn., and finished the course in 1896, but spent the following year as a student in the University of Nashville. From 1897 to 1902 was principal of one of the graded schools in Jackson, Tenn. It was there he met Miss Bessie Ross, to whom he married in 1903. In 1902 he was elected superintendent of Thomasville (N. C.) City Schools and there for twenty-five years he gave his best efforts. He resigned in 1927 to be superintendent of Lincoln County Schools, in which position he served for four and one-half years. Then in 1935 he was called back to serve as superintendent of the Thomasville City Schools, where he is now employed.

Dr. William Sumner Jenkins, son of Blair and Mary (Sumner) Jenkins, graduated from Lincolnton High School, and from the State University with A.B. degree in 1924, and received M.A. degree in 1925, also the Ph.D. degree in history and government from the same institution in 1927. Studied law at Harvard in 1928 and at our State University Law School, 1929-1931, and received the LL. B. degree in 1931; was admitted to the bar in August, 1930. His professional career: Teaching Fellow in Department of History, University of North Carolina, 1924-25; Research Assistant with the Institute for Research in the Social Sciences, 1925-1927; Instructor in History, University of Tennessee, 1927-29; Instructor in Political Science, University of North Carolina, 1929-30; Assistant Professor, 1930-35; Associate Professor from 1935.

Dr. Holland Thompson, a distinguished author, historian and college professor, son of the late D. Matt Thompson, grew up in Lincoln County, was intimately associated with her people and we claim him as an honored Lincoln man.

The County has enriched this and other States by furnishing this long line of notable educators.

At the camp meeting held at St. Matthews Reformed Church, six miles north of Lincolnton, in 1851, the education of young men for the ministry and the heavy expense of sending to Northern colleges was discussed, when Judge M. L. McCorkle, then a young lawyer, asked the question, "Why not found a college of our own?" A minister present later stated that "from this germ Catawba College sprang," for money was soon raised in various Reformed Church circles and in 1851 a building was erected in Newton and Catawba College opened for students, and then for 72 years, until 1923, when the college was moved to Salisbury, it exercised a high educational influence in this section.

CHAPTER XXV

Newspapers and Authors, Physicians and Lawyers
Newspapers

The Newspapers of the County have contributed their full share in the education of the people. In 1831 Peregrine Roberts, a Lincolnton lawyer, established the *Lincoln Herald*, the first newspaper published in the County. It is difficult now to find a copy of that pioneer sheet.

In 1836 the *Lincoln Transcript* was published by A. R. Porter and Company. The subscription price was $2.00 a year cash, or $2.50 to credit subscribers. From 1836 to 1840 the *Lincoln Republican* was edited by L. E. Thompson, a Lincolnton lawyer, but he sold it to Robert Williamson, another Lincolnton lawyer, in 1840. The *Western Whig-Banner* was established in 1839 by Haywood W. Guion, and continued through 1840, as indicated by two copies dated June 27 and July 18, 1840, found in Duke University newspaper files.

The *Carolina Republican*, founded in 1848 by J. M. Newsom (a teacher by profession and a native of Maryland), was still published in 1853, according to newspaper files in the State University Library.

The *Lincoln Courier* was established as a Democratic paper in 1845 by Thomas J. Eccles (he was a printer born in Ireland in 1823, who came with his parents to Charleston, S. C., in 1824), and he published it certainly until 1853. Files of the paper dated July 30, and August 5, 1845, and May 10, 1851, are among newspaper files in State University Library.

In 1867 and probably 1868 another paper called the *Lincoln Courier* was printed in Lincolnton by E. H. Brittain, and then discontinued. A third paper called the *Lincoln Courier* was founded in Lincolnton by J. M. Roberts in 1883 and edited and published by him until 1895 when it was sold to F. S. Starrett and continued by him for several years. It does not appear in the 1904 Ayers American newspaper annual. Two copies of this paper dated February 7, 1890, and January 4, 1895, mutilated, are in Duke University Library.

The *Lincoln Progress*, established in 1873 by Monroe Seagle and James H. Smith (a Charlotte printer), was published by the founders until about 1877, when John T. and Francis H. DeLane bought it and continued in control until about 1881 when

Beverly C. Cobb assumed editorial control. It was finally discontinued. William M. Warlick published the *Lincolnton News* from about 1878 to 1880 when it was discontinued. The *Lincoln Press* was published by Col. John C. Tipton in 1884. One copy, dated December 5, 1884, is in State University Library. The *Lincoln Journal*, founded in 1894, was published by Col. John C. Tipton from 1894 to 1904. Copies, dated July 2, 1898, and March 24, 1899, are among the newspapers filed in the State University Library.

The *Lincoln Democrat* was established as a weekly paper in 1896 by Dr. Chas L. Coon, who was the brilliant editor, and espoused the cause of the Gold Democrats in the political campaign of 1896. He was succeeded by S. G. Finley, who continued it for only two years. The *Lincoln County News* was first edited, from 1907 for several years, by W. A. Fair. Volume 4-1910 indicates that Milton Tiddy had become the owner and editor and he continued in control for probably ten years when he sold his interest to John T. Perkins, who has published it since that time. Complete files of the *News*, a semi-weekly paper, from 1907 to 1928 (and probably later) are found in the State Library in Raleigh.

The *Lincoln Times* was chartered in 1907 with John M. Rhodes, Chas. H. Rhodes, C. Z. Hoyle, D. L. Yount, Samuel Yount, J. P. Mullen, Chas. A. Jonas, W. H. Hoover, A. S. Yount, L. B. Thompson, G. S. Mullen, C. A. Jonas, Sr., A. P. Sain, B. E. Sain, S. A. Whitener, R. L. Mullen, J. M. Hoyle and A. S. Scronce as stockholders. L. B. Thompson, a Northern man, was editor for two years, later Chas. A. Jonas edited it for two years, then J. F. Click became editor until F. A. Slate took charge. In 1919 the late Jonas W. Mullen and his son, John M. Mullen, became owners of the paper. Since 1925 it has been managed and edited by Miss Maude R. Mullen.

It should not be forgotten that Dr. Collier Cobb, in 1872, when but ten years old, published a little paper in Shelby called the *Home Journal*, and three years later, in 1875, it was published in Lincolnton. (See 1934.) The following appeared in the issue of July, 1875:

THE HOME JOURNAL

Published by Collier Cobb, Printer, Pressman and Proprietor, at fifty cents per annum, in advance.

Advertisements 25 cents an inch for each insertion.

Subscribers will please add ten cents postage. Those in town will add ten cents for carriage. Lincolnton, N. C., July, 1875.

To the business men of Lincolnton:

I commenced publishing the *Home Journal* in this place with high expectations. I obtained a few subscribers in town and a great many "promised" advertisements. When the time came for the paper to be gotten out I called on the gentlemen who had "promised" me, for their advertisements. The first one said, "Oh, I don't believe I will advertise until your paper has a little larger circulation." Another said, "Money is too scarce." And it was just that way every time. I started with only one advertisement; the next month I had none. Oh, business men of Lincolnton, I say to you, as I did to the men of Shelby, "Any man who can't afford to pay twenty-five cents to advertise his goods ought to shut up shop and quit business."

Advertisement

Have your work done at the *Home Journal* office. Pamphlets, blanks, circulars, posters, letterheads, bill heads, and all kinds of job work, neatly and promptly executed at this office.

For Sale. A good milk cow. For particulars apply at this office.

Description of Prize Picture in "Home Journal"

No. 1—The only one received.

"This seems to be a beautiful place—a kind of swamp, and the little boy seems to be asleep. He has curly hair and is lying in some weeds and the little birds are flying above his head. There are some kind of cattle grazing about him. A snake is crawling up to him and is about to bite his hand. The place looks as if it were a good place for snakes. The weeds are very high and the snakes can hide themselves. It seems as if it were Spring or Summer when the little birds began to fly all around you and the snakes began to show themselves.

"Lincolnton, N. C., July, 1875.

"Nettie Johnston, age 11 years."

Lincoln County Authors

Col. John H. Wheeler, when residing at Beatties Ford from 1850 to 1853, wrote *The History of North Carolina*.

THE ANNALS OF LINCOLN COUNTY 463

The Comet by Haywood W. Guion, a work of fiction, written in elegant literary style, appeared prior to the Civil War, and deserves a place in every library, but it is now a rare volume, difficult to secure.

The Common School Arithmetic, written by Rev. Samuel Lander, Jr., during the Civil War, was a text book in North Carolina Schools for some years. He was also the author of *Lander's Primer*, a text book for beginners, used during the war period, when, on account of the blockade, books could not be secured from the outside. These books were printed by the Sterling Co., Greensboro.

Dr. Cyrus L. Hunter was the author of *Sketches of Western North Carolina* in which is recorded much valuable Revolutionary history made by the patriots of Rutherford, Lincoln, Mecklenburg, Cabarrus, Iredell and Rowan Counties, during the eventful years from 1775 to 1783.

The Life of General Joseph Graham, by his grandson, Major William A. Graham, is a volume of Literary merit and preserves history of the Revolution in which Gen. Graham was active, along with the record of his later life. Major Graham was also the author of the *History of the South Fork Baptist Association*, a valuable contribution to local church history.

North Carolina, 1780-81, by the late Judge David Schenck, is a noble defense of the North Carolina troops and the courageous service they rendered in the Battle of Guilford Court House.

A Documentary History of North Carolina Schools and Academies, 1790-1840, by Dr. Charles L. Coon—one volume, and *Public Education in North Carolina, a Documentary History, 1790-1840*—two volumes, by the same author were issued by the State Historical Society. The author did much research work to secure the valuable facts embraced in these volumes, and assembled them in chronological order.

A concise history of Lincoln County, written by Alfred Nixon, appeared in the North Carolina Booklet about 1910. It covered the period from the Revolutionary to the Civil War, and is a well-written and valuable production, which contains much local history of that era.

Marriage Bonds of Tryon and Lincoln Counties, by Curtis Bynum, a volume of 184 pages, contains a vast body of information in small space, of interest to many people in Western Carolina. Mr. Bynum gave much time and money to this work and deserves grateful thanks for his unselfish service.

Pro-Slavery Thought in the Old South, a volume of 381 pages, was issued in 1935 by the University of North Carolina Press. Dr. William S. Jenkins, a Lincoln man, now Professor of Political Science in the State University is the author of this interesting historical volume and we have the right to expect other volumes by this gifted scholar.

Lincoln County Physicians

Among those who practiced medicine in the eastern part of the County were: Dr. Daugherty, Dr. William Johnston, Dr. Henry M. Pritchard, Dr. Joel Houston, Dr. Cyrus L. Hunter, Dr. William B. McLean, Dr. Sidney Connor, Dr. Sidney Harris, Dr. Calloway, Dr. Crider and Dr. S. P. Abernethy, of earlier days, and Dr. Sidney X. Johnston, Dr. Henry Y. Mott, Dr. Robert A. McLean, Dr. Ephraim A. Brevard, Dr. Chas. S. Rozzelle, Dr. J. D. Munday, Dr. Chas. L. McCaul, Dr. J. E. S. Davidson, Dr. Henry N. Abernethy, Dr. O. W. Shellem, and probably others.

West of the South Fork River were Dr. Eli Crowell, Dr. A. J. Fox, Dr. L. D. Black, Dr. W. A. Thompson, Dr. R. B. Killian, Dr. C. H. Hoover, of Crouse, and probably others.

Lincolnton physicians: Dr. S. P. Simpson, Dr. Z. Butt, Dr. Alex Ramsour, Dr. David W. Schenck, Dr. Elam Caldwell, Dr. J. C. Rudisill, Dr. J. M. Richardson, Dr. M. L. Brown, Dr. J. M. Abernethy, Dr. George M. Hoke, Dr. John M. Lawing, Dr. T. H. Means, Dr. R. A. McLean, Dr. John D. McLean, Jr., Dr. Robert J. Brevard, Dr. J. A. Reedy, Dr. Sumner McBee, Dr. W. L. Crouse, and more recently Dr. Lester A. Crowell, Dr. Albert C. Fox, Dr. J. M. Pressly, Dr. Thomas F. Costner, Dr. Gordon B. Crowell, Dr. L. A. Crowell, Jr., Dr. W. F. Elliott, Dr. A. M. Cornwell, Dr. J. W. Saine, Dr. J. S. Wise, Dr. Henry L. Sloan, Dr. George Costner, Dr. R. W. Petrie, Dr. W. C. Kiser, Dr. W. G. Bandy, Dr. J. R. Gamble, Dr. J. F. Gamble, Dr. C. D. Thompson, Dr. W. V. Costner, Dr. B. M. Bradford, Dr. R. E. Lee, and probably others.

Dr. Michael Hoke, son of Gen. R. F. Hoke and Lydia (Van Wyck) Hoke, was born in Lincolnton, June 28, 1874. He was graduated in 1893 at the University of North Carolina, where he will always be remembered as a distinguished athlete. He then studied medicine at the University of Virginia, attain-

Top left: Dr. Michael Hoke (1874-   ). See 1912 and Chap. 25.
Top right: Dr. Cyrus L. Hunter (1807-1881). See 1881.
Center left: Dr. R. B. Killian (1858-1935). See 1935 and 1896.
Center right: Dr. J. R. Gamble (1884-   ). See 1930.
Lower left: Dr. Lester A. Crowell (1867-   ). See 1907.
Lower right: Dr. William L. Crouse (1852-1902). See 1902.

ing his doctorate in 1895. He was married to Laurie Hendree Harrison of Atlanta, April 20, 1904, and has two children, Laura Hendree and Lydia Van Wyck. He has lived in Atlanta since 1897, and is an orthopaedic specialist of wide repute. Some years ago he was persuaded by President Roosevelt to give up his extensive practice in orthopaedic surgery in Atlanta and assume medical direction of the widely known Warm Springs Foundation in Georgia. He has gained national fame through his work of medical adviser and chief surgeon at the institution and through his achievements in the general practice. In 1931 the University of North Carolina recognized his distinction, awarding him the degree of LL.D. (See also 1912.)

Lincolnton Lawyers

Judge Robert H. Burton, Alfred M. Burton, Robert Williamson (State Senator), James Graham (Member of Congress from Rutherford district), Henry Y. Webb (late Federal Judge in Alabama), Bartlett Shipp (Legislator and member of Constitutional Convention of 1835), James R. Dodge (State Solicitor and Clerk Supreme Court), Judge Theodorus W. Brevard, Haywood W. Guion, L. E. Thompson, James P. Henderson (Diplomat, Governor of Texas, United States Senator, General in Mexican War), Peregrine Roberts, Michael Hoke (Legislator and Democratic Candidate for Governor in 1844), William Lander (State Solicitor, member Constitutional Convention of 1861, and of the Confederate Congress), Augustus W. Burton (Legislator and State Solicitor), Col. John F. Hoke (Adjutant General and Legislator), W. P. Bynum (State Solicitor and Justice of the Supreme Court), Thos. N. Herndon, V. A. McBee, A. F. Brevard, B. S. Guion, William Williamson, Robert Williamson, Jr., David Schenck (Judge Superior Court and member of Convention of 1861), John D. Shaw, Samuel Lander, III, B. C. Cobb, W. S. Bynum, A. J. Morrison, R. J. Shipp, S. G. Finley, Theodorus H. Cobb, Bartlett Shipp, Jr., C. E. Childs, W. A. Hoke (Chief Justice of Supreme Court), Lemuel B. Wetmore, David W. Robinson, R. J. Mauser, A. L. Quickel (Legislator and Judge Superior Court), Charles A. Jonas (State Legislator and Member of Congress), Kemp B. Nixon (State Senator), H. A. Jonas, W. M. Nicholson, S. M. Roper, Chas. R. Jonas, L. E. Rudisill, Waverly Rudisill, W. H. Childs (State Senator), M. T. Leatherman, Kenneth Goodson, H. E. Rees, L. Berge Beam and Bruce F. Heafner.

CHAPTER XXVI

The Church in Lincoln County

The Church is entitled to a prominent place in history for we owe a mighty debt to the great and good men, who have sacrificed and labored to build up the church. We can never pay the debt we owe to John Gottfried Arndt, Andrew Loretz, Humphrey Hunter, James Lewis, Robert Johnston Miller and Daniel Asbury, the pioneer preachers, who established the early churches of the Lutheran, German Reformed, Presbyterian, Baptist, Episcopal and Methodist denominations west of the Catawba River and they will ever be remembered by a grateful people for their devotion to the Master, whose spirit impelled them to follow our fathers into the wilderness, preach the gospel of reconciliation and plant the church beside the cabin of the humblest pioneer.

These missionaries were the saving salt when men sorely needed the gospel to deliver them from the wickedness of that period. The truth they preached has been handed down to the succeeding generations and still abides as a saving power. Others as good as they have since been faithful ministers in this territory but Arndt, Loretz, Hunter, Lewis, Miller and Asbury laid the foundations upon which the laborers west of the Catawba have builded since these early missionaries have passed to their reward.

Among the earlier settlers were the Pennsylvania Dutch, who were Lutheran and German Reformed in faith. They had much in common, were the same stock and spoke the German language. They established a church in the several communities where they settled, for the use of both denominations. The first of these union churches, Emanuels, commonly known as the old White Church in Lincolnton was built about 1788.

An interesting and comprehensive history of Emanuels was written by the late Judge David Schenck and published in the *Lincoln Progress*, July 12, 1873, as follows:

Emanuels Church

This venerable building, known in the community as the "Old White Church," of Lincolnton, has clustered around it so many local and personal reminiscences, interesting to the citizens of the County, that we give a short historical sketch of it. The incidents and facts have been collected from such meagre records as we can find, and from the memory of our fellow-citizens, Henry Cansler, B. S. Johnson, Daniel Seagle, Jacob Bisaner and others who have long known and worshipped in it.

The Town of Lincolnton was chartered in 1786, and under its provisions a deed was made on the 10th of January, 1788, by Joseph Dickson to Christian Reinhardt and Andrew Hedick for two acres and sixteen poles of land in the Southeast square of Lincolnton which they were to hold "as agents for the Dutch Presbyterians and Dutch Lutherans, for the purpose of building thereon a meeting house for public worship, school houses, both Dutch and English, and for a place for the burial of the dead; the said societies having, at their joint expense already built a house for public worship thereon." This deed is registered in Lincoln County, book 3, page 362, and was drafted and witnessed by Waightstill Avery, Esq. The church which was, at that date, on the premises, is the portion which constitutes the lower part of the present building. It was built of logs; the southeast corner of it was "carried up" or fitted by Philip Cansler (father of Henry Cansler, Esq.) and Adam Reep. We have not been able to find any record of the church older than 1794. We have the register of baptized children, commencing in that year and running down to 1822, and in this there are occasional entries of other matters. It is all written in German and rather difficult to translate, but by the assistance of General Daniel Seagle, we have been able to extract a few prominent facts. The title page informs us, that at that date John Gottfried Arends was the pastor of the Evangelical Lutheran congregation, and Andrew Loretz was pastor of the "Reformed" congregation, which at that time seems to have been synonymous with Dutch Presbyterians. The first entry made is the baptism of Anna Maria Koch, 7th June, 1794, the next of Catherine Ganzler, daughter of John Ganzler, then follow Hokes, Fingers, Botzs, Summerows, Reinhardts, etc., all ancestors of our present population. It is curious to see how names have been changed, "Hock" is now "Hoke," "Butts" now, was "Botz" then, "Cansler" now, was "Ganzler" then, "Rahmsaur" then, is "Ramsour" and "Ramseur" now. These two faithful ministers, Arends and Loretz, each served their respective congregations until they died. Rev. John Gottfried Arends died 9th July, 1807, aged 66 years, 6 months, and 28 days, and was for 35 years a minister of the

Gospel. He was buried under the church; the floor was taken up and an excavation made, which was walled with brick, and in this vault his coffin was placed. In the year 1810 a tombstone commemorating his service, was placed outside of the church against its walls by his congregation. It is in German and was prepared by a neighbor of Mr. Arends, named Stochinger, an old school master. This venerable minister had left a reputation for piety, humility and zeal in his work, of which his worthy descendants may well be proud.

(See 1912 for the paragraph referring to Rev. Andrew Loretz taken from this article.)

The burial ground attached to this old church contains some of the ancestors of nearly every old family in the County, and the names of the seniors who lie buried there are still familiar in our own generation.

The first person ever buried there was killed by a fall from the old court house window. A rude stone still marks the grave, but there seems to be some discrepancy in the memory of parties as to his name. Mr. Cansler thinks it was Thomas Perkins, while others say it was Thomas Hawkditch. There are some old tombstones of the Summerow family, which show dates as far back as 1722, but it is evident these bodies were removed to this graveyard long after that date, as there was neither church, town or graveyard here in 1722.

After the death of Rev. Mr. Arends in 1807, Philip Henkel became pastor of the Lutheran congregation. On the 14th April, 1808, we find his name as pastor, among the list of communicants, and 28th Feb., 1809, he baptized a child, as pastor of the church.

Philip Henkel lived for a while on the lot where the new jail now stands and preached to several congregations in the surrounding country; he afterwards removed to Lyles Creek, in Catawba County, thence to Tennessee. He was a worthy man and much respected by the people.

Rev. Daniel Moser succeeded Philip Henkel in 1815. We find his name as pastor, among the list of communicants, October 15, 1815, which continues on the list until the 17th May, 1818, the year previous to the time when the Tennessee Synod seceded from the North Carolina Synod.

After the death of Rev. Mr. Loretz, the Presbyterians of Concord Presbytery seem to have occupied the church jointly with the Evangelical Lutherans, and were organized under the ministrations and pastoral care of Rev. Humphrey Hunter. We have no record of his pastorate, and have only the memory of those living who heard him preach there.

The division of the Tennessee Synod from the North Carolina Synod, took place in Emanuels Church, in the year 1819. Rev. David Henkel, who was a man of learning, spirit, and resolution, differed with the North Carolina Synod in regard to certain doctrines of the Church, which he urged with great zeal and pertinacity, but being unable to convince his brethren he separated from them, and with his followers, constituted the Evangelical Lutheran Tennessee Synod, whose first meeting was held on the 17th July, 1820. A spectator of the debate, in the old church, describes it as very warm and exciting and at times bitter and personal, and finally after all efforts to effect harmony had failed, Mr. Henkel and those agreeing with him, left the Synod and met that evening in the present "Johnson Hotel," then occupied by John B. Harry, Esq., to take preliminary steps for a separate organization. Rev. David Henkel was a younger brother of Philip Henkel; he also had another brother, Ambrose Henkel; all were Lutheran preachers, and afterwards became members of the Tennessee Synod. After this unfortunate division in the Church the Lutheran congregation seems to have lost much of its strength and organization. There was no regular pastor for perhaps ten years, and a great many of its members joined the Presbyterian organization under the pastoral care of Rev. Joseph E. Bell. The North Carolina Synod held the legal title to the church and sent occasional supplies to that portion of the congregation which adhered to their Synod. Rev. John Graber, of the North Carolina Synod, and perhaps others preached in the church.

In the year 1819, the log church was raised a story higher and weatherboarded, and a new pulpit erected and other material alterations and improvements made on the church, constituting the building as it now stands. Col. John Hoke was at that time Treasurer of the congregation, and we have, in his handwriting the subscription list for the work, and his final settlement with the session of the church, showing the cost to have been

$573.06. At that time there was a school taught in the church by a Mr. Quinn, and we find this entry on the subscription list for the church—"School boys paid first money of all, $2.12½.

The bell of the church was not put up until 1827. Daniel Shuford's and J. M. Jacob's receipts for the work are filed. The carpenter's work on the church was done by Daniel Shuford. The church was painted in 1830; there is a voucher of that date filed for $175.00 for painting and repairs.

It will be necessary now, to trace as nearly as possible the Presbyterian organization which grew up in this old church, and which finally separated and built the present Presbyterian Church in 1839.

After Mr. Loretz's death, Rev. Humphrey Hunter, a member of Concord Presbytery, preached for some years in the church, and the members of Mr. Loretz's congregation, or nearly all of them became enrolled as Presbyterians, and we find their first church record beginning Feb. 14th, 1823, Joseph E. Bell, Moderator, and John Hoke, David Ramsour, Peter Summey, and Michael Reinhardt, Elders.

Mr. Bell came to Lincolnton from Tennessee, and was first a school teacher at Lincolnton and a member of the Lutheran church; he was under the patronage of Philip Henkel and soon became a Lutheran minister and was at the Synod of 1819 when the separation took place. Soon after this, in 1821 or 1822, he joined the Presbyterian Church and became the first regular pastor of the congregation. In 1823 Peter Summey and Michael Reinhardt were relieved from "the active duties of the eldership," and Charles E. Reinhardt was chosen as Elder. The session, then composed of Joseph E. Bell, pastor, John Hoke, David Ramsour, and Charles E. Reinhardt, continued down to March, 1828. In August, 1827, the session resolved to prefer charges against Mr. Bell, before the Presbytery which met at Morganton in September of that year, and which resulted in silencing Mr. Bell as minister, and shortly thereafter, in his expulsion from the Church. The charge against him was that he removed a landmark, or corner of a survey of land which he had purchased from David Ramsour; this charge was fully sustained by the testimony of Henry Cansler, Esq., who was the surveyor, and B. S. Johnson and Lemuel Moorman, who were the chainbearers. Mr. Bell having been silenced, the congregation called the Rev. Patrick J. Sparrow, who was ordained by the Presbytery, in the Church, Nov. 15th, 1828, and immediately installed as pastor of the congregation. Mr. Sparrow continued as pastor until the 18th March, 1833, when by resolution of the session, the pastoral relation was dissolved, at his request. In 1834 Rev. William B. Davis became stated supply for a short time, and in July of that year, Rev. Albertus W. Watts, was engaged as stated supply and continued until July, 1836, when he was installed as pastor.

In the year, 1829, as near as we can ascertain, Rev. John G. Fritchey, a German Reformed minister, came to Lincolnton and soon created a division in the Presbyterian congregation, and induced the majority of them to organize into a separate congregation of the German Reformed Church, and claimed that he and they were the Dutch Presbyterians, meant in the deed of conveyance. The list of the original members of the Presbyterian Church was revised and a formal separation took place, and in 1832, the record of the German Reformed congregation begins. Mr. Fritchey not only created discord in the Presbyterian Church, but he violently assailed the Lutheran doctrines, and made charges against Martin Luther, which drew from Michael Rudasill, in July, 1830, a most caustic and severe letter to Mr. Fritchey's session, in which the not very polite epithet of "calumniator" is applied to the reverend gentleman, in reply to his strictures on Mr. Rudasill's church.

Mr. Fritchey seems to have been fond of controversy. He obtained considerable popularity at first, but in 1839, having run his course, he returned to Pennsylvania, where he was still living in 1867.

The Presbyterian congregation, proper, held their first service in the new Presbyterian Church on the southwest square, on the 4th Sabbath of June, 1839, when Mr. Watts preached a sermon from Haggai, second chapter and ninth verse.

The German Reformed congregation continued its organization under Rev. J. H. Crawford, Rev. David Crooks and others, until about 1850, when they became so reduced in number that they ceased to have service. The North Carolina Lutheran Synod also ceased to send a minister to the church and their organization has become extinct and no members of it remain.

The Tennessee Synod for a while kept together a considerable congregation under the ministration of Rev. Adam Miller, about 1840 and subsequently and after his fall, they too became scattered and joined other churches, and now the church is used by the Baptists, who have organized lately, under the pastoral care of the Rev. Needham B. Cobb. So that we see that in 1873, there are no Dutch Lutherans, or Dutch Presbyterians to hold title to the property and the German Reformed congregation being almost extinct and the Presbyterians having erected a new place of worship, it becomes the descendants of the former members of the church to preserve this old and venerable landmark of the past.

D. S. (These are the initials of David Schenck.)

The old White Church was destroyed by fire in December, 1893. It had been the place of worship for all the denominations until individual churches were built in the town. After the fire a new brick church was built by the Lutherans on the site of the old one, but in recent years it was abandoned as a place of worship and converted into an undertaker's establishment, when the Lutherans built the beautiful church just across the street from the old one.

The pastors of this new church, which was completed in 1920, have been Rev. W. J. Roof, under whose leadership the building was erected, Rev. V. C. Ridenhour, Rev. Voigt R. Cromer and the present pastor, Rev. L. A. Thomas.

In 1910 the German Reformed congregation in Lincolnton was reorganized and built a new church on East Main street under the pastoral leadership of Rev. W. H. McNairy.

The charter members were E. D. Fox, Mrs. Laura Fox, P. D. Hinson, Jacob Holbrooks, Pearl Holbrooks, Ethel Holbrooks, T. J. Keever, Mrs. M. C. Keever, Mrs. B. E. McNairy, Wyatt McNairy, Miss Minnie Michael, Mrs. Kitty Rudisill, Miss Marie Rudisill, R. J. Ramseur, John J. Ramseur, K. M. Ramseur, D. A. Seagle, Mrs. Catherine Seagle, Miss Vera Seagle, Miss Ruth Seagle, Craig Seagle, Mrs. E. C. Shuford, Jas. A. Shuford, A. P. Willis, Mrs. Della Willis.

Those who have served as pastor from 1910 to date are: Rev. W. H. McNairy; Rev. J. B. Swartz, Jan. 8, 1922, to April 30, 1922 (supply); Rev. B. J. Peeler, May 6, 1922, to May 1, 1924; E. Warner Lentz, May 4, 1924, to July 24, 1924 (supply); H. W. Black, May 24, 1925, to August 31, 1925 (supply); Rev. H. C. Kellermyer, June 6, 1926, to April 15, 1929; Rev. Hoy L. Fesperman, Sept. 1, 1930, to 1935; Rev. Huitt R. Carpenter, Sept. 1, 1935—.

Daniels Church

Daniels Church was organized about 1786, though the old records date back only to 1809.

The original pioneers to this section were Daniel Warlick and Derrick and John Ramsour. They were followed by the Lantz, Summerow, Hoke, Reinhardt, Kistler, Coon, Coulter, Heedick, Seagle, Houser, Shuford, Carpenter, Quickel, Anthony, Clay, Motz, and other families. On July 15, 1768, Matthew Floyd in consideration of ten pounds sterling conveyed to Nicholas Warlick, Frederick Wise, Urban Asherbraner, Peter Stotler, Peter Summey and Peter Hafner, trustees of the United Congregation of the Lutheran and German Reformed Churches, 50 acres of land.

To remove all doubt as to who should share the property Cephas Quickel and David W. Ramsour again entered the Daniels Church land and a grant was made by Governor Vance, dated January 20, 1863, and on July 26, 1863, they conveyed same to George Coon, Jacob Kistler, Maxwell Warlick, Jacob Lantz, Daniel Seagle and Geo. S. Ramsour, trustees of Daniels Lutheran and Reformed Churches.

The second Daniels Church was built in 1844 and used by both congregations until 1889, when the Lutherans decided to build a new and separate church.

The Reformed congregation in the same year agreed to do likewise and both churches were completed about 1894. The Reformed pastors were Andrew Loretz, until his death in 1812; J. R. Reilly, Jacob Scholl, J. S. Ebaugh, John Rudy, W. C. Bennett, John G. Fritchey, 1828-1840; G. A. Leopold, 1840-1841; J. H. Crawford, 1841-1842; S. S. Middlekauf, 1842-1845; David Crooks, 1846-1859; Jeremiah Ingold, 1859-1874; Julius Shuford, 1874-1876; J. C. Clapp and J. A. Foil, 1876-1878; Julius Shuford, 1878-1883; A. P. Horn, 1883-1884; G. D. Gurley, 1884-1885; J. L. Murphy, 1885-1890; J. L. M. Lyerly, 1891-1893; J. C. Clapp, 1894-1897; T. C. Hesson, 1897-1902; C. B. Heller, 1902-1906; O. B. Michael is the present pastor.

Among the Lutheran pastors were Philip Henkel, David Henkel, Daniel Moser, Adam Miller, Polycarp Henkel, Alfred J. Fox (1854 to 1884); Jesse R. Peterson, M. L. Little, J. A. Rudisill, E. J. Sox, M. L. Pence, L. L. Lohr and Rev. W. J. Roof, the present pastor. This is not a complete list.

Salem Church

Salem Church was established prior to 1814 by John Ramsour, Henry Ramsour and David Carpenter, of the Reformed, and Jacob Killian, Anthony Hallman, Henry Creasmore, Jonas Rudisill, Henry Grose, John Cline and Jonas Heedick, of the Lutheran Church. The first church was built of logs prior to 1814.

At a meeting, August 27, 1814, Capt. Henry Ramsour, Col. John Reinhardt, and Joshua Wilson were appointed to collect funds to repair the old building and direct the work on it. The cost of improvement was $338.94. It was used until 1845, when a brick church was built on the same site. Jacob Ramsour, (M. W.), Wm. McCaslin, and David Heedick, were commissioned to raise the funds and superintend the construction. John Coulter assisted David Heedick in making the brick, while Jacob Ramsour furnished pine trees and Ambrose Ramsour the door sills. The new church cost $628.39. In 1875 further improvement was made at a cost of $284.37, under direction of Noah Summerow and William Ramsour (Reformed) and Abel Seagle and Hosea Yount (Lutheran).

On July 18, 1896, the two congregations celebrated the Centennial of the building of the original church. Among the ministers present were Dr. R. A. Yoder, Dr. J. C. Moser and Dr. W. P. Cline, of the Lutheran Church, and Dr. J. C. Clapp and Dr. J. L. Murphy, of the Reformed Church. The pastors of Daniels Church have generally served the two congregations at Salem.

St. Matthews Church

This church was organized on May 3, 1837, by the German Reformed people under the leadership of Rev. John G. Fritchey, from members of the old White Church in Lincolnton, and was built on land donated by John Ramsour, who with John Coulter, was elected trustee. They with Joseph Finger, John Blackburn, and Jacob Summerow were appointed a committee to build a church, size 30 by 40 feet. Joseph Finger was the lowest bidder and the first church was built for $265.00. The first elders were John Carpenter, Jacob Ramsour, (M. W.), John Ramsour and Daniel Finger.

Annual camp meetings were held under a brush arbor until 1845 when a substantial wood arbor was built and large crowds gathered for these meetings. The Reformed pastors at Daniels and Salem Churches have generally served at St. Matthews Church.

The Lutherans have eight congregations in the County with 1,463 members and church property valued at $141,365, according to recent church statistics.

Prominent laymen were Peter Hoyle, Cephas Quickel, Ambrose Costner, George Coon, Daniel Seagle, Titus Rhodes, Melchi Rhodes, John M. Rhodes, Chas. H. Rhodes, Daniel E. Rhyne, Jonas Rudisill, Jacob Killian, Jonas Heedick, David Heedick, Abel Seagle, John B. Smith and others.

Rev. David Henkel, a notable preacher, married Catherine, daughter of Hon. Peter Hoyle. Among their children were Rev. Dr. Polycarp and Dr. Socrates Henkel, both of whom were brilliant preachers. Rev. Dr. A. J. Fox, for thirty years a pastor of Daniel, Salem and Trinity Churches, had two sons, Rev. Luther A. Fox, D.D., and Rev. Junius B. Fox, who spent their lives in the service of the church in Virginia. Other native ministers of note were Rev. Dr. W. A. Lutz and Rev. Dr. L. L. Lohr.

The following excerpts are taken from *Bernheim's History of the Lutheran Church:*

The early churches were owned jointly by German Reformed and Lutherans with union Hymn Books. In the old Bibles frequent notes are entered of their colonization, with dates of settlement.

Pennsylvania, and not Germany, furnished North Carolina with these sturdy citizens. Williamson's *History* gives us a reason why the Scotch came to this State and the same applies to the Dutch.

Land could not be obtained in Pennsylvania without great difficulty because the Proprietors of that Province purchased the soil in small parcels from the natives and the best land was soon taken up. No one then ventured to cross the Alleghanies for the savage Indians were a menace, so they went south rather than west until they found unoccupied and fertile land, which was cheap, and where welcome was given to people of all faiths.

The Scotch Irish and Germans dwelt together peaceably, and coming South long before railroads or even decent dirt roads were opened, they stowed away every useful article for house or farm in wagons and brought them along. The cavalcade moved on, the men on foot with women and children in wagons. Cattle, sheep and hogs were driven on before. They usually left the North in Autumn after crops were gathered and disposed of.

The first pioneer teams arrived in Rowan about 1745, and in Lincoln a few years later. This is certified by tradition, family records and old deeds, which were dated some time later. They were industrious, thrifty and economical, not afraid of, or ashamed to work and Providence smiled upon their efforts.

They were generally farmers, lived in the country, ignorant of the English language, not shrewd enough for merchants, well read in the Bible and other German devotional books, lived at home and were good farmers. Their churches were therefore in the country. In the absence of pastors in the early days they had the school teacher to read prayers and sermons on Sunday and self-appointed missionaries preached now and then and administered the Sacrament, while the school teacher generally read burial service for the dead and in urgent cases baptized children.

Rev. Dr. George William Welker, of the German Reformed Church, in Colonial Records wrote of the tide of German immigration to North Carolina as follows:

"The German immigration to America grew out of the fearful results of the Thirty Years' War that had desolated their native land and made existence there intolerable. After this came the French invasion of the Rhine territory. By this the grand home of the Palatines, who were Protestants, was made a houseless waste. For these sufferers the new world opened an asylum. William Penn gave the heartiest invitation to his colony. Queen Anne of England, offered a refuge and means of succor. Thousands left their native land by way of England to reach a home in the wilderness. Most of these were aided to reach the colony of Pennsylvania, which for a time, seemed to become largely Germanized. Among them were also French Huguenots, who on the revocation of the edict of Nantes, fled to Germany, and came with their co-religionists to America.

"This influx of German, Swiss and French into Pennsylvania began about 1707. Many had come over previous to this and as early as 1682. During the period from 1727 to 1775 the archives of the colony of Pennsylvania record the names of more than thirty thousand persons who landed at the port of Philadelphia. It is from this colony that the German immigrants to North Carolina to a great extent came."

The best lands in Pennsylvania, east of the Alleghanies, were taken up and the Proprietors of Carolina offered very advantageous terms to settlers. Its climate and soil fertility attracted these industrious people, and in 1785 the German population in North Carolina from Pennsylvania was over fifteen thousand.

Morse, in his "American Universal Geography" in 1789 says: "The Germans compose about one-fourth of the population of Pennsylvania. They consist of Lutherans (who are most numerous), Calvinists or Reformed, Catholics and Mennonites. These are all distinguished for their temperance, industry and economy."

Rupp quotes Governor Thomas (1738): "This province has been for some years the asylum of the oppressed Protestants of the Palatinate and other parts of Germany, and I believe it may truthfully be said that the present flourishing condition of it is in a great measure owing to the industry of these people; it is not altogether the fertility of the soil, but the number and industry of the people, that makes a flourishing country."

These were the Pennsylvania Dutch, whose descendants today are substantial, progressive citizens of Lincoln, Gaston, Catawba, Rowan and other counties of North Carolina.

The Episcopal Church

The Mother Church of the Episcopal faith in Lincoln was White Haven, in the eastern part of the County. In 1786 a congregation was organized and a vestry elected. It was located a mile south of Lowesville, in what is now Gaston County. Bishop Cheshire, when rector of Saint Peter's Church (Charlotte) visited the spot where the old church stood, one hundred years after it was first organized. At the Diocesan Convention of 1890 he read a paper about the old church and Reverend Robert Johnston Miller, the minister, stating that, "A few of the older inhabitants on both sides of the Catawba River remember when the old church was standing and a few recall the fact that they were baptized by 'Parson Miller,' as he was called ... An old graveyard surrounded by a stone wall identifies the spot."

Names associated with the parish are those of Abernethy, Burton, Forney, Fite, Hager, Nance, Robinson, Shipp and others.

Rev. Robert Johnston Miller was a Scotch Episcopalian and a soldier of the Revolution. In 1785 he came with Bishop Thomas Coke to the Methodist Conference in Franklin County, held at the home of Green Hill, became a Methodist preacher and served that year on Tar River circuit. He was not ordained and withdrew from that church within a year, and settled on the west side of the Catawba, where he organized White Haven congregation, composed of people attached to the Episcopal form of worship. Among these was the family of David Abernethy, whose wife was Mary Turner, from Aberdeen, Scotland, and a Scotch Episcopalian. A daughter of this couple married Peter Forney and a son married Susan, a sister of Peter Forney.

Mr. Miller was lay leader at White Haven, and also catechised the children. He was ordained by the Lutheran clergy, distinctly reserving his Episcopal belief, on May 20, 1794 in Saint John's Church in Cabarrus County. In his application for orders he stated that he was "obliged to obey the rules, ordinances and customs of the Christian Society, called the Protestant Episcopal Church in America."

Dr. Bernheim in the History of the Lutheran Church, says:

"The first English Lutheran preacher in North Carolina was the Rev. Robert Johnston Miller. Although licensed to preach by the Methodist Conference, yet not having authority to administer the Sacraments, his people of White Haven Church, Lincoln County, sent a petition to the Lutheran preachers of Cabarrus and Rowan Counties, with recommendations, praying that he might be ordained by them, which was accordingly done . . . On the reverse side of the certificate the Lutheran ministers gave the reason why they had ordained a man who was attached to the Episcopal Church as a minister of that denomination."

In 1787 Mr. Miller married Mary Perkins, daughter of "Gentleman" John Perkins, a wealthy citizen of Lincoln County, and in 1806 moved from Lincoln to Burke County. In 1817 at the Episcopal Convention held in Raleigh he presented his certificate of Lutheran orders and on May 1, 1817 was regularly ordained deacon and advanced to the priesthood of the Episcopal Church.

The parish of White Haven, Smyrna and Saint Peter's was admitted into the Convention of the Diocese in 1822, and in 1824 Robert H. Burton and Daniel M. Forney were appointed lay readers. Bishop Ravenscroft preached there in 1824 and confirmed sixteen persons. When he returned in 1828 he found it a hopeless task to collect the scattered membership into one congregation. He preached at Beatties Ford in 1828 and baptized three children of the Burton family. After Mr. Miller moved to Burke his many ministerial duties there made it impossible for him to give the required attention at White Haven. When Bishop Ives visited the parish in 1833 he could find only three or four persons who were Episcopalians.

In 1849 the Rev. Joseph Huske in charge of Saint Luke's Church, Lincolnton, held a service at White Haven, which was perhaps the last one held there. "Parson Miller" filled a high niche in the early religious life of Lincoln County as well as in Burke and Caldwell, where many of his honored descendants have lived. He died May 13, 1834 in Burke County and his body was buried at Mary's Grove where he had lived for many years.

After the death of Mr. Miller the Rev. Dr. Moses Ashley Curtis was sent as a missionary to Lincoln and Mecklenburg Counties and was the first resident Episcopal minister in Lincolnton. Dr. Curtis brought with him to his first charge his bride who had been Miss Mary DeRossett, of Wilmington. Their daughter, Mary, became the wife of the Rev. William Shipp Bynum and was for many years a resident of Lincolnton, while her mother and sisters in later years made Lincolnton their home. In 1837 Dr. Curtis was transferred to another field and was succeeded here by the Rev. T. S. W. Mott, until 1841 when Rev. E. M. Forbes was given charge of this mission field. Rev. J. S. Kidney was his assistant and preached in Morganton, Lenoir and Rutherfordton.

On March 2, 1842 Col. John Hoke conveyed to E. M. Forbes, Jeremiah W. Murphy, Michael Hoke, Thomas N. Herndon, Haywood W. Guion and L. E. Thompson, Trustees of Saint Luke's Episcopal Church, the lot on which the present church stands. Haywood W. Guion drew plans for the church and supervised the work of building. When it was remodeled (or rebuilt) some forty years ago, according to plans drawn by Silas McBee, nothing of the old church was left, except the tower which had been rebuilt in 1859.

In 1843 Bishop Ives confirmed twelve persons in Lincolnton and at the same time ordained Rev. J. S. Kidney to the priesthood and A. F. Olmstead as a deacon.

The late Chief Justice R. M. Pearson was one of the twelve confirmed at that time. Mr. Olmstead was ordained Priest by Bishop Ives, July 20, 1844.

Jeremiah W. Murphy came to Lincolnton about 1840 and taught in the Male Academy, was an active Episcopalian, lay leader and one of the first delegates to the Diocesan Convention. He had a leading part in planting the Episcopal Church in both Lincolnton and Charlotte. Three of his sons, Joseph W. Murphy, William Murphy and Reginald Heber Murphy, became Episcopal clergyman. Others prominent in the Episcopal faith that came to Lincolnton about that time were the Sumner, Guion, Thompson and Alexander families, who were active in religious work. Descendants of Benjamin Sumner, the teacher, who became leaders in church work were: Rev. Benjamin McKenzie, an Episcopal Archdeacon in Texas; Rev. Hoke Ramsour, a consecrated young man who died in the African mission field; Rev. Sumner Guerry and his brother Rev. Moultrie Guerry, Episcopal ministers, the former a missionary in China; Mr. Silas McBee, one of the most widely known Episcopal laymen in America; his daughter, Dr. Vardrine McBee, the principal of a high grade private school in Charleston; Misses Mary Wood Sumner, Mary Ramsour and Sallie Sumner, workers in the Young Women's Christian Association.

From 1841 to 1862 the Rectors of Saint Luke's Church were Reverend E. M. Forbes, A. F. Olmstead, J. C. Huske, T. S. W. Mott, H. H. Hewitt, C. T. Bland, and G. F. Everhardt.

St. Luke's was made an independent parish about 1860. Rev. W. R. Wetmore was called to St. Luke's as rector in 1862. His useful service in Lincolnton as a minister and educator have already been elaborately portrayed in these ANNALS. He was a consecrated and tireless worker until he fell asleep in March, 1904. A great, good man, who left a noble record! During the Civil War many refugees came to Lincolnton. Prominent among these were Bishop Lay and members of the Calder family of Charleston. Before the war Bishop Lay (who married a daughter of Bishop Atkinson) had been a missionary bishop of the Southwest, which included Arkansas. Shortly after the surrender he was arrested by Federal authorities while robing in the vestry of Saint Luke's Church, suspected of having papers belonging to President Davis. He was taken to Washington, cleared of all charges and returned to Lincolnton. He and his family lived there from February to November, 1865. He held some confirmation services at request of Bishop Atkinson and took prominent part in many other services. Later he became Bishop of the Eastern Maryland diocese. His son, Rev. George Lay, was one time Rector of St. Mary's School at Raleigh.

Rectors of Saint Luke's after the death of Dr. Wetmore were Reverends D. T. Johnson, W. R. Dye, J. Crosby, C. S. Parker, C. E. Bently, Saunders Guignard, John C. Seagle and J. C. Grainger who in July, 1936 entered upon the work.

Since it was established in 1843 many prominent people have been members of St. Luke's, including Michael Hoke, Col. John F. Hoke, Haywood W. Guion, Judge W. P. Bynum, Judge W. M. Shipp, Gen. R. F. Hoke, William Julius Alexander, Judge W. A. Hoke, Major John D. Shaw, Major A. W. Burton, V. A. McBee, Dr. J. M. Richardson, Capt. C. C. Wrenshall, B. H. Sumner, J. C. Cobb and others.

Among ministers who went out from this parish are William Shipp Bynum, Charles L. Hoffman, B. M. Lackey, Thos. C. Wetmore, Norvin Duncan and Frontis Anthony.

The Presbyterian Church

The early settlers in the eastern part of Lincoln County were largely of Scotch-Irish and English background and Unity Presbyterian Church was the pioneer religious organization in the Beatties Ford community. It was established about 1796 or earlier. John Beatty was one of the charter members and Rev. Humphrey Hunter, the pastor from 1796 to 1803, was the first Presbyterian preacher to serve a church west of the Catawba River, and he laid the foundation at Unity and Goshen upon which the Presbyterian Church has been built in Lincoln and Gaston Counties.

The first structure at Unity was a log building used until 1808 when a new church was erected, at which time James Connor, Gen. Joseph Graham, Alexander Brevard and Captain John Reid were the Trustees. In 1833 a third church was built on the same site under the direction of John D. Graham, John Knox and Daniel M. Forney, Trustees. These churches were all plain wooden structures, but served the needs for the long period from 1796 to 1931, when the present pastor, Rev. W. T. Smith, led a movement for the modern brick church, which is now used by that growing congregation.

Prior to the Civil War no rural community in the Southern States had a finer type of citizens or a higher average of intelligence than the Beatties Ford section. Gen. Joseph Graham, Capt. Alexander Brevard, Capt. John Reid, Capt. James Connor, Robert Johnston, John Hayes, Dr. Cyrus L. Hunter, Dr. William Johnston, Dr. Sidney X. Johnston and many others were officials in Unity Church.

Among those buried in Unity graveyard are Gov. Hutchins G. Burton, one time Governor of North Carolina and the families of Judge Robert H. Burton, Alfred M. Burton, Capt. John Reid, Henry Connor, John Hayes, Dr. Sidney X. Johnston, Robert Johnston, Nixons, Barkleys, Luckeys, Kings, Derrs and many others.

Among the pastors who served that church after Rev. Humphrey Hunter were Henry N. Pharr, Patrick J. Sparrow, James Adams, Frederick Nash, Thomas Espey, Dr. James McRee, Dr. Robert Hall Morrison, Dr. S. H. Chester, R. W. Boyd, C. H. Little, F. B. Rankin, T. G. Tate, W. E. Furr, and Rev. W. T. Smith, the present pastor (1936).

In 1801 Gen. Joseph Graham and Capt. Alexander Brevard established the Graham and Brevard family graveyard, where Machpelah Church was finally built in 1848 for the convenience of people in that community. The contract for this church was let in 1847 and the Building Committee was composed of Dr. C. L. Hunter, Col. William Johnston, Chas. Connor Graham, E. A. Brevard and David Dellinger.

Rev. Dr. Morrison was the pastor there and at Unity during that period. It was abandoned as a preaching place in 1865 but in recent years it has been served by the pastors of Unity Church. Gen. Joseph Graham, Rev. Dr. R. H. Morrison, Rev. Alfred J. Morrison, Judge Theodorus W. Brevard, Maj. William A. Graham, Dr. C. L. Hunter, Capt. Alexander Brevard, Dr. E. A. Brevard, Dr. William Johnston, Dr. Calloway, Capt. Joseph G. Morrison, and many other prominent citizens are buried at Machpelah.

Rev. Humphrey Hunter was the first Presbyterian minister to preach in Lincolnton. Long before the Presbyterian Church was organized there he preached for several years at stated times in the old "White Church," which was then the only house of worship in the town. A congregation was organized in 1823 with Rev. Joseph E. Bell as pastor. Col. John Hoke, David Ramsour, Peter Summey, Michael Reinhardt and Chas. E. Reinhardt were the Elders. In 1827 Isaac Erwin and Jonas Ramsour were ordained Elders and they, with Jacob Ramsour, were chosen as Trustees. Mr. Bell was succeeded as pastor in 1827 by Rev. Patrick J. Sparrow, who served until 1833.

Early in 1834 Rev. William B. Davis served as supply until July of that year and was succeeded as pastor by Rev. Albertus W. Watts. During his pastorate Paul Kistler conveyed to David Ramsour and J. Taylor Alexander the lot on West Water street where a brick church was built costing about $1,800. In 1840 Rev. Lemuel Murray succeeded Mr. Watts and served as pastor for ten years, when in 1850 Rev. Robert N. Davis was installed and served as pastor until his death in 1871. The body of Mr. Davis was buried in front of the church on West Water street, but when a new church was built in 1892 on West Main street the body was taken up and buried under the new church. The tablet which marked his grave was placed in the vestibule of the new church. Those who served as elders during the pastorate of Mr. Davis were J. Taylor Alexander, Abner McCoy, Jacob A. Ramsour, William Tiddy, John F. Phifer and William H. Michal.

On April 9, 1872, Rev. R. Z. Johnston accepted the call to the Lincolnton Church for half of his time and so continued until March 12, 1903, when he gave full time service to the church which he served with fidelity until December 9, 1906, when on account of age and ill health he resigned. During this long pastorate of thirty-four years he preached part time at Shelby, Dallas, Goshen, Stanley, Mount Holly, Iron Station, and other points. He was constant in service and made a record for faithfulness and consecration which has borne and will continue to bear good fruit. During the latter part of his pastorate he was assisted by Rev. W. A. Murray.

The elders who served during that long period were Judge David Schenck, Capt. Geo. L. Phifer, Dr. J. A. Reedy, S. D. Burgin, Col. W. L. Davidson, Thos. H. Hoke, R. M. Roseman, Alfred Nixon, J. A. Abernethy, S. W. McKee and Edgar Love.

Those who served as church school superintendents were Col. W. H. Michal, Thos. H. Hoke and S. W. McKee.

The Presbyterian Churches at Iron Station and at other points were organized through the labors of Mr. Johnston.

On December 16, 1906, Rev. Dr. W. R. Minter, a grandson of Jacob A. Ramsour, one time Elder of this church, was called to succeed Mr. Johnston and served as pastor until March 13, 1915. Dr. Minter was a preacher of superior gifts, a fine pastor, loved by all the people when he resigned to accept the call to the First Southern Presbyterian Church of Austin, Texas.

The Elders during this period were Alfred Nixon, R. M. Roseman, S. W. McKee, Edgar Love, Augustus M. Hoke and R. A. McNeely.

Dr. Minter was succeeded by Rev. Dr. W. S. Wilson, who served as pastor from September 15, 1915, until 1922. During that period the church prospered and in 1917 the old church on West Main street was torn down and the present handsome structure was built on the site of the old building. This Building Committee was composed of Dr. Wilson, the pastor, who was Chairman, and R. M. Roseman, R. F. Beal, J. A. Abernethy, R. S. Reinhardt and J. W. Mullen. Upon the resignation of Dr. Wilson he was succeeded by Rev. W. W. Akers in June, 1922, who served until 1929 when he accepted a call to another church. Additional elders elected during this period were R. F. Beal, P. M. Keever, J. M. Reinhardt, E. A. Ballard and E. M. Browne.

Then the congregation extended a call to Rev. Dr. W. S. Wilson, who had served them from 1915 to 1922. This call was accepted and he is now closing the seventh year of his second pastorate in this church.

The pastors of this congregation since the service rendered in the start by Rev. Humphrey Hunter are in the order mentioned: Joseph E. Bell, 1823-27; Patrick J. Sparrow, 1827-33; William B. Davis, supply to July, 1834; Albertus W. Watts, July, 1834 to 1840; Lemuel Murray, 1840 to 1850; Robert N. Davis, 1850 until his death, April 24, 1871; R. Z. Johnston, April 9, 1872, to December 9, 1906; W. R. Minter, December 16, 1906, to March 13, 1915; W. S. Wilson, September 15, 1915, to 1922; W. W. Akers, 1922 to 1929; W. S. Wilson, 1929 to 1937. Note: On account of ill health Dr. Wilson resigned and retired in March 1937.

Lincoln County has furnished some notable native sons as ministers of the Presbyterian Church. Rev. Patrick J. Sparrow was pastor in Lincolnton and at Unity, Professor in Davidson College and President of Hampden-Sydney College in Virginia. Rev. Alfred J. Morrison was a brilliant young minister, who died after only a few years of service. Young men who have recently entered the ministry are Rev. Wm. C. Robinson, Professor in Columbia Theological Seminary, Decatur, Ga., Rev. Henry S. Robinson, son of the late Henry S. Robinson, and Rev. Joseph G. Morrison, son of Joseph G. Morrison, II, of Lincoln County.

Note: Some material in this historical article was taken from the well-prepared brief history of the Lincolnton Presbyterian Church written by the pastor, Rev. Dr. W. S. Wilson.

The Baptist Church

The oldest Baptist Church in old Lincoln County was Long Creek, located two miles east of Dallas, in the present County of Gaston. Its earliest history was not preserved. Some claim that this church was organized in either 1772 or 1777, but later records prove that it was reorganized in 1794 and that the members were Lemuel Sanders, Charles Jones, Samuel Swanengam, James Weathers, John Weathers, Isaac West, James West, Ralph Cobb, Cornelius Rodgers, Reuben Jenkins and Julius Holland, but the membership increased to sixty-three before the year closed. Julius Holland later became a preacher and died in 1814.

James Lewis, of Lincoln County, one of the early pioneer preachers of the Baptist Church in this section, was pastor of Long Creek Church. When a youth he went to Virginia where he was converted and united with the Baptist Church. He had a good English education and was a fair Latin scholar; was ordained as a minister at Mill Creek Church, York, S. C.; was pastor of Long Creek and Hebron Churches. He married to Annie, daughter of James Witherspoon, of Lincoln County. Among his children was John G. Lewis, a prominent citizen and for some years Register of Deeds in Gaston County and also Clerk of the Catawba River Association of the Baptist Church in 1863 and 1864. He died in 1883.

James R. Lewis, a prominent member of the Dallas Baptist Church, and leading merchant until his death in 1929, was a son of John G. Lewis. The pioneer preacher, James Lewis, died in 1834. Long Creek is now a large congregation with a handsome brick church.

Sharon Church, located at Iron Station, was erected about 1831, size 20 by 24, on land donated by the father of Rev. John Lowe. There were about fifty members, but growth in membership has never been large. From 1831 to 1841 the pastors were D. L. Farr, John Lowe, Jeptha Clark, Alex Abernethy and others.

Rev. John Lowe, an active preacher for many years, was a man of high integrity and served his church faithfully. He had been pastor of Sharon, Hebron, Long Creek and Rocky River Churches; was a delegate to the Association from Sharon in 1830, 1831 and 1832. He moved to Mecklenburg in 1833 and was a delegate from Rocky River in 1833-34-35 and 36. He died in 1836. Aaron Lowe and Mrs. James Mullen, late of Lincoln County, were his children.

Mount Zion, five miles north of Sharon, was served before the Civil War by Rev. A. J. Cansler, G. J. Wilkey and R. H. Moody, but a church was not built until 1870, near the home of the late Rev. J. H. McClure, under the leadership of Rev. G. J. Wilkey, with sixty-one members. Among those who were members in its early history were D. Frank Abernethy, J. H. McClure, Smith McAllister, John Black, Bartlett Stroup and the Upton and Hansell families.

Macedonia Church was organized about 1835 with twenty-five members. It was first called "Sign Board" Church and was located on the old Beatties Ford road, nine miles from Lincolnton. Randolph Barnett was one of the early members. In 1835 Jeptha Clark was ordained as a minister there and was an active preacher until his death in 1872. He preached at Macedonia, Mt. Ruhamah, Lebanon, Olivet, New Bethany and many other churches in Lincoln and Catawba Counties.

In 1832 the Macedonia congregation built a new church about two miles from the site of the original church. Rev. G. J. Wilkey preached there in 1869-70, when the church was reorganized. The prominent members then were Ivey H. Laney, Alexander Goodson, Alfred Dellinger, W. E. Keener, Johnson Burke, Thomas J. Saunders, James Mullen and his wife, who was a daughter of Rev. John Lowe.

It has grown in recent years and the handsome brick church stands on the new Lincolnton-Mooresville highway nine miles from Lincolnton.

THE ANNALS OF LINCOLN COUNTY 487

In August, 1934, the one hundredth anniversary of Macedonia Church was celebrated. A great crowd was present. Rev. S. W. Bennett, a former pastor, delivered the historical address and Rev. A. A. Lockee, the present pastor, Rev. L. A. McClure, and Rev. T. H. Roach, also spoke. Rev. Dr. R. J. Redwine preached a sermon appropriate to the occasion.

Salem Church, four miles south of Lincolnton, was established about 1847 by Rev. Wade Hill.

Alexander Stroupe heard him preach at Long Creek and told his mother about his eloquent sermon, so she invited him to come and preach. He came and preached at High Shoals and Stroupe's school house regularly for two years. In 1845 a brush arbor was built and camp meetings were held at Salem annually until about 1870. Mrs. Stroupe, before her marriage to Moses Stroupe, was Susan Masters and was said to be in her community "a beacon light of Baptist principles."

The leading members at Salem were in those days the Stroupe, Abernethy, Garrison, Smith, Robinson, Harrell and Clanton families.

In 1868 there were 219 members, but in 1934 the membership was reduced to 134.

Lower Ruhamah, located near the residence of the late J. F. Reinhardt, was first established as a preaching place for negro slaves and Rev. John Ruker held occasional services there until his death in 1819. Later Randolph Barnett led the movement to build a church, but religious services were abandoned there about 1852.

Mrs. Polly Kids and many other useful members were baptized there.

Olivet was organized near Sherrill's Ford, August 17, 1833. Hugh Quin and Paul Phifer preached at Smyrna, "a free meeting house" (now German Reformed), until Olivet was built. Wade Hill was pastor from 1847 to 1851; A. J. Cansler, 1852-53; R. P. Logan, 1854-57; Isaac Oxford, 1857-58; L. M. Berry, 1858-67; E. Allison, 1868; J. K. Howell from 1869 until it was abandoned.

David Setzer, John and James Clarke and James Bynum and their families were early members there.

Kids Chapel, five miles from Beatties Ford was named for Mrs. Polly Kids, a saintly woman and an ardent Baptist. She was the mother of James M. Kids, who in his day was a merchant and influential citizen.

Rev. J. T. Shell, of Caldwell County, held a meeting there many years ago and 34 candidates were baptized, seventeen of whom were descendants of Mrs. Kids.

The church was organized by Rev. G. J. Wilkey and Rev. J. H. McClure. Among those baptized was Rev. J. A. Huggins of the Northern Methodist Church and he was then ordained as a Baptist minister.

Leonard's Fork, five miles west of Lincolnton, was organized by Rev. A. L. Stough in 1882. W. H. Hoover, T. J. Hoover, L. A. Houser and T. M. Foster were active members. In 1934 the membership was 59.

Zion Hill or Reepsville, seven miles northwest of Lincolnton, is a growing congregation. The present membership is 121.

The earlier records of the Baptist Church in Lincoln County show that James Lewis, Wade Hill, John Lowe, Alexander J. Cansler, George J. Wilkey, L. M. Berry, A. L. Stough, J. H. Booth, and others, did enduring work in laying foundations upon which the Baptist Church has grown strong and become a great religious force in the County, where they now have about 25 congregations, with a total membership of around 3,000 and church property valued near to $200,000.

The early settlers in the central and western part of the County held to the faith of the Lutheran and German Reformed Churches and the first church in Lincolnton was built jointly by these congregations and called Emanuel's Church. Later on the Presbyterians and Methodists came and they were followed by the Episcopalians, but the Baptists were slow to organize there. Hugh Quin preached in Lincolnton and other nearby points from 1825 to 1835 when he moved to Georgia and J. Alonzo Webb, known as the "Wandering Pilgrim" preached there for a short time about 1850, but the Baptists were not organized as a church there until 1859, when Rev. L. M. Berry, a native of Buncombe, and Rev. Wade Hill, of Cleveland, called a meeting in the "Old White Church," May 28, 1859, and a congregation was organized with ten white members: Rev. L. M. Berry, Martha Berry, Catherine Johnson, Florence Cansler,

Rhoda Crawford, Nancy Crawford, Maria Parker, Frances Courtney, John Killian and E. N. Shuford. Besides these were nine colored persons: Benjamin Hoke, Isaac Cansler, Holland Cansler, Charles Quickel, Jane Abernethy, Betsy Hoke, Kessiah Abernethy, Nancy Alexander and Mina Cansler. In November, 1866, after the negroes were freed, the colored members were dismissed to form a church of their own.

The first deacons were John A. Parker, and John Killian, who were elected March 25, 1860, and ordained in July following. Robert W. Cauble was the first clerk. Rev. L. M. Berry was the first pastor and served from 1859 to 1867. He was followed in 1869 by Wade Hill for one year and J. K. Howell succeeded Mr. Hill and served one year. About this time the church was reorganized at a meeting held in the home of Mrs. Amanda M. Finch, February 12, 1872. Those present were Rev. Dr. N. B. Cobb, Mrs. Finch and her mother, Mrs. Calvert, R. W. Cauble, H. P. Crawford, and others. Rev. Dr. Cobb accepted the call as pastor at a salary of $150 per year. In April J. W. Bean was appointed to raise money to build a church and in October reported that he had collected and paid to B. C. Cobb $250 for a lot on Water Street, and that good subscriptions amounting to $475 for building purposes were yet to be collected. The first revival meeting was held in July, 1875.

From October, 1875, to June, 1879, the record shows no meetings, and only occasional preaching services by visiting ministers. In the summer of 1879 Rev. A. L. Stough secured the help of Rev. F. M. Jordan, a successful evangelist, and a revival meeting was held in the "Old White Church," many were added to the church and plans for a church building were made. J. L. Wilkey, L. T. Wilkey, and Eben Childs were chosen as a building committee and five years later the church on Water street was completed; regular services meanwhile were held in the "Old White Church." About 1920 the Water street property was sold to Edgar Love and the present handsome church on the corner of Main and Cedar streets was built at a cost of about $40,000. The Building Committee was composed of T. J. Ramsour, D. C. Wilson, J. O. Allen, M. H. Hoyle, Thorne Clark, C. H. Harrill, J. L. Putnam, J. A. Suttle, J. T. Perkins, G. W. Cauble, C. L. Goodson, A. Bumgarner, L. V. Padgett, W. L. Mustain, and the pastor, Rev. J. A. Snow.

The congregation has grown steadily as the town has grown and the membership in 1934 was 278.

Among the early members were John A. Parker, John Killian, R. W. Cauble, Judge T. W. Brevard and his wife, Mrs. Carolina Mays Brevard, Mrs. Amanda M. Finch and her mother, Mrs. Calvert, J. L. Wilkey, L. T. Wilkey, H. P. Crawford and others.

Those licensed to preach and ordained in this church were J. J. Paysour, C. A. Caldwell and G. W. Rollins.

The pastors to date were: 1859-1867, L. M. Berry; 1869-70, Wade Hill; 1871, J. K. Howell; 1872-75, N. B. Cobb; 1878, J. H. Booth; 1879-82, A. L. Stough; 1883-87, J. K. Faulkner; 1888, F. C. Hickson; 1889, M. P. Matheny; 1890-94, C. E. Gower; 1895-98, D. M. Austin; 1899-1905, D. P. Bridges; 1906-08, Baylus Cade; 1908-14, S. W. Bennett; 1915, E. R. Stewart; 1916, C. C. Wheeler; 1917-23, J. A. Snow; 1924-27, Eph Whisenhunt. Since 1927, Elbert F. Hardin.

Church Clerks from 1859 to 1930 were R. W. Cauble, J. A. Parker, H. P. Crawford, Judge T. W. Brevard, C. E. Childs, T. J. Dellinger, Baylus Cade, Jr., J. T. Perkins, W. E. Padgett, Claude Williams, R. H. Harrill and E. T. Childs, Jr.

Sunday School superintendents covering that period from 1859 to 1930 were L. T. Wilkey, J. L. Wilkey, Carey Wells, J. O. Allen, L. V. Padgett and R. H. Harrill.

The following have served as Deacons during some portion of the same period: J. A. Parker, John Killian, J. L. and L. T. Wilkey, E. H. Cauble, James Gaston, F. A. Tobey, J. T. McLean, Sr., W. W. McCutcheon, Weldon Bridges, L. V. Padgett, J. A. Suttle, C. L. Goodson, T. J. Ramsour, Dr. J. C. Whitesides, G. W. Cauble, J. O. Bumgarner, J. L. Putnam, D. C. Williams, Dr. W. F. Elliott, J. T. McLean, Jr., T. P. Honeycutt, E. T. Childs, Jr., T. V. Banks, M. H. Hoyle, Hal Hoyle, S. D. Lineberger, R. H. Harrill, W. E. Garrison, M. T. Leatherman, Lonnie Robinson, Puett Lawing, J. O. Allen, W. L. Abernethy and N. W. Williams.

The Methodist Church

The pioneer preachers were fully consecrated to the task of carrying the gospel to the last man. The early circuit rider was a missionary without a mission board to support him, or an official board to receive him on a new charge. When he arrived in new territory he stopped at the first cabin, told his business, requested that the neighbors be called in to hear him preach, delivered a fervent message to the assembled group, organized a small congregation and departing left an appointment to preach four weeks later. The circuit rider then had a wide field in which to labor, preaching somewhere every day to meet the twenty-five or thirty monthly appointments.

Probably the first Methodist to preach west of the Catawba was a young local preacher named Brown, who visited the colony of Virginia Methodists that settled near the village of Terrell, some 18 miles east of Lincolnton, prior to 1788. The colony was composed of the Turbyfill, Wilkinson, Mayhew, Abernethy, Stacy, Edwards, Harvell, Morris, and other families.

In 1789 Daniel Asbury was sent to preach in this territory. He was an earnest and persuasive preacher and labored heroically to plant the church in this section. He never spared himself but through cold and heat he rode, braving the perils of the wilderness to carry the gospel to the early pioneers.

Before a church was built he established the first camp ground in America at Rehoboth. John McGee assisted in the preaching at this camp meeting. Later a log church was built and called Rehoboth. Following this a camp meeting was held at Bethel. As it was easy to build a brush arbor the camp meeting was moved from place to place. For some years following 1815 it was held annually at Robey's Church near Catawba Springs, but Joseph M. Munday conveyed to Freeman Shelton, Richard Proctor and Dr. James Bivens for ninety dollars a tract of land containing forty-five acres for a camp ground for the Lincoln circuit. This land was near Bethel Church and the deed was dated August 7, 1830. This was Rock Springs camp ground where meetings have been held annually since it was established.

Rehoboth was the first Methodist Church west of the Catawba and built in 1791. The third church building was erected on the same site in 1890.

Daniel Asbury, the pioneer preacher, was born in Fairfax County, Virginia in 1762, and died in Lincoln County in 1825. He married Nancy Morris, a member of the Virginia colony, which settled at Rehoboth. She was converted in Brunswick County, Virginia, with Enoch George and William McKendree and others.

Bishop Asbury, "the prophet of the long road," visited his cousin, Daniel Asbury, near Rehoboth, and preached there

Oct. 27, 1814. Jonathan Jackson (1758-1831) for a long time an active itinerant, located and settled in the Rehoboth community. He willed all his property to Rev. Jacob Hill, who lived near by. His nephew wrote that Jonathan Jackson and Stonewall Jackson both came from Western Virginia, both were of Methodist birth, both were named Jonathan and probably related.

The bodies of Daniel Asbury, Jonathan Jackson, Jacob Hill and Henry Asbury (son of Daniel and for many years a useful local preacher) are buried at Rehoboth.

Next to Rehoboth was Bethel, also one of the older churches west of the Catawba. Rev. Jeremiah Munday, a soldier of the Revolution, was a useful local preacher and member of Bethel Church. He was the ancestor of the numerous Munday families of Lincoln County. He died about 1835.

Among other members of Bethel Church were W. W. Munday, Matthias and Spencer Munday, Freeman, Meacom and Spencer Shelton, John and Thomas Thompson, Isaac Lowe, J. W. Lowe, Osborne Robinson, Freeman Kelly, Richard Proctor and many descendants of these faithful men. Among other prominent churchmen in that section were Henry Asbury, Dr. J. A. Sherrill, David Kincaid, Captain J. B. Shelton, Gilbert M. Beatty, J. Madison Smith, and Frank Howard.

The Rock Springs circuit was organized about 1865 and among the earlier pastors were John Finger, A. P. Avant, T. Page Ricaud, J. W. Puett, M. V. Sherrill, George W. Ivey, Jesse H. Page, T. A. Boone, R. S. Webb, T. S. Ellington and P. L. Terrell, all of whom have passed to their reward. But their children have honored the names of their fathers.

The Circuit was divided in 1896, when Salem, New Hope, Snow Hill and Hill's Chapel were grouped and called Lowesville Circuit. D. M. Litaker was the first pastor and Beverly Wilson is the present pastor of this charge.

Rock Springs camp ground near Bethel has been for more than a hundred years noted for great religious meetings. Vast multitudes still gather there annually and the good results can never be estimated. While many of the old camp meetings have been abandoned Rock Springs still carries on and does effective work. This writer in his youth heard great sermons there and one on "Hell" preached by Rev. Dr. W. M. Robey will never be forgotten. It was more than two hours long but he held the multitude spellbound all the way to the end.

In those days, more than sixty-five years ago, the preacher lined out the hymns, Captain J. B. Shelton raised the tunes and the great throngs sang the old hymns of the church with spirit and understanding.

Among the pastors of the Rock Springs Circuit special mention should be made of Rev. George W. Ivey, who possessed sanctified common sense and was a preacher who always proclaimed a mellow gospel and exercised a high spiritual influence. He had five sons: Dr. William P. Ivey, a skilled physician; Rev. Dr. Thomas N. Ivey, a brilliant preacher and editor of church periodicals; J. B. Ivey, a great merchant; George F. Ivey, a successful manufacturer; and Eugene C. Ivey, a genius as an electrician; all were prominent church officials. All these sons lived in the parsonage at Denver when their good father served Rock Springs Circuit.

McKendree Church was organized in 1836. The Quarterly Conference appointed on April 2, 1835, as Building Committee, Jacob Hoyle, Robert Blackburn and Henry Carpenter, to erect a church on the Island Ford road north of Lincolnton to be called McKendree Chapel. The Conference on February 17, 1838, elected Benedict Jetton and John Schenck to serve in place of Henry Carpenter, who had died and Jacob Hoyle, who had moved away. A log church was first built and fifty years later a frame building was erected on the same site. This was used until 1936, when the present beautiful stone church was built to take the place of the frame building. The Blackburn, Carpenter, Haynes, Shrum and other families, who were charter members a century ago, have left descendants, who still carry on the work their fathers began in earlier days.

Wesley Chapel is another one of the older churches on the original Lincolnton Circuit and located in the western part of old Lincoln County. It was a preaching place where camp meetings were held as early as 1824, but the first church was not built until 1834. Among the early members were Rev. D. E. Warlick, Lewis Warlick, Alfred Ramsour, George Deitz, David Clay, Martin Shuford, John Dellinger, Daniel Whitener, Berry Abernethy and Turner Abernethy. The great preacher and teacher, Rev. Dr. Robert L. Abernethy, who founded Rutherford College, was a son of Turner Abernethy, and was brought up in this congregation. This church is now on South Fork Circuit, and among many who have served as pastors since the Civil War were John Watts, J. C. Hartsell, G. W. Callahan, R. M. Hoyle, M. T. Steele, M. V. Sherrill, Albert Sherrill, J. F. Armstrong, H. G. Stamey, W. M. Boring, J. N. Randall, W. J. Miller, R. A. Taylor, C. M. McKinney, and G. L. Wilkinson.

Palm Tree on the same circuit furnished seven ministers to the Conference: P. F. W. Stamey, W. I. Hull, M. W. Boyles, C. A. Gault, H. G. Stamey, J. J. Heavner, and R. L. Bass. Rev. P. F. W. Stamey, Rev. M. W. Boyles and Rev. C. A. Gault from Palm Tree congregation were admitted to the North Carolina Conference at Goldsboro, N. C., in 1873.

Zion, located seven miles west of Lincolnton, was the church where Captain John F. Hill, Lawson H. Hill, Isaac R. Self, Burton C. Wood, the Houser, Sain and other good families worshipped. Rev. James Hill, father of Capt. John F. Hill, preached the first sermon in the Lincolnton Methodist Church about 1828 and his body now sleeps in the Methodist graveyard in Lincolnton.

The five congregations, Crouse, Antioch, Laboratory, Pleasant Grove and Lander's Chapel, constitute the Crouse Circuit of which Rev. A. L. Latham is now (1936) the pastor.

The Lincolnton congregation was organized in 1824 and the first church, a wooden structure, was built about 1828 on South Aspen street, then in the suburbs of the town. Michael Schenck, Dr. James Bivens and Samuel Lander were three of the early members. From an historical paper on "Early Methodism in Lincoln" written by Rev. W. B. West, the following excerpts are taken:

"The tradition is that Lorenzo Dow, the eccentric evangelist, preached in the home of Michael Schenck in Lincolnton in 1798 . . . Mr. Schenck was an active member of the Methodist Church and his house became the home of the weary itinerant. His four daughters married Methodist ministers. Elizabeth, married Rev. D. G. McDaniel; Barbara, married Rev. Allen Hamby; Louvenia, married Rev. Angus McPherson; and Catherine, married Rev. J. J. Richardson. Mrs. McDaniel was one of the charter members of the Lincolnton Church in 1824 . . . Mr. Schenck, at the time of his death in 1849, was in his 78th year and the oldest citizen of Lincolnton.

"An old newspaper published in 1881, carried *The Reminiscenses of a Methodist Preacher* in which the writer said: 'I spent a Sunday in Lincolnton and was entertained by a very pious family, consisting of a widowed father, Michael Schenck, three sons and four daughters, who later married Methodist ministers. I preached in the old frame church, which has long since disappeared, giving place to the present handsome brick church.'

"Among the men of stalwart stature, who were officially connected with the early history of Lincoln Methodism, Samuel Lander was a prominent pillar in the Lincolnton Church and circuit. He was powerfully converted at Robey's camp meeting in 1828 under the preaching of Malcolm McPherson and Hartwell Spain, and he and his wife joined the Methodist Church. In 1833 he was licensed to preach and was soon recognized as a power in the pulpit. He was the moving spirit in founding McKendree Church four miles north of Lincolnton in 1836 and of Lander's Chapel, which was organized about the same time."

Six of his descendants became Methodist ministers: his son, Dr. Samuel Lander, who founded Lander College; three grandsons, Dr. Samuel A. Weber, of the South Carolina Conference, Dr. John M. Lander, Missionary to Brazil, and William L. Sherrill, of Western North Carolina Conference; and two grandsons, Dr. John L. Weber, late of the Memphis Conference, and Norman Lander Prince, who died early.

Three ministers have come out of Lincolnton Church: Paul F. Kistler, who was for fifty years a member of the South Carolina Conference; Dr. Samuel Lander, the educator; and William L. Sherrill, of the Western North Carolina Conference.

Dr. James Bivens was a prominent citizen and active Methodist official. He was one of the first trustees of Rock Springs camp ground. At the Quarterly Conference in August, 1836, Henry Asbury and Samuel Lander were appointed to settle with Dr. Bivens, the Commissioner of Church Property, which was effected most satisfactorily.

As Dr. Bivens was planning to move elsewhere, resolutions expressing high regard and best wishes for him and gratitude for his untiring and indefatigable performance of the duties devolving on him in the relation he sustained to our church were passed, and the Secretary was directed to transmit by letter this expression of our regard to Dr. Bivens.

Besides Michael Schenck, Dr. Bivens and Samuel Lander and their families, many others including Paul Kistler, his son Lawson H. Kistler, Dr. David W. Schenck, Henry F. Schenck,

John Schenck, Peter Wingate, Milton and Benedict Jetton, James C. Jenkins, William T. Shipp, John E. Boger, S. P. Sherrill, Thomas Wells, H. W. and R. H. Abernethy, the McDaniel, McPherson and Templeton families were active in the church.

The Lincolnton Church was set apart as a station in 1902 and the other churches now constitute the Lincoln Circuit.

Goodsonville (now Boger City) was made a station in 1923, has about 250 members and is a growing church.

Among ministers not already mentioned who came from Lincoln County are, Dr. Albert M. Shipp, a great preacher and educator; C. G. Little, J. A. Scronce, J. F. Armstrong, T. W. Hager, W. O. Rudisill, A. S. Abernethy, D. C. and E. D. Ballard, W. L. C. Killian and Beverly Wilson.

The following interesting items are found in the old Lincolnton Circuit Quarterly Conference Records:

May 18, 1838—"It was moved by S. Lander and seconded by Henry Asbury that the church in the suburbs of Lincolnton be moved to some convenient lot in town for the accommodation of our people and those who may attend our church, as soon as a suitable lot may be obtained, and that plans for a parsonage on same lot be made. Adopted."

January 1, 1841—"Albert M. Shipp came duly recommended from Friendship Church for license to preach and after due inquiry as to his qualifications he was licensed and recommended for admission into the South Carolina Conference."

October 16, 1841—"The Committee appointed to arrange for a camp ground near Lincolnton was thanked for its service and a new committee consisting of Henry Cansler, Milton Jetton and Peter Wingate was appointed to care for the ground, sell lots, receive money and appropriate it as they deem necessary."

October 16, 1841—"It was unanimously resolved that the thanks of this Conference be tendered by our Secretary to Henry Cansler, Esq., for the kind disposition he has manifested toward the church by assisting us so efficiently in preparing for our meeting, and the liberal manner in which he gave us plank and other material."

August 10, 1844—"Resolved that we endorse the call for a General Conference of the Church in the South at Louisville next May, and we are willing to commit the interest of our Zion to their united wisdom, under the guidance of God, and that this resolution be published in the Church papers."

August 2, 1845—"Paul F. Kistler was granted license to preach and recommended for admission into the South Carolina Conference."

August 4, 1846—"Reports from various Sunday Schools on the Circuit were made and the school in Lincolnton is large and interesting with a large Bible Class. There being no other school in the place, makes this larger than it would otherwise be. There are nine teachers and fifty scholars."

Balls Creek camp ground was established in 1853 and large crowds gather there annually. It is in the bounds of Balls Creek Circuit in Catawba County.

March 27, 1856—"Samuel Lander, J. C. Jenkins, J. E. Boger, Lawson H. Kistler, and E. Blackburn were elected Trustees of the Lincolnton Church. Samuel Lander, J. C. Jenkins, J. E. Boger, H. W. Abernethy and W. H. Michal were named as the Building Committee for Lincolnton Church."

October 29, 1864—"Samuel Lander, Jr., was recommended for admission into the South Carolina Conference."

In the pioneer days the salary of a preacher (bishop or pastor) was fixed at $64.00 a year, but the records of the Circuit show that in 1829, with twenty-five preaching points, the pastor and presiding elder received $160.09; in 1830 it was $188.27; in 1851 it had grown to $358.46.

In 1935 the seven pastoral charges in the County paid for ministerial support $12,665.00.

The present membership of the church in Lincoln County is (1935) about 3,400 and the value of church property is $220,000.00.

The pastors who have served on the old Lincolnton Circuit were Daniel Asbury, George McKenny, John Bonner, James King, Moses Matthews, William Gassaway, Oscar Rogers, Samuel Miller, John Porter, Robert Porter, James Hill, Jonathan Jackson, Hugh McPhail, Jesse Richardson, John Taylor, J. Freeman, Z. Williams, J. L. Jerry, Josiah Freeman, Joseph Moore, Z. Dowling, Hartwell Spain, Jacob Hill, D. G. McDaniel, Elisha Calloway, T. C. Smith, J. Covington, J. B. Anthony, S. Armstrong, J. H. Robinson, W. A. Gamewell, A. B. McGilvary, A. H. Richardson, T. S. Daniel, J. M. Bradley, Colin Murchison, J. H. Zimmerman, L. M. Little, H. M. Mood, W. C. Patterson, Landy Wood, J. S. Ervin, E. W. Thompson, John Finger, G. W. Ivey, O. A. Darby, E. G. Gage, Samuel Lander, II, E. W. Walker, M. A.

Connelly, W. D. Lee, V. A. Sharpe, R. G. Barrett, J. T. Harris, G. F. Round, J. W. Jenkins, F. A. Dishop, J. W. Wheeler, J. B. Bailey, M. H. Hoyle, M. T. Steele, W. F. Womble, A. E. Wiley, T. T. Salyer.

In 1902 Lincolnton Station was created and the pastors there have been R. M. Courtney, J. E. Gay, F. L. Townsend, T. J. Rogers, Z. Paris, D. M. Litaker, J. T. Mangum, W. B. West, R. S. Truesdale, P. W. Tucker, W. A. Rollins, Carlock Hawk, R. B. Templeton and A. L. Stanford, the present pastor (1936).

Among those who served as Presiding Elders prior to 1900 were Daniel Asbury, Isaac Lowe, Jonathan Jackson, Jesse Richardson, Malcolm McPherson, Hartwell Spain, Chas. Betts, Allen Hamby, W. A. Gamewell, Albert M. Shipp, H. H. Durant, J. W. Kelly, John T. Wightman, F. A. Mood, R. P. Franks, J. W. North, E. J. Maynardie, E. W. Thompson, L. S. Burkhead, J. S. Nelson, H. T. Hudson, M. L. Wood, J. R. Brooks, C. W. Byrd, J. J. Renn and W. R. Ware.

In preparing the notes on the church history of the County space has been given to the Lutheran, German Reformed, Episcopal, Presbyterian, Baptist and Methodist denominations, because these religious bodies have been constant in service almost from the time when the pioneers first settled west of the Catawba River. Much more could be written of them all, but for lack of space the facts have been condensed, though from what has been written the reader may gather some almost forgotten religious history.

The history of some of the older congregations has been given briefly and it was out of these that many of the present-day congregations sprang.

Aside from the six religious bodies mentioned there are in the County several smaller religious groups, but those referred to started with the early pioneers and have for a hundred and fifty or more years filled a high place in the religious life of the people.

APPENDIX
COUNTY COURT CLERKS

Ezekiel Polk, April, 1769, to July, 1772.
Andrew Neel, October 28, 1772, to (about) April, 1776.
William Graham, (about) April, 1776, to July, 1777.
Andrew Neel, July, 1777, to April, 1780.
David Dickey, October 23, 1780, to April, 1781.
Joseph Dickson, April 16, 1781, to October 8, 1788.
John Dickson, October 8, 1788, to October 3, 1804.
Lawson Henderson, October 3, 1804, to April 13, 1807.
Daniel M. Forney, July 7, 1807, to May 22, 1812.
Vardry McBee, July 21, 1812, to July, 1833.
Miles W. Abernethy, October 28, 1833, to September 4, 1837.
Henry Cansler, September 4, 1837, to June, 1844.
Cyrus L. Hunter, June, 1844, to September, 1845.
Robert Williamson, Jr., September, 1845, to October, 1853.
John A. Huss, October, 1853, to October, 1857.
William R. Clark, October, 1857, to June, 1865.
A. Sidney Haynes, June, 1865, to January 31, 1866.
William R. Clark, January 31, 1866, to 1868, when county court was abolished.
(See "Bynum's Marriage Bonds of Tryon and Lincoln Counties.")

CLERKS OF THE SUPERIOR COURT

Lawson Henderson, 1807 to 1837, when he resigned.
John Michal, 1837 to 1841.
Franklin A. Hoke, 1841 to 1843.
Robert Williamson, 1843 to 1845. Died in office, July, 1845.
Franklin A. Hoke, 1845 to 1847.
Vardry A. McBee, 1847 to 1853. Resigned.
Robert Williamson, Jr., 1853 to 1859. Died in office in 1859.
Vardry A. McBee, 1859 to 1861. Resigned.
S. P. Sherrill, 1861 to September, 1874.
W. M. Reinhardt, 1874 to 1880. Resigned.
Vardry A. McBee, 1880 to 1886.
Charles E. Childs, 1886 to 1894.
G. A. Barkley, 1894 to 1898.
Alfred Nixon, 1898 to March, 1924. Died in office.
G. L. Heavner, March, 1924, to December, 1924.
M. T. Leatherman, December, 1924, to 1930.
J. L. Hunter, December, 1930, until his death, May 12, 1936.
James A. Abernethy, Jr., May 14, 1936, to August 19, 1936. Resigned.
Thomas E. Rhodes, August 19, 1936.

SHERIFFS OF LINCOLN COUNTY

1779-1780—Probably Thomas White.*
1781-1782—Thomas White.
1782-1792—Joseph Henry.
1792-1796—William Rankin.
1796-1801—Lawson Henderson.
1801-1803—David Shuford.
1803-1808—Robert Patterson (resigned).
1808-1812—John Allen.
1812-1813—Robert Patterson.
1813-1816—Martin Shuford.
1816-1818—Isaac Holland.
1818-1824—John Coulter.
1824-1826—Jacob Forney.
1826-1829—Henry Cansler.
1829-1831—John Coulter.
1831-1836—Thomas Ward.
1836-1840—James Quinn.
1840-1844—John R. Stamey.
1844-1846—Benjamin Morris.†
1846-1847—H. N. Gaston (resigned).
1847-1848—B. S. Johnson.
1848-1854—J. W. Lowe.
1854-1858—Caleb Miller.
1858-1868—Logan H. Lowrance, died in office.
Sept., 1868, to Sept., 1872—J. H. King.
Sept., 1872, to Dec., 1880—J. A. Robinson.
Dec., 1880, to Sept., 1883—A. S. Haynes.
Sept., 1883, to Dec., 1890—Alfred Nixon.
Dec., 1890, to Aug., 1891—I. B. Luckey, died in office.
Aug., 1891, to Dec., 1892—Alfred Nixon.
Dec., 1892, to Dec., 1894—John K. Cline.
Dec., 1894, to Dec., 1898—Chas. H. Rhodes.

---

* The Minute Book for 1779-1780, makes no reference to the Sheriff, but in an old trial docket covering that period the initials "Sheriff T. W." appear which makes it probable that Thomas White was the first Sheriff of the County.

From record found in Minutes of July Court, 1781:

"Thomas White, Sheriff, John Barber, Thomas Espey, James White and Joseph Dickson to His Excellency, Thomas Burke, Esq., Governor, etc., for $50,000.00 for a bond for the said Sheriff faithfull discharging of his duties in office, dated 18th July, 1781, was signed, sealed and delivered in open Court . . ."

† From the record, September, 1844:

"It appearing to the satisfaction of the Court that some informality existed in the election of Sheriff by the people, whereupon Benjamin Morris, Sheriff-elect, came into Court and surrendered his claim to said election and a majority of the Justices being present, the said B. Morris was unanimously appointed Sheriff of Lincoln County for two (2) years from this term."

THE ANNALS OF LINCOLN COUNTY

Dec., 1898, to Dec., 1908—John K. Cline.
Dec., 1908, to Dec., 1914—G. L. Heavner.
Dec., 1914, to Dec., 1918—A. P. Willis.
Dec., 1918, to Dec., 1920—G. B. Goodson.
Dec., 1920, to Dec., 1928—W. B. Abernethy.
Dec., 1928, to Dec., 1936—A. F. Reinhardt.
Dec., 1936—Geo. E. Rudisill.

REGISTERS OF LINCOLN COUNTY

1779-1796—John Wilson.
1796-1847—William J. Wilson.
1847 to March, 1866—J. T. Alexander.
March to August, 1866—Samuel Lander, III.
1866-1868—P. A. Summey.
1868-1870—T. W. Robinson.
1870-1873—P. A. Summey.
1873-1874—D. R. Hoover.
1874-1884—W. R. Edwards.

1884-1888—H. E. Ramsaur.
1888-1894—B. C. Wood.
1894-1898—J. F. Killian.
1898-1908—H. A. Self.
1908-1914—W. H. Sigmon.
1914-1920—B. C. Wood.
1920-1926—J. E. Hoover.
1926-1928—R. E. Sigmon.
1928-1930—W. A. Abernethy.
1930 to date—W. H. Boring.

COUNTY TREASURERS
The office was created in 1868.

1868-1870—W. T. McCoy.
1870-1872—Andrew Roseman.
1872-1880—James C. Jenkins, died in office.
1880-1886—Andrew Heedick.
1886-1890—L. T. Wilkey.
1890-1894—John C. Quickel.
1894-1898—D. L. Yount.
1898-1902—L. B. Camp.

1902-1908—R. F. Beal.
1908-1914—J. O. Allen.
1914-1916—G. B. Goodson.
1916-1918—County National Bank.
1918-1924—M. T. Leatherman.
1924-1928—H. B. Camp.
1928-1930—D. L. Yount.
1930-1934—Ezra Mace.
The office was then abolished.

LINCOLN COUNTY RECORDER'S COURT—ESTABLISHED IN 1925

Judge
L. E. Rudisill, 1926 to 1928.
Harvey A. Jonas, 1928 to 1930.
S. M. Roper, 1930 to 1936.
Kemp B. Nixon, 1936—.

Solicitor
W. H. Childs, 1926 to 1928.
W. M. Nicholson, 1928 to 1932.
L. Berge Beam, 1932 to 1936.
Bruce F. Heafner, 1936—.

MAYORS OF LINCOLNTON

All town records prior to 1867 seem to be lost, but before the Civil War Charles C. Henderson was Mayor, for according to an old story, a drunk man staggered into the store of Mr. Henderson, the Mayor, and when asked by the Mayor where he got his whiskey, said he bought it from Presnel. A warrant was issued for Presnel, and when the drunk man on the witness stand testified that he did not buy liquor from Presnel, the Mayor asked, "Didn't you tell me you bought it from him?" the witness replied: "Yes, but Mr. Henderson, I was talking then, but I am swearing now." The Mayors who have served since the Civil War were:

1867-	—V. A. McBee.	1900-	—A. L. Quickel.
1868-	—S. P. Sherrill.	1901-	—John L. Cobb.
1869-1872	—inclusive, not known.	1902-	—Henry E. Ramsaur.
1873-	—Dr. Robert J. Brevard.	1903-1904	—J. Thomas McLean.
1874-1877	—Augustus W. Burton, who died in office.	1905-1906	—A. J. Bagley.
		1907-1908	—Edgar Love.
1878-1879	—B. F. Grigg.	1909-1910	—Capt. C. C. Wrenshall.
1880-1881	—J. L. Wilkey.	1911-1912	—R. J. Mauser.
1882-1883	—J. Logan McLean.	1913-1914	—Charles E. Childs.
1884-	—William T. Shipp.	1915-1918	—Edgar Love.
1885-1886	—W. T. Massey.	1919-1920	—J. T. Perkins.
1887-1888	—Capt. E. W. Ward.	1921-1922	—Dr. J. R. Gamble.
1889-	—Beverly C. Cobb.	1923-1924	—Fred Ramsaur.
1890-1891	—Henry E. Ramsaur.	1925-1926	—C. Guy Rudisill.
1892-	—J. M. Roberts.	1927-1928	—J. F. Love.
1893-	—Alfred Nixon.	1929-1930	—J. A. Abernethy, Jr.
1894-1895	—S. W. McKee.	1931-1932	—Thorne Clark.
1896-	—Henry W. Burton.	1933-1934	—C. Guy Rudisill.
1897-1899	—W. E. Grigg.	1935-	—E. M. Browne.

POSTMASTERS, LINCOLNTON, LINCOLN COUNTY, N. C.

(Secured from the Post Office Department, Washington, D. C.)

Joseph Morris, Appointed January 1, 1795.
James Campbell, Appointed October 1, 1796.
John Dobson, Appointed January 1, 1802.
Joseph Black, Appointed April 1, 1803.
Vardry McBee, Appointed April 1, 1806.
David Reinhardt, Appointed October 1, 1812.
Chas. C. Henderson, Appointed June 29, 1829.
Rufus R. Templeton, Appointed April 11, 1851.
Benjamin H. Sumner, Appointed May 8, 1855.
John E. Boger, Appointed August 23, 1865.
B. F. Grigg, Appointed September 21, 1865.
Mrs. Harriett E. Bomar, Appointed October 20, 1865.
Miss Ann E. Henderson, Appointed April 22, 1870.
James H. Marsh, Appointed May 2, 1870.
Miss Nannie C. Hoke, Appointed April 7, 1885.
John P. Mullen, Appointed January 11, 1893.
Miss Eva G. Sumner, Appointed April 5, 1893.
Franklin A. Barkley, Appointed April 4, 1897; Re-appointed January 28, 1899; Re-appointed February 5, 1904.
Charles A. Jonas, Appointed March 18, 1907; Re-appointed January 14, 1908.
D. Luther Yount, Appointed March 4, 1910.

THE ANNALS OF LINCOLN COUNTY 503

John K. Cline, Appointed March 11, 1914; Re-appointed September 5, 1918.
Clyde G. Mullen, Appointed January 10, 1923.
Giles B. Goodson, Appointed April 1, 1927.
James F. Seagle, Appointed March 1, 1936.

DELEGATES TO CONSTITUTIONAL CONVENTIONS

1788—Robert Alexander, John Sloan, James Johnston, John Moore, William McLean.
1789—Joseph Dickson, John Moore, William McLean, John Caruth, Robert Alexander.
1835—Bartlett Shipp, Henry Cansler.
1861—William Lander (resigned 1862). Succeeded by David Schenck.
1865—William P. Bynum.
1868—Joseph H. King.
1875—Caleb Motz.

GOVERNORS

William A. Graham, North Carolina, 1845-1849.
James P. Henderson, Texas, 1846-1848.
Joseph F. Johnston, Alabama, 1897-1901.
Hoke Smith, Georgia, 1907-08; 1911-12.

JUDGES

Robert H. Burton, 1818.
W. P. Bynum, Justice Supreme Court, 1873-79.
W. M. Shipp, Superior Court, 1865-68 and 1881-1890.
David Schenck, Superior Court, 1874-1881.
W. A. Hoke, Superior Court, 1891-1904; Justice Supreme Court, 1905-1924; Chief Justice, 1924-1925.
Augustus L. Quickel, Superior Court, 1932.

STATE SOLICITORS

Joseph Wilson, 1823.
W. J. Alexander, 1833.
James R. Dodge, 1837.
Hamilton C. Jones, 1845.
Daniel Coleman, 1848.
William Lander, 1853 to 1862.
W. P. Bynum, 1862 to 1873, resigned to accept appointment to Supreme Court.
J. L. Carson, 1873 to 1874.
W. J. Montgomery, 1874 to 1882.
F. I. Osborne, 1882 to 1892.
J. L. Webb, 1892 to 1905.
Heriot Clarkson, 1905 to 1913.
H. T. Newland, 1913 to 1916, died in office.
R. L. Huffman, 1916 to 1926.
L. S. Spurling, since 1926.

STATE COMMISSIONERS OF AGRICULTURE

William A. Graham II., 1899 to 1923, when he died and was succeeded by his son, William A. Graham III., who served from 1923 to the end of 1936.

UNITED STATES SENATORS

William A. Graham, 1841-1843.
J. P. Henderson, Texas, 1857-1858.
Joseph F. Johnston, Alabama, 1903-1913.
Hoke Smith, Georgia, 1911-1921.
William L. Hill, Florida, 1936.
H. R. Revels (colored), Mississippi, 1870-1871.

MEMBERS OF CONGRESS

Joseph Dickson, 1799-1801.
Peter Forney, 1813-1815.
Daniel M. Forney, 1815-1818.
Henry W. Connor, 1821-1841.
Green W. Caldwell, 1841-1843.
William Lander, Confederate Congress, 1862-1864.
Charles A. Jonas, 1929-1931.
James Graham, Mountain district, 1833-1843 and 1845-1847.
William H. Forney, Alabama, 1875-1893.

CABINET OFFICERS

James Pinckney Henderson, Attorney General and Secretary of State in the Cabinet of Samuel Houston, who was the first President of the Republic of Texas; then Minister to France and England from that Republic and secured the recognition of Texas by the French Government. Later, through his diplomatic work, Texas was admitted into the Union.

William A. Graham, Secretary of the Navy under Filmore, 1850-53, and under his administration the hermit nation of Japan opened her doors to the world after 300 years of seclusion.

Hoke Smith, Secretary of the Interior under President Cleveland, 1893-96.

LINCOLN COUNTY MEMBERS OF GENERAL ASSEMBLY

Year	Senate	House of Representatives
1779	William Graham	Robert Abernethy, Miles Abernethy
1780	James Johnston	Valentine Mauney, John Sloan
1781	James Johnston	Robt. Alexander, John Sloan
1782	James Johnston	John Moore, John Sloan
1783	Robert Alexander	Dan'l McKissick, John Sloan
1784 (Apr.)	Robert Alexander	Dan'l McKissick, John Sloan
1784 (Oct.)	Robert Alexander	Dan'l McKissick, John Sloan
1785	Robert Alexander	Dan'l McKissick, John Sloan
1786	Robert Alexander	Dan'l McKissick, John Sloan
1787	Robert Alexander	Joseph Jenkins
1788	Joseph Dickson	John Moore, William McLean
1789	Joseph Dickson	John Moore, William McLean
1790	Joseph Dickson	John Moore, William McLean
1791	Joseph Dickson	John Moore, William McLean

THE ANNALS OF LINCOLN COUNTY 505

Year	Senate	House of Representatives
1792	Joseph Dickson	John Moore, Nathaniel Alexander
1793	Joseph Dickson	John Moore, Nathaniel Alexander
1794	Joseph Dickson	John Moore, Peter Forney
1795	John Perkins	David Robinson, Peter Forney
1796	Wallace Alexander	David Robinson, Peter Forney
1797	Wallace Alexander	John Ramsour, Peter Forney
1798	Wallace Alexander	John Moore, John Ramsour
1799	Wallace Alexander	John Moore, John Reinhardt
1800	Peter Forney	John Moore, John Reinhardt
1801	Peter Forney	John Moore, Jesse Robinson
1802	Peter Forney	John Moore, Peter Hoyle
1803	Henry Hoke	John Moore, Peter Hoyle
1804	Henry Hoke	John Moore, Peter Hoyle
1805	Ephraim Perkins	John Moore, Peter Hoyle
1806	David Shuford	John Moore, Peter Hoyle
1807	Andrew Hoyle	Jones Abernethy, Peter Hoyle
1808	Andrew Hoyle	Jones Abernethy, Peter Hoyle
1809	Andrew Hoyle	Daniel Hoke, Robert Patterson
1810	John Reid	Daniel Hoke, Peter Hoyle
1811	John Reid	Daniel Hoke, Peter Hoyle
1812	David Shuford	Daniel Hoke, Peter Hoyle
1813	David Shuford	Daniel Hoke, Peter Hoyle
1814	William McLean	Robert Patterson, John Ramsour
1815	David Shuford	Daniel Hoke, Peter Hoyle
1816	David Shuford	Daniel Hoke, Peter Hoyle
1817	John Reid	Henry Y. Webb, Peter Hoyle
1818	John Reid	Robert Williamson, J. F. Brevard
1819	Peter Hoyle	Robert Williamson, Dan'l Conrad
1820	David Shuford	Wm. Johnston, Dan'l Conrad
1821	Robert Williamson	O. W. Holland, Peter Hoke
1822	Robert Williamson	Daniel Conrad, Peter Hoke
1823	Daniel M. Forney	Daniel Conrad, O. W. Holland
1824	Daniel M. Forney	Daniel Conrad, Bartlett Shipp
1825	Daniel M. Forney	Daniel Conrad, O. W. Holland
1826	Daniel M. Forney	Bartlett Shipp, O. W. Holland
1827	Michael Reinhardt	Daniel Conrad, Alex J. M. Brevard
1828	Michael Reinhardt	Bartlett Shipp, Andrew H. Loretz
1829	Daniel Hoke	Bartlett Shipp, Andrew H. Loretz
1830	Daniel Hoke	Bartlett Shipp, Andrew H. Loretz
1831	Daniel Hoke	M. W. Abernethy, Henry Cansler
1832	Daniel Hoke	M. W. Abernethy, Henry Cansler
1833	Daniel Hoke	Peregrine Roberts, Henry Cansler
1834	Bartlett Shipp	Michael Hoke, Henry Cansler
1835	John B. Harry	Michael Hoke, Henry Cansler

Legislators were elected biennially after 1835

1836	Michael Reinhardt	Michael Hoke, Henry Cansler O. W. Holland, Thomas Ward

Year	Senate	House of Representatives
1838	Michael Reinhardt	Michael Hoke, John Killian
		O. W. Holland, W. W. Munday
1840	Thomas Ward	Michael Hoke, John Killian
		O. W. Holland, W. W. Munday
1842	A. Ray	Larkin Stowe, James H. White
		Nathaniel Wilson, John Yount
1844	Larkin Stowe	James H. White, Nathaniel Wilson
		F. D. Reinhardt, Richard Rankin
1846	Larkin Stowe	James H. White, Nathaniel Wilson
		F. D. Reinhardt, John Webster
1848	Henry W. Connor	James H. White, F. D. Reinhardt
		Samuel N. Stowe, Andrew H. Shuford
1850	John F. Hoke	Henderson Sherrill, Samuel N. Stowe
		F. D. Reinhardt, Richard Rankin
1852	John F. Hoke	Henderson Sherrill, William Lander
		John H. Wheeler, James A. Caldwell
1854	John F. Hoke	Henry Cansler
1856	James H. White	Adolphus P. Cansler
1858	Franklin D. Reinhardt	Ambrose Costner
1860	Jasper Stowe	John F. Hoke, resigned 1861
		V. A. McBee
1862	James H. White	Ambrose Costner
1864	M. L. McCorkle (Catawba)	Ambrose Costner
1865	W. P. Bynum	John F. Hoke
1866	M. L. McCorkle (Catawba)	Dr. M. L. Brown
1868	Lawson A. Mason (Gaston)	A. C. Wiswall
1870	Dr. Eli Crowell	David Kincaid
1872	Dr. J. R. Ellis (Catawba)	A. J. Morrison, resigned 1873
		Ambrose Costner
1874	William A. Graham	Dr. W. A. Thompson
1876	S. M. Finger (Catawba)	B. C. Cobb
1878	William A. Graham	B. C. Cobb
1880	S. M. Finger (Catawba)	J. G. Morrison
1882	Ambrose Costner	Dr. W. L. Crouse
1884	Miles O. Sherrill (Catawba)	Dr. W. L. Crouse
1886	Dr. W. L. Crouse	T. H. Proctor
1888	Dr. Josephus Turner (Catawba)	W. A. Hoke
1890	J. W. A. Paine	C. L. Wilson
1892	Miles O. Sherrill (Catawba)	Dr. W. L. Crouse
1894	A. Y. Sigmon (Catawba)	John F. Reinhardt
1896	R. H. W. Barker	Luther A. Abernethy
1898	D. A. Lowe	John F. Reinhardt
1900	J. O. McIntosh	John F. Reinhardt
1902	John F. Reinhardt	A. L. Quickel
1904	C. L. Turner (Catawba	William A. Graham
1906	John F. Reinhardt	Walter N. Keener
1908	J. D. Elliottt (Catawba)	Henry D. Warlick

Year	Senate	House of Representatives
1910	John F. Reinhardt	A. L. Quickel
1912	W. B. Council (Catawba)	Dr. R. B. Killian
1914	Chas. A. Jonas	John A. Hoover
1916	Chas. A. Jonas	Edgar Love
1918	W. A. Reinhardt (Catawba)	Edgar Love
1920	W. A. Reinhardt (Catawba)	A. L. Quickel
1922	William A. Graham III.	A. L. Quickel
1924	A. A. Shuford, Jr., (Catawba)	G. B. Goodson
1926	W. H. Childs	Chas A. Jonas
1928	J. C. Sigmon (Catawba)	C. L. Eaker
1930	Kemp B. Nixon	W. H. Sigmon
1932	J. W. Aiken (Catawba)	W. H. Sigmon
1934	Kemp B. Nixon	Chas. A. Jonas
1936	B. B. Blackwelder (Catawba)	Thorne Clark

(For Officials of Tryon County, see 1778.)

CORRECTIONS

Page 178, line 32
Read Rev. W. I. Langdon.

Page 220, line 38
Read Confederate States Senate 1864; elected by General Assembly of 1866 to United States Senate, but was denied his seat.

Page 221, line 36
Rev. William S. Bynum was ordained Deacon by Bishop Lyman in St. Barnabas' Church in Greensboro.

Page 232, line 12
One daughter of John and Fannie D. Ramseur Minter, Josephine, married Nathaniel B. Dial.

Page 259, line 22
Dr. Sumner McBee married June 30, 1874, died August 31, 1892.

Page 268, line 13
Read *became,* not *become.*

Page 270, line 24
J. F. Reinhardt defeated Capt. E. W. Ward in 1894.

Page 294, line 4
Minerva May Crouse, who married John Malcus Merritt.

Page 300, line 22
Dr. Sumner McBee (died August 31, 1892), married Anna Cameron Shipp (born 1853, died 1923).

Page 301, lines 8-9
Read Prof. W. M. Pickens, the present Superintendent, was first elected in 1926.

Page 368, line 3
See note above correcting page 301, lines 8-9.

Page 422, line 26
Read (See 1921).

Page 464, illustration
Dr. R. B. Killian—read (1853-1935).

INDEX

A

	Page
Abbott, Joseph C.	207
Abernethy	8
Abernethy, Arthur T.	266
Abernethy, A. W.	142
Abernethy, Hon. Chas. L.	265
Abernethy, Dr. Claude	265
Abernethy, David	117
Abernethy, Eric	265
Abernethy, Elizabeth	60, 63
Abernethy, Ethel	265
Abernethy, Fannie Whitener	263
Abernethy, Felix M.	117, 142
Abernethy, Irene	265
Abernethy, Dr. James	120, 231, 421
Abernethy, James Alonzo	182, 231, 248, 421, 422
Abernethy, James Alonzo, Jr.	422, 423, 432, 433
Abernethy, Janie Campbell	231
Abernethy, John	120, 231, 265
Abernethy, John D.	119
Abernethy, John Daniel	422
Abernethy, Rev. John T.	265
Abernethy, Jos.	68
Abernethy, Rev. L. Berge	265
Abernethy, Lula	422
Abernethy, Mary A. Hayes	265
Abernethy, Mary Elizabeth	422
Abernethy, Mary Rankin	231, 421
Abernethy, Mattie Smith	231
Abernethy, Miles W.	107, 112, 116, 117, 119, 231
Abernethy, Moses T.	122
Abernethy, Nancy	54, 109
Abernethy, R. H.	159, 265
Abernethy, Robert	24, 54, 91
Abernethy, Robert Laban	42, 54, 86, 263, 264, 265, 266
Abernethy, Robert Sidney	422
Abernethy, Sarah	231, 421
Abernethy, Susan M. Forney	119
Abernethy, Theodore R.	231
Abernethy, Thomas C.	312
Abernethy, Turner	57, 58, 109, 117, 263
Abernethy, Mrs. W. C.	191, 231
Abernethy, Washington Clay	231
Abernethy, Rev. William E.	265
Adair (Gov.)	112
Adams, Mr.	164
Adams, Francis	14, 16
Adams, J. M. H. (Rev.)	108, 126
Adams, Julia	164
Adams, Pinckney Henderson	164
Adams, Robert	15
Aderholt, John M.	363
Aderholt, Margaret	364

	Page
Aitkin, Isabel	375
Akers, Effie	415
Akers, W. W. (Rev.)	87
Alderman, Sidney Sherrill	355
Alexander, A. C.	191
Alexander, Abram	62
Alexander, Agnes	191
Alexander, Allen	116
Alexander, Anna	191
Alexander, Anna Taylor	190
Alexander, Ann Dobson	194
Alexander, Barbara L. Summey	190, 431
Alexander, Catherine	132, 147
Alexander, Charlotte Hill	191
Alexander, Dr. Eben	293
Alexander, Elias	73, 175, 190, 191, 192, 193
Alexander, Elias James	190, 431
Alexander, Ella	190
Alexander, Francis	191
Alexander, Harriet Clark	190
Alexander, Isabella	139
Alexander, J. F.	191
Alexander, J. T.	87, 121, 123, 159
Alexander, James Taylor	190, 192, 214
Alexander, Jane	175, 191
Alexander, Jane Alexander	194
Alexander, Jane McBee	191
Alexander, John	55
Alexander, John Taylor (Capt.)	104, 112
Alexander, Lawson Henderson	194
Alexander, Lena	410
Alexander, M. W. (Dr.)	139
Alexander, Margaret	191
Alexander, Margaret McClung	293
Alexander, Margaret Rebecca	191
Alexander, Mary Royal Robinson	190
Alexander, Mary Wood (Miss)	108, 240
Alexander, McK.	194
Alexander, Moses W. (Dr.)	114
Alexander, Nathaniel	194
Alexander, Patsy Blanton	191
Alexander, R. M.	123
Alexander, Robert	19, 20, 21, 23, 24, 26, 55, 112
Alexander, Ross, Jr.	191
Alexander, Major Ross, Sr.	191
Alexander, Sarah Caroline	194
Alexander, Summey	190, 431
Alexander, Sydenham B. (Capt.)	114
Alexander, Wallace	38, 194, 214, 324

	Page
Alexander, Wallace Henderson	190
Alexander, William	191, 194
Alexander, William Julius	54, 107, 112, 126, 145, 147, 161, 166, 194, 376
Allston, Lemuel J. (Col.)	176
Alston, William	23, 24
Anderson (Rev. M.)	143
Anderson, Esley O.	151
Andrew, James O. (Bishop)	106
Andrews, A. B., Jr.	272
Andrews, Graham H.	272
Andrews, John H.	272
Andrews, Samuel	31, 125
Andrews, William Johnston	272
Anthony, Frontis H. (Rev.)	356
Anthony, John P.	75
Anthony, Philip	75
Arends, John Gottfried (Rev.)	71
Armistead, Katherine Eloise	268
Armstrong, Capt.	37
Armstrong, Col. C. B.	203
Armstrong, Rev. J. Frank	410
Armstrong, William	46
Arndt, Catherine	71
Arndt, Elizabeth	71, 84
Arndt, Frederick	71
Arndt, Hannah	71, 104
Arndt, Jacob	71
Arndt, Rev. James Allen	317
Arndt, John	71
Arndt, John Allen	57
Arndt, John Gottfried	16, 56, 57, 70, 72, 75, 84, 104, 260, 307, 317, 373
Arndt, Mary	71
Arndt, Susan	71
Asbury	9
Asbury, Daniel	59, 61, 89, 90, 218
Asbury, Henry (Rev.)	61, 218
Ashe, Capt. Samuel A.	330
Ashley, John	23, 24
Avery, Alphonso C.	168
Avery, Isaac Erwin	323
Avery, John Morehead	239
Avery, Sudie	300
Avery, W. W. (Hon.)	151
Avery, Waightstill	14
Aycock, Gov. Chas. B.	230, 284

B

Babington, Benjamin B.	202
Babington, Buenavista Biggerstaff	202
Babington, Elisha B.	202
Babington, Hattie McLurd	202
Babington, Robert B.	202, 203, 204, 205
Badger, Allison L.	308
Badger, Judge George E.	101, 103, 301, 308

	Page
Baggett, Jesse	25
Bagwell, Dr. J. T.	266
Baird, James	20, 21
Baird, Robert	106
Baker, Catherine	132, 133
Bandy, Dr. J. F.	399
Bandy, James M.	190, 217, 325, 326, 327
Bandy, Martha Leonard	190, 326
Bandy, Martha Lynn	326
Bandy, Wesley	326
Bangle, Alice	393
Bangle, Elizabeth	392, 393
Bangle, Luther	393
Banister, James	104
Barber, John	23, 24, 25
Barineau, Mrs. J. W.	232, 355
Barkley, Senator A. W.	396
Barkley, Archibald C.	395
Barkley, Avis	395
Barkley, David A.	331
Barkley, Eleanor Cathey	395
Barkley, Henry	395
Barkley, James	395
Barkley, Mary	395
Barkley, Robert	395, 396
Barnhardt, J. M.	39, 411
Barr, Rev. J. S.	214
Barrett, Mrs. E. S.	162
Barringer, Daniel M.	125, 179
Barringer, Mrs. Eugenia Morrison	164
Barringer, John	418
Barringer, Joseph (Gen.)	86
Barringer, Matthias	128
Barringer, Paul	116
Barringer, Rufus	164, 252
Bartlett, George L.	209, 331
Baskerville, Wm. S.	309
Battle, Dr. Kemp P.	200
Baxter, John	127
Beam, Michael	81, 82
Beard, John	15
Beattie, Elizabeth	299
Beatty, Abel	21
Beatty, Charles	106
Beatty, John	7, 8, 32, 62
Beatty, Thomas	19, 20, 21, 23, 24
Beatty, William	62
Beeman, John	20, 21
Bell, John	168
Bell, Joseph E. (Rev.)	87, 88, 94
Bennett, Judge Risden Tyler	234
Bergner, Maria	32, 69
Berry, L. M. (Rev.)	169
Best, Bastian	409
Best, Daniel	364
Best, Marie Elizabeth	409
Bethel, Battle of	169
Beulow, Joachim	70
Bird, Jos. L. C.	268

THE ANNALS OF LINCOLN COUNTY 511

	Page
Bisaner, Jake	226, 227
Bisaner, Susan	71
Bissell, E. H.	112
Bivens, James	83, 102, 132
Bivins, Nancy	132
Black, George	20, 21, 23
Blackburn, Robert	14, 15, 16, 54
Bland, C. T. (Rev.)	169, 178, 310
Bland, Chas. T., Jr.	178
Blanton, George	14
Blount, William	136
Blythe, J. L.	63
Blythe, Joseph (Dr.)	99
Blythe, S. J.	63
Boger-Crawford Company	428
Boger, John E.	43, 287
Boger, Mary Ann Ramseur	287
Bolinger, Mary	88
Bolinger, S. L.	309
Bomar, Mrs. Harriet	107, 153
Bone, Harland	167
Boone, Daniel	98
Bost, Marcus L.	76
Bost, Dr. T. C.	398
Boyd, J. D.	103
Boyd, John	81
Boyd, M. T.	201, 309
Boyd, Mary Reinhardt	201, 309
Boyden, Willard	117
Boylan, William	282
Boyles, Augustus C.	258
Boyles, Mrs. Blanche Carr Sterne	259
Boyles, Frank C.	259
Boyles, Franklin C.	259
Boyles, John	258
Boyles, Joseph H.	259
Boyles, Marcus M.	259
Boyles, Rev. Marcus W.	258, 259
Boyles, Pitman A.	259
Boyles, Susan Wood	258
Branch, John	110
Brandon, Capt.	37
Brandon, Elizabeth	62, 63
Brandon, Margaret Locke	62
Brandon, Richard	62
Branson, John	15
Breckinridge	168
Brem, Charles F. (Dr.)	76
Brem, Jacob	76
Brem, T. R.	77
Brem, Thomas H. (Col.)	76
Brem, Thomas H., Jr.	76
Brem, Walter	77
Brevard, A. F.	65
Brevard, Adam	25
Brevard, Alexander (Capt.)	33, 57, 58, 63, 82, 100, 101, 109, 140, 227
Brevard, Capt. Alexander F.	228, 318

	Page
Brevard, Caroline Mays	225, 308
Brevard, E. A. (Col.)	107
Brevard, E. J.	65
Brevard, Ephraim	100, 225
Brevard, Franklin	100
Brevard, Harriet	82, 100, 140
Brevard, J. H. (Maj.)	107
Brevard, J. Franklin	101
Brevard, John	100
Brevard, Joseph	100
Brevard, Mary	100
Brevard, Mary Call	225
Brevard, Rebecca (Davidson)	101
Brevard, Robt. A.	58, 100, 227, 228, 318
Brevard, Robert H.	148
Brevard, Dr. Robert J.	225, 308
Brevard, Judge Theodorus W.	100, 225, 308
Brevard, Theodorus W., Jr.	225
Brittain, Barbara	365
Broadfoot, William Wilson	177
Brooks, Elizabeth	94
Brooks, W. W.	381
Brown, Ella	410
Brown, George A.	373
Brown, John	46
Brown, John E.	252
Brown, Dr. M. L.	222
Brumby, Harriet Brevard	101
Brumby, Mary Brevard	101
Brumby, Richard T.	100, 101
Bryan, William J.	270
Bryant, Ed.	31, 125
Bryant, Eva Sumner	187
Bryant, H. E. C.	187
Bryden, Barbara Glen	131
Buchanan, James	21
Buffalo Academy	97
Buffalo Shoals School	100
Bullock, Zachary	14
Bulwinkle, Cong. A. L.	385
Burgin (Miss)	174
Burgin, Sam D.	305
Burton, Mrs. Alfred	166
Burton, Alfred M.	70, 93, 114, 127, 162, 165, 166
Burton, Augustus W.	126, 135, 153, 223
Burton, Eliza	126
Burton, Elizabeth	125, 162
Burton, Fanny (Miss)	166
Burton, Frances	106, 126, 132
Burton, Frank O.	224
Burton, Henry W.	126, 207, 274, 433
Burton, Mrs. Henry W.	162
Burton, Hutchins Gordon (Gov.)	114, 115, 116
Burton, Mrs. Hutchins Gordon	115
Burton, James M.	102
Burton, Julia L. Olmstead	223

	Page
Burton, Robert (Col.)	126, 165
Burton, Robert H.	45, 80, 82, 93, 103, 106, 112, 114, 123, 125, 126, 132, 140, 166, 223
Burton, Mrs. Sarah Hoyle Keenan	207
Burwell, Judge	307
Busbee, Hon. Fabius H.	276
Butler, Harriet Ford	177
Butts, Elizabeth	96, 269
Butts, John	75, 117, 140, 269
Butts, Margaret	140, 269
Byerly, D. H.	157
Bynum, Ann Eliza Shipp	278, 318
Bynum, Bartlett Shipp	281
Bynum, Curtis Ashley	281, 387, 388
Bynum, Eliza Shipp	281
Bynum, Florence Helen Boyd	281
Bynum, Gray	318
Bynum, Hampton	318
Bynum, John Gray (Gen.)	125
Bynum, Katharine Fullerton	281
Bynum, Margaret Hampton	318
Bynum, Mary Coleman Martin	318
Bynum, Mary deRosset	281
Bynum, Mary Louisa Curtis	280
Bynum, Mary Preston	319
Bynum, Minna (Barbara)	281
Bynum, Susan Allan (Suzanne)	281
Bynum, Judge W. P., Jr.	337
Bynum, William Preston, Jr.	280
Bynum, William Preston (Judge)	84, 127, 138, 165, 166, 179, 184, 189, 202, 217, 278, 318, 319, 320, 321, 322, 323
Bynum, William Shipp (Rev.)	214, 217, 221, 234, 278, 279, 280, 281, 319

C

Caldwell, (Judge)	158
Caldwell, Angie	388
Caldwell, Prof. B. P.	301
Caldwell, Elam (Dr.)	124, 388
Caldwell, Green W.	68, 125, 145, 178, 179
Caldwell, Hannah	77
Caldwell, J. A.	155
Caldwell, John W.	148
Caldwell, Joseph	185
Caldwell, Joseph P.	146, 337
Caldwell, Kittie	168
Caldwell, Pinckney C. (Dr.)	104, 120, 261
Caldwell, R. B.	168
Caldwell, Tod R. (Gov.)	77, 123, 211, 214, 274
Calloway, Joseph W. (Dr.)	158, 161

	Page
Calvert, J. S.	369
Cameron, Hon. John A.	255
Camp, Stephen	191
Campbell (Col.)	43
Campbell, James	175
Cancelor, Barbara	67
Cancelor, Elizabeth	67, 86
Cancelor, George	67
Cancelor, John	67
Cancelor, Uly	67
Canipe, Adam	392
Cansler, A. P. (Col.)	155
Cansler, Abel T.	208
Cansler, Adelaide	209
Cansler, Mrs. Adelaide M.	155, 208
Cansler, Adolphus P.	208
Cansler, Alex. Jacob	208
Cansler, Andrew J.	149
Cansler, Barbara	209
Cansler, Barbara Rudisill	207
Cansler, Conrad	66, 68
Cansler, Daniel	209
Cansler, Edwin T.	94, 96, 208, 209
Cansler, Fanny J.	209
Cansler, Fanny Shuford	207
Cansler, George	305
Cansler, George W.	208
Cansler, Henry	31, 71, 86, 95, 110, 111, 116, 121, 125, 133, 149, 159, 168, 202, 207, 208, 209
Cansler, Jane E. Long	208
Cansler, John P.	208
Cansler, Katie	270
Cansler, Kate Murphy	208
Cansler, Mary A. Marshall	208
Cansler, Mary J. Morrow	208
Cansler, Mary Quickel	207
Cansler, Nancy McNeely	208
Cansler, Philip	30, 56, 65, 66, 67, 71, 83, 86, 207, 270
Cansler, Philip, Jr.	58, 67, 68, 83, 86, 207
Cansler, Mrs. T. H.	356
Cansler, Thomas J.	209
Cansler, William H.	208
Carolina Republican	143
Carpenter (Capt.)	38
Carpenter, Annie	128
Carpenter, Catherine	83, 365, 418
Carpenter, Christian	14, 21
Carpenter, Christopher	17, 18, 29, 36
Carpenter, David	83
Carpenter, Elizabeth	94
Carpenter, Jacob	83, 366
Carpenter, John	134
Carpenter, Samuel	21, 388
Carson, Hon. Joseph McDowell	193
Caruth, Elizabeth	60, 130
Caruth, John	29, 30, 52, 55

THE ANNALS OF LINCOLN COUNTY 513

	Page
Cashwell, Claudia	261
Castles, William	118
Catawba College	156
Presidents of	156
Faculty of	157
Removal of	157

Catawba County:
Magistrates of (1843) 128
Select Court of 128

Catawba River:
Territory west of 7
Early Settlers (see also Pioneers) 7

Catawba School 87
Catawba Springs 103, 104
Cathey, William 46
Cauble, Ephraim H. 282
Charlotte Mint 120, 122, 179
Chase, James 131
Chase, Salmon P. 105
Cheshire, Bishop 279
Childs, Albertus D. 244, 284
Childs, Bessie 403
Childs, Capt. Charles E....284, 403
Childs, Chas. E., Jr..............403
Childs, Eben 284, 403
Childs, Edward T. 284
Childs, Fred Sherwood 403
Childs, Katie Motz 403
Childs, L. D. 83, 132, 159, 284
Childs, Marietta Sheldon 403
Childs, Susie 403
Childs, Wade Hampton 403
Childs, William G. 420
Christ School 305
Chronicle, William
  (Maj.) 33, 44, 81
Cincinnati (N. C.) Society
  of the 99, 100, 184
Clapp, Rev. Dr. J. C. 324
Clapp, Joshua 156
Clark, David 221
Clark, Henry 13, 14
Clark, Thorne 221
Clark, W. A. Graham.............221
Clark, Mrs. W. R. 107
Clark, Walter, Judge
  (also Chief Justice) 181, 221
Clark, William Rufus 220
Clary, Robert 69
Cleaveland, Benjamin 30, 125
Cleveland (Col.) 43
Cleveland, Grover 125, 240, 258, 262
Cline, Catherine 67
Cline, John K. 401
Cline, Thomas F. 317
Cline, W. P. 57
Cloyd, Uriah 142
Cobb, Barbara Henderson 306

	Page
Cobb, Bartlett	430

Cobb, Beatrice (Morganton
  News-Herald) 289
Cobb, Beverly C. 269, 284, 299
Cobb, B. Y. 206, 306, 332
Cobb, Chas. C....202, 230, 236, 239, 332, 333, 385, 398
Cobb, Collier 213, 411, 412, 413
Cobb, Ella Kincaid 289
Cobb, Ellen 430
Cobb, Ellen V. Johnson....228, 332
Cobb, Fannie Helton 288
Cobb, Mrs. J. C. 75
Cobb, James 288
Cobb, Joseph C. 140, 269
Cobb, John L. 269, 292
Cobb, Matilda Falls 288
Cobb, Nancy Fairley 333, 385, 398
Cobb, Dr. Needham B. 213, 333, 411
Cobb, Robert Alexander....288, 289
Cobb, Gen. T. R. R. 401
Cobb, Theodore G. 288, 289
Cobb, Theodorus H....202, 221, 228, 244, 248, 306, 307, 332, 430
Cobb, Thomas Lee 332
Cobb, William 209
Coburn, James 20, 21
Coke, (Bishop) 33
Coleman, Daniel 143
Coleman, Mrs. Lucy Ann 120
Coleman, Mark 149
Collins, Abraham 69
Collins, Elvira 133
Collins, Evaline 133
Conley, George 155
Connor (Mrs.) 166
Connor, Ann 189
Connor, Ann Epps 60, 187
Connor, Betsy 114
Connor, Charles (Capt.)...60, 63, 64, 110
Connor, Charles D.
  (Capt.) 64, 114
Connor, Charles T., Lt....182, 187, 188, 189
Connor, Charlie 189
Connor, Cornelius 106
Connor, Eliza 65
Connor, Elizabeth 64
Connor, Dr. Francis 200
Connor, Harriet 65
Connor, Henry 33, 60, 63, 64, 65, 88, 110
Connor, Henry William....64, 102, 103, 105, 107, 117, 120, 135, 142, 145, 147, 187
Connor, Henry Workman 64
Connor, Henry Workman,
  Jr. 65, 189

	Page
Connor, James	33, 63, 64, 65, 110
Connor, John	64
Connor, Dr. LeGree	200
Connor, Mrs. Lucy Hawkins	147, 188
Connor, Luetta	189
Connor, Margaret	65
Connor, Mary	189
Connor, Nancy	65
Conner, Peter	15
Connor, Samuel (Dr.)	65
Connor, Sarah	178, 200
Connor, T. F.	189
Conrad, Bettie	245
Coon, Betty	356
Coon, Frances Hovis	382
Coon, Carrie Louise Sparger	384
Coon, Charles Lee	197, 355, 382, 383, 384
Coon, Charles Lee, Jr.	384
Coon, David A.	174, 197, 355, 356, 382
Coon, Frances Elizabeth	384
Coon, Mary Moore	384
Cope, R. F.	98, 141
Cornelius, H. R. (Rev.)	63
Cornelius, James	167
Cornwallis (Lord)	22, 38, 40, 43, 45, 92
Corpening, Catherine	133
Corpening, Mary	124
Costner, Adam	327
Costner, Ambrose	91, 94, 138, 147, 168, 217, 327, 328, 329, 431
Costner, Anna Rudisill	327
Costner, Barbara	410
Costner, Catherine Malinda Quickel	327
Costner, Emmeline	410
Costner, Dr. George H.	328, 422
Costner, Dr. Henry A.	329
Costner, Jacob	15, 21, 24, 36, 327
Costner, Jacob (Maj.)	95
Costner, James A.	329
Costner, Margaret	95
Costner, Martha	329
Costner, Michael	327
Costner, Robert E.	329
Costner, Thomas	18, 327
Costner, Dr. Thos. F.	329, 431
Costner, Dr. W. V.	399
Costner, William A.	328
Coulter, D. J.	107
Coulter, John	123, 168
Counties:	
Formation of	7
Reorganization of	26, 29, 31, 52
New boundary lines of	30, 138
Creation of new	30, 52, 125, 127, 138, 141

	Page
County Court of Pleas and Quarter Sessions	18
Courts, Daniel W. (Hon.)	105
Cowan (Capt.)	44
Cowan's Ford	45
Cox, Frances	131, 163
Cox, John	163
Coxe, Francis S.	191
Coxe, Col. Frank	191, 192
Coxe, Jane McBee Alexander	191
Cozart, James	15
Craig, John H.	244
Craig, Gov. Locke	230
Craige, Burton	145, 159, 163, 179, 219, 221
Craige, David	219
Craige, Elizabeth Erwin	219
Craige, Kerr	219
Cranford, J. H.	156
Crawford, Dan G.	315
Crawford, J. H. (Rev.)	56, 125
Creasemore, Rebecca	417
Crider, Dr.	415
Crockett, David	15, 115
Crockett, John	115
Crockett, William	15
Cromer, J. L.	364
Cromer, Voigt	57, 364
Crook, Andrew B.	132
Crooks, David (Rev.)	56
Crouse, David	293
Crouse, David Stowe	294
Crouse, Josephine	305
Crouse, Mattie Anna Stowe	294
Crouse, Minerva May	294
Crouse, Prue	294
Crouse, Sallie Bright	294
Crouse, Dr. W. L.	234, 293, 294, 337
Crowell, Dr. Eli	167, 311
Crowell, Frances Geitner	381
Crowell, Frank Hull	312
Crowell, G. Edward	364, 365
Crowell, Georgia Corinne	312
Crowell, Dr. Gordon Bryan	310, 312, 381
Crowell, Katie Rhodes	364, 365
Crowell, Dr. Lester A.	310, 311, 312, 430
Crowell, Dr. Lester A., Jr.	311, 312
Crowell, Mae	365
Crowell, Mary Beatrice	312
Crowell, Mary Beatrice Lowrance	311
Crowell, Mary Jane Hull	312
Crowell, Maude	365
Crowell, Michael	311
Crowell, Nina	365

THE ANNALS OF LINCOLN COUNTY 515

	Page
Cuban War	274
Cumberland (Capt.)	38
Curtis, Rev. Dr. M. A.	280

D

Dale, Dr. J. Y.	305
Dale, Katherine	305
Dallas, Catherine	32
Dallas, George M.	31
Dalley, L. Les (Dr.)	130
Daniel, Louise	261
Dargan, Atlas J.	127
Davenport, A. W.	142
Davenport, Mary E.	138
Davenport, William	138
Davidson College	86
Davidson (Gen.)	113
Davidson, Isabella	113
Davidson, John	59, 99, 100, 113
Davidson, Mary	59, 99
Davidson, Rebecca	100
Davidson, W. L. (Lt. Col.)	25, 34, 45
Company Roll of	25
Davis, D. A.	419
Davis, George L.	206
Davis, J. S.	172
Davis, James H.	172
Davis, R. N. (Rev.)	87, 165, 167, 169, 211
Davis, Richmond Pearson (Gen).	105
Davis, Robert	16
Davis, W. B. (Rev.)	87
Day, W. A. (Capt.)	39
Day, William H. (Capt.)	115, 319
Deal, C. H.	367
Deal, Jacob	86
Deaton, John	209
DeBerry, Grace	422
Deihl, Eli	86
Deitz, J. C.	57
DeLane, Francis H.	333
DeLane, John T. (Jack)	333
Dellinger, Chester	353
Dellinger, George	36
Dellinger, Henry	18, 19, 30, 84, 353
Dellinger, John	18, 36
Dellinger, Marsh	353
Denver Seminary Commencement	229, 230
Denver Seminary Gazette	229
Derr, Jonas W.	58, 234
Detter, John R.	312
Detter, Mary	126
Detter, Sarah A.	129
Devepaugh, Margaret Cancelor	67
Devepaugh, Philip	68
Dewey, P.	104
Dews, Martha	102
Dews, Thomas	72, 149
Dews, Thomas, Jr.	72, 102, 119, 150

	Page
Dickson (Col.)	37
Dickson, John	29, 44, 52
Dickson, John B.	92
Dickson, Joseph	30, 32, 55, 60, 73, 92
Dillard, H. K.	245
Dillard, Judge John H.	290
Dobbs, James R. (Col.)	72
Dobson (Capt.)	37, 38
Dobson, Nancy	392
Dockery, Alfred	110
Dockery, Oliver H.	234
Dodge, James R.	127, 166, 197, 198, 229
Doggett, E. Ross	191
Donnell, R. S.	127
Dorsey, A. B.	267
Dow, Alonzo (Rev.)	108
Dowd, Dr. Jerome	266, 282
Dry Pond P. O.	116
Duke, William	185
Dunavant, Ann	131
Durham, Achilles	31, 125
Durham, L. N.	209
Dusenberry, E. L. (Dr.)	173
Dutch Meeting House (Old White Church) Pastors of (1828-1859)	56

E

Eaker, John	18
Earhardt, Abram	57, 109
Earle, John	26
Earney, John	106
Eddleman, Peter	117
Edison, Charles	308
Edison, Thomas A.	308
Edney, B. M.	117
Edwards, William R.	129, 240
Ehringhaus, Gov.	293
Elder, Samuel	34
Elliott, Dr. William F.	150, 310
Ellis, (Gov.)	93, 168, 251, 272
Ellis, Elizabeth	93
Ellis, John W.	145
Elms, William W.	148
England, Wilson	155, 156
Epperson, T. M.	309
Epps, Mary Ann	64
Epps, Peter	64
Ervin, Isaac	87
Erwin, Col. James	219
Espey, Thomas	20, 21, 23, 34, 55
Eutaw Springs, Battle of	44
Ewart, Robert	14

F

Fair, County and State	347, 348
Fair, W. A.	41
Fairley, Henry	333, 334

	Page
Fairley, Sallie Glenn Shaw	333, 385
Falls, Capt.	37
Farney, Jacob	21, 69
Farrior, Mrs. Kittie McMullen	315
Ferguson, James	142
Ferguson, Patrick (Col.)	32, 38, 43, 81
Ferrier, Lorenzo	220
Ferry, Thomas	101
Fey, Jacob	418
Finch, Mrs. Amanda Calvert	370
Finch, George	370
Finch, Capt. K. S.	227
Finger, Beatrice	410
Finger, Caty Cancelor	67
Finger, Daniel	72, 270
Finger, Daniel, Jr.	270
Finger, Henry	270
Finger, John	270
Finger, Joseph	270
Finger, Mrs. Joseph	143
Finger, Mary	270
Finger, Michael	270
Finger, Peter	270
Finger, Sarah	270
Finger, Sarah Hoyle Rhyne	271
Finger, Sidney M. (Maj.)	72, 270, 271
First National Bank, Directors of	294
Fisher, Charles	135
Fisher, Jacob	191
Fite, H.	209
Fitzsimmons, Elizabeth	369
Flack, W. Edgar	365
Fleming, Samuel	151
Flow, Eunice	431
Foard, Osborne G.	139
Forbes, E. M. Rev.	125, 126, 129
Forney, A. J.	112
Forney, Abram (Maj.)	33, 57, 63, 69, 109, 112, 117, 146
Forney, Abram E.	146
Forney, Catherine	69
Forney, Christina	69
Forney, Daniel M.	54, 82, 100, 107, 109, 140
Forney, E. J.	387
Forney, Eliza	140
Forney, Elizabeth	69
Forney, Jacob	8, 13, 19, 20, 33, 45, 51, 69, 87, 108, 124, 146, 202, 261, 373, 387
Forney, Jacob, Jr.	82, 107, 111, 112, 124
Forney, John H.	111
Forney, John W.	146
Forney, Lavinia	93
Forney, Maria Bergner	387

	Page
Forney, Monroe	162
Forney, Nancy	84, 158
Forney, Peter (Gen.)	33, 51, 54, 57, 58, 62, 69, 81, 84, 93, 100, 108, 109, 111, 140, 158, 201, 354
Forney, Polly	63
Forney, Sarah Hoke	87, 261
Forney, Sophia	108
Forney, Susan	69, 82, 202
Forney, William H.	87, 162, 261
Forsyth, John	14
Fort Sumter	168
Fox, Dr. Albert C.	374
Fox, Alfred J. (Rev.)	239, 374
Fox, Alfred J. (Dr.)	82, 167, 239, 240
Fox, Dr. Claude B.	239
Fox, Dr. J. Frank	239
Fox, Rev. Junius B., D.D.	239
Fox, Rev. Luther A., D.D.	239
Fox, Lydia Bost (Mrs. A. J.)	239
Frazier, Sarah	328
Freeman, Rev. James Otis	219
French, James	15
Friday, Anna Mariah	82
Friday, John C.	410
Friday, Lee A.	410
Friday, Martin	85
Friday, Michael	82
Friday, Nicholas	23, 29, 30, 52, 55, 86
Fritchey, J. G. (Rev.)	56
Froneberger, Jacob	173
Frontis, Stephen (Rev.)	102
Fulenwider	93
Fulenwider, Eli H.	157, 162, 164, 178
Fulenwider, Elizabeth	73, 93, 107, 140, 162, 166
Fulenwider, Esther	93
Fulenwider, Henry	93, 123, 127, 129
Fulenwider, Jacob	93, 107
Fulenwider, John	65, 73, 92, 126, 140, 166
Fulenwider, John, Jr.	93
Fulenwider, Mary	93, 126, 140
Fulenwider, Roxanna	134, 162
Fulenwider, Sarah	93, 162
Fulenwider, William	93

G

	Page
Gabriel, Rachel	63, 146
Gabriel, Ruanna	60
Gaffney, Nancy Riley	131
Gaither, Thos. H.	162
Gamble, J. F. (Dr.)	153, 398, 399
Gamble, J. R. (Dr.)	153
Gamble Clinic, Inc.	398, 399
Gantzler, Philip	68

THE ANNALS OF LINCOLN COUNTY

	Page
Gardner, Col. Junius P.	308
Gardner, Pearl	308
Gaston, William	31, 110, 118
Gaston College, Dallas, N. C.	258
Gaston County:	
Record of First Court	141
Officers elected	141
Gates, (Gen.)	100
Gatewood, Dora	329, 431
Gattis, Annie Belle	268
Geisler, Arthur H.	164
George III, (King)	21
George, Enoch	59
Gheen, Warren	236
Gibson, L. T.	391
Gilbert, Richard	15
Gilbert, William	19, 25, 26
Gillespie, Mary Jane	138
Gilliam, Robert B.	30, 125
Gilliland, Alexander	23, 24
Givens, Thomas (Capt.)	97
Glass, Joseph	69
Godfrey, Miss	365
Godwin, John	25
Goforth, Andrew	15
Goodson, James	25
Goodwin, Polly	60
Gordon, John	13
Goshen Church	98
Graham, Adelaide	116
Graham, Alfred	112
Graham, Alice Caldwell	369
Graham, Augustus W.	221
Graham, Caroline Brevard	369
Graham, Charles Connor	123, 140
Graham, Eliza P.	155
Graham, Elizabeth Hill	369
Graham, Ellen	369
Graham, Florence Lane	369
Graham, George Franklin (Dr.)	114, 221, 272
Graham, Dr. George W.,	221
Graham, James	60, 113, 114, 150, 166, 312
Graham, James A.	221
Graham, John	108
Graham, John D.	112, 113, 114, 119, 140, 155
Graham, John W.	221
Graham, Joseph	33, 57, 60, 63, 100, 106, 109, 111, 112, 113, 114, 119, 150, 178, 188, 220, 252
Graham, Joseph Mrs.	369
Graham, Dr. Joseph	221
Graham, Joseph M.	134
Graham, Julia Evalin	369
Graham, Julia Robertson Lane	369
Graham, Martha	369
Graham, Martha A.	272

	Page
Graham, Mary	114
Graham, Moses	116
Graham, Sophia	369
Graham, Susan Wash'ton	220, 369
Graham, Violet	114
Graham, William	19, 20, 21, 23, 24, 25, 29, 34, 44, 55, 68, 109, 369
Graham, William A. (Gov.)	65, 113, 114, 116, 119, 132, 133, 134, 155, 220, 221
Graham, William A., Maj.	221, 368, 369
Graham, William A., III	369, 420
Grant, Henry	106
Grant, U. S.	197, 241
Granville, Earl	13
Gray, David	31, 125
Green, Joseph	14
Green, William	192, 193
Greene, (Gen.)	44, 100
Greene, Bishop Wm. M.	146, 251
Grier, Addie Ramseur (Mrs.)	232, 354
Grier, Calvin E.	232, 354
Grier, Sadie	232
Grier, Thomas	165
Grier, Mrs. Thomas	162
Grigg, B. F. (Capt.)	174, 206, 211, 338
Grigg, Mary McCoy	338
Grigg, W. E.	208
Grimes, William	24, 29, 223, 299
Gryder, J. L.	309
Guerry, Dr. Alexander	300
Guerry, Anne	300
Guerry, Rev. Edward Brailsford	300
Guerry, Rev. Moultrie	300
Guerry, Rev. Sumner	300
Guerry, Rt. Rev. William A. Guerry	300, 387
Guignard, Elizabeth	261
Guion, Alex. H.	261
Guion, Alice	261
Guion, Benjamin S.	158, 260, 261
Guion, Caroline	158
Guion, Catherine Caldwell	104, 261
Guion, Dr. Connie M.	261
Guion, Effie	261
Guion, H. W.	121, 126, 145, 155, 157, 158, 160, 165, 237, 261
Guion, Josephine Wilson	261
Guion, Katie	261
Guion, Laura	261
Guion, Louis	261
Guion, Mary Wood	261
Guion, Ridie Justice	261
Guion, Vivian Q.	261
Gullett, Jonathan	29
Gullick, Jonathan	26, 54

H

	Page
Guthrie, Thomas C.	379
Gwyn, Annie Joyce	300
Hafer, Lewis	71
Hager, Barbara	418
Hager, George	418
Halifax Convention	28
Hall, Rev. Frank	263
Hall, John	263, 325
Hall, Maude	403
Hallman, Daniel	76
Hallman, Fanny	86
Hallman, John	76
Hambright, Frederick	15, 18, 19, 20, 21, 22, 23, 24, 29, 32, 44, 51, 52, 54, 95
Hamilton (Gov.)	96
Hamilton, H. C.	332
Hammerskold, Charles W.	167
Hamby, Allen (Rev.)	108
Hampton, Andrew	14, 19, 20, 23, 24
Hampton, Anthony	318
Hampton, Jonathan	90
Hand, J. G. (Col.)	102
Hank, Michael	418
Hanks, Adeline	392
Hanks, William	127
Happoldt, J. M. (Dr.)	129
Hardin, Benjamin	19, 20, 21, 23, 26, 29
Hardin, Joseph	19, 20, 21, 23, 24, 25
Hardin, John	393
Harrell, Lucy	340
Harris, Ann Eliza	114
Harris, Charles	114
Harris, Edna	422
Harris, Martha A.	114
Harrison, Benjamin	251
Harry, John B. (Capt.)	112, 117, 118, 163
Hart, Oliver J.	300
Haselip, Robert	21
Haskell, A. C.	261
Hasselbarger, Susan	70
Hauss, Prof. J. N.	432
Hauss, John	135
Hauss, Peter	135
Hawkins (Gov.)	112, 113, 120, 187, 188
Hawkins, Benjamin (Gen.)	59
Hayes, John	88, 93, 137
Hayes, Leonidas B. (Rev.)	42
Hayes, Martha	93
Hayes, Mary	42
Hayes, William J. (Dr.)	138, 139
Haynes, Capt. Albert Sidney	202, 234
Haynes, Elizabeth Carpenter	202

	Page
Haynes, Isabella	202
Haynes, John	202
Haynes, Robt. G.	202
Heavner, Effie	365
Hedrick, Philo	156
Heedick, Andrew	56
Heedick, Bessie Irene	367
Heedick, Elizabeth	43
Helderman, George	106
Helderman, Margaret M.	143
Helderman, Susanah	414
Henderson (Gov.)	160
Henderson (Maj.)	101
Henderson, Ann E. (Miss)	2, 206, 287
Henderson, Archibald	281
Henderson, Mrs. Elizabeth	146
Henderson, Barbara M.	206
Henderson, Charles Cotesworth	130, 131, 147, 155, 160, 161, 165, 168, 206, 287, 332, 333
Henderson, Frances	164
Henderson, Frances E.	206
Henderson, Franklin (Dr.)	146
Henderson, George William	131
Henderson, Hugh L.	106, 131
Henderson, James	129
Henderson, James Pinckney	101, 103, 107, 112, 117, 118, 130, 131, 160, 161, 163, 164
Henderson, John Caruth	131
Henderson, Julia	164
Henderson, Lawson	60, 70, 85, 97, 106, 107, 111, 129, 130, 146, 206
Henderson, Logan	119
Henderson, Logan Barry	131
Henderson, Lawson Franklin	131, 163
Henderson, Lawson P.	206
Henderson, Margaret B.	165, 206
Henderson, Mary Graham	131
Henderson, Mary Helen	206
Henderson, Richard	98
Henderson, Theodora	206
Henderson, Wallace Alexander (Dr.)	130
Henderson, Wallace Alexander Irwin	131
Henderson, Walter Caruth	131
Henderson, Willie Caldwell	206
Henderson, William	90
Henkel, David (Rev.)	95
Henkel, Polycarp (Rev.)	94
Henry, Isabella	98
Herndon, Stephen	263
Herndon, Thomas N.	108, 112, 126, 131
Hickle, Emma Bell	282
Hildebrand, Elizabeth	270
Hill, Gen. A. P.	179

The Annals of Lincoln County 519

Hill, D. H. (Maj.) 143, 179, 252
Hill, Frances Carpenter 429
Hill, Jacob (Rev.) 59, 142
Hill, Mrs. Jacob 143
Hill, James (Rev.) 100, 429
Hill, John 17
Hill, Capt. John F. 397, 429
Hill, Lawson Logan 429
Hill, Louisiana Elizabeth Zetrouer 429
Hill, Margaret 108
Hill, Mary E. 397
Hill, Mary Hoffman 429
Hill, Precious Stokes 429
Hill, Robert Hoffman 429
Hill, William Logan 429
Hill, William Luther 429
Hillsborough (Lord) 13
Hiltz (Consul General) 75
Hite, Enoch 57
Hobson, Richmond Pearson 105
Hoffman, Charles L. 245
Hoffman, Daniel 142
Hoffman, F. D. 127
Hoffman, Jonas 413
Hoffman, Laban Miles 413
Hoffman, M. L. 66, 70, 96, 328
Hoffman, Martha Jenkins 413
Hoffman, Myra 365
Hoffman, Sarah Alice 367
Hoffman, Ural L. 312
Hoffman, W. H. 244
Hoffstetler, Michael 18
Hogg (Gov.) 96
Hoke, Ann 119
Hoke, Annie Michal 209
Hoke, Augustus M. 315
Hoke, Barbara Quickel 251, 376
Hoke, Catherine Alexander 161, 251, 376
Hoke, Daniel 82, 91, 103, 104, 111, 112
Hoke, Daniel, Jr. 112
Hoke, David 132
Hoke, Elizabeth 82, 147
Hoke, Francis 132, 329
Hoke, Franklin A. 117, 121
Hoke, Franklin H. 112
Hoke, Frederick 91
Hoke, George 103, 104
Hoke, George M. (Dr.) 133, 189
Hoke, Georgiana 209
Hoke, Georgiana Sumner 209
Hoke, Henry 82, 92
Hoke, John 72, 83, 86, 91, 92, 104, 111, 112, 117, 126, 132, 251, 376
Hoke, John Burton 138
Hoke, John D. 104, 107, 111, 112, 130
Hoke, John E. 135

Hoke, John F. (Col.) 132, 145, 147, 158, 159, 161, 189, 207, 251, 376
Hoke, Katharine 263
Hoke, Lollie 209
Hoke, Lydia Van Wyck 331
Hoke, Marcus L. 116, 117, 119, 132, 133
Hoke, Mary 209, 300, 377
Hoke, Mary Brent 133, 157
Hoke, Mary McBee 300, 377
Hoke, Michael 102, 104, 105, 106, 119, 126, 132, 133, 138, 157, 166, 189, 329, 401
Hoke, Michael (II) 209, 224
Hoke, Dr. Michael 331
Hoke, Nancy 209, 365
Hoke, Nancy Childs 132, 251, 259
Hoke, Robert Frederick (Maj. Gen.) 119, 133, 180, 329, 330, 331, 433
Hoke, Sabina 91, 111
Hoke, Sallie Badger 251, 259
Hoke, Sarah 82, 91, 111, 132
Hoke, Thomas H. 209, 263
Hoke, Virginia 209
Hoke, William Alexander (Chief Justice) 108, 194, 214, 251, 300, 301, 370, 376, 377, 378, 379, 380
Hoke, Col. William J. 132, 209
Holcomb, Philip 339
Holcomb, Wesley 339
Holden, W. W. (Governor) 197
Holland, E. B. (Dr.) 105
Holland, James 60
Holland, Margaret 131
Holland, O. W. 112
Holland, W. F. 173
Holsclaw, James 112, 117
Holt, Governor 254
Holton, Thomas J. 108, 168
Hood, Fraser (Dr.) 42
Hooper, E. A. 117
Hooper, William 184, 335
Hoover, Dennis 393
Hoover, Edney 393
Hoover, Eve 76
Hoover, Herbert 387
Hoover, John T. 267
Hoover, Solomon 71
Hoover, Mrs. T. H. 409
Hoover, Tom 393
Hopkins, S. H. 230, 247
Horse Shoe, Battle of 114
Horton, John 25
Houser, E. A. 339
Houston (Capt.) 37
Houston, Sam 163, 164
Houston, Theodore 134
Hovis, J. J. 339
Hovis, Martin 267

	Page
Hovis, Sarah	59
Hoyle, Abel (Rev.)	95
Hoyle, Alfred E.	161
Hoyle, Andrew	15, 94, 95, 123, 142, 161, 165
Hoyle, Catherine	95
Hoyle, E. M. (Rev.)	94
Hoyle, Eli	31, 125, 129, 162
Hoyle, Mrs. Eli	166
Hoyle, Elizabeth	95
Hoyle, Fanny	95
Hoyle, Fitzhugh	385
Hoyle, Jacob	94, 95, 364
Hoyle, John	15, 18, 51, 95
Hoyle, John (Rev.)	95
Hoyle, John B.	228
Hoyle, L. J.	94, 169
Hoyle, Laban A.	162, 206, 228
Hoyle, Lemuel J. (Capt.)	95
Hoyle, M. H. (Rev.)	94, 95
Hoyle, Margaret	95, 133
Hoyle, Mary	162, 267
Hoyle, Michael	18, 94
Hoyle, Noah	95
Hoyle, Peter	32, 51, 59, 94, 161, 409
Hoyle, Peter, Jr.	94
Hoyle, Philip	95
Hoyle, R. M. (Rev.)	94
Hull, J. Haywood	422
Huff, S. W.	369
Hunt, Elizabeth Duke	185
Hunt, Memucan	185
Hunt, Sara Duke	185
Hunt, Dr. Thomas	185
Hunter (Maj. Gen.)	117
Hunter, Cyrus L. (Dr.)	98, 102, 108, 112, 233
Hunter, Humphrey (Rev.)	31, 75, 97
Hunter, John Lindsay	423
Huss, George A.	364
Hutchison, J. M.	172

I

Icem, Edward	167
I. O. O. F. (Mountain Lodge No. 19)	148, 149, 153, 154
Indian Creek Trestle, 1881	232
Ingram, Charley	282
Irwin, Alexander	46
Irwin, Isaac	104, 107
Irwin, James P.	252
Ivey, George W. (Rev.)	42, 169
Ivey, J. B.	229
Ivy, Ann Connor	189
Ivy, J. M.	189

J

Jackson, Andrew (Gen.)	114
Jackson, T. J. (Maj.)-Gen. Stonewall	161, 174, 175, 179, 337

	Page
Jackson, Mrs. Thomas Jonathan	337, 338
James, Mrs. Augustus P.	107
Jarvis, Thomas J., Gov.	231, 290
Jenkins, Aaron	106, 244
Jenkins, Aaron D.	244
Jenkins, Addie	230
Jenkins, Alice	230, 234
Jenkins, Barbara Schenck	230, 401
Jenkins, Bessie	230
Jenkins, Blair	230, 273, 401, 402
Jenkins, Blair, Jr.	231, 402
Jenkins, David	19, 20, 21, 24
Jenkins, David A.	244, 413
Jenkins, David H.	245
Jenkins, Elmira	244
Jenkins, Hugh	157, 165, 230
Jenkins, Hugh, Jr.	231, 402
Jenkins, J. H. C. (Miss)	157
Jenkins, James C.	143, 165, 207, 230, 234, 245, 247, 401
Jenkins, James Campbell	230, 402
Jenkins, Laban L.	245
Jenkins, Lodema Holland	244
Jenkins, Margaret	108
Jenkins, Martha	244
Jenkins, Mary	244
Jenkins, Susan	230, 247
Jenkins, Dr. William Sumner	184, 230, 287, 402
Jenkins, Wm. W.	244
Jetton, B.	120
Jetton, F. J.	241
Johnson, Annie	41
Johnson, B. S.	41, 104, 129, 155, 159, 234, 310, 324
Johnson, Cyrus (Rev.)	140, 155
Johnson, Prof. E. D.	268
Johnson, Ellen	248
Johnson, Frances Ann	41
Johnson, Jennie	41
Johnson, Jesse (Capt.)	44
Johnson, Mary	41
Johnson, Pinkie	41
Johnson, Susan Forney Shipp	248
Johnson, Capt. V. Q.	202, 247, 248, 332
Johnston, Alice Graham	312
Johnston, Anne Eliza Graham	272
Johnston, Annie	158, 161
Johnston, Bartlett Shipp	159, 385
Johnston, Bessie D.	315
Johnston, Caroline Brooks	385
Johnston, Catherine	137
Johnston, Catherine Caldwell	313
Johnston, Cora	272
Johnston, Eleanor Gillespie	312
Johnston, Elizabeth Dickey	312
Johnston, Evans	354
Johnston, Frank G.	272

ANNALS OF LINCOLN COUNTY 521

Johnston, Harriet 126
Johnston, Mrs. Harriet Connor 138, 241
Johnston, Henry 32, 68
Johnston, James 19, 25, 32, 34, 54, 57, 68, 137, 158, 159
Johnston, James A. 112
Johnston, James F. (Capt.) 158
Johnston, Jane E. 125, 241
Johnston, Jennie S. 315
Johnston, John R. 72, 158
Johnston, Joseph B. 316
Johnston, Joseph Forney (Gov.) 84, 158, 334, 335
Johnston, Julia 272
Johnston, Kate C. 315
Johnston, Lida W. 315
Johnston, Lizzie Johnston Evans 354
Johnston, Mary 68, 272
Johnston, Mary Knox 316, 422
Johnston, Miriam 403
Johnston, Nancy Forney 334, 354
Johnston, Nettie W. 315
Johnston, R. Z. (Rev.) 87, 168, 214, 244, 312, 313, 314, 315, 316
Johnston, Robert 72, 84, 88, 126, 142, 158, 312
Johnston, Robert (II) 312
Johnston, Robert Caldwell 244, 315
Johnston, Robert D. (Gen.) 84, 158, 272, 312, 335, 354
Johnston, Robert Henry 138
Johnston, Rufus M. 72, 158
Johnston, Capt. Rufus Z. 315, 316
Johnston, Samuel 59, 127
Johnston, Sidney X. 65, 72, 138, 148, 158, 241
Johnston, Theresa Hooper 335
Johnston, William 312
Johnston, William (Col.) 114, 123, 158, 172, 271, 272, 273
Johnston, William (Dr.) 58, 84, 125, 158, 159, 161, 334, 354, 385
Johnston, William A. (Capt.) 158
Johnston, Wm. R. 272
Johnston, William Sidney 138
Jonas, Abel 392
Jonas, Alice 392
Jonas, Amy 392
Jonas, Andrew 392
Jonas, Celeste 391
Jonas, Cephas A. 372, 388
Jonas, Charles A. 310, 372, 388, 389, 390, 391, 392, 393, 396, 399
Jonas, Charles Raper 391
Jonas, Daniel 392
Jonas, Donald 391
Jonas, Effie 393
Jonas, Euphronia Lohr 392
Jonas, Harvey A. 393

Jonas, Henry 392, 393
Jonas, John 392, 418
Jonas, John, Jr. 392
Jonas, Dr. Justus 391
Jonas, Kate 393
Jonas, Katie 392
Jonas, Lucy 393
Jonas, Martha Scronce 388
Jonas, Mary Killian 392
Jonas, Perry 393
Jonas, Rebecca 392
Jonas, Robert 393
Jonas, Rosa Petrie 390, 393
Jonas, Simon 391, 392
Jones, Hamilton C. 143, 145, 251, 354
Jones, Hamilton C., Jr. 378
Jones, Rachel 108
Joyner, Andrew 30, 125
Jugnot, Charles 103
Justice, Elizabeth 223, 299
Justice, Jennie McBee 223, 299
Justice, Capt. John Guion 223, 236, 299
Justices of Peace (Tryon County) 28

K

Kanceller, Philip 30, 55
Kelly, John W. (Rev.) 161
Keenan, Mrs. Sarah Hoyle 126
Keener, Elijah W. 407
Keener, Walter Ney 406, 407
Kerr, A. D. 135
Kerr, John 156
Kibler, Rebecca 91
Kiddoe, David 97
Killian, Abraham 418
Killian, Andreas 416, 417, 418, 419
Killian, Andrew, Jr. 418
Killian, Bunia 418
Killian, Caroline 365, 418
Killian, Christiana 418
Killian Clan Officers 419
Killian, Crete 418
Killian, Elizabeth 418
Killian, Emma 328
Killian, Fanny 86
Killian, George 418
Killian, J. Yates 416, 419
Killian, Jacob 417, 418
Killian, Jacob, Jr. 418
Killian, Jean 418
Killian, John 15, 112, 416, 417, 418
Killian, Leonard 417
Killian, Marellis 418
Killian, Margaret 417
Killian, Mary 365, 417, 418
Killian, Mathias 417
Killian, Phillip 418
Killian, Polly 270

522   Annals of Lincoln County

Killian, Dr. R. B. 269, 270, 365, 419
Killian, Samuel 418
Killian, Sarah 123, 147, 418
Killian, William 417
Kincaid, Margaret Conley 289
Kincaid, Nancy 414
Kincaid, Robert N. 289
Kincaid, Susannah 414
Kinder, Conrad 15
King, J. H. 197, 254
King, James 104
Kings Mountain, Battle of 30, 31, 38, 40, 43, 44, 98
   Centennial Celebration 231
Kings Mountain Men 48, 49
Kirkpatrick, J. L. (Rev.) 168
Kiser, Annie 410
Kiser, Lawrence 18
Kistler, Lawson H. 117, 143, 197
Kistler, Nancy 270
Kistler, Paul 73, 87, 121, 143, 197
Kistler, Paul F. (Rev.) 126, 143
Knox (Capt.) 37
Kuhn, Herbert 431
Ku-Klux-Klan 210
Kurkendall, Abram 14, 17, 19, 23, 26
Kuykendall, Abram 19

L

Laboon, Peter 18, 19
Laboratory 102, 132
Lacy, Drury (Rev.) 161
Lafferty, R. H. (Rev.) 150
Lambeth, Daisy Hunt Sumner 187
Lambeth, J. Walter, Jr. 187
Lambeth, John W. 187
Lambkin, Samuel 26, 29
Lamkin, George 53, 54
Lander, Agnes 200
Lander, Alice Jenkins 200
Lander, Angus M. 298
Lander, Ann 110, 178
Lander, Bruce Ramsay 432
Lander, Clara 431
Lander, Ella 200
Lander, Eliza 178
Lander, Eliza Ann Miller 294
Lander, Ernest M. 298
Lander, Frank 200, 304, 431
Lander, Dr. Frank 297
Lander, Frank T. 431
Lander, George 178
Lander, John Lawing 432
Lander, Dr. John M. 297
Lander, Kathleen 297
Lander, Laura Ann McPherson 297
Lander, Lou Templeton 200, 304, 431
Lander, Malcolm M. 298
Lander, Margaret 133, 178
Lander, Martha 157, 162, 178, 297
Lander, Nora McPherson 431
Lander, Rufus Jackson 432
Lander, Samuel (Rev.) 110, 133, 135, 142, 157, 161, 169, 178, 197, 294, 332, 380, 425
Lander, Samuel, Jr. (Rev.) 106, 157, 174, 178, 182, 196, 294, 295, 296, 297, 298
Lander, Samuel, III 200, 234
Lander, Samuel William 432
Lander, Sarah C. 161, 178, 200, 431
Lander, William 82, 121, 136, 145, 147, 155, 157, 166, 168, 172, 178, 189, 197, 198, 199, 200, 263, 290, 353
Lander, Dr. Wm. Tertius 297
Lane, Evelyn 403
Langdon, W. I. (Rev.) 133, 157, 165, 178
Langford, George P. 157, 158
Lawing, Agnes Lander 263, 353
Lawing, Connor 263
Lawing, Dr. J. M. 200, 262, 263, 353, 416
Lawing, Karl L. 263, 416
Lawing, Lander 263
Lawing, William 418
Lawson, Henry 76
Lay, Nancy 108
Lee, (Gen.) 175, 179, 180, 207
Lee, Annie Elliott 391
Lee, Bertha M. 211
Lee, Dr. R. E. 391
Lee, Hon. T. Bailey 211
Lee, Rev. William B. 211
Lee, Rev. and Mrs. W. D. 211
Lehman (Miss) 74
Lemley, Ann 142
Lemley, Jacob 142
Leonard, Andrew 365
Leonard, Charles 104
Leonard, Chas. A. 393
Leonard, Elcanah 326
Leonard, Emma 326
Leonard, Mamie 393
Lewin, William 418
Lewis, James 60
Lincoln, Abraham 168, 181
Lincoln, Benjamin (Gen.) 29
Lincoln Courier 131, 214, 256, 269, 286, 432
Lincoln Herald (The) 107
Lincoln Hospital 310, 311
Lincoln Lithia Inn 432, 433
Lincoln Lodge, No. 137, (A. F. & A. M.) 151, 152, 153
Lincoln Progress (Paper) 143, 214, 215, 216, 217, 222, 227, 333

Annals of Lincoln County

Lincoln Republican (The) ___122
Lincoln Transcript (The)_117, 118
Lincolnton Chapter Royal
  Arch Masons ___156
Lincolnton Female Academy___86,
  88, 89, 93, 94, 96, 104, 116, 118,
  124, 145, 156, 186, 452-455, 457
Lincolnton High
  School ___316, 317, 425, 426
Lincolnton Male Academy_86, 147,
  186, 211, 212, 213, 303, 376, 454
Lineberger, Catherine ___129
Lineberger, Frederick ___117
Lineberger, J. Laban ___420
Linkhorn, Thomas ___364
Little, (Rev. Mr.) ___157
Little, Bridget ___108
Little, Hua ___174
Little, John G. ___367
Little, Rev. M. L. ___258
Lloyd, Frank E. ___308
Locke, Elizabeth ___246
Locke, Francis ___37, 40, 70, 84
Locke, Matthew ___26, 46, 246
Lofton, James ___106
Logan, James ___19, 20, 21, 23, 24
Logan, William ___16
Lohr, George ___70
Lohr, Valentine ___392
Long, Andrew ___24
Long, Irva ___41
Long, Thurman B. ___41
Long, W. Locksley ___41
Long, Wallace (Dr.) ___41
Long Shoals, Cotton Mill ___104
Lore, George M. ___160, 161
Lore, James A. ___315
Loretz, (Rev.) Andrew___56, 60, 70,
  72, 73, 74, 75, 76, 86, 97, 423, 424
Loretz, Andrew H.___75, 76, 86, 103
Loretz, Anne ___76
Loretz, Barbara ___76
Loretz, Catherine ___72, 75, 76
Loretz, D. P. ___74
Loretz, Daniel ___76
Loretz, Elizabeth ___76
Loretz, Frederick ___76
Loretz, John F. ___76
Loretz, Judith ___76
Loretz, Mary ___76
Loretz, Mary H. ___76
Loretz, Mary J. E. ___76
Loretz, (N—) ___76
Loretz, Polly ___76
Loretz, Salome ___76
Loretz, Sarah ___76
Love, Edgar___248, 362, 408
Lowe, Alexander ___414
Lowe, Cora Henderson___415
Lowe, Col. D. A. ___329, 414, 415

Lowe, David Schenck___413, 415
Lowe, Ed ___413, 415
Lowe, Elizabeth ___414
Lowe, Ella ___415
Lowe, Emily ___147
Lowe, Frances ___414
Lowe, Franklin ___414
Lowe, George ___415
Lowe, Greenbury ___414
Lowe, Haywood ___415
Lowe, Isaac ___138, 414
Lowe, Isaac C. ___415
Lowe, Isaac McLean ___415
Lowe, James ___415
Lowe, Jane C. ___415
Lowe, John F. ___116
Lowe, John Washington___413-416
Lowe, Laura ___415
Lowe, Martha ___415
Lowe, Mary ___416
Lowe, Mrs. Mary A. Cole___415
Lowe, Meacom ___415
Lowe, Milton ___415
Lowe, Nancy ___415
Lowe, Rufus ___414
Lowe, Samuel D. ___415, 416
Lowe, Sidney Houston ___415
Lowe, Sidney J. ___415
Lowe, Thomas ___413, 414
Lowe, Thomas L. (Lieut.) ___134
Lowe, Tullius ___415
Lowe, William ___415
Lowe, Willie Ellen ___134
Lowrance, Elizabeth ___91
Lowrance, Logan H.___108, 197, 254, 311
Lowrance, M. B. ___167
Lowrance, Rhoda ___
Lutheran Pastors (1900-1928)_ 57
Lutz, Ambrose ___402
Lutz, Daniel ___402
Lutz, David ___402
Lutz, Eli ___402
Lutz, Ephraim ___402
Lutz, Ephraim (II) ___402
Lutz, George ___402
Lutz, Jacob ___402
Lutz, Jacob, Jr. ___402
Lutz, Manlius ___402
Lutz, Mary ___267
Lutz, Rev. W. A. ___402, 403
Lyerly, Christopher ___16
Lytle, Alexander (Col.) ___113
Lytle, Archibald (Col.) ___99
Lytle, James ___29, 52

Mc

McAfee, James ___23
McAlpine, Sarah ___132
McArver, J. L. (Capt.) ___102

524 ANNALS OF LINCOLN COUNTY

	Page
McBee (Mr.)	106
McBee, Alexander	177
McBee, Alphonso Avery	300
McBee, Anne	300, 387
McBee, Elizabeth	300
McBee, Emma Estelle	300, 371
McBee, Hannah Echols	177
McBee, Jane	299
McBee, Jane Alexander	298
McBee, Joseph Gallishaw	176
McBee, Louise J. Post	300, 372
McBee, Luther Martin	177
McBee, Malinda Penelope	176
McBee, Martha Adeline	177
McBee, Martha Turner	300
McBee, Mary	300, 377
McBee, Mary Elizabeth Sumner	177, 299
McBee, Sarah	299, 421, 429
McBee, Silas	236, 300, 370, 371, 372
McBee, Silas, Jr.	300, 371
McBee, Silas Leroy	176
McBee, Dr. Sumner	255, 259, 300
McBee, Thomas	300
McBee, Dr. Vardrine	300, 371
McBee, Vardry	300
McBee, Vardry A.	83, 85, 86, 90, 104, 123, 146, 147, 165, 168, 175, 177, 187, 190, 191, 223, 259, 298, 299, 300, 332, 387, 421, 429
McBee, William Pinkney	177
McCall, Susan B.	177
McCarty, Daniel	15
McCombs, Dr. Annie Parks	261
McConnell, Mrs. Mary C.	164
McCorkle, Alexander	31, 123, 125, 129, 138
McCorkle, Alberta	282
McCorkle, Alexander Work	62
McCorkle, Anna	282
McCorkle, Betsy Brandon	404
McCorkle, Catherine	282
McCorkle, Lt. Col. Charles M.	282
McCorkle, Elizabeth	63
McCorkle, Francis	25, 40, 62, 63, 404, 422
McCorkle, Francis M. (Dr.)	63
McCorkle, Frank W.	282
McCorkle, George	63, 282, 404
McCorkle, Henry W.	282
McCorkle, Isabella	62
McCorkle, Dr. J. Macon	282
McCorkle, James Marshall (Col.)	63
McCorkle, Jane	62
McCorkle, John	63
McCorkle, John R. (Dr.)	63
McCorkle, Martha Ann Wilfong	281
McCorkle, Mary Locke	282

	Page
McCorkle, Matthew	62
McCorkle, Matthew Locke (Judge)	63, 156, 254, 281, 282
McCorkle, Rebecca	62
McCorkle, Richard	63
McCorkle, Sarah	63
McCorkle, Thomas	63
McCorkle, Wm. A. (Dr.)	63
McCorkle, William Brandon	63
McCoy, Abner	153, 174, 246
McCoy, Mary	174
McCoy, William S.	135
McCulloh, G.	90
McCullough, George	107
McCutchan, Mrs. J. S.	121
McDaniel, Daniel G. (Rev.)	106, 138
McDaniel Spring	289
McDavid, Patrick	14
McDowell (Col.)	43
McDowell (Gen.)	52
McDowell, Miss	415
McDowell, Charles	149
McDowell, F. Brevard	101, 189
McDowell, John	31, 125
McEntyre, James	22
McEwen, Margaret	92
McFee, James	20
McIntosh, Mrs. C. E.	134
McIntyre, James	14, 19
McKee, Mrs.	44
McKee, James	44
McKendree, William	59
McKenzie (Dr.)	130
McKenzie, Charles Hampton	187
McKenzie, Ellen Sumner	187
McKenzie, Margaret Stokes	273
McKenzie, Sallie Hunt	402
McKezick, Daniel	46, 55
McKinley, William	284, 287
McKinney, John	19, 23, 24
McKissick	54
McKissick, Daniel	29, 37, 51, 52, 55, 56
McLean, Alexander	99
McLean, Anne	261
McLean, Augustus A. (Maj.)	59, 99
McLean, Carrie L.	243
McLean, Charles	14, 17, 19, 20, 21, 23, 24, 25, 26, 44, 57, 68
McLean, Ephraim	14, 15
McLean, J. Thomas	243
McLean, James Logan	242, 243
McLean, John D. (Dr.)	59, 99
McLean, John D. B.	261
McLean, Margaret Ann Smith	242
McLean, Mary L.	243
McLean, Mattie	243

ANNALS OF LINCOLN COUNTY 525

McLean, R. D. S. (Gen.) 102
McLean, T. B. (Maj.) 102
McLean, William (Dr.) 33, 59, 81, 99, 130
McMann, Robert 26
McMinn, Robert 23
McMullen, Rev. John C. 315
McMullen, Nettie 315
McMullen, Rev. Robert Johnston 315
McNairy, Rev. W. H. 56
McNeel, Andrew 34
McNeil (Col.) 113
McRae, Duncan K. 127
McPherson, Angus (Rev.) 105
McPherson, Laura 157, 178
McRee, Martha 150

M

Mackness, Perrygreen 21, 23
Magness, Perrygreen 14, 19, 21
Mahoon, William S. 103
Mangum, Nannie 244
Mangum (Sen.) 111
Marsh, James H. 353
Marshall, Mary 63
Martin, Alexander 14, 52, 53
Martin, Emmaline 133
Martin, John 318
Mason, Abigail 129
Mason, Lawson A. (Col.) 129, 310
Mathias, H. J. 57
Matthews, Lucretia 93, 94
Matthews, William M. 135, 172
Mattocks, John (Capt.) 81
Mauney, Christian 17, 19, 20, 21, 23, 24, 25, 26
Mauney, Christy 19
Mauney, Elizabeth E. 366
Mauney, Fetty 23
Mauney, Jacob 18, 36
Mauney, Valentine 20, 21, 29, 36
Mauney, W. A. 22, 248, 408
Mecklenburg Declaration of Independence 97, 113
Melchor, Margaret 414
Mellon, Mary Neal 415
Merrimon, James G. 307
Merritt, John Malcus 294
Michael, John (Maj.) 104, 117
Michael, O. B. (Rev.) 76
Michal, Annie 263
Michal, Catherine 263
Michal, Conrad 91
Michal, Jacob 91
Michal, John 76
Michal, Robert 263
Michal, Sarah 263
Michal, W. H. 43, 91, 147, 148, 263, 287, 331

Middlekauf, S. S. (Rev.) 56, 135, 174
Mikell, Mary 300
Mikell, Thomas Price 300
Mikell, William E. 300
Mikell, William E., Jr. 300
Miller, Adam (Rev.) 120
Miller, Caleb 121, 155
Miller, J. F. A. 135
Miller, J. M. (Dr.) 172
Miller, James 36
Miller, John 308
Miller, John F. (Dr.) 94
Miller, Robert Johnston (Rev.) 32, 106, 108, 132
Miller, W. J. T. (Dr.) 107, 162
Milligan, Gilbert 62
Minter, Harriet Marie Smith 232
Minter, John 232
Minter, Josephine 232
Minter, W. R. (Rev.) 87, 232
Mitchell, Dr. Elisha 185
Monday, Martha 414
Monday, Pinckney 416
Monday, W. W. 117
Moore, Alexander 41
Moore, Amanda M. 131
Moore, Annie 41
Moore, John 26, 33, 36, 40, 52, 54, 68, 69, 159
Moore, Bishop John J. 260
Moore, Mary 41, 159
Moore, Moses 19, 21, 26
Moore, Rosannah 142
Moore, William 14, 15, 16, 17, 18, 19, 23
Morehead, Col. James T. 180
Morgan, Permenter 90
Morris, Amos 138
Morris, Benjamin 142
Morris, John 19, 20, 21, 23, 60
Morris, Joseph 117, 175
Morris, Nancy 59, 90
Morrison, Alfred J. 211, 214, 217, 221, 252
Morrison, Alston 308
Morrison, Anna 337, 338
Morrison, Anna Jackson 308
Morrison, Elizabeth Davis 308, 419
Morrison, Eugenia 252
Morrison, Harriett 252
Morrison, Isabella 143, 252
Morrison, Joseph G. 252, 308, 419
Morrison, Joseph G., Jr. 308, 419
Morrison, Laura 252
Morrison, Louise 308
Morrison, Lucy Reid 368
Morrison, Mary Anna 175, 252
Morrison, Mary Graham 252, 308
Morrison, R. H. (Rev.) 60, 104,

Morrison, Dr. Robert H., 114, 125, 139, 143, 164, 168, 178, 221, 251, 252, 253, 308, 338, 368 Jr. 252, 368
Morrison, Dr. Reid 368
Morrison, Col. Robert Hall......308
Morrison, Stella 376
Morrison, Susan 168, 252
Morrison, Wm. M. 252
Morrow, Benj. (Maj.) 140
Morrow, John W. 142
Morrow, Sarah E. 140
Morton, Henry W.
Moseley, Gov. Wm. D. 251
Mosteller, D. 129
Mosteller, Geo.......104, 129, 132, 155
Mott, Dr. Henry Y. 200
Mott, Dr. J. J. 201
Mott, Mrs. Susan 154
Mott, T. S. W. (Rev.)...154, 157, 200
Mott, Dr. Walter B. 200
Motz, Alda McDowell 268
Motz, Andrew...75, 112, 116, 148, 153
Motz, Aubrey 268
Motz, Benjamin J. 324
Motz, Caldwell 324
Motz, Caleb 75, 220, 268
Motz, Caleb Carson 268
Motz, Caroline Matilda 268
Motz, Catherine 324
Motz, Catherine Loretz......268, 324
Motz, Charles H. 190, 324
Motz, Edna Easterday 268
Motz, Elizabeth 124
Motz, Elizabeth Hampton 268
Motz, Ella Alexander 190
Motz, Emmaline Almira Carson 268
Motz, Enoch Marvin 268
Motz, Frederick Victor 268
Motz, George W. 75, 112
Motz, Guy 268
Motz, Jane Johnson 324
Motz, Jennie 324
Motz, John......73, 75, 76, 112, 124, 155, 268, 324
Motz, John Carson 268
Motz, John M. 324
Motz, Margaret 324
Motz, Mary Catherine Stribling 268
Motz, Mary Helen Sherrill......268
Motz, Matilda Ellen 268
Motz, Samuel Cochrane 268
Motz, Wade H. 75, 324
Motz, William Wilson 268, 332
Motz Hotel 155
Mull 146
Mull, Henry 106

Mull, Peter 118
Mullen, Chas. G. 309
Mullen, Clyde G. 309
Mullen, Edwin F. 309
Mullen, Elizabeth 309
Mullen, Ellie Reid 309
Mullen, Emily Lowe 309
Mullen, George S. 309
Mullen, James 147, 309, 310
Mullen, John M. 309, 356
Mullen, John P. 309
Mullen, Jonas W. 309, 381
Mullen, Josephine 309
Mullen, Earl 309
Mullen, Lucy 309
Mullen, Mary 309
Mullen, Mary Keever 308
Mullen, Maude 201, 309
Mullen, Patrick 308, 309, 310
Mullen, Paul J. 309, 356
Mullen, Virginia Shipp Boyd..309
Mullen, S. L. 309
Mullen, William C. 309
Murray, (Capt.) 38
Murray, C. E. (Rev.) 63
Murray, W. A. (Rev.) 87

N

Nash (Judge) 157, 223
Nash (Gov.) 34
Neal, Selina 42
Neal, Susan Spratt 162
Neel, Andrew 16, 19, 20, 21, 23
Neel, Thomas 13, 15, 16
Newsom, J. M. 143, 145
Newspapers:
　Charlotte Democrat 200
　Western Whig Banner 237
　Gastonia Gazette 237
　Shelby New Era 247
　Southern Christian Advocate.250
　Lincolnton News 268
　Lincoln Journal 282
　Lincoln Times 314, 349, 416
　Charlotte Chronicle 331
　Charlotte News 337
　Charlotte Observer 337, 396
　Durham Sun 407
Newton, Mrs. J. H. 382
Newton, S. D. 261
Ney, Peter S. 138
Nicols, Sarah 54
Nixon, Alfred......7, 14, 15, 32, 159, 233, 234, 275, 372, 397
Nixon, Iola Robinson 372
Nixon, James 385
Nixon, Joseph R. 372, 425
Nixon, Kemp Battle......372, 400
Nixon, Milley Womack 372

	Page
Nixon, Robert	159, 372
Noland, Dr. W. W.	340
North Carolina Orthopedic Hospital	204
Nuckles, John	16
Nussman, Adolphus (Rev.)	16, 70
Nuttall, Mary Ann	142

O

Oates, Samuel	104
Oats, William	123
Ochiltree, Judge William B.	333
O'Hara, (Gen.)	45
Olds, Fred (Col.)	30, 127
Olds, Lewis P.	127
Old White Church	56, 75, 87, 97, 102
Pastors of (1828-1859)	56
Olmstead (Prof.)	103
Olmstead, Rev. A. F.	223
Olmstead, Julia L.	126, 223
O'Reilly, M.	91
O'Reilly's School	91
Orman, Benjamin	54
Osborne (Judge)	126
Osborne, Adlai	25
Osborne, Edmund	117
Osborne, Judge Frank I.	321
Osborne, James W.	126, 145, 172, 189
Overman, Lee S.	294
Owen (Gov.)	110
Owen, Portia L.	308

P

Pack, Betsy	364
Padgett, M. C.	308
Page, Harry	385
Paine, Isaac E.	58
Paine, J. W. A.	63
Palmer, Gen. John C.	181, 182, 246
Parker, (Rev. Mr.)	147
Parker, James P.	369
Parker, Mamie	329
Parks, Robert	23, 24
Pasour, E. Grant	366
Patrick, John	29
Patterson, James	18
Payne, Dr. Bruce Ryburn	42, 94, 95, 268
Payne, J. N.	268
Paysour, Hannah	410
Pearson, Richmond M.	105, 136, 142, 223
Pearson, Wm. S.	318, 322
Pee, George	34
Peed, Cyrus	146
Peeler, Mattie	339
Pegram, E. L.	173

	Page
Pegram, Frank	173
Pegram, Mary	173
Pegram, Miles P.	173
Pegram, Theodore	173
Pegram, Violet	173
Pegram, W. W.	173
Pegram, Winchester	83, 173
Pensioners:	
Lincoln County	49, 50
Perkins, Elisha	32
Perkins, Ephraim	60, 68
Perkins, Frances	41
Perkins, John	8, 32, 33, 60, 68
Perkins, Mary	32
Perkins, Nancy	133
Peterson Jesse R. (Rev.)	143
Petrie, Annie Rhyne	430
Petrie, Eliza Yoder	393, 430
Petrie, Eva Wilkie	430
Petrie, Michael	393, 430
Petrie, Dr. R. W.	430, 431
Phifer, Caleb	119, 129
Phifer, George	93, 246
Phifer, Capt. Geo. L.	246
Phifer, John	81, 93, 109
Phifer, John F.	120, 129, 182, 240, 245, 246, 425
Phifer, Mrs. John F.	43, 240, 245
Phifer, Martin, Jr.	246
Phifer, Mary Wilfong	246, 425
Phillips, Samuel F.	207
Pickens, (Gen.)	44, 52
Pickens, Prof. W. M.	301, 368, 428
Pioneers:	
Early	8, 9
Pennsylvania Dutch	9
Plank Road	298
Pleasant Retreat Academy	80, 81, 131, 194, 451, 452, 453, 454, 457
Plonk, Calvin	399
Plonk, Jacob	399
Plonk, Peter	399
Polk, Ezekiel	14, 16
Polk, James K.	14, 84, 115, 251
Porter, A. H.	117
Porter, Robert	23, 24
Postelle, Cornelia Wilson	400
Postelle, Rev. James C.	400
Postelle, Rev. John	400
Postelle, Martha Frances	400
Potts, J. M.	172
Potts, John	26
Powell, Robert	86
Pressley, W. A.	230
Price, Michael	417
Price, William	110
Prince, George E.	297
Pritchard, Claudia	244
Pritchard, C. H. (Rev.)	142

ANNALS OF LINCOLN COUNTY

Pritchard, Henry M. (Dr.) 140
Pritchard, Jeter C. 273
Pritchett, James 418
Propst, (Mrs.) 107
Propst, Jacob 104
Puckett, Mrs. W. L. 382

Q

Queen's Museum 99
Quickel, Addie Gay 423
Quickel, Anna Mariah 83
Quickel, Judge Augustus L. 306, 400, 423, 430
Quickel, Barbara 72, 83, 92, 132
Quickel, Caroline 305
Quickel, Catherine 83, 305
Quickel, Cephas 123, 147, 305, 306
Quickel, Elizabeth 83
Quickel, Hoke 365
Quickel, Dr. John C. 305, 306, 423
Quickel, Levi H. 305
Quickel, Malinda 138, 147
Quickel, Mary 58, 86
Quickel, Michael 72, 82, 86, 132, 138, 147, 305
Quickel, Michael C. 364
Quickel, Michael, Jr. 147, 305
Quickel, Sarah Killian 305
Quickel, Dr. Thomas C. 306, 423
Quinn, Hugh 107
Quinn, James 116, 142
Quinn, John 14

R

Rabb, Elizabeth 134
Rabb, William 81
Ramsay, James G. (Dr.) 125
Ramsay, Dr. W. B. 189
Ramseur, Addie 354, 355
Ramseur, Burgin 230
Ramseur, Charles 232
Ramseur, Ellen Richmond 180, 231
Ramseur, Fannie Dodson 232
Ramseur, Harvey 232
Ramseur, Jacob A. 179, 231, 354
Ramseur, Lucy (Dodson) 179, 231
Ramseur, Mary Badham 232
Ramseur, Mary Dodson 181
Ramseur, Sarah Wilfong 231
Ramseur, Gen. Stephen Dodson 179
Ramsour, Alex 209
Ramsour, Alfred A. 173
Ramsour, Alice 173, 245
Ramsour, Alexander (Dr.) 43, 153, 173, 245
Ramsour, Andrew 43
Ramsour, Anne 43, 93
Ramsour, Annie 129
Ramsour, Barbara 91, 111

Ramsour, Carolyn Elizabeth 129
Ramsour, Catherine 92
Ramsour, Cynthia 129, 162
Ramsour, D. 104
Ramsour, Daniel 43
Ramsour, Daniel F. 117, 173
Ramsour, David 43, 68, 76, 77, 87, 93, 107, 119, 120, 123, 128, 245
Ramsour, Diedrich 42, 43, 77, 92, 128, 173
Ramsour, Edmund G. 43, 174, 240
Ramsour, Elizabeth 76, 86, 120, 245
Ramsour, Eliza S. 173
Ramsour, George 70
Ramsour, Harriet E. 173
Ramsour, Harriet L. 125
Ramsour, Henry 43, 76, 269
Ramsour, Henry E. 240
Ramsour, Isabella 43
Ramsour, J. T. 129
Ramsour, Jacob 18, 43, 92, 112, 125, 128, 173, 187
Ramsour, Jacob, II 43, 91, 104, 106, 128, 155, 173
Ramsour, Jacob A. 43, 129, 153, 165, 179, 290, 294
Ramsour, John 43
Ramsour, Jonas 133
Ramsour, Martha A. 173
Ramsour, Mary Adeline 119, 129
Ramsour, Mary A. E. 174
Ramsour, Melvin 43
Ramsour, Myra Avery 174
Ramsour, Oliver A. 43
Ramsour, Polly 76
Ramsour, R. A. 39, 411
Ramsour, Sallie 165
Ramsour, Sarah 43, 70, 269
Ramsour, Solomon 43
Ramsour, Susan 41
Ramsour, Theodore J. 43
Ramsour, Thomas J. 43
Ramsour, Walter 43
Ramsour, William 43, 153, 173, 284
Ramsour's Mill, Battle of 36, 37, 38, 40, 44, 310, 399, 411
Randleman, Christopher 16
Rankin, Benj. Theodore 142
Rankin, Ellen 73, 92
Rankin, J. D. 127, 142
Rankin, Jane 120
Rankin, Mary 120
Rankin, Richard (Col.) 127, 142, 159
Rankin, Watson S. (Dr.) 63
Rankin, William 92, 159
Ransom, Gen. M. W. 207, 235
Ransom, Matt 282
Raynal, Chas. E. 308

ANNALS OF LINCOLN COUNTY 529

Reel, Jacob B. 143
Reep, Adam 40, 56
Reep, Adolphus 18
Reep, John 157
Reep, Minnie 393
Reep, P. A. 393
Rees, Mrs. John 385
Rehoboth Church, Organization of 90
Reid, David S. (Hon.) 147, 149, 155, 156
Reid, Elizabeth 69, 135
Reid, James 106
Reid, John (Capt.) 63, 69, 70, 72, 85, 135, 158, 159
Reid, Mary 72, 158
Reid, Rufus 85, 159
Reinhardt (Mrs.) 40
Reinhardt, A. Forney 382
Reinhardt, Abram Forney 41, 201
Reinhardt, Allie Abernethy 335
Reinhardt, C. E. 104
Reinhardt, Charles 76, 87
Reinhardt, Christian 14, 16, 30, 40, 41, 54, 56, 63, 65, 201, 310, 373
Reinhardt, Christian B. 106
Reinhardt, D. 85, 106, 107
Reinhardt, Col. David 191
Reinhardt, Edna 336
Reinhardt, Elizabeth 76
Reinhardt, Emanuel 103
Reinhardt, Fannie Wilson 382, 388
Reinhardt, Mrs. F. M. 84, 382
Reinhardt, Frances Johnson 310
Reinhardt, Franklin D. 41, 145
Reinhardt, Franklin M. 41, 58, 108, 201, 202, 335, 382
Reinhardt, Hettie 336
Reinhardt, J. 104
Reinhardt, J. Ed. 201, 382
Reinhardt, J. Ed., Jr. 382
Reinhardt, J. M. 336, 385
Reinhardt, John 41
Reinhardt, J. F. (Jack) 41, 201, 270, 335, 336
Reinhardt, Lawson 133
Reinhardt, Leckie Smith 335
Reinhardt, Lena 373, 388, 399
Reinhardt, Louise 336
Reinhardt, M. W. 105
Reinhardt, Mary Forney 201
Reinhardt, Melvin 41
Reinhardt, Michael 41, 87, 107, 310
Reinhardt, R. R. 336
Reinhardt, Robert P. 41
Reinhardt, Robert S. 201, 373, 408
Reinhardt, Stephen 373
Reinhardt, W. A. 41
Reinhardt, W. B. 336
Reinhardt, W. H. 336

Reinhardt, W. P. 41
Reinhardt, Wallace M. 41, 310
Republic of Texas, Volunteer emigrants to 118
Revels, Rev. Hiram Rhodes 284, 285, 286, 287
Rhodes, Ada 364
Rhodes, Annie 366
Rhodes, Charles H. 401
Rhodes, Caleb 363, 366
Rhodes, Caleb 365
Rhodes, Caroline 367
Rhodes, Carrie 365
Rhodes, Catherine 365, 366
Rhodes, Cecelia Elizabeth 367
Rhodes, Charles H. 365, 401
Rhodes, Mrs. Charles H. 410
Rhodes, Christian 365
Rhodes, Christian (II) 365
Rhodes, Christian William 366
Rhodes, Clarence K. 367
Rhodes, Clary Hire 364
Rhodes, D. P. 363, 422
Rhodes, Dora C. 367
Rhodes, Dora Emily 366
Rhodes, E. Titus 365
Rhodes, Edward R. 367
Rhodes, Elizabeth 364, 366
Rhodes, Ella 365
Rhodes, Frederick 364, 365, 366, 367
Rhodes, George P. 365
Rhodes, Georgia Agnes 364
Rhodes, Henry 83, 364
Rhodes, Henry, Jr. 365
Rhodes, Jacob 364
Rhodes, Jacob Henry 365
Rhodes, John 365
Rhodes, John M. 363, 366, 408, 422
Rhodes, Katie 365
Rhodes, Lillie May 364
Rhodes, Lucinda 366
Rhodes, Mabel Rosalie 364
Rhodes, Mamie 365
Rhodes, Margaret Aderholdt 363
Rhodes, Mary 267, 364, 365
Rhodes, Melchi 365, 366, 367
Rhodes, Nancy 83, 365
Rhodes, Nina Crowell 364
Rhodes, Oliver P. 367
Rhodes, Peter 364
Rhodes, Robert 365
Rhodes, Rudolph 365
Rhodes, Sarah Jane 366
Rhodes, Solomon 365
Rhodes, Sophia 366
Rhodes, Susan 364
Rhodes, Titus 364
Rhodes, Violet Almetta 364
Rhyne, Abel P. 410
Rhyne, Ambrose 410

Rhyne, Daniel E.	248, 408, 409, 410, 421, 433
Rhyne, Ellis	410
Rhyne, Frank	410
Rhyne, Jacob	409
Rhyne, Jacob II	409
Rhyne, Jacob K.	410
Rhyne, Jonas	410
Rhyne, M. H.	127, 231
Rhyne, Madalene	365
Rhyne, Mary	410
Rhyne, Moses H.	410, 421
Rhyne, Robt E.	325
Rhyne, Sarah	410
Rhyne, Simon	108
Rhyne, Thomas	410
Rhyne, William	410
Richardson, Alice Ramsour	245
Richardson, Catherine Schenck	245
Richardson, James J. (Rev.)	104, 106, 245
Richardson, John M. (Dr.)	173, 245
Richardson, Julia	245
Richardson, Leonard	245
Richardson, Lila	245
Richardson, Malvina	245
Richardson, Mary	245
Richmond, Ellen	180, 231
Ridenhour, V. C.	57
Riggs, Timothy	14, 26
Ritzhaupt, John	16
Roberts, John F.	267
Roberts, Peregrine	107
Robertson, Julia	272
Robertson, Thos. R.	272
Robertson, Maj. W. R.	272
Robeson, John	14, 19, 20
Robinson, A.	117
Robinson, Alice	305, 420
Robinson, Charles	275
Robinson, David W.	275, 419, 420
Robinson, David W., Jr.	420
Robinson, Dr. Edith	420
Robinson, Edith Childs	420
Robinson, Henry S.	275
Robinson, Holly	71
Robinson, John	23
Robinson, John (Rev.)	130
Robinson, John A.	83, 275, 419
Robinson, Mary Royal	190
Rabinson, Nancy Rhodes	275, 419
Robinson, Robert	275
Robinson, Sarah	95
Robinson, Susan	98
Robinson, Rev. William	420
Rock Springs Camp Ground, Incorporation of	150
Trustees of	150
Rock Springs Masonic Lodge	218
Rock Spring Seminary	222
Roderick, Marcus	392
Rodes, Jacob	15
Rodrick, Lewis P.	117
Roof, W. J.	57
Roosevelt, Franklin D.	403
Roosevelt, Theodore, Pres.	287, 301, 305, 354
Roseman, Andrew	419
Roseman, Robert M.	419
Ross, J. M. (Dr.)	172
Rowell, Isaac	25
Rozzell, Mrs. Richard	143
Rozzelle, S. C. (Rev.)	143
Rozzelle, Richard	148
Rucker, Mrs. Elizabeth Hoyle	95
Rudisill, Anne	86
Rudisill, Barbara	66
Rudisill, Eliza	86
Rudisill, Fanny	86
Rudisill, Hannah	71
Rudisill, Hettie	108
Rudisill, J. C. (Dr.)	167
Rudisill, Jonas	77, 86, 117
Rudisill, Judge L. E.	385
Rudisill, Marcus	86
Rudisill, Mary	86
Rudisill, Michael	66, 71
Rudisill, Pattie P.	167
Rudisill, Philip	86
Rudisill, Philip, Senior	86
Rudisill, Solomon	270
Rudisill, William	86
Ruffin (Chief Justice)	107, 130, 223
Rutherford (Gen.)	26, 36, 37, 84, 92, 109, 113
Rutledge, James	54
Rutledge, Jane	71
Rush, Jacob	157
Rusk (Sen.)	163
Russell, George	23
Russell, Lewis J.	101
Russell, Richard Brevard (Judge)	101
Russell, Richard Brevard, Jr.	101
Ryan, Lt. D. L., U. S. N.	299
Ryan, D. L., Jr.	300
Ryan, Elizabeth Sexton	300
Ryan, Sallie McBee	300
Ryburn, Robert L.	94

S

Sadler, John	71
Sain, Catherine	392
Sain, Israel	39, 367, 411
Sain, Sarah Jane	410
Saine, Jacob	393
Saine, John W.	315
Saine, Zeb	393
Sane, Elijah	157
St. Luke's Episcopal Church	126, 302, 303, 371, 435

ANNALS OF LINCOLN COUNTY 531

	Page
Saunders, Romolus M.	112
Saunders, Samuel G.	250
Scales, Gen. Alfred M.	240
Schaffer, (Mrs.)	74
Schenck, (Mrs.)	120
Schenck, Barbara	143
Schenck, Barbara Warlick	108, 289
Schenck, Catherine	99, 104
Schenck, David (Judge)	60, 75, 165, 172, 189, 231, 233, 267, 289, 290, 291, 292, 293
Schenck, David, Jr.	292
Schenck, D. W. (Dr.)	123, 143, 172, 230
Schenck, Dr. David Warlick	267, 289, 290
Schenck, Dodson	292
Schenck, Elizabeth	106
Schenck, Maj. H. F.	267
Schenck, Henry	267
Schenck, J. W.	312
Schenck, John F.	267
Schenck, J. Simpson	292
Schenck, John R.	292
Schenck, Rev. Lewis J.	292
Schenck, Louvenia	105
Schenck, Lucy	292
Schenck, Michael	81, 82, 83, 104, 105, 108, 132, 145, 267, 289
Schenck, Judge Michael	267, 292, 293
Schenck, Mrs. Michael	81
Schenck, Paul W.	293
Schenck, Rebecca	292
Schenck, Rose Few	293
Schenck, Sallie Wilfong Ramsour	290
Schenck, Susan R. Bevens	290
Schenck, Weldon E.	292
Schools	186, 194, 243, 404, 405, 420, 425, 426, 427
Schwartz, Edith Robinson	420
Scott, Abram	18
Scott, James	112
Scott, Mary	112
Scott, Moses	68
Scruggs, Susie	245
Seagle, Andrew Jackson	241
Seagle, B. F., Jr.	242
Seagle, Benj. Franklin	241, 242
Seagle, Catherine	95, 241
Seagle, Catherine Hoover	241
Seagle, Dallas Polk	241
Seagle, Daniel (Col.)	117
Seagle, Daniel (Gen.)	88, 112, 120, 241, 242, 324
Seagle, David	122
Seagle, George Washington	241
Seagle, James Madison	241
Seagle, Mrs. John A.	399

	Page
Seagle, Martin Van Buren	241
Seagle, Mary	365
Seagle, Mary Elizabeth Bollinger	241
Seagle, Monroe	174, 241
Seagle, Nathaniel Macon	241
Seagle, Polly	77
Seagle, Sarah Ann	241
Seagle, Thomas Jefferson	241
Self, Alda Malinda	340
Self, Hilary Augustus	339
Self, Ila Rebecca	339
Self, Dr. Isaac Ruffin	339, 340
Self, Dr. Lester L.	339
Self, Rev. Marvin Y.	340
Self, Mary Lula	339
Self, Mary Young	339
Self, Susan Etta	339
Settle, Judge Thomas	223
Setzer, George	156
Setzer, Reuben	156
Sevier, John	24, 42, 43
Shady Grove Female Academy	121
Shaw, A. C.	334
Shaw, Angus Clifton	206
Shaw, Bettie Thomas	334
Shaw, Easdale	334
Shaw, John D. (Maj.)	165, 333, 334
Shaw, John D., II	206, 334
Shaw, John D., III	206, 334
Shaw, Margaret Henderson	333
Shaw, Sallie Glenn	334
Shaw, Mrs. T. S.	232
Shelby, Isaac	31, 43, 52, 125
Shelton, Abigail	414
Shelton, Henry	414
Shelton, Lucinda	119
Sherrill, Absalom (Col.)	132
Sherrill, Adam	8, 24, 32, 42, 395
Sherrill, Agnes	63
Sherrill, Alexander	60, 106
Sherrill, Aquilla	23, 42
Sherrill, Barbara Henderson Cobb	332
Sherrill, Bettie Lee	332
Sherrill, C. F. (Rev.)	42, 293
Sherrill, Casey	63
Sherrill, Catherine	41
Sherrill, Col. Clarence O.	355
Sherrill, Dr. Coite L.	190
Sherrill, Elizabeth McCorkle	190
Sherrill, Elizabeth Wilkinson	332
Sherrill, Frank	42
Sherrill, Henderson	63, 155, 190
Sherrill, Hiram	106, 189
Sherrill, Isaac	41
Sherrill, J. A. (Dr.)	63
Sherrill, Dr. J. Garland	355
Sherrill, Jacob	41
Sherrill, James H.	190

	Page
Sherrill, Jeptha	63, 106, 190
Sherrill, John	190
Sherrill, John B.	42, 293
Sherrill, Lawson L.	332
Sherrill, Lewis J. (Rev.)	42
Sherrill, Luetta Connor	189, 239, 332
Sherrill, M. V. (Rev.)	42, 246, 293
Sherrill, Mahala Long	190
Sherrill, Dr. Mary	355
Sherrill, Mary Helen	332
Sherrill, Miles O.	355
Sherrill, Moses	41
Sherrill, Oscar	190
Sherrill, Powell	63
Sherrill, R. D. (Rev.)	42
Sherrill, Richard E.	125
Sherrill, Samuel	24, 42
Sherrill, Samuel Pinckney	63, 161, 178, 206, 274, 332
Sherrill, Sarah Catherine Lander	332
Sherrill, Uriah	13, 42
Sherrill, Walter L.	190
Sherrill, William (Capt.)	16, 42
Sherrill, Wm. L.	189, 228, 238, 239, 332, 395, 404
Sherrill, William M.	42
Shetley, Sophia	365
Shipp, Albert M. (Dr.)	90, 123, 138, 146, 249, 250, 254
Shipp, Albert W.	250
Shipp, Anna	255, 404, 405
Shipp, Ann Eliza	138, 202
Shipp, Bartlett	56, 58, 82, 102, 103, 110, 111, 121, 127, 166, 201, 208, 248-49, 254-55, 294, 318, 337
Shipp, Cameron	337
Shipp, Catherine	189
Shipp, Catherine (Miss Kate)	255, 387, 388, 399, 404, 405, 406
Shipp, Catherine Cameron	255, 275
Shipp, Elizabeth Oglesby	249
Shipp, Fabius Busbee	276, 278, 373
Shipp, Hannah Joyce	201
Shipp, Harriett Elizabeth	250
Shipp, J. Thornwell	250
Shipp, John	249
Shipp, John Wilds	250
Shipp, Margaret Busbee	422
Shipp, Margaret Iredell	255
Shipp, Mary Gillespie	250
Shipp, Mary Preston	255
Shipp, Mary Wade	250
Shipp, Robert J.	269
Shipp, Samuel W. G.	250
Shipp, Sarah W.	250
Shipp, Susan	202
Shipp, Susan Forney	254

	Page
Shipp, Susan V.	250
Shipp, Thomas	201
Shipp, William Ewen	255, 275, 276, 277, 278, 282, 283, 422
Shipp, William Ewen, Jr.	276, 277, 278
Shipp, William M. (Judge)	123, 129, 189, 202, 207, 233, 249, 254, 255, 275, 337
Shipp, William T.	126, 249, 269
Shitle, Henry	392
Shuford, A. A.	94, 96
Shuford, Abel	133
Shuford, Abel A.	134
Shuford, Alonzo Craige	134
Shuford, Andrew	133
Shuford, Andrew H.	134, 145
Shuford, Catherine	134
Shuford, Daniel	106, 143
Shuford, David	134
Shuford, Elcanah L.	112
Shuford, Eli	133
Shuford, Eli P.	134
Shuford, Elizabeth	133
Shuford, Elkanah	133
Shuford, Eve	133
Shuford, Fanny	86, 95, 133, 207
Shuford, Frances	43
Shuford, George A.	134
Shuford, George P.	134
Shuford, Jacob	95, 133, 134, 157, 207
Shuford, Jacob, Jr.	96, 134
Shuford, Jacob H.	133
Shuford, Jacob L. (Rev.)	134, 162
Shuford, James Monroe	134, 153
Shuford, John	95, 133, 134
Shuford, John J.	133
Shuford, Lemuel	365
Shuford, Magdelene	43
Shuford, Margaret	96, 133, 134, 207
Shuford, Martin	95, 134
Shuford, Martin P.	133
Shuford, Mortimer (Rev.)	134
Shuford, Poindexter	94, 96
Shuford, Sidney A. (Capt.)	173
Shuford, Susan	133, 134
Shuford, Thomas R.	96, 121, 157
Sides, Adam	36
Sigmon, (Capt.)	43
Sigmon, Elias	366
Sigmon, Jesse Caleb	366
Sigmon, Rev. Paul Cromer	366
Sigmon, Rev. Robert Bruce	366
Sigmon, Dr. William	366
Simons, Eugene	282
Simonton, Mary	65
Simonton, W. S.	65, 104
Simonton, William S.	103

	Page
Simpson, Daniel	14
Simpson, S. P. (Dr.)	103, 104, 107
Simpson, William	39, 51
Skelly, John	143
Slade, Mary	151
Slade, William	112, 117, 151
Slaughter, E. R.	300, 377
Slicer, Henry (Rev.)	120
Sloan (Capt.)	37
Sloan, Henry T.	115
Sloan, John	108
Sloan, William (Dr.)	163, 168
Smith, (Capt.)	37
Smith, Amy	73
Smith, Birdie Cobb	401
Smith, Burton H.	166
Smith, Catherine	91
Smith, Campbell	191
Smith, David	41, 71, 84, 108
Smith, Hannah Bess	71
Smith, Harriet	132
Smith, Hoke (Gov.)	133, 401
Smith, Prof. Hosea Hildreth	96, 133, 157, 201
Smith, Dr. Thos. C.	191
Smith, J. Madison	58, 108
Smith, James Madison	335
Smith, John Barnett	307
Smith, John Bartlett	84
Smith, Joseph C.	191, 415
Smith, Margaret Rebecca Alexander	191
Smith, Rev. Campbell	191
Smith, Mazie Crawford	401
Smith, Nathaniel N.	87
Smith, Peter	51, 71, 84
Smith, Rev. R. A.	240
Smith, Sarah	41, 108
Smith, Stephen	246, 425
Smith, Stephen O.	41, 191
Smith, Whiteford	106
Smyer, J. F.	366
Smyer, John	133
Smyer, Mrs. S. J.	382
Soldiers:	
Whig (at Ramsour's Mill)	38
Revolutionary	38, 46-50
War of 1812	77, 78, 79, 80
Mexican War	143, 144, 179
Civil War	169, 170, 171, 182, 183, 184, 210, 247
Southern Stars Military Co.	226
World War, 1914	336, 338-340, 341, 342, 343, 344, 345, 346, 347, 348, 349, 350, 351, 353, 356, 357, 358, 359, 360, 361, 363, 385, 386, 387, 393, 394
Sohn, Lucinda C.	134
Sorber, Annie N.	282
Sowers, Robert	206

	Page
Spaight, Richard Dobbs	116, 136
Spain, Hartwell (Rev.)	107
Sparrow, Patrick J. (Rev.)	87, 97
Spencer, (Judge)	34
Spencer, Samuel	14, 24
Spencer, Zack	18
Stacy, Chief Justice	380
Stacy, J. (Rev.)	138
Stacy, L. E. (Rev.)	42
Stamey, Daniel	257
Stamey, Harriet E. Wyant	257
Stamey, John	257
Stamey, John R.	148
Stamey, Rev. Paul Franklin Winfield	257
Stamey, Peter	257
Stanley (Congressman)	124
Starrett, F. S.	269
Staudenmyer, Mrs. L. R.	65
Steele, John	68, 69, 112
Steele, Joseph	30, 55
Stewart, Josiah	135
Stirewalt, Elizabeth	91
Stirewalt, W. J.	364
Stowe, E. B.	162
Stowe, Elizabeth	163, 168
Stowe, Jacob	173
Stowe, James	162
Stowe, Jasper	153, 162
Stowe, Larkin	83, 102, 107, 132, 142, 162, 163, 168
Stowe, Leroy	127
Stowe, Margaret Abernethy	294
Stowe, Mary	83, 173
Stowe, Mattie Anna	294
Stowe, Samuel N.	132, 142, 145, 159, 162
Stowe, Stephen Decatur	294
Stowe, Whiten	127, 142
Stowe, William A. (Col.)	163
Strange, Col. Robert	220
Stroup, B. L.	325
Stubbs, Elbridge W.	274
Stubbs, Col. Seth W.	273, 274
Sullivan, Elijah	135
Sullivan, Nancy J.	135
Sully, Ellen	120
Sully, Thomas	120
Summerow, Catherine	72
Summerow, David	227
Summerow, W. A.	227
Summey, Barbara	43, 173
Summey, Catherine	95
Summey, J. J.	117
Summey, Peter	87, 104, 178, 190
Sumner, Benjamin	184, 185, 186, 273, 299, 454
Sumner, Mrs. B. H.	43, 174, 187, 273

Sumner, Benjamin Hunt 174, 187, 209, 215, 229, 273, 402
Sumner, Bettie Shannonhouse 187
Sumner, Charles McBee 273
Sumner, Charles Wadsworth 187
Sumner, Daisy Hunt 187
Sumner, Edward Everett, Lt. 187
Sumner, Elizabeth Turner 184
Sumner, Ellen 187
Sumner, Eva 187
Sumner, Georgiana T. 132, 187, 209
Sumner, Jacob 224, 273
Sumner Jennie Loftin 187
Sumner, Jethro, Colonel 184
Sumner, Jethro (Gen.) 34, 184
Sumner, John 184
Sumner, Julian 187
Sumner, Laura 187
Sumner, Mary Elizabeth 177, 187, 273, 299
Sumner, Sarah 187
Sumner, Sarah Duke Hunt 185, 299
Sumner, Thomas Jethro 185, 186, 187, 273, 299
Sumner, William Hoke 273, 281
Suttlemire, Martin 418
Sutton, Estelle 300
Swain, David L. 110, 111

T

Taggart, John 14
Taylor, James H. 243
Templeton, Alfred J. 404
Templeton, Frances McPherson 431
Templeton, James M. 403, 404
Templeton, R. H. 209
Templeton, Rufus B. 431
Tharp, James 25
Thomas, Jane Grimes 299
Thomas, John 14
Thomas, Mason 299
Thomason, B. (Capt.) 102
Thompson, (Miss) 173
Thompson, (Mr.) 122
Thompson, Amelia 104, 255
Thompson, Bartholomew 422
Thompson, Prof. D. Matt 374, 375, 376
Thompson, Dorman 376
Thompson, E. W. (Rev.) 164, 415
Thompson, F. W. 366
Thompson, Henry 29, 52
Thompson, Holland 375
Thompson, Howard R. 63, 366
Thompson, John 422
Thompson, L. D. (Rev.) 63, 366
Thompson, L. E. 117, 125, 126, 153, 155

Thompson, Mrs. L. E. 43
Thompson, Leonard E. 173, 255-56
Thompson, Mary Elizabeth Rice 374
Thompson, Pinckney A. 422
Thompson, Walter (M. Emily Gregory) 375
Thompson, William 23
Thompson, William T. 189
Thurston, Henrietta R. (D'Oyley) 177
Tiddy, Lucy Mayfield 294
Tiddy, Martha 294
Tiddy, Richard 104
Tiddy, William 104, 105, 167, 172, 294
Tin Mine (Corp.) 429, 430
Tingen, John 117
Tipton, John C. 283
Tobey, Isabel 340
Tompkins, D. A. 65
Townsend, Thomas 23, 24
Troutman, David 106
Truesdale, W. H. 403
Tryon County: Articles of Association 94
Tryon, William (Gov.) 7, 13, 26, 29
Tuckaseege Ford 18, 19, 112
Turbyfill 63
Turner, Josephus (Dr.) 63
Twitty, Allen 69
Tygart, John 16

U

Unity Church 98

V

Valentine, Peter 25
Van Buren, Martin 117, 123
Vance, David 52
Vance, Robert B. 99
Vance, Zebulon B. 173, 189, 207, 213, 214, 223, 227, 235
Vanhom, (Lt.) 43
Vanzant, Jacob 15
Vanson, S. J. 261
Von Preuschen, (Baron) 164

W

Waddell, Christie 230
Wagner, J. H. (Rev.) 145
Wahab, J. S. 369
Walke, Casper 369
Walker, Felix 98, 99
Walker, James Reuben 98
Walker, John 17, 18, 19, 20, 21, 26, 29, 98, 172
Walker, John, Jr. 98, 99
Walker, Joseph 99
Walker, Thomas 99

ANNALS OF LINCOLN COUNTY 535

	Page
Walker, William	98
Walkup, S. H.	127
Wallace, J. A.	117
Ward, Bettie Lee Sherrill	274
Ward, Capt. Edward W.	274
Ward, H. N.	173
Ward, J. H. (Rev.)	142
Ward, Thomas	103
Ward, Gen. W. T.	274
Warlick, Absalom	81, 82
Warlick, Anna	267
Warlick, Anne	268
Warlick, Barbara	40, 95, 267
Warlick, Catherine	270
Warlick, Catherine Coulter	267
Warlick, Catherine Seagle	268
Warlick, Daniel	13, 41, 267
Warlick, Daniel, II	267
Warlick, Daniel, III	267
Warlick, David	39, 411
Warlick, David C.	267, 363
Warlick, Eli	94, 95, 241, 268
Warlick, Elizabeth	41, 43
Warlick, Eliza Jane	267
Warlick, George A.	268
Warlick, Henry	39, 411
Warlick, Henry D.	267
Warlick, Jacob	39, 411
Warlick, Jacob R.	267
Warlick, John C.	267
Warlick, Lewis	95, 267
Warlick, Lewis Franklin	95, 268
Warlick, Margaret	267
Warlick, Mary Hoyle	267
Warlick, Mattie Wilson	268
Warlick, Maxwell	95, 155, 172, 266, 267, 268
Warlick, Nicholas	38, 39, 267, 411
Warlick, Phillip	267, 411
Warlick, Rachel	270
Warlick, Sallie	267
Warlick, Sarah Balina Robinson	268
Warlick, Solomon	95, 267
Warlick, Thomas	268
Warlick, William M.	268
Warlick, Wilson	63, 94, 95, 268, 387, 399, 404
War Saving Stamps	351, 352, 353
Washington, George	43, 58, 60, 61, 75
Washington, John	116, 134
Washington, Mary	134
Washington, Susannah	114, 116
Wasson, Joseph	37
Watson, William	13
Watts, A. L. (Rev.)	119
Watts, A. W. (Rev.)	471, 483
Waynick, Capus	300
Weathers, Sarah	364
Webb, Albert Micajah	250

	Page
Webb, Henry Y.	83, 140
Webb, John M.	250
Weber, Rev. Dr. John Langdon	380
Weber, John W.	110
Weber, Rev. Dr. Samuel A.	380
Weber, Dr. William Lander	380
Webster, J.	127, 142
Weidner, Henry	8, 9, 32
Welborn, James	112
Welch, Thomas	26
Welker, Mrs. Abigail	149
Welker, George W. (Rev.)	129, 149
Western Whig Banner (The)	121
Wetmore, Clara Lander	304, 431
Wetmore, Elizabeth Ann Badger	301
Wetmore, Ichabod	301
Wetmore, Lemuel Bingham	304, 353, 431
Wetmore, Mary Bingham	304
Wetmore, Nellie Jarrett	304
Wetmore, Silas McBee	305
Wetmore, Susan Allan	304
Wetmore, Thomas Cogdell	304
Wetmore, W. R. (Rev.)	103, 201, 211, 212, 213, 261, 301, 302, 303, 304, 305, 333, 353, 435
Wetmore, William Robards, Jr.	305
Wharton, Betty	267
Wharton, Emma	267
Wheeler, Ellen Sully	236
Wheeler, John H. (Col.)	120, 122, 123, 124, 135, 145, 149, 155, 235, 236
Wheeler, Mary Brown	236
Wheeler's History of N. C.	149, 235
White, Benjamin	145
White, Elvarna	414
White, Hugh Lawson	117
White, James H.	108, 127, 142, 145, 237, 238, 239
White, John B.	238
White, Margaret Jenkins	238
White, Philip S.	150
White Church	259
Whitener, Henry	106
Whitener, Sidney J.	381
Whitesides, Davis	19, 20
Whitney, Eli	59
Wightman, W. M. (Dr.)	106
Wilfong, Catherine	161
Wilfong, George	24, 43, 161
Wilfong, John	43, 106, 112, 116, 117, 119, 128
Wilfong, Sarah	43, 68, 128
Wilfong, Mrs. Susan	388
Wilkes, Charles (Admiral)	65
Wilkes, Isabelle Roanoke	160
Wilkes, J.	160
Wilkey, J. L.	226
Wilkey, L. T.	226, 430

	Page
Wilkinson, Ibby	418
Wilkinson, John	63
Wilkinson, Reuben	25
Wilkinson, Thomas	71
Wilkinson, William	25
Williams, Anne Marshall	299
Williams, Elizabeth Cleveland	299
Williams, James T.	299, 421, 428, 429
Williams, James T., Jr.	299
Williams, John C. (Col.)	105
Williams, Kathryn	299
Williams, L. S.	172
Williams, Margaret C.	105
Williams, Mary Elizabeth	299
Williams, Sarah McBee	299
Williams, Silas	299
Williams, Sumner McBee	299, 421
Williams, Sumner McBee, Jr.	299
Williams, Vardry McBee	299
Williams, William	65
Williamson, Albert C.	124, 136
Williamson, Dallas (Dr.)	136
Williamson, Elizabeth	69
Williamson, Hugh	136
Williamson, James	136
Williamson, John	136
Williamson, Joseph	136
Williamson, Robert (Col.)	69, 84, 90, 122, 127, 129, 135, 136, 146, 159, 166
Williamson, Robert, Jr.	136, 145, 159, 165
Williamson, Rufus R.	136
Williamson, Sarah A.	129
Williamson, Thomas	104, 136, 165
Williamson, Wm.	110, 112, 136, 159
Willis, Annie	391
Willis, Sheriff A. P.	391, 423
Willis, Robert H.	423
Willis, Sarah Coon	423
Wills, Elizabeth	409
Wilson, David	46
Wilson, J. H.	172
Wilson, John	52, 55
Wilson, John C.	297
Wilson, John M. (Rev.)	130
Wilson, Joseph (J. P.)	42, 104, 201, 376, 400
Wilson, Lilis	64
Wilson, Nathaniel	155
Wilson, Ronald B.	308
Wilson, Sarah R.	104
Wilson, Thomas	125
Wilson, W. A.	102
Wilson, W. J.	106
Wilson, W. S. (Rev.)	87
Wilson, Woodrow, Pres.	331, 338
Wingard, Mary	126
Wingate, Jesse	414
Wiseman, Nancy	187
Wiswall, A. C.	104
Withers, Benjamin	189
Wolfe, Drayton	403
Womack, Milly	159
Wood, A. F.	397
Wood, Burton Craige	397
Wood, Emma Hudson	397
Wood, O. O.	261
Woodcock, Mrs. J. A.	241
Work, Alexander	62
Work, Sarah	62
Workman, (Miss)	64
Workman, Pinckney	392
Wray, William	18
Wrenshall, Capt. C. C.	324
Wrenshall, Charles N.	294
Wright, David Milo	353
Wright, Mr. and Mrs. J. A. J.	353
Wright, John B.	364
Wyatt, James	15

Y

	Page
Yancey, John	268
Yancey, William	13, 23, 24
Yates, W. J.	172, 200
Yeates, Thomas	15
Yoder, Blanche	325
Yoder, Charles	365
Yoder, Eliza	393
Yoder, Lela	325
Yoder, Margaretta	325
Yoder, Dr. Paul E.	325
Yoder, R. A.	57
Yoder, R. A., Jr.	325
Yoder, Rev. Dr. R. A.	324, 325
Yoder, Rosa Fisher	325
Yoder, Sarah Seagle	324
Yoder, Solomon	324
Yorktown	43
Young, Alfred Burton	166, 219
Young, Ephraim	106
Young, James	135
Young, Mrs. Sarah V.	166
Yount, Jacob	418

Z

Zimmerman, John (Col.)	102
Zimmerman, Elizabeth	417